P9-BYV-631

Advance Praise for *Brand New*

"*Brand New* felicitously blends biography, business history, and conceptual analysis in a book that gives the vogue word *branding* a rich and surprising past. Koehn writes with lively prose and has the historian's eye for illuminating detail. From Wedgwood and Heinz to Estée Lauder and Dell, her entrepreneurs created lasting brands, but always in a context of their own choosing. While giving due credit to their enterprise, Koehn brings out the interplay between vision and the historical forces that make it realizable."

—**Jack Beatty,** Senior Editor, *Atlantic Monthly* and Author, *Colossus: How the Corporation Changed America*

"*Brand New* is absolutely essential reading for anyone who has ever aspired to build a successful business. Countless "new new thing" technologies end up not making it to companyhood because their creators fail to appreciate basic lessons of businesses and brands past. In all moments of great economic change, technology matters. But understanding customers and meeting their needs effectively and meaningfully matter just as much—sometimes more. Using a range of compelling historical and modern companies, *Brand New* lays out a series of critical lessons that no businessperson operating in today's turbocharged environment can afford to ignore."

—**Jonathan Bush,** Chairman, CEO, and Cofounder, Athenahealth

"Koehn has opened a new field of business history—one that focuses on the demand side rather than the supply side in technologically new industries. She brilliantly records the careers of six entrepreneurs who, by defining customer needs, became leaders in their rapidly growing markets. By combining past and present, she joins her talents as a historian, case writer, and teacher to provide a new perspective on branding."

—**Alfred D. Chandler Jr.,** Straus Professor of Business History, Emeritus, Harvard Business School

"Today's literature on brand building is replete with simpleminded platitudes and prescriptions generally divorced from any context other than someone's most recent success story. With *Brand New,* Koehn has successfully described the complex evolution of modern consumer brands. In viewing contemporary business behavior through six of the world's great brand developers, she provides the reader with an interesting set of tales with significant take-home value. A superb read!"

—**Len Schlesinger,** Executive Vice President, The Limited, Inc.

"In a world where many companies are built to sell, *Brand New* shows how companies can be built to last—and that is where value is created. Unlike the recent spending frenzy, history shows that brands are built by giving value to customers, suppliers, capital sources, and employees—and by doing so at a margin that preserves the economic engine. The entrepreneurs in this book built enduring best-of-class businesses by creating change *and* living through it. Their stories contribute to an inspiring book."

—**Howard Stevenson,** Senior Associate Dean and Sarofim-Rock Professor of Business Administration, Harvard Business School

"Nancy Koehn understands how markets reward quality brand names, which is the essence of honorable capitalism. Indeed, in this field of study she is the quality brand name."

—**Ben Wattenberg,** Senior Fellow, American Enterprise Institute and Moderator, PBS's weekly discussion program *Think Tank*

BRAND NEW

Henry Heinz, age 64, paying an unexpected visit to
one of his company's cucumber fields in 1908.
Courtesy of H. J. Heinz Company.

BRAND NEW

How Entrepreneurs Earned Consumers' Trust from Wedgwood to Dell

Nancy F. Koehn

Harvard Business School Press
Boston, Massachusetts

Printed in the United States of America
05 06 07 08 01 5 4 3 2 1

Chapter 2: Nancy Koehn, "Josiah Wedgwood and the First Industrial Revolution." Case 796-079. Boston: Harvard Business School Publishing, 1995, edited version.

Excerpts of Chapter 3, "H. J. Heinz 1844–1919," were previously published in "Henry Heinz and Brand Creation in the Late Nineteenth Century: Making Markets for Processed Food," *Business History Review* 73, no. 3 (Autumn 1999).

Excerpts of Chapter 5, "Estée Lauder," were previously published in "Estée Lauder: Self Definition and the Modern Cosmetics Market." Copyright © 2000 from *Beauty and Business: Commerce, Gender, and Culture in Modern America,* edited by Philip Scranton. Reproduced by permission of Taylor & Francis Inc., http://www.routledge-ny.com.

Library of Congress Cataloging-in-Publication Data

Koehn, Nancy F. (Nancy Fowler), 1959–
Brand new : how entrepreneurs earned consumers' trust from Wedgwood to Dell / Nancy F. Koehn.
p. cm.
Includes bibliographical references and index.
ISBN 1-57851-221-2 (alk. paper)
1. Entrepreneurship. 2. Businesspeople.

HB615 .K64 2001
658.4'21--dc21

00-063224

The paper used in this publication meets the requirements of the American National Standard for Permanence of Paper for Publications and Documents in Libraries and Archives Z39.48-1992.

TEXT DESIGN BY JOYCE C. WESTON

For Sally Koehn,
a woman of keen commercial imagination and many other gifts

Contents

CHAPTER 1

Entrepreneurs and Consumers

This book first took shape for me as a series of questions about entrepreneurs and their relationships with consumers. As a historian at the Harvard Business School watching the Information Revolution unfold in the 1990s, I was struck by the sheer number and variety of new goods and services being brought to market: technology-based cellular phones and Internet access, specialty coffee shops and cappuccinos, and so on. Most consumers in the 1980s had not even heard of e-mail or caffe lattes. Yet in less than a decade, millions of people not only became familiar with these and other novel products, they also made them part of their daily lives.

What, I wondered, motivated buyers to embrace specific goods or services of which they had little or no experience? The consumers past and present that I had studied were careful shoppers—initially skeptical of offerings they had not previously encountered. Consciously or not, they were using their money as ballots, choosing products that they perceived to be at least as valuable as the prices paid for those items. Why, in the countless elections of the marketplace, did some offerings attract consumers' attention while others did not?

The more I thought about these issues, the more interested I became in the connections between entrepreneurs and consumers. How did individual entrepreneurs and companies translate a few buyers' curiosity about new products into widespread customer loyalty?

If entrepreneurial inspiration were to move out of the garage and into a successful company operation, it obviously had to include making quality goods at reasonable prices. Well-organized manufacturing, however, was seldom enough to ensure a new firm's prosperity. Building a better mousetrap has almost never, by itself, been sufficient for success in business. Unless the company could also communicate the virtues of its products to potential buyers in effective ways, it could not maintain and grow a viable customer base. Unless young businesses listened carefully to consumers, gauged their reactions, and responded accordingly, early victories in a market would not likely endure. How did individual entrepreneurs, especially those working in the midst of intensified social and technological transitions, deal with these imperatives? What kinds of organizational capabilities did they develop to learn about consumers and earn their trust?

This book addresses all of these questions from a *historical* perspective. It is about six illustrative entrepreneurs in six different industries, all working to create new markets for their wares. They are "illustrative" rather than "typical" because the typical entrepreneur does not usually succeed, especially in his or her first try. Many never succeed at all.

The book opens in late-eighteenth-century Britain, when Josiah Wedgwood tried to pique widespread consumer interest in fine china. It then moves on to investigate—100 years later in the United States—the efforts of Henry Heinz and Marshall Field to develop markets in food processing and mass retailing. The book then analyzes three twentieth-century businesspeople and the new sectors in which they worked: Estée Lauder in prestige cosmetics, Howard Schultz of Starbucks in specialty coffee, and Michael Dell in personal computers. It concludes with a number of historical and strategic lessons drawn from all six entrepreneurial experiences.

Supply, Demand, and Changing Historical Contexts

Economists and businesspeople often divide the market into two sides: the supply side, where goods, services, companies, and physical capital originate, and the demand side, where household priorities and consumers' decisions are shaped. Obviously, economic and social change always affects both sides, altering how businesspeople produce their goods and services and how consumers perceive new needs for themselves and their families.

The six entrepreneurs analyzed in this book had many things in common. Perhaps the most important was a powerful understanding of what rapid social and economic change meant for consumers' needs and wants. They used their knowledge of both the supply and demand sides of the economy to create high-quality goods, meaningful brands, and other connections with customers—and they built elite organizations that worked to *satisfy* and then to *anticipate* buyers' changing preferences.

Four of these people *made things:* Wedgwood's earthenware, Heinz's bottled pickles, Lauder's cosmetics, and Dell's personal computers were, and of course still are, tangible products. The other two entrepreneurs *created "encounters"* that proved appealing to consumers: Field's department store environment and Schultz's café experience. In addition, Wedgwood's showrooms, Dell's customized ordering process, and Lauder's in-store demonstrations added an important element of experiential shopping to the sale of the things they made and sold.

Most of the existing research and writing on economic change—on the Industrial Revolution and similar movements—has concentrated on supply-side developments: technological, financial, and managerial innovations aimed at producing goods and services. Much of this excellent work has analyzed the efficiencies and resulting cost savings achieved by specific business leaders, companies, and industries in adopting particular technologies or organizational systems.

By contrast, my book is focused on entrepreneurial action directed mostly at the demand side. As the six individuals analyzed here well understood, economic expansion and social transformation affected what consumers want, have, and can afford as well as what companies choose to make. Each of the six *pursued new business opportunities relentlessly, without becoming deterred by the limited resources that he or she initially controlled.* (This italicized phrase happens to be one of the best existing definitions of "entrepreneurship."[1]) Exploiting available opportunities depended on comprehending consumers' emerging needs, developing a product that met these needs, communicating back and forth with customers, and actually delivering the product or service effectively. It also depended—crucially—on building a company that could perform all of these disparate functions well.

In 1759, for example, Josiah Wedgwood founded his own pottery workshop with the idea of developing a large market for dinner plates, vases, and other china. He had ambition, experience, and imagination, but virtually no cash and few connections. Yet he recognized that rising incomes in eighteenth-century Britain meant that many men and women now had more money to spend on nonessential goods such as china. He also saw that large numbers of people directed their spending toward social emulation. This meant aping the habits and purchases of the income class directly above them—what in the twentieth century would come to be called "aspirational consumption." Wedgwood used his knowledge to create not only an excellent product but also a widely recognized brand name and other significant connections with his customers. As the market for china expanded, he assembled additional resources, constructing the most innovative and successful firm in his industry.

Like Wedgwood, the other five central characters in this book developed particular tools to take advantage of the possibilities they confronted. These tools included rigorous quality-control measures, focused employee training policies, innovative selling and distribution methods, and strong brands. All of these initiatives were coordinated toward one goal: *making a market for novel goods and services.*

Each of these six entrepreneurs, of course, operated within a particular historical context, as all human beings must. By the late nineteenth century, for example, Henry Heinz and Marshall Field had access to transportation possibilities and mass markets that Josiah Wedgwood could scarcely have imagined 100 years earlier. Then, after still another 100 years, Michael Dell employed the telephone and the Internet to sell personal computers and network servers, using a business model and product mix that would have confounded both Henry Heinz and Marshall Field.

Much of what these six entrepreneurs accomplished, especially early on, was a result of improvising—of making it up as they went along. In starting their own businesses, they had few employees, meager revenues, and only rudimentary management systems. Two of the six made their first products out of their kitchens. A third worked from his college dorm; a fourth from a room in the back of his café. But all six shared an obsession with creating a quality offering, a determination to bring it to large numbers of customers, and an ability to appreciate how social and economic shifts affected consumers' wants. In a sense, each was lucky in confronting new business opportunities growing out of major societal changes. But in every case, as the oft-stated business principle puts it, the harder each one worked, the luckier he or she became.

Organizations and Brands

Each of the six also created specific institutions—that is, companies—which in five of the six cases still bear the name of the founding entrepreneur. Each also made ingenious use of specific marketing tools, perhaps the most significant of which was the *brand.*

Today, a brand is usually defined as a name, logo, or symbol intended to distinguish a particular seller's offerings from those of competitors. Great brands—Coca-Cola, American Express, McDonald's, IBM, Rolls-Royce, Chanel, Sony—command awareness and esteem from consumers around the world. Strong, relevant identities for specific branded offerings enhance a firm's profitability and influence the terms of competition in its industry. Brands also greatly facilitate the introduction of additional products by companies in possession of popular brands—Coca-Cola's Diet Coke, Caffeine-free Coke, Sprite, Fresca, and so on.

All of the brands I discuss were developed during periods when demand-side shifts were altering consumers' priorities. This kind of thing happens in all historical epochs, of course, but in each of the six cases, social and economic changes were racing forward more rapidly than usual. The brands analyzed here thus offered quicker potential connections between consumers' shifting wants, on the one hand, and increasing entrepreneurial possibilities, on the other.

Back-and-Forth Communication

The six entrepreneurs did not often think in terms of bridges between the supply and demand sides of the economy or—at least initially—about brands and organization building. What they did think about was how to attract broad interest in new products that they had reason to believe would fit well into the changing social and economic environments. Their convictions and self-confidence grew so strong that they were willing to stake their own futures and those of their young companies on their own personal insights about changing conditions and new opportunities. These insights, in turn, flowed from constant two way communication between each entrepreneur and his or her customers.

Since the eighteenth century, when the Industrial Revolution gave rise to rapidly expanding business opportunities, ambitious manufacturers and distributors have attempted to reach beyond local markets. Similarly, on the demand side, consumers have tried to obtain information about the burgeoning world of new goods and services that industrial capitalism constantly makes available. Many of these goods and services were originating far away, of course. And personal, face-to-face, two-way communication between producers and consumers was becoming more and more difficult. As the scale and speed of economic activity accelerated, it became progressively harder, and ultimately almost impossible, for buyers to base their connections with sellers on personal interactions. Brands, salespeople, new forms of distribution, and advertisements therefore became surrogates for firsthand familiarity with local producers. At the same time, some of these same channels steadily funneled information from consumers back to producers, in early forms of what later became known as "market research."

But how this happened—and what form this two-way communication took—changed radically over time. In the eighteenth century, Josiah Wedgwood built powerful, strategically advantageous connections with eighteenth-century households through personal contact, printed circulars, and modest newspaper ads. Today, the emergence of mass media such as television and the Internet has allowed Estée Lauder, Starbucks, Dell, and many other present-day companies to "speak" with millions of potential buyers simultaneously, a possibility that earlier entrepreneurs could not have contemplated. In our own time, companies such as Procter & Gamble and Mattel create and promote new brands for specific products almost as a matter of course. Internet start-ups devote huge resources to reaching and acquiring new buyers whom they hope will become loyal customers over the long term. And constant customer feedback has become part of the essence of modern marketing.

On the Shoulders of Giants

In writing this book, I have had the advantage of a rich storehouse of previous work by outstanding scholars and writers in several disciplines. The names of these scholars are too numerous to list here, but they make abundant appearances in the endnotes of the book. As mentioned, numerous business and economic historians have concentrated on the supply side of the economy. With great insight, these writers have examined the technological, managerial, and organizational innovations of the eighteenth and nineteenth centuries with reference to specific individuals and firms. Much of their research has focused on the evolution of big businesses in the middle and late decades of the nineteenth century. A smaller but no less talented group of business and cultural historians has studied the emergence of mass markets and national advertising in the late-nineteenth and early-twentieth centuries and the challenges that individual companies faced in distributing their goods.[2]

Meanwhile, a very perceptive group of marketing scholars, working mostly in business schools, has concentrated on current business practice. They have produced detailed analyses of the objectives, initiatives, and effectiveness of brand creation, advertising, and distribution strategies.[3] In addition to marketing specialists, scholars of modern consumerism—including historians, anthropologists, and economists—have been equally industrious. Particularly since the early 1980s, they have scrutinized the origins and development of modern consumer culture.[4] At the same time, scholars of entrepreneurship have examined the managerial, financial, and technological underpinnings of new businesses, analyzing how individuals and organizations marshal resources in order to exploit specific opportunities.[5]

In my own work, I kept being drawn back to the *connections* among all of these issues. I wanted to understand the role that particular entrepreneurs played historically in making new markets and affecting modern consumption—subjects that have not yet received a lot of attention.

This book is not, of course, a comprehensive history of all types of new product development or of marketing. Nor can it be an exhaustive reconstruction of entrepreneurship since the Industrial Revolution. Rather, it is a close investigation of six instances of entrepreneurial commitment and the development of two-way communication with consumers. The book analyzes the evolution of these phenomena within the larger context of six exemplary entrepreneurs making their marks in young industries, summarizing the relevance of these experiences for today's readers. It begins in mid-eighteenth-century Britain with Josiah Wedgwood's remarkably "modern" innovations in new product development, brand creation, strategic marketing, and organization building.

PART ONE

THE PAST

CHAPTER 2

Josiah Wedgwood, 1730-1795

Prologue: The Catherine Service

In June 1774, members of London's social elite made their way through the bustling streets of the West End to a stately Georgian building called Portland House. Here in five commercial showrooms, earls, dukes, and Queen Charlotte, wife of George III, mingled with prosperous merchants and traders. They had all come to see the most famous set of china in England.

Commissioned by Catherine the Great of Russia at a price of £3,000 (about $280,000 today), the fifty-person dinner and dessert services consisted of 952 pieces, each hand-painted with a distinctive British scene.[1] It was an impressive sight. One of Queen Charlotte's attendants commented that "three rooms below and two above" were filled with china, "laid out on tables, everything that can be wanted to serve a dinner." The china was in pale creamware, the drawings in purple, the borders a wreath of leaves, and "the middle of each piece a particular view of all the remarkable places in the King's dominions."[2] Drawn from engravings and firsthand sketches, most of the scenes were detailed renderings of provincial mansions and elaborate gardens. The men and women crowding into Portland House were anxious to see whose properties had been reproduced for the Russian empress.

In contrast to the rest of the set, a few pieces pictured canal locks, a colliery, a paper mill, and a dockyard. These few plates, teapots, and cups offered glimpses of an emerging England, inventive, industrial, and busy, a new world mixing with the traditional order.[3] Overall, this new china service that London elites clamored to see in mid-1774 was both a symbol and a product of the nation's evolving economy. Novel manufacturing methods and organizational arrangements of the Industrial Revolution had been used for the expeditious production of the unadorned pieces. But the unique decoration on each piece, applied by skilled artisans using long-established practices, had taken fifteen months to complete. So the whole project symbolized a fusion of old and new industrial processes.

The men responsible for the project were Josiah Wedgwood and his partner, Thomas Bentley. They owned and managed Wedgwood & Bentley, one of the most innovative and successful firms in Britain's expanding pottery industry. Both men had worked hard to obtain the Russian royal commission. They had earned smaller profits on the sale than projected, but their company and its wares had captured significant aristocratic attention and, therefore, prestige.[4] From Josiah Wedgwood's vantage point, elite sanction was a critical component in selling both luxury goods and more essential pottery to an expanding range of customers. As he wrote to his partner:

> It is really amazing how rapidly . . . [our china] has spread almost over the whole Globe, & how universally it is liked. How much of this general use, & estimation, is owing to the mode of its introduction & how much to its real utility & beauty? are questions in which we may be a good deal interested for the government of our future Conduct. . . . For instance, if a Royal, or Noble Introduction be as necessary to the sale of an Article *of Luxury,* as real Elegance & beauty, then the Manufacturer, if he consults his own interest will bestow as much pains, & expence too if necessary, in gaining the former of these advantages, as he would in bestowing the latter.[5]

Wedgwood and Bentley understood that in the emerging consumer society, marketing was as important as manufacturing.

What else did it mean to do business in an age when widespread economic and social change was altering the range of possibilities available to consumers and suppliers? What kinds of opportunities did such transition present for creative, ambitious entrepreneurs? How were these individuals going to manage the challenges presented by new goods, markets, mechanical contrivances, and labor relations? The story of Josiah Wedgwood is that of a man living at an inflection point in the history of capitalism. Over the course of his career, organized manufacturing and marketing became much more significant in Britain's economic structure. Industrial productivity increased. At the same time, agricultural and commercial productivity grew. The nation's international trading patterns shifted.[6]

Most of these changes were gradual. A few were dramatic. Taken together, they altered irrevocably the pace, tenor, and scope of British life.

As English novelist Henry Fielding, author of *Tom Jones*, commented in 1751, "Nothing has wrought such an Alteration in this Order of People, as the Introduction of Trade. This hath indeed given a Face to the whole Nation, hath in great measure subverted the former State of Affairs, and hath almost totally changed the Manners, Customs and Habits of the People."[7] Josiah Wedgwood wanted to understand and profit from this transformation.

Wedgwood was born on or about July 12, 1730 (which was the date of his baptism), in Burslem, a Staffordshire village 150 miles northwest of London. He was the thirteenth and last child of Mary and Thomas Wedgwood. Thomas Wedgwood was a man of moderate means from a long line of potters and owned a potworks near the Burslem churchyard. Along with most babies born in England and Europe at that time, Josiah's chances of dying in the first year of life were about one in six.[8] If he survived his first twelve months, he could be expected to live another thirty-nine years. Actually he proved remarkably hearty in body and mind, living to the age of sixty-five and defying the demographic odds.

The young Josiah, from his earliest years as a potter's apprentice, used his own substantial gifts of intellectual curiosity, aesthetic sensitivity, and commercial imagination to make sense of his world. He wanted to exploit the opportunities offered by scientific progress and economic expansion. But he was motivated by more than money.[9] Throughout his life, he was also drawn to scientific experiment, politics, literature, philosophy, and even botany.

Josiah's dedication and creativity eventually paid handsome rewards. He became the most successful and respected potter in Europe. He played a major role in transforming social attitudes toward earthenware, expanding its markets, and implementing a host of organizational and production innovations. The British statesman William Gladstone said in 1863, looking back over the early years of the Industrial Revolution, "Wedgwood was the greatest man who ever, in any age, or in any country . . . applied himself to the important work of uniting art with industry."[10]

Such accolades might have embarrassed Josiah, but would not have surprised him. Throughout most of his life, he remained sure of his purpose and confident of his abilities to elevate himself and his world. He wrote Bentley in 1766, before their partnership was formalized, that if Bentley himself "could really fall in love with, and make a Mistress of" this new pottery business, "I should have little or no doubt of our success." He went on to declare that "we have certainly the fairest prospect of enlarging this branch of Manufacture to our wishes, and as Genius will not be wanting, I am firmly perswaded that our *proffits* will be in proportion to our *application.*"[11] As Josiah understood, inspiration was a necessary, though not sufficient, condition of success. It was going to take a lot of work to make the most of the opportunities afforded by the Industrial Revolution.

The Pottery Industry and the Eighteenth-Century Economy

In 1730, when Josiah Wedgwood was born, pottery manufacture and commerce were the principal occupations in his home village. Burslem had a population of 1,000 and was well on its way to becoming a town.[12] More than two-thirds of the residents earned their livelihood in nonagricultural occupations, up from one-half three decades earlier.[13] Burslem's inhabitants lived and worked in 150 thatched cottages, many of which were surrounded by hollows from which potters dug their clay and into which they carted ash piles and other waste from their kilns. The tradesmen of Burslem included two blacksmiths, a baker, cobbler, butcher, and barber. Two general shops sold tobacco, soap, candles, sugar, buttons, and thread. One of them also sold cloth, books, knitting needles, and groceries such as rice, prunes, and spices.[14] At least eight alehouses, with names such as the "Jolly Potters," provided libations to quench the community's thirst.[15]

Several primitive roads connected Burslem with London, Liverpool, and other markets. The roads were rough, and in the winter often impassable even by packhorse.[16] In 1730, the nearest canal was twenty miles away and still under construction.

Burslem was an important community in the Staffordshire region, which was (and still is) the center of earthenware production in England. Earthenware, another name for pottery, is china made of slightly porous clay. Earthenware differs from porcelain, which is made from a compound of refined clay, fusible rock, and flux, an oxide added to ceramic bodies to promote fusion during firing. Porcelain is usually fired to the point where it becomes translucent. Consequently, it is usually more fragile than earthenware.[17]

In sixty small Burslem workshops, most of them employing fewer than a dozen men and children, master earthenware craftsmen and their assistants made butter-pots, pitchers, and mugs from the red, brown, and orange clays available locally. Known as coarseware, these simple, durable products were usually coated in colored salt-based glazes. As consumer products, they were fast replacing the wood and pewter dishes that most Britons had used for centuries. Coarseware was sold to wholesalers and retailers in local and London markets. British demand for finer wares was met by European and Far Eastern imports or by the delftware potteries in London and Bristol. Delftware was an elaborately decorated form of earthenware, vulnerable to scratches and breakage.[18]

By modern standards, a potter's tools were very simple. Most workshops had one or two wheels and at least one lathe to scrape the surface of the ware after the potter had "thrown," molded, and dried the clay. In the 1730s, both wheels and lathes were powered by human energy, as they had been for centuries. Earthenware manufacture at this time was a labor-intensive process, more dependent on individual craft and energy than on capital equipment or organizational capabilities. Even so, the necessary tools and inputs represented a substantial financial investment for most households.

The majority of potworks had at least one oven, fueled by coal and usually measuring eight feet long by ten feet wide and standing fifteen feet high. Some potters also had special molds. A potter's oven cost £15, a wheel approximately £1, and a high-quality lathe £2 10s.[19] Counting raw materials and existing stock, a midsized workshop such as that inherited by Josiah's father was valued at about £40 (approximately $4,500 in today's dollars), exclusive of rent for the shop.[20] This was almost three times the annual income of a farm laborer and almost twice the yearly earnings of a collier.[21] Financial barriers to entry, plus the long training required, prevented most of the Staffordshire labor force from obtaining any kind of ownership stake in the pottery business.[22]

The industry was broadly representative of the national economy. Manufacturing in early-eighteenth-century Britain was diverse, small in scale, and regionally concentrated by industry. Manufacturing output was spread across a broad range of industries: baking, milling, brewing, distilling, pottery, leather processing, building materials, and woolen textiles.[23] The last three sectors probably accounted for close to two-thirds of all industrial output before 1750. The famous technological leaders of the Industrial Revolution—cotton, textiles, iron smelting, and engineering (machine tool manufacture)—made up less than 10 percent.[24]

Still, as early as 1740, almost 40 percent of men over the age of twenty labored in commercial or manufacturing enterprises, a higher fraction than was true for the rest of Europe. About 30 percent of British families farmed, and most of the remaining 30 percent were servants and other laborers.[25] During the middle decades of the eighteenth century, the British economy became even more industrialized, but agriculture and commerce steadily expanded along with manufacturing. Through a series of cost-reducing innovations, including the introduction of fodder crops into the rotations, agricultural output grew an average of 0.6 percent each year in the first half of the century.[26] Industrial output climbed an average 0.7 percent annually before 1760.[27] Though not high by twentieth-century criteria, these were significant gains at the time.

The starting date for the Industrial Revolution is a hotly debated subject.[28] Historians and economists argue about the relative importance of labor, capital, and technological change in industrialization as well as about the contribution of agriculture and international trade in accounting for Britain's rising national product.[29] Most scholars agree, however, that in the mid-eighteenth century England's traditional and newer sectors experienced steady growth (see Table 2-1). The expansion of agricultural output slowed after 1760.[30] But output in commerce and manufacturing sectors—wool, iron, silk, cotton, beer, leather, soap—increased by more than 1 percent each year in the two decades after 1760, accelerating to 1.8 percent

TABLE 2-1

Growth of British Gross Domestic Product and of Industrial and Agricultural Output, 1700–1801
(% per year)

Years	1700–1760	1760–1780	1780–1801
GDP	0.7	0.6	1.4
Industry	0.7	1.3	2.0
Agriculture	0.6	0.1	0.8

Source: Adapted from Nick Crafts, "The Industrial Revolution," in Roderick Floud and Donald McCloskey, eds., *The Economic History of Britain since 1700,* 2d ed. (Cambridge: Cambridge University Press, 1994), 1, p. 47.

annually in the last twenty years of the century.[31] By eighteenth-century standards, this was very rapid growth.

After 1780, cotton and iron manufacture became more significant components of industrial output, which itself was becoming an ever-larger part of national product. During the second half of the eighteenth century, the number of weavers more than doubled, and the number of men in the textile trades as a whole more than tripled.[32] By 1800, industry, commerce, and services made up more than half of Britain's national product.[33] Britain was one of the first countries in the world to pass the benchmark of having less than half its workforce deployed in agriculture.[34]

Businessmen and politicians working during Josiah Wedgwood's lifetime had no access to national income and productivity figures such as the ones quoted above. Such measurements are twentieth-century innovations, and the numbers cited here have been carefully calculated retrospectively, on the basis of incomplete data. By modern criteria, the growth figures mentioned are not very impressive, but they did represent quite a large increase at the time, and they underscore the far-reaching inventiveness and improvement that characterized the British economy.

As noted earlier, eighteenth-century manufacturing was usually centered in specific regions. Pig and bar iron were smelted in Shropshire and Worcestershire. Metalware was produced in factories and workshops around cities such as Birmingham, Wolverhampton, and Sheffield.[35] Woolens, linens, fustians (mixes of cotton and linen), and other cotton goods were made in northwest England.

Mining, too, had regional centers. Copper was centered in Cornwall, slate in North Wales, lead in Cumberland and Derbyshire. But the most important of all mining sectors was coal. Because Britain was richly endowed with coal reserves, these were broadly dispersed, and they played a critical role in the nation's industrialization. Coal was used in smelting iron and in many other manufactures. It was mined in Shropshire, Worcestershire, Yorkshire, South Wales, and Staffordshire. Coal mining, like the production of textiles, earthenware, and ships, engendered subsidiary trades, which grew up to serve the principal occupations in a particular area. Grindstone production drew artisans to Sheffield to make equipment for the ironware industry. The making of spindles, needles, combs, and cards developed in the textile regions. Crate manufacturing proliferated in

Staffordshire as the earthenware sector expanded. Figure 2-1 locates Staffordshire and other regions in the United Kingdom.

Many industries and regional economies became much more efficient during the eighteenth century. Few sectors, however, underwent the range of operational advances that earthenware manufacture did. In the decades surrounding Josiah Wedgwood's birth, a series of important developments in raw materials, casting processes, and firing methods increased the potential quality, quantity, and range of output. Before 1730, Staffordshire potters had begun working with white clays imported from southwest England, eventually combining them with local clays to produce a cream-colored ware, often called creamware, that was smoother to work with and more appealing to the eye.[36] These innovations marked the first stages in the production of earthenware that could compete with high-priced porcelain and delftware.[37]

In Burslem and other pottery centers, manufacturers experimented further with molds and casting processes to shape "useful" earthenware—products used for domestic functional purposes, such as plates, cups, basins, and pitchers. Techniques for shaping the earthenware expanded to include not only *press molding*—the pushing of flat pieces of damp clay into brass or alabaster molds—but also a larger number of shapes made from plaster of Paris.[38] This development proved crucial to the evolution of *slip-casting,* which offered potters a much wider range of shapes than those possible on the wheel or through press molding.[39] Slip-casting entailed pouring *slip,* a creamy clay solution, into plaster molds, allowing the solution to dry, and then removing the unfired clay.

In the 1740s, Staffordshire potters also experimented with new firing and glazing methods for cream-colored earthenware. They combined fluid glaze mixtures with novel firing techniques. Instead of firing the clay once after a powdered glaze had been applied, a few master craftsmen began firing their clay unglazed. Then, while the ware was still in a porous or "biscuit" condition, they dipped it in the glaze, then fired it again to fuse the glaze.[40] As Josiah Wedgwood and other potters quickly realized, the two firings produced pottery more evenly finished and with less resultant waste.

By the mid-eighteenth century, the Staffordshire pottery industry blended traditional skills and practices with novel processes, products, and organizational forms—the fusion of old and new that was to be so neatly symbolized by Wedgwood & Bentley's exhibition at Portland House some

FIGURE 2-1

The United Kingdom

years later. Many of these early innovations produced quick, visible results: whiter, more smoothly polished plates and cups. Others took longer to bear fruit. Whether they occurred gradually or swiftly, the improvements were cumulative, with each feeding on and often encompassing recent discoveries. Taken together, these innovations played a critical role in transforming the industry to which Josiah was to devote his life.

Josiah's Early Years

Josiah Wedgwood's childhood seems to have been a happy one. His mother, Mary, was a small, organized woman of uncommon sensitivity and kindness.[41] When Josiah was born, she already had twelve children, including six under age ten. Mary was relatively well educated, and she passed to her children her faith in the ethical and practical power of human industry. Josiah's father, Thomas, was a potter like his ancestors, many of whom had accumulated sizable resources. But he himself was not particularly ambitious or prosperous. The family was neither rich nor poor by eighteenth-century standards.[42] Like other contemporary manufacturers, the Wedgwoods were of the "middling" sort, part of Britain's heterogeneous and growing commercial classes.[43]

Josiah spent his early boyhood as other potters' children did. Before he was old enough to begin learning the family craft, he did washing, dairy work, and other chores. When he was not working, he had time to ride the cratemen's packhorses as they waited for their loads and to explore the countryside surrounding Burslem, collecting fossils and pottery shards. In his father's workshop, Josiah put his hands in clay, forming imitations of all kinds of objects that interested him.[44] He was a lively, joyful child.

At age seven, he was sent to school in Newcastle-under-Lyme, west of Burslem, where he studied reading, writing, figures, and chemistry. According to his teacher, Josiah was "a fair arithmetician and master of a capital hand."[45] In 1739, when he was nine, his father died, and the pottery works passed to Josiah's eldest brother, Thomas. Cash became short, and Josiah left school. He probably began work in the pottery at this time.[46]

In 1742, smallpox broke out in Staffordshire, infecting the twelve-year-old Josiah and other Burslem children.[47] He spent many weeks in bed, his body covered with sores. In this illness, some biographers have seen the origins of his adult passion for books.[48]

The disease left Josiah's face pockmarked and his right knee weak and unreliable. Often he could not walk without crutches or a cane. Pain dogged him, limiting his ability to operate the foot pedal on the potter's wheel. So he took up modeling, glazing, and other parts of earthenware production in his brother's workshop, mastering a wide range of tasks.[49]

In 1744, the fourteen-year-old Josiah was formally apprenticed to his eldest brother. In exchange for room, board, and training in the "art, Mistery, Occupation or Imployment of Throwing and Handleing," Josiah bound himself for five years to a standard series of conditions: "At Cards Dice or any other unlawful Games he shall not Play, Taverns or Ale Houses he shall not haunt or frequent, Fornication he shall not Commit—Matrimony he shall not Contract—from the Service of his said Master he shall not at any time depart or absent himself without his said Masters Leave."[50]

Josiah completed his apprenticeship and worked for his brother an additional three years as a journeyman.[51] Constantly tinkering with various stages of pottery making, Josiah tested different oxides that imitated a more vibrant marbled finish on the ware. He also developed his own variations on tortoiseshell ware, named for its mottled glaze, which faintly resembled a turtle's shell. His brother's workshop manufactured primarily useful goods. But Josiah also tried his hand at making ornamental goods—vases, snuffboxes, and decorative knife handles.

In 1752, Josiah left the workshop. He may have been frustrated by his brother's lack of ambition or the limitations of the family business. Most likely he sought a wider realm in which to nurture and develop his gifts. He worked for two years in a pottery in nearby Stoke. Then, when he was twenty-four, he entered into a partnership with Thomas Whieldon, an experienced potter of the nearby town of Fenton, who had a large workshop and was on his way to amassing a considerable fortune.[52] Whieldon, thirty-five years old when Josiah began working with him, employed more than twenty assistants who made stoneware, tortoiseshell, and creamware in a wide range of pieces.[53] He oversaw a larger and more diversified operation than any Josiah had previously known. In the mid-1750s, Whieldon's annual sales rose to £900 (about $95,000 today).[54] Josiah spent five years in Whieldon's pottery, working extensively with colors and glazes. He also traveled regularly to sell snuffboxes and knife handles to the metalware and cutlery industries in Birmingham and Sheffield.[55]

In the 1750s, both of those cities were booming. A center for the growing metalware and iron industries, Birmingham had almost tripled its population since 1700. With almost 30,000 people, it was now the fifth largest city in England, behind London, Bristol, Norwich, and Newcastle.[56] In 1754, Sheffield had 12,000 inhabitants (by 1801 it would have 46,000).[57] In both Birmingham and Sheffield, Josiah could see the power of industrial capitalism unleashed: crowded, busy streets, sprawling growth, and an expanding number of consumer goods—brooches, tankards, toys, French pottery, books, and much more.[58] Table 2-2 shows the pattern of urban growth in England before and during the Industrial Revolution.

Josiah also observed the social changes that accompanied urban expansion. He and other contemporary observers were particularly struck by how quickly fortunes could be made (and lost) in this environment. The British statesman Lord Shelburne, after visiting Birmingham in the 1760s, noted that "it is not fifty years since the hardware began to make a figure [in the city], from thence begun by people not worth above three or four

TABLE 2-2

Urban Growth in Early Modern England

	Population Totals (thousands)			
	c. 1600	c. 1700	c. 1750	1801
England	4,110	5,060	5,770	8,660
London	200	575	675	960
Ten historic regional centers[a]	73	107	126	153
Eight established ports[b]	53	81	128	190
Four "new" manufacturing towns[c]	11	27	70	262

Source: E. Anthony Wrigley, "Urban Growth and Agricultural Change: England and the Continent in the Early Modern Period," in Robert I. Rotberg and Theodore K. Rabb, eds., *Population and History: From the Traditional to the Modern World* (Cambridge: Cambridge University Press, 1986), p. 133.

a. Norwich, York, Salisbury, Chester, Worcester, Exeter, Cambridge, Coventry, Shrewsbury, Gloucester.
b. Bristol, Hull, Colchester, Newcastle, Ipswich, Great Yarmouth, King's Lynn, Southampton.
c. Birmingham, Manchester, Leeds, Sheffield.

hundred pounds a-piece, some of whom are now worth three or four hundred thousand."[59] There is no evidence that Josiah exulted in the changes he witnessed. But apparently the symptoms of industrialization neither frightened nor dismayed him. For Josiah, economic transformation was to be understood and exploited.

By his mid-twenties, he realized that success in earthenware manufacture demanded precise, systematic knowledge of production techniques and attention to changing customer wants. So in Whieldon's workshop he spent most of his time on the development of handling and glazing processes. At age twenty-eight, still working for Whieldon, he began keeping the first of many notebooks, which he called Experiment Books, to record the state of his own innovations. As Josiah noted, the firm's manufacture of earthenware at that time stood in great need of improvement. With "the demand for our goods decreasing daily, and the trade universally complained of as being bad and in a declining condition" something new was wanted, he wrote, "to give a little spirit to the business."[60]

Using his own secret code to log specific formulas, Josiah kept these detailed notebooks for the rest of his career.[61] In them, he meticulously laid out the results of his ongoing experiments, always attempting to organize his thoughts on a systematic basis and to apply science to the manufacture of pottery.

On His Own

In May 1759, Wedgwood left Whieldon's workshop and established himself as an independent potter. He was twenty-eight, ambitious, and eager to test his talents. His new establishment at Burslem consisted of a cottage, two kilns, sheds, and workrooms, all of which he rented from his cousin John Wedgwood for £15 a year (about $1,350 today).[62] For additional rent of £2.6 per year, he acquired a potter's wheel. He hired as a journeyman another cousin, Thomas, at an annual salary of £22. Thomas was twenty-four, and his experience centered around porcelain manufacture, enameling, and transfer printing, areas that complemented Josiah's own expertise.

It is not clear how Josiah financed this first venture. Perhaps he borrowed funds from wealthier relatives. He seems to have been short of money. He was six months late paying rent for the pottery works, and almost a quarter of the total rent was paid in goods.

For the next three years, Josiah, his cousin Thomas, and several hired hands manufactured tortoiseshell and other ware. Josiah began coating creamware in the new green and yellow glazes he had perfected while working with Whieldon. He applied these brilliant glazes to teapots and plates molded or pressed in many shapes, such as pineapples, cauliflowers, cabbages, and pears. He bought the ornate molds needed to produce these elaborate pieces from one of Whieldon's potters.

Pineapple and cauliflower wares were eye-catching, functional, and, most important, *novel.* These ornate pieces were immediately popular and are still manufactured today. Of course, not all Britons in the mid-eighteenth century could afford to care about the fashionability of new products.[63] But as per capita and family incomes climbed, increasing numbers of consumers from the upper and middling ranks acquired new possessions.[64]

The rich built magnificent houses, sometimes demolishing Elizabethan and Jacobean mansions to make room for them. To fill their new homes, they commissioned furniture from Chippendale, Hepplewhite, Sheraton, and other designers. They created orangeries, greenhouses, and sumptuous gardens. Some wealthy households even had private menageries stocked with exotic animals.[65]

Within their means, Britons from the middling orders were no less zealous consumers. They bought clocks, linens, window curtains, books, cutlery, pottery, tobacco, chocolate, and tea. Some types of goods, such as table linens and books, had been used by the rich in the seventeenth century, but by 1750 were much more common. Tea, coffee, and chocolate were new products introduced from the Far East and the New World. Like espresso drinks in the late twentieth century, these new hot beverages took Great Britain by storm. In 1730, Britons had consumed 1.4 million pounds of tea each year, or about one fourth of a pound per person. By 1800, annual tea consumption had risen to over 12 million pounds, or about 1.5 pounds per person.[66] Increased spending on new and established goods begat still more spending. Preparation of coffee, tea, and chocolate called for specialized equipment: cups, pitchers, pots, sugar bowls. Tobacco required pipes and snuffboxes. As households acquired books, they needed bookshelves. Table linens and pottery required new sideboards and china closets with glass doors. Most of these items, as the political economist Josiah Tucker noted in 1758, were goods that middle-class consumers in past centuries or other nations could scarcely have dreamed of. Farmers, freeholders, tradesmen, and manufacturers, he wrote, "have better Conveniences in their Houses and affect to have more in Quantity of clean, neat Furniture, and a greater Variety (such as Carpets, Screens, Window Curtains, Chamber Bells, polished Brass Locks, Fenders, etc. Things Hardly known abroad among Persons of such Rank) than are to be found in any other country of Europe, Holland excepted."[67] In London and provincial cities, some items that had formerly been considered luxuries among various classes were now perceived as essentials.[68]

Throughout all this consumption ran a strong thirst for novelty. In furniture, pottery, fabrics, and millinery, consumers insisted on new fashions. The desire for novelty was so pervasive that the great wit Dr. Samuel Johnson grumbled that nowadays men were even "to be hanged in a new way."[69]

Josiah Wedgwood understood all of this quite well. By the early 1760s, he was hard at work developing an improved creamware, the attractive white pottery made possible by earlier innovations. While working with Whieldon, he had experimented extensively with creamware. He was aware of the problems in its dipping and firing but also recognized its potential as both useful and ornamental ware. In color, it could compete with porcelain and delftware. But its durability and lower cost might appeal to a much broader market. Consumers who could not afford the expense of porcelain or the replacement cost of fragile delftware might scoop it up.

His chief technical problem seems to have been consistency of quality and color. His early creamware, like that of other potters, had varied from straw color to deep saffron. Josiah was certain that the market would be more efficiently served with a single pale color, a shade that did not vary across firings and that closely resembled porcelain.[70]

By 1762, he had made great progress using a body composed of ground flint and pipe clay and covered with a lead glaze. He had developed what he described as a "species of earthenware for the table quite new in its appearance, covered with a rich and brilliant glaze bearing sudden alterations of heat and cold, manufactured with ease and expedition, and consequently cheap."[71]

Josiah sent some of his creamware to Liverpool, where it was decorated by a new process now becoming fashionable for porcelain. This technique, called transfer-printing, allowed a wide array of intricate scenes or characters to be applied smoothly to any kind of china.[72] After printing, the ware was shipped back to Burslem for firing and often enameling.[73]

The demand for Josiah Wedgwood's goods outstripped his potworks' capacity even before he made these improvements to creamware.[74] In late 1762, he moved production to the larger Brick House Works in Burslem. These rented premises consisted of five or six workshops, five ovens, and a brick dwelling for him as master potter.[75] He employed sixteen paid hands. Three years later, now thirty-five years old, he acquired even more workshop space from his cousin John.

The Partnership of Wedgwood & Bentley

In the early 1760s, Wedgwood rode frequently to Liverpool to do business with Sadler & Green, sales agents and merchants. He did not relish the forty-mile journey. Since his childhood bout with smallpox and the deterioration of his knee, riding had been difficult. Although as an adult he was hypochondriacal about other aspects of his physical condition, he was remarkably stoic about this handicap.[76] Like the twentieth-century U.S. president Franklin D. Roosevelt, who was stricken with polio, Josiah Wedgwood sought to conquer his infirmity through sheer will. Throughout his life, he routinely subjected himself to grueling physical exercise.[77] These regimes also helped him control his appetite and weight, both of which he often worried about. He took care with the rest of his appearance, favoring unostentatious dress and a simple wig. His gray-blue eyes were resolute and full of humor. He carried his 5-foot, 6-inch frame and 12 stones (about 168 pounds) gracefully.

One day in early 1762, the thirty-one-year-old Wedgwood set out on one of his arduous journeys to Liverpool. By the time he reached the port city, he had damaged his bad knee even more and had to lie in bed for many weeks. While he was recuperating, his physician introduced him to Thomas Bentley. This meeting was a fortuitous one for both men. It inaugurated a long friendship of depth and intimacy, as well as one of the most important business partnerships of the eighteenth century.[78] In 1769, Bentley formally became Wedgwood's partner in manufacturing and selling ornamental china. But from the time they met in 1762, the two men collaborated closely on a range of managerial issues. Until his death in 1780, Bentley brought his commercial experience, mercantile connections, social grace, and entrepreneurial skills to bear on the business. He oversaw the firm's London operations, developed new markets, and channeled Josiah's boundless enthusiasms in productive directions.[79]

At the time they met, Bentley was thirty-two, about the same age as Wedgwood. The son of a Derbyshire gentleman, Bentley was classically educated. He was also well traveled and solidly established as a leading local merchant. A member of the Liverpool Philosophical Club, he had helped found the Public Library and the Nonconformist Academy.[80] Bentley was active in the movement to abolish slavery in England and its colonies. His mercantile and intellectual contacts spanned the Atlantic world. He was friends with the chemist Joseph Priestley, and when Benjamin Franklin was in Britain in the 1760s, he spent time with Bentley.[81]

Wedgwood and Bentley liked each other immediately. They sat up late night after night, smoking their pipes, discussing religion, commerce, art, chemistry, and poetry. As soon as Josiah was well enough, Bentley introduced him to some of his own circle of friends: the scientist Priestley, the portrait painters Chubbard and Caddick, the well-known watchmaker John Wyke, and other artistic and commercial men. After eight weeks' convalescence for his bad knee, Wedgwood was finally ready to go home. Back in Burslem, he wrote Bentley a lengthy letter, the first installment in what became a rich correspondence that spanned eighteen years and covered a variety of subjects. National politics, romance, pottery prices, the latest London plays, Wedgwood's weight, all were fair game.

Like Wedgwood, Bentley was an active supporter of additional turnpikes and canals for the economic development of Britain. In the second half of the eighteenth century, Parliament approved hundreds of miles of turnpike construction, much of it initiated and funded regionally by local businessmen.[82] During the 1760s, Wedgwood lobbied aristocrats and politicians for road construction between Burslem and the ports of Chester and Liverpool. He himself invested heavily in several turnpike trusts, and he urged his brother John to do so as well: "We have another Turnpike broke out amongst us here betwixt Leek and Newcastle," he wrote. (Leek is seven miles northeast of Burslem.) Wedgwood said that "£2000 is wanting for this road" and that he had subscribed £500, intending that John would put up two or three hundred of it.[83]

At the same time, Wedgwood and Bentley began recruiting political and financial support for a canal that would link the port cities of Liverpool and Hull with the Staffordshire potteries. The Trent-Mersey canal, as the proposed waterway was to become known, was part of a large system of canals that would connect the four major rivers of England: the Trent, Mersey, Thames, and Severn. To increase public support for the project, Bentley published a pamphlet that set out the case for the new canal in which he argued that the waterway would decrease travel time and carriage costs, encourage new and existing manufactures, and raise property values along the proposed route.[84] Wedgwood traveled across the Midlands drumming up commercial support for the canal.[85] On July 26, 1766, after more than six months of lobbying and negotiation among business interests and politicians, Josiah cut the first sod of earth on the Trent-Mersey canal. From this time on, politics became yet another of Wedgwood's passions, and somehow in the midst of twelve-hour workdays he made room for it.

Marriage had broadened his world still further. In 1764, he wed his distant cousin Sarah Wedgwood, the daughter of a wealthy cheese maker from Cheshire.[86] Four years younger than Josiah, she was a kind, practical, and spirited woman, devoted to her husband and, later, their eight children. (In 1796, the Wedgwoods' eldest child, Susannah, married the son of scientist Erasmus Darwin, Robert. Their child [Wedgwood's grandson], Charles Darwin, was born in 1809. When Charles Darwin was thirty, he married his first cousin, Emma Wedgwood, the daughter of Josiah II and granddaughter of Josiah Wedgwood. The Wedgwood family fortune then helped underwrite Darwin's famous voyage aboard the *Beagle,* which comprised a critical part of his research for *The Origin of Species.*)[87]

The marriage between Josiah and Sarah seems to have been a harmonious, satisfying partnership.[88] She helped with his experimental work, discussed commercial finances, and advised him on pottery design, helping him to anticipate what women buyers wanted. Sarah suggested, for example, that he decorate the lids of transfer-printed teapots and sugar bowls, which had previously been plain.[89] "I speak from experience in Female taste," Josiah told Bentley, "without which I should have made but a poor figure amongst my Potts, not one of which, of any consequence, is finished without the approbation of my Sally."[90]

Sally Wedgwood and Thomas Bentley were both involved in Josiah's most significant expansion plans. By early 1765, sales of useful ware were booming, and it was clear that the business was outgrowing the Brick House facilities in Burslem. In 1769, Wedgwood sold about £7,000 of tableware and other useful goods (approximately $700,000 today).[91] The market for vases, cameos, and other ornamental ware seemed promising. Creamware exports were climbing, helped significantly by Bentley's work as a wholesale agent. Table 2-3 shows the statistics for the ornamental ware part of the business as it developed in the late 1760s and early 1770s.

In 1766, Josiah paid £3,000 ($225,000 today) for 350 acres located close to Burslem and in the path of the projected Trent-Mersey canal. Construction began immediately on the factory and a nearby mansion for Josiah and Sally.[92] Wedgwood named the factory and estate "Etruria" after the region in central Italy where beautiful ancient pottery was then being excavated.[93] At the same time, Josiah took his cousin Thomas Wedgwood into partnership to oversee production of all useful ware manufacture. This partnership allowed Josiah to concentrate on market expansion and his experiments, including the search for a new clay body for ornamental ware.[94]

TABLE 2-3

Profit and Turnover, Wedgwood Ornamental Ware, 1769–1775
(pounds sterling)

Fiscal Year	Goods Sold	Expenses of Manufacturing and Selling	Goods on Hand at End of Year	Profit[a]
Aug. 1769–Aug. 1770	2,404	1,921	3,164	2,561
Aug. 1770–Aug. 1771	3,955	2,372	4,411	2,830
Aug. 1771–Aug. 1772	4,838	2,924	8,187	5,691
Aug. 1772–Aug. 1773	4,244	2,303	9,069	2,823
Aug. 1773–Aug. 1774	6,168	2,937	10,144	4,307
Aug. 1774–Dec. 1774	2,065	946	10,261	1,235
Jan. 1775–Dec. 1775	6,481	3,804	11,190	3,545

Source: Financial Accounts, 1775, W/M 1713, Moseley Collection, Wedgwood Manuscripts, Keele University Library.

a. Profit figures also reflect receivables collected—often after a long lag—in a particular year, but do not capture carrying costs on inventory.

In 1765, Wedgwood had opened an office in a small wholesale warehouse in London. Three years later, he began looking for showroom space there. He envisioned a distinct selling environment from that found in many other shops. Most eighteenth-century merchants did not devote great time or money to displaying goods. Many had no cupboards or shelves, and goods were often heaped in back rooms and attics, then brought out for interested customers.[95] Wedgwood, by contrast, wanted facilities for retailing as well as premises large enough to show various table and dessert services completely set out. Such displays, as he wrote Bentley, would both attract and entertain female consumers:

> Six or eight at least such services are absolutely necessary to be shewn in order to *do the needful* with the Ladys in the neatest, genteelest & best method. The same, or indeed a much greater variety of setts of Vases should decorate the Walls, & both these articles may, every few days, be so alter'd, revers'd, & transform'd as to render the whole a new scene, even to the same Company, every time they shall bring their friends to visit us. I need not tell you the many good effects this must produce, when business & amusement can be made to go hand in hand. Every new show, Exhibition, or rarity soon grows stale in London, & is no longer regarded after the first sight, unless utility, or some such variety . . . continue to recommend it to their notice.[96]

In March 1768, Wedgwood found the space he wanted. Over the next few years, he moved his showrooms to premises in nearby Portland House and opened additional selling space in Bath and Dublin. Wedgwood proposed to pay his salespeople in the showrooms on commission. As he pointed out to Bentley, this compensation scheme would help ensure that stock was not wasted, that business was conducted at "a moderate expence," and that "as great a quantity of goods as possible" was sold.[97]

Expansion plans were interrupted in May 1768 when Wedgwood's right knee collapsed, a serious recurrence of the old ailment. Erasmus Darwin and others recommended amputation, which was a fairly common procedure at that time. The operation was performed in Wedgwood's home without anesthetic, while Josiah remained conscious. Although he had frequently been depressed at the onset of one of his psychosomatic illnesses, he was stoic and resilient during this operation and recovery. Within three weeks, he was directing his business from bed and reporting to Bentley on his recuperation: "I am well even beyond my most sanguine expectations, my leg is allmost healed, the wound is not quite 2 inches by one & ½, I measur'd it with the compasses this morning when I dress'd it."[98] Soon he was fitted with a wooden leg, joking that next year he planned to throw a party to celebrate St. Amputation Day.[99]

The Etruria factory was completed in mid-1769, the same year that Bentley officially became Wedgwood's partner in the production of ornamental ware.[100] At the heart of the factory's organization was Wedgwood's insistence on specialized manufacture based on a carefully planned division of labor.[101] He was certain that the "same hands cannot make fine & coarse—expensive and cheap articles so as to turn to any good account to the Master."[102] He thus separated the production of useful ware from that of vases and other ornamental ware, allocating workshops and kilns to each. The shops were arranged in sequence in order to provide an efficient production line and to avoid unnecessary movement of workers or goods.[103]

The shops for both useful and ornamental ware incorporated the latest technology, including the engine-turning lathe, which used eccentric or elliptical motion to produce uniform, vertical fluting and other patterns on the pottery. Wedgwood's first engine-turning lathes were modeled on those he had seen in a Birmingham foundry and were built to his specifications for use in earthenware manufacture.[104] In 1782, Josiah installed a steam engine, manufactured by the nationally famous foundry, Boulton & Watt, to grind flint and colors. When a French industrial spy visited Etruria in the mid-1780s, he described the factory and village of workmen's cottages as a small town unto itself, "a marvel of organization."[105]

Marketing

By the early 1760s, when the popularity of Wedgwood china was surging, the market for Staffordshire pottery was rapidly becoming a national one. Finished goods traveled by horse, ship, and canal barge to dealers in Newcastle, Yarmouth, Liverpool, Bath, and Bristol. Useful ware and small quantities of ornamental goods were sold in Leeds, which was a hub for cotton textile production, Birmingham, and other industrial areas. But the overwhelming bulk of all pottery was sent directly to London, where large wholesale dealers bought earthenware in growing quantities, primarily for distribution to small retailers.[106] From Liverpool and Bristol, merchants shipped Staffordshire pottery to continental Europe and increasingly to America and the West Indies.[107]

Pottery exports reflected the broad outlines of British commerce. Throughout the eighteenth century, and especially after 1750, international trade became ever more important. Total imports into Britain climbed by 500 percent between 1700 and 1800, reexports (commodities imported into Britain and then exported) by 250 percent, and exports by more than 560 percent.[108] The composition of this trade reflected the economic transformation under way. Agricultural goods fell markedly as a fraction of exports, and by 1750, Britain had become a net importer of grains.[109] By contrast, manufactured exports, including woolens, metalwares, glass, cottons, and pottery, grew sixfold over the course of the century.[110] In 1700, over 80 percent of Britain's exports had gone to Europe. Seventy years later, European customers purchased only 30 percent of Britain's exports, while colonists on the North American mainland and in the West Indies took almost half. The remainder of exportable goods went to India, Ireland, and the Far East.[111]

Wedgwood was keen to sell his creamware internationally. By 1769, he could hardly contain his excitement about France's market potential: "Do you really think that we may make a *complete conquest* of France? Conquer France in Burslem? My blood moves quicker, I feel my strength increase for the contest."[112] Two years later, as domestic sales became sluggish and as stock piled up, Wedgwood concluded that "nothing but a *foreign market*" would ever keep the stock "within any tolerable bound."[113] His production had now grown so efficient that he needed new outlets. "Every *Gentle & Decent* push," he wrote, "should be made to have our things *seen & sold* at Foreign Markets."[114]

Toward this end, in 1771 Josiah sent unsolicited parcels of his pottery to 1,000 members of the German aristocracy and nobility. Each package cost about £20 and was accompanied by a circular letter advertising his products . . . and an invoice. This strategy was one of the earliest recorded examples of "inertia selling," that is, marketing to selected customers by shipping them unsolicited goods and offering them the opportunity either to purchase the items at set prices or return them to the manufacturer at no cost to themselves. It was a precursor of the practice of modern book and music clubs. Wedgwood's plan cost £20,000 ($1.8 million today) and involved significant financial risk.[115] But, as he remarked, "We know that nothing great can be done without some risque, nor is there any *absolute certainty* in trade."[116] It was a successful gamble, as a majority of the selected customers purchased Wedgwood's goods.[117]

In the mid-1760s, however, Wedgwood's primary focus was still the domestic market. He sought a buoyant, growing demand for his useful pieces. Many of these products were new. Others had been available for years. How was one to create and sustain customer interest in the wares of a particular workshop or firm? What kind of competitive advantage could a company construct with customers when other suppliers were producing similar goods?

He had few precedents to follow in creating and sustaining customer loyalty. One of his responses to the challenge was to build his brand systematically. Brand marketing was virtually unheard of in the mid-eighteenth century. Only a handful of luxury goods, such as Chippendale furniture or Meissen porcelain, were known by their manufacturers' names. Until about 1770, most potters did not mark their products. The few earthenware and porcelain manufacturers that did, such as the Chelsea porcelain factory, generally used signs, symbols, or the location of the factory as identifying marks. Wedgwood changed this practice in the late 1760s by impressing his own name in the unfired clay. His works were thus much less vulnerable to forgery than those of other makers, and, as Josiah understood, every piece advertised the Wedgwood name.[118] By 1772, everything made at Wedgwood's pottery, useful or ornamental, carried his name.[119]

Josiah realized that many Britons now had more money to spend on nonessential or luxury goods than had their counterparts in previous generations.[120] He also understood that much of this spending was directed toward social emulation. Eighteenth-century Britons, like modern consumers all over the world, tended to put their money where their aspirations were. They spent as the rich did, or at least as the income class directly above them did. In 1767, the English political economist Nathaniel Forster bemoaned "the perpetual restless ambition in each of the inferior ranks to raise themselves to the level of those immediately above them," causing "fashionable luxury" to spread "like a contagion."[121]

Even so, there was not much movement toward economic parity. Although average per capita income increased almost 30 percent during the eighteenth century, the Industrial Revolution did not distribute this income equally.[122] In 1688, the wealthiest 10 percent of Britons had received 44 percent of total income. By 1801, this group received 53 percent. At the same time, the fraction of income that went to the bottom 40 percent of the population held steady at between 10 and 11 percent.[123] But, as the U.S. experience in the 1980s and 1990s demonstrated, rising equality is not a necessary condition of the habit of emulative spending. The two may even be inversely correlated.

Josiah Wedgwood could not measure income distribution with any precision in the 1760s. He did not need to. He knew that the middling ranks wanted to ape their social betters, and he planned his sales strategy accordingly. In 1763, he presented George III's wife, Queen Charlotte, with a breakfast set of his finest creamware. Two years later, he produced a tea set for her, a sale that resulted in his appointment as "Potter to Her Majesty." His creamware quickly became known as Queensware. A young entrepreneur (he was thirty-five at the time) could hardly have hoped for more. In Josiah's eyes, nobility, aristocrats, and to a lesser extent the gentry were the principal conductors of fashion diffusion. By the late 1760s, Josiah had opened an office and showrooms in London to serve his growing clientele. In 1770, he instructed Bentley to scan the English peerage for additional "lines, channels and connections."[124] These groups, he noted, were the "legislators in taste."[125]

Josiah actively sought aristocratic and noble commissions and the explicit and implicit endorsements that accompanied these sales.[126] Like sportswear and cosmetics manufacturers today, Josiah understood the value of celebrity sanction. He worked hard to obtain it, absorbing significant costs in time and money in order to produce highly specialized individual commissions. While other potters avoided such orders, Wedgwood actively sought them.[127]

Once he had completed an aristocratic sale, Josiah lost no time in advertising it to a much larger, more profitable market. As he wrote his partner about the growing market for Wedgwood vases, "The Great People have had their Vases in their Palaces long enough for them to be seen and admired by the Middling Class of People, which Class we know are vastly, I had almost said, infinitely superior in number to the Great."[128] Wedgwood took out ads in London newspapers to celebrate his royal patronage. His company catalogues emphasized upscale potential at reasonable prices. His traveling salesmen carried samples of goods endorsed by aristocrats along with a sales manual of sorts, with specific marketing and collection guidelines.[129]

Specific Wedgwood pieces were named for members of the nobility. In 1779, Josiah suggested calling a set of flowerpots after the Duchess of Devonshire. These and other techniques, he said, "complete our notoriety to the whole Island" and help greatly in the sale of goods both useful and ornamental, by showing that "we are employ'd in a much higher scale than other Manufacturers."[130] Competitors, such as John Turner, Humphrey Palmer, and others followed Wedgwood's marketing lead. These manufacturers used newspaper advertising and urban showrooms to sell their wares. Some sought aristocratic endorsements. But none deployed a marketing strategy that rivaled the scope, effectiveness, and sustainability of Wedgwood's.

The middling-class customers were to be won with quality and fashionability, rather than low prices.[131] From the mid-1760s on, Wedgwood priced his most successful useful line, Queensware, as much as 75 to 100 percent higher than competing products from other potteries.[132] His entire line of useful ware was more expensive than those of rivals. In 1770, for example, the wholesale price for a top-quality Wedgwood dinner plate was 8 pence (about $27 today).[133] By contrast, other Staffordshire potters priced their best table plates at 2 pence each.[134]

Josiah was willing to reduce prices when the spread between his and competitors' prices became too great or when he wanted to expand sales of a product already popularized at a high price.[135] But he generally kept his prices noticeably above the industry average. "*Low prices,*" he wrote Bentley in 1772, "must beget a *low quality* in the manufacture, which will beget *contempt,* which will beget *neglect, & disuse,* and there is an end of the trade." But if any one manufacturer will continue to keep up the quality of its manufacture, or improve it, "that House may perhaps keep up its prices." In such a case, an economic downturn "will work a *particular good* to that house," for it "may continue to sell *Queensware at the usual prices* when the rest of the trade can scarcely give it away."[136] When Josiah thought that demand for one of his products was becoming saturated, he discontinued it, and reintroduced it only when he thought the market was once more ripe.

In exchange for the premium they paid, Wedgwood's customers received free shipping anywhere in England and compensation for damage that occurred in transport. They also received a satisfaction-or-money-back guarantee, the first recorded example of such product support.[137]

Josiah's marketing strategy toward international outlets was similar to his domestic strategy. He paid special attention to British ambassadors and their wives, who were likely to be moved from one European capital city to another. He courted aristocrats, nobility, and gentry in France, Germany, Turkey, Portugal, Italy, and even China.[138] Wedgwood's expanded show-rooms displayed wares ordered by the crowned heads of Europe. The order from Catherine the Great for a 952-piece set of Wedgwood china, so impressively displayed to Londoners in 1774, was a conspicuous example. He charged premium prices for what was fast becoming some of the most fashionable china in the world. When the political economist Arthur Young visited the Wedgwood factory and other Staffordshire potteries in 1771, he noted that "some of the finest sort went to France" and that large quantities of creamware were sent to Ireland, Germany, Holland, Russia, Spain, the British colonies in the East Indies, and "much to America."[139] By 1783, Wedgwood was exporting almost 80 percent of his total production of ornamental and useful ware.[140]

Organizing the Workforce

The organization of work at Etruria and other late-eighteenth-century factories imposed new standards on craftsmen and laborers.[141] They were required to be punctual. They had to appear every day, six days a week, at the same time. They had to labor until the clock or the bell tolled. These rhythms contrasted sharply with those imposed by the sun and seasons or the requirements of a specific task, all of which determined the nature and pace of agricultural labor. Factory work was also much more routinized than that of preindustrial enterprise, which alternated between bouts of intense effort and idleness, like modern student life.[142]

Wedgwood devised several schemes to increase his craftsmen's and laborers' punctuality and attendance. From his days at the Brick House, he had used a bell to summon workmen. According to his instructions, the bell was to be rung at 5:45 in the morning or a quarter of an hour before the men could see to take up their jobs; then at 8:30 for breakfast, at 9 to recall workers from the meal, at noon for dinner, at 12:30 to return to their tasks, and on until "the last bell when they can no longer see."[143] Josiah also hired a Clerk of the Manufactory, who was to arrive at Etruria before anyone else. The clerk's job was to

> settle the people to their business as they come in—to encourage those who come regularly to their time, letting them know that their regularity is properly noticed. . . . Those who come later than the hour appointed should be noticed, and if after repeated marks of disapprobation they do not come in due time, an account of the time they are deficient in should be taken, & so much of their wages stopt as the time comes to.[144]

To keep track of his workers' time, Wedgwood devised a primitive clocking-in system, the first in the history of business. He described it in precise terms. To save the trouble of the porters going round, tickets were printed with the names of all the workers. Each person took two of these tickets with him when he left work every evening. He delivered one of them into a box when he went through the lodge the next morning, and the other when he returned from dinner. The porter then "looks over these tickets only; & if he finds any deficiency, goes to such places only where the defiance appears. If the persons have neglected or refused to deliver their tickets on going through, they are to be admonished the first time, the second time to pay a small fine to the poors box."[145] By the end of the eighteenth century, this innovative system had given way to the kind of punch clock that is still in wide use today throughout the world.[146]

The overarching authority of the clock was not the only novel aspect of industrialization. Factory work also demanded precision, avoidance of waste, and obedience to an evolving managerial hierarchy. The challenge, according to Josiah, was to "make such *Machines* of the *Men* as cannot Err."[147] Early-eighteenth-century potters had worked by rule of thumb under dirty, inefficient, and arbitrary conditions. The mess and waste were natural companions to the craft.[148]

To encourage cleanliness and careful working habits, Wedgwood issued a detailed set of "Potters' Instructions" and "Rules and Regulations." The clerk or overseer in each workshop, plus the five to ten general managers, such as the Clerk of the Manufactory and the Clerk of Weights and Measures, received guidelines encompassing almost every aspect of the manufacturing process and of factory discipline. The regulations prohibited workers from carrying ale or liquor into the manufactory, scaling the gates, writing obscene or other language on the walls, playing games, and "striking or otherwise abusing an overlooker."[149] Most of these offenses carried stiff financial penalties.[150] Striking a manager resulted in instant dismissal.

In addition to disciplining all his workers to function effectively under the new regime, Josiah had to find the skilled artists and craftsmen essential to the production of useful and, especially, ornamental ware. To do this, he decided to train his artists rather than rely on workers from outside. The task, he wrote Bentley, was to make artists of "mere men."[151] It made no sense to rely on the local labor market because

> few hands can be got to paint flowers in the style we want them. I may add, nor any other work we do. *We must make them.* There is no other way. We have stepped forward beyond the other Manufacturers & we must be content to train up hands to suit our purpose.[152]

Although Wedgwood instituted policies to retrain existing hands, he was much more successful working with new hires. In the early 1770s, he established a drawing and modeling school for his apprentices. Eventually more than a quarter of the firm's total of 290 workers in the early 1790s were apprentices. About 10 percent of these young artists and potters were women—a large proportion relative to other earthenware manufacturers.[153]

Product Management and Finance

By the time Etruria was in full operation, Wedgwood & Bentley had become as renowned for ornamental ware as for Queensware. In 1772, Josiah reported that the firm was producing "upwards of 100 Good Forms of Vases," many of which were manufactured with interchangeable handles and ornaments.[154]

He and Bentley always monitored their product lines carefully, at times restricting output of various styles to keep them relatively scarce and thus more desirable. The designs were mostly derivative, drawn from a range of contemporary sources on classical and ancient pottery. Wedgwood modeled his Etruscan vases, in which red wax-based paint was applied to black basalt, on the extensive collection of ancient Egyptian, Roman, and Greek vases owned by Britain's ambassador to the Court of Naples, Sir William Hamilton.[155]

Although Wedgwood & Bentley produced library busts, decorative candlesticks, portrait medallions, and cameos, the firm's most popular ornamental products were vases. In 1769, these vases were suddenly in great demand. Wedgwood noted that at the London showrooms there was "no getting to the door for Coaches, nor into the rooms for Ladies & Gentlemen. . . . Vases was all the cry. We must endeavor to gratify this *universal passion.*"[156] A visitor to Etruria described a similar "violent *Vase madness*" breaking out in Ireland.[157]

The surge in demand took the firm by surprise. Writing from London in late spring 1769, Wedgwood told Bentley to assign all "hands that can be spared" to vase production and ordered a large number in two different styles. He said he could sell £1,000 worth of such vases ($98,000 today).[158] That order was filled within two months, but the firm still could not keep pace with the demand from London. To speed production, Wedgwood simplified decoration processes and ordered some vases to be finished by the firm's engine-powered lathes rather than by hand. But unmet orders continued to pile up:

> Strange as it may sound [Wedgwood wrote Bentley] I should be glad never to receive another order for *any particular kind* of Vases, & I should wish you to avoid taking such orders as much as you *decently* can, at least till we are got into a more methodical way of making *the same sorts over again,* & there is no other way of doing this but by having models & moulds of every shape & size we make.[159]

By late 1769, Wedgwood & Bentley had significant cash-flow problems. The firm was spending larger-than-anticipated sums on raw materials, wages, and other costs, without collecting its bills fast enough to finance expanded production.[160] Wedgwood urged Bentley "Collect. Collect," and "set all your hands & heads to work."[161] At the end of the year, despite having manufactured more than £12,000 worth of pottery in 1769 (almost $1.2 million today), the firm had debts totaling £4,000 (about $400,000 today) in addition to weekly wage costs of £100 ($9,800). Wedgwood complained of being "poor as a Church mouse."[162]

His response to this crisis was to initiate a thorough analysis of the firm's cost structure for vase production. This effort resulted in the preparation of Wedgwood's Price Book of Workmanship, which included "every expence of Vase making," from the crude materials to the retail counter in London, for each sort of vase.[163]

For Wedgwood, the most important discovery of his analysis was the distinction between fixed and variable costs. He advised Bentley to notice how large a share of the cost of manufacturing was borne by modeling and molds, rent, fuel, and bookkeepers' wages. "Consider," the potter said, "that these expences move like clockwork, & are much the same whether the quantity of goods made be large or small." Thus, said Josiah, "you will see the vast consequence in most manufactures of *making the greatest quantity possible in a given time.*"[164]

In this context, he revised his earlier policy of actively soliciting special commissions. Such orders often involved high labor and materials costs for a small one-time increase in output. He cautioned Bentley to avoid made-to-order sales unless they had significant marketing value, such as the huge sale to Catherine the Great in 1774.[165] Wedgwood also lengthened production runs for certain ornamental wares, reduced stocks in market downturns, and kept careful tabs on sales and marketing costs.

Wedgwood and Capitalism

By the mid-1770s, Josiah Wedgwood and his partners, Thomas Bentley and Thomas Wedgwood, were the preeminent British pottery manufacturers. They were market leaders at home and important players in outlets abroad. Josiah's mounting commercial success reinforced his ardent belief in the logic and integrity of industrial capitalism. In 1783, he published his views on this subject in a short pamphlet, *An Address to the Young Inhabitants of the Pottery,* excerpts of which follow:

> I would request you to ask your parents for a description of the country we inhabit when they first knew it; and they will tell you, that the inhabitants bore all signs of poverty to a much greater degree than they do now. Their houses were miserable huts; the lands [were] poorly cultivated and . . . yielded little of value for the food of man or beast. . . .
>
> Compare this picture, which I know to be a true one, with the present state of the same country. The workingmen earning nearly

> double their former wages—their houses mostly new and comfortable, and the lands, roads and every other circumstance bearing evident marks of the most pleasing and rapid improvements. From whence, and from what cause has this happy change taken place? You will be beforehand with me in acknowledging a truth too evident to be denied by any one. Industry has been the parent of this happy change—A well directed and long continued series of industrious exertions, both in masters and servants, has so changed for the better the face of our country, its buildings, lands, roads, and notwithstanding the present unfavourable appearances, I must say the manners and deportment of its inhabitants too, as to attract the notice and admiration of countries which had scarcely heard of us before; and how far these improvements may still be carried by the same laudable means which have brought us thus far, has been one of the most pleasing contemplations of my life.[166]

Josiah's workforce did not always share his unabashed faith in industrial capitalism. Many workers resented the enforced specialization of the factory system. Others found the training tedious and the rules of behavior overly restrictive. Some refused to take orders from factory foremen. Almost all workers resented their own dependence on the ebb and flow of market forces. These and other grievances led workers into confrontations with Wedgwood on several occasions between 1769 and 1790, when Josiah withdrew from active management of the business. In 1782 and 1789, Etruria workers staged demonstrations.[167]

These uprisings always surprised Josiah. He considered himself a benevolent employer. He supplied housing for his workers and subsidized a sick club, a kind of primitive health insurance. The factory he had developed was the first standardized production system to be applied to pottery. He wanted to use his organizational, production, and marketing innovations not only to increase profits, but to achieve what he called "constant employment" for his workforce and capital equipment.[168] In return for these efforts on the workers' behalf, Josiah expected loyalty, punctuality, and consistently high performance. To the end of his life, Josiah could not understand why many of his workers were less than content with the social contract he had established at Etruria.

Conclusion

Josiah died in 1795, leaving a fortune estimated at £500,000 (about $30 million today).[169] The business, which had been incorporated in 1790 as Josiah Wedgwood & Sons, passed to his second son, Josiah II, and his nephew, Thomas Byerly. Neither proved equal to the task of running the firm efficiently. Production standards declined. The company's financial condition deteriorated. Market conditions worsened as the Napoleonic Wars dragged on and Continental markets were frequently unavailable. But sales remained relatively robust, climbing to over £43,000 in 1810 ($2.5 million today). Under often-reluctant family management, the firm survived the nineteenth century, although revenues rarely exceeded their 1810 level.

In 1903, U.S. President Theodore Roosevelt commissioned a 1,300-piece dinner service for the White House, which was made in the Etruria factory. In 1940, production was moved to new, larger premises in nearby Barlaston, where it is still located today. In 1986, Waterford Crystal acquired Josiah Wedgwood & Sons, which continued to produce china in the Barlaston factory under the Wedgwood name.

Modern china manufacture is a blend of state-of-the-art technology, including robotics, and craft skills, some of which are virtually unchanged since the eighteenth century. At the end of the twentieth century, about 1,400 craftspeople worked in the Wedgwood Group factories in Stoke-on-Trent. In 1999, Waterford Wedgwood PLC earned operating profits of 82.9 million euros ($70 million) on sales of 879.6 million euros ($746 million). The premium brand that Josiah Wedgwood had helped to create 240 years earlier continued to command widespread consumer recognition and loyalty in china, housewares, and giftware markets around the world, symbolizing quality and fashionable elegance.

Preview to Chapter 3: H. J. Heinz

THE PRECEDING CHAPTER analyzed how Josiah Wedgwood made a market for fine china in the midst of the First Industrial Revolution in Britain. More than 100 years after Wedgwood founded his company in 1760, entrepreneurs in the United States encountered even more challenging potential markets of all kinds. The United States was, of course, a much larger country. Then, too, beginning in the mid-nineteenth century, a range of supply-side innovations, including improved transportation, communication, and technological developments, greatly expanded the productive capacity of the U.S. economy. These innovations helped transform the production and distribution of countless goods and services, creating a host of new industries.

At the same time, rising incomes, population growth, and urbanization were changing the demand side of the economy, affecting the wants and needs of consumers. These developments, taken together with those on the supply side, irrevocably altered the very nature of the American economy, ushering in widespread industrialization, national markets of unprecedented size, and mass consumption on an entirely new scale. Scholars often refer to the period between about 1850 and 1930 as the "Transportation and Communication Revolution" or the "Second Industrial Revolution." These labels, in themselves, speak to the far-reaching nature of the changes.

Henry Heinz (1844–1919), living in the rapidly growing city of Pittsburgh, recognized that intensified socioeconomic transition afforded vital opportunities to create a new mass market for the kinds of processed vegetable foods that he had been experimenting with since he was a boy. He understood that this objective entailed a number of significant supply-side initiatives, including using new technology effectively and constructing a specific set of organizational capabilities.

But this, he realized, was not enough. To develop new outlets for his goods, Heinz would also have to think hard about the demand side of the economy. With remarkable insight, he began to recognize that increasing incomes, urban expansion, and women's shifting roles presented new strategic possibilities. His subsequent success in manufacturing, branding, and distributing bottled and canned goods, many of which consumers had previously prepared in their own kitchens, helped create a mass market for processed foods—and in Heinz's case, one of the largest companies in the industry.

Henry Heinz was one of thousands of entrepreneurs who entered the food processing business in the late-nineteenth century. Most ventures were small-scale operations located in agricultural regions and focused on canning corn, tomatoes, and other produce. Some companies specialized in preserved meats, such as corned beef and, after the development of refrigerated railroad cars in 1875, in meatpacking—shipping freshly dressed meat by rail to distant markets. The vast majority of these early food manufacturers did not succeed. But a few, such as Joseph Campbell, Gail Borden, Arthur and Charles Libby, Gustavus Swift, Philip Armour, and Henry Heinz, defied the odds. They translated initial victories in their young industries into sustained competitive advantage for their organizations—and their names became well-known national brands.

The story of Henry Heinz epitomizes their success, but it is important to remember that most ventures by most businesspeople (of that time or any other) do not necessarily prosper. And even those that do often undergo traumatic struggles, as we shall see in the roller-coaster career of Heinz himself.

CHAPTER 3

H. J. Heinz, 1844-1919

Prologue: The 1893 Columbian Exposition

On May 1, 1893, the World's Columbian Exposition opened in Chicago with great fanfare. Held to commemorate the four hundredth anniversary of Columbus's voyage to America, the Exposition promised to be the most extravagant and memorable world's fair ever held on U.S. soil.[1] Although it included exhibitions from around the globe, the fair was organized to celebrate the unprecedented achievements of American civilization.[2] These accomplishments were not lost on most fairgoers, even in the face of the depression plaguing the national economy in 1893.[3] With characteristic irony, the philosopher William James captured popular perceptions of the event: "Everyone says one ought to sell all one has and mortgage one's soul to go to [the Chicago Exposition], it is esteemed such a revelation of beauty. People cast away all sin and baseness, burst into tears and grow religious, etc. under its influence!"[4]

Sprawling across almost two square miles in Jackson Park on Chicago's South Side, the exhibition grounds and buildings were laid out by Daniel Burnham, Richard Morris Hunt, Charles McKim, Stanford White, and other renowned architects. Frederick Law Olmsted designed the lagoons around which the Exposition's 400 buildings were erected. The main structures—the Transportation Building, Machinery Hall, Manufacturers, as well as the Women's Horticultural, Art, and Agricultural Buildings—were planned to represent the major categories of human knowledge. Other exhibits included the Blue Grotto of Capri, Lapland Village, and life-sized models of the *Niña*, the *Pinta*, and the *Santa Maria*. More than thirty-five countries and forty states, one contemporary guidebook reported, helped "transform a wilderness into a garden of palaces" by contributing inventions, prizes, and other testaments to man's accomplishments.[5] Over five months, more than 27 million people, a daily average of over 175,000, crowded onto the grounds to experience the wonder and bewilderment of the Exposition.[6]

A few visitors, such as the historian Henry Adams, puzzled over the larger meaning of the fair. What did all the progress on display portend and how was it to be understood?[7] After more than two weeks on the grounds, he concluded that "the Exposition itself defied philosophy. . . . Since Noah's ark, no such Babel of loose and ill-joined, such vague and ill-defined and unrelated thoughts and half-thoughts and experimental outcries as the Exposition, had ever ruffled the surface of the [Great] Lakes."[8] Adams was deeply troubled by the potential implications of this incongruity. "Chicago," he wrote, "asked in 1893 for the first time the question whether the American people knew where they were driving."[9]

Henry Heinz entertained none of this uncertainty as he walked around the Exposition grounds. The fair, he asserted, was a "wonderland and a great educator."[10] The 48-year-old entrepreneur from Pittsburgh had come to the Exposition to expand national awareness of his company's brand and products. His assigned exhibition space on the second or gallery level of the Agricultural Building was the largest allotted to any U.S. food manufacturer, and Heinz had taken out a bank loan to finance it.[11] Surrounded by the displays of Knox Gelatin, Schlitz Brewery, American Cereal, Swift meats, and other producers, the Heinz exhibit was a "magnificent pavilion of antique oak, hand carved and oil polished," according to the Rand McNally guidebook to the fair. "At each end of the four corners is a small pagoda," the guidebook continued. "These are tenanted by beautiful girls—one French, one English, one German, and one Spanish."[12] From this pavilion, as many as ten Heinz employees dispensed samples of all company products: pickles, ketchup, relish, horseradish, celery sauce, mustard, and more.

During the opening days of the fair, hordes of visitors streamed through the main level of the Agricultural Building. But few ventured up to the gallery level, where Heinz and the other U.S. food manufacturers' exhibits were located. After watching this disappointing traffic flow for several hours one morning, Henry Heinz devised a solution. He arranged to have tens of thousands of small tickets printed and dropped around the fair grounds. Resembling a baggage check card, each ticket promised the bearer a free souvenir at the Heinz exhibit.

This tactic paid off. Over the next five months, more than a million people stopped at the company's exhibit to claim their souvenir: a pickle-shaped charm with the Heinz name stamped on one side. Chicago police regulated crowd control until the gallery floors could be strengthened to support the unexpected weight.[13] In haste to find the Heinz exhibit, many visitors no longer lingered on the main floor of the Agricultural Building, where foreign food manufacturers—Lea & Perrins, Crosse & Blackwell, and others—had display space. Some of these producers charged Heinz with unfair competition. But the other U.S. food exhibitors were grateful for the crowds that filled the gallery level. At the close of the fair, they hosted a dinner in Henry's honor, presenting him with an inscribed silver loving cup.

For Heinz and the business he had founded, the World's Columbian Exposition had been a marketing tour de force that promised to extend the company's leadership in the young, booming market for processed foods. Huge numbers of potential customers had been exposed firsthand to the Heinz name and its products. The national recognition that the company's founder had been working to build for over ten years had been significantly enhanced. Thousands of men, women, and children who had not previously encountered the brand now associated pickles with Heinz.[14] Those that had sampled company products at the world's fair knew Heinz produced a wide range of condiments, jellies, and preserves similar to those many American women made at home. The exhibition had also augmented retailer interest in company products, strengthening the firm's influence in the rapidly expanding distribution channel for processed foods. All these advantages, Henry Heinz reasoned, would fuel more sales, already growing at a compound rate of 25 percent annually since the company's founding.[15] All in all, he had reason to be proud. But Heinz never allowed himself to take full stock of his business accomplishments, lest such success prove short-lived. His most prolific diary entry concerning the Exposition acknowledged the company exhibit as "a great hit. We hear it from all sources."[16]

It was altogether fitting that one of Henry Heinz's most important marketing triumphs unfolded at an event held to highlight the United States' newfound economic preeminence. Heinz was born and came of age at a critical moment in the development of American capitalism. He never made the time to write down an assessment of his work in a broader historical context. For such an ambitious entrepreneur, the opportunity cost of such analysis was simply too high. But he knew instinctively that he was living through unprecedented change and embraced most of what he saw.[17]

By the time of the world's fair, Heinz understood that his own business success was closely intertwined with the marvels of the Transportation and Communication Revolution. Over the course of his life (1844–1919), the agrarian origins of the U.S. economy gave way to widespread industrialization. Beginning in about 1850, technological and organizational innovations altered the production and distribution of many goods. In new industries, such as steel, telephony, and food processing, and traditional ones, such as tool and furniture production, output increased significantly.[18] Between 1870 and 1920, real gross national product (GNP) expanded more than five times. Measured on a per capita basis, it grew 250 percent.[19] Much of this output was produced for expanding markets, some of them national in scope.

At the same time, a host of transitions—demographic, social, and perceptual—was altering the demand side of the U.S. economy. Between 1860 and 1920, the country's population grew more than threefold, climbing from 31.5 million people to almost 107 million.[20] As the economy became more industrialized, increasing numbers of Americans depended on manufacturing, commerce, and service industries, rather than farming, for their livelihoods.[21] To secure jobs in the growing industrial and commercial sectors, people poured into cities: burgeoning young communities such as Pittsburgh and Chicago as well as older, established urban centers. When Henry Heinz was born, less than 10 percent of Americans lived in towns of 2,500 or more. Seventy-five years later, more than half lived in urban communities, and about one in five lived in cities of more than 250,000 residents.[22] In Chicago and other large towns, Americans encountered people, activity, and products they had not previously known. Their ideas about work, consumption, and the rhythms of daily life changed markedly.

What were households and companies to make of the expanded possibilities of industrialization? What did it mean to start a business when economic and social changes were affecting not only what manufacturers produced but also what consumers needed, wanted, and could afford? How were entrepreneurs to create markets for novel products manufactured in unprecedented quantities?

Henry Heinz understood that exploiting the tremendous supply-side developments of the Transportation and Communication Revolution entailed correspondingly large shifts on the demand side of the economy. To make the most of the opportunities in food processing, consumers across the country would have to be satisfied that all food need not be made at home, that pickles produced in a factory were a good alternative to those that housewives bottled each August. For Heinz to succeed, these same Americans would also need to have ready access to such new products and consistently choose to buy them. It was going to take substantial strategic and organizational innovation to change consumer perceptions and behavior in important, lasting ways.

Heinz devoted much of his life to meeting these challenges. By the time he died, the food processing industry he had helped create had revolutionized the nation's cooking and eating habits, transformed U.S. agriculture, and established itself as one of the country's most important.[23] The company he built became one of the largest and most successful food processors in the world, and it remains a leading global manufacturer in our time.

Laying the Foundations

When Heinz was growing up there was no national market for processed food. In the early nineteenth century, most households grew or made most of their food at home. What they could not produce themselves, they bought on a local or regional basis. Most of the foods that consumers purchased were commodities such as coffee, flour, spices, and rum. But some prepared foods were also exchanged. For example, many merchants carried horseradish and other locally produced foods that they had accumulated as customer payments.[24] Virtually all of these goods were undifferentiated within their respective categories. Consumers bought sugar, butter, crackers, and cocoa in bulk. They knew little beyond what the storekeeper told them about a given item's attributes or origins.

Henry Heinz was born on October 11, 1844, in Birmingham, Pennsylvania, a small industrial community near Pittsburgh. He was the eldest of eight surviving children of Anna and John Henry Heinz, both German immigrants.[25] The father, John Henry, came from a long line of once-prosperous farmers and vineyard owners in Bavaria.[26] By the early nineteenth century, the family lands had been subdivided into small tracts, and in 1840, John Henry sailed for America and wider opportunities. With other recent German immigrants, he settled in the raw, smoky town of

Birmingham, just south of Pittsburgh, which had a growing number of glassmaking factories. Here in 1843, he met and married Anna Schmitt, who had recently emigrated from Kruspis, a small village near Frankfurt, Germany.[27]

John Henry and Anna remained in Birmingham for the first seven years of their marriage.[28] When Henry was six, they moved their family to Sharpsburg, a German community of 1,400 inhabitants, six miles northeast of Pittsburgh. Sharpsburg encompassed rich farmland, young industry, and a stretch of the Main Line Canal linking western and eastern Pennsylvania. Like most of the new towns bordering the intersection of the Ohio, Monongahela, and Allegheny rivers, Sharpsburg's economy fed off that of Pittsburgh.

Pittsburgh, known as the "Iron City" or the "Birmingham of America" for its reliance on iron and metalware production, was booming in the 1840s and 1850s.[29] A fast-growing frontier town, it was becoming an industrial and commercial nexus between the eastern states and developing western lands.

Transportation improvements powered Pittsburgh's growth. By 1854, two railroads, the Pennsylvania and the Baltimore and Ohio, linked the city with Baltimore and Philadelphia to the east and Cleveland to the west. The region's three rivers connected it with other areas north and south as well as east and west. Raw materials such as coal, iron ore, and cotton entered the city, leaving it as manufactures: iron rails, glass, and cloth. In the middle of the century, Pittsburgh was producing more than $26 million annually in manufactured goods—about 3 percent of the nation's total.[30]

The region's growth and vigor impressed contemporary visitors. "Nowhere in the world is everybody so regularly and continually busy," observed one Frenchman. "There is no interruption of business for six days in the week, except during the three meals, the longest of which occupies hardly ten minutes."[31] A reporter for the *Atlantic Monthly* echoed these perceptions: "What energy, what a fury of industry! This surpasses Chicago. What would luxurious St. Louis say of such reckless devotion to business as this?"[32]

Employment possibilities in this thriving economy lured men and women from the eastern seaboard as well as the Old World. More than a third of Pittsburgh's residents in 1860 were immigrants who, like John Henry and Anna Heinz, came in search of a better life.[33] Some of the largest contingents of newcomers arrived from Ireland, Scotland, Germany,

Britain, and France.[34] As recent immigrants and other Americans moved inland from the seaboard, Pittsburgh's population climbed, from fewer than 5,000 in 1810 to more than 50,000 at the century's midpoint.[35]

The construction business in and around Pittsburgh was heady, and in 1850, John Henry Heinz purchased a brickyard in Sharpsburg. He was not particularly ambitious, but his business grew with the surrounding economy.[36] Within four years, John Henry could afford to design and build a small, two-story house on four acres of land near the town center. Here, Anna Heinz raised and fed a growing family, using some of the land for a large garden. She was a deeply religious, highly organized woman, who managed an immaculate household and expected strict obedience from her children. When Henry was born, she had resolved that he would become a Lutheran minister, and she devoted herself to teaching all her children the Bible's most important lessons.[37] She expected them to attend church every Sunday. If a family member missed the services, she "was accustomed to sit down after dinner and go over the entire sermon from memory."[38]

Bursting with energy, Henry internalized his mother's discipline and work ethic.[39] He attended school nearby.[40] Before and after school hours, Henry helped in his father's brickyard. He also led horses along the canal's towpath and dug potatoes for a neighboring farmer, earning twenty-five cents a day and meals for his time. He loved virtually all farming activities. From an early age, he had helped his mother in the family garden, first tending it and later selling its surplus to local grocers. Among a community of meticulous gardeners, the Heinz plot was known for its clean, straight rows, varied produce, and consistent bounty.[41] Fascinated by the effects of weather, soil, light, and the farmer's efforts on the final harvest, Henry was a talented gardener and a gifted salesman.[42] By the time he was twelve, he had his own personal plot, a horse, cart, and a growing list of customers.

Henry finished school at age fourteen, and for a time enrolled in Sharpsburg's recently established Allegheny Seminary. He was not an exceptional student or a particularly reflective young man. He found it difficult to sit still, and his exuberance for work, especially that involving physical activity, did not extend to reading.[43] Before long, Henry left the seminary, ending his family's hopes for his career in the church. One can only speculate about why he did this. Perhaps he decided the ministry was not suited to his talents. His father may have needed additional help in the brickyard. Most likely Henry recognized that his true calling was business.

He began working as his father's assistant.[44] Henry also enrolled in an accounting course at Duff's Business College in Pittsburgh, learning double-entry bookkeeping and other skills. Like John D. Rockefeller and Pierre Du Pont, he had a facility with numbers. He soon took over the bookkeeping duties in the brickyard. During the winter when the construction trades closed down, he cut ice. In the summer and early autumn, he continued to expand the produce business, hiring some of his siblings to help.

In addition to vegetables, he also began to sell food his mother had long prepared for the family table. Like many other contemporary women, Anna Heinz made her own horseradish, grating the homegrown root by hand, packing it in vinegar and spices, and sealing it in jars or pots. It was a time-consuming chore. Most nineteenth-century American women worked long, full days in their homes: minding children, cooking, sewing, cleaning, and more.[45] As they do today, women in the 1850s and 1860s balanced their varied domestic responsibilities, devoting the lion's share of their time and energy to those deemed most pressing. Cooking meals, caring for infants, and nursing the sick took precedence over laundry and cleaning.[46] In this context, few women welcomed the tedious task of making horseradish, one less essential to the household economy than other cooking duties.

But in mid-nineteenth-century Pittsburgh, horseradish was a popular condiment. Some considered it a remedy for indigestion and respiratory ailments. Many more people used it to flavor dull food—potatoes, cabbage, bread—as well as to improve meats and fish. Horseradish root grew well in the rich soil of western Pennsylvania, and by the early 1860s, a local trade had grown up in the condiment. More than a score of small manufacturers and wholesalers sold prepared horseradish in green or brown glass bottles. The greater proportion of these goods, a contemporary business writer observed, "was of a very inferior quality, and the dealers had adulterated it to so great an extent [by adding turnip and wood fibers as filler] that its use was rapidly diminishing."[47]

The safety and quality of various foodstuffs was a growing concern in many mid-nineteenth-century cities.[48] These issues were not new. Various local laws had mandated inspection of meat and flour exports since the colonial period. Other ordinances had regulated bread prices and ingredients, banning adulterants, such as chalk and ground beans. But as urban areas and the sources of food supplying these areas expanded, older controls weakened. Public anxiety about contaminated food, including milk, meat, eggs, and butter, mounted. So, too, did worries about adulterated chocolate, sugar, vinegar, molasses, and other foods.[49] Journalists, reformers, and legislators began calling for tighter oversight of the nation's food supply in the late 1840s.[50] These demands intensified as the scale and scope of food manufacturing increased in the late nineteenth century.[51]

Henry Heinz realized that consumers were suspicious of food they did not know and could not see. But he believed he could reinvigorate and expand the young horseradish market. Using his mother's recipe, he began bottling unadulterated horseradish in clear glass. A tireless, exuberant salesman, he peddled his product to individual housewives, local grocers, and hotel owners, emphasizing its purity, encouraging potential customers to examine and sample his goods, and comparing his to other bottled horseradish packed in colored glass. The young entrepreneur's sales of horseradish and vegetables rose steadily. In 1861, he had more than three and a half acres under cultivation. His revenues for that year totaled $2,400 (about $43,000 today).[52]

By the time he was twenty-one, Henry Heinz had saved enough money from his food business to buy a half interest in his father's brickyard. As the young man's ambitions for the brickyard grew, so too did his managerial role. To enable the yard to run through the winter and accumulate inventory for the spring construction rush, Henry installed heating flues and drying equipment. He also sought out new customers and collected payment on debts that his father had written off. In 1868, using some of the money he had obtained from the brickyard's debtors, Henry designed and constructed a new, larger house for his family. He did this without consulting his father, who at the time was in Germany visiting relatives. When John Heinz returned, he took up residence in a larger, more comfortable and elegant home than that he had left. There is no record of how the older man reacted to Henry's architectural choices or generosity. But it was doubtless clear to both men that the balance of power in the family and business had shifted from father to eldest son.[53]

Although the brickyard filled much of Henry's time, he did not neglect his food business. Each spring, he experimented with seeds, planting conditions, and watering regimes, keeping notes on what worked and failed. Heinz loved the weather, and his diary entries and correspondence are strewn with observations on prevailing temperatures and seasonal patterns.

During the late summer and autumn months, the young entrepreneur continued to expand his produce and horseradish business.

In the late 1860s, Henry extended his sales routes to include the new oil towns of western Pennsylvania. Centered around Titusville, about eighty-five miles north of Pittsburgh, the region had seen explosive growth since Edwin Drake's 1859 discovery of oil.[54] For much of the next decade, men, money, and equipment streamed into the Allegheny Valley in search of "black gold."[55] Heinz and other entrepreneurs who traveled to the area watched oil output and capital investment soar.[56] In 1860, western Pennsylvania produced 450,000 barrels of oil; by 1862, the number had climbed to over three million barrels. Processing capacity grew in lockstep with crude oil extraction. There were five refineries in Pittsburgh when the decade opened; by 1870, there were more than fifty.[57] In Pittsburgh, Titusville, Pithole Creek, and other oil towns, the possibilities for profit seemed boundless. Andrew Carnegie never forgot his 1861 visit to the oil regions:

> Good humor prevailed everywhere. It was a vast picnic. . . . Everybody was in high glee; fortunes were supposedly in reach; everything was booming.
>
> On . . . the derricks floated flags on which strange mottoes were displayed. I remember . . . seeing two men working their treadles boring for oil on the banks of the stream, and inscribed upon their flag was "Hell or China." They were going down no matter what.[58]

To service the frenetic activity of oil extraction, a range of businesses sprung up, including Heinz's produce sales. In Oil City, Tarentum, and other towns, Heinz called on hotel owners, boardinghouse managers, general merchants, and grocers. He returned to Sharpsburg with a suitcase full of orders.[59]

Oil exploration and refining were not the only businesses that were thriving. Railroad construction, interrupted by the Civil War, began again in earnest in the late 1860s. In the seven years after the war ended, more than 30,000 miles of new road opened, including the first transcontinental railroad, completed in 1869.[60] The pace of expansion accelerated in the next two decades, and railroads spread like wildfire across western Pennsylvania and much of the country.[61] Figure 3-1 illustrates this growth.

A burgeoning railroad and telegraph network, as the historian Alfred D. Chandler Jr. has written, "provided the fast, regular, and dependable transportation and communication so essential to high-volume production and

FIGURE 3-1

Regions Served by the U.S. Railroad System, 1850–1889

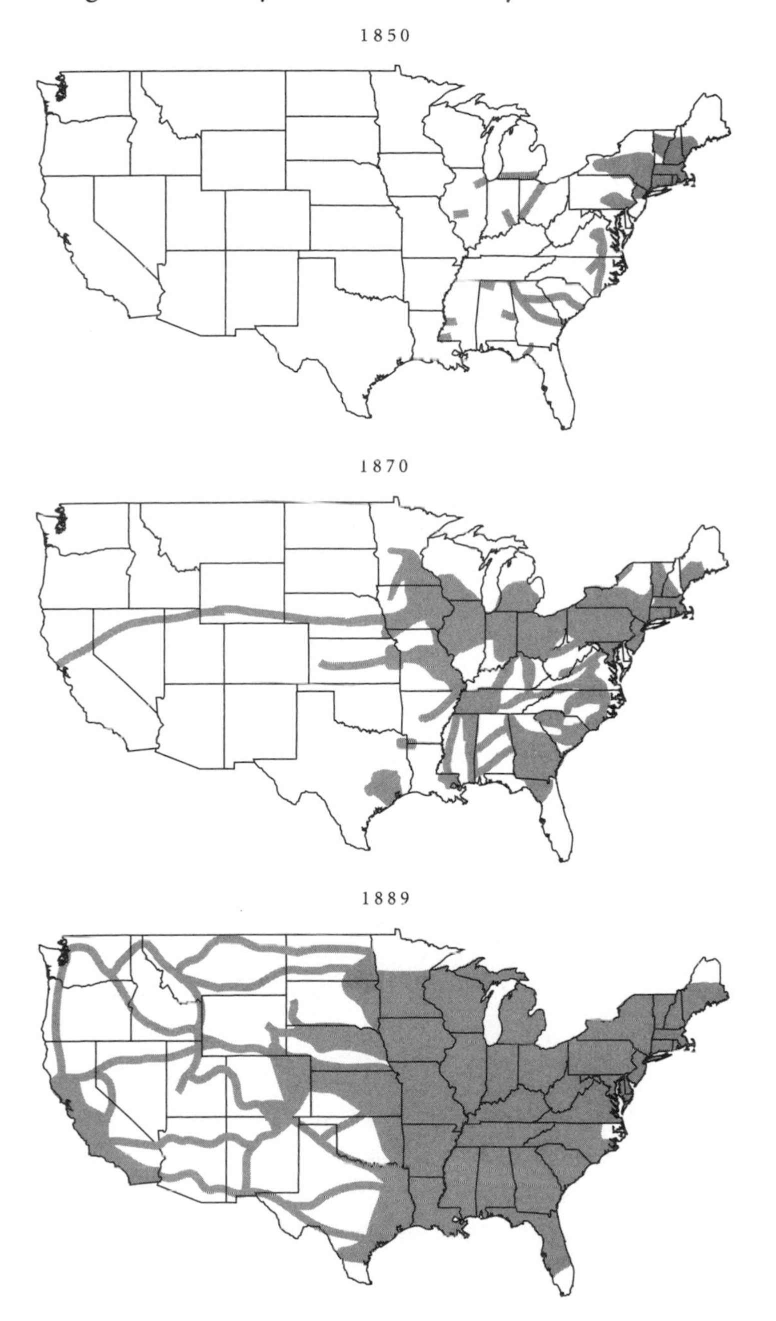

Sources: 1850 map adapted from Fletcher W. Hewes, *Scribner's Statistical Atlas of the United States* (New York: C. Scribner's, 1883), plate 15; 1870 and 1889 maps adapted from *Railways of America: Their Construction, Development, Management, and Appliances* (London: John Murray, 1890), pp. 431, 433.

distribution."[62] In Pittsburgh and other regions, new businesses emerged to exploit the advantages of scale and scope made possible by a large-scale railroad and telegraph network. For example, Andrew Carnegie's success in bridge construction, locomotive manufacture, as well as iron and later steel production was predicated on the development of such innovations. So, too, was that of the American Iron Works, owned by the Pittsburgh partners Benjamin Jones and Henry Laughlin. At the close of the 1860s, these works sprawled for twenty acres along the banks of Monongahela. With a coal mine behind it and an iron mine on Lake Superior, this was one of the fastest growing plants in the city, employing 2,500 people.[63]

Iron manufacture and the young steel industry generated a huge demand for coal and coke, and the production of these inputs accelerated significantly after 1865.[64] In 1869, George Westinghouse received a patent for his locomotive air brake and formed the Westinghouse Air Brake Company shortly thereafter. The same year, Thomas Mellon made plans to open a private banking house, T. Mellon & Sons, to finance Pittsburgh real estate transactions and extend credit to local entrepreneurs such as Carnegie and Henry Clay Frick.[65] In finance, heavy industry, and other sectors, Pittsburgh, by the end of the 1860s, was on its way to becoming one of the preeminent cities of the Transportation and Communication Revolution.[66]

Heinz, Noble & Company

What did Heinz make of the economic changes he witnessed? How, if at all, did the growth of so many new industries and fortunes affect his thinking about the future? In 1869, the young businessman had neither the time nor the inclination to synthesize his observations on paper. But that year, at the age of twenty-five, Heinz made two of the most important decisions of his life. He married Sarah (Sallie) Sloan Young, whose parents had emigrated from Ulster and established a successful mill in Pittsburgh.[67] She was an industrious, religious woman supportive of her husband's ambitions and involved in many of his business decisions. During the early part of their marriage, Sallie was a calming presence in the face of Henry's exuberance and anxiety. In her later years, she frequently suffered from physical illness and depression. But when she was able, Sallie remained at the center of a large family, which included four children, Henry's parents, and some of his brothers and sisters.[68]

Heinz also decided to devote his energies entirely to food production. He relinquished his interest in the brickyard and formed a partnership with L. Clarence Noble, a member of a wealthy Sharpsburg family.[69] Heinz and Noble chose an anchor as their company's symbol and began marking their labels, trade cards, invoices, and advertisements with it.[70] Keen to capitalize on the reputation Heinz had already established, the partners began production with bottled horseradish, using pure homegrown root. In their first year, they planted three quarters of an acre of horseradish root in Sharpsburg and took over one of the rooms and the basement of the house from which Heinz's family had recently moved. Here they set up a small—and by modern standards, very primitive—food factory, hiring two women and a boy to make and pack their product. To preserve the horseradish, the entrepreneurs used a technique pioneered in France during the Napoleonic Wars and widely known in the United States by the 1860s. The condiment was packed in airtight glass bottles and then immersed in boiling salt water for as long as thirty minutes.[71] This minimized the chances of spoilage; it also sustained and helped broaden the reputation for quality that Henry Heinz had already begun to create.

Noble took charge of manufacturing and bottling operations in Sharpsburg. Heinz devoted the bulk of his energies to sales. He extended his earlier sales routes, heading east to New York City, Baltimore, Philadelphia, and Washington, D.C., as well as the Oil Regions, where he called on grocers, jobbers, and hotel and restaurant owners. Heinz also went to Ohio, stopping regularly in Cleveland, Cincinnati, and Akron.[72] With few exceptions, he traveled by train, and his early notebooks contain numerous references to rail schedules, journey times, and destinations.[73] His sales routes tracked the rail network rapidly growing up around Pittsburgh in the 1860s and 1870s. When a train route opened from Pittsburgh to another eastern or midwestern city, Heinz was often one of the first regular passengers, carrying his sample case and trade cards to a new set of potential customers in the grocery, restaurant, and wholesale trade.

At times, his pace was almost manic. In a three-day period in early 1875, Heinz traveled from Pittsburgh to Philadelphia, then on to New York City and Baltimore, and back home.[74] Later that same month on a whirlwind trip to Illinois, Heinz found time during a short buggy drive to "talk religion to the bachelor driver [for] half an hour. [I] hope he may have benefited."[75] The rest of the midwestern visit was packed with business, as he tried to broaden company sales and increase capacity in Chicago and St. Louis.

Demand for Heinz & Noble products increased "with a rapidity seldom witnessed," observed one contemporary business writer.[76] In 1870, the partners had taken over a second room in the old Heinz family house for processing purposes. A year later, they had expanded their product line to include celery sauce, prepared brown mustard, and sweet-and-sour pickles. At the time, a few small American producers made dill pickles.[77] The market for sweet pickles or gherkins belonged to Crosse & Blackwell, a British company with an established presence in the U.S. market.[78] In introducing these new offerings to customers, Heinz continued to stress the Anchor brand's commitment to food purity and taste. He also compared his products to competing ones, many of which were made by small producers.

Like the growing urban outlets for prepared horseradish, condiments markets included a number of dubious goods. "Probably half the vinegar sold in our cities was rank poison," remarked one food reformer in the late nineteenth century. Peppers and mustard were often adulterated with lead, he continued, while sugar, molasses, and some syrups also frequently contained harmful additives. Several mills in New England, he added, "were grinding white stone into fine powder of three grades, called *soda, sugar,* and *flour.*"[79] In the 1860s, there were also a few larger condiments makers that imposed high quality standards on their products and had good reputations, such as Crosse & Blackwell and William Underwood & Company of Boston, which manufactured pickles, sauces, and ketchup.[80]

Why did Heinz and Noble decide to broaden their product line? How did they settle on celery sauce, mustard, pickles, and other condiments, goods that Americans had historically produced at home or bought in small quantities from European manufacturers? Both supply- and demand-side considerations affected the young businessmen's choices. As the market for Anchor products grew in the early 1870s, so too did the company's need for specific inputs, especially vinegar of specific strengths. Heinz and Noble decided to integrate backward and begin producing their own vinegar to ensure adequate supplies.[81]

Expanding the Market

By 1873, Heinz & Noble was selling vinegar as a final product to a growing number of customers, including other food processors and potential competitors.[82] Within three years, the company's vinegar production capacity was more than 400 barrels a week.[83] Concerned to utilize this capacity as fully as possible while extending the market for his goods, Heinz was constantly on the lookout for new products. He experimented frequently with different recipes for pickles, mustard, cider vinegar, pickled cauliflower, curry powder, pickled cabbage, and other condiments. He kept track of what ingredient combinations, cooking times, temperatures, and utensils worked well and what did not.[84] Heinz and Noble had no consumer surveys, focus group analyses, or market research to guide their decisions on new product development. These are managerial tools of the twentieth century, of a mass market and consumer culture that were only beginning to emerge in 1870.

But, as a boy, Henry Heinz had spent hundreds of hours in his mother's kitchen; as a young man, he had made food preparation his business. Like countless women, he knew from firsthand experience that a small number of ingredients, used creatively, yielded a range of different dishes and meals. During the early years of his company's life, horseradish root, vinegar, cucumbers, onions, cabbages, and a few spices were the core inputs. Heinz & Noble's first product line developed directly from inventive reliance on these makings. In the early 1870s, the company added vinegar, sauerkraut, and pickled cauliflower to its offerings. New products such as gherkins and mustard were combined to create still other goods.

Today we might point to Heinz and Noble's skills in exploiting economies of scope, in developing additional goods that made use of existing inputs and organizational capabilities.[85] But neither man thought in theoretical terms about what he was doing. Like other entrepreneurs at other times, they were working to expand a fledgling business operating in a new, as yet largely undefined, market. In the early 1870s, Heinz and Noble believed that they had no time to lose. To make the most of the opportunity they saw before them, they would have to use their limited financial resources and more ample creativity as efficiently as possible. Increasing the company's product line was a potentially quick, inexpensive way to build a nascent market for processed food.

It was also a means, Heinz reasoned, of building the brand. In the 1870s, branding was a new commercial concept.[86] Before that time, as business historian Richard Tedlow has written, "most manufacturers were unknown to the people who bought their products."[87] Heinz would not have used the words "brand creation" to describe his initiatives. This term is a product of the mid-twentieth century. But the entrepreneur understood the strategic rationale of branding and its importance to competing effectively on the demand side of the economy. In a young market, he realized, consumers had to be able to identify a particular product's source, functional attributes, and perceived quality relative to rival goods. Customers also needed to be made to appreciate the intangible aspects of a good—the associations and expectations that they attached to it.

Heinz knew from selling bottled horseradish that women and men would not buy a completely new product, especially a good they could make themselves, unless its quality was assured. Through careful packaging, unadulterated ingredients, and savvy salesmanship, Heinz had provided such assurance. Grocers, wholesalers, and their customers—Heinz's end users—now associated his name and the anchor symbol with superior horseradish, manufactured outside the home. "The brand of the Anchor Pickle and Vinegar Works," a business writer noted at the time, "is known to consumers throughout the country as a guarantee of a first-class quality of goods."[88]

Heinz wanted to extend this brand association to other related goods. He suspected that the potential demand for pure, savory condiments and sauces was enormous. Rising incomes fed this demand and that for other goods, such as toothpaste, packaged cigarettes, ready-made shirts, and watches. Between 1869 and 1899, real per capita income grew at a compound annual rate of 2.1 percent, climbing to $1,000 (about $19,100 today) at the end of the century.[89]

Henry Heinz had no access to these statistics. These numbers are based on economic concepts developed in the twentieth century. What Heinz *could* observe in the 1870s was that men and women in Pittsburgh, Titusville, New York, and other growing areas had more money to spend. He could also see that in addition to being affordable to large numbers of Americans, standardized, branded condiments would also be appealing. As cities grew, fewer households had access to their own food supplies: the family cow or garden. Many consumers in urban areas, Heinz reasoned, might turn to mass-produced foods, such as packaged meat, bottled sauces, and condiments. Not only would Heinz's products save women time and energy, they would also enhance the flavors of other foods. Horseradish, pickles, and Worcestershire sauce were already popular with English and

German-origin peoples. Pickles and horseradish were also commonly used in Jewish cuisine.[90]

In the early 1870s, Heinz saw an important opportunity to develop a larger market for his products. Most existing canneries and condiment manufacturers were small enterprises that sold their products locally. From Heinz's perspective, these companies had not yet begun to tap the possibilities of a broad national market. By concentrating initially on growing cities, he intended to expand his young business westward across the country.

Commercial traffic in prepared foods was not new to the late nineteenth century. Rural consumers had long bartered butter, eggs, horseradish, and other foodstuffs with storekeepers in exchange for sugar, coffee, and other items that could not be made at home.[91] Retailers used these in-kind payments as capital, reselling them to other store customers or trading them to urban wholesalers and jobbers for needed supplies. Bartering reduced storekeepers' dependence on currency. It also created informal distribution networks for locally produced goods. For instance, Philadelphia consumers could often find butter at their local grocers. These and other such products were made by farm households in Devon, Berwyn, and other surrounding areas. Although these foodstuffs bore no name or other information, urban retailers could generally vouch for their quality.

In the 1870s, horseradish, mustard, pickles, and other condiments enhanced meals that were often monotonous. Until the last quarter of the century, most foodstuffs, except meat on the hoof and grains, did not travel from one region to another. Except during harvest months, many nineteenth-century farm families subsisted largely on bread, potatoes, root vegetables, dried fruits, and smoked or salted meat.[92] In many rural households, fresh fruits and vegetables were relatively rare, eaten only when they were ripening.[93] Even in cities, many of the foods that today are considered staples were not consistently available or affordable in the nineteenth century. Many consumers in the 1870s, for example, regarded lemons, oranges, and tomatoes as luxuries.

Whatever ingredients were used, nineteenth-century cooking was a labor-intensive and time-consuming task. On farms, food supplies had to be stockpiled and menus carefully planned for a family to eat well year-round.[94] Men, women, and children all helped harvest produce, tend animals, stoke the fire, and prepare and clean various tools.[95] But in the city as well as the country, cooking itself fell principally to women. Then, as now, it was rarely easy. Before industrialization, wood fires had to be kept going, larger families had to be fed, raw materials often had to be made from scratch, bread had to be baked several times a week. Cooking and related chores spread out across the entire day, from preparing breakfast before sunrise to washing supper dishes by lamplight.[96]

Processed foods could potentially save women time and add variety to many families' diets. But, as Heinz realized, most people, including grocers, did not trust bottled or canned food. Its taste was inconsistent and it often spoiled. Heinz hoped to convince households and storekeepers that Anchor products were of better quality and more reliable than competing goods. In 1870, he did not have a laboratory in which to analyze the content of Anchor or competing products. The science of nutrition began to develop in the 1890s; the presence of vitamins in food and the relationship between diet and disease are twentieth-century discoveries. But as he and his partner expanded their business in the early 1870s, Heinz made an important strategic bet on potential consumer attitudes toward processed food. He believed that a "wide market awaited the manufacturer of food products who set purity and quality above everything else in their preparation."[97] Heinz also suspected that women would be willing to pay a reliable source to take over some of their cooking duties.[98]

Throughout the company's early years, Heinz and Noble tried to manage both sides of the market: to build customer awareness of their products and increase capacity to meet this nebulous, emerging demand. In 1872, they moved the business from Sharpsburg to the center of Pittsburgh, where they leased a four-story factory, office, retail store, and warehouse.[99] The same year, they also took in a third partner, E. J. Noble, Clarence's brother, who purchased a 25 percent stake in the business. The firm, now known as Heinz, Noble & Company, acquired more land outside the city; by 1875, the manufacturer was growing produce on 160 acres near Pittsburgh, the largest garden in the state.[100] During harvest season, Heinz, Noble & Company employed 150 people. To meet bigger payrolls and finance new facilities, Heinz took out short-term bank loans, borrowed money from friends, and bought a $15,000 mortgage on his father's brickyard and house.[101]

Relying on Heinz's energetic salesmanship, a burgeoning railroad network, and the young Anchor brand's growing reputation, the company expanded westward. The three partners wanted to establish a series of beachheads for serving the rapidly growing markets west of Ohio: Indianapolis, St. Louis, Chicago, Omaha, Detroit, and other cities. In 1873, Heinz, Noble & Company opened a sales office and warehouse in St. Louis. Within two years, the firm added a vinegar factory in St. Louis and a distribution warehouse in Chicago. Heinz sensed that Chicago was well on its way to becoming a vital commercial center, calling it "a second New York City, a great city indeed." "Those that have little ambition," he continued, "must move along or get out altogether."[102]

By extending the company's business in the west, Heinz and the Noble brothers also hoped to increase the firm's proximity to specific inputs, such as cucumbers and cabbages. They located a canning company in Woodstock, Illinois, some fifty miles northwest of Chicago, in 1875. The business had over 600 acres of cultivated land and was situated on the Chicago & Northwestern Railroad. Heinz and his partners contracted to buy the tract's produce at a set price of sixty cents a bushel for cucumbers and ten dollars a ton for cabbages in return for use of the Illinois firm's salting and packing facilities as well as outbuildings.[103]

In 1875, at thirty-one years old, Heinz had much to be optimistic about. Despite the lingering nationwide depression that had set in two years earlier, Heinz, Noble & Company continued to enjoy significant success. Sales had grown markedly in each year since the firm's inception. Productive capacity had kept pace. In 1871, the business had manufactured 60 barrels of pickles; four years later, it made over 15,000.[104] Vinegar production climbed equally quickly, to over 50,000 barrels in 1875.[105] The young organization was on its way to establishing a regional presence in a number of fast-growing markets.

Clarence Noble managed the company's interests in Woodstock, Illinois; his brother ran the St. Louis facilities. Heinz, based in Pittsburgh, oversaw operations there. The bulk of his time, however, was devoted to building recognition for the business and its products. In the spring of 1875, he arranged to have the firm's wagons painted with "pea green running gear and plum colored bodies." Heinz had never seen "or heard of such colors in running gear."[106] Nor had his potential customers, who, he believed, were likely to remember the flamboyant wagons with company signs and anchor logos. With an aim to increasing retailers' and end users' awareness of the brand, he entered pickles, horseradish, and several other products in the Cincinnati Exposition, where they were recognized for their quality.[107]

Marketing had always come easy to Heinz, and he often took his seemingly innate ability to understand and attract customers for granted. But he was outwardly proud of his other business accomplishments. "I have more ambition and confidence," Heinz wrote in the diary he began keeping that year, "in my ability to manage the Pittsburgh house, gardens, finance, etc. than I have had for two years past."[108]

Financial Crisis

The entrepreneur's ebullience proved short-lived. Despite growing sales, by late spring of 1875 the business was short of operating capital. In a depressed economy, credit was tight. Pittsburgh banks and other potential lenders could offer only limited assistance to the young enterprise. On April 20, Heinz noted, "My bank account [is] short about $3,000 . . . and [I] know not how to get it."[109] The company's financial position did not improve. "I had the hardest day I ever had," the entrepreneur wrote four days later. "I could eat no dinner owing to worry and hurry and planning. I had to raise $4,000, mostly by exchanging checks and by many new, yet honest, plans and favors of friends and cashiers."[110] Through spring and early summer, Heinz hustled for funds, borrowing money on his father's house and other assets to pay employees and short-term creditors. He described July 3 as "one of the hardest and worst days to finance." The company had three large notes due, and more than fifty hands working on the Sharpsburg plots were owed biweekly wages. But Heinz had "little to meet them with."[111] The strain began to tell. "I am wearing brain and body out," he wrote in a diary entry headed "Panic Times." "I fear I shall break down if times don't soon change."[112]

The late summer harvest only compounded the company's financial difficulties. Growing conditions were ideal, and crop yields were huge.[113] Cucumbers began to rain down at the firm's salting stations in late August, arriving at the rate of 2,000 bushels a day.[114] Other vegetables were harvested in record numbers. Heinz and his partners confronted a new, urgent problem: how to mobilize productive capacity in the face of a surging supply of perishable inputs? The entrepreneur pushed himself harder, extending his usual fourteen-hour workday to eighteen hours. Heinz, Noble & Company hired additional workers to process the huge harvest. Purchasing and payroll costs soared, exacerbating the business's liquidity crisis.

Heinz grew more and more anxious. As during other moments of professional stress, his health gave out. Boils erupted over his body; gastric fever plagued him. "I have been nearly killed and crazed at times," he noted in late October, "meeting and protecting checks, which [Clarence Noble] would issue on me from Woodstock."[115] Since the first of the month, Heinz had "paid out an average of $1,000 per day."[116] Through a combination of short-term bank loans and family funds, he again managed to finance the most pressing debts and prevent checks from bouncing. "I thank God I have lived through it," he sighed at the end of the month.[117]

Even in the midst of financial chaos, Heinz allocated time and money to marketing. In October 1875, the company erected a "grand display" at the first Pittsburgh Exposition.[118] Funded by local business leaders and billed as a "Tradesmen's Industrial Institute," the Exposition was organized as a five-week advertisement of the city's industrial and commercial accomplishments.[119] Visitors to the booths and displays had a chance to see, sample, and purchase a variety of products. As the Exposition opened, Heinz, Noble & Company had more than a thousand bottles of horseradish, mustard, pickles, and celery sauce on hand at the 10-by-24-foot exhibit. Heinz took out an $800 insurance policy on the display and its inventory.[120]

The company's fine showing at the fair and strong autumn sales did not solve its financial problems. Short-term expenses continued to mount, outpacing Heinz's access to credit. In November, he noted, "I have two thousand dollars [of debt] to meet tomorrow, and not a penny to meet it with."[121] Heinz borrowed money for as long as he could. By the end of the month, however, he had exhausted available sources. He bounced his first check.[122] Bedridden by boils in mid-December, the entrepreneur realized the business was doomed. "Oh, what a thought," he wrote in his diary, "to give up all after working hard for ten years, besides getting many friends and parents into trouble with us. The pen cannot describe all our feelings."[123]

News of the company's crisis spread quickly. Angry local creditors levied charges of fraud against the firm and had Heinz, the only partner resident in Pittsburgh, arrested.[124] Although he was released on bail, the county sheriff placed a levy on Heinz's household goods, his father's house, furniture, brickyard, and all of the business's assets. The St. Louis and Chicago operations were quickly closed down. "Trio in a Pickle," announced *The Pittsburgh Leader*'s headline. On December 17, Heinz, Noble & Company filed for voluntary bankruptcy, one of more than 5,000 businesses that failed in 1875.[125]

The founder was deeply depressed. The firm's horses, wagons, boiler, equipment, and stock at hand were all sold to pay outstanding debts. His parents' furniture and home were also appraised and advertised, filling the entrepreneur with shame. "Oh, what a feeling came over me, words can't find the language [to describe it]. . . . I never went near [the sale] as I could not bear it."[126] The holidays were especially hard: "No Christmas gifts to exchange," Heinz wrote in his diary. "Sallie seemed grieved, and cried, yet said it was not about our troubles; only she did not feel well. It is grief. I wish no one such trials. I have no Christmas presents to make. . . . I feel as though people were all pushing us down because we are bankrupt."[127] There is no historical evidence of how neighbors and colleagues actually treated Heinz in the wake of the bankruptcy. But by the close of 1875, he perceived himself to be the object of sudden, widespread disapproval.[128] "A man is nowhere," he observed on December 30, "without money."[129]

A New Beginning

As 1876 opened, Henry Heinz surveyed his prospects. They could not have been encouraging. His business was gone. He was heavily in debt to Heinz, Noble & Company creditors. Assuming personal, family, and company assets could be liquidated at their market value, Heinz himself was still liable for at least $20,000. His personal financial crisis was more pressing. By early January, he was so short of cash, he could not buy groceries. Ashamed of the pain the bankruptcy had cost his family and friends, Heinz refused to ask them for help.[130] Instead, he sought credit at three local merchants. All turned him down. He grew increasingly bitter:

> I tried these [three] parties to learn human nature and shall try more. I feel confident I can get the groceries at Gibson's. I shall ask him to trust us until it is in my power for me to pay him. I would rather ask for such a favor than ask my [wife] or my wife's relatives for money. Besides, I learn more of nature and see how far people are friends.

> Majority of friends are seemingly [so] as long as it costs them nothing or they have no sacrifice to make. This I could not have believed.[131]

Heinz was also disappointed with Clarence and E. J. Noble. Neither man, he concluded, appreciated the support, financial and otherwise, that the Heinz family had lent the company.[132] Moreover, the founding partner believed, each of the Noble brothers had allowed him to shoulder a disproportionate amount of the responsibility and blame for the company's failure.[133] In the months after the bankruptcy, Heinz's relationship with his former colleagues cooled markedly.[134]

Seemingly isolated from onetime associates and friends, Henry Heinz considered his next move. He knew that when business conditions improved, he could probably go back to the construction trade, working for one of the many brickyards springing up around Pittsburgh in the 1870s. There is little evidence, however, that he seriously considered this possibility. His heart was in farming and food manufacturing. He believed his recent experience was valuable, his initial business vision sound. He hoped to put these to work again. By early January, he had been offered a position as an operating agent for two neighboring farms.[135]

Yet like many other entrepreneurs, Heinz resisted going to work for somebody else. He did not wish to follow another person's direction. He wanted control over the fruits of his own labor and ingenuity.[136] Perhaps he also believed that the food processing and farming business owed him something. But how was Heinz to exploit what he had learned over the last seven years while simultaneously creating a successful independent venture? He was penniless. Legal restrictions prohibited him from entering into another partnership until he was discharged from bankruptcy.

The only course open was to seek assistance from his family. He approached his brother John and cousin Frederick Heinz about helping him finance a new food processing business. Each relative advanced him $1,600; Henry raised an additional $1,400 from assets his wife owned. Under the terms of the agreement between the three men, John and Frederick would rent nearby acreage, form a new company, and pay Henry to run the enterprise. Henry would have a right to half interest in the concern when his bankruptcy was discharged.[137] On February 6, 1876, the F. & J. Heinz Company was launched.

The business began operations on a shoestring. Henry used as much as he dared of the firm's $3,000 capitalization to buy back some of the equipment and stock he had liquidated in the bankruptcy. He secured the premises his earlier company had occupied in downtown Pittsburgh, convincing the owner to let his new firm take occupancy several months before paying the first rent check.[138] Heinz persuaded former employees to work for half pay for several weeks, telling them he intended to use the balance of their salaries to buy back additional equipment from creditors.[139]

The new company's product line included bottled horseradish, pickles, gherkins, and celery sauce. Sallie Heinz packed the horseradish. Frederick Heinz oversaw the firm's growing operations on rented land, while John took charge of manufacturing. Henry assumed responsibility for marketing, finance, and the overall direction of the business. He hired one salesman, reserving the most challenging sales routes for himself. With "satchel in hand," he "started out to hunt up trade . . . such as our man could not sell to."[140] Drawing on rich reserves of energy, Heinz resumed the grueling pace of travel he had kept up several years earlier. On February 18, for example, he arrived in Philadelphia at 9 in the morning to call on former trade connections: wholesalers, jobbers, restaurant owners, and grocers. At 11:30 that evening, he took the train to Baltimore, where he hoped to expand the company's presence on the eastern seaboard. By late the next day, he was on his way back to Pittsburgh.[141] Trips such as this one also doubled as scouting expeditions for the entrepreneur. Heinz surveyed various locations with an eye to establishing distribution points—sales offices and warehouses—as the company expanded and future revenues grew.

At home in Pittsburgh, he worked long days and nights, often with Sallie and their children helping. In spite of such efforts, early revenues were not encouraging. June sales were "fearful dull," Heinz noted on a trip to Philadelphia. "Here no one wants goods in our line, and if you force them, you can only do it at a loss."[142] In late summer, the company confronted significant cash-flow problems. "Very close run for money," Heinz nervously observed. "Can't see how to get along and not a man or friend will give us a cent."[143] He worried about how to finance over forty-five acres of cabbage and horseradish that had not yet been harvested. "We manage with a little capital to do a business of about $3,000 to $4,000 a month, but it requires managing. [I write] checks and then hope in some way to meet them. . . ."[144]

As his anxiety mounted, Heinz's health deteriorated. Headaches set in, accompanied by painful boils. At such times, self-doubt and depression plagued him. "I feel as though every person had lost confidence in me."[145]

Periodic despondency did not smother Heinz's commercial imagination. He had long suspected that business success depended on much more than overseeing the supply side of the market. To be effective, his organization needed broader capabilities than those involved in obtaining cucumbers and manufacturing pickles.[146] Sustained growth and market power depended critically on his and his partners' capability to harness productive capacity to the changing parameters of demand. This involved more, Heinz realized, than understanding consumer needs. It also involved clarifying household priorities, applying the organization's technical know-how to the creation of new, customer-satisfying offerings.[147]

The bankruptcy drove home the importance of staying in close touch with household concerns. After 1875, Heinz was determined to lead his new company toward serving and affecting customer demand. This goal would become paramount. Other strategic decisions about manufacturing, product development, and organizational structure would be made with this ultimate end in mind. He resolved to build an organization that, as marketing scholar Theodore Levitt has written, would "feel the surging impulse of commercial mastery."[148]

Heinz worked to extend the brand reputation he had built in the early 1870s. To expose potential customers to his products, Heinz mounted an exhibit at the Pittsburgh Exposition of 1876. The company's display highlighted pickles. But it also included horseradish and celery sauce. The stand featured free samples and souvenir cards. "We hear people say," Heinz noted, that "it surpasses anything in [the] way of a pickle display at [the] Centennial [Exposition]," held in Philadelphia the same year to commemorate the nation's founding.[149] In November, the entrepreneur sent four wagons to take part in a huge Pittsburgh parade for presidential candidate Rutherford B. Hayes. The wagons carried signs with the company name and trademark. One read: "We Will Pickle Tilden."[150]

In the last quarter of 1876, sales began to improve. Heinz was pleased with the company's $400 glass bill (for bottling) for the month of October, "the biggest since F. & J. Heinz started," and a sound indicator of growing demand. Two months later, he was able to record in his diary that "trade is good and we are working hard."[151] After busy days in the company office and factory, Heinz used his evenings to write letters and handle orders. On December 14, for example, there was no time to go home. He and his brother Peter, who helped manage the firm's wholesaling operations, spent the night in the company office. Henry roused his brother at five the next morning and "started him off for Wheeling at 6 A.M. to start selling there."[152] For 1876, F. & J. Heinz recorded revenues of $44,474 (about $665,000 today).[153] Rising wholesale and retail revenues served to vindicate Heinz's business vision. "Truly," he observed of the company's first year of operations, "it is starting life over."[154]

The next five years were busy, successful ones for Heinz and his company. Revenues expanded rapidly, growing at a compound annual rate of 45 percent.[155] As sales increased, Heinz and his colleagues introduced new products under the company's brand. In 1876, the firm started manufacturing tomato ketchup.[156] British households had used ketchup in many varieties as a flavoring sauce for fish, meat, vegetables, and gravies since the early eighteenth century. North Americans imported a number of culinary tastes from Britain, including ketchup. By the mid-nineteenth century, walnut, mushroom, and tomato ketchup had all become established seasonings in the United States. Most general cookbooks published in the decades before the Civil War contained several ketchup recipes.[157]

During the war, the production of bottled and canned foods proliferated, spurred on by technological developments and military demand.[158] Commercial ketchup manufacture grew in tandem.[159] Scores of small- and medium-sized factories in Pennsylvania, New York, Ohio, Indiana, and Missouri were soon making ketchup as a by-product of canning tomatoes.[160] But few companies manufactured a consistent product. Overcooking, spoilage, and large quantities of camouflaging spices often destroyed taste and appearance.[161]

From Heinz's vantage point in 1876, the potential ketchup market was not unlike those he had faced years earlier for processed horseradish or pickles. Consumers, he reasoned, would buy ketchup made outside the home if they were sure the condiment was delicious and unadulterated. A major opportunity thus existed for the company that could make and sell such ketchup on a large scale. Using his young brand's reputation for quality and his company's manufacturing capabilities, Heinz hoped to capitalize on this possibility before other firms did. His early advertisements pronounced the product "a blessed relief for mother and other women in the household."[162]

Three years later, Heinz brought out red and green pepper sauce. The new condiment was "keyed to high-spiced tastes," according to company documents, and "was greatly in demand in fish, oyster, and clam bars."[163] F. & J. Heinz introduced Worcestershire sauce in the same year. The market for this condiment was a fast-growing one, dominated by the British manufacturer Lea & Perrins.[164]

Using the latest technology, Heinz also began production of canned foods, including baked beans, vegetables, and other products. The majority of the company's condiments and sauces sold to restaurants and hotels continued to be packed in glass jars and bottles; those marketed to grocers were usually stored in crocks, wooden tubs, and barrels. But from the company's first sale of canned goods in 1877, Henry Heinz and his brother John, who oversaw manufacturing, understood that canning technology had the potential to significantly reduce breakage as well as packaging and transportation costs.[165] Both men wanted to use this and other supply-side innovations to augment the market they were helping to create for processed foods.

Five years after the founding of F. & J. Heinz, sales exceeded $284,000 ($4.7 million today).[166] Led by pickles, product revenues grew quickly in almost all of the firm's markets, fueling more expansion possibilities and allowing Heinz to repay his personal bankruptcy debts a year earlier than anticipated.[167] At times, the entrepreneur was surprised by the company's fine performance. In September 1881, he struggled to reconcile his own growing success with the tragedy of President James Garfield's assassination. A day after the president's funeral, Heinz observed, the firm's trade "again goes on." It was, he continued, "[part] of a strange but true year of steadily increasing business."[168]

Sales continued their rapid climb. Business, Heinz concluded, had obtained a kind of critical momentum, taking on a life of its own. "We never saw such an amount of orders," the 37-year-old entrepreneur jotted in his diary in October. "Our trade is very good. [We're] not able to get orders filled and scarce see how ever to catch up."[169] Despite its founder's worry, the company did fill its orders. At the end of the decade, sales topped $800,000 annually ($14.1 million today).[170] Table 3-1 tracks the manufacturer's sales in its first five decades.

TABLE 3-1

H. J. Heinz Company Sales, 1876–1925

Year	Total Dollars
1876	44,474
1881	284,000
1888	779,836
1893	1,890,911
1899	3,788,439
1904	5,882,648
1909	6,134,196
1914	12,010,558
1919	20,684,782
1925	37,071,868

Source: H. J. Heinz Company Sales, H. J. Heinz Company Collection, MSS 57, box 2, folder 14, Historical Society of Western Pennsylvania, Pittsburgh, PA.

Marketing

Between 1865 and 1880, Heinz had established a reputation for high-quality condiments. In Pittsburgh, Philadelphia, Baltimore, and Chicago, retailers and households associated his company with flavorful, healthy condiments and sauces. How was Heinz to expand regional recognition and interest into nationwide customer loyalty? How was he to convince millions of potential consumers that food produced in his Pittsburgh factory was comparable, even superior, to that made at home? What competitive advantages could he construct over other companies manufacturing similar products?

One of the entrepreneur's most powerful tools in meeting these challenges was the Heinz brand. The entrepreneur wanted to build a more distinctive identity for his offerings than that he had begun to develop before his first business went bankrupt. He intended to put his experience with reaching consumers to use on a much larger scale. He wanted to forge a national brand that would distinguish his offerings from those of competitors and provide households with important information about Heinz foodstuffs. This information would focus on his products' taste, variety, and overall quality. He also intended to earn customers' and retailers' trust, to convey confidence and familiarity to the women and men who bought his products. To do this, he would continue the company's emphasis on purity in manufacturing. He would also try to link Heinz products with the values most people placed on homemade food: wholesomeness, care, goodness, and consistency. The Heinz brand, he reasoned, would become a critical tool in how loyal and potential customers came to know processed foods. As such, it might be a critical strategic asset in growing markets for processed foods.

How was Heinz to construct a preeminent national and perhaps international brand? In most of his regional markets, he faced local competition from smaller canneries and food processors. On a larger scale, U.S. companies such as Campbell Soup Company, Libby, McNeil & Libby, William Underwood & Co., Van Camp Packing Company, and Borden's Condensed Milk were struggling to secure growing domestic markets for a range of canned and bottled goods, including soups, meats, produce, preserves, sauces, and milk. Several British firms, including Crosse & Blackwell, were jockeying for stakes in the American vinegar and condiments business. In the manufacture of virtually all these products, Heinz also faced rivalry from his potential customers—women who could choose to make their own pickles.[171]

To differentiate his goods from those of other firms and those made at home, Heinz pursued an ambitious brand creation strategy. It was built around imaginative advertising, aggressive promotion, a carefully managed company image, an organized sales force, and supporting manufacturing methods. It was designed to exercise as much influence as possible over the distribution channel.[172] Most of the large food processors in the late 1800s relied heavily on advertising.[173] A few invested in a trained sales force before the turn of the century. But no other manufacturer took the brand so seriously, devoting so many organizational resources to its construction and subjugating other managerial priorities to its maintenance.

Advertising and Promotion

Since his first years in the food business, Heinz had devoted significant company resources to advertising and promotion. As the firm's market presence expanded in the 1880s, the founder extended the scale and reach of its advertising initiatives. F. & J. Heinz continued to sponsor elaborate exhibits and food tastings at local and state fairs all over the country.[174] The company used these displays, such as that at the Columbian Exposition in 1893, to expose customers—households as well as retailers—to its product line and distribute samples and souvenirs.

The company's presence at fairs and parades introduced thousands of consumers to the Heinz brand. The details of each display, including its appearance, signage, merchandising, souvenirs, and staffing, were coordinated to emphasize taste, purity, cleanliness, and convenience. In the last two decades of the nineteenth century, for example, the company handed out thousands of free souvenirs: calendars, spoons, show cards, and souvenir books.[175] Each item carried the Heinz name. Most also emphasized an important brand attribute, such as "Pure Food for the Table." Beginning in the 1890s, the business also mounted exhibits at trade shows and grocers' picnics. These demonstrations were directed specifically at retailers.[176] Like the company's exhibits at public festivals, these promotions stressed the brand's reliability, including its money-back guarantee.

As the firm's market presence grew, the founder extended the scale and reach of its advertising initiatives.[177] By the early 1890s, the company name and its eight-sided keystone symbol, which also appeared on virtually all product labels, were covering delivery wagons, railroad tank cars, and billboards in major U.S. cities.[178] Signs along main-line railroads promoted the firm's most popular goods. Company cards, complete with a four-line verse, dotted the interiors of streetcars. Heinz spent heavily on newspaper ads, although he prohibited any appearing on Sundays.

In 1896, the 52-year-old Heinz devised what would become the brand's most enduring logo. Riding an elevated train in New York City, he noticed a shoe sign publicizing 12 styles. His company manufactured varieties of goods rather than styles. But he was intrigued by the advertised number. "Counting up how many [products] we had," he later recalled, "I counted well beyond 57, but '57' kept coming back into my mind. 'Seven,' 'seven'—there are so many illustrations of the psychological influences of that figure . . . that '58 varieties' or '59 varieties' did not appeal at all."[179] Within weeks, "57 Varieties" was appearing everywhere—on billboards and product labels, as well as in major newspapers. Before long, the new slogan had been emblazoned in concrete on prominent hillsides along main rail routes. In the early twentieth century, the company newsletter pointed to the prominence of these symbols: "The King's Highway of California picks its way across mountainous 57s. Most spectacular of these is a ground sign with 125-foot figures. Illuminated with powerful floodlights, it glistens out through the night, to be read by automobilists and patrons of the railroads."[180] One rail passenger, who spotted the numbers from the dining car, queried the waiter as to their meaning. "I don't know, Ma'am," he replied. "But I think they are numbering the hills along this road!"[181]

Heinz himself designed the most famous example of this advertising. In 1900, the company erected Manhattan's first electric sign at the corner of Fifth Avenue and 23rd Street. The sign was six stories high with a forty-foot-long pickle bearing the Heinz name and the "57 Varieties" slogan. Lit by 1,200 bulbs, it rang up an electricity bill of ninety dollars a night.[182] During a period when an individual light bulb was an unusual novelty, this represented a significant investment. In the display room below the sign, daytime visitors and passersby could watch company employees packing miniature pickles in bottles.[183]

The Heinz Pier in Atlantic City was another splashy marketing innovation designed to introduce consumers to Heinz products and the company. Henry Heinz had first visited the resort in 1880 and had been impressed by the summer crowds.[184] Eighteen years later, he paid $60,000 for a 900-foot pier along the boardwalk there. A huge glass pavilion was constructed at the end of the pier. On top of the building was an electric sign, seventy feet tall, announcing "Heinz 57 Varieties." The central area of the pavilion was exhibition space, given over to a collection of paintings and curios. Busts, bronzes, even an Egyptian mummy and a panel from one of Admiral Horatio Nelson's warships, were on display. The building also housed a large display booth, a demonstration kitchen, a reading room, a sun parlor, and rest rooms. The pavilion's assembly hall seated 125 persons.

Here a company employee delivered regularly scheduled lectures on Heinz production techniques, complete with seventy-five stereopticon slides of the Pittsburgh factory. These presentations emphasized the cleanliness, efficiency, and quality-control standards of Heinz manufacturing policies. The slides showed Heinz's female employees packing pickles, strawberries, and other produce into bottles by hand. These women were dressed in dark blue uniforms, spotless white aprons, and mobcaps. Some were seated, two by two, at small tables with wooden spoons and crockery bowls. These slides conveyed an unmistakable aura of domesticity.

These presentations concluded with an invitation to the audience: "You are cordially invited to sample the 57 Varieties and will not be asked to buy.

If, however, you wish an assorted case you can leave your order and it will be delivered to your home, through your grocer, at less than wholesale price. Only one case to any one home."[185] More than 15,000 people a day went through the Heinz Pier each summer. In the winter months, the main pavilion closed. But 4,000 came daily to the sun parlor. During the forty-six years that the company maintained the pier, over 50 million people walked through. Every visitor was offered a pickle pin.[186]

Heinz opened its Pittsburgh factory to the public in the 1890s. Within a decade, more than 20,000 people a year were touring the manufacturing facilities.[187] A company guide led visitors through the company stables, printing department, box and can factories, female employee dining room, Baked Bean Building, preserving kitchens, and pickle bottling facilities. Employees distributed samples of Heinz products and a souvenir pickle pin to each visitor. The factory tour concluded with a brief lecture. This presentation summarized the company's manufacturing techniques and product lines, emphasizing the brand's purity and commitment to quality.[188] Like the manufacturer's other promotions, factory tours were intended to put the Heinz name and offerings in front of customers.

But the company founder hoped to do more with his advertising than appeal to passive consumers. He wanted to involve these people in extending his brand's reputation. "We keep our shingle out," he wrote in mid-1892, "and then let the public blow our horn, and that counts. But we must do something to make them do this."[189] Virtually all of the company's advertising was designed to excite general attention, to get people interested in and talking about Heinz offerings. Some ventures, such as the Atlantic City pier, also encouraged participation. Pickle pins turned men, women, and children into walking announcements of the Heinz brand and its most famous product.[190] In the modern language of service management, the Pittsburgh entrepreneur worked to enlist his customers as committed spokespeople or disciples for the company.[191]

Most of these initiatives were directed toward increasing brand recognition among retailers and end consumers. But Heinz and his colleagues also promoted the company to employees. As the organization expanded rapidly in the late 1880s and 1890s, it established annual sales meetings, a company newsletter, and a range of social and educational activities for staff. These forums served a number of objectives, including increasing brand awareness *within* the organization itself. Sales conventions, newsletter articles, and other communication channels emphasized the company's reputation and accomplishments. The 1893 sales convention, for example, opened with an elaborate celebration. As Heinz noted in his diary:

> About 100 Branch managers and salesmen are here [in Pittsburgh]. . . . The Western men came in one car and the Eastern men in two cars with streamers over the Pennsylvania Railroad. [They] were met by our H.J. Heinz Company Brass Band of 21 pieces and were led from the hotel to the works this morning. The men were highly pleased.[192]

This and other venues also highlighted the brand's commercial potential. The Heinz Auditorium, built for lectures, plays, and other employee events, was completed in 1900. The stained-glass dome atop the 1,500-seat theater represented the globe. Emblazoned on the glass was the company motto "The World Our Field." Around the base of the globe were inscribed eight requisites for business success: integrity, courage, economy, temperance, perseverance, patience, prudence, and tact.[193]

Sales Organization

Heinz had been building a company sales force since the late 1870s. During the late 1870s and early 1880s, Henry Heinz endeavored to reconstruct and extend the distribution network that he had built with his first business partners. It was a slow process, and by 1881, only five employees, including Henry and his brother Peter, peddled goods for the firm. Henry was the firm's most successful and widely traveled sales agent. His sales calls took him to East Coast cities such as Philadelphia, New York, and Washington, places where the Heinz name was already known among grocers and other retailers. His routes also stretched west to Des Moines, Louisville, Kansas City, and Buffalo. Figure 3-2 sketches Heinz's sales trips between 1869 and 1910.

By the mid-1880s, the business had a more permanent sales presence in Chicago, St. Louis, Baltimore, Cincinnati, Cleveland, Richmond, and Philadelphia. Company salesmen who dealt exclusively in F. & J. Heinz goods staffed a few of these distribution points, such as that in Baltimore. In Chicago, Cincinnati, Cleveland, and Philadelphia, however, the company sold its line through independent wholesalers or jobbers, many of whom also traded in competing goods. Henry Heinz would have preferred not to deal with wholesalers. Their selling efforts were often spread thinly across rival products. Heinz also resented having little influence over jobbers'

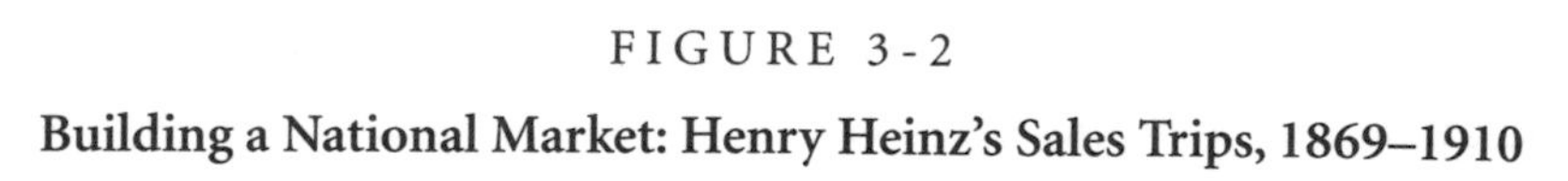

FIGURE 3-2

Building a National Market: Henry Heinz's Sales Trips, 1869–1910

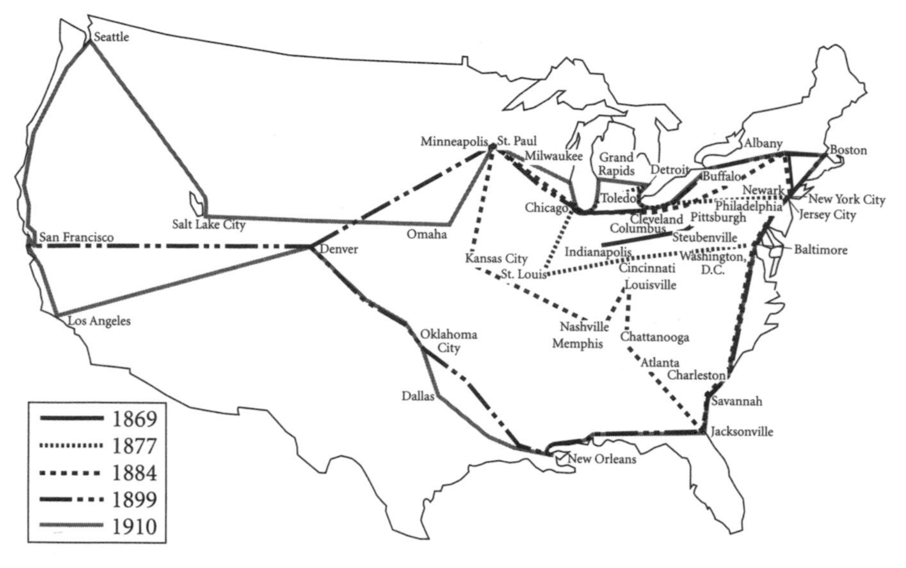

Sources: "The Personal Diaries of H. J. Heinz," Heinz Family Office, Pittsburgh, PA; "The Private Diary of H. J. Heinz," Robert C. Alberts, ed., Alberts MSS 37, box 4, folder 2, Historical Society of Western Pennsylvania, Pittsburgh, PA; H. J. Heinz Co., "57 Varieties," privately printed, 1910, p. 2; Henry John Heinz Notebook (1876–1877), Heinz Family Office; "Outline of the H. J. Heinz Company," MSS 57, H. J. Heinz Company Collection, box 2, folder 7, Historical Society of Western Pennsylvania; 1869 Order Book, Heinz Family Office.

Note: Sales trips in each year include new cities visited by H. J. Heinz.

customers—grocers, hotel owners, and others—and how they promoted company products. Finally, manufacturers like Heinz had no control over which "fastening" techniques were used in peddling their goods.[194]

But Heinz had no choice. He needed to get his goods to customers and convince them of the foods' quality, convenience, and value before competing producers reached the best markets. As significantly, the entrepreneur wanted his name to be the first and only one that retailers and households associated with healthy, delicious mass-produced condiments. Heinz knew he could not always accomplish all of his goals simultaneously. In the late 1870s and early 1880s, his own sales force was too small to reach most U.S. consumers directly. But the young organization could not afford more representatives. It certainly could not finance a company-owned sales organization that was national in scope.[195] Heinz decided then it was more important to make his goods accessible to customers in growing regions, to try to secure these markets, than to exercise additional control over the distribution channel.

As business boomed in the mid-1880s, however, Heinz significantly reduced his reliance on jobbers. He and his partners began to expand the company's sales organization, establishing a series of regional agencies and company-owned warehouses.[196] They staffed these offices and warehouses with trained, full-time employees, significantly reducing the independent wholesaler's role and increasing Heinz's potential influence over distribution.[197] Table 3-2 demonstrates the expansion of Heinz's sales organization.

TABLE 3-2

H. J. Heinz Company Permanent Salesmen, 1877–1919

Year	Total Salesmen
1877	2
1881	5
1888	50
1893	125
1899	273
1901–02	357
1904	450
1909	450
1915	700
1919	952

Sources: "The Private Diary of H. J. Heinz," Robert C. Alberts, ed., Alberts MSS 37, box 4, folder 2, Historical Society of Western Pennsylvania, Pittsburgh, PA, 18 Oct. 1878, 8 Nov. 1878, 1 Oct. 1880; "Three Decades," *Pickles* 3, no. 1 (1 March 1899), pp. 1–3; "Brief Outline of H. J. Heinz Company," p. 9, H. J. Heinz Company Collection, MSS 57, box 2, folder 7, Historical Society of Western Pennsylvania; "Managers' Fifteenth Annual Convention," *Pickles* 6, no. 9 (Jan. 1903), p. 5; "Looking Backward," *Pickles* 5, no. 5 (n. d.), p. 12 ; "A Foreign View of Heinz Methods," *The 57* 7, no. 9 (Feb. 1904), p. 7; "Forty Years of Progress," *The 57* 10, no. 9 (1909), p. 11; Edward Purinton, "The Plant That Made the Pickle Famous," *The Independent* 101, no. 3705 (17 Jan. 1920), p. 95; John W. Jordan, ed., *Genealogical and Personal History of Western Pennsylvania* (New York: Lewis Historical Publishing, 1915), 1, p. 36.

Heinz management strongly encouraged each sales representative or "traveler," as they were known in the company, to establish ongoing, personal relationships with the retailers in his territory. "The confidence of the grocer," observed the Heinz employee newsletter in 1904,

> should first be gained by the salesman. When once a salesman has established such relations between himself and the dealer that the merchant believes in him, almost any suggestion made by the salesman will be accepted by his customer as a good one, because he believes that the salesman is working for the interests of both.[198]

It was critical, noted a Heinz sales manager, "to make the buyer understand correctly that we have his best interests at heart, that our interests are mutual, that we must help him if we would help ourselves."[199] Company salesmen helped individual retailers manage their inventory flow, choose advertising, and enhance merchandising displays, responsibilities that had previously belonged to independent wholesalers.[200] In the late 1880s, travelers began emphasizing point-of-sale marketing to retailers. For example, the salesmen showed grocers how to display Heinz products and signage. They also distributed company paraphernalia for public distribution. By 1906, they were providing free ad copy, designed by the company's Retailers' Advertising Service, to interested retailers.

These relationships were intended to help expand sales to the trade. The connections that Heinz travelers established with grocers also enhanced the flow of information along the distribution channel. Heinz sales representatives reported back to Pittsburgh on changing demand, competitors' actions, and the performance of specific grocers.[201] In 1898, for example, a Heinz traveler making routine calls on grocers in his territory found company goods at one store "scattered from one end of the place to the other." He spoke with the grocer, suggesting that the products would be more effectively displayed by consolidating them. This was followed, the salesman recalled,

> by an offer to help arrange them, which was immediately accepted; the change was made to the satisfaction of the grocer. A few labels were mailed to him to replace those that were dirty; chutney, euchred figs and India relish were added to his line, making it very presentable and a good advertisement.

The proud traveler exhorted other Heinz salesmen to get the grocer "to give you a tier of shelves and devote them to our line; you can do it."[202]

Heinz salesmen received ongoing instructions and training. Company publications and regular sales meetings detailed job responsibilities, sales techniques, and travelers' dress codes.[203] The *57 Sales Manual* from the early twentieth century listed seven steps to be followed when calling on grocers. Adhering to these fundamentals, the handbook promised, "will result in a well-rounded sales presentation, which will build the business on your territory and insure your success."[204] On Saturdays, for example, each sales representative was required to set a table with linen and china in one of his region's better grocery stores. All day, he offered samples of the "57 Varieties," telling customers about the Heinz brand, manufacturing processes, and product line.[205] Each traveler was required to wear a derby hat, stiff collar, and company pin. He carried a sample case equipped with materials to tack up a printed ad anywhere. He was also required to carry a clean white cloth for dusting Heinz products on the store shelves. This allowed each salesman to rearrange displays, placing competitors' products behind and under Heinz foods. By the early twentieth century, Heinz's sales network had assumed many of the responsibilities previously belonging to wholesalers.

Annual conventions and regular regional meetings were scrupulously organized to help Heinz travelers increase sales and expand the company's presence in the distribution channel. During the three-day annual convention in 1902, for instance, sales representatives attended sessions on such subjects as "Broader Salesmanship" and "Pickling Vinegar—The Most Effective Way of Selling to the Merchant." They also toured the main factory, ate dinner in the employee dining room, and met with senior management and manufacturing workers. In between, the travelers heard lectures on "Our Seed and Vegetable Farms and Salting Houses" and other subjects.[206]

Like the corporate retreats and seminars held today, the purpose of the Heinz conventions transcended revenue growth. These late-nineteenth- and early-twentieth-century gatherings were baptisms in the organization's values and, by extension, in the Heinz brand. In the words of an 1898 company newsletter, the conventions were the firm's "training schools of success." At these assemblies, the newsletter observed,

> men are practically reborn into salesmanship. Men are taught to unlearn and relearn. . . . The swift communication and intermingling

> of nations produce marvelously keen competition. Only the brightest of minds in the healthiest bodies can produce success. Information, knowledge of one's subject, must be thorough. In consequence, business absolutely requires its representatives to possess the best natural qualifications, which may be readily molded to the requirements of enterprise.[207]

Annual conventions also provided educational opportunities for senior management. As the company founder remarked at the Fourteenth Annual Meeting of Managers and Travelers in 1902,

> You come here to sharpen us up, you don't appear to know that you come here for that purpose; you imagine you come here to learn . . . [To] hear what other managers do, [to listen to] other travelers from other parts of the world. . . . This is all well and good. But you come here to teach us, and if we don't learn something from you, gentlemen, before you go away from here, it will be our fault, not yours.[208]

Product Development and Manufacturing

Product development played a key role in Henry Heinz's brand building efforts in the 1870s and 1880s. Even in the wake of the 1875 bankruptcy, he was confident that most customers associated his name with pure, tasty pickles.[209] To enhance these perceptions and build the market for manufactured condiments, Heinz worked constantly to extend his company's product line.[210] In 1880, for example, the company began production of cider vinegar, distilled white vinegar, apple butter, and mincemeat.[211] Not long after, Heinz added chili sauce, sweet onions, East India chutney, and chow-chow to his product line.[212] Backed by aggressive and innovative marketing, most of these introductions quickly became well-established products.[213] Many were market leaders.

During the first decade of his new company, Heinz also devoted considerable time to the development of canning technology and raw material supplies. As a means of preserving food, canning dated back to early-nineteenth-century France. In 1809, Nicolas Appert, a wine maker and chef, had answered a government appeal to devise a means of ensuring wholesome foods to itinerant French armies. Appert's method was simple: meat, vegetables, eggs, and fruit were packed in airtight bottles, then placed in boiling water for varying lengths of time. This process preserved foods longer than other techniques.[214] In 1810, Appert published his methods in *The Book for All Households, or the Art of Preserving Animal and Vegetable Substances for Many Years.* By the second decade of the nineteenth century, a variety of American entrepreneurs were using Appert's techniques to process and preserve food that they sold on a regional basis.[215]

But it wasn't until 1875 that canning processes and technology were sufficiently advanced for efficient, large-scale food processing. During the 1860s, the introduction of calcium chloride to boiling water cut sterilization times for meats, fish, vegetables, and fruits from as much as five hours to twenty-five minutes. This difference increased a well-run factory's potential output from 2,500 cans of food a day to over 20,000 cans.[216] After 1868, can-making became increasingly mechanized, resulting in expanded production and efficiency.[217] The 1874 invention of the pressure cooker further reduced cooking times for food processors and prevented accidents caused by the buildup of force during heating. Heinz was quick to adopt such innovations, and in the mid-1870s his company began preserving foods in cans as well as jars, bottles, and sealed crocks.[218] A few years later, the company began using continuous canning technology, which significantly increased the efficiency of operations.[219]

Like Heinz, other commercial food processors embraced the new technology and techniques. By 1885, can production had emerged as a secondary industry dependent on, but separate from, food processing. Canning technology continued to improve rapidly in the last two decades of the century. In 1900, Carnation introduced the hole-in-cap can.[220] The sanitary can was invented three years later and quickly replaced its predecessors; these new containers were the first airtight cans that did not need to be soldered in sealing.

Advances in canning technology helped expand the scale of Heinz's production. So, too, did increased coordination of raw materials and output. In 1890, Heinz added additional capacity, moving manufacturing facilities to the company's present-day location on Pittsburgh's north side. He maintained the Sharpsburg plantation and throughout the 1880s and 1890s purchased hundreds of acres in Pennsylvania, Indiana, and Iowa.[221] He also contracted with farmers to supply additional cucumbers and other produce at prearranged prices. Most vegetables were delivered to Heinz facilities in company-owned freight cars, where they were preserved in bottles made at an adjacent company facility. In Pittsburgh, for example, a spur of the Baltimore and Ohio Railroad ran directly into the factory's Vinegar Building. Other food manufacturers followed suit, integrating backward and forward. By 1920, almost all of the major American food processors that had been founded in the preceding four decades had concentrated production in a few large factories. Like Heinz, these companies operated their own buying, selling, distributing, and marketing systems.[222]

The Heinz organization grew with its capacity and markets. In the late 1870s, Heinz employed less than 100 permanent workers. Most of these worked in the factory. A handful of others were salesmen. A few others, such as John Heinz, had managerial responsibilities. Employment expanded quickly over the next three decades as the company established production and distribution facilities across the United States and in more than twenty other countries. During the peak planting and harvesting periods each year, the company also hired thousands of temporary workers. At the turn of the century, for example, Heinz had 20,000 people on its payroll. More than half were working on 16,000 acres of U.S. farmland devoted exclusively to producing fruits and vegetables for the Pittsburgh food processor.[223] Figure 3-3 shows the growth of permanent employees.

Food Adulteration and the Pure Food Law of 1906

By the end of the nineteenth century, food manufacturing was a highly integrated, capital-intensive industry. In 1900, it was the largest component of the U.S. manufacturing sector, accounting for almost $3.6 billion in economic activity and comprising almost a third of all finished commodities produced in the nation.[224] As increasing numbers of Americans depended on large, often distant corporations for various foodstuffs, long-standing concerns about product quality and safety intensified. Doctors and food safety experts pointed to several issues. Food processors, wrote one observer,

> may deliberately offer for sale food which has begun the process of decomposition. Second, they may treat food with preservatives which, while they destroy or prevent the action of microorganisms, are injurious to the human frame. Third, they may adulterate or substitute cheaper, poorer foods for better, more nutritious foods.[225]

FIGURE 3-3

H. J. Heinz Company Permanent Employees, 1878–1919

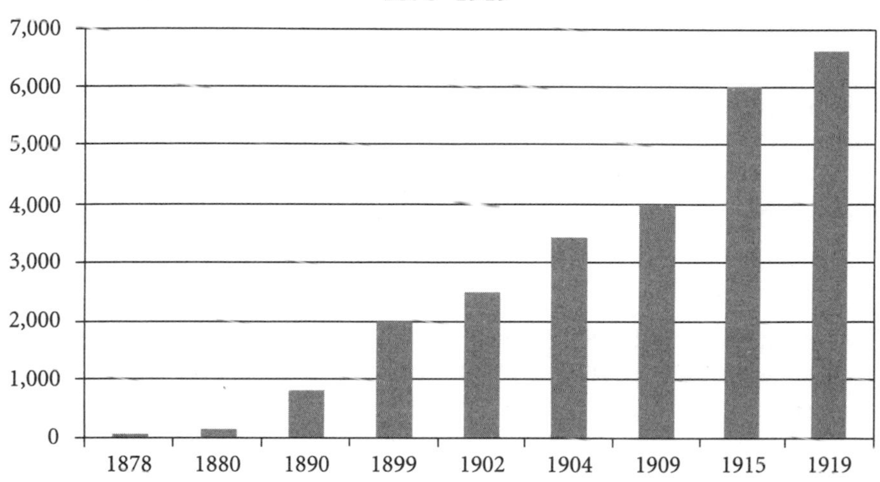

Sources: "The Private Diary of H. J. Heinz," Robert C. Alberts, ed., Alberts MSS 37, box 4, folder 2, Historical Society of Western Pennsylvania, Pittsburgh, PA, 18 Oct. 1878, 8 Nov. 1878, 1 Oct. 1880; "Pay Roll Book 1890, for H. J. Heinz Company," Accession 53.41, box 55, folder 1, Henry Ford Museum, Dearborn, MI; "Three Decades," *Pickles* 3, no. 1 (1 March 1899), pp. 1–3; "Outline of the H. J. Heinz Company," p. 9, H. J. Heinz Co., MSS 57, box 2, folder 7, Historical Society of Western Pennsylvania; "Managers' Fifteenth Annual Convention," *Pickles* 6, no. 9 (Jan. 1903), p. 5; "Looking Backward," *Pickles* 5, no. 5 (n. d.), p. 12; "A Foreign View of Heinz Methods," *The 57* 7, no. 9 (Feb. 1904), p. 7; "Forty Years of Progress," *The 57* 10, no. 9 (1909), p. 11; Edward Purinton, "The Plant That Made the Pickle Famous," *The Independent* 101, no. 3705 (17 Jan. 1920), p. 95; John W. Jordan, ed., *Genealogical and Personal History of Western Pennsylvania* (New York: Lewis Historical Publishing, 1915), 1, p. 36.

Beginning in the 1880s, the American Medical Association and a few state agriculture officials had begun campaigning for federal oversight of food safety. Over the next twenty years, public interest in the possibility grew substantially. Women played an important role in the early-twentieth-century movement for government regulation. The National Consumers' League founded a food investigating committee.[226] The General Federation of Women's Clubs petitioned Congress for legislation.[227] As public awareness increased, progressive reformers championed the campaign, clamoring for a national pure food law. In early 1906, Senator Porter James McCumber from North Dakota contended:

> The Government cannot prescribe a dietary course for every individual, but it ought to protect the individual against all character of imposition and fraud, so that entering into the markets he may purchase those things without fear which he knows to be conducive to his health and comfort, and above all that he may avoid those things which he knows to be detrimental.[228]

Food processors and distributors were divided over the issue of federal regulation. The National Food Manufacturers' Association opposed government oversight. Retail grocers and many canning companies generally supported the possibility. Henry Heinz was one of the most outspoken proponents of a strong law governing food production, labeling, and sales. In early 1905, he sent three company executives, including his eldest son Howard Heinz, to seek President Theodore Roosevelt's backing for federal action.

As a candidate for reelection in 1904, Roosevelt had not endorsed such regulation. But extensive lobbying by food experts, such as Department of Agriculture chemist Harvey Wiley, helped change the president's public position. In late 1905, Roosevelt advised Congress to enact a law "to regulate interstate commerce in misbranded and adulterated foods, drinks, and drugs. . . . [Such legislation] would protect legitimate manufacture and commerce, and would tend to secure the health and wealth of the consuming public."[229] The legislature took up the issue in early 1906. After months of committee hearings, the Fifty-ninth Congress passed the Pure Food and Drug Act on June 29, 1906.[230] Roosevelt signed it into law the next day. The law marked the first national attempt to improve food safety and nutritional standards.

Undoubtedly, Heinz's involvement in the campaign for food regulation grew out of his personal commitment to producing safe, healthy food. But he also had strategic reasons for championing federal regulation. Heinz believed that such legislation would help increase consumers' confidence in processed foods, legitimating the broader industry and guaranteeing its survival.[231] Stringent guidelines for food manufacturing and labeling, he believed, would enhance the reputation of the overall business. Such guidelines might also focus public attention on his brand's core attributes of purity and quality. Heinz's standards for ingredients, production processes, and cleanliness were among the highest in the industry. The entrepreneur welcomed another opportunity to promote his products and his company's identity.

From Heinz's perspective, there were other advantages to endorsing federal regulation. Government-imposed standards for food manufacturing, labeling, and distribution would alter the terms of competition in the industry, forcing some companies to change their operating policies, usually at higher costs. Other manufacturers would be driven out of business. Both possibilities, Heinz realized, would enhance the Heinz Company's competitive position.

International Markets

In 1886, the forty-two-year-old Heinz took his first trip to Europe for a vacation. But Heinz could not resist combining business with pleasure. Intending to explore potential overseas markets, he carried a suitcase containing at least one of each of his company's products.[232] Heinz saw no pickle displays as he inspected store windows in central London.[233] He decided to approach Fortnum & Mason, a large food retailer known for its quality and sales to British royalty. Heinz entered the store without a contact or a letter of introduction and asked for the head of grocery purchasing.

Heinz introduced himself as a food manufacturer from America and delivered a well-rehearsed presentation. He opened seven different company products, including ketchup, horseradish, and chili sauce. The Fortnum & Mason's agent tasted the condiments while Heinz readied himself to meet a rebuff with his prepared counterattack. He was astonished to hear the purchasing manager say, "I think, Mr. Heinz, we will take all of them."[234] Heinz's diary entry for that day opens "1st Sale in England."[235] When Heinz returned to Pittsburgh, he moved quickly to build British sales. In less than a decade, the company had established a London branch office to serve fast-growing markets in England and other European countries. By the early twentieth century, the business was selling its products in Norway, Sweden, Denmark, Germany, Spain, Belgium, Holland, and Russia.[236]

For the next twenty-five years, Heinz traveled around the globe, visiting Europe almost every year between 1890 and 1915 and journeying through Asia, the Middle East, and northern Africa. Wherever he went, he worked to exploit potential sales opportunities, visiting food brokers, glass manufacturers, farmers, and factories. By 1910, the company distributed its products through more than forty international agencies, located in twenty-five countries ranging from South Africa to India to New Zealand.[237] On the eve of the First World War, sales from these markets represented 13 percent of the company's $12 million in annual revenues.[238] At a time when many industrial leaders were learning how to expand distribution domestically, Henry Heinz was setting his sights overseas. "Mountains and oceans in this day," he wrote in his diary, "do not furnish any impassable barrier to the extension of trade. . . . Our market is the world."[239]

Conclusion

By 1900, the H. J. Heinz Company was the largest food processor and one of the first multinational businesses in the United States. In 1905, the company was incorporated, with $4 million worth of stock owned by the founder, his sons (Howard, Clifford, and Clarence), and two associates (cousin Frederick and brother-in-law Sebastian Mueller). Henry Heinz became the first president of the corporation and held that office until he died in 1919.

At the time of the entrepreneur's death, the H. J. Heinz Company had 6,523 employees; 25 branch factories; 85 pickle-salting stations; its own bottle, box, and can factories; and its own seed farms.[240] The company harvested over 100,000 acres and operated in more than 25 countries in 1919. It was a major player in one of the nation's most vital industries. Its brand was one of the best known in the growing landscape of consumer goods.[241]

Heinz's life and work mirrored the economy that he helped shape. He got his start in business as a farmer peddling produce to his Pittsburgh neighbors. In Pittsburgh, he witnessed the rise of industrial capitalism and big business on an unprecedented scale. He understood that rapid economic transition altered what households needed, wanted, and could afford. The young Henry was determined to harness the opportunities presented by such demand-side shifts and set about creating a market for bottled condiments.

The brand was Heinz's most powerful tool. It was his principal means of reaching customers, earning their trust, and establishing a lasting, dynamic connection with them. It was thus a vital means of breaking open new consumer markets, of encouraging households to change their behavior in small but important ways. Henry Heinz was one of the first U.S. entrepreneurs to pursue such a consistent, innovative, and multifaceted brand-building strategy.

But he was by no means the last great brand creator. A host of companies followed in Heinz's wake. Between 1890 and 1920, businesses such as Eastman Kodak, Waterman's Fountain Pen Company, Beech-Nut, and Gillette began to develop relevant, distinctive brands. Many of them relied on creative advertising, trained sales forces, and influence in the distribution channel to develop large markets for their offerings. But few deployed a brand-creation strategy that surpassed the scope, effectiveness, and sustainability of Heinz's.

After the founder's death, his eldest son, Howard Heinz, took the reins of the family business. A trained chemist, he worked to apply scientific methods to food processing and strengthen the organization's commitment to research and development. Taking a lesson from his father's bankruptcy in 1875, Howard Heinz pursued a conservative financial strategy, paying down debts and postponing dividends. During the Depression, he instituted a range of policies to protect the company's competitive position, adding staple products such as baby food and ready-to-serve soups and expanding the sales force. In order to keep prices low without lowering employee wages, Heinz cut production costs. While sales declined markedly from their levels in the 1920s, the firm remained profitable throughout the long economic downturn. The company continued to build its international presence, founding the H. J. Heinz Company Australia in 1935 to manufacture goods for this market.

When Howard Heinz died in 1941, management of the business passed to his son, Henry John "Jack" Heinz II. Under his leadership, the firm undertook several important organizational innovations, establishing controller and personnel divisions, instituting a modern cost-accounting system, and making its first public stock offering in 1946. During the late 1950s and 1960s, the H. J. Heinz Company grew rapidly, acquiring food companies around the world and manufacturing a diverse portfolio of products including tuna, pet food, and frozen entrees.

Heinz family members ceased leading the organization in 1966. During the ensuing decades, the company made new acquisitions in existing markets, established joint ventures in developing countries, augmented its product lines, and continued to align its organizational structure with its evolving competitive strategies. In the early 1990s, the business launched a vigorous ad campaign to defend its core brands in the face of emerging challenges in the food processing and grocery retailing industries. A new restructuring process included both strategic acquisitions and divestitures. In 1995, Chief Executive Officer Anthony J. F. O'Reilly declared that the changes of the past two decades had left Heinz "with the right brands in the right categories in the right countries."[242]

In 1998, William R. Johnson became CEO, becoming only the sixth person to hold this position in Heinz's 129-year history. He continued Heinz's global expansion, acquiring new businesses in Indonesia and the Philippines. He also initiated a reorganization plan to focus on the core categories of ketchup, condiments, and sauces; pet food; tuna; infant foods; frozen food; convenience meals; and organic and nutritional foods. As the twenty-first century began, Heinz remained one of the world's leading food processors, supplying supermarkets, eating establishments, and other retail and food service channels. Its family of brands included StarKist, Ore-Ida, Weight Watchers Foods, 9-Lives, Budget Gourmet, Guloso, Olivine, and Linda McCartney Meals. In 2000, the flagship Heinz brand accounted for about one-third of the company's $9 billion in annual sales.

Preview to Chapter 4: Marshall Field

THE NEXT CHAPTER analyzes the efforts of Marshall Field (1834–1906) to develop a market for mass retailing in late-nineteenth-century Chicago. Like Henry Heinz, Field understood that improved communication and transportation as well as rapid industrialization offered unprecedented business opportunities. Some were to be found on the supply sides of new markets. Economies of scale in machine-based mass production had lowered the costs of countless products. And by moving goods quickly, reliably, and cheaply, the railroad and telegraph were revolutionizing distribution, permitting merchants to buy and sell goods in much larger volumes.

In the middle and late decades of the nineteenth century, hundreds of entrepreneurs rushed to take advantage of these possibilities. Some of the successful ones built large new wholesale and retail organizations: mail-order businesses such as Montgomery Ward and Sears, Roebuck and Co. and chain stores such as the Great Atlantic and Pacific Tea Company (A&P) and the F. W. Woolworth Company.

The department store, which sprung up in several fast-growing urban markets during the 1860s, was one of the most significant of these retail innovations. By 1900, most major cities (and many smaller ones) boasted at least one major department store: A. T. Stewart's, Macy's, and Lord & Taylor in New York; John Wanamaker in Philadelphia; Sanger's (later Sanger-Harris) in Dallas; Filene's and Jordan Marsh in Boston; and Marshall Field and Carson Pirie Scott in Chicago. Each of these stores was very successful at the time, and many endured into the twenty-first century. But their success was exceptional, in the literal sense. Most of the early department store entrepreneurs—like early entrants in other young industries, such as H. J. Heinz—failed. R. H. Macy himself went bankrupt in at least one retailing venture and floundered in several others before moving to New York in 1858, where he established what eventually became one of the preeminent retail operations in the world.

Marshall Field, from his early days as a clerk in a general store, realized that creating a successful distribution business involved more than efficient management of merchandise, accounts, and supplier relationships. To build a prosperous wholesale and especially retail operation in Chicago at a moment when other entrepreneurs were trying to do the same thing, Field would have to attract consumer interest in *his* company: first earn their trust, then convert it into long-term customer loyalty.

Field understood that department stores offered potential new benefits to nineteenth-century women over and above the mere presentation of a large assortment of goods. He and his business partners believed that female shoppers wanted an elegant atmosphere, the latest fashions, and courteous service—preferably from other women. During the late nineteenth century, Field and his colleagues developed a range of initiatives, including sophisticated buying by New York and European agents, innovative marketing, and close attention to customer service. These steps were designed not only to meet but also to enhance consumer expectations and to create a special position for Field's company in the emerging world of mass distribution.

In the last decades of the nineteenth century, the Marshall Field brand emerged as a vital marketing tool for the company. The department store itself *became* the brand, in an era when shoes, clothing, and other goods were not commonly branded by their manufacturers. By 1900, Field's had become a powerful player in U.S. department store merchandising. And a century later, at the advent of the twenty-first century, Marshall Field's remained a premier retailing name.

CHAPTER 4

Marshall Field, 1834-1906

Prologue: The 1902 Grand Opening

On September 29, 1902, Marshall Field & Company celebrated the grand opening of its new department store after having been in business since the mid-nineteenth century. Located in the center of Chicago's commercial district, the twelve-story structure greatly expanded the company's selling space. Shoppers could now roam more than half a million square feet spread over three retail buildings. This made Marshall Field's the largest retail store on earth. The bargain basement alone, at 136,000 square feet, was the largest single salesroom.[1]

"Colossal in size; magnificent in appointments; magical in service" is how one contemporary trade journal described the company's enlarged premises.[2] The public agreed. More than 150,000 people poured into the store on opening day, jamming the twelve entrances and fifty elevators and at times slowing business to a standstill.[3] Serenaded by six orchestras and surrounded by fresh flowers, visitors trooped wide-eyed through the store. They took away over $10,000 (or about $194,000 today) in silver spoons, gold-plated bowls, and other free souvenirs.[4] As crowds continued to fill the store, the opening was extended to six days. All told, over half a million people passed through during the celebration.[5]

Marshall Field himself, the senior partner and founder who had begun his career in a small country store, joined the throng roaming the premises. A perfectionist, he had a keen eye for retail mistakes—inattentive clerks, sloppy counter displays, and disgruntled customers—and a reputation for quick reprisals. But even Field could not fail to have been impressed with what he and his colleagues had achieved in opening this store.

Inside the new building, Field's visitors strolled through a long central arcade, framed by rows of Corinthian columns. Electric Tiffany chandeliers lit the interior, casting brilliant light across the mahogany display cases and French glass counters. A vast open atrium, culminating in a massive skylight, reached up through the twelve stories. In the style of an Italian palazzo, each floor opened onto the atrium. On all but the ground level, Oriental rugs and other carpeting covered the floors. Green leather furniture and walnut paneling lined the library, where weary shoppers could read the latest newspapers and magazines—or poetry and other literature—before returning to the sales floors.

There were four restroom suites for women, each consisting of a sitting room, lavatory, and forty toilet rooms. Each sitting room, with its Madras window hangings and willow rockers was "large, airy and inviting, a veritable haven of rest," in the words of one reporter.[6] The lavatory featured individual vanities, each with an electric curling iron, brush, and comb. Attending maids polished the enamel fixtures and "supplied patrons with soap, face and talcum powder, individual flannel cloth for powdering, hair pins, safety pins, needles, thread, tape, shoe laces, shoe buttons, pearl buttons, button hooks, scissors, sewing silk and hooks and eyes"—all free.[7]

Maids were a small fraction of the store's 7,000 workers.[8] More than a third of the staff were salespeople and floor managers. Almost half worked in merchandising, receiving, and accounting. The remaining employees delivered purchases, cleaned the premises, worked in one of the store's two restaurants, or provided miscellaneous customer services. Over two dozen men served as store greeters and ushers. Several nurses staffed the medical room. Stenographers in the Information Bureau helped customers send telegrams, while other attendants made theater, railroad, and steamer reservations for interested patrons. Guides provided information on local cultural and recreational activities.

Marshall Field employees aimed to provide responsive, courteous service to all store visitors, whether they purchased goods or not.[9] "We have built this great institution for the people," explained Harry Selfridge, the general manager of retail, "to be their store, their downtown home, their buying headquarters—where, in the quality of the merchandise, as well as the price, their best interests will always be considered."[10]

Selfridge was particularly proud of the vast assortment of items for sale. Shoppers found things from all over the globe: American sewing machines, Russian furs, Japanese screens, French gloves, South African diamonds, and more. Many of the product lines had been purchased from the company's own wholesale division; some lines, including umbrellas and linens, had been made in Field factories. Some goods came from U.S. and international manufacturers. One early-twentieth-century visitor to the store was amazed by the

> truly universal contact, which the store has with the people and industries of the world. One might easily fancy that threads, leading from every nook and corner of the globe, are gathered here in great skeins, and passing through the doors, separated and led out again to the houses of the people.[11]

The new building had cost $1.75 million ($34 million today).[12] The company's wages, advertising, and other operating expenses in 1902 totaled $3.8 million, and the cost of goods sold amounted to over $9 million.[13] Meanwhile, total sales in Marshall Field's retail division grew by 21 percent between 1901 and 1902, climbing to more than $17 million ($330 million today) in the later year.[14] The store earned $845,000 on these sales—almost 5 percent.[15] Mr. Field did not sit back and merely reap his profits. Instead, he plowed much of this money into nearby real estate to preempt competitors and create additional sales space.

Retailing had changed significantly since the early 1850s when Field worked in a country store. In the second half of the nineteenth century, the business of buying and selling was transformed by rapid industrialization, rising incomes, the development of a national market, and urbanization. New transportation networks created opportunities for entrepreneurs to distribute goods faster and in unprecedented volume. These same innovations brought millions of Americans into contact with a number and variety of things that their counterparts a century before could hardly have imagined.

Field spent his life successfully exploiting the possibilities presented by the economic changes. By 1902, his department store's achievements made him the most famous commercial name in Chicago and one of the best known in the country. According to the Chicago magazine *Saturday Evening Review*, the company was "a giant among giants" and its retail establishment was not only the largest in the world, but "also the most solid and exclusive."[16] Even Philadelphia merchant John Wanamaker, owner of another famous department store, was intrigued. During a 1903 trip to Chicago, he toured the new Marshall Field's store, making notes on the building and its operations. He was impressed with the merchandise mix, especially the more expensive goods. "Send our people to study their china department," he wrote in his diary, singling out one of many product categories in Marshall Field's store known for its quality, fashion, and attentive customer service.[17]

The Background: Retailing in the Nineteenth Century

Early Retail Trade

In the early 1800s, most commercial connections within the United States were local. New England peddlers, for example, hawked Bibles, almanacs, and hymnals to farmhouses in rural Vermont and other nearby states. Plantation owners in eastern Georgia traveled to Savannah to buy buckwheat, crackers, lard, and tea, using credit on their future cotton sales. And towns everywhere had general stores where goods could be bought or bartered. For example, in one general store located in Louisville, Kentucky, sixty-six different customers were noted in the ledger during a nine-month period. Most of these patrons were white men, but several women and African-American slaves shopped there as well. They made two visits a month, on average, bought thread, shoes, hats, chamber pots, spectacles, and other goods, and paid for their purchases with cash, store credit, skins, and wood.[18]

The inhabitants of cities such as New York and Boston had more choice in goods and outlets. Hundreds of general stores filled urban streets, offering an assortment of groceries, dry goods, glassware, medicines, and even paint. In 1806, for example, a retailer in greater Boston advertised paint, glassware, and more than forty grocery items, including West India rum, chocolate, and salt fish.[19] In the 1820s, as city populations grew, specialty shops appeared, and by 1850 urban consumers could find stores dedicated to narrow lines of goods, such as books, carpeting, tea and coffee, china, cutlery, and hats.[20] Nearly all stores were small, measuring a few hundred square feet. Many were operated informally from the owners' homes without elaborate displays or much advertising. Specie was frequently in short supply during the first half of the century, and large numbers of city dwellers, like their counterparts in the country, paid for their purchases with other goods or on credit.

Most Americans did not have material affluence or comfort. Before the Civil War, the majority of people lived in what today would be considered cramped quarters, without adequate sanitation. The United States was still predominantly agricultural, and as late as the 1830s, most farm families lived in three or four rooms without basements or flooring. On average, these households probably spent less than $200 a year (about $3,200 today) for all expenses except housing.[21]

Before 1850, the majority of Americans could count the number of durable manufactured items they owned on the fingers of two hands. Some of these items, such as a Wedgwood vase, a grandfather clock, or silver spoons, occupied special places in households, prized symbols of gentility or, for those on the frontier, of people and places once close by and now distant. Recounting her family's move to Lowell, Massachusetts, in the antebellum period, one middle-class woman remembered

> familiar articles [that] journeyed with us: the brass-headed shovel and tongs, that it had been my especial task to keep bright . . . the two china mugs, with their eighteenth-century lady and gentleman figures, curiosities brought from over the sea. . . . Inanimate objects do gather into themselves something of the character of those who live among them, through association. . . . They are family treasures, because they are part of the family life, full of memories and inspirations.[22]

Mass Distribution

Beginning in the mid-1800s and accelerating in the late decades of the century, the United States developed a *national* market. Borne along by the dramatic expansion of the telegraph and railroad after the Civil War, people, livestock, and goods crisscrossed the continent faster, cheaper, and more reliably than had been possible before. In 1830, it took three weeks to move calico or imported earthenware from New York to Chicago. In 1860, it took only three days, and by 1880, people and goods could make the journey in less than twenty-four hours.[23]

The Transportation and Communication Revolution knit together an economy of unheard-of scale. Previously scattered and localized transactions gave way to more frequent commercial connections that spanned regions, industries, and the nation. By the 1880s, many settlers, even in the remote Dakota territory, no longer produced most of the foods they consumed. Instead, increasing numbers of farmers in the West concentrated on wheat or cattle for sale to eastern markets. For foodstuffs such as flour, bottled pickles, salt, spices, fruit, and some vegetables, these men and women increasingly relied on distant manufacturers.

The development of an integrated national market helped fuel mass production. In 1869, more than half of the goods produced in the United States were agricultural commodities, and about a third were manufactures. Thirty years later, the ratio had flip-flopped: 33 percent of all commodities produced were agricultural, and 53 percent were manufactures. The remaining 14 percent came from mining and construction.[24]

Industrialization stimulated economic growth and rising incomes. Rising incomes helped fuel more retail trade. From 1869 through 1900, per capita income adjusted for price changes rose by a compound annual average of 2.1 percent.[25] Although the late nineteenth century was punctuated by depressions in 1873, 1884, and 1893, the long-term trend was strongly upward. This was the most significant growth that the U.S. economy had undergone to date. One obvious consequence was the mass production of hundreds of new goods: canned baked beans, ready-made jackets, mechanical reapers, and many more items. Using technological and other improvements, American factories also turned out larger quantities of existing goods—such as clocks, carpets, shotguns, boots, and buttons—better and cheaper.

Households encountered many of these goods in novel forms and from new sources. For most of the century, clerks had poured, weighed, or scooped bulk items—such as vinegar, soap, and crackers—into desired quantities, at times advising customers on quality. After about 1880, however, rapidly growing companies began branding and packaging a wide range of products for national distribution. Examples include Heinz, Procter & Gamble, National Biscuit Company (Nabisco), American Tobacco, Singer Sewing Machine, Kellogg, Eastman Kodak, and Pillsbury. These manufacturers used their brands and marketing initiatives to build direct relationships with end users and to create large markets for their offerings.[26]

As the scale and scope of national distribution expanded, households relied progressively less on the local retailer's assessment of a product. Instead they came to know and trust goods in the way the new brands were advertised. Heinz's condiments were "good things for the table." Coca-Cola, invented in 1886, was a "Delightful, Palatable, Healthful Beverage."

Ads claimed that Singer sewing machines had helped bring the "women of the world into one universal kinship and sisterhood."[27] Many of these branded products were sold through established distribution channels—urban specialty shops, country merchants, and "drummers" or traveling salesmen.[28]

In the third quarter of the century, several important new outlets exploded onto the American scene: chain stores, mail-order houses, and department stores.

Chain stores. One of the first and most important chain stores was the Great Atlantic & Pacific Tea Company (A&P), which began in 1859 as a small store selling hides and feathers in New York City. Within a few years, the founder, George Francis Gilman, decided to specialize in tea. He and his partner, George Huntington Hartford, opened new stores and gradually broadened their lines to include groceries. By the end of the century, the chain had nearly 200 stores in twenty-eight states. Other chains quickly followed. The Jones Brothers Tea Company, which later became Grand Union, began operations in 1872. F. W. Woolworth opened his first "five and ten cent store" in Lancaster, Pennsylvania, in 1879. And in 1882 the Great Western Tea Company of Cincinnati (later the Kroger Company) opened its doors. These chains gradually homogenized the U.S. grocery market, exposing millions of Americans to a growing and roughly similar array of goods.

Mail-order houses. A. Montgomery Ward was one of the first entrepreneurs to sell things by mail. In 1872 he published his first mail-order catalogue. It was a single sheet, listing cloth, glass, and notions intended to reach Western farm families that would not otherwise have access to these goods. Ward's venture was a huge success, and within two decades his catalogue totaled more than 1,000 pages and had a circulation of 730,000 with an average of two and a half orders per catalogue.[29] The arrival of the Ward's book, one customer remembered, "was like having Christmas come three or four times a year."[30] Other retailers, such as Sears, Roebuck, also began offering goods by mail in the 1880s and 1890s. By 1900, according to historian William Leach, almost 1,200 mail-order concerns were competing for the patronage of six million customers.[31] For households, especially those in remote locations, mail-order catalogues were a vital link to an expanding world of goods.

Chain stores and mail-order houses relied on centralized buying and management, high inventory turnover, and modern accounting systems. These practices made possible lower unit costs than those faced by most local merchants. Chain stores passed some of these savings to customers by offering national brands and private label goods at prices below those of independent retailers.

Department stores. Beginning in the middle decades of the century, a number of these big new emporiums, including A. T. Stewart's, Macy's, Wanamaker's, Gimbels, Jordan Marsh, and Marshall Field's, opened for business in eastern and midwestern cities.[32] Successful department stores became busy places, aimed at sustaining a high volume of sales and rapid inventory turnover across a variety of product lines.

The rise of mass marketers, as historian Alfred D. Chandler Jr. has written, exploited the economies of scale, scope, and speed made possible by the Transportation and Communication Revolution.[33] Department stores depended critically on the expanding telegraph and railroad networks. Retailers such as Field used this infrastructure to coordinate the movement of growing quantities of information and goods between individual producers and thousands, eventually millions, of ultimate consumers. The same distributors quickly learned that by buying directly from manufacturers or, in the case of Field's company, from its own wholesale division, they could move more goods faster, at lower costs, and improve profits.[34]

Marshall Field, the entrepreneur, was part of this new world and embraced the opportunities that were opening up. He was keen to use the technological, logistical, and manufacturing possibilities of his age to build a large, enduring retail enterprise. However, he also knew that commercial success in the upheaval taking place in transportation, communication, and the broader economy depended on more than managing its supply-side developments. To build a competitive distribution business, Field had to comprehend and influence the demand-side shifts that came with industrial capitalism. This entailed understanding a range of economic, demographic, and social transitions.

Field's Chicago career began in 1856. During the forty-six years between that time and 1902, when he presided over the grandest of his several "grand openings," per capita income in the United States, adjusted for price changes, more than doubled. Table 4-1 charts this growth.

TABLE 4-1

U.S. Per Capita Income, 1869–1929
(2000 dollars)

Year	Per Capita Income
1869	2,528
1879	3,684
1889	3,784
1899	4,760
1909	6,140
1919	6,669
1929	7,954

Sources: U.S. Department of Commerce, *Historical Statistics of the United States, Colonial Times to 1970* (Washington, DC: U.S. Government Printing Office, 1976) 1, p. 224. For price indexes, U.S. Department of Commerce, *Historical Statistics of the United States,* 1, pp. 211–212; Council of Economic Advisers, *Economic Report of the President* (Washington, DC: U.S. Government Printing Office, 2000), p. 310.

During the same period, the country's population almost tripled, from twenty-eight million to over seventy-nine million.[35] Cities grew rapidly as industrialization accelerated. Table 4-2 shows the pattern of urban growth during the Transportation and Communication Revolution.

Chicago's growth was extraordinary, climbing from 86,000 in 1856 (when Field arrived) to 1.7 million in 1900.[36] From all over the nation and many parts of the globe, people poured into the city. In the 1890s, a visiting Englishman described Chicago as "the child of steam, electricity, and world-wide exchange" and "the very embodiment of the world-conquering spirit of the age."[37] To the writer George Steevens, it was "the queen and guttersnipe of cities."[38] Swedish novelist Frederika Bremer was more explicit and critical: "Chicago is one of the most miserable and ugly cities, which I have yet seen in America, and is very little deserving of its name, 'Queen of the Lake;' for, sitting there on the shore of the lake in wretched dishabille, she resembles rather a huckstress than a queen."[39]

Urban streets were "largely unpaved," according to historian Robert Twyman, "and as a result were always deep in mud or sending up choking clouds of dust as horses and wagons rumbled by." During the summer

TABLE 4-2

Urbanization, 1850–1910: Population of Selected U.S. Cities

	1850	1870	1890	1910
Pittsburgh	46,601	86,076	238,617	533,905
Chicago	29,963	298,977	1,099,850	2,185,283
Washington	40,001	109,199	230,392	331,069
Philadelphia	121,376	674,022	1,046,964	1,549,008
New York	515,547	942,292	1,515,301	4,766,883
San Francisco	34,776	149,473	298,997	416,912

Sources: Campbell Gibson, "Population of the 100 Largest Cities and Other Urban Places in the United States: 1790 to 1990," *Population Division Working Paper No. 27* (Washington, DC: U.S. Bureau of the Census, 1998), Tables 8–15.

Note: In 1910 and after, Pittsburgh includes Allegheny City. Starting with 1900, New York City includes all the five boroughs.

months, "garbage, dead rats, and animal excrement fermented together beneath the wooden sidewalks, and made walking or shopping something less than a pleasure." Most of the buildings sitting in this sticky soil were made of timbers that were often slapped together to keep pace with Chicago's rapid expansion.[40]

Field recognized that the city's growth was part of the nation's movement west. "Everything was coming this way," he recalled in an 1898 interview with the journalist and novelist Theodore Dreiser, "immigration, railways, and water traffic, and Chicago was enjoying what was called 'flush' times. There were things to learn about the country, and the man who learned the quickest fared the best."[41]

One of the things Field and his partners had to learn was how to create a market for their wholesale and retail offerings. How was the company to interest both merchants and consumers in an unprecedented variety of novel products? What strategic position should Field take in order best to exploit the tremendous opportunities he faced? How could the entrepreneur and his colleagues manage the demand-side transitions of the Transportation and Communication Revolution for their own lasting competitive advantage?

Their fundamental response to these imperatives was to build an ambitious and enduring *brand.* Field realized that creating a meaningful reputation that appealed to buyers and distinguished his offerings from those of competitors was a complex process. To accomplish it, he and his colleagues had to understand how economic change was altering what consumers wanted and could afford. They also needed to figure out what, in turn, merchandisers could do to affect customer preferences for new goods, services, and distribution outlets.

Beginning in the 1860s, the entrepreneur and his partners committed time, energy, and money to acquiring this knowledge, using it to craft an attractive, relevant reputation for the company and its offerings. Based on sophisticated merchandising, rapid vertical integration, ambitious marketing, and innovative customer service, Marshall Field's brand provided a critical source of competitive strength in the wholesale business and particularly the retail division. By the early 1900s, Field's had become one of the most powerful names in department store merchandising, commanding strong customer loyalty, sustained margins, and substantial influence with manufacturers.

Marshall's Early Years

Marshall Field was born on August 18, 1834, in Conway, Massachusetts, a village of several hundred inhabitants in the Berkshire Mountains. He was the third son of John and Fidelia Field. John was a farmer of moderate means, who scratched out a living among the rocks and hills of western Massachusetts. "My father," Marshall remembered, "had good judgment. He made a success out of the farming business."[42] His mother was a determined, religious woman who raised her children to attend church, avoid liquor, and keep their word. She passed on her work ethic and ambition to young Marshall.[43] Both parents, he recalled, "were anxious their boys should amount to something in life."[44] But his mother was a particularly strong influence on the entrepreneur. As an adult, he attributed much of his business success to her.

In 1851, the father turned the family farm over to his eldest son, Chandler. Marshall, then seventeen, certain that he stood no chance of inheriting the property and not having a love of farming in the first place, left home and obtained a clerkship in a dry goods store in Pittsfield, a town near the western border of Massachusetts. From early childhood, he had been interested in what he later called "the commercial side of life."[45] In Pittsfield, he had an opportunity to develop his interests and to discover whether this was an area in which he had any talent.

For four and a half years, Marshall worked for Deacon H. G. Davis, one of Pittsfield's leading merchants. The quiet, slender Field proved to be a natural salesman. He had a quick mind for numbers and a fine memory. In those times, most prices were determined by negotiations between clerk and customer. Payment was often in kind. In this environment, Field learned how to bargain effectively with townspeople and farmers. Most came to trade milk, butter, eggs, and produce for groceries and other staples. He discovered how to judge individual wants and how to relate these interests to the price he charged a customer for coffee, flour, nails, and calico. An old friend of Field remembered his quiet concentration and uncanny ability to understand female customers:

> We called him "Marsh," and he did not resent the nickname, but he mingled with few of the young men of the town. He was not afraid of work, but he always appeared to be turning something over in his mind. As a clerk, he was one of the best Pittsfield ever had, but his popularity was with the women folk. He seemed to know just what they wanted and if it was not in stock he was able without deceit to sell them something else.[46]

Field also dealt well with men, impressing Davis with his poise and salesmanship. When the wealthy New York banker Junius Spencer Morgan and his teenage son, John Pierpont, visited Pittsfield on a business trip in the mid-1850s, the storekeeper asked Field to escort the two visitors around the town. Field and the young J. P. Morgan got on amicably.[47]

In 1856, Davis offered the twenty-two-year-old Field a quarter interest in the business. Field declined because he wanted a wider range of opportunity. That was the moment when Field, swept up in what he later described as "the prevalent fever to come West," fixed on Chicago, a city he believed had "plenty of ambition and pluck."[48] Gathering his savings and a few belongings, he left Massachusetts, determined, as he later put it, "not to remain poor."[49] His only connection in Chicago was his older brother Joseph, who was working for the largest wholesale dry goods house in the city, Cooley, Wadsworth & Company.[50]

Learning the Business

Chicago had hardly existed before the 1830s. At midcentury, its population was 30,000 and rising rapidly.[51] The recent entrance of several major railroad lines hinted at a great economic future. By late 1856, 104 trains a day entered or departed Chicago.[52] But to Field, as he later put it, the "possibilities of greatness were hardly visible."[53] In 1856, the city was still on the frontier.[54] In these rough environs, however, business was booming. People came to Chicago, one contemporary visitor commented, "merely to trade, to make money, and not to live."[55]

With his brother's help, Marshall Field obtained a position as a clerk for Cooley, Wadsworth & Company, earning $400 a year (roughly $7,500 today).[56] He worked twelve to fourteen hours a day loading wagons, clearing docks, and arranging merchandise. To save money, he slept in the store. Marshall was not a naturally ebullient or warm person, and he made few friends at the firm. But after several months, it became clear to his superiors that the serious, focused clerk had a first-rate instinct for merchandising. John Farwell, the senior partner at Cooley, Wadsworth & Company recalled:

> It did not take us long to find out that he had no bad habits, that his word was always good, and that he was with us to make money. Yet these were the characteristics of many other good clerks. But it was discovered in a very short time that he was an extraordinary salesman. He could find out quicker what a woman wanted and sell her quicker than any other clerk in the establishment. . . . He knew how to show off a stock to its best advantage and he always knew what was in stock. . . . The store and the stock was his life.[57]

To capitalize on Field's talents, the company's owners sent him out on the road. With two large sales cases, Marshall traveled through southern Iowa on horseback, stopping in one village after another to talk patiently with local merchants. Almost everywhere he went, he saw the effects of swift migration and economic growth: railroad construction, young towns, new stores. Field was as successful at drumming as he had been selling cloth behind a counter in Pittsfield. He earned a reputation as one of the most winning and trustworthy sales agents in Chicago.[58]

In 1860, at age twenty-six, Field was made a junior partner in the firm (by then called Cooley, Farwell & Company). He was unable to contribute any capital at that time, but in 1862, the senior partners invited him to invest $15,000.[59] He contributed $5,000 that he had saved since coming to Chicago and borrowed an additional $10,000 from one of the senior partners. In exchange, Field became entitled to one-sixth of the firm's profits.

Business conditions during the Civil War "were something extraordinary," recalled John Farwell. Buoyed by military purchasing, demand for many goods skyrocketed. Consequently, he added, "any one who had a stock of goods on hand was practically certain to sell them at an advance over what he had paid for them."[60] Rising prices and handsome profits enabled Field to repay his loan quickly. By 1863, he knew that he was on his way. He would not be poor again.[61]

That same year, he married. He had met Nannie Scott, the daughter of a prosperous Ohio ironmaster, while she was visiting friends in Chicago. Field accompanied Nannie to the train on her way out of town, and with uncharacteristic impulse, he leaped on board as the train was pulling out of the station. By the time Field got off at the next stop, he had proposed, Nannie had accepted, and they had begun planning the wedding. The ceremony took place in June 1863.[62]

But Field had little time for domestic life. Business was too absorbing, its possibilities too urgent and short-lived to accommodate other aspects of life. In 1864, the firm's senior partner, Francis Cooley, retired, and the company was reorganized as Farwell, Field, and Co.[63] Business continued to thrive, nourished by military demand and Chicago's growing population—up to 200,000 in 1864.[64] The firm quickly expanded its sales space.[65]

Despite strong revenues and profits, Field became restless. He did not get along well with John Farwell. He wanted more autonomy. He began recruiting potential colleagues to join him in his own venture, one of whom was Levi Leiter, the company's brilliant young accountant. Leiter had joined the firm in the same year as Field, worked his way up through the bookkeeping department, and earned a partnership stake at the same time as Field. Both men were ambitious, and their skills—Leiter's financial acumen and Field's sales and merchandising talents—complemented one another.[66] Together, they had a capital pool of more than $300,000.[67] They knew they would need more to start their own business, so the two merchants began casting about for other investors.[68]

Just before Christmas in 1864, a tremendous opportunity presented itself. Potter Palmer, owner of Chicago's largest and most fashionable dry goods house, offered to sell his business to Field and Leiter. Palmer's health was poor. He planned to leave merchandising, take a long vacation, and turn his full attention to Chicago real estate. In the twelve years since he had first come to Chicago, Palmer had created a formidable operation. He sold velvets, calicoes, and other dry goods at both the retail and wholesale levels.

Potter Palmer & Company, located in a four-story building at the corner of Lake and Clark Streets, in what was then the city's commercial center, was known for its inviting displays, high-quality goods, money-back guarantees, and splashy advertisements.[69] Palmer targeted his retail merchandise to the wives and daughters of Chicago's newly wealthy, a group largely ignored by other dry goods businesses.[70] However, reasonable prices on a range of stylish goods pulled customers into the store from other social and economic classes as well.[71] Palmer's retailing success and relentless salesmanship fed interest in the wholesale branch of the business. "I always hunted for customers," Palmer said. "If I learned of a man two hundred miles away, buried in a clearing in the forest, who might buy, I got the name of my establishment to him and invited him in. After he once got acquainted with the store, we rarely lost him."[72] By 1864 Palmer was a millionaire and the most famous merchant in the Midwest.

The offer Palmer made to Field and Leiter was an attractive one. In January 1865, partnership agreements were drawn up for the firm of Field, Palmer & Leiter to be capitalized at $750,000.[73] Field supplied $250,000 of this amount and Leiter $120,000. Potter Palmer agreed to remain as a "special partner," contributing $330,000.[74] The remaining $50,000 was supplied by Palmer's brother Milton.[75] Confident about the new company's future, Field and Leiter agreed to repay Potter Palmer about a third of the money he had invested within a year.[76] The partners also agreed to a broad division of responsibility. As stipulated in the original documents, Field was to "have charge of buying all goods for the firm and a general supervision of the entire business." Leiter was to oversee the company's finances, while Potter Palmer's brother, Milton, managed its retail division.[77]

Field, Palmer & Leiter

Although Potter Palmer had already created a successful company and a fine reputation before this new venture, Field and Leiter knew that capitalizing on the opportunities before them would be a challenge. In the mid-1860s more than a dozen dry goods houses vied for consumers' attention and money. Several of these houses, such as Carson, Pirie & Company and Mandel Brothers, were young firms that had been founded since 1860. Others, such as Allen & McKay and Field and John Farwell's business, had been in operation for more than a decade. All these firms served the rapidly expanding regional economy, selling wholesale goods to country merchants in the Midwest. Others offered goods at the retail level. A few, like Field, Palmer & Leiter, operated both wholesaling and retailing divisions.[78]

Competition was fierce, and price wars commonplace. So, too, were bankruptcies, as wholesale houses struggled to unload their stocks, often extending credit to unreliable merchants. Economic downturns, such as that precipitated by a financial crisis in 1857, exacerbated the difficulties of buying and selling goods in a young regional economy. So did the huge price changes that accompanied the Civil War. But in 1865, Field and Leiter were determined to manage the risks they faced. They also were resolved to make the business their own—to use their experience and intelligence to expand the business that Palmer had built.

Assembling a group of skilled merchants, accountants, and salesmen to help them manage the company was a top priority. Several of these men, such as Lorenzo Woodhouse, an experienced buyer, and Harlow Higinbotham, a credit expert, came from Farwell & Company. A few others, including Lafayette McWilliams, were business associates from other Chicago firms. McWilliams, who was an outstanding salesman, had returned from the Civil War battlefields to join the venture. Field also wanted to work with at least a few people whom he trusted completely. Two of his brothers, Joseph and Henry, had mercantile experience, and they now assumed places in the business. To staff the vast majority of sales, clerk, and operational positions, Field and Leiter retained Palmer's employees.[79]

During the first twelve months of the partnership, the policies that Palmer had instituted remained in place. Nevertheless, Field, Leiter, and their colleagues worked tirelessly to enhance the reputation that Palmer had created. The new proprietors hoped to increase the retail operation's appeal to prosperous women. Dubbed "the carriage trade" by retailers because many were driven to the city's shopping area in horse-drawn buggies, such women represented a growing group of potential customers. Field and Leiter hoped to attract them with stylish new products. Shortly after opening for business, for example, Field and Lorenzo Woodhouse started expanding the sewing notions department, adding parasols, cloaks, and other accessories to the buttons, thread, and thimbles that the store already carried. To increase wholesale customers' interest in the firm's offerings, they bought colored worsteds, cassimeres (cashmeres), and new, ready-made goods for the division's woolen department, which they advertised as "greatly enlarged and improved."[80] Field moved to New York City to oversee all purchasing. There, he bought a wide assortment of items, ranging from gingham to shawls to men's collars. He took pains to obtain fashionable products, which he believed would attract both wholesale and retail customers.[81]

Leiter remained in Chicago to manage the company's finances. He and Harlow Higinbotham drew up the broad outlines of the company's purchasing and sales terms. In order to command the best possible prices with manufacturers and wholesale agents ("jobbers"), the business paid cash for all its purchases. In turn, Field, Palmer & Leiter sold the bulk of their wholesale goods to merchants on terms of ten, thirty, or sixty days. Merchants who paid for their purchases within ten days received a 10 percent discount, payment within thirty days earned a 5 percent discount, and sixty days earned 4 percent. Field, Palmer & Leiter's wholesale sales terms were similar to those retailers face today. By nineteenth-century standards, however, these were tight deadlines, but they were necessary to ensure predictable payments to the company and thus financial liquidity.

These and other policies were designed to restrict the firm's wholesale patrons to well-managed, established retail outlets.[82] "Credit and confidence," Higinbotham explained, "go hand in hand and are a bulwark of commerce. . . . To refuse time to some is to refuse their trade." The success of selling on credit, he continued, "depends upon the class of trade [the merchant] deals with, or his environments, and most of all, upon his own ability as a business man and a financier."[83] He and Leiter knew that to grant credit successfully to a growing number of patrons in both the wholesale and retail divisions, they would have to have a way of accurately evaluating each customer's situation, financial integrity, and long-term value to the company. At the beginning of the twenty-first century, credit-rating agencies provided banks, retailers, and other businesses with this information.

But in 1865, Leiter and Higinbotham had to make these assessments themselves. To do so, they began building the organizational capabilities to grant, administer, and refuse credit to a wide spectrum of retailers and final customers.[84] The business partners relied on several information sources to determine a potential wholesale or retail customer's creditworthiness. Field, Palmer & Leiter traveling salesmen reported back to headquarters on the local economy, condition of crops, and population changes. Lawyers, bankers, and station agents in midwestern communities offered their own assessments of nearby merchants. Leiter, Higinbotham, and Field took all such dependable information into account in deciding whether and how much time to grant purchasers in paying for what they bought.[85]

The economic conditions of 1865 tested the young company's position on credit. Wholesale prices had doubled over the first three years of the Civil War, but between 1864 and 1867, they dropped more than 20 percent.[86] Merchants who had purchased inventories months—even years—earlier suffered significant losses in the deflation of 1865.[87] Scores of Field, Palmer & Leiter's small wholesale customers were short of cash. Many faced the prospect of bankruptcy. Rather than let them fail or turn to other wholesalers, Field and Leiter decided to grant extra time to specific retailers. Their market held. By the end of 1865, business was brisk. During that first year of operations, Field, Palmer & Leiter earned $240,000 on sales of $8 million (or about $2.6 million on sales of $88 million today).[88] In 1866, sales climbed 15 percent. By 1867, Field and Leiter were ready to buy out the Palmers' interest in the company. Field was thirty-three years old, Leiter thirty-two.

Field, Leiter & Company

On January 1, 1867, a reorganized partnership, Field, Leiter & Company, opened for business. The early years were hectic. In 1868, the firm left its Lake Street location and moved to larger premises on the corner of State and Washington Streets. There, Potter Palmer had erected a showy six-story building complete with Corinthian columns, large windows, and a marble facade. He now rented the structure to his former partners for $50,000 a year, a price that many other businessmen regarded as astoundingly high.[89]

But Field and Leiter were glad to pay it. It was an elegant, well-situated building that both men believed would suit their growing image and clientele. The upper levels housed the wholesale business. In the late 1860s, the firm's wholesale operations rose steadily as the center of the country developed and thousands of merchants opened for business all over the Midwest. Word of Field and Leiter's merchandise selection, fashionability, and reasonable prices spread. Within a few years, the company was regarded as one of the finest and most reputable dry goods wholesalers in Chicago.

Such success, in turn, enhanced Field and Leiter's retail business, which was located on the main or first floor and in the basement of the building that the partners rented from Palmer. Departments on the main floor included cloaks, shawls, gentlemen's furnishings, and other dress goods. The "Ladies Suit" department on the same floor offered the most recent styles from Paris, including a black velvet ensemble with blue satin piping for $160 (about $2,000 today).[90] On all floors, Field and Leiter offered a diverse collection of fashionable merchandise: gloves, furs, hoop skirts, perfumes, imported linens, and more. The partners also displayed a few unique, prohibitively expensive products, such as a shawl of Persian cashmere, priced at $175, or point lace at $300.[91] These "prestige pieces," like their modern-day counterparts in the Neiman Marcus Holiday catalogue, were unlikely to sell. But Field and Leiter recognized that such goods attracted substantial consumer interest and enhanced the store's identity as a purveyor of fine things.

The entrepreneur and his colleagues paid much attention to the building's furnishings. Gloves, ties, and handkerchiefs were laid out on walnut counters, which lined wide aisles. Gas fixtures cast light on the displays and the store's frescoed walls. The whole effect, wrote one observer, was "enough to turn almost any female head." "From now on," the writer continued, "if an inquiring lady should ask 'Oh, Julia, where did you get that superb shawl?' the reply will be, 'At Field and Leiter's, my dear!'"[92]

With much fanfare, the store celebrated its grand opening on October 12, 1868, which, according to the *Chicago Tribune*, was "a Dazzling Assemblage of Wealth, Beauty and Fashion." The paper reported, "The formal opening by Field, Leiter & Company of Potter Palmer's new marble palace was the grandest affair of its kind which ever transpired even in Chicago, the city of grand affairs."[93] The 1868 festivities were the first in a series of gala celebrations held to commemorate the company's occupancy of new—often larger—quarters. These events culminated in the opening of 1902.

At the time Field and Leiter moved, State Street was on its way to becoming a commercial center. Under Potter Palmer's development, the avenue had been widened, rundown frontage had been destroyed, and a building boom had commenced. Determined to create the "Broadway of Chicago," Palmer helped finance the construction of several marble-fronted buildings, including the elegant Palmer House Hotel.[94] In the 1870s, wholesale houses and department stores, including Charles Gossage & Company, The Fair, Carson, Pirie & Company, and Mandel Brothers, had constructed or leased buildings on State Street.[95] By the 1880s, the "Ladies Half Mile"—the section of State Street between Randolph and Adams Streets—was one of the greatest concentrated shopping districts in the world.[96]

Chicago's and Marshall Field's development, however, was not an uninterrupted ascent. The Great Fire of October 8–9, 1871, stopped Chicago dead in its tracks, devastating thousands of wooden sidewalks, dwellings, and businesses, including State Street.[97] Field, Leiter & Company's elegant building burned to the ground. More than $2.5 million in merchandise was destroyed.[98]

Field and his partners made plans to reopen quickly. Within a week, they had posted a sign amidst the ruins saying, "Cash Boys & Work Girls will be Paid what is due them" and listing where and when employees should report. Operating out of a large, two-story barn at the corner of State and Twentieth Streets, the wholesale business resumed three weeks after the fire. A week later, the retail division reopened in the same structure. In March 1872, the wholesale division relocated permanently to a huge new building on the city's West Side.[99] It was the first time that the two divisions had not been housed in the same building. In the future, they would remain separate to comply with insurance restrictions.

In 1873 on the second anniversary of the fire, Field and Leiter opened a new five-story retail store on the State Street site of their former one. The building, with light wells, skylights, and floor-to-ceiling windows on the ground floor, had 30 percent more square footage than its predecessor. It had been built to display larger stocks of increasingly varied product lines, including carpets and upholstery. More than 500 employees staffed the new establishment, double the number that had worked in retail five years earlier.[100] Table 4-3 illustrates the growth in the department store's workforce.

To help salesclerks and other staff appeal to store visitors and convert them into loyal customers, the management issued its first official set of rules in 1873. Clerks must "never misrepresent any article, or guarantee wear or colors." They were required to "be polite and attentive to rich and

TABLE 4-3

Marshall Field & Co. Retail Employees, 1868–1902

Year	Employees
1868	200
1877	700
1882	900
1894	3,000
1902	7,000

Sources: Robert W. Twyman, *History of Marshall Field & Co., 1851–1906* (Philadelphia: University of Pennsylvania Press, 1954), p. 69; "Marshall Field & Company, Retail," *Chicago Evening Journal* (26 Sept. 1903), p. 2.

Note: Field, Leiter & Co. was renamed Marshall Field & Co. in 1881.

poor alike, and have patience in serving customers" and to show goods "willingly and pleasantly."[101]

Four years later, in 1877, a second terrible fire gutted Field and Leiter's State Street property. Again, the company swiftly reopened in the best temporary quarters available—an exposition building known as the Crystal Palace, situated near the lakefront. To lure customers out of the city's main retail district to this location, Field and Leiter ran free coaches every five minutes between the commercial district and their store. In April 1879, the business moved back once again to its location on State Street, occupying a new six-story building.

Designed in the style of the French Second Empire, this structure had a mansard roof, crowned with eight cupolas. A large, central skylight surrounded by a rotunda illuminated all the sales floors. Corinthian columns and ornate cornices around the light well supported each floor. Specific features such as a waiting room with comfortable chairs and commodious restrooms invited women to linger on the premises. Field's aim was to open a beautiful store that was inviting to female shoppers—a goal he accomplished. A contemporary trade directory said it was "the best arranged retail store on the continent."[102] This "new marble palace" swiftly became a popular destination for Chicago residents and for visitors from all over the world.[103]

Building the Brand

When Field and Leiter took up the reins of their own company in the late 1860s and early 1870s, they faced both opportunities and challenges. Most of these concerned the ever-changing environment in which they did business. In the third quarter of the century, rising population, improved connections to the rest of the country, especially New York, and accelerating industrialization fueled growth and created a host of new, large-scale enterprises.[104] Railroad construction, agricultural machinery, grain storage, commodity exchange, and meatpacking were some of the major industries in Chicago. Wholesaling, banking, and retailing also proliferated.

Immigrants to the city hustled to find jobs and social identities in these expanding sectors.[105] Some of them became wealthy; a few, such as Philip Armour and George Pullman, incredibly so. But most did not. Few could fail to notice the effects of swift economic and social change: the striking contrasts between rich and poor, the ever-present allure of material advantage, the speed with which money was made and lost. In late-nineteenth-century Chicago, as novelist Theodore Dreiser remembered,

> the rancidity of dirt, or the stark icy bleakness of poverty [in some neighborhoods] fairly shouted, but they were never still, decaying pools of misery. On wide bleak stretches of prairie swept by whipping winds one could find men who were tanning dog or cat hides but their wives were buying yellow plush albums or red silk-shaded lamps or blue and green rugs on time. . . . There were vice districts and wealth districts hung with every enticing luxury that the wit of a commonplace or conventional mind could suggest. Such was Chicago.[106]

Economic downturns, such as the one that hit the city and the nation in 1873, added uncertainty to the lives of workers and managers. To many contemporaries, the world seemed to be traveling in new and, at times, frightening directions at breakneck speed. Yet the variety and rapidity of transition did not intimidate Field and his partners. They hoped to harness these waves of change.

In the early 1870s, Field and his colleagues saw enormous potential in the new metropolis. In addition, they realized that Chicago's growth pulled other midwestern cities and towns along with it.[107] This regional expansion extended Field and Leiter's customer base, especially for wholesale, far beyond northeastern Illinois. As Leiter noted, Chicago was becoming "the point of distribution for the Mississippi Valley." Merchants that established a solid base in Chicago had access to customers in "Milwaukee, Detroit, Lafayette, Peoria, St. Paul, Minneapolis, Kansas City, St. Joseph, Omaha, Quincy, Madison, Springfield, Louisville and even as far south as New Orleans." He concluded with satisfaction that "all come to Chicago."[108] It was the mercantile, transportation, and financial nexus of the central United States.

By the 1870s, the firm's owners understood that they were in the thick of the commercial action. But how were they to exploit the possibilities of the expanding Midwest? How could Field and Leiter interest consumers in the new, diverse goods coming out of the nation's workshops and being shipped through Chicago?

They also faced a range of management issues. They had acquired two successful lines of business: wholesale and retail. In 1875, their combined revenues totaled $18 million (about $275 million today).[109] To remain successful, they wanted to determine the existing strengths and weaknesses of each division and to decide which was more important. They then needed to resolve how the two activities should be coordinated to improve the company's long-term profitability and effectiveness.

One of their most important answers to these challenges was to build a strong, consistent, and comprehensible brand for the firm. Field and his colleagues had few models to rely on in building and sustaining such an identity. Up until the last quarter of the nineteenth century, most goods were exchanged as undifferentiated commodities. The majority of merchants selling calico and crackers in rural areas, men such as Marshall Field's first employer, Deacon Davis of Pittsfield, Massachusetts, worked in family-run shops. These stores offered little variety in product mix or service.[110] Even in cities, most stores were known by little more than the owner's name. Although many urban wholesalers and retailers advertised before 1860, few attempted to identify their operations on any basis other than price or product availability. A smaller number of jobbers and retailers conceived of meeting customer needs as a means of distinguishing their operations. Virtually none could imagine using such priorities as an organizing principle in their business.

Inside the warehouse or store, buyers had little to fall back on in deciding whether and what to purchase. Service was limited. In the mid-nineteenth century, caveat emptor ("let the buyer beware") was standard operating procedure between merchants and the people to whom they sold their goods.[111] The customer knew that he or she was liable for faulty merchandise. As a result, a mutual distrust often prevailed between merchant and customer. By the standards of modern consumer culture, the context was often capricious, unappealing, and frustrating—something akin to buying a used car today.

In the third quarter of the 1800s, a score of department store entrepreneurs began to change the terms of retailing.[112] Many of these merchants, such as A. T. Stewart, Potter Palmer, and Rowland Macy, also developed innovative selling policies.[113] The Philadelphia merchant John Wanamaker and Chicago's Potter Palmer, for example, offered money-back guarantees. Macy established a one-price policy that eliminated haggling and uncertainty. These practices attracted shoppers.

Few, however, devoted the organizational attention and resources to piquing and satisfying customer interest that Marshall Field did. From the time he and his partners acquired Palmer's business, they recognized the importance of building a credible, engaging brand for their company—one that wholesale and especially retail consumers associated with the store's name, merchandise, and service.[114] Field and, later, Harry Selfridge, who joined the firm as a stock boy in 1879, worked as a salesman, and became general manager of the retail division in 1887, did not use this terminology, however. The language of branding, like the emergence of corporate brand managers, was an early-twentieth-century innovation.

Field and his colleagues realized early that a carefully crafted reputation was critical to managing the demand side of the Transportation and Communication Revolution. An effective brand would help wholesale and retail customers distinguish Field and Leiter from other stores competing for midwestern markets. It would command consumer loyalty, thus shielding the firm from excessive price competition. Equally important, a viable brand would help the business define its markets by identifying which potential customers the company wanted (and did not want) to serve. Field knew that a strong reputation, prudently maintained, might affect other company initiatives as well. It might serve as a vital criterion for managers evaluating a range of possible actions. Company decisions, including hiring, merchandising, even credit availability, would have to be made with attention to supporting the company's identity and to sustaining its intended meaning to consumers.[115]

The pillars for building such an identity, as Field conceived it, were dependability, high quality, and style. The entrepreneur recognized that in Chicago's burgeoning economy, many people had more money to spend.[116] Some had become fantastically rich almost overnight. Others were on their way to wealth. Many were in the middling ranks. The majority was working class and lived in or near poverty. But, at almost all economic levels, Chicago residents saw their real incomes rise over the second half of the nineteenth century.[117] Field could not measure purchasing power, as twentieth-century economists can; but in the late 1860s and early 1870s, he could see that the city and surrounding region were thriving. It was "a merchant's *beau ideal* of paradise," according to the nineteenth-century writer and clergyman Henry Ward Beecher. Chicago, he continued, "fairly smokes and roars with business." Everyone there was obsessed with "buying and selling, buying and selling, buying and selling."[118]

Field was certain that even in this heady environment, customers would be much more likely to purchase goods, especially new items, if they trusted both the products and seller. For this reason, he and his partners decided to continue Palmer's policy of specializing in better-quality goods. "It was a rule of the house," explained Field,

> that an exact scrutiny of the quality of all goods purchased should be maintained, and that nothing was to induce the house to place upon the market any line of goods at a shade of variation from their real value. Every article sold must be regarded as warranted, and every purchaser must be enabled to feel secure.[119]

Security was not all that Midwesterners desired. Field believed that men and women in the region's young, raw communities hungered as well for style: for goods and services that reflected established standards of taste and social legitimacy. Consumers in nineteenth-century Peoria, Madison, and Chicago wanted more for their money than coats and shawls that kept them warm. They sought products and perhaps, Field reasoned, a shopping environment that helped them define their place in a changing economic and social order.

Identifying which goods and what kind of store surroundings played these roles for customers was a critical task for Field and his partners. During the 1870s, they worked to establish a reputation that would stimulate and guide public taste.[120] In early 1881, after fourteen years in partnership,

Field bought out Leiter's interest in the business.[121] The concern was again reorganized, and its name changed to Marshall Field & Company.

The firm continued to invest in what Field and his colleagues believed were the key components of the company's identity to consumers: product quality and desirability; an appealing shopping environment; and responsive, unpretentious service. By the mid-1880s, the Field's brand—represented by the name "Marshall Field"—had become a symbol of integrity for customers, leading them to prudent buying decisions that they saw as consistent with their rank and aspirations. For wealthy Chicago women, this meant purchasing kid gloves imported by Field from Paris. Retail customers from the middle elements chose factory "modifications" of European-styled linens from the store's less costly merchandise. As the department store's reputation and customer base developed, its sales climbed steadily, accelerating at the turn of the century. Table 4-4 shows this increase. The company enjoyed significant gross margins and healthy operating returns on these sales.[122] The wholesale division also benefited from growing awareness of the brand as mercantile customers from all over the region demanded particularly popular or stylish goods for their retail establishments.[123]

TABLE 4-4

Marshall Field & Co. Retail Sales, 1867–1905
(millions of dollars)

Year	Retail Sales
1867	1.4
1875	3.1
1880	3.6
1885	4.5
1890	6.6
1895	7.6
1900	12.5
1905	25.3

Source: Accounting Ledgers, Marshall Field & Co. Archives.

Josiah Wedgwood, portrait by Sir Joshua Reynolds in 1782, when Wedgwood was 52 and a renowned national figure.

By courtesy of the Trustees of the Wedgwood Museum, Barlaston, Staffordshire, England.

Line engraving of the Ivy House Works at Burslem, where Wedgwood set up as an independent potter in 1759. He rented the cottage, as well as the kilns and pottery behind it, from his cousin John Wedgwood for £15 a year.

By courtesy of the Trustees of the Wedgwood Museum, Barlaston, Staffordshire, England.

Pineapple ware tea canister and cover and slop basin, with green and orange-yellow glaze, from the early 1760s. Wedgwood's early pineapple ware was prized for its shape, color, and, above all, novelty. As demand for these goods grew in the 1760s, Wedgwood probably contracted out the production of some of this ware to local potters.

Victoria & Albert Museum; copyright V&A Picture Library.

Queensware vases on pedestals, with engine-turned decoration, from about 1765. Named for Queen Charlotte, wife of George III, Queensware was immediately popular when it was introduced in the mid-1760s.

By courtesy of the Trustees of the Wedgwood Museum, Barlaston, Staffordshire, England.

Thomas Bentley, Wedgwood's business partner and close friend. Portrait attributed to Joseph Wright of Derby, 1775. Bentley's artistic influence, commercial experience, and social contacts were instrumental to the success of the firm.
By courtesy of the Trustees of the Wedgwood Museum, Barlaston, Staffordshire, England.

An illustration of Wedgwood's showrooms in St. James's Square, London, from Ackerman's *Repository of Arts*, 1809. In 1774, the Catherine Service was displayed in similar Wedgwood showrooms in Portland House, near Soho Square. "We must have an Elegant, Extensive and Convenient showroom," Josiah insisted. The display cabinets, tables, and wide aisles for customer movement were all retailing innovations in the late eighteenth century.
Hulton Getty/Liaison Agency.

Thirteen-inch oval dish in the Catherine Service, decorated with a view of Kew Gardens in Surrey, southwest of London. Its bucolic imagery is characteristic of much of this 952-piece creamware dinner and dessert service commissioned by Catherine the Great of Russia in 1773. The Catherine Service is also known as the "Frog Service" for the empress's palace, which was located on a frog marsh. Each piece bears a green frog crest.

The State Hermitage Museum, St. Petersburg.

Catherine Service flat plate with a scene of an iron foundry in Colebrookdale, Shropshire. The foundry depicted was important in the early Industrial Revolution, and Shropshire became a center of iron production in the eighteenth century. This plate is one of several pieces in the Catherine Service that portrayed England's growing industrialization.

The State Hermitage Museum, St. Petersburg.

Josiah Wedgwood and his family on the grounds of Etruria Hall, painted by George Stubbs, 1780. From right to left: Josiah Wedgwood (I), his wife, Sarah, and their children John, Josiah II, Susannah, Catherine, Thomas, Sarah, and Mary Ann.

By courtesy of the Trustees of the Wedgwood Museum, Barlaston, Staffordshire, England.

A "first edition" Portland Vase, Wedgwood's most celebrated masterpiece of Jasperware, 1793. Wedgwood's vase was a copy of a famous Roman antiquity from the first century B.C. and owned in the late eighteenth century by the Duke of Portland, who lent it to Josiah to copy in Jasper in the late 1780s. Wedgwood and at least three of his modelers made several defective copies before completing what Josiah regarded as a near perfect vase in mid-1789. By early 1790, more than twenty customers had requested a first edition of the vase. But production of the vases continued to be slow, difficult, and costly. In his lifetime, Josiah probably completed ten such pieces. These rank among the greatest technical achievements of European pottery.

By courtesy of the Trustees of the Wedgwood Museum, Barlaston, Staffordshire, England.

Wedgwood cameos were one of the many new product lines developed from Josiah's Jasperware. This jewelry became very popular in the late eighteenth century, especially among the middling classes. On the supply side, it was a product of Wedgwood's friendship and professional alliance with highly successful Birmingham iron-master Matthew Boulton. To increase the decorative and practical applications of Wedgwood cameos, they were mounted in cut steel at Boulton's Birmingham foundry in a variety of shapes, including buckles, brooches, rings, and buttons.

Victoria & Albert Museum; copyright V&A Picture Library.

Wedgwood's Etruria factory in the mid-twentieth century. From 1772 until 1940, all of Wedgwood's production took place in this facility. The bell tower, which summoned Wedgwood's laborers to work, is visible over the center door, left of the ship's mast in this photograph. The Trent-Mersey canal, promoted by Wedgwood and Bentley, ran in front of the factory. Etruria was demolished in the 1960s.

By courtesy of the Trustees of the Wedgwood Museum, Barlaston, Staffordshire, England.

Henry Heinz was 36 when he sat for this photograph in 1880. His confidence had been badly shaken by his bankruptcy in 1875. But his enthusiasm and energy returned swiftly in the late 1870s when his second venture, F. & J. Heinz, began to take off. In the late 1880s, Heinz changed the company's name to the H. J. Heinz company.

Courtesy of the Heinz Family Office.

Horses pull a dray wagon loaded with H. J. Heinz Company products for delivery. Heinz was always keen to take advantage of advertising opportunities, and this wagon bears several bold company signs. Even the boxes of products in the wagon are on display, advertising Heinz India Relish, Chow Chow, Baked Beans, and Keystone Dressing.

Courtesy of H. J. Heinz Company.

A photograph of Heinz Preserved Sweet Onions and Pearl Onions used in a 1910 company publication. Heinz's early product lists, which included horseradish, celery sauce, and chutney, reflected the nation's diverse culinary tastes. Sweet and pearl onions were a common accompaniment to meat and vegetables in English, German, and other turn-of-the-century immigrant communities. Heinz products were always bottled in clear glass to demonstrate their purity and quality to consumers.
Courtesy of the Heinz Family Office.

The H. J. Heinz Company exhibit at the World's Columbian Exposition, 1893. The Heinz name and the Keystone and pickle logos were displayed prominently, and the "57 Varieties" meticulously arranged for maximum advantage. The Heinz pavilion was made of polished antique hand-carved oak, with a pagoda at each corner, where women of different nationalities offered samples of Heinz products to visitors.
Courtesy of H. J. Heinz Company.

Inside the Heinz Print Shop, 1901, where artists created appealing advertisements for Heinz products. Hanging from the artist's worktable is a Heinz sign from the World's Columbian Exposition, "See Our Exhibit at World's Fair, Section 10B, Agricultural Building." All the signs include the "57" logo.

Courtesy of H. J. Heinz Company.

New York City's first electric sign was put up by Heinz at the corner of Fifth Avenue and 23rd Street in 1900. It used 1,200 lightbulbs and cost $90 a night in electricity charges. The sign shows both the familiar pickle logo, here 40 feet long, and the slogan "57 Good Things for the Table." It also promoted the Heinz Pier in Atlantic City.

Courtesy of H. J. Heinz Company.

Heinz's promotion of his brand included pouring "Heinz 57" in concrete on hillsides along major railways and rivers.

Courtesy of H. J. Heinz Company.

The H. J. Heinz Company main plant in Allegheny (now part of Pittsburgh), pictured circa 1900 in an illustration by Charles Graham. The factory began operations in 1890 and was situated on the Allegheny River with access to the B&O Railroad along the river and the Pennsylvania Railroad at the rear of the plant. Today, this plant is the oldest of the H. J. Heinz Company factories and is the headquarters for Heinz U.S.A.

Courtesy of the Heinz Family Office.

The Heinz company opened its manufacturing facilities to the public in the 1890s, using the tours to support its brand and advertise its reputation for quality, purity, and cleanliness. More than 20,000 people toured the Pittsburgh factory each year. Visitors would have encountered a scene much like this—a large packing room full of uniformed women bottling pickles. *Courtesy of the Heinz Family Office.*

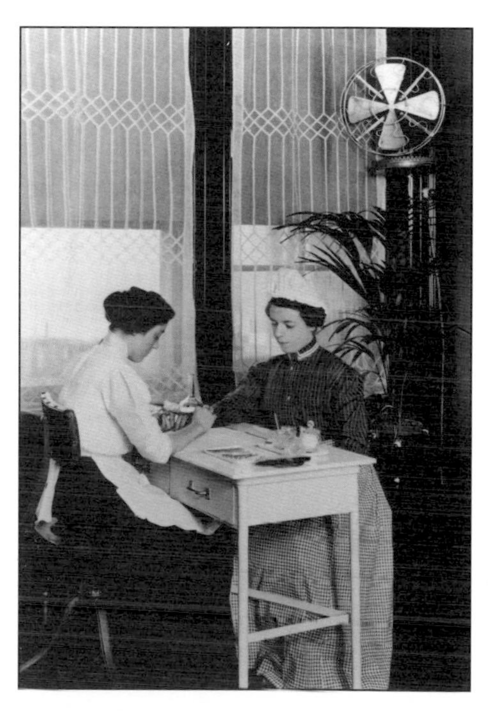

Every employee who handled food at the Heinz factory was required to have a manicure at least once a week. Few workers objected; this practice not only upheld the quality standards that were a hallmark of the Heinz brand, but also inspired employee loyalty and satisfaction. The H. J. Heinz Company was generally considered a good, if paternalistic, employer, and worker turnover rates were consistently lower than those of many other turn-of-the-century Pittsburgh factories.
Courtesy of H. J. Heinz Company.

The young Marshall Field in about 1860, when he would have been 26 years old and about the time he became a junior partner in the Chicago dry goods firm Cooley, Farwell & Company. Five years later, he and Levi Leiter took over Potter Palmer's business, giving Field his first opportunity to head a dry goods concern.
Courtesy of Marshall Field's.

The site of Field and Leiter's once-elegant store at State and Washington Streets after the devastating Chicago fire of 1871. Destruction was complete, and more than $2.5 million in merchandise was destroyed. Field and Leiter, however, were determined not to let the fire put them out of business. Within the week, they had tacked up the rough board sign in this photograph, announcing "Cash Boys & Work Girls will be paid what is due them" and the appointed time and place for employees to report. Within a month, both the wholesale and retail divisions were back in business at a temporary location. On the second anniversary of the fire, Field, Leiter & Co. reopened a beautiful new retail store on the site of the old.
Courtesy of Marshall Field's.

The corner entrance of Marshall Field and Company at the intersection of State and Washington Streets, 1895. The store's attractive window displays (at right) were designed to catch the attention of passersby. This hustle and bustle of smartly dressed Chicagoans was commonplace in the commercial center of the city.
Courtesy of Marshall Field's.

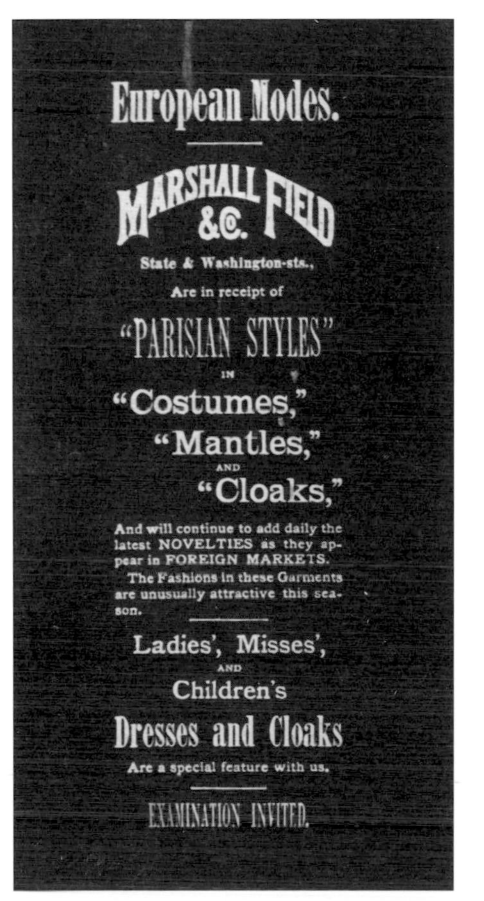

European Modes.

MARSHALL FIELD &Co.

State & Washington-sts.,

Are in receipt of

"PARISIAN STYLES"

IN

"Costumes,"

"Mantles,"

AND

"Cloaks,"

And will continue to add daily the latest NOVELTIES as they appear in FOREIGN MARKETS.

The Fashions in these Garments are unusually attractive this season.

Ladies', Misses',

AND

Children's

Dresses and Cloaks

Are a special feature with us.

EXAMINATION INVITED.

A newspaper advertisement for Marshall Field & Co.'s "European Modes," 1882. Field made sure that his store carried the latest styles from Europe, advertising that Field's would "continue to add daily the latest NOVELTIES as they appear in FOREIGN MARKETS." The store's European offerings contributed to its reputation for high quality, status, and fashion.
Courtesy of Marshall Field's.

The retail rug department in Marshall Field's State Street store, 1893. Great attention was paid to the interior appearance of each department. The retail rug department displayed not only a profusion of luxurious and colorful merchandise, but also ornate architectural detail. *Courtesy of Marshall Field's.*

The retail women's stocking department in the State Street store, 1895. Marshall Field's built a reputation for courteous, gracious service. Customers were invited to be seated at stools along the counters, while comely, well-dressed sales clerks waited on them. *Courtesy of Marshall Field's.*

Horse-drawn Marshall Field's delivery wagons, lined up in Holden Court, the alley that divided the store, running north-south between Randolph and Washington Streets, 1897. The wagons are ready to deliver customers' purchases.

Courtesy of Marshall Field's.

A promotional illustration of Marshall Field & Co.'s new 1902 retail store. It was 12 stories high and covered more than one million square feet of floor space. The store offered customers a variety of services: reading rooms, an infirmary, a nursery, restaurants, luxurious lavatories, a check-cashing bureau, and a theater ticket booth.

Courtesy of Marshall Field's.

The rotunda at Marshall Field's State Street store, circa 1927. The Tiffany dome was made of richly colored iridescent glass. Reminiscent of a cathedral's vault, the design was intended to convey a sense of opulence, awe, and wonder to shoppers.
Courtesy of Marshall Field's.

Merchandising and Vertical Integration

Field understood that building a powerful, profitable brand required a systematic undertaking involving most of the firm's operations. At the center of the effort was the firm's merchandising strategy. All goods offered by wholesale and retail had to be trustworthy. In the department store, company standards dictated that they should be "dignified, progressive, thoroughly up-to-date."[124] In the next three decades, the business broadened its stocks. In 1877, for example, the retail store had 34 departments, including dress goods, notions, and gloves. Seven years later, there were 42 departments, counting jewelry, suits, gents' hosiery, and other product categories; by 1898, the number had climbed to 74, including Japanese bric-a-brac, cut glass, and stationery departments.[125] At the time of the store's gala opening in 1902, shoppers had more than 100 departments from which to choose.[126] In each of these categories, the firm's partners and designated buying agents worked to ensure the quality, stylishness, and appeal of store merchandise.

In the late 1860s and early 1870s, Field and Leiter obtained the bulk of its goods from New York jobbers. Marshall Field himself oversaw purchasing until 1868, when Lorenzo Woodhouse moved east to take over buying. There, the firm's large volume and policy of paying cash for its purchases commanded sizable discounts.[127] The company used these discounts as competitive weapons, passing on some of its savings to mercantile customers in the Midwest. "Why patronize New York wholesalers?" An 1870 wholesale catalogue of Field, Leiter & Company asked that question and answered it: "We guarantee to offer you a superior stock and at as low prices as can be had in any Eastern market for the same class of goods, thereby saving freight and other expenses to the purchaser."[128]

As the wholesale and retail divisions expanded, Field and his partners began bypassing jobbers, purchasing goods directly from individual manufacturers in order to cut costs and enhance the brand's image. Dealing directly with producers allowed the firm to eliminate other wholesalers' markups. It also kept the company in close contact with the latest styles and design innovations.

To increase the appeal and distinction of company merchandise, Field, Woodhouse, and other managers tried to get exclusive distribution rights with specific makers. In the 1870s, for instance, the wholesale division became the sole western agent for Imperial Rugs, American Hosiery

Company, Quaker City clothes, and other suppliers. The Chicago distributor also contracted with manufacturers to produce goods under the Field's label.[129] "We are now prepared to offer for the Fall trade," a Field's wholesale circular declared, "a full line of carpets, mattings, oil cloths, etc. Having the control, and taking the production of several Mills, enables us to offer an extensive variety of private designs, especially adapted for a fine retail trade."[130]

In the early 1870s, Field established several in-house specialty workshops, many of them located in the retail store. These small manufactories produced fur coats, cloaks, suspenders, and other goods for both the wholesale and retail divisions. In the early twentieth century, the firm built even greater manufacturing capabilities, establishing Fieldcrest Mills to supply cotton textiles. Most items produced by these manufacturing arms were marked with the company name and distributed as exclusive designs.[131]

Expanding operations to include additional value-adding processes such as manufacturing—what today is known as *vertical* or *upstream integration*—fed the brand's image of stylish distinctiveness. As Field realized, it offered other advantages as well: Controlling the sources of supply reduced distribution costs and allowed both the wholesale and retail divisions to exercise more control over consumer preferences and to respond rapidly to unforeseen changes in fashion. "The modern merchant must be more than a purveyor of goods," according to a Field's wholesale catalogue. "He must be an authority on styles. He must be a source of supply where the needs of his community must be fully satisfied. Marshall Field & Company are in constant touch with the latest fashions in merchandise."[132]

The wholesale division grew fast in the late 1800s, increasing from eight to forty departments between 1870 and 1890. By the latter year, it offered products as diverse as copper rivets, tea strainers, and infant teething rings. The goods were displayed in over half a million square feet of floor space in the company's wholesale store in North Chicago.

To market these expanding product lines, Field and his colleagues established a traveling sales force. These men ventured as far west as the Dakota territory to sell products to urban and rural merchants. Most traveled by rail or horse. But in the winter months, some resorted to bobsleds to reach customers in remote areas. Many of these salesmen stayed with the company for years, honing their selling techniques and developing long-term relationships with specific retailers. For example, W. F. Hypes, one of

Field's most successful salesmen and a gifted singer, routinely gave concerts to customers.[133] But the most important asset that the company's traveling representatives had in closing most deals was Field's reputation, including the quality of its merchandise and its commitment to customer satisfaction.[134] Wholesale revenues increased quickly, climbing from $11 million in 1870 to $26 million in 1890.[135]

The retail operation also benefited from this growth. Throughout Field and Leiter's business partnership (1865–1881), most retail goods were purchased from their wholesale operation. Buyers from each retail department were able to replenish their stocks daily, paying 6 percent over cost for goods.[136] The integration of the two divisions offered the company significant advantages relative to many Chicago department stores, which did not have in-house wholesale divisions and bought merchandise from independent jobbers. Field's retail buyers always had first choice of new products.

Vertical integration also helped speed inventory turnover by ensuring quick delivery and rapid replacement of retail stocks. Other factors, including close attention to consumer demand, also helped move stocks of goods in both divisions. Table 4-5 illustrates Field's inventory turns (known also as *stock turns*—the number of times per year that the company sold its average inventory) for retail dry goods and the larger retail and wholesale divisions.

TABLE 4-5

Marshall Field & Co. Average Stock Turn: Dry Goods, Retail, and Wholesale, 1885–1905

Year	Dry Goods Retail	Retail Average	Wholesale Average
1885	5.9	4.6	4.5
1890	6.3	5.1	4.9
1895	5.8	4.9	4.8
1902	6.4	5.1	4.8
1905	7.5	5.4	4.8

Sources: Accounting Ledgers, Marshall Field & Co. Archives; Robert W. Twyman, *The History of Marshall Field & Co., 1852–1906* (Philadelphia: University of Pennsylvania Press, 1954), p. 119.

Relative to the performance of modern department stores, Field and his colleagues achieved rapid inventory turns in many product categories, such as silks, gloves, and dress goods. In the 1880s and 1890s, for example, turnover for all dry goods averaged almost six. This meant that Field's sold its average dry goods inventory six times a year. (At the end of the twentieth century, by comparison, most department stores had inventory turns of about three on apparel).[137] Some items such as cloaks, suits, handkerchiefs, and quilts sold especially quickly. In 1879, for example, Field's stock of cloaks and suits turned over more than eight times a year; that is, these products remained in the store an average of forty-four days. Handkerchiefs turned over faster—more than eleven times, with the average handkerchief staying in the store about a month. Quilts were especially popular, turning over twenty-one times in 1879 and staying in the store an average of only seventeen days.[138]

Field scrutinized such numbers, constantly admonishing department buyers and his partners to "keep stocks turning."[139] He realized that the faster inventory turned over, the more efficiently his firm was using its financial capital. He also recognized that turnover provided some measure of how accurately the firm was projecting and—in the case of specially advertised goods—stimulating consumer demand.

In buying from the company's own wholesale division, Field's retail store paid less for its inventory than stand-alone Chicago department stores, such as Schlesinger & Mayer and the Boston Store. Buyers at Field's used some of these savings to undersell the competition on carefully selected staple items. Ready-to-wear hats, notions, and women's cotton underwear were advertised at prices that "were unquestionably the lowest in Chicago."[140] Such goods acted as nineteenth-century "loss leaders," drawing customers from all classes into the store, broadening the potential appeal of the Field's brand, and increasing the store's conversion rate—the percentage of people walking through the store who made a purchase.

The bargain basement achieved similar ends. In the late nineteenth century, most department stores did not have a separate sales floor devoted to lower-priced goods. The brainchild of Harry Selfridge, Field's bargain basement was introduced in the mid-1880s. The underground salesroom carried a wide assortment of discounted merchandise, most of it drawn from slow-moving retail stock. From its inception, the basement was heavily advertised and immensely popular. "Realizing the Growing Demand for

Lower Priced Goods!" proclaimed one early ad, "And to meet the wants of our Rapidly Increasing Business, We have enlarged our Salesroom on [the] Basement Floor." The notice announced the availability of underwear, hosiery, linens, embroideries, cloaks, shawls, dress goods, and other items.[141] By the early 1890s, sales in Field's bargain basement were so high that Selfridge could no longer stock the floor solely with less popular goods from the main retail sections upstairs. He began buying separate lots of merchandise for the basement, most of which were less expensive versions of products found upstairs. In 1900, basement sales topped $3 million, almost a quarter of retail's total.[142] The basement salesroom did more than draw traffic into the store and augment sales. As a dumping ground for slow-moving goods from upstairs, the basement helped keep higher-margin offerings on the main levels orderly and attractive. By relegating specific products to the basement, buyers from individual departments freed up valuable shelf space for faster-turning, higher-margin items.

Attracting Consumers

Although Field's offered low prices on goods in its bargain basement and on specific items upstairs, most of the store's merchandise, including its pricing and layout, was aimed at the carriage trade. In the late 1860s, Field had realized that these consumers had income, influence, and time. He also recognized that they were generally not well served by other retailers. Working from Potter Palmer's policies, he directed his product lines, store displays, fixtures, and employee guidelines at the growing numbers of prosperous Chicago women.[143]

Beginning in the 1870s and 1880s, many of Field's customers were prominent social and political figures. Bertha Palmer, the city's leading hostess and Potter Palmer's wife, was a frequent patron; so was Mary Todd Lincoln. Grover Cleveland visited several times. Ida McKinley, wife of President William McKinley, had her gown for the 1896 inaugural made at the Chicago store. At the turn of the century, the struggling young dancer Isadora Duncan successfully applied for credit to buy a gown at Field's.[144] By the early 1900s, Field's was firmly established as a top-tier department store. Other Chicago retailers, such as Carson Pirie Scott and Schlesinger & Mayer, served the middling ranks; The Fair, the Bee Hive, and the Boston Store catered to working- and lower-middle-class customers.[145] A contemporary child's rhyme captured Field's upscale image:

All the girls who wear high heels
They trade down at Marshall Field's.
All the girls who scrub the floor,
They trade at the Boston Store.[146]

After 1887 when Harry Selfridge became head of the retail division, he, Field, and the division's buyers worried at times that the firm's brand was becoming too exclusive. They used loss leaders, the bargain basement, and advertisements announcing "Less Expensive but Reliable Grades of Goods" to broaden the store's appeal to middle- and working-class shoppers.[147] Some of the store's merchandise, such as an imported Italian lace tablecloth priced at $800, remained beyond the means of all but the wealthiest households. But as the Field brand developed, regularly priced items in the store became symbols of social achievement for the broader ranks of consumers. For example, thousands of Chicago parents purchased children's shoes and other essentials at second-tier stores such as Carson Pirie Scott. Some of the same people saved up to buy a special item—a graduation dress or a first communion suit—at Field's.[148]

The company's reputation for high quality, status, and fashion grew out of a series of initiatives, especially its buying decisions. From the time he and Leiter struck out on their own in the mid-1860s, Field was determined to offer new, distinctive goods to both wholesale and retail customers. In the late 1860s, he made several buying trips abroad. An 1867 advertisement highlighted the foreign goods in the retail store, "selected with much care by our Mr. Field, now in Europe, with especial view to the wants of our public."[149] Four years later in 1871, the business established a permanent buying office in Manchester, England. Field's brother Joseph ran the outpost, overseeing the purchasing and transportation of increasing quantities of international goods. In 1873, for example, the firm imported $1.2 million in dry goods inventory. Seven years later, this amount climbed to $2 million, accounting for 65 percent of all dry goods imported into Chicago that year.[150] By 1900, Marshall Field's had buying offices in Britain, Germany, Belgium, France, and Japan. Six years later, the business bought $6 million in foreign goods abroad, making it the single largest importer in the United States.[151]

Company buyers traveling abroad purchased some goods from international wholesalers, but many lines, including Spanish lace, British cutlery, and Japanese silks came straight from foreign manufacturers. By dealing directly with suppliers and eliminating the jobber, Field's buyers cut costs on their inventories. They also obtained new, stylish goods before other U.S. wholesalers and department stores. When possible, Field's buyers and partners negotiated exclusive distribution contracts with manufacturers abroad. These agreements enhanced the Field's brand, solidifying its position as a broker of fine taste. They were also a source of competitive advantage. In seeking out such arrangements, Field's representatives targeted suppliers of prominent, high-margin goods; for example, Field's negotiated a contract for sole U.S. distribution rights with Fortin Fils, a Parisian glove manufacturer.[152] For most of the 1870s, the French company had sold its famous kid gloves exclusively through A. T. Stewart in New York. In 1880, Field became its sole distributor in the United States.

As Field's scale of operations expanded, however, other international suppliers were interested in doing business with the Chicago company. In the 1890s, for example, Selfridge obtained exclusive Western rights to distribute goods designed by the British painter and poet William Morris. He constructed a "Morris Room" in the retail store, complete with wallpaper, fabrics, and furniture inspired by the artist. Marshall Field & Company heavily promoted the Morris Room and other international exclusives. These and other initiatives helped draw thousands of consumers a day into the State Street store, increasing sales and brand recognition. In 1892, retail sales totaled $7.4 million. Ten years later, when the new building opened, retail sales exceeded $17 million.[153]

Marketing and Customer Service

From the company's inception, Marshall Field and his partners used innovative marketing and customer-service policies to develop and maintain the Field brand. The money-back guarantee was one of the most important of these policies. Though a few New York merchants had begun to offer guarantees in the 1860s, such policies were unprecedented in contemporary Chicago. Yet Potter Palmer realized that to sell his goods, many of them unfamiliar and relatively expensive, he had to create customer trust in his selections. As a result, the merchant began offering a "guarantee of satisfaction" to customers. This guarantee served as a promise to refund the purchase money to any customers who were unhappy with "price, quality, or style."[154]

As with many of Palmer's ideas, Field adopted it, then expanded upon it. This guarantee was one of the distinguishing features of his young brand. Most Chicago merchants during this period had strict return policies; for example, those of J. V. Farwell & Co. announced, "Positively No Goods Will Be Taken Back Unless Damaged When Delivered." But Field, Leiter & Company promised customers that "if not entirely approved," purchases were to be "returned at our expense."[155] Not only were dissatisfied customers to receive a prompt refund, they were to be treated as if they were making a purchase.[156] Although the firm did have a few restrictions governing returns, its policy was the most liberal in the city. By 1900, competitors complained, charging the company with unfair competition.

Despite these accusations, Field maintained his company's guarantee, backed by courteous, unquestioning service. He knew that the policy increased returns and thus operating costs.[157] However, its benefits were substantial. A consistent guarantee inspired customer confidence in the company and its merchandise. The return policy allowed customers to change their minds and encouraged them to buy new, high-priced goods, the majority of which were not returned. In tandem with free delivery, the return policy expanded Field's retail customer base. By the 1890s, shoppers living outside the city center sent for specific goods, sight unseen, and charged the sale. They felt safe in making these purchases because they knew that if they were not satisfied, they could return the items to the store free of charge. Because customers could always return an unwanted purchase, clerks had less incentive to use aggressive sales tactics. This reinforced Field's reputation for gracious service.

The organization offered a range of other services to retail customers. Beginning in the 1870s, company greeters met shoppers at the State Street entrance. These men were trained to welcome all patrons to the store, helping make each visitor feel that she or he was valued by the institution. Greeters took care to call as many customers as possible by name. As one Field's employee recalled:

> I'd get a name, write it down, and at night I'd go over the names, fixing them with faces in my memory. . . . I could only write down the names the way I heard them. If a lady would come two or three times I'd remember her. They'd be surprised when I'd call them by name, and pleased. . . . After autos came it was much easier for I'd get their licenses

> and check up [on their names] that way. . . . My job has been to be the same to everybody, to make them feel that Marshall Field's has been polite.[158]

Management set similarly high standards of service for clerks in the individual departments. Salespeople were instructed to be attentive and courteous to every patron they encountered. Field's clerks, said a woman customer at the end of the nineteenth century, "have a way of making me feel that the whole store is there for my convenience, whether I come to buy, or to return goods I don't want, or just look around."[159] Employee guidelines instructed salespeople to afford customers immediate attention, great patience, and constant respect. Goods should be shown "willingly and pleasantly without asking too many questions as to price, width, size, or color wanted."[160] Clerks were prohibited from using aggressive sales techniques or otherwise pressuring shoppers to buy. A notice from the retail manager's office in the 1890s warned employees not to "neglect a customer who happens to be poorly dressed."[161]

Other service innovations helped make the shopping experience more appealing to consumers. One of the most important of these was Marshall Field's decision in the 1880s to hire women salesclerks. Most department stores in the late nineteenth century employed girls and women to help stock shelves, count cash, keep records, and sew garments, but few retailers hired and trained women to wait on customers. But Field believed that women consumers would welcome female clerks—and perhaps buy more from these representatives than they would from men. The store's first women clerks worked in lingerie and other clothing departments. As Field's retail business and product lines expanded, so did the number of female salespeople, many of whom rose to become department heads.

Another key innovation, inspired by Harry Selfridge, was the tearoom, which opened in 1890. Here, hungry shoppers could eat chicken pie, corned beef hash, and pastries on dainty china and fine linen. This was not the first department store restaurant in Chicago, but it was the most elegant. In 1885, The Fair had started serving meals. But Field's entered the restaurant business a notch higher with its tearoom, which quickly became famous for its food, service, and decor. By 1892 the restaurant was serving over 1,200 people a day and earning an annual profit of $12,000.[162]

Three years later, the store opened a check-cashing bureau. Like the tearoom, the facility made the shopping experience more convenient. The bureau was specifically targeted at school teachers and other working women, who could not cash their paychecks at local saloons. In 1896, a *Chicago Tribune* editor speculated on Field's rationale for opening the facility:

> Given a school teacher, who finds herself in the downtown district with a check in her possession which makes her feel [rich]; given also an easily accessible spot where the check may be cashed without delay; given, too, certain surroundings to that spot, consisting of all the alluring fabrics and bewitching knick-knacks most dear to a woman's heart. What will be the result? Certainly it will not end in the sudden death of trade.[163]

Other services helped create a leisurely, refined atmosphere. Reading and writing rooms, stocked with books and free stationery, were sanctuaries for tired shoppers. The building that was opened with much celebration in 1902 housed a "silence room" for "quiet rest for women and children" and an infirmary staffed by a trained nurse.[164] Parents could leave their children in the store nursery, where trained employees provided free supervision.

To heighten public awareness of its services, merchandise, and brand, Field's advertised heavily in Chicago newspapers. Although its 1860s newspaper ads were indistinguishable from those of other retailers, the tone changed markedly as Field and his partners started developing the company's brand. The ads in 1865 had been small announcements of available merchandise, such as: "Low Prices for Merinos, Dress Goods, Silks . . . Shawls, Embroideries [etc.]. Wishing to make room for Spring Goods, we are offering our entire stock at largely reduced prices."[165] As Marshall Field and his partners began creating a stylish, elegant image for the company, however, their new ads reflected these changes. In 1867, Field, Leiter & Co. announced: "a choice and full assortment of SILKS, selected in Europe expressly for the RETAIL TRADE, comprising all the best grades and consisting in part of Plain Taffetas . . . Velours . . . Moire Antiques . . . Scotch Plaids, Drap de France."[166] Over the next two decades, the company avoided the sensationalism of competitors such as The Fair, which commanded readers to "LOOK, SEE and BEHOLD! THE GREATEST STORE on

EARTH."[167] Instead, Field's ads became progressively more understated, inviting the public to examine its exclusive merchandise.

In the late 1880s, the store's advertising increased in scope and frequency. Selfridge helped to create bigger ads that marketed the entire institution, its competitive performance, buildings, and service, as well as its merchandise. Field's retail linen sale of 1892 proved "phenomenally successful," announced a notice in the *Chicago Tribune*. "In amount of sales, in amount of stock displayed (all of which was new and fresh), and in beauty . . . and variety of patterns . . . offered, this sale has . . . surpassed by a very large percent, any similar effort ever made in America."[168] The next year, the store ran scores of ads to coincide with the World's Columbian Exposition held in Chicago: "Our Retail Store, owing to its enormous size, its perfect arrangements, its wonderful variety of merchandise, and its great stocks is a continual and ever-changing exposition."[169] Many of these ads appeared in the same paper with other Marshall Field notices. By 1902 and the much-heralded store opening, Field's was spending 1.4 percent of sales on advertising, six times its expenditures in 1880.[170]

Conclusion

Marshall Field died in 1906, leaving a fortune estimated at $100 million (the equivalent of about $1.9 billion today). Under Field's successor, John Shedd, sales and earnings continued to rise. By the mid-1920s, its retail division had higher sales than any other single department store in the world. In 1928 the company opened branches in two Chicago suburbs, Oak Park and Lake Forest. The same year, the firm began construction on the Merchandise Mart, a four-million-square-foot wholesale marketplace intended to serve a wide range of retailers. In 1929, Marshall Field's purchased Frederick & Nelson, Seattle's largest department store.

Sales in both the wholesale and retail divisions fell considerably during the Depression, and in 1932 Marshall Field's suffered its first loss. In 1946, Joseph P. Kennedy purchased the Merchandise Mart from the company, and by 1950 the business had sold most of its wholesale and manufacturing interests. It continued to open department stores in the Midwest and, through Frederick & Nelson, in Washington state. The beautiful building in downtown Chicago that Field himself had helped design at the turn of the century remained the company's flagship store, and the

Marshall Field's brand continued to connote quality, service, and style for millions of consumers.

Buffeted by intense competition from specialty retailers, such as The Gap, and mass discounters, such as Wal-Mart, many American department stores closed their doors for business in the last quarter of the twentieth century. Others merged with similar retailers, forming large operating companies, such as Federated Department Stores, which managed several different chains encompassing hundreds of individual stores. Some department stores were acquired by unrelated businesses, and in 1982 Marshall Field's became part of British American Tobacco Industries but kept its name and upscale reputation.

Eight years later, the Minneapolis-based retailing company Dayton-Hudson (later renamed Target Corporation) purchased Field's, which continued to operate under its own brand in more than two dozen midwestern locations. Almost 100 years after Marshall Field had presided over his final "grand opening" in 1902, the Chicago store—complete with its distinctive merchandise, responsive salespeople, Tiffany dome, and other elegant fixtures—remained a destination spot for countless consumers. At the end of the twentieth century, many of the innovations that he helped pioneer, including fashionable, fast-moving offerings, an appealing shopping experience, and a meaningful store identity had become the bulwarks of retailing success.

Preview to Part Two: Past and Present

IN THIS BOOK about business leaders operating in different historical eras, there is a special relevance to the familiar saying that the past informs the present and the present illuminates the past. Obviously, the book is a work of history, but its contents also reflect its origins in the distinct milieu of the Harvard Business School. In the decade that I spent doing research and exposing my students to the book's evolving contents, I brought my historian's knowledge of long-term capitalist development to bear on current issues of business leadership. At the same time, I learned a great deal from both students and colleagues about how today's consumers think and how entrepreneurs and their organizations work. This understanding proved useful in analyzing specific questions about the very different worlds of eighteenth- and nineteenth-century business history—that is, about Wedgwood, Heinz, and Field, who together comprise Part One of the book.

Part Two is about business leaders in the latter half of the twentieth century, and the text ends close to the present time. Part Two opens with Estée Lauder, who helped build a vibrant market for prestige cosmetics after 1945. The next chapter analyzes Howard Schultz's creation of the successful Starbucks organization during the 1980s and early 1990s. Chapter 7 investigates how a very young Michael Dell used his precocious knowledge about the demand side of the personal computer market to construct powerful relationships with business and household consumers.

From the historian's viewpoint, of course, it is far too early to assess whether the three twentieth-century companies analyzed here will endure as Wedgwood's, Heinz's, and Field's have done. This is why many historians, myself included, tend almost reflexively to avoid writing about the recent past. For good reasons, historians prefer the long perspective to the short, and in that respect Part Two is an unorthodox endeavor. But in researching the book, it became clear to me that for my topic the past can inform the present (and vice versa) to an unusual degree. So I am willing to assume the risk that some of my interpretations of Estée Lauder, Howard Schultz, and Michael Dell may be shown by future scholars (who may be aided by access to personal and corporate archives not yet available) to have been slightly awry in this or that particular.

And yet, however the personal stories of Lauder, Schultz, and Dell turn out, and whatever the ultimate fate of their companies, several facts are already indisputable. In a relatively short time, these three innovators and their companies have made large and influential markets for their offerings. They have profoundly influenced customers' expectations and, not incidentally, also the ways in which other firms in their industries have had to compete. These three twentieth-century entrepreneurs share these characteristics in full measure with the three from longer ago analyzed in Part One.

Before 1750, for example, most Britons ate off wood or pewter plates. Then came Josiah Wedgwood. In antebellum America, the majority of women made their own pickles. Then came Henry Heinz. Until the Civil War, urban retailing was a specialized activity with a wide variety of small shops offering particular kinds of goods. Then came department store entrepreneurs such as Marshall Field. Before 1945, few American women wore premium lipstick or facial creams, and those who did bought them in beauty shops along with elaborate treatments administered by trained cosmeticians. Then came Estée Lauder. Prior to the late 1970s, Americans bought ground coffee mostly in one-pound cans sold in supermarkets and supplied by large food processors. Then came Starbucks. Before 1980, most businesses used only typewriters and copy machines for paperwork. Large companies relied on mainframe and midsized computers to handle extensive calculations and data processing. Only a small number of households owned a personal computer or printer. Few if any of these users expected to be able to specify a particular computer's configuration. Then came Apple, IBM, Compaq, and Michael Dell.

Like other men and women with appealing ideas for new products, the six entrepreneurs analyzed in this book had sound intuitions about what economic change meant for consumers' wants and needs. But these six were more than savvy marketers. They were also *institution builders*, who oversaw the conversion of entrepreneurial inspirations into viable organizations.

The opportunities and challenges that these individuals confronted suggest a number of important lessons. I close the book with a survey of the historical comparisons and contrasts among these entrepreneurs' approaches and strategies as they evolved from Wedgwood's experience in the late 1700s through that of Dell at the beginning of the twenty-first century. I conclude with an extended commentary about the relationship between historical forces and entrepreneurial agency, emphasizing common themes about entrepreneurship, communication with consumers, the role of brands, and the importance of functional coordination within organizations.

Part Two begins with Estée Lauder, whose remarkable career illustrates these themes with exceptional vividness.

PART TWO

THE PRESENT

CHAPTER 5

Estée Lauder

Prologue: The Launch of "Beautiful"

In the summer of 1985, Estée Lauder Incorporated, an American company, prepared to launch "Beautiful," its latest fragrance. It was the company's first new perfume in seven years and was intended to enhance the cosmetic manufacturer's leadership position in the $3.8 billion U.S. fragrance market.[1] Estée Lauder herself, the organization's cofounder and chairwoman, then seventy-seven, had created the scent. "I wanted a new fragrance," she said, "so I started mixing the finest oils and essences. I worked on one, and that came out lovely. I worked on another and *that* came out lovely. I put them together and that came out beautiful."[2]

Developing an interesting, appealing perfume was just the beginning. Once she was satisfied with her creation, Lauder began working with senior colleagues to fashion an ambitious marketing plan. She left no aspect of this process to chance, deliberating over the new product's image, packaging, accompanying cosmetics, and store rollout. She devoted particular attention to choosing a name for the fragrance. Major scents had traditionally been labeled with nouns rather than adjectives. For example, Chanel's "Coco," also introduced in 1985, was named after the company's founder, French designer Coco Chanel. Calvin Klein's "Obsession," launched the same year, was named for the times, according to company president Robin Burns. "Today, women are obsessed," she explained. "They're obsessed with diets, obsessed with careers, obsessed with equality, obsessed with marriages, obsessed with bringing up children."[3]

Lauder knew that whatever name she chose, it had to reflect an image that female consumers considered attractive and relevant to their lives. This vision, like the fragrance itself, had to be consonant with the meaning of the Estée Lauder brand. Toward this end, she and other company executives had considered calling the new perfume Elle, E.L., and Fleurs 2000. They floated these possibilities with scores of women. Lauder offered samples of the scent to friends and associates. When she asked for their reactions, some said the fragrance was beautiful. The entrepreneur realized she had found a name. "That's good enough for me, we'll call it Beautiful," Lauder remembered, saying, "I'm so tired of all those sexy names that are being used to sell perfume. If you're beautiful, you're also going to be sexy—you just don't have to talk about it."[4]

Estée Lauder not only named her perfumes—she named herself. The European sounding "Estée" evolved from a succession of earlier names she used, including Esther, Esty, and others. Lauder was her married name, though initially it was spelled Lauter and was changed on her initiative.

She was born Josephine Esther Mentzer in New York City in 1908, of Hungarian immigrant parents. Even as a teenager, she showed remarkable talents in preparing and selling face creams. In 1929, at age twenty-one, she married Joseph Lauter, of Austrian descent. In the 1930s, self-employed in the beauty business, she steadily gained experiences with skin care products, makeup, and sales methods. In 1946, when she was thirty-eight, she founded Estée Lauder Cosmetics with her husband, Joe.

The company's introduction of Beautiful in 1985 had several strategic objectives. Most obviously, it was intended to capture consumer interest in a crowded category. More than 80 percent of American women used fragrance in the mid-1980s.[5] They had a bewildering array of colognes, perfumes, and toilet waters from which to choose. In 1985, more than 700 fragrances were distributed in the United States.[6] Most of these scents were sold through mass merchandisers and drugstores. But the more expensive, prestigious fragrances, such as Chanel No. 5 and Estée Lauder's White Linen, were available primarily in department stores. In all of these outlets, competition was fierce.

Scores of manufacturers from Avon to Chesebrough-Pond's to Yves St. Laurent (owned by Squibb Corporation) competed to offer scents that best met women's evolving needs and wants. Most relied heavily on product launches to help them do this. In the mid-1980s, new fragrance introductions averaged about seventy a year. The majority of these—more than three-quarters—failed.[7] Purchasers seemed to use their choice of fragrance as many used the purchase of a car or piece of clothing—to express themselves. Consumption of certain goods served as a means by which women and men explored their own self-images, including their identities, creativity, fantasies, and fears.[8] By addressing the priorities of a particular market segment, product launches offered fragrance makers a crucial opportunity to reach new customers and expand their existing share.

Some of this increase would come from perfume sales. But Estée Lauder Inc. also planned to introduce body lotion and powder under the Beautiful name, and these new products would drive additional revenues. Just as important, sales of other Estée Lauder cosmetics were likely to grow after a fragrance launch. Consumers who had not previously bought a company's products often became interested in its broader offerings after buying a specific perfume for the first time.[9]

Priced at $150 an ounce, Beautiful was targeted at women in their late twenties.[10] This was something of a departure for the cosmetics manufacturer, which had generally concentrated its original and most popular brand of cosmetics, the Estée Lauder line, on female buyers thirty-five years and older. Lauder managers projected that younger women were more likely to buy Beautiful for themselves than wait to receive it as a gift.[11]

The new launch was directed toward other strategic goals as well. It was intended to help establish a credible, differentiated position for the new scent. Why should consumers choose Beautiful rather than Coco, Obsession, Yves Saint-Laurent's Opium, or other competing products? All facets of Beautiful's introduction, from the pink and gold packaging to the counter decorations in department stores, were coordinated to present the product as a premium fragrance that was unabashedly romantic. Lauder executives selected a bride as the advertising symbol for the new perfume. "In almost every woman's life," noted a marketing vice president, "there's a moment when she's said to be beautiful. The imagery of the bride is timeless, classic, an integral part of every culture's traditions."[12]

This positioning stood in marked contrast to that of many popular perfumes. Obsession, Opium, Revlon's Scoundrel, and Dior's Poison had overtly sexual associations, many of which bordered on the risqué. But her own customers, Estée Lauder maintained, "were too fine, and more important, too smart, to be taken in by crudeness." These women, she continued, were "elegant achievers." They were independent and wanted something more than sex appeal.[13]

In addition to establishing the perfume's position in the marketplace and attracting specific consumers, the launch campaign was also intended to enhance the broader Estée Lauder brand. In 1985, Estée Lauder Inc. was a privately held company, selling a range of skin care products, makeup, and fragrances under the Estée Lauder name.[14] The enterprise had also developed three other cosmetics brands—Aramis, Clinique, and Prescriptives. In the United States and more than seventy other countries, all four of these names had become household words. Each of the brands commanded strong consumer recognition, premium prices, and significant market share in their respective segments. Company sales totaled over $1 billion in 1985.[15] The flagship Estée Lauder brand or line of products, sold primarily through department stores, accounted for the most revenues.[16] To millions of women, the Lauder name represented quality, elegance, individual control, and self-respect.

To bring these associations home to consumers, the company developed an extensive marketing campaign based on in-store promotions, direct mail, and print advertising. The manufacturer had not used television to introduce earlier fragrances. But company executives decided to have a thirty-second commercial made for Beautiful's launch. The ad featured a top fashion model wearing a $15,000 wedding gown. Filmed in a bucolic setting with a rendition of the song "You Are So Beautiful" playing in the background, the commercial closed with the tag line "This is your moment to be beautiful."

All marketing efforts were carefully coordinated to coincide with the perfume's fall rollout in selected stores. Neiman Marcus, for example, was scheduled to be the first retailer to offer Beautiful. Shortly after Labor Day, Estée Lauder arrived in Dallas to promote the fragrance at the retailer's headquarters store. This was the first of a series of personal appearances she made to help launch the new perfume. Wherever she went, listeners were struck by her energy and missionary-like zeal.[17] "Every one of you can be an Estée Lauder," she told Neiman Marcus saleswomen. "You're beautiful. No matter how old you are, you can always feel like a bride. Now I am going to show you my new commercial. It's going to be on every television throughout the world!"[18]

The manufacturer worked closely with retailers to market Beautiful. Each store that distributed Estée Lauder cosmetics received detailed guidelines on the appearance of sales counters, banners, windows, and personnel. The colors pink, gold, and the company's signature blue were to be featured in these venues. Each sales representative for the cosmetics maker was required to wear a pink smock and matching scarf during the launch.

Some retailers planned in-store events to promote the new fragrance. Kaufmann's department store in Pittsburgh, for example, staged a mock wedding on the sales floor while customers feasted on free cake. Other retailers hired models to distribute pink cloth flowers scented with Beautiful. Some stores arranged for instant photographs to be taken of shoppers and placed in pink frames.[19] Whether stores orchestrated an elaborate event or not, nearly all of them that sold Lauder products distributed large numbers of samples to promote the new perfume. Estée Lauder had long believed in the importance of using samples to build consumer interest in her products. For the Beautiful launch alone, the company planned to give away 25 million samples of the product.[20]

Advertisements by direct mail and in print encouraged women to visit the Estée Lauder counters in local department stores. Scented sachet cards went to thousands of charge-account holders at specific retailers. Newspaper and magazine ads were coordinated to appear with the perfume's arrival in individual stores.

Extensive advertising, like the rest of the Beautiful launch, represented a substantial expenditure for Estée Lauder Inc. The company did not release its marketing costs for the new fragrance. But it is reasonable to assume that the manufacturer spent at least $10 million introducing its new perfume.[21] From the perspective of the senior management team, this expenditure was a smart bet. Estée Lauder had a strong track record anticipating what would appeal to consumers. If she was right about the appeal of her latest perfume, the costs of launching the scent would quickly be repaid in thousands of repeat sales. Many of these customers would also buy other company products.

During the next fifteen years, Estée Lauder executives had reason to be satisfied with their investment in Beautiful. The perfume was enormously popular in its inaugural year, and it continued to sell well in U.S. and international markets.[22] Through most of the late 1980s and the 1990s, Beautiful was a leading product among prestige fragrances distributed in the United States. In 1998, for example, it was the second most popular scent in the category. The top seller was Pleasures, an Estée Lauder fragrance introduced in 1995.[23] These and other products helped expand the company's sales to almost $4 billion in fiscal 1999.[24] As the decade closed, the manufacturer's product lines, including those recently developed and acquired, accounted for 46 percent of U.S. prestige cosmetic sales.[25]

The markets for beauty products—which included makeup, skin care products, fragrances, and toiletries (dental care products, shaving items, and deodorants)—had changed substantially since the early 1920s when, as a teenager, Estée Lauder first started experimenting with skin creams. At that time, the U.S. cosmetics and toiletries business was a fledgling sector with retail sales totaling about $130 million (or $1.9 billion today).[26] On a per capita basis, the average American spent $1.20 ($10.10 today) annually on all goods such as lipstick, hand lotion, cologne, toothpaste, and razors.[27] Working women in cities probably spent more than this, most rural consumers less. Regardless of where they lived or what they did for a living, the majority of women in 1920 would not have considered perfume, facial cleansers, or after-shave essential goods.

By the mid-1990s, cosmetics production was a thriving global industry with estimated worldwide revenues of more than $60 billion a year.[28] More than half of these sales were generated in the United States.[29] The average American at the close of the twentieth century spent about $100 annually on cosmetics.[30] The bulk of these expenditures was for makeup, fragrances, and products for skin care, hair care, and oral hygiene. Unlike their counterparts in the early twentieth century, most consumers in the 1990s viewed these expenses as routine components of the cost of living.

How did female and male consumers come to make such products a part of their everyday lives? What role did entrepreneurial brand creation play in the evolution of consumers' attitudes toward these goods and the larger market? How were these changes related to broader economic and social shifts?

Estée Lauder probably did not focus on these larger historical issues. She was interested in understanding *current* happenings and what they meant for her life, professional and personal. Growing into adulthood in the 1920s, she realized that the possibilities confronting women were changing. On average, most American women then had more disposable income than their mothers. More held jobs outside the home. Many played larger roles in getting and spending household resources than had previous generations of women.

These changes accelerated in the 1940s during and after World War II. Rising incomes, population growth, increases in the female workforce, and women's expanding public roles influenced consumers' priorities, creating new desires and underscoring existing ones. Such transitions, Lauder realized, presented significant strategic opportunities. Acting on her own intuition about the demand side and input from her customers, the entrepreneur constructed a meaningful identity for her products, one that women associated with quality, self-expression, reinvention, elegance, and control. Relying on tightly controlled distribution, imaginative marketing, and careful merchandising, she and her colleagues built a brand that, by 1970, had become one of the most powerful in the business.

As her company grew in the 1960s, Lauder and her colleagues worked to translate the founder's entrepreneurial knowledge of the demand side into a range of *organizational* capabilities.[31] These efforts were very successful. Many of the specific initiatives that they pioneered to interest and earn the trust of consumers—women and men alike—such as gift-with-purchase and on-site sales training, quickly became industry standards. At the end of the twentieth century, experts recognized the company as the premier creator and manager of prestige cosmetic brands in the world.[32] Most observers also applauded management's long-term perspective, distribution control, and ability to anticipate and respond to shifts in consumer behavior.

The Beauty Business

Ancient Origins

Estée Lauder's start in the cosmetics industry began in the 1920s in her home country, the United States. But the use of cosmetics had a long history that dated back at least 5,000 years. Archeological evidence has revealed that in ancient Egypt, men and women painted their eyes, used perfumed oils, and applied softening ointments to their skin. Egyptian nobles were often buried with makeup, wigs, and mirrors to ensure adequate supplies for their passage into the next world. Jars found in the tomb of Tutankhamen, for example, contained skin creams.[33]

Ancient peoples in Persia, Assyria, Japan, and Phoenicia, among others, also applied cosmetics.[34] Both sexes in classical Greece and Rome rubbed perfumed oils, including that from wool (known today as lanolin), into their skin. Upper-class women in both societies used makeup. In the second century A.D. Greek physician Galen warned his peers about the dangers of contracting mercury poisoning from face paint.[35]

Many early Christian writers opposed the use of makeup and hair color, regarding these practices as deceitful or wanton. Powdering one's face or "lying Blush on the Cheeks" altered God's creation and must be the work of the Devil, declared St. Cyprian, the third-century bishop. Writing a century later, St. Ambrose was more virulent: "O woman," he wrote, "thou defacest the picture if thou daubest thy countenance with materiall whitenesse or a borrowed red. . . . Do not take away God's picturing and assume the picture of a harlot."[36]

In spite of such objections, women and men continued to use cosmetics during the Middle Ages and Renaissance. Queen Elizabeth I, who reigned from 1558 to 1603, helped popularize perfume, powder, rouge, and other cosmetics in England. She used lead paint to create her famous lily-white complexion. The monarch usually wore a red wig, and her courtiers marveled that as she grew older, "her hair was of a light colour never made by nature."[37]

The use of cosmetics gradually spread over the next two centuries. By the 1700s, large numbers of wealthy European men and women whitened their faces. Women also colored their cheeks and lips, penciled their eyebrows, and applied beauty spots made of silk or velvet. Clergymen and other observers criticized such practices as tools of artifice, warning men to examine beautiful women carefully. One eighteenth-century British writer was initially enamored of his lover's "fair Forehead, Neck, and Arms, as well as the bright Jet of her Hair." But "to my great Astonishment," he continued, "I find that they were all the Effects of Art. Her Skin is so tarnished with this Practice, that when she first wakes in a Morning, she scarce seems young enough to be the Mother of her whom I carried to Bed the Night before."[38]

Early U.S. Markets

Upper-class women and men in North American cities also used cosmetics. In the eighteenth century, both sexes wore fragrance, whitened their faces, and applied patches to their faces—small bits of gummed silk cut into crescents, stars, circles, and other designs.[39] Many women and men, including George Washington, sported powdered wigs.[40]

Elite enthusiasm for cosmetics began to abate in the late 1700s. During the American Revolution, men and women were expected to shun the most obvious trappings of aristocratic society, including wigs and luxurious clothes. As ambassador to France, Benjamin Franklin made a point to discard his wig for a fur cap and his court finery for plain dress.[41] The use of face color and other cosmetics also fell out of vogue.

Opposition to cosmetics continued into the nineteenth century. Equating external appearance with inner morality, social observers in the United States criticized the use of face paint, rouge, and lip and eye colors. Such practices, many argued, were a form of hypocrisy that effectively concealed a person's true virtue.[42] Some nineteenth-century observers associated the use of face color with prostitution and sexual brazenness.[43]

Despite such strictures, women and, to a lesser extent, men continued to use cosmetics. Many households made their own, drawing on rich oral and written traditions. Native Americans had long blended plants as remedies for skin problems. West African slaves crushed berries to redden their cheeks.[44] Some white women produced face powder from pulverized flour or starch. Women from varied ethnic backgrounds made their own simple toilet waters and lotions. Most of these practices became part of a store of collective beauty knowledge, passed by word of mouth among female family members, friends, and neighbors. In making beauty potions, women also relied on early cookbooks or household manuals, which frequently contained recipes for ointments and curative waters to treat dyspepsia (or what is known today as indigestion) and other ailments.[45]

Americans' interest in cosmetics extended to few commercial products. Most nineteenth-century consumers remained wary of face powder, skin whitener, rouge, and other items sold in general stores or urban druggists. In addition to long-standing moral and social concerns, many doubted the safety of various products. Doctors, advice writers, and others cautioned buyers to avoid formulas that contained lead, mercury, or arsenic. In 1858, for example, actress Lola Montez published a book of cosmetics recipes, advising every woman "to become *her own manufacturer*—not only as a matter of *economy,* but of *safety.*" Patent cosmetics, she continued, "have ruined the finest complexions and induced diseases of the skin and of the nervous system."[46]

Although a handful of larger companies such as Colgate-Palmolive (founded in 1806) sold their products in bigger markets, most cosmetics makers were small concerns that distributed their goods in local or regional outlets. For much of the nineteenth century, the beauty business was a tiny sector of the economy. In 1879, for example, the total value of cosmetics, toiletries, and perfumes made in the United States was about $3 million. In the same year, the early food processing industry exceeded over $1 billion in output.[47]

The Market Grows

The cosmetics industry grew quickly between 1890 and 1910, fueled by changes on both the supply and demand sides of the U.S. economy. On the supply side, female entrepreneurs helped create the first large American market for beauty products. Madame Celeste J. Walker, Elizabeth Arden, Helena Rubinstein, Harriet Hubbard Ayer, Annie Turnbo, and others got started in the cosmetics business a generation or more before Estée Lauder. Each of these earlier entrepreneurs sold her own line.[48] Most worked outside the established wholesale and retailing systems, distributing their products by mail order, through the growing number of beauty salons, and door-to-door. Many of these women advertised their abilities to understand women's needs and wants better than male doctors or manufacturers.[49]

Some, such as the African-American entrepreneur Celeste Walker, were proud of overcoming humble beginnings. Madame Walker, as she became known, was a daughter of former slaves. Orphaned in childhood, she built up a hair-care and hot-comb business that catered to African-Americans. Walker employed hundreds, and later thousands, of African-American women as agents to sell her products door-to-door, urging them to show others how to be independent.[50] Her salespeople responded enthusiastically.[51] When Walker died in 1919, she had amassed a personal fortune of several million dollars. At the time, her company had 25,000 agents, almost all women.[52] (At the century's end, the Walker Company still used the founder's original formulas.)

Elizabeth Arden and Helena Rubinstein took a different tack in creating their public lives. Arden was born in 1884 to a poor Canadian farming family. Rubinstein was born in 1870 in Cracow, Poland, and grew up in a middle-class home. Each woman deliberately obscured her own origins. Both tried to project an image of aristocratic glamour, believing that this would help them sell beauty services and products. Arden, for example, regarded her given name, Florence Nightingale Graham, as inappropriate for an elegant beauty salon. She chose *Arden* from a Tennyson poem, believing it had a sophisticated sound when paired with *Elizabeth.* She furnished her Fifth Avenue beauty parlor with French antique chairs, Oriental carpets, and fresh flowers to simulate elegant drawing rooms. As her business grew and her fame spread, she was careful to hide her childhood poverty.[53]

Rubinstein followed a similar business strategy to that of Arden, establishing beauty salons in U.S. cities before starting to manufacture her own line of skin care products and cosmetics. She encouraged women to join her company and the larger beauty industry, saying it offered them "a field that is their own province—working for women with women, and giving that which only women can give—an intimate understanding of feminine needs and feminine desires."[54] Like Arden, Rubinstein obscured her origins, claiming to have been born into a wealthy European family. Within two decades of starting out, both entrepreneurs created multimillion-dollar companies.[55]

Men, too, entered the cosmetics business. In 1886, David Hall McConnell founded the California Perfume Company (later renamed Avon).[56] Twenty years later, Max Factor, a Russian-born wigmaker and cosmetician, began selling theatrical makeup to actors in Los Angeles and gradually transformed his brand into one for the mass market. In the next decade, his children expanded the company's distribution by promoting the products in retail drugstores. By 1927, Max Factor's makeup was available coast to coast. The next year, the company's ads ran in movie and romance magazines.

At the turn of the century, several larger, established companies began producing skin care products. Most of these firms, such as Pond's, which was founded in 1846 to produce household remedies, applied methods of mass production and distribution to the manufacture of skin care products. At the same time, enterprising pharmacists transformed private formulas, once sold locally, into trademarked, advertised products for a national market. In 1914, for example, George Bunting created a formula to soothe sunburn and "knock eczema," hawking it on Maryland beaches. Noxzema, as his new product was named, was soon sold across the country.

Through corporate initiatives and especially by entrepreneurial efforts, the growth of the cosmetics industry accelerated after 1910. Retail sales of skin care products, makeup, and fragrances reached $129 million in 1920.[57] Per capita output of cosmetics, perfumes, and toiletries rose 56 percent in the 1920s.[58] The beauty business, wrote a reporter for the *Saturday Evening Post* in 1926, "is a husky infant, and growing so rapidly that only now is the Government surveying it for the purpose of standardizing it and learning just how big it really is."[59] By 1930, industry sales totaled $336 million. Adjusted for price changes, this was a threefold increase over revenues a decade earlier.[60]

Despite innovation and growth on the supply side in the 1920s, many consumers initially had been slow to embrace beauty products. As late as 1914, the average person spent only about 40 cents annually (or about $6.70 in 2000) on any kind of toiletries, including makeup, shaving supplies, and dental products.[61] An early trade journal estimated in 1916 that only one in five Americans used toilet preparations of any kind.[62] Modern attitudes toward personal appearance and their attendant buying habits did not take sudden hold at the beginning of the new century.[63]

But older objections to makeup and toiletries were eroding, and this was an important start in laying the demand-side foundations of a mass market. Urban consumers, especially those in New York City, led the way. They were the first large group to purchase commercial skin care products and beauty services such as those made by Madame Walker, Elizabeth Arden, and Helena Rubinstein.[64] Not surprisingly, they were among the earliest buyers of makeup, including eye shadow and lipstick. Observers in major cities were struck by how many women from all social classes wore makeup.[65] Skin care rituals, such as daily use of an astringent, facials and other beauty services, as well as specific products came more slowly to smaller urban centers. So, too, did makeup. By the 1920s, many middle-class women in cities such as Cleveland, Baltimore, and Atlanta had begun to use commercial skin care products, including cold cream and hand lotion. But large numbers of consumers in these places had not tried mascara, lipstick, or any other makeup.[66]

Among poorer urban women and those in small towns or farming areas, beauty products were less common. Low-income women frequently lacked the means or interest to buy cosmetics. Through the 1920s, many retailers in small towns and rural communities did not carry lipstick, mascara, or other similar goods.[67] Farm households, which made up almost half the U.S. population in 1920, often did not have ready access to beauty products. Before radio advertising became commonplace in the

1920s, many consumers in the countryside had little information about cosmetics.[68]

Beginning in the 1910s and accelerating over the next twenty years, manufacturers, cosmetologists, and others tried to enhance the appeal of beauty and personal care products. Advertising expenditures for drugs, cosmetics, and toiletries in leading magazines grew almost threefold in real terms between 1915 and 1925, amounting in the latter year to more than $10 million (about $96 million today).[69] By the mid-1920s, toiletries were the second most heavily advertised category of products in national magazines.[70] With the advent of radio broadcasting in the 1920s, cosmetics manufacturers began to advertise across the airwaves. In the last three years of the decade, annual industry expenditures for radio advertising rose from $300,000 to $3.2 million.[71] Hundreds of how-to books and magazine articles also appeared during those years.[72] These and other early twentieth-century developments in the cosmetics business helped set the stage on which Estée Lauder would play an important role.

Estée Lauder's Early Years

Josephine Esther Mentzer was born on July 1, 1908, in Corona, a section of the borough of Queens in New York City.[73] She was the second and last child of Rose Schotz Rosenthal Mentzer and Max Mentzer.[74] Max had immigrated to the United States from Hungary in the 1890s. He was a large, kind Jewish man with a ruddy complexion who worked as a storekeeper when his youngest daughter was born.

Josephine's mother, Rose, was also a Hungarian Jew. She had left her native country in 1898 to join her first husband, Abraham Rosenthal, in America, bringing their five children with her.[75] A total of 299,000 immigrants entered the United States in 1898.[76] Most, like the Rosenthal family, came in search of a better life. The Rosenthals settled in or around New York City. The historical record is silent on what became of Rose's first marriage, but within seven years of arriving in the United States, she had married Max Mentzer.[77]

Rose and Max had two daughters: Grace, born in 1906, and Josephine Esther, two years later. The older child was called Renee and the younger, Esty, presumably after her middle name. The two sisters grew up in a busy household, surrounded by their half siblings.[78] While Rose cared for the children and kept house, Max opened a hardware store on Corona Avenue. Like many turn-of-the-century merchants, he lived with his family above the store.

Corona in the first decades of the twentieth century was a working-class neighborhood of about 40,000 people.[79] Located in northeastern Queens between Elmhurst and Flushing, Corona had been settled in the mid-nineteenth century by developers who hoped to attract immigrants from the Lower East Side.[80] By the early decades of the twentieth century, the community was growing rapidly, caught up in the whirl of New York City's expansion. Construction for industry and for government projects such as subway lines and bridges went on incessantly. In 1909 the Queensboro Bridge was completed, tying Corona more closely to Manhattan and expanding the town's commercial prospects. Garment making, ceramics, and other light manufacturing proliferated. Small retail businesses, like Max Mentzer's hardware store, opened to serve the town's growing population. When Esty was growing up in the 1910s, Corona was heavily Italian, although Germans, Irish, Jews, and some African-Americans also lived there.[81]

The changes that caused Corona's expansion also made it ugly. Roads remained unpaved long after old farmsteads had been sold, subdivided, and developed. Chickens and goats from family plots intermingled on many streets with pushcarts and pedestrians.[82] Barges plowed into Flushing Bay, near the present La Guardia Airport, at Corona's docks for delivery to farms in outlying areas. The Brooklyn Ash Company and other businesses from nearby boroughs dumped ash and other refuse in the town's eastern meadows. By the 1920s, most of Brooklyn's garbage traveled by rail to Corona. There it was piled in huge heaps, some reaching over sixty feet in height. Residents referred to the refuse piles as "Corona Mountain."[83]

Esty spent her childhood in Corona.[84] She was a bright, active child. Like many little girls, she enjoyed experimenting with her mother's skin creams and fragrances. But Esty's interest in beauty products and other symbols of femininity extended beyond trying them on herself. From her earliest days, she wanted to alter other people's appearance, to pat cream onto their faces, brush their hair, and apply lip rouge (called lipstick today). Esty started at home, applying what she called "treatments" to her family members and friends. Max Mentzer admonished his daughter to stop "fiddling with other people's faces."[85]

But Esty could not obey her father. She was obsessed with the possibilities that cosmetics afforded women. She said in her autobiography, "I want to paint a picture of the young girl I was—a girl caught up, mesmerized by pretty things and pretty people."[86] How, if at all, was this commitment to external beauty related to Esty's upbringing in Corona? Did her strong interest in altering other people's faces connect with her lifelong desire to reinvent herself? Lauder recalled that as a schoolgirl, she was ashamed of her parents' heavy accents, their European manners, and her mother's age. She yearned "to be 100 percent American." She remembered being torn. "I loved them both so much—their beauty and their character, but I didn't love feeling different because of their old country ways."[87]

Meanwhile, after school and on weekends, she helped her father in his store. She learned to keep track of merchandise, talk with customers, and arrange tools in the display windows. During the December holiday season, for example, she would place hammers, saws, and other gift possibilities under an artificial Christmas tree, wrapping them in satin ribbon. Sales rose immediately, and Esty came to appreciate the importance of attractive packaging and merchandising.[88]

She took part in another family business as well, a small Corona department store called Plafker & Rosenthal run by Fanny Rosenthal (the wife of Esty's older half-brother, Isidor Rosenthal) and Fanny's sister, Frieda Plafker. Both women were savvy merchants who worked to understand and meet customers' needs. For example, the sisters spoke Yiddish with many Jewish shoppers and also learned Neapolitan Italian. They kept the store open six and a half days a week, stocking it with an array of merchandise from menorahs to communion dresses and extending credit to Jews and gentiles alike. They earned a reputation for being intelligent and trustworthy storekeepers, and their business thrived.[89]

What did the young girl make of Plafker & Rosenthal and its merchants? Like most department stores, it was a public arena in which women predominated.[90] Female shoppers tried on clothes, talked over potential purchases, hushed crying babies, and exchanged neighborhood gossip. Esty took part in the commercial and social activity of the store, running errands, laying out merchandise, and waiting on customers. She was an enthusiastic, gifted salesperson, and she realized it: "I whetted my appetite for the merry ring of the cash register. . . .The ladies in their furs came to buy, and bought more when I waited on them. I knew it. I felt it."[91]

When she was not working, Esty ventured into the clothing department, trying on new garments and identities. Plafker & Rosenthal, Lauder wrote in her autobiography, "was my gateway to fancy." She loved to dress up in fancy clothes: dresses, gloves, and lace scarves.[92]

Esty's interest in fine clothes was not unusual. Children have long enjoyed dressing up, imagining lives to match their costumes. What was noteworthy about Esther Mentzer's developing identity was her determination to shape this sense of self actively without regard to existing circumstances, to become the person that she *wanted to be,* and make this identity public. Before she was twenty, for example, Esther had changed her first name at least twice, from her childhood name, Esty, to Estelle and then to Estella.[93] (She would go back to calling herself Esther before settling permanently on Estée in her early thirties.)[94]

Discovering the Beauty Business

As she experimented with different names, Esty explored her interests. She dreamed of being an actress. But she continued to be drawn to beauty products and the art of applying makeup. She was intrigued by the possibilities for self-improvement and reinvention that cosmetics offered women. She also associated some products, particularly fine skin care creams, with European spas and an older, elite, almost magical world. Some of these images may have originated in a trip that she took with her mother to the baths at Saratoga Springs in upstate New York. She remembered being "vastly impressed" with the environment at the springs. There were "steaming vapors. Plush terry cloth towels. Face creams that smelled like heaven. My mother's cream, in particular, was divine." Her mother called it "the Formula." It was "something from Europe. A mystery."[95]

How was Esty to use her strong interest in cosmetics? As she approached adulthood in the mid-1920s, there were plenty of opportunities to earn a living in the beauty business.[96] In New York City alone, 12,000 women worked as hairdressers, manicurists, and skin specialists.[97] Thousands of others sold toiletries and cosmetics door-to-door. Female entrepreneurs opened their own hairdressing shops or beauty parlors. For all these women, employment in the cosmetics business held out the possibility of flexible working arrangements. This was particularly attractive for women with families and other responsibilities. "The profession of Beauty Culture," wrote the toiletries manufacturer William Woodbury,

> is the easiest for a woman of good sense to learn and establish herself in. . . . Most of the necessary preparations can be made at home, as the best formulas for them are exceedingly simple. Practice can be begun in the home of the operator, or the homes of her patrons.[98]

Esty may have considered working in a beauty parlor or opening her own shop. But in 1924 a different opportunity opened up in the cosmetics industry. Her mother's brother, John Schotz, started a small business in Manhattan, New Way Laboratories, to manufacture and distribute beauty products and other compounds.[99] His product list included several skin care preparations: "Six-in-One Cold Cream," "Dr. Schotz Viennese Cream," and "Flory Anna's Eczema Ointment," which was named for his wife, Flora Anna.[100] New Way Laboratories also made several fragrances, lip rouge, freckle remover, poultry lice-killer, Dog Mange Cure, embalming fluid, and Hungarian Mustache Wax.[101]

Esty was fascinated by the beauty side of the business. At sixteen, she began spending all her free time with Schotz, learning from him as he worked. Her uncle, she remembered, "produced miracles." She watched "as he created a secret formula, a magic cream potion," which he poured into jars, vials, and flagons. She was impressed by how his creams improved women's faces, softening skin and smoothing imperfections.[102]

Like anyone passionate about what she is studying, Esty was a fast learner. She instinctively appreciated both the science and art of the cosmetics business. She took careful note of how her uncle prepared each product, and she learned how to combine oils, wax, borax, lanolin, and other ingredients.[103] She began experimenting with formulas. As a student in high school, she became known among her peers for her cosmetic applications—what today are called "makeovers." "After school," she recalled, "I'd run home to practice being a scientist."[104] She was interested in how effective each formula was. How quickly did a particular compound clear up blemishes? How well did a certain cream moisturize dry skin? Esty talked with her schoolmates, gauging their reactions to Schotz's formulas and taking the results of her school makeovers back to New Way Laboratories where she and her uncle used them to improve his products.[105]

Schotz reinforced his niece's interest in hands-on selling. He was an expert at demonstrating his creams and other skin care products on customers' faces. He passed these skills on to his apprentice, teaching her to massage a woman's face quickly and soothingly. Esty learned to apply cleansing oil, cream, rouge, powder, lip color, and often eye shadow to a potential customer's face in three or four minutes.

Rise of the Consumer

While Esty was learning, the world was changing. In the mid-1920s, not only the young cosmetics business but automobiles, radios, cigarettes, and other consumer goods boomed.[106] The United States had endured a short, intense recession after World War I. But beginning in 1922, there was a strong economic expansion marked by mass production, mass distribution, and mass marketing. Over the 1920s, gross national product (adjusted for inflation) grew at a compound average of more than 3 percent per year. Per capita, it increased from $710 to $857, or about 20 percent.[107]

Esty did not think in terms of national product. What she *could* observe around her were substantial changes in the demand side of the economy. She had watched firsthand as the boroughs of New York City expanded and solidified their preeminence. Immigrants, African-Americans, and others moved to the city, attracted by employment possibilities, advances in transportation, and the sheer excitement of urban life. Greater New York's population grew 23 percent in the ten years after 1920, climbing to almost 7 million in 1930.[108] Each time she traveled from Corona to her uncle's Manhattan office, Esty could observe the results of such growth: constant construction, busy streets, new goods, novel retail outlets, and stylish women wearing the latest clothes and makeup.

Other metropolitan areas were growing rapidly too. Attracted by new economic and social possibilities, people of all sorts poured into Chicago, St. Louis, Los Angeles, and other cities. Between 1920 and 1930, the nation's urban population rose by 15 million people, a 28 percent increase. In contrast, the number of Americans living in rural areas grew by only 5 percent.[109] More Americans lived in closer contact with new objects, fashions, socioeconomic distinctions, and each other than in the past.

Esty herself had seen the standard of living change substantially for her own family. Her father had begun work in the United States as a journeyman tailor. By the time his youngest daughter was twenty, Mentzer owned a successful business and a small vacation home in Mohegan, New York. He may also have kept horses.[110] As the family's means increased, they purchased novel goods and services. Rose bought beauty services and saved for a refrigerator. Max had indoor plumbing installed at the family's summer-house.

The young woman's experience was hardly unique. Millions of Americans acquired new products and services in the 1920s, changing their material conditions. At the beginning of the decade about one in five families had indoor plumbing; in 1930, more than half had flush toilets in their homes. Nine percent of families owned a vacuum cleaner in 1920; as the decade closed, this fraction rose to 30 percent. About a quarter of American households owned a car in 1920; ten years later, more than half did.[111]

Many of the goods that a majority of Americans owned in 1930, such as automobiles, electric lighting, or indoor plumbing, would have been considered luxuries in the late nineteenth century. Other products that were becoming more widely available, such as radios or vacuum cleaners, would have been almost inconceivable two generations earlier. In this sense, the 1920s were a critical period in the evolution of U.S. consumption. A number of developments, including rising incomes and the growth of advertising, installment credit, and chain stores, influenced what many households owned and how Americans thought about getting and spending.[112]

The breadth and depth of postwar prosperity struck contemporary commentators. More people, it seemed, had more discretionary income and more possessions than in any other period in U.S. history. According to some scholars working in the 1920s, a revolution had occurred, comparable in its significance to Russia's Bolshevik revolution. The U.S. economic transformation centered on the newly available world of goods. It "had little to do with politics, embodied no particular theory, brought forth no striking incidents," noted one historian late in the decade. But, he continued, it altered the daily existence of the "average American citizen almost as profoundly as the revolution of 1917" altered the daily existence of the Russian peasant.[113]

Not all Americans, however, participated equally in the emerging consumer society of the 1920s. Working-class and farm families ate less canned food, made fewer telephone calls, and drove fewer and smaller cars than white-collar households. A 1928 survey of Kentucky mountain families, for example, revealed that these consumers spent almost 70 percent of their incomes on food, leaving 30 percent for all housing, clothing, fuel, furnishings, and other expenses.[114] In *Middletown,* Robert and Helen Lynd's 1929 study of Muncie, Indiana, a quarter of families had no running water. Almost half of the working-class households in the study did not have a telephone.[115] Modern consumption and the behaviors and attitudes that underlie it did not take hold firmly or en masse in the 1920s.

As a young woman, Esty probably was not interested in such historical analysis. She knew, however, that many families had access to more things than her parents had when they first arrived in the United States. She also realized that women played increasingly important roles in decisions about household consumption. This influence dovetailed with other changes in women's political, social, and economic status. After ten years of political organization, women had earned the vote in 1919. This was a critically important advancement. But it was by no means the only arena in which early-twentieth-century women struggled for more freedom. They also demanded easier and more equitable divorces, cigarettes, alcohol, and better, more accessible birth control. The "flapper" of the 1920s came to symbolize many of the new possibilities that women saw for themselves.

Long-term advancements in education and economic power underlay some of this assertiveness. Single women had begun entering the paid workforce in large numbers in the 1880s and 1890s. By 1900, 5 million women or about 20 percent of the eligible female labor pool worked outside the home.[116] This proportion grew steadily in the early twentieth century as large numbers of married women began working outside the home. In 1930, more than 10 million American women, or about a quarter of the possible labor force, were employed in paid occupations.[117] Whether they worked in an office, store, school, or hospital, women in the 1920s often assumed larger public roles than their grandmothers had. As women spent more time in the public eye, many devoted more time and attention to their appearance.[118]

Esty did not have ready access to employment numbers or data on consumer behavior. Her uncle's company was too small and strapped for cash to tap into the expanding advertising or market-research businesses.[119] Her views of the cosmetics market grew out of working in the business in New York City. She had seen firsthand countless urban women wearing cosmetics. She had also observed that scores of consumers who had not previously worn makeup were curious about it. The beauty industry, Esty believed, was here to stay. Like refrigerators and automobiles, cosmetics in the 1920s were about to become part of the daily lives of millions.

Plunging In

As Esty approached her twentieth birthday, she considered her future. She was very interested in the beauty business, but she also was considering an acting career. In the midst of such deliberations, she met Joseph Lauter, a gentle, handsome, and down-to-earth man with a quick sense of humor. Six years older than Esty, he had a similar background. The child of Austrian immigrants, Joe had grown up on Manhattan's Lower East Side, where his father worked as a tailor. When Esty met Joe, he had been in and out of several commercial ventures, including silk manufacturing.[120] In January 1930, after a three-year courtship, Josephine Esther Mentzer and Joseph Lauter were married in a formal Jewish ceremony.[121]

For the next several years, Esty worked to balance the demands of family life with her own ambitions. In March 1933, she and Joe had their first child, a son whom they named Leonard Alan Lauter. Esty continued her involvement in the beauty business. In between making meals for her family, she tinkered with Schotz's formulas and cooked up pots of cream on her kitchen stove. She tried her skin care creations out on anyone willing: friends, family, and even passersby. Neighbors remember her approaching strangers on the street—working women, shoppers, even Salvation Army volunteers—to criticize their makeup and suggest how to correct it. In the process, Esty would often recommend her own products, and many women bought them.[122]

The Beauty Parlor Circuit

By 1933, in the New York telephone directory, she listed her home-based business as Lauter Chemists.[123] She marketed goods in her apartment. Some of her sales may also have come through the mail. But the bulk of her revenues were earned in nearby Manhattan beauty parlors. In 1935, there were 61,355 beauty shops in the United States, more than 4,400 in New York City alone.[124] The majority of these businesses were owned by women and operated primarily as hair salons.

Esty herself was a regular customer at one such shop, the House of Ash Blondes on Manhattan's Upper West Side. For Esty, and many of the other customers, beauty parlor visits were more than a necessary errand. They were a welcome respite from the workaday routine. Such appointments offered a pocket of time in which to savor the rituals of beauty: a new hairstyle, a shampoo and wave, a manicure, or facial. These visits often had a social component. Women exchanged insights, humor, and gossip as they sat in hairdressers' chairs or at the manicurist's station.[125]

Esty used these moments at the salon to talk with other customers about beauty. These one-on-one encounters convinced her that consumers, especially those who did not have extensive experience with cosmetics, needed guidance and encouragement in navigating the expanding world of beauty. They also needed enough time to ask questions of the salesperson, experiment with different products, and, if possible, have a makeover.

When Florence Morris, the owner of the House of Ash Blondes, asked Esty about her skin care products, the entrepreneur seized her opportunity. She returned to the shop, Lauder remembered, with "four jars, on which only *everything* rested." After applying cleansing oil, creams, powder, rouge, and lip color to the owner's face, "I showed Mrs. Morris a mirror. She was a raving beauty."[126] Morris immediately gave her a concession at another Manhattan salon.

For the next several years, Esty sold her products in beauty parlors. She quickly developed an effective strategy for connecting with female consumers in these outlets. She offered makeovers to women while they waited. Esty realized that a woman sitting under a hair dryer or waiting for her nails to dry was often bored. The entrepreneur used this restlessness, offering individual beauty parlor patrons a free makeover. "Of course, she would agree. She had nothing else to do."[127] Esty would soften the woman's skin and apply makeup. By the time the client's hair was dry, she had a whole new look. If the woman was pleased, she usually bought one or more products.

As Esty traveled between beauty parlors, she always carried extra supplies of her offerings and wax paper. She would leave samples of her products with the women she met—a shaving of lipstick, a dollop of All-Purpose Crème, a spoonful of turquoise eye shadow. This practice was unusual at the time. In the 1920s and 1930s, cosmetics makers did not generally hand out products. But the entrepreneur believed strongly in the quality of what she made and the power of giving women something for nothing.

In distributing samples or applying makeup, Esty listened to consumers. She solicited their opinions about her offerings, adjusting specific products and her selling techniques to suit them better. For example, if several women complained about a specific cream's texture, she tinkered with the formula. Analogously, when women reacted negatively to a particular sales approach, she jettisoned it. Esty learned never to greet a potential customer with the question "May I help you?" The entrepreneur saw this as a redundant and possibly off-putting opening. Instead, she approached women in beauty parlors by saying, "I have something that would look perfect on you, madam. May I show you how to apply it?"[128]

Attracting Consumers

Most of Esty's early products were based on Schotz's formulas. But in starting her own business, she wished to distinguish her offerings from those of her uncle and other chemists who made cosmetics. Since childhood, Esty had been convinced that how a product *looked* affected consumers' interest in it. When she began selling her products at New York beauty parlors, she decided not to use the medicinal jars and tin lids in which Schotz had distributed his creams. These were not feminine enough for the image Esty wanted to project. Instead, she chose opal white jars with black lids.

She debated long and hard about what to call her line of products. Schotz had sold his formulas under the Flory Anna and Florana labels, both named for his wife.[129] Esty wanted none of this. The entrepreneur's products *had* to reflect her involvement. "I wanted to see my name in lights," she said. "But I was willing to settle for my name on a jar."[130] Esty's yearning for public recognition did not overwhelm her business objectives. Whichever name she chose for her products, it would have to appeal to the women whom she was targeting.

She rejected her formal married name, Josephine Lauter, as being too long. She experimented with variants of her middle name, Esther, and nickname, Esty, eventually settling on Estée with an accented second "e." In the mid-1930s, she also changed her married name from Lauter to Lauder. The name Estée Lauder first appeared in the phone book in 1937.[131] In the future, she would be known by that name, and her products would be sold under that label. The person and the offerings were intertwined. "Estée Lauder made her first public appearance," the businesswoman recalled, "on a little black and white container."[132]

From a marketing perspective, the name was a smart choice. Estée Lauder was distinctive. But it was also easy to say and remember.[133] It sounded unquestionably womanly and vaguely European, an association reinforced by the mandatory acute accent in Estée. Feminine and worldly were connotations that Lauder wanted attached to her products, key attributes of the identity that she was creating for her offerings and perhaps herself. She knew instinctively that how a product looked, including what its label said, communicated a range of information to consumers. Some of this information concerned the product's functional properties—what it was, what tangible benefits it provided, and how it was to be used. A label for a moisturizing cream, for example, would include Estée Lauder's name as well as that of the product. It might also briefly describe how the cream softened skin or minimized facial lines and give instructions for use.

Some of the information conveyed by the product's name and packaging appealed to female consumers' sense of themselves. Estée believed that women in the 1930s wanted "confidence-building beauty."[134] In the midst of widespread economic uncertainty, she reasoned, they wanted to feel feminine and attractive. Perhaps they also wished to exert more control over aspects of their lives, including how they looked. Lauder tailored her packaging, sales approach, and makeover techniques to these insights, emphasizing how quickly and easily women could incorporate a beauty routine into their daily lives. She also stressed that her products provided good value. "You can use this wonderful all-purpose cream in the morning or in the evening," Lauder explained as she demonstrated her skin care products. "No going crazy with four separate creams!"[135]

Estée Lauder knew that most consumers in the 1930s had less money to spend than ten years earlier. In the first four years of the Great Depression, real gross national product per capita fell precipitously—more than 32 percent. Unemployment soared to 25 percent over the same period. Almost 13 million people were out of work in 1933. As the economy deteriorated, investment declined swiftly, by about 87 percent between 1929 and 1933.[136]

Consumption of food, fuel, and other daily essentials fell less than investment expenditures. In the midst of economic crisis, Americans continued to cook meals, heat their homes, and wash themselves. Millions of people also purchased small luxuries: movie tickets, candy, and alcohol. These expenditures, Estée realized, bought people moments of enjoyment, an escape from everyday problems, or just a means to pass the time. Consumers had long valued such benefits. They might be especially vital in economic downturns, as Lauder appreciated. Per capita movie sales in the 1930s, for example, were about six times as high as in the 1990s.[137]

Going to the movies offered Americans more than a respite. This experience also fed individual and collective conceptions of well-being—material, aesthetic, and emotional. As the popularity of movies increased in the 1930s, millions of women took at least some of their fashion cues from stars such as Bette Davis, Carole Lombard, and Claudette Colbert. Their looks and lifestyles set influential, glamorous, and inevitably unrealistic standards. But moviegoers in the 1930s, like those today, probably did not agonize about the ultimate accessibility of cinematic ideals. Instead, many tried to emulate specific aspects of their favorite stars' lives.[138] For countless women, this meant copying the hairstyles and makeup of Carole Lombard or other famous actresses. The growth of the film industry in the 1930s and 1940s thus indirectly fed that of the cosmetics sector.

Going to the beauty parlor or buying a lipstick was, as Lauder understood, more than an exercise in the latest fashions. It was also a means for an individual woman to assert self-confidence at a moment when her family's economic opportunities seemed limited. Even in the Depression, Estée contended, women would buy cosmetics. Skin and beauty care, Lauder believed, was an essential part of many consumers' lives. "A woman in those hard times would first feed her children, then her husband, but she would skip her own lunch to buy a fine face cream."[139]

Lauder may have overstated the significance of beauty products in women's consumption priorities. But sales figures for the 1930s indicate that the cosmetics industry, like many other consumer-goods sectors, suffered less than banking, housing, and other businesses. Even in 1933, one of the worst years of the Depression, cosmetics sales (adjusted for deflation) were actually *higher* than they had been before the downturn. They continued to climb as economic conditions slowly improved during the decade. By 1939, cosmetics revenues were 35 percent higher in real terms than they had been ten years earlier.[140]

Estée's experience selling beauty products in the late 1930s and early 1940s proved a fertile training ground. She learned how to produce effective, appealing goods, what consumers cared about, and how to reach them. This understanding did not come through formal training.[141] The bulk of Estée's education was a result of trial and error, of making it up as she went along. Day-to-day experience, customer input, and her own instincts about the demand side shaped her early offerings and selling model.

Reinventing Her Marriage

Estée's growing commitment to the business put strains on her marriage. In 1939, she decided to leave Joe Lauder. In her autobiography, she was vague about her reasons. Perhaps she wanted a more successful, wealthier partner. She may have desired additional latitude to pursue long-standing dreams of fame. Whatever the rationale, Estée divorced Joe on April 11, 1939, citing grounds of mental cruelty. She took custody of their son Leonard and moved to Miami Beach, Florida, then a thriving, upper-middle-class resort.

Over the next three years, she shuttled between the southern resort and New York City, selling her products at beauty parlors, bridge parties, and hotels. For a time, she had a concession at the swank Roney Plaza Hotel on Collins Avenue in Miami Beach. In this and other venues, Estée learned as much from certain wealthy customers as they from her. She learned to dress, speak, and comport herself as a member of Palm Beach high society. Like Elizabeth Arden or Helena Rubinstein, Estée had long dreamed of transcending her immigrant roots and acquiring the perquisites of wealth. In Florida and New York, she met scores of well-connected women. Estée kept track of these contacts, determined to build a reputation for herself as an elegant and nationally recognized socialite.[142]

In 1942, after almost four years apart, Estée and Joe Lauder reunited. It is not clear exactly why the couple got back together. Most likely, she reassessed her husband, deciding he was a good match. They were married for a second time on December 7, 1942, in a quiet ceremony. On the wedding license, Joe listed his profession as "salesman." She described hers as "housewife."[143] She vowed that her primary identity would be Mrs. Joseph Lauder, rather than Estée Lauder. In early 1944, the couple's second child, Ronald, was born.

The Beauty Business during World War II

Retail sales of cosmetics and toiletries had totaled $425 million in 1939.[144] With the onset of war in 1941, writers, government officials, and others had debated the role of the industry.[145] Some, such as novelist Fannie Hurst, regarded the pursuit of beauty in the midst of global conflict as frivolous.

The spectacle of "hordes of fur-bearing women," she wrote in a 1942 *New York Times* article, "emerging from mornings dedicated to massage, facials, coiffuring, manicuring, and pedicuring is at shocking variance with our national crisis." The history of women's role in "this desperate struggle for the free and good way of life," she concluded, "will not be written in lipstick."[146]

Others disagreed. The beauty shop or "whatever it is which contributes to one's well-being," one housewife responded to Hurst's article, "definitely offers a service to humanity." The woman "who gets a lift from a new 'hairdo,'" Mrs. Horace Harrison added, "may just be the one who makes a commendable contribution in any great crisis."[147] According to an editor for the *American Perfumer,* shaving razors, toothbrushes, hand cream, and makeup were "*essential* to our way of living, just as much so as an orange or a dish of spinach." Cosmetics, the writer continued, "have been with mankind from the beginning of time" and have withstood "every social, political, and religious change in history."[148]

Physicians and efficiency experts offered other reasons for women to use cosmetics during wartime. Psychiatrists suggested that interrupting daily routines, such as beauty practices, would produce a "wholesale sense of insecurity."[149] Some medical authorities argued that using cosmetics had positive physiological effects for women. Applying lipstick, one psychiatrist noted, stimulated the thyroid and adrenal glands, restored blood sugar, and counteracted fatigue and depression.[150] Efficiency experts in Britain and the United States argued that working women were more productive when they had access to cosmetics.[151] Industrial engineers used these and similar findings in redesigning plants for mobilization, adding primping rooms, makeup tables, and large mirrors to female workers' facilities.[152] Some companies, interested in maximizing output, urged women workers to look good on the job. For example, Martin Aircraft's monthly newsletter, *Martin Star,* offered beauty tips. Lockheed had beauty salons and cosmetics stations installed in its factories.[153]

In 1939, the nation began mobilizing for war, imposing huge demands on the working population and drastically reducing unemployment.[154] Men and women took war-related and other jobs in record numbers.[155] Between 1939 and 1944, more than 3 million women entered the labor force, including 200,000 who joined the military.[156] Figure 5-1 shows working patterns during the twentieth century.

FIGURE 5-1

Women and Men in the U.S. Workforce, 1920–2000
(% of women and men)

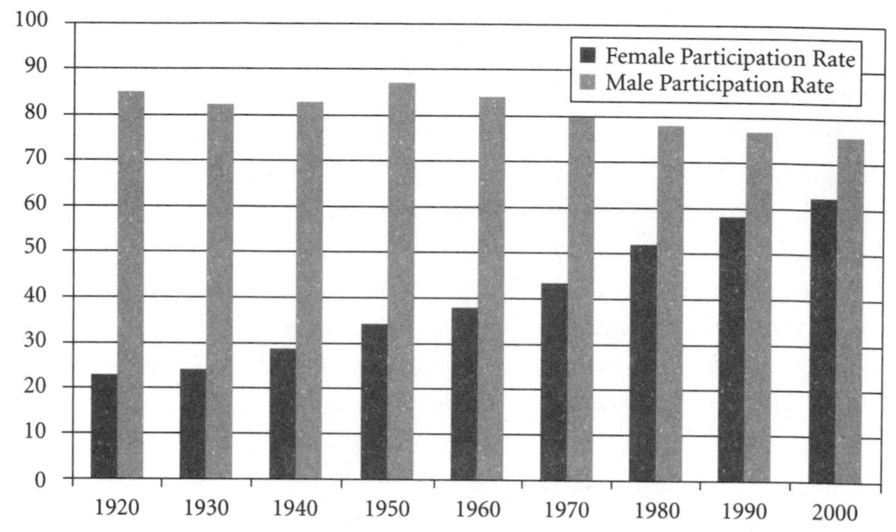

Sources: U.S. Department of Commerce, *Historical Statistics of the United States: Colonial Times to 1970* (Washington, DC: U.S. Government Printing Office, 1976), 1, p. 132; U.S. Department of Commerce, *Statistical Abstract of the United States, 1998* (Washington, DC: U.S. Government Printing Office, 1998), p. 408; U.S. Department of Commerce, *Statistical Abstract of the United States, 1995* (Washington, DC: U.S. Government Printing Office, 1995), p. 399.

Notes: The figure for 2000 is projected. *Statistical Abstract of the United States, 1995*, p. 399. "Participation Rate" is defined as the percentage of the civilian noninstitutional population of each specified group in the civilian labor force.

In or out of uniform, millions of working women had larger public roles and personal income than in the past. Many also attended more to their appearance. Working women purchased beauty products for a number of reasons: to help define their public identities, assert their independence, enjoy themselves, and spend some of the money they earned. Female wage earners, commented cosmetics executive Charles Revson in 1942, "have the money to indulge themselves in beauty products they've heard so much about: the cosmetics their bosses' wives use, the good grooming preparations their rich friends buy."[157] Perhaps some working women, as historian Kathy Peiss has noted, used makeup to maintain their femininity as they took up jobs historically belonging to men.[158]

Whatever their rationales, women spent heavily on cosmetics during the war. In 1940, retail sales of makeup, fragrances, and toiletries totaled about $450 million. Five years later, these revenues had climbed to $711 million, rising 23 percent in real terms.[159] This was substantial growth for a consumer industry in a wartime economy regulated by government rationing.

The beauty industry, like most sectors, had been affected by mobilization. In July 1942, officials of the federal War Production Board (WPB) issued Order L-171 restricting the manufacture of specific products and banning production of new goods. Industry representatives and female consumers opposed the measure. Faced with widespread objections and concerned to sustain female workers' morale, the WPB rescinded its earlier action, calling instead for voluntary limits on cosmetics. From the perspective of WPB members, beauty products had become sufficiently important in women's lives to affect their commitments to the war effort.[160]

Although the beauty industry was not as heavily regulated as many others, it was plagued by war-induced shortages. Severe limitations on alcohol supplies restricted the manufacture of fragrance and other products. Rationing of some fats and oils meant that substitutes had to be found for a variety of formulas. Shortages of plastic, glass, and metal reduced packaging supplies.[161]

In spite of these constraints, cosmetics manufacturers continued to advertise heavily during World War II, spending about 20 percent of industry sales on print and radio messages.[162] Some of these advertisements, such as those for Helena Rubinstein's products, emphasized the importance of glamour during a national crisis. Others stressed the need for war workers to look their best. A 1943 print ad for a new line of Cutex nail polish, for example, pictured women in military uniforms saluting with painted fingernails. The product line was called "On-Duty."[163] A 1943 ad for Jergens Hand Lotion addressed women's new, broader responsibilities while asserting the primacy of traditional commitments. The ad pictured a typical user engaged in several activities: changing a tire in a volunteer motor corps, running her hands through her husband's hair, and drying dishes. The tag line read "Our marriage comes first, so though I work hard for victory, I keep my hands attractive."[164]

Building a National Brand

As World War II ended, Estée Lauder's products were popular in New York beauty shops. But the entrepreneur was becoming restless. She wanted a larger market than she believed she could build in these outlets. She also wanted to sustain a strong marriage with Joe.

How was she to balance these two goals? After long discussions, the couple decided to enter the cosmetics business together. They hoped to exploit Estée's formulas, selling skills, and commercial imagination along with Joe's financial and manufacturing knowledge to create a nationally known company. So the couple divided responsibilities. They opened an office at 39 East Sixtieth Street in Manhattan, relying on savings and on loans from Max Mentzer, Estée's father, to help finance early operations. In 1946, they founded their company, calling it Estée Lauder Cosmetics.[165]

The first product line was based on that which Estée had been refining and selling for years. It consisted of several skin creams, a cleansing oil, face powder, a turquoise eye shadow, and one shade of lipstick, called "Just Red."[166] (The original line did not include perfume, cologne, or any other type of fragrance.) The couple made most of their products in a former restaurant on West Sixty-fourth Street in Manhattan, mixing Estée and Schotz's formulas on gas burners, sterilizing containers, and attaching labels. She remembered that in the first years of business, "We did everything ourselves. We stayed up all night for nights on end, snatching sleep in fits and starts."[167]

Using her local contacts, Estée sold their products in Manhattan and Brooklyn beauty shops. Joe staffed the small office and expanded his role in looking after the couple's sons.[168] Revenues at the end of the Lauders' first year in business totaled $50,000.[169] Operating expenses ate up virtually all of this.

A Booming Market

Despite little profit to show for their hard work, Estée remained optimistic. Surveying the postwar cosmetics business, she saw several important developments.

On the supply side of the market, government rationing had ceased, and raw materials had once again become widely available. Scores of new companies entered the cosmetic industry. Established firms whose sales had risen steadily during the war—such as Helena Rubinstein, Elizabeth Arden, Max Factor, and Coty—planned to expand production and increase advertising expenditures in the late 1940s. So, too, did younger companies such as the Revlon Nail Enamel Company, founded in 1932.[170] Competition among cosmetics manufacturers intensified.

On the demand side, cosmetics consumption grew slowly in the immediate postwar years, then accelerated. Among 50 million American women, noted a reporter for the *New York Times* in 1946, "the glamour market is solid." A recent survey, the article continued, demonstrated the breadth of consumer interest. In a sample of 1,000 women, 99 percent used lipstick, 95 percent nail polish, 94 percent face powder, and 73 percent perfume. Given such consumption patterns, the writer analyzing the survey predicted that beauty products would soon be a billion-dollar business.[171]

These projections turned out to be sound. In 1946, Americans bought $758 million in makeup, fragrances, skin care products, and toiletries. Seven years later, total purchases exceeded $1 billion. By 1957, they had risen to $1.4 billion, and in 1960, almost $1.8 billion.[172]

Economic and demographic shifts underlay such consumption patterns. World War II had jolted the U.S. economy out of the Depression. When the conflict ended, many Americans worried that a general business downturn was unavoidable. But these fears quickly faded. Gross national product, powered by enhanced productivity in the private sector, government stabilization policies, and huge international markets, continued to climb rapidly. Between 1946 and 1970, real GNP increased 230 percent. Per capita income rose more slowly, climbing 60 percent in real terms during this period.[173]

Millions of Americans used their expanded means to buy new things, as Table 5-1 demonstrates. Some of these goods, such as big cars, phonographs, and imported perfume, had been available for decades, but had been beyond the financial reach of most households. Others, like televisions, frozen foods, and antiperspirant, were relatively novel.

Population growth also enlarged the postwar cosmetics market. After falling off in the 1930s, U.S. birthrates began to surge in the mid-1940s. Within a decade, they had climbed to 122.9 per 1,000 women, creating a "baby boom" that was to exert significant economic, political, and social influence for the rest of the century.[174] Cosmetics manufacturers in the late

TABLE 5-1

U.S. Material Standards of Living, 1910–1997
(% of households owning selected amenities)

Amenity	1910	1920	1930	1950/1953	1970	1997
Inside flush toilets	17[a]	20	51	71	96	99
Central heating	0	1	42	50	78	83
Home lighting with electricity	15	35	68	94	99	99
Mechanical refrigerators	0	1[b]	8	82	99	97
Washing machines	0	8	24	70	70	77
Vacuum cleaners	0	9	30	54	92	98[c]
Radios	0	0	40	94	96	98
Automobiles	1	26	60	65	79	92[d]

Sources: Stanley Lebergott, *The American Economy: Income, Wealth and Want* (Princeton: Princeton University Press, 1962), pp. 248–299; U.S. Department of Commerce, *Statistical Abstract of the United States, 1999* (Washington, DC: U.S. Government Printing Office, 1999), p. 729; *U.S. Consumer Electronics Industry Today* (Arlington, VA: Consumer Electronics Manufacturers Association, 1997), p. 7; U.S. Department of Commerce, *Statistical Abstract of the United States, 1954* (Washington, DC: U.S. Government Printing Office, 1954), p. 565; "The Saturation Picture," *Appliance* (September 1997), p. 86; Nationwide Personal Transportation Survey Symposium, FHA, U.S. DOT 29–31 Oct. 1997 (published February 1999), p. 103.

a. Author's estimate
b. Less than 1 percent
c. 1996 number
d. 1995 number

1940s and early 1950s did not use the term *baby boom.* But they monitored demographic changes, particularly projections of female population, and assessed their likely impact.[175] Figure 5-2 illustrates the growth of the U.S. population.

Beauty companies also followed employment trends.[176] The end of the war put thousands of women out of work. Many lost their jobs in military industries. Others found that seniority rules and informal norms favored returning soldiers. Some women stopped working when their husbands returned from war and economic circumstances changed.[177]

But many stayed. Frankie Cooper, a shipyard worker, said,

> My husband would have been happy if I went back to the kind of girl I was when he married me and that was a little homebody there on the farm, in the kitchen. [But] I wasn't that person anymore. . . . I tried it for a couple, three years. . . . I did all the things—churned butter, visited the neighbors. I became president of the PTA—I did all the things, but I wasn't satisfied. I just had that restlessness. . . . I wanted to go back to work.[178]

Others, who had not held paying jobs during the war, entered the labor market between 1944 and 1950.[179] Overall, the number of working women increased during the 1940s, climbing to 16 million by the decade's end.[180] Measured in absolute terms or as a fraction of the eligible, interested population, this was the highest level of labor force participation by women in the country's history to date.

No matter which job they held, the women who entered the paid workforce during and after World War II comprised a growing, dynamic group of economic performers. They had more disposable income, more choices regarding their private and public lives, and in general, greater potential for individual self-expression than women of earlier periods.

FIGURE 5-2

U.S. Population, 1920–1998
(millions of people)

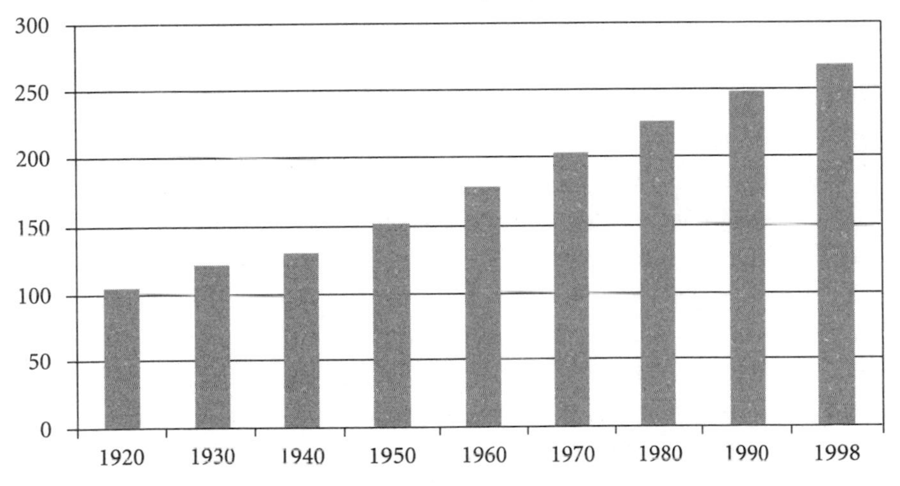

Source: U.S. Department of Commerce, *Statistical Abstract of the United States, 1999* (Washington, DC: U.S. Government Printing Office, 1999), pp. 8, 9.

Estée Lauder was interested in understanding what these changes meant for female consumers. How, for example, were women to balance family obligations with their needs for a broad sense of self-worth and perhaps economic independence?[181] What did occupational success mean for women's sense of their own femininity? As unprecedented numbers of women assumed more responsibility outside the home in the 1940s, they grappled with such issues.

Estée believed that in the prosperous postwar economy women would, within their means, use consumption to help express themselves and their aspirations. For twenty years she had consistently tried to tailor her products to consumers' priorities. But in the late 1940s, she saw a new and much greater opportunity. She was fairly certain that female consumers wanted beauty offerings that made them feel feminine, sophisticated, and elegant. She was equally sure that women from a variety of social classes could and would pay premium prices for such products. They would do this *not* because female consumers were gullible or careless with their money. The women that she had known and worked with were neither. Rather, consumers would purchase upscale, relatively expensive cosmetics only if the advantages that buyers expected to receive from these offerings were equal to or greater than the price.

How were Estée and Joe to provide women with superior skin care products and makeup that addressed their desires and needs at what they regarded as reasonable costs? In the aftermath of the war, how was the couple to build a national market for premium beauty products? To address these challenges, the chief strategic tool that the couple had was the brand. In the late 1940s, they set about enhancing the image of Estée Lauder products.

First, Estée selected new packaging. Her existing glass containers were "too medicinal," she decided. She was selling "pure glamour," and her products "had to be dressed for the part."[182] For several months, she examined other cosmetics packages. She also noted the bathroom interiors of friends and colleagues. Estée eventually settled on a pale, cool turquoise color for her jars. She was drawn to the color not only because she found it luxurious but also because she was certain it would look elegant on most bathroom counters or medicine chest shelves. Women, she believed, would not buy cosmetics in ugly jars or containers that clashed with the décor of their bathrooms. "I wanted them to be proud to display my products."[183] This signature shade eventually became known as "Estée Lauder blue." Even into the twenty-first century, it was still being used in most packaging for the company's flagship brand, the Estée Lauder line of products.

Distribution

A second key decision that Estée and Joe made about the brand concerned distribution. She believed that *where* her products were sold, in which outlets consumers encountered her cosmetics, would have significant consequences for the brand's future and the company's larger prospects. She ruled out drugstores, supermarkets, and five-and-tens as being at odds with the upscale image that she had already created and to which she was strongly committed. Even if the Lauders had wanted to sell in chain stores, they could not afford the large sales force necessary to service such outlets.[184]

Because she wanted to reach women who may not have had extensive experience with makeup, Estée believed she could not confine the Lauder line to beauty shops and other outlets that sold only cosmetics. Moreover, the entrepreneur thought most consumers would rather learn to make themselves more beautiful than pay expensive beauticians to do this.[185] She thus avoided the early selling strategies of Elizabeth Arden, Helena Rubinstein, and other manufacturers that distributed their products through company-owned salons.

Estée decided to focus her efforts on getting the company's products into premium department stores. Several issues were critical in her thinking. First, she wanted to reach large numbers of middle-class and wealthy consumers, women with sufficient means to buy premium-priced products associated with sophistication and elegance. She also hoped to locate her goods in high-traffic locations, where consumers felt free to make on-the-spot, "impulse" purchases. From her earliest days selling her uncle's creams, Estée had understood the power of spontaneous decision making. She had seen how women responded to her products once she had made up their faces. Her business must have outlets where such point-of-purchase buying was encouraged.

This meant the surroundings must be beautiful, exclusive, and comfortable for consumers. Department stores, like beauty parlors, often conjured up pleasurable associations for women. They were destinations that transcended the routine stops that most women made each week to the grocery store, druggist, or dry cleaners. In the three decades following

World War II, it was not uncommon for a pair of women—friends, family members, or neighbors—to devote an afternoon to a particular department store such as Filene's in Boston or Rich's in Atlanta. Many consumers, Estée realized, started on the store's main level and worked their way up through the upper levels, stopping for lunch or tea in the restaurant. The entrepreneur knew from her own experience that women felt freer in these settings to try on new looks: dresses, hats, handbags, and beauty products. The Lauders hoped to use the novelty and leisurely enjoyment that women connected with upscale department stores to demonstrate their products and stimulate impulse buying.

In the late 1940s, department stores offered another advantage: Most allowed consumers to buy on credit. Many, such as Marshall Field's, issued a charge card to good customers. Credit options had been effective in encouraging households across income categories to purchase both durable and nondurable goods. Installment sales and other forms of consumer credit had expanded quickly in the 1920s. During that decade, some 70 percent of new automobiles were bought on installment plans. Three out of four radios, eight out of ten appliances, and nine out of ten pianos were purchased with credit.[186] In the early years of the Depression, households had reduced their dependence on such debt. But after 1934, consumers again began buying goods on credit. By the eve of World War II, credit sales accounted for 41 percent of U.S. department stores' total revenues.[187]

Charge cards and other possibilities for buying cosmetics on credit were particularly attractive to Estée Lauder. At the beauty salon or drugstore counter, consumers had to pay for merchandise with cash. This, the entrepreneur believed, precluded a consumer from making a spontaneous purchase when she had not intended to buy anything and had not brought extra cash.[188] Estée's customers in New York beauty shops had asked repeatedly if her line was available at stores that issued charge cards.

Where could Estée find such outlets? There were no universal bank credit cards such as MasterCard, Visa, American Express, or Diners Club.[189] Consumer debt was usually issued by individual retailers or by manufacturers or sales finance companies.[190] Estée therefore targeted a small number of fine department stores that sold merchandise on credit, including Saks Fifth Avenue, Neiman Marcus, Bloomingdale's, and Marshall Field's.

In the late 1940s there were over 2,500 different department stores in the United States. Three years after the war ended, the annual sales of department stores totaled $9.5 billion, an average of about $4 million a store.[191] Most of these retailers, such as Kaufmann's in Pittsburgh, were regional operations. A smaller number of companies had created national distribution networks and brands. Macy's and Gimbels, for example, were recognized throughout the country for their broad selection of merchandise, reasonable prices, and splashy advertising. Macy's most famous slogan in the postwar era was "It's Smart to be Thrifty." "Nobody but Nobody Undersells Gimbels" was so well known as an advertising tag line that Winston Churchill once asked his friend Bernard Baruch if this was true.

Estée Lauder, however, was not interested in middle-market department stores that competed on low prices. She wanted to work with retailers such as Saks or Neiman Marcus. This objective probably owed something to the social aspiration that drove her. She was especially interested in Saks Fifth Avenue, which she saw as one of the most elegant American stores.[192] She may even have associated the possibility of placing her products in the store with social elevation for herself. Estée "resolved to break the rules that sheltered this traditional and exclusive store from experimental merchandisers who would sell their souls to sell from Saks."[193]

Her interest in such upscale stores was also strategic. The entrepreneur suspected that her young brand would benefit from association with established, prestigious retailers.[194] Since consumers outside Manhattan did not know anything about her products in 1946, she had to find ways to increase their willingness to try them. She believed that when women once used Lauder cosmetics, they would become loyal customers and her brand recognition would grow.

Leading Companies

At that time, hundreds of other cosmetics manufacturers were trying to sell beauty products to American women.[195] Most of these firms were small organizations with local markets. But a handful of large players had brands that commanded name recognition and market shares on a nationwide basis. These leading firms fell generally into three groups: dedicated cosmetics makers, large consumer-products companies, and proprietary drug producers.

The cosmetics companies included older houses such as Avon Products, Max Factor, Coty, Elizabeth Arden, and Helena Rubinstein, and newer firms like Revlon.[196] Each had a significant cash flow and a large advertising budget. Avon's 1952 sales exceeded $40 million, Coty's were $19 million, Helena Rubinstein's $18 million, and Revlon's $25 million.[197] Most of these companies devoted between 20 and 25 percent of net sales to advertising.[198]

Consumer-products companies such as Chesebrough-Pond's, Alberto-Culver, Helene Curtis, and Lever Brothers produced a range of cosmetics offerings in the postwar period, including cold creams, makeup, and hair colors. Like the established cosmetics houses, these were multimillion-dollar companies. In 1955, for example, Chesebrough-Pond's revenues totaled $29 million.[199]

The third category consisted of large drug manufacturers, such as Warner-Lambert and Lehn & Fink, that produced cosmetics. Lehn & Fink, for example, marketed its makeup under the Dorothy Gray and Tussey lines.

The leading companies distributed cosmetics through several different channels. Avon employed thousands of agents to sell its offerings directly to consumers. The largely female sales force was an itinerant one, traveling door-to-door to demonstrate Avon makeup and fragrances to American women. As the suburbs expanded in the years following World War II, this tactic was extraordinarily effective.[200]

Most cosmetics makers, however, sold their products through retail outlets, including drugstores, department stores, five-and-tens, and supermarkets. Max Factor, Maybelline, and other mass-market lines were distributed in drugstores, variety stores, and supermarkets. In retail sales, drugstores were the beauty industry's chief channel in the immediate postwar years, accounting for 37 percent of total sales in 1950. Variety stores and five-and-tens such as Woolworth's accounted for about 15 percent that year, supermarkets about 6 percent.[201] Higher priced, prestigious brands, such as Germaine Monteil and Lanvin, were sold primarily in department stores.

Breaking into Department Stores

How was Estée Lauder to compete with nationally known names controlled by established, multimillion-dollar companies? Without a large advertising budget, how could she attract consumer interest in her offerings? Selling through fine department stores was a potential answer. Prestigious retail brands, such as Saks or Marshall Field's, served as information sources and quality safeguards for consumers, assuring shoppers that the merchandise sold by the store met its high standards. Upscale store brands encompassed other positive associations for consumers: social status, worldliness, and fashion cachet.[202]

Estée hoped to use the appeal of specific stores to help build her brand. She believed that women would be more willing to try her skin creams and other products in elegant department stores than in drugstores or middle-market retailers like Gimbels. Beginning in the mid-1940s, Estée visited scores of department store buyers. In 1948, she was intent on getting her brand into Saks. The store's buyer for cosmetics, Robert Fiske, was not initially interested. Saks was already devoting significant selling space to cosmetics, most of them well-known brands. When Estée told the buyer that Saks shoppers wanted her line, he responded that he and store salespeople had seen no evidence of this. "In the absence of that demand," Fiske said, "we're not going to give any further consideration to your product."[203]

Estée set out to prove him wrong, telling Fiske that she would demonstrate Saks customers' interest in her products at a charity luncheon where she was speaking. The event was to be held at the Starlight Roof of the Waldorf-Astoria Hotel in midtown Manhattan. She donated over eighty of her lipsticks to be distributed as table gifts at the luncheon. Unlike most lipsticks made during and right after World War II, these were housed in metal cases. Lunch guests noticed not only the product's unusual packaging but also its color and texture. As the event broke up, Fiske recalled, a line of women entered the store from across Park Avenue, all "asking for these lipsticks, one after another." This convinced us, he continued, "that there was a demand for the Lauder product."[204] Saks placed an initial order for $800 worth of cosmetics, becoming the manufacturer's first department store account.[205]

Estée also wanted to distribute her products in Neiman Marcus. Stanley Marcus, head of the Texas-based department store, first met her on one of her sales calls. "She came to see me late one afternoon as I was on my way home, and she introduced herself," he recalled. "'I'm Estée Lauder and I have the most wonderful beauty products in the world and they must be in your store.'" Marcus tried to put the entrepreneur off. "We already had Elizabeth Arden and Germaine Monteil and Charles of the Ritz. We didn't need another line." But Lauder was persistent. When Marcus asked her when she could have her merchandise in the store, Estée produced a big bag of her products. "The very next day she set it up and she was in business at Neiman Marcus. Stopping everyone who came in the store, she said, 'Try this. I'm Estée Lauder and these are the most wonderful beauty products in the world.'" She was, Marcus concluded, "a very determined salesperson; she pushed her way into acceptance. She was determined—and gracious and lovely through it all. It was easier to say yes to Estée than to say no."[206]

The entrepreneur designed and opened her counters in Saks and other department stores. She had long thought "ambience counted deeply" in attracting consumers. She was determined to make each sales post for the brand "a tiny, shining spa" that whispered elegance and enjoyment.[207] Her signature blue color was everywhere: on the product packages, the paper that lined counter shelves, the window banners, and counter fixtures that held open lipsticks and other product testers. She chose the lighting and mirror placement carefully so they would flatter rather than intimidate consumers.

None of these features came cheaply. Constructing and maintaining a cosmetics counter in a department store was expensive.[208] So were hiring and training sales representatives, buying advertising space, creating window displays, and running regular promotions. In exchange for purchasing a given beauty line and allocating selling space to it, department stores usually expected manufacturers to bear the bulk of these expenses.[209] The initial terms of the sales agreement were hammered out between department store buyers and representatives for the manufacturer. The agreement was usually renegotiated annually. If the cosmetics brand sold well, manufacturers could often demand better terms from retailers.

In its first five years, Estée Lauder Cosmetics' annual revenues were well below $500,000.[210] The costs associated with department store distribution were formidable outlays for a start-up business trying to manage its cash flow. Estée and Joe, however, had no choice but to try to finance such expenditures. They were determined to sell their products in upscale department stores. They believed this distribution strategy was critical to reaching consumers and presenting them with the company's offerings—the intangible benefits of Lauder cosmetics as well as the physical products. In this context, the costs of doing business with department stores represented critical investments in the company's brand. Estée believed that as the brand developed and sales expanded, her bargaining position with individual retailers would improve. She set out to promote the young brand as quickly and effectively as she could.

Promotion and Advertising

Over the next decade, the entrepreneur crisscrossed the United States talking to department store buyers and trying to create a large market for her products. She hired an experienced saleswoman, Elizabeth Patterson, to work closely with her as she opened counters, made women up, and trained sales representatives. "We traveled from Dallas to Seattle, from Chicago to San Francisco," Estée said, "the length and breadth of the country."[211] The work was often tiring, the days long, and the separation from her family painful. "One year," Leonard Lauder remembered, "my mother was away twenty-five weeks."[212] Estée worried about what she was missing at home and how to balance her family commitments with those to her company and brand.[213]

Despite her worries, she was obsessed with building the business. "I was unstoppable, so great was my faith in what I sold," Estée said, describing her weeks on the road.[214] By the early 1950s, Estée Lauder Cosmetics was distributing its products through Saks, Neiman Marcus, Bonwit Teller, and other nationally known retailers. The beauty manufacturer also targeted department stores with a strong regional presence such as I. Magnin in California, Himmelhoch's in Detroit, and Sakowitz in Houston. Estée quickly developed a routine that she followed at each new store. First, she tracked consumers' movements in the store. For example, she stood at the main entrance for a week watching women enter. Nine out of ten times, she noticed, shoppers' eyes moved to the right rather than the left or straight ahead.[215] Next, Estée fought for the best possible space on the retailer's cosmetics sales floor—or "real estate," as it is known in the trade. This meant placing the Lauder counter close to and to the right of the entrance to keep the brand in consumers' line of vision. She was confident that an attractive counter located to the right of a store's entrance would draw women to her products before they went anywhere else."[216]

The entrepreneur spent a week at each store in which her line was introduced. She devoted most of this time to working the counter. This included overseeing the sales representatives, tweaking the merchandise layout, and especially, talking with and touching potential consumers. "I'd make up every woman who stopped to look," Estée remembered. "I would show her that a three-minute makeup could change her life." The energetic businesswoman wanted consumers to understand that applying cosmetics was not a lengthy, mystical process but rather "one that should be as automatic and quick as breathing."[217]

Estée tried to create awareness of her brand outside the cosmetics department. Hoping to increase the likelihood of salespeople recommending Lauder products, she introduced herself to clerks who sold dresses, hats, and shoes. She also gave each of the saleswomen whom she met a gift of Estée Lauder makeup or cream. If a woman in the millinery department liked the beauty products, Lauder reasoned, she might mention the possibility of a free makeover at the Estée Lauder counter to her customers.[218]

To draw women into the store, Estée generally worked with the advertising manager. In its early years, the company could not afford a large mass media campaign, such as that which would support the Beautiful launch in 1985. Instead, Estée and department store managers sent mailings to targeted local consumers. When she first began selling her products at Saks, for example, all the store's charge account customers received a small, white printed card with gold letters that read: "Saks Fifth Avenue is proud to present the Estée Lauder line of cosmetics: now available at our cosmetics department."[219] Estée herself would occasionally take to the airwaves. In the late 1940s, for example, she did a radio interview to publicize her brand and its introduction in Neiman Marcus. "Start the year with a new face," she told Texas listeners.[220] (This slogan was so successful that Estée Lauder and the retailer used it for decades as part of their annual New Year's campaign.)

One of the Lauders' innovative marketing strategies involved *giving* the company's products away. Since her early days offering beauty parlor customers a dollop of free cream in wax paper, Estée had believed that distributing samples was "the most honest way to do business."[221] Consumers who liked a particular product's quality would buy it. Their choices would be based on their personal experience rather than on the indirect allure of advertising. Estée thought that such experience would do more than motivate women to buy her products. It would also encourage consumers to tell others about the Estée Lauder brand. The entrepreneur had seen firsthand how powerful the customers' word-of-mouth endorsements had been in enhancing her reputation in Manhattan beauty salons.[222] She hoped to exploit this same communication channel in building her brand on a larger scale in the late 1940s and 1950s.

How exactly was the young company to do this? How many resources should the enterprise commit to such an effort? At what point in a brand's development should the business try to enlist their customers as spokespeople? Estée and Joe recognized these important issues, but in the intense activity of running a young business, they did not always have time to address these questions systematically.

A decision about the company's advertising budget forced their strategic hand. Early in the 1950s, the couple began looking for an ad agency that could represent their business. For an advertising campaign, they had set aside $50,000 from company profits. They were quickly rebuffed. A representative from BBD & O, a large national agency that handled accounts for Revlon, Campbell's Soup, and Lucky Strike, told the Lauders that $50,000 was far too little to finance an effective campaign.[223] This amount was tiny compared to that being spent by the leading cosmetics companies. In 1955, for example, Revlon's advertising, promotional, sales, and administrative expenditures totaled $22 million or almost 40 percent of total revenues.[224] Revlon's sponsorship of the new television game show, "The $64,000 Question," accounted for a large proportion of these costs.[225]

Estée and Joe decided to put their advertising fund into free samples. This, they reasoned, could prove to be a better investment in the brand than an ad agency. Perhaps it would create a more direct, personal connection with consumers. They ordered huge quantities of samples: lipstick, rouge, eye shadow, and creams. They also had mailers printed to inform potential customers that a gift awaited them at the Estée Lauder counter at a specific department store.

In the early 1950s, distributing large quantities of cosmetics samples was a novel idea. Some beauty executives scoffed at the female entrepreneur's efforts. "She'll never get ahead," said a manager from Charles of the Ritz observing a Lauder giveaway at Lord & Taylor. "She's giving away the whole business."[226] But her samples worked very well. Women flocked to Estée Lauder counters all over the country to receive a free gift, learn more about the brand's products, and purchase what they needed. The giveaways and the later gift-with-purchase that Estée pioneered created an excellent opportunity in which to exercise her sales approach, encourage spontaneous buying, and increase customer loyalty. "People trooped in to get the free sample," explained Leonard Lauder, "liked it and bought it again."[227] Competitors began to copy the innovation. By the late 1960s, most major cosmetics manufacturers regularly used samples and the gift-with-purchase to drive traffic to their counters.

The promotional strategies that Estée exploited, including direct mail and gift-with-purchase, are commonplace in cosmetics marketing today. But in the late 1940s and early 1950s, most department stores did not rely on mail inserts to advertise beauty products. Few used female businesswomen to publicize a product line. Virtually no other cosmetics manufacturers or retailers appealed to consumers by distributing free samples.

In the 1940s and early 1950s, the Lauders lacked the resources, name recognition, and market power to reach consumers through mass advertising. They had to find other ways of building connections with women. One was giving away samples. Estée also reached consumers indirectly through the press. During the week that she spent at each counter's opening, for example, she met with editors or reporters from local magazines and newspapers. Most of these journalists were women. If they were impressed with a particular line, they would write about it. How was Estée to capture the attention of the beauty press? She used the same strategies she employed at the sales counter, distributing samples and offering a makeover to every female journalist with whom she met. Some were struck by her charisma and natural warmth.[228] Many liked her products and were glad to see a woman trying to make a mark in the cosmetics industry. Most thought that she and her business generated good copy for their columns.[229]

Product Development

In the early 1950s, Estée began to experiment with fragrances, hoping to develop a signature scent to complement her cosmetics. She had always enjoyed wearing perfume, cologne, or bath oil and looked forward to creating and selling a fragrance that was appealing to other women. But she was also motivated by financial and strategic reasons. Fragrance was more profitable than skin care products or makeup. Gross margins—the difference between cost of the inputs and the selling price—averaged 80 percent for perfume and cologne, about 70 percent for skin care and makeup products. If a scent was popular, it would have a relatively large impact on the company's bottom line.

Moreover, a signature fragrance could be marketed with accompanying beauty products, including skin care items and makeup. This, as Estée recognized, created sales opportunities at the company's counters. Customers looking for a specific perfume might also become interested in scented body lotion or dusting powder. Impulse or point-of-purchase buying might increase considerably with a new fragrance introduction. Estée and Joe had made relatively large investments in setting up and supporting their department store counters. They wanted to leverage these expenditures by selling as much merchandise as possible through each of these distribution points.

Finally, the entrepreneur hoped to use a new fragrance product to expand the market and enhance the Estée Lauder name. She developed a sweet, diffusive scent that she thought would have broad appeal. It was more assertive and longer lasting than the leading prestige perfumes such as Chanel No. 5 or Evening in Paris.[230] She had always considered fragrance as integral a component of her everyday beauty routine as lipstick or moisturizer. Estée intended to show other women how to use scent to express themselves and feel more beautiful. She was confident that in the prosperous postwar economy the potential demand for a distinctive, appealing, and glamorous scent was high.

But how was she to stimulate demand among women? In the mid-1950s, fragrance sales were a tiny fraction of the larger beauty business, amounting to less than 1 percent of the $1 billion cosmetics and toiletries market.[231] (In the late 1990s, by contrast, fragrance revenues accounted for more than 15 percent of the market.)[232] Most female consumers viewed perfume and cologne as luxuries, to be used on special occasions. Few women purchased fragrance for themselves. Most, as Estée observed, waited for men to buy perfume for them, often receiving scents that their husbands or boyfriends liked. It was considered "self-indulgent, narcissistic, and even decadent" for a woman to buy perfume for herself.[233]

Estée realized that to create a successful perfume, she would have to do two things: motivate women to buy their own fragrance and convince female consumers that her fragrance was a daily necessity rather than a luxury.

The entrepreneur devised an ingenious solution to both challenges. She decided to market her fragrance not as perfume but as bath oil. This would be acceptable to women, Estée reasoned, "because it was feminine, all-American, very girl-next-door to take baths." A woman could buy herself a bottle of bath oil the way she would buy a lipstick "without feeling guilty, without waiting for her birthday, anniversary, graduation, without giving tiresome hints to her husband."[234] In 1953, she introduced a dark, rich oil that could be poured in bath water or directly on the skin and called it Youth Dew. It was priced at $5.00 a bottle, well below prestigious scents such as Elizabeth Arden's De Luxe On Dit perfume, which sold for $65, or Rochas's Femme priced at $40 an ounce.[235] Unlike most perfumes, Youth Dew was packaged in unsealed containers. Women were free to lift any bottle's stopper and take a whiff, often leaving the bath oil on their hands. When an individual consumer left the cosmetics counter, Estée reasoned, the scent would linger on her hands, reminding her of Youth Dew and potentially leading her back to Lauder.[236]

Because the company could not afford a large-scale advertising campaign for its new product, it relied on its evolving promotional strategy, one rooted in direct contact with consumers. Estée again visited department stores, spraying Youth Dew on countless women and in elevators and throughout the selling areas. She trained the sales staff in each store to cross-sell the fragrance with the brand's broader line of cosmetics. When women came to a Lauder counter looking for Youth Dew, sales representatives emphasized the scent's connection to skin cream, lotion, or lipstick.

To lure consumers into the stores and to the Lauder counters, Estée worked with individual department stores to advertise the bath oil and its availability at her counters. Some retailers inserted scented blotters into monthly statements, inviting women with charge accounts to sample the new fragrance. Like using samples, these were new promotional techniques in the mid-1950s. Most department store customers, for example, had never received a scented insert with their charge bill. Even fewer women had been offered an attractive gift when they bought something at a cosmetics counter.

Youth Dew was the beauty company's first big success. "Middle America," remembered one industry observer, "went bananas" for Youth Dew.[237] Women gathered at Estée Lauder counters to try the new fragrance. Consumers, according to the cosmetics expert, liked Youth Dew's strong, long-lasting scent. They liked buying bath oil that doubled as a perfume. They also liked choosing their own perfume. "It was a whole new direction" in fragrance, and "it was affordable."[238] Women around the country sampled Youth Dew, discovering a new scent and the Estée Lauder brand.

They responded enthusiastically to both, buying not only bath oil but also other Lauder products. Over the next few years, retail demand for the cosmetics line increased rapidly, climbing from a weekly average of $300 in stores such as Neiman Marcus to more than $5,000.[239] In helping to open the fragrance market to female consumers, the product became the foundation of the business.

By the late 1950s, the Estée Lauder brand had passed an important inflection point in its development with consumers. According to the Saks buyer Bob Fiske, the company was becoming "a very dominant factor on the cosmetics scene." Lauder's line, he added, "was probably the number-three treatment line" behind those of Helena Rubinstein and Elizabeth Arden.[240] Thousands of women understood the appeal of the Estée Lauder brand—its combination of core products and specific associations. This offering was so distinctive, interesting, and relevant that it had earned a place in consumers' thinking about beauty products. This, as Estée realized, gave the brand and the company critical momentum. She was committed to using this momentum to build one of the leading beauty companies in the country.

Creating the Organization

The business grew steadily during the next five years. But the rough division of managerial responsibility between Estée and Joe Lauder remained unchanged. Estée focused on expanding the company's distribution network of upscale department stores. For most of the 1950s, she kept up a grueling travel schedule—visiting retail buyers, opening counters, and training sales representatives. She also oversaw promotion, merchandising, and product development. Joe remained in New York to manage the firm's manufacturing and finances.

In 1957, the business sold $800,000 in beauty products. In 1958, this figure climbed to $1 million, a twentyfold increase over the company's sales in its first year.[241] But the organization was still a relatively small, family-run operation with a Manhattan office and production facility in nearby Nassau County on Long Island.[242] Three employees staffed the office. Ten worked in the manufacturing plant.

In 1958, the Lauders' older son, Leonard, officially joined the business. He was twenty-four and had been involved in the company almost since its inception, working after school, on weekends, and during summers.[243] As a boy, he filled jars, delivered packages, typed invoices, answered phones, and eventually worked in the factory.[244] As an undergraduate at the University of Pennsylvania's Wharton School, he stayed in touch with developments at the family business. After he graduated from college in 1954, he worked days in the manufacturing facility and attended evening classes at Columbia's Graduate School of Business.[245] In late 1955, Leonard enlisted in the Navy, where he served as a supply officer on an aircraft carrier and later a destroyer. After completing his tour of duty, Leonard decided to commit his experience and energies to his parents' company.

One of his first responsibilities was to help his mother sell.[246] In the late 1950s and early 1960s, he worked to extend the firm's distribution network, visiting a large number of upscale department stores. He met buyers, surveyed sales floor space at new retail outlets, and evaluated the firm's existing counters. Leonard was not as charismatic or outgoing as his mother. But he was a gifted salesperson in his own right. In conversations with department store buyers, he emphasized the quality of Estée Lauder products, the growing popularity of Youth Dew, and the expanding consumer awareness of the company's brand. He also spent time with customers, taking note of what they liked and disliked about specific offerings, promotions, or sales techniques and bringing this information back to the company headquarters.[247]

In 1959, Leonard married Evelyn Hauser, an elementary school teacher. She, too, worked in the family business, helping train behind-the-counter sales representatives and advising her husband and in-laws on product development and package design.[248] Like Estée and Joe Lauder, the newlyweds worked hard to take advantage of a good economy and the flourishing beauty market.

Between 1955 and 1965, U.S. retail cosmetic and toiletry sales rose from $1.2 billion to $2.9 billion.[249] Figure 5-3 illustrates the expansion of the beauty business.

Established companies, such as Avon, Revlon, and Helena Rubinstein, and younger firms, like Estée Lauder and Hazel Bishop, experienced strong revenue gains. Avon's annual sales, for example, more than doubled in the late 1950s and early 1960s, climbing to $168 million in 1960 and to $352 million in 1965.[250] Estée Lauder's sales also rose rapidly, rising from $1 million in 1958 to $14 million in 1965.[251]

As the company grew, the Lauders recruited managerial talent. To become a major player in the cosmetics industry, Leonard reasoned, the

FIGURE 5-3

U.S. Retail Sales of Toiletries and Cosmetics, 1915–1995
(millions of 2000 dollars)

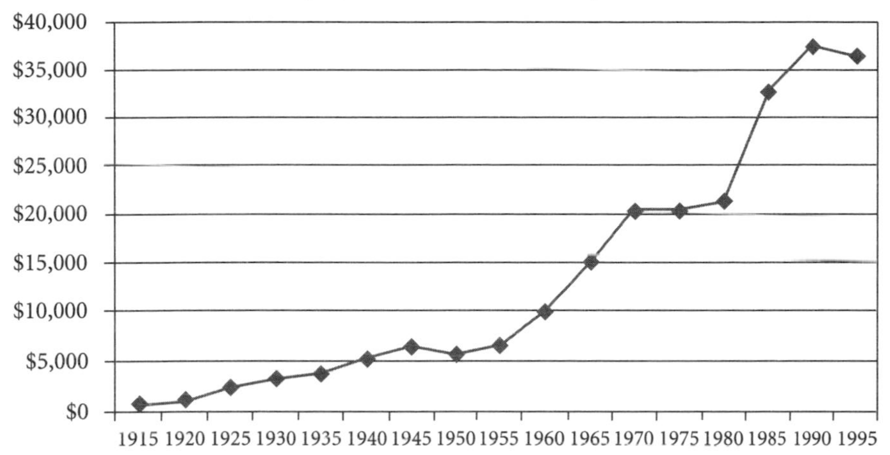

Sources: "Perfume, Cosmetic and Toilet Preparations Sales at Retail, 1914–1960," *Advertising Age* 32, no. 42 (16 October 1961), p. 88; Toilet Goods Association, "Toiletry Sales," *Oil, Paint and Drug Reporter* (6 July 1964, 20 June 1966), p. 45 and p. 50, respectively; "Cosmetics '81," *Chemical Marketing Reporter* 219, no. 9 (2 March 1981), p. 38; Ali Khan, Kline & Co., Inc. (27 October 1999). Price indexes are from U.S. Department of Commerce, *Historical Statistics of the United States, Colonial Times to 1970* (Washington, DC: U.S. Government Printing Office, 1976), 1, pp. 210–211, and the Council of Economic Advisers, *Economic Report of the President* (Washington, DC: U.S. Government Printing Office, 2000), p. 373.

family enterprise needed a range of capabilities, including expertise in advertising, sales, design, and production. In a fast-growing market, there was no time to develop and nurture these skills *in-house.* Estée Lauder Inc. would have to acquire them by hiring experienced managers from other companies and industries. The Lauders and their colleagues sought individuals with abilities that they were lacking. "If I was going to help build a business," Leonard Lauder said, "I was going to do it with people smarter than I."[252]

During the 1960s, the cosmetics manufacturer hired men and women from Saks Fifth Avenue, Bergdorf Goodman, Pan American Airways, Bristol Myers, *Vogue,* and Revlon. "We needed smart people, the right people, for a growing organization," Leonard Lauder remembered. "I sought men and women who were refugees from the tyranny of our competitors.

If someone had a fight with Charles Revson, I was there waiting for that person."[253]

Between 1960 and 1971, the number of employees working in the Manhattan headquarters increased from 8 to 225 people.[254] More than a third of these were managers. To motivate executives, the company offered high salaries, consistent respect, and substantial responsibility. "The areas that my parents knew other people were good at," Leonard Lauder said, "they let other people do."[255] He and his family, he explained, "look upon ourselves as winders of the clock and directors of the symphony orchestra who try to stimulate our group of talented and brilliant people to do the best we can."[256] This stimulation included creating and maintaining an ambitious company culture. "We believe in a hungry organization," Leonard said in 1973, "hungry for sales, hungry for income, hungry for the amenities of life."[257]

Employee motivation, however, did not extend to any kind of equity ownership.[258] (Until the company's initial public offering [IPO] in 1995, the Lauder family controlled all stock.) But managerial turnover in the organization remained relatively low. Some of the people hired in the early and mid-1960s—such as Robert Barnes, who joined the company as a regional sales manager, Robert Worsfold, who headed the company's international operations, and Ira Levy, who, with Estée, oversaw package design and product aesthetics—stayed with the business for decades.

Even as the company expanded, the Lauders remained involved in most major decisions. As the organization's president, Estée continued to manage product development and promotional initiatives. Joe still focused on manufacturing, logistics, and finances. In the mid-1960s, the couple's younger son, Ronald, joined the company, working in its Belgian facility. Leonard shared some responsibilities with his mother and some with his father. Using the experience of other executives, he also began to systematize the firm's activities. "I started out with a schizophrenic approach to the business," Leonard remembered. "On the one hand, I was concerned to preserve the intuitive, gutsy feel of Mrs. Estée Lauder. On the other, I was dedicated to having the right things done in the right way by the right people in the organization." Over time, he added, "this schizophrenia became a kind of symbiosis."[259]

During the 1960s, Leonard worked to build an organizational structure, develop a national sales force, create advertising initiatives, and establish long-term, professional relationships with retailers. Leonard's planning mechanism with stores, said Richard Salomon, former head of Charles of the Ritz, was crucial to the Estée Lauder Inc. performance:

> He would sit down with store heads, set a goal for the year, and plan how it was that they would reach that goal. It was reduced to writing. It wasn't a legal contract, but an understanding of what would govern next year's operations. . . . Stores were impressed not only by the method but by the volume achieved, and by the fact that they consistently reached those increased goals.[260]

Sales continued to climb, increasing at a compound annual rate of 45 percent in the ten years after 1958. In the late 1960s, annual sales hit $40 million.[261] Relative to the leading cosmetics companies, Estée Lauder Inc. was still a small player. In the late 1960s, for example, Revlon's yearly revenues exceeded $314 million, and Avon's $558 million.[262] Estée Lauder Inc., however, had staked out a position in the U.S. cosmetics market distinct from that of Avon, Revlon, and large consumer-product companies such as Chesebrough-Pond's. The Lauder products, brand, marketing initiatives, and distribution strategy were directed at consumers who wanted beauty offerings with a feminine, elegant, and upscale image.

Other companies, most notably Helena Rubinstein and Elizabeth Arden, maintained a prominent presence in the evolving market for prestige cosmetics. Both commanded wide consumer recognition and price premiums. Each was represented by its female founder, who had cultivated a glamorous image for herself and her products. Each brand appealed to a widening cross-section of American women who were interested in using cosmetics to express themselves and their aspirations. Each was sold in company-owned beauty salons, department stores, and drugstores. In the 1950s and early 1960s, both companies enjoyed healthy sales growth. By the mid-1960s, Helena Rubinstein's annual revenues exceeded $30 million; Elizabeth Arden's were $60 million.[263]

But in 1965, at age ninety-five, Helena Rubinstein died. Elizabeth Arden, eighty-one, died the following year. For the next several years, each company struggled to define its brand's strategic objectives, identity, target customers, and distribution channels. The president of Helena Rubinstein said in 1973, "It's been a tradition in this industry that when the founding genius or guiding light of a company dies, the marketing structure of that company falls apart."[264] In 1970 the pharmaceutical manufacturer Eli Lilly acquired Elizabeth Arden. In 1973, consumer-products giant Colgate-Palmolive bought Helena Rubinstein. Under new ownership, each cosmetics maker began concentrating on the mass market, reducing its commitment to the prestige segment.[265] (In the 1980s, both companies changed corporate hands several times. At the century's end, the cosmetics maker L'Oreal owned Helena Rubinstein. Elizabeth Arden was a subsidiary of Unilever, the consumer-products manufacturer.)

Estée Lauder Inc. benefited significantly from both companies' fortunes in the late 1960s and early 1970s. The deaths of founders Helena Rubinstein and Elizabeth Arden increased public interest in Estée, the only remaining female beauty entrepreneur. As the younger firm's sales climbed, the press devoted much attention to her business and social activity, thus generating free publicity for the company.[266] Moreover, the rivals' ownership changes and strategic confusion provided Estée Lauder Inc. with opportunities in the burgeoning market for upscale cosmetics.

The Lauder family and its management team worked to take full advantage of this possibility, making huge investments in the company's product lines, brands, and distribution network. Revenues continued to escalate, reaching $100 million in 1972.[267] The privately held company did not release earnings information. But industry observers estimated profitability at between 6 and 12 percent of sales.[268] During the 1960s and early 1970s, Estée Lauder Inc. poured the vast majority of its earnings back into the business, using the funds to finance product development, marketing initiatives, international expansion, manufacturing facilities, and new hires.

These efforts paid off. By 1973, when Estée relinquished the presidency of the company to Leonard, the family firm had emerged as one of the leading cosmetics makers in the United States. Measured by annual sales, Estée Lauder Inc. was considerably smaller than Avon or Revlon. But, as Figure 5-4 shows, the younger manufacturer was catching up quickly.

In 1973, the three players were pursuing distinct strategies. Avon, with over $1 billion in sales, sold its products door-to-door. Although Revlon distributed its premium lines, such as Ultima, through department stores, most of its $506 million in annual sales came through drugstores and other mass-market outlets.[269] In 1973, Revlon had more than 15,000 distribution points in contrast to Estée Lauder's 2,000 store counters.[270] Even in department stores, Revlon priced its cosmetics and skin care products lower than

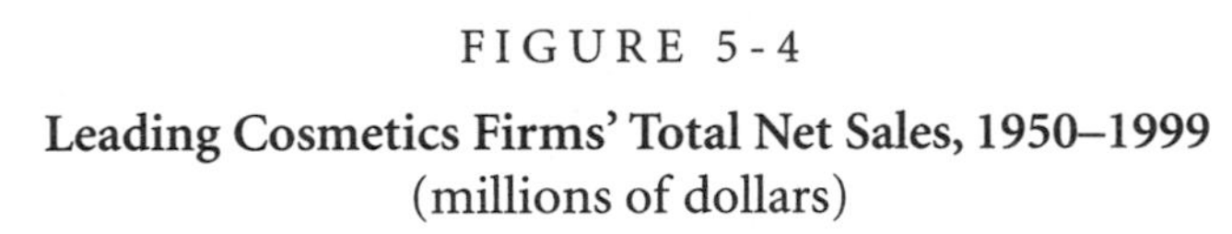

FIGURE 5-4

Leading Cosmetics Firms' Total Net Sales, 1950–1999
(millions of dollars)

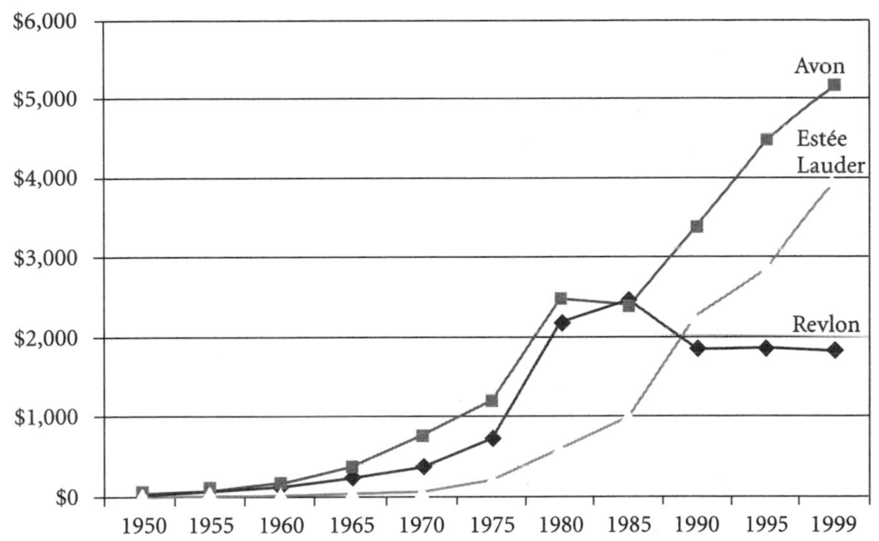

Sources: Revlon figures are from *Moody's Industrial Manual* from the following years: 1956, p. 1665; 1961, p. 1983; 1966, p. 647; 1971, p. 1992; 1976, vol. 2, p. 2413; 1981, vol. 2, p. 4129; 1986, vol. 2, p. 4325; Revlon, *Annual Report 1996,* p. 1; "Revlon Professional Unit Revenue Allocated toward Debt Payment," *The Rose Sheet,* 28 Feb. 2000. Avon figures are from *Moody's Industrial Manual:* 1951, p. 612; 1961, p. 697; 1971, p. 1535; 1981, vol. 1, p. 756; 1986, vol. 1, p. 1009; and 1991, vol. 1, p. 2624; Avon, *Annual Report 1995,* p. 1; Avon Products Inc. Investor Relations, "Corporate Overview," www.corporate-ir.net/ireye/ir_site.zhtml?ticker=AVP&script=2100 (accessed 30 June 2000). Estée Lauder figures are from "About the Size of It," *Beauty Fashion* (October 1971), p. 34; Lee Israel, *Estée Lauder: Beyond the Magic* (New York: Macmillan, 1985), p. 106; Anthony Ramirez, "Asset Sale by Revlon Called Near," *New York Times,* 10 April 1991, p. D1; Estée Lauder Companies Inc., *Annual Report 1996,* p. 7; Estée Lauder Investor Information, "Financial Highlights, 1998–1999," www.elcompanies.com/investor/fin_high. html (accessed 30 June 2000).

Note: All of the total sales figures include both domestic and international sales.

those of Estée Lauder. For example, in 1973 an Ultima II lipstick retailed for $2.85; an Estée Lauder lipstick sold at $3.50 to $4.00.[271]

Despite higher prices, Estée Lauder's profit margins were generally smaller than many of its competitors.[272] Frequent distribution of samples, elaborate promotions, and training of counter representatives increased the premium manufacturer's selling costs. But, from the perspective of senior management, these costs were a necessary condition of enhancing brand identity—brand identity that depended critically on the environment in which consumers encountered the company's products. "Sure I could pick up another million in earnings by breaking our traditional distribution pattern," Leonard Lauder said in 1973. "But we are the keystone of department store cosmetics and if we weaken that we will undo ourselves."[273]

Expanding the Market

During the 1950s and 1960s, the Lauders and their colleagues built a reputation for producing fine cosmetics. By 1973, millions of consumers associated the Estée Lauder name with elegance and femininity. How was the company to exploit this recognition? As the market developed, how should the manufacturer respond to changing customer needs and wants? What kind of competitive advantage could Estée Lauder Inc. construct over other firms producing premium cosmetics?

The organization used its flagship line and other brands to address these issues. Senior management continued to invest substantial resources in the Estée Lauder line. Between 1965 and 1990, the company also built four new brands: Aramis, Clinique, Prescriptives, and Origins. Each of these lines was developed in response to evolving consumer priorities and was targeted at distinct market segments. Each was intended to increase women's and men's interest in the company's offerings. Each was supported by stringent quality control, frequent product introductions, and strategic human resource management. Several of the brands lost money in their early years. But each, like the company's flagship brand, Estée Lauder, ultimately became a market leader. Each remained so at the beginning of the twenty-first century.

Manufacturing and Quality Control

When Estée and Joe founded the company in 1946, they made the company's skin care products themselves, working out of a former Manhattan restaurant.[274] As the business expanded in the 1950s and early 1960s, they outgrew their informal factory, moving manufacturing to much larger premises in Nassau County on Long Island. Joe oversaw operations there, including production, packaging, and shipping. In the late 1960s, more than 300 employees worked in the manufacturing facility.[275]

In 1967, the expanding company constructed a 150,000-square-foot plant in Melville, Long Island, about thirty-three miles east of New York City. The factory cost $2 million to build and was designed to provide manufacturing flexibility for increasing product lines and demand fluctuations.[276] In 1970, the company doubled the size of this plant. It had 700 employees.[277] Managers and other staff monitored quality control at the facility, ensuring that individual offerings met company and federal standards.

In the early years of the business, Estée and Joe had been responsible for creating new products. But in the early 1960s Leonard established a research and development laboratory. Here, chemists and other experts, in consultation with marketing executives, worked to develop beauty offerings that met consumers' needs. Once a prototype formula was developed, senior and other managers tested it with potential customers, gauging their reactions and adjusting ingredients accordingly.[278] At times, the firm sought outside research and advice about product possibilities. For example, Clinique, a line of allergy-tested, fragrance-free cosmetics introduced in 1968, was developed in consultation with a well-known New York dermatologist.

Product Innovation

The success of Youth Dew, the company's first fragrance, had lasting consequences for Estée Lauder Inc. Financially, the fragrance remained an important source of company revenue. In 1985, thirty-two years after its introduction, Youth Dew accounted for $30 million in annual sales.[279] Strategically, the scent's popularity underscored the efficacy of using new products—skin care treatments, makeup, and especially fragrances—to attract consumer interest in the company's flagship brand. Youth Dew was consistently effective in driving traffic to Estée Lauder counters, where trained sales representatives introduced customers to other cosmetics.

Senior management continued to rely on product introductions to enhance the original brand, build new lines, and increase sales.[280] In 1957, for example, the manufacturer introduced Re-Nutriv, a moisturizing cream, intended to compete with upscale European and American skin care products such as Helena Rubinstein's Tree of Life cream made with placenta. Most of these treatments, packaged in 4- or 8-ounce jars, sold for under $30.00.[281] By contrast, a 16-ounce jar of Re-Nutriv retailed for

$115—a pricing strategy designed to attract consumer interest, move the brand upmarket, and deepen its associations with female identity and self-worth. To promote the new product, the manufacturer took out full-page advertisements in fashion magazines such as *Harper's Bazaar* and *Vogue.* The ads featured an elegantly beautiful model, a list of the cream's "costliest" components, such as turtle oil, royal jelly, and silicone, and the question "What Makes a Cream Worth $115.00?" as a headline. "Re-Nutriv by Estée Lauder," the ad replied and continued:

> Rare ingredients. Rare Formula. But above all the rare perception of a woman like Estée Lauder who knows almost better than anyone how to keep you looking younger, fresher, lovelier than you ever dreamed possible. She has created what she likes to think of as "a goldmine of beauty"—her Crème of Creams Re-Nutriv . . . Costly? Yes, but so rewarding![282]

In the next four decades, the company launched scores of other skin care treatments, makeup, and fragrances under the Estée Lauder name. All of the products were developed to attract consumer interest in the brand and its broader offerings. Like Youth Dew, Re-Nutriv, and Beautiful perfume, these innovations were also intended to enhance the brand's image and position in the prestige market, deepening Estée Lauder's reputation as a purveyor of elegant, fashionable cosmetics. A wide range of company initiatives surrounding product introduction—from packaging to the timing of a new good's arrival in specific department stores to a focused advertising campaign—was coordinated to communicate this identity to retailers and, especially, to ultimate consumers.

New fragrances played a major role in supporting the Estée Lauder brand. The launch of each new perfume provided opportunities to attract new consumers to the Lauder line and deepen the loyalty of existing customers. Between Youth Dew's debut in 1953 and the introduction of Beautiful in 1985, the company introduced six successful fragrances under the Estée Lauder brand: Estée, Azurée, Aliage, Private Collection, Cinnabar, and White Linen. Senior management relied on samples, in-store events, trained sales representatives, and national advertising to promote these products. By the mid-1980s, Estée Lauder's scents attracted more users than those of any other U.S. company except Avon.[283]

To introduce new scents and other products, the Lauders began to advertise on a broad scale. Estée and Joe had not relied on national media in their first decade in business. But as sales increased in the early 1960s, the company reversed its earlier policy of not using advertising agencies and embarked on a campaign overseen by the AC & R agency, a large firm based in New York City. At any given time, Estée said, "Our competition used many models to speak for them." But "we decided to personify our products in the vision of one woman—the same model."[284] Estée and her colleagues wanted a model who would represent the brand's fundamental attributes and associations, who, over time, would come to symbolize "the Estée Lauder woman" for millions of consumers. In relying so heavily on a single image, they were taking a risk, Lauder remembered, that consumers would become tired of one face.[285]

Senior management decided to take the risk. Between 1962 and the end of the century, the Estée Lauder brand has had seven successive spokeswomen. Most served as the brand's representative for at least five years. During her tenure, each has appeared in virtually all the brand's print ads, which have run in *The New Yorker, Town and Country, Vogue,* and other magazines. As the brand's most publicized image, each woman was chosen very carefully. In 1971, for example, Karen Graham became the third model to represent the brand. Her face, Estée explained, was "selected from a thousand faces" as epitomizing

> a young, sophisticated woman with charm and éclat. She was sensual rather than sexy. She was strong and smart. She seemed in charge of her life, which was perceived as the good life by millions of women who identified with her and strove to be like her.[286]

During the ensuing decades, marketing executives have tried to keep "the Estée Lauder woman" relevant to changing consumer priorities. The woman in the early ads, Estée explained, "was more formal, more involved in dressed-up elegance." Since that time, Lauder continued, the brand's representative has achieved "a more relaxed richness that reflects today's world. She's become less status-conscious. Our Estée Lauder woman is within reach."[287] (In 1995, actress and model Elizabeth Hurley became the brand's latest representative.)

Executives also worked to develop brands to complement the flagship Estée Lauder line.

Aramis. In the mid-1960s, the company introduced a new brand developed for men.[288] Named for a Turkish root with aphrodisiac properties, Aramis was largely Estée's creation. Surveying the market in the early 1960s, she believed that it "was barren in the men's toiletries field." The available products, she continued, "were mediocre at best and irritating at worst."[289] She set out to develop an appealing line of toiletries for men, using Leonard and eight coworkers as guinea pigs. Aramis was launched in 1965 around a woodsy scent offered as a fragrance, cologne, and aftershave lotion.[290]

The first two years of sales were disappointing, and in 1967 the company relaunched a broader line of Aramis products including aftershave moisturizers, facial masque, eye pads, and cologne. Backed by a sophisticated advertising campaign and extensive promotions, the brand attracted consumers' interest and helped break open a growing market for men's prestige toiletries. Industry sales of men's fragrances, skin care treatments, and shaving products increased quickly—as fast as 12 percent annually—during the late 1960s and 1970s.[291] By 1978, Aramis sales totaled $40 million or about 14 percent of Estée Lauder's total sales.[292]

Clinique. In 1968, Estée Lauder Inc. launched Clinique, a new line of skin care products and makeup. Targeted at women who were knowledgeable about and interested in their skin, the Clinique brand was introduced as a state-of-the-art, medically sound, and accessible offering. The products were packaged in sleek, pale green casings accented with silver and were designed to appeal to consumers younger than those traditionally attracted to the flagship Estée Lauder brand. Like products in the original line, Clinique offerings were distributed through a controlled number of upscale department stores. Behind-the-counter saleswomen for Clinique wore white lab coats and carried penlights to examine consumers' skin types and recommend a specific regime. To promote the line, the manufacturer distributed samples as usual, including a gift-with-purchase, and conducted a print advertising campaign. The most famous Clinique ad, appearing in the *New York Times Magazine* in 1974, featured a toothbrush leaning in a glass and the tag line "twice a day." Photographed by Irving Penn, the image was clean and ultramodern, emphasizing the simplicity and necessity of using

Clinique products. The ad ran for more than two decades. In the late 1990s, it occasionally appeared worldwide.

The company did not market its new brand under the Estée Lauder name. Within individual department stores, the manufacturer located Clinique counters far from those selling Estée Lauder products. To develop and manage the new line, senior management established a separate division within the organization and hired Carol Phillips, the former managing editor of *Vogue,* to head the creative effort within the new business. Ronald Lauder became the division's executive vice president. Senior management, according to Estée, had three reasons for separating Clinique from its better-known sister brand:

> We didn't want to confuse the customer. We were offering something new; we didn't want her to think she'd ever tried it before. Second . . . it would have hurt Estée Lauder to have anyone make the very wrong assumption that we'd come out with a hypoallergenic line because there was something allergenic about our main line. Third, combining two different lines under one umbrella wouldn't allow for each to grow strongly as a separate entity. Leonard was quite correct when he said we would be our own best competition. The best way of competing was with two companies, not two products under a parent name.[293]

Clinique lost money for several years. But Phillips and Ronald Lauder believed that the new brand would ultimately succeed. So did other senior executives. In the late 1960s, the company invested millions of dollars in marketing initiatives and production facilities for the line.[294] Within five years of the brand's launch, these commitments began to bear fruit. Clinique sales increased rapidly in the mid-1970s, climbing to $80 million in 1978—almost 30 percent of Estée Lauder's total revenues that year.[295] Three years later, *Forbes* magazine pronounced Clinique the "walkaway winner" among skin care products in the prestige market.[296] Consumer awareness of the brand continued to expand. So did its popularity. In the mid 1990s, Clinique ranked first or second in sales among all products in virtually every U.S. outlet in which Estée Lauder products were sold.[297]

Industry experts recognized the role that managerial patience had played in creating the brand. The women who bought Clinique, said a cosmetics manager in the early 1980s, "liked the scientific, therapeutic attitude behind it." Building these associations and conveying them to consumers "was costly," the executive added, "but the Lauders spent the money, took the losses for a while, and nourished the business."[298] The company could only do this, Leonard Lauder realized, because it was privately held and thus relatively immune to capital market pressures for rapid growth and profits. "If we had been public, I would never have launched Clinique," he said looking back on the brand's first years. "We took a bath before it started paying off. The same with Aramis."[299]

Prescriptives. In 1979, Estée Lauder Inc. introduced Prescriptives, a high-tech line of skin care treatments and makeup. Like Clinique, the new brand was sold through upscale department stores and emphasized the science of healthy skin care. But Prescriptives offerings were priced higher, their image was tonier, and they were directed at consumers older than the average Clinique customer, who was typically in her twenties. Prescriptives was targeted at career women between thirty and forty-five, who were interested in an individualized regime of skin care and cosmetics. Behind-the-counter salespeople, encouraging customers to have a lengthy consultation, tailored their product recommendations to each woman's complexion.

Consumers were initially slow to embrace the brand. Many women found the long makeover off-putting. Some thought Prescriptives products were too complicated. Others did not clearly understand the brand's distinctive benefits. In the early 1980s, Estée Lauder's senior management tried to address these concerns, clarifying Prescriptives' identity, streamlining its sales approach, and shifting the product mix. The manufacturer invested nearly $40 million in the brand during its first decade. In the mid-1980s, the line began to take off with consumers. At the end of the decade, it had become the parent company's fastest growing brand with estimated annual sales of $42 million.[300]

Origins. In 1990, Estée Lauder Inc. introduced Origins, a line of botanically based products for skin care, makeup, and sensory therapy. The new brand was targeted at consumers of both sexes interested in natural, environmentally friendly offerings. It included products such as Salt Rub Smoothing Body Scrub, Clear Head Mint Shampoo, and Happy Endings Conditioner. To oversee the development of Origins, the parent company created another separate division, headed by Leonard Lauder's son, William. He and other executives carefully controlled the young brand's distribution, establishing company-owned stores and "store within a store" formats in major retailers. In 1993, the first Origins store, dedicated solely to the brand's offerings, opened for business in Cambridge, Massachusetts. Within five years, Origins was sold in 30 freestanding stores and more than 200 other distribution points worldwide.[301] The brand enjoyed early success and in the mid-1990s was one of the fastest growing cosmetics lines in the United States.[302]

International Markets

In the late 1950s, Estée Lauder was convinced that her company's brand and supporting strategies would appeal to consumers in other countries. She decided to begin in England, setting her sights on that nation's premium department stores, such as Harrod's. "If I could start with the finest store in London," she reasoned, "all the other great stores would follow."[303] In 1960, the company opened its first international outlet in Harrod's. As sales and brand awareness increased, other upscale retailers, including Fortnum & Mason and Selfridge's, agreed to sell Estée Lauder products. Until the beauty company created an executive position to oversee British markets, Estée herself traveled from one department store to another, talking to buyers, making up customers, and training saleswomen.

In the 1960s and 1970s, Lauder visited other European retailers, setting up counters in Austrian, Italian, and French department and specialty stores. The cosmetics buyer at Galeries Lafayette, the Paris department store, was initially uninterested in the Estée Lauder line and refused to see the company's founder. To attract French consumers' interest, Estée spilled Youth Dew on the sales floor. Over two days, shoppers repeatedly asked Galeries Lafayette saleswomen where they could purchase the scent. Some of these conversations took place in the presence of the store's cosmetics buyer, who was impressed with women's enthusiasm for Youth Dew. Within a few weeks, Estée Lauder opened her first counter in Galeries Lafayette.[304]

For the next twenty years, Estée and other senior managers traveled around the world, seeking to expand markets. As sales grew, the company established a separate division, Estée Lauder International, Inc., to manage growth outside the United States. Executives such as Jeanette Sarkisian Wagner, president of this division from 1986 to 1998, devoted considerable time and attention to understanding consumers' priorities in different markets. "You cannot nurture global brands and keep them consistently relevant," she said, "unless you immerse yourself in local cultures. This means you cannot run the business from an office in a single city. You have to be out in the markets, staying close to the customer."[305]

In the mid-1990s, the manufacturer distributed its products in more than 100 countries, including Germany, Hong Kong, Russia, Australia, Canada, Singapore, Mexico, the Ukraine, Malaysia, and Venezuela.[306] International revenues accounted for more than 40 percent of the company's total sales. Most of that volume, Leonard Lauder noted, was "concentrated in Western Europe and Japan." As economies expand, he continued, "so do opportunities in Asia, Eastern Europe, and Latin America. We have a disciplined but aggressive approach to expanding our presence in those areas. As always, our philosophy is to have demand precede supply."[307]

Conclusion

In the late 1990s, Estée Lauder Inc. was one of the largest cosmetics companies in the world with 15,000 employees and annual sales of almost $4 billion.[308] The company was widely recognized for its market leadership and consistently strong financial performance. In 1996, for example, it ranked 727 on *Business Week*'s Global 1000 of the world's most valuable companies.[309] Estée, the company's cofounder, retired from active public life in 1994, having served as president and chairman of the board for many years. By the late 1990s, she had become one of the country's wealthiest self-made women.[310] *Time* magazine chose the cosmetics entrepreneur as one of the twentieth-century's 100 most influential business geniuses.[311]

In the late 1990s, the organization that Estée and Joe had started fifty years earlier was a major player in the worldwide cosmetics industry. Seven global corporations—L'Oreal, Procter & Gamble, Unilever, Shiseido, Estée Lauder, Avon, and Johnson & Johnson—accounted for almost half of global revenues, competing intensely for market share in established and emerging markets.[312] Most of this rivalry was directed at the demand side of a given market as companies jockeyed for customer attention and loyalty. Each of these players tried to affect customer interests and decision making, using product introductions, promotions, advertising, merchandising, service, and other initiatives.

In this competitive environment, successful brands played critical roles. They educated consumers about a particular firm's products, increasing customer confidence and reducing risk in making purchasing choices. Cosmetics brands, as Estée Lauder had long understood, also offered women and men a means of exploring and asserting their identities, social as well as individual. She and her colleagues had devoted most of their efforts to understanding these and other consumer priorities in a changing market, using this knowledge to create a series of relevant, appealing brands and the organizational capabilities that supported them.

In the late 1990s, the company acquired several cosmetics brands such as Aveda, Bobbie Brown, *jane,* Jo Malone, La Mer, M.A.C, and Stila. The manufacturer also signed licensing agreements to make and distribute fragrances and other cosmetics under the Tommy Hilfiger and Donna Karan names. Each of these brands was targeted at a particular market segment. Each was intended to increase customer awareness of and loyalty to the line. Each was managed and promoted with rigorous quality control, limited distribution, and imaginative marketing. Each owed its future to an organization that was founded on its ability to anticipate and respond to consumers' changing wants and needs.

Preview to Chapter 6: Howard Schultz and Starbucks

THE PRECEDING CHAPTER examined how Estée Lauder helped make a large market for prestige cosmetics. The next chapter on Howard Schultz and Starbucks looks at another new market—for specialty coffee and local cafés—created in the midst of late-twentieth-century economic growth and social change.

Howard Schultz, who built Starbucks into a nationally known brand name, was born in 1953, the same year in which Estée Lauder introduced Youth Dew. He came of age under very different social and economic conditions from those Lauder had experienced in the 1920s and 1930s. But like Lauder, Schultz had a keen appreciation for how socioeconomic change affected consumers' wants and needs. And he used this understanding to create Starbucks distinctive strategy: its products, brand, retail presence, and overall operating policies.

Schultz recognized that the men and women born after World War II, particularly those who came to represent the "baby boom," had, on average, more education and higher incomes than earlier generations. In the 1980s, Schultz observed that "boomers" and other Americans had begun to reject many prepackaged foods and beverages in favor of those they regarded as of higher quality and more "natural": organic fruits and vegetables, breads baked only hours before, and freshly roasted coffee beans.

At the same time, millions of Americans were beginning to complain more and more of having too little time for their families, friends, homes, and selves. Schultz believed that overworked, time-constrained consumers were increasingly interested in "authentic" products and experiences, especially those that seemed to have some kind of meaningful social component. He was also certain that Americans were becoming more interested in a higher level of service than was generally available in most retail outlets.

Schultz used this understanding of the changing demand side—in tandem with a range of operating policies—to develop premium coffee products and appealing retail environments. (By the 1980s, per capita coffee consumption in the United States, which was based largely on supermarket sales of one-pound cans from Maxwell House and other mass marketers, had been declining for twenty years.) Beyond the high quality of Starbucks products themselves, the keys to Schultz's success were responsive customer service and a powerful brand. These innovations helped create a mass market for specialty coffee—including cappuccinos and caffe lattes—that altered consumers' tastes and expectations about a commodity beverage that previous generations of Americans had regarded simply as a "cuppa Joe."

CHAPTER 6

Howard Schultz and Starbucks Coffee Company

Prologue: International Expansion

On August 2, 1996, Starbucks Coffee Company opened its first store outside North America. Like many of its U.S. and Canadian outlets, this was located in a busy district of a prominent city—Tokyo. Starbucks managers had devoted much time to selecting the site, designing the store's layout and fixtures, training its staff, and publicizing its introduction. A series of events, including receptions and public samplings, attracted consumer interest in the new store's specialty coffee drinks, whole (unground) coffee beans, and pastries. For example, a man with a container of iced coffee in his backpack and a long hose poured shots of the cold beverage for passersby on the sidewalk.[1] CEO Howard Schultz flew in from the company's Seattle headquarters to celebrate the opening and observe consumers' reactions.

The Starbucks store, really a small café measuring 1,500 square feet, was situated at a prime corner in Tokyo's swank Ginza district. Surrounded by commercial activity, the establishment was bound to attract attention from thousands of pedestrians each day. In keeping with established practice, the company relied on consumer word of mouth rather than traditional advertising. The Starbucks brand had developed quickly in the United States and Canada, gaining widespread recognition and interest among consumers in these countries. In entering Asia, Schultz and his colleagues were betting that the company's reputation would have broader appeal. As the store opening approached, however, the CEO could not avoid some last-minute worries about Tokyo customers' response. "What," he asked himself, "could the name Starbucks possibly mean to the Japanese?"[2]

Actually, Starbuck was the mate on the whaler *Pequod* in Herman Melville's novel *Moby Dick.* The Seattle-based founders of the company in 1971 had adopted this name, adding an *s* to it, because it had associations of high seas adventure and indirect connections to the history of the Northwest.[3] By 1996, the name they chose had become a conspicuous feature of American cities.

August 2 in Tokyo was a hot day—95 degrees Fahrenheit with almost 100 percent humidity. But Japanese customers, Schultz could see, were not deterred. Customers filled the store from opening to closing, lining up forty to fifty people deep to try Starbucks coffee. Businessmen in suits came, as did elegantly dressed women and students with books and backpacks. Some customers bought Frappuccinos® blended coffee drinks, which Starbucks had invented a year earlier. "We had been warned that, culturally, the Japanese refuse to carry to-go food or beverages on the street. Yet many customers were walking out the door proudly carrying their Starbucks cups—with the logo showing."[4]

Over the following days and weeks, consumers of all ages continued to crowd into the new store and, at lunchtime, overflowed onto the sidewalk. Some came to buy coffee beans. Some came to experience the ambience in the city's newest coffee bar. Others, who had heard of Starbucks, wanted to learn more about the brand and its offerings. Most people standing in line intended to buy a caffe latte, cappuccino, or other specialty coffee drink that they associated with the young company. Schultz was impressed by the customers' enthusiasm. The Starbucks brand, he realized, "had the same power in Tokyo that it had in New York and Seattle. It had taken on a life of its own."[5]

Schultz had bought the company in 1987, when it was still a small Seattle retailer, mainly selling coffee beans. By 1996, it had become the nation's largest purveyor of specialty coffee, selling the beverage served in various ways, along with coffee beans and related food and merchandise. Between 1992 and 1996, annual revenues had skyrocketed 650 percent, climbing to almost $700 million.[6]

Most of this increase had been driven by the swift proliferation of company-owned stores with the rest of it coming from two thriving divisions—mail order and specialty sales (which sold coffee to restaurants and other institutional purchasers). In 1987, Starbucks had 11 outlets; nine years later, over 1,000. In fiscal 1996 alone, the company opened 330 outlets, an average of almost one a day.[7] As the business moved into new U.S. and Canadian urban markets, consumer awareness of specialty coffee and the Starbucks brand widened considerably. By the mid-1990s, millions of North Americans associated the company's name with superior dark roast coffee, customized espresso drinks, responsive customer service, and an appealing store experience.

More recent alliances with corporations such as Dreyer's Grand Ice Cream, Pepsi-Cola Company, Barnes & Noble, and United Airlines promised to broaden the Starbucks product line, distribution channels, and name recognition. Marketing experts and financial analysts, impressed with the company's growth and impact on the broader coffee industry, regarded Starbucks as one of the strongest young consumer brands in North America.[8]

In the mid-1990s, Schultz and other executives sought to use this reputation to create new international markets. After much discussion, senior management decided to enter Asia, concentrating initially on Japan. "We looked at Europe and felt that there was opportunity in the region," said Howard Behar, the first president of the Starbucks International Division, "but we believed there were more possibilities" in the East.[9] "We needed to focus," Behar added. "We cannot be everywhere at once." The decision to invest in Pacific Rim countries, he explained, ran "counter to what others might do. But there is a large, growing middle class in Asia, over 500 million people."[10] Company executives believed that many of these potential consumers would be interested in Starbucks offerings. In early 1996, the company announced plans to open the store in central Tokyo. Working in partnership with Sazaby, a Japanese retailer, Starbucks opened seventy-six more stores in Tokyo and another thirty-one nationwide during the next five years.[11]

The Tokyo and larger Japanese market presented big opportunities for the U.S. company. Many of these, such as a significant, expanding middle class, were on the demand side of the coffee market. Japanese households not only enjoyed relatively high per capita incomes but also were apt to be enthusiastic coffee drinkers.[12] Japan was the third largest coffee-consuming nation in the world behind the United States and Germany.[13] Japanese consumers drank instant or traditional American-style hot coffee at home. They also bought iced and hot canned coffee dispensed from more than a million vending machines across the country.[14] Many stopped regularly at coffeehouses.

Whether they drank coffee or not, millions of Japanese consumers had encountered the Starbucks brand on business trips or leisure travel to the United States.[15] Company executives believed that such exposure, coupled with Japanese interest in coffee, meant that the Seattle business would not start from ground zero in trying to build a national market for specialty coffee drinks and beans. "There is not a lot of education to do," Behar said. "We are not the first place to serve lattes."[16]

Behar and Schultz realized, however, that the existence of a strong coffee culture also posed competitive challenges. In 1996, Tokyo seemed to have a coffee shop on nearly every corner, and several were located in the same block as the new Starbucks store.[17] Some of the city's coffee shops were small mom-and-pop operations that also sold snacks and sandwiches. Others were upscale Parisian-style cafés. A growing number of discount coffee bars were run by large Japanese chains, such as Doutor Coffee Company, with 453 stores, or Pronto Corporation with 94.[18] In the mid-1990s, such outlets, many of which sold hot dogs, spaghetti, and fried noodle sandwiches in addition to coffee, had become increasingly popular in urban Japan. In mid-1996, Pronto charged ¥160 (about $1.50) for a small, regular coffee. Starbucks, by comparison, priced its small coffee at ¥250 (about $2.30).[19] In such an environment, Schultz recognized, "the odds against success were formidable."[20]

Intense competition was not the only obstacle that the company faced. Starbucks also had to construct an operational and managerial infrastructure 5,000 miles west of Seattle. This involved practical and cultural challenges. How was the business to supply its Asian stores, choose specific menu items, and train new employees? How was it to select joint-venture partners? How should the young, growing enterprise allocate management time between issues related to the American market and those in emerging outlets halfway around the world? When Starbucks started expanding in the United States in the late 1980s, Behar explained, "few people had well-defined expectations about the company." Now, he continued, "we have to go into each new market and deliver on a set of consumer expectations that is much, much higher."[21] How, he and other senior executives wondered, was the company to accomplish this?

Starbucks also faced financial hurdles. By mid-1996, the company and its retail partner Sazaby had each invested $5 million in setting up Japanese operations. Both partners expected to invest considerably more money in the project, and soon.[22] Making markets for specialty coffee in other Asian countries would entail still more expenditures.

But given Starbucks strategic objectives, senior management viewed the potential benefits of international expansion as greater than the possible risks. Schultz and his management team wanted to use the firm's resources—its assets and capabilities—to build a *global* business. One of the most important of these assets was the Starbucks brand.

The brand was the appealing, distinctive identity that consumers associated with the company's offerings. It was an identity that commanded broad awareness and strong buyer loyalty. In 1995, for example, the average Starbucks customer in North America visited a company store eighteen times a month.[23] Such loyalty, as Schultz and his colleagues understood, constituted a vital source of advantage in the increasingly competitive markets for specialty coffee.

Consumers' attachment to the Starbucks brand was not based on mass advertising or promotion. It was based, Schultz believed, on their experience in company stores: on their reactions to the coffee, the people who made and served it, and the stores' atmosphere and sense of community. This experience, he said, "earned customers' trust by speaking to their hearts as well as their heads."[24] As they debated international expansion in 1995 and 1996, he and other managers were fairly confident that the appeal of the Starbucks brand extended beyond North America and that consumers around the world would respond enthusiastically to the store experience. Senior executives were willing to bet time, talent, money, and even the future integrity of the brand, on these assessments.

Building a global brand, as Schultz realized, involved new imperatives. "We have created a set of expectations around an intimacy of experience that lies at the heart of what we are as a company and brand." To be successful in the future, Starbucks must "continue to meet these expectations and sustain the trust that we have earned as we grow, as the scale, people, and complexity involved all increase." How, he wondered, does an organization "get big and at the same time, stay small?"[25]

The Rise of Coffee

The commercial market for coffee probably originated after A.D. 500 when Arab traders brought the *Coffea arabica* tree from its native Ethiopia to the

Middle East for cultivation.[26] A variety of legends surrounds the plant's discovery. One popular legend tells of an Ethiopian goatherd who, noticing that his goats became energized after eating red berries from a nearby bush, tried some himself and soon was frisking with the animals. Whether or not the story is true, coffee became an established part of Ethiopian diets.[27] Early users chewed the leaves and beans. Later, people put the leaves and beans in boiling water. They also ground the beans, mixing them with animal fat, in effect creating one of the first "energy bars."[28]

The invigorating powers of coffee also appealed to Arabs. During the Middle Ages, many believed that coffee had medicinal powers, and for the next several centuries, coffee consumption spread throughout the Islamic world.[29] By the sixteenth century, people of various ranks in Turkey, Persia, Egypt, and North Africa were drinking it daily.[30] In 1587, an Arab aristocrat praised coffee as "the common man's gold," for it "brings to every man the feeling of luxury and nobility. . . . Where coffee is served there is grace and splendour and friendship and happiness."[31] Coffeehouses sprang up in Constantinople (now Istanbul) and other places throughout the Ottoman Empire.[32]

Coffee's popularity took a big leap in the early 1600s when Dutch and Venetian merchants introduced the product to Europe. Men, women, and some children initially embraced the beverage for its supposed health benefits, but as coffee drinking spread across the continent, its perceived benefits gradually widened to include taste and sociability.[33] Before and during the eighteenth century, coffeehouses flourished in Italy, England, Austria, and France and were popular forums for political and literary debate.[34] In Italy's leading cities, for example, men and women crowded into simple, low-ceilinged rooms for companionship, news, and gossip. Parisians met at a growing number of cafés, including the Café Procope and the Café de la Régence.[35] In London, John Dryden, Alexander Pope, Joseph Addison, and other public figures were devotees of particular coffeehouses.[36] In 1668, Edward Lloyd opened a coffeehouse that attracted merchants involved in overseas trade. He often prepared lists of ships' schedules and contents for underwriters who met there. Lloyd's of London, the insurance company, grew out of this enterprise.[37]

Meanwhile, European imperialism took coffee to Indonesia, South America, the Caribbean, and other parts of the world. Coffee probably reached North America in the early 1600s. By the last quarter of that century, coffeehouses had opened in Boston, New York, and other colonial cities. These establishments quickly became centers of commercial, political, and social activity.[38] North Americans drank increasing amounts of both coffee and tea in the eighteenth century. Tea was probably the preferred beverage.[39] But coffee got a boost in 1773, when colonists boarded British ships anchored in Boston and pitched tea cargoes overboard to protest the mother country's economic policies. This "Boston Tea Party" led many Americans to reject tea for patriotic reasons. "I must be weaned," John Adams noted in 1774, "and the sooner the better."[40]

Coffee consumption climbed slowly after the American Revolution, more rapidly in the early 1800s. By the mid-nineteenth century, the commodity had surpassed tea in popularity.[41] In 1859, Americans consumed about eight pounds of coffee a year, per capita.[42] Many city dwellers enjoyed the drink in coffeehouses. But most men and women, as the industry historian Mark Pendergrast noted, "drank coffee at home or brewed it over campfires heading west."[43] In the city or on the frontier, the beverage was generally prepared by boiling ground beans in water. Some users added eggs or fish skins to the mixture to clarify it, helping the grounds settle to the bottom. To mask the fishy taste and bitterness of the finished product, many added milk and sugar.[44]

During the Civil War, coffee was a staple in Union soldiers' daily diets. The federal government purchased more than four million pounds of coffee, allocating each soldier up to thirty-six pounds of beans a year.[45] After the war, John Billings, a former Massachusetts artilleryman, put coffee second only to bread in its importance to troops: "It was coffee *at* meals and *between* meals; and men going on guard or coming off guard drank it all hours of the night.[46] Most soldiers drank their coffee black, and one veteran remembered that it was "strong enough to float an iron wedge."[47]

A National Market

Coffee consumption in the United States spread after the war, spurred not only by returning soldiers' interest in the drink but also by supply-side developments. The invention in 1864 of the self-emptying roaster enabled industrious manufacturers such as John Arbuckle of New York City and Jim Folger of San Francisco to distribute ground coffee on a regional or even national scale.[48] In 1878, Caleb Chase and James Sanborn of Boston introduced canned ground coffee.[49] They advertised the Chase & Sanborn product heavily, and consumers responded enthusiastically to its quality and convenience. The partners built a North American sales force that eventually numbered 25,000.[50]

Other players entered the growing industry. In 1881, for example, brothers Austin and Reuben Hills acquired a retail coffee store in San Francisco. During the next two decades, they expanded their markets in the western United States, incorporating new technologies such as vacuum packing. At the same time, another team of brothers, Max, Mannie, and Eddie Brandenstein, also of San Francisco, founded a tea, coffee, and spice company. By the turn of the century, their principal product, MJB coffee, competed directly with that of Folger and Hills Brothers. In 1901, Nashville entrepreneurs Joel Cheek and John Neal went into business together to produce Cheek's special Maxwell House blend, named for the local hotel in which it became popular. Six years later, President Theodore Roosevelt, sampling the coffee on a trip through Nashville, proclaimed it "good to the last drop."[51]

The proliferation of chain stores in the late nineteenth and early twentieth centuries also helped enlarge U.S. coffee markets. One of the most successful chains was the Great Atlantic & Pacific Tea Company (A&P), established in Manhattan in 1859 by George Francis Gilman.[52] During the next four decades, this retailer gradually widened its grocery offerings, including coffee. It also expanded its store locations. In 1900, A&P had 198 stores; thirty years later, it had 15,737, selling over one billion dollars of groceries annually. The chain's Eight O'Clock brand of coffee beans, which customers could buy freshly ground, was one of its best-selling products.[53]

World War I, like the Civil War before it, increased Americans' demand for coffee. Yearly per capita consumption of preroasted beans, ground coffee, and newly developed "instant" coffee rose from just under nine pounds in 1913 to almost twelve in 1919.[54] Soldiers stationed overseas were especially heavy users.[55] Many veterans arrived home with a permanent taste for the beverage. "It shall not be forgotten," a coffee roaster declared as the war ended, "that a good cup of coffee is one of the vital blessings of everyday life which should not and must not be denied to them, our boys, the unbeatable happy warriors of a coffee-loving nation!"[56]

Stimulated by national advertising, U.S. consumption climbed through most of the 1920s and again in the late 1930s. In 1939, the average American consumed more than fourteen pounds of coffee a year. According to market surveys, 98 percent of families drank the beverage.[57] Why was the beverage so popular? One industry observer cited the "big boost" that Prohibition gave coffee drinking, "high-pressure advertising plus cheap retail prices," and "the nervous national tempo." "It may also be," the same writer reasoned, "that when depression nips an average man's buying power, he finds a 5¢ cup of coffee a sort of emotional *ersatz* for more expensive things."[58]

By the onset of World War II, three large companies led the U.S coffee industry. A&P, Maxwell House, and Chase & Sanborn together controlled almost 40 percent of annual revenues. The rest of the market belonged to Folgers, Hills Brothers, Nestlé, and more than a thousand medium-sized and smaller roasters.[59] The large manufacturers profited during the war by supplying soldiers with all the coffee they could drink.[60] On the other hand, government actions such as naval warfare, rationing, and price controls also disrupted coffee companies' operations.[61] Consolidation in the U.S. coffee industry had begun early in the century, and this continued during and after the war. In 1915, 3,500 firms supplied the American market. Thirty years later, there were 1,500. Only a small fraction of these—57 roasters—were producing more than 50,000 bags a year.[62]

As the war ended, U.S. coffee executives were optimistic.[63] Despite the growing popularity of soft drinks, particularly Coca-Cola and Pepsi, most industry analysts expected coffee usage to rise.[64] And indeed it did, at first. The end of rationing increased Americans' demand for a wide range of goods, including coffee. In 1946, the average person consumed almost twenty pounds, which, when brewed, produced approximately forty gallons of coffee.[65] By the early 1960s, per capita consumption had increased to about forty-eight gallons a year, or about three cups a day.[66] The prevalence of coffee in the mid-twentieth century spawned its own cultural icons and social institutions: the New York or San Francisco café patronized by writers, artists, and musicians, the stark diner depicted in Edward Hopper's painting *Nighthawks,* and the coffee break in business and household schedules.

Large Processors

Regional roasters proliferated in the 1940s and 1950s, selling their beans through local grocery stores and other outlets.[67] By the early 1960s, however, supermarkets had become the dominant distribution channel for coffee. Competition for shelf space forced many small suppliers out of business and spurred further consolidation among others.[68] Large suppliers, such as General Foods, which owned the Maxwell House, Yuban, Sanka, and Maxim brands, increased their capacity and market share. In 1960, a handful of big companies, including General Foods, Hills Brothers, Folgers, Standard Brands, and A&P, controlled more than half of industry sales.[69]

These and other large suppliers used blends of beans from *Caffea arabica* (also known as "arabica") and *canephora* (also known as "robusta") coffee plants. Cultivated in Colombia, Brazil, Indonesia, Kenya, Ethiopia, and other countries, arabica plants produced beans that were flavorful and aromatic when brewed. These beans were more expensive than those from robusta plants, a hardy, higher-yielding strain of coffee grown primarily in central and West Africa. Robusta beans produced a harsh, bitter taste when brewed.[70] But large manufacturers realized that they could be mixed with arabica beans to produce lower-cost blends for canned and instant coffee.

To gain market share and supermarket shelf space, the big processors clashed in frequent price wars, using coupons, discounts, and other promotions. In the decade after World War II, price emerged as the primary means of differentiating what had essentially become a standardized product.[71] The large manufacturers, such as Maxwell House and Chase & Sanborn, Pendergrast noted, "offered roasted ground coffee containing a blend based largely on average Brazilian beans, and they all tasted pretty much the same. The all-arabica cans weren't bad, but they weren't terribly good either."[72]

As price competition and pressure on profit margins intensified, the major rivals sought ways to cut costs. A few companies started packing coffee in fourteen-ounce cans and selling these at prices that previously had applied to one-pound containers. Most began adding larger quantities of cheaper robusta beans to their existing blends. Makers of instant or soluble coffee relied on the less expensive beans.[73]

The large manufacturers invested heavily in print and television advertising, and the vast majority of these messages were targeted at women. Many ads emphasized the importance of pleasing other family members—especially husbands. They equated good coffee with domestic harmony and female accomplishment. According to a 1960 review of industry marketing practices,

> Women approach the career of homemaker with a wide variety of notions as to what constitutes success in marriage. In general it may be safely assumed that once a woman accepts the numerous responsibilities that are part and parcel of maintaining a home, she can be expected to go about her chores in such a manner as to incur the least possible adverse criticism. Regardless of any other considerations, such as availability and price, a woman can be expected not to purchase any given brand of coffee if she believes that her husband and other coffee-drinking members of her family will express displeasure with it, perhaps even to the point of casting doubt on her ability to cook.[74]

Starting from these and other similar premises, coffee ads played on women's fears and fantasies. For example, when Procter & Gamble bought Folgers in 1963, it inaugurated an ambitious series of television commercials featuring a coffee-brewing busybody named Mrs. Olsen, who berated countless housewives for serving substandard coffee and ruining their husbands' happiness.[75] A 1962 print ad for Chock Full o' Nuts showed a woman with a cup overturned on her head and coffee spilling down her face. The message: "Men! Don't let it come to this! Win your fight for a decent cup of coffee without losing your temper!" The tag line at the bottom of the ad proclaimed "every man's right . . . every wife's duty."[76]

During the next two decades, the large roasters continued to spend huge advertising budgets fighting for shares in a shrinking market. Per capita coffee consumption began to fall in the mid-1960s, declining from a postwar peak of 3.1 cups per day in 1963 to less than 2 cups in the mid-1980s.[77] Americans, especially teenagers who had historically drunk coffee, increasingly consumed other beverages, especially soft drinks such as Coke and Pepsi. By the late 1980s, about half the U.S. population over the age of ten did not consume coffee.[78] Long the nation's number one beverage (excluding tap water), coffee had dropped to a distant second behind soft drinks.

Several factors underlay Americans' falling interest in coffee. Some consumers worried about the long-term health effects of caffeine. Others preferred the convenience of soft drinks or bottled juice. Younger buyers regarded coffee as an older generation's choice. Many simply did not like the taste of coffee. Expensive advertising campaigns did not significantly allay these concerns. Nor did aggressive promotion. The large processors' "shift to massive couponing," noted an industry observer in 1990, "only further eroded the product's image."[79] Supermarket coffee sales reflected Americans' disenchantment with canned and instant coffee, the consumption of which decreased almost 48 percent during the 1980s to $4.7 billion at the decade's end.[80] Figure 6-1 shows drinking patterns for several beverages.

FIGURE 6-1

U.S. Beverage Consumption, 1950–1995
(gallons per capita per year)

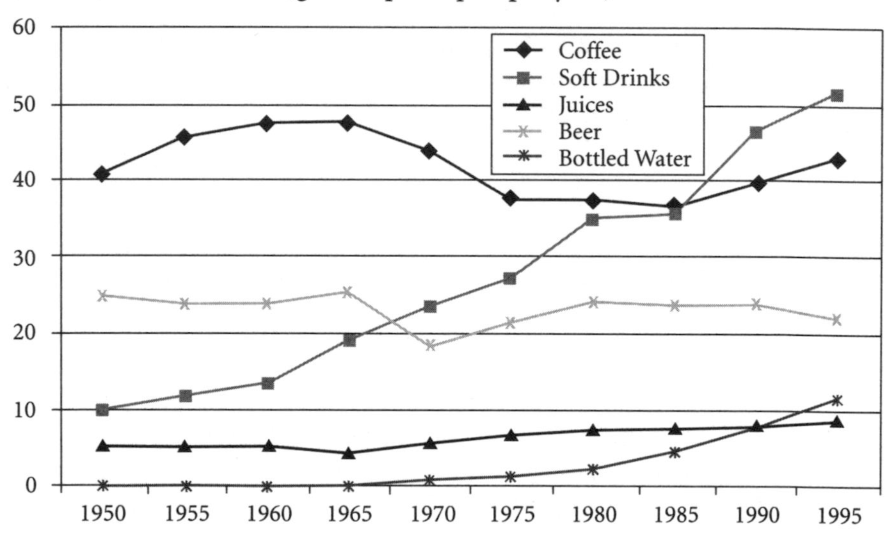

Sources: Coffee consumption figures are based on per-cup data from National Coffee Association of USA, Inc., "National Coffee Drinking Trends" (1998), Annex Tables, pp. 49–53. Conversion figures for 1950–1975 assume a six-ounce container. Conversion figures for 1980–1995 reflect the increasing use of coffee mugs, which, on average, hold eight to twelve ounces. Other consumption figures are from Judith Jones Putnam and Jane E. Allshouse, *Food Consumption, Prices, and Expenditures, 1970–1997* (U.S. Department of Agriculture Statistical Bulletin 965), pp. 34, 79; U.S. Department of Commerce, *Statistical Abstract, 1971* (Washington, DC: U.S. Government Printing Office, 1971), pp. 82, 702; *Beverage Industry Annual Manual* (Cleveland: Magazines for Industry, 1984), p. 12.

Note: Juices were originally in pounds per capita for 1950–1965 and have been recalculated to gallons.

The Growth of Specialty Coffee

While the larger coffee business stagnated in the 1970s and 1980s, the specialty segment took off. Unlike Procter & Gamble or the other large manufacturers, specialty coffee producers were usually small, independent distributors selling only higher-quality arabica beans. In the early 1980s, the retail price of specialty beans averaged five to seven dollars a pound, about twice the price of traditional coffee.[81] Despite the higher price, self-appointed enthusiasts around the country had been buying specialty coffee for decades from independent coffeehouses and regional roasters such as Zabar's in New York City.

Until the late 1970s and early 1980s, however, these consumers were a tiny minority of U.S. coffee drinkers. Most households in the postwar period had little knowledge of where the coffee that they purchased through supermarkets originated. Most had never tasted an espresso-based beverage. Most did not own a coffee grinder. The vast majority of Americans spent little time thinking about, preparing, or savoring their coffee. The specialty coffee business, based on interested, educated buyers who cared about quality coffee and how it was served, remained a fragmented niche of the larger market in the 1950s and 1960s.[82]

This began to change as growing numbers of coffee aficionados opened their own roasters to sell fresh, full-bodied arabica beans in scattered locations around the country. Some of these men and women followed in the tradition of Alfred Peet, whose passion for and knowledge of fine coffee was well known among devotees. Peet's father had been a roaster in the Netherlands, and Alfred inherited his interest in quality coffee. After arriving in San Francisco in the 1950s, Peet worked for an importing company that supplied beans to Hills Brothers and Folgers.

But he became disillusioned: "I couldn't understand why in the richest country in the world they were drinking such poor quality coffee."[83] In 1966, he opened his own store in Berkeley to roast and sell whole-bean coffee directly to consumers. The Dutch coffee connoisseur, as Howard Schultz later noted, "treated coffee like wine, appraising it in terms of origins and estates and years and harvests" and also "created his own blends."[84] Peet recognized that helping Americans develop an appreciation for fine-roast coffee involved educating them about specialty coffee: its origins, aromas, flavors, and preparation. He had stools in his store installed so customers could leisurely sample brews from various beans. He also trained the people who worked with him to appreciate different coffees, encouraging them to share their own enthusiasm with buyers. Peet's store quickly became a northern California institution, attracting first-time customers and loyal fans alike.

Other coffee lovers got into the business. Inspired by Peet's work, Gordon Bowker, Jerry Baldwin, and Zev Siegl opened a store in Seattle to roast and sell quality whole beans in early 1971. Each partner invested $1,350 and took out a bank loan for $5,000.[85] The store, which was located in Pike Place Market in Seattle, also offered bulk tea, spices, and supplies; it did not sell coffee by the cup. The three partners chose a logo based on an old Norse woodcut—a bare-breasted mermaid or siren surrounded by the store's original name: Starbucks Coffee, Tea and Spice.[86]

Seattle in 1971 was in the midst of a severe economic downturn. Boeing, the city's largest employer, had cut over half its workforce—more than 60,000 jobs—since the late 1960s. Other employment prospects, real estate prices, and business possibilities deteriorated. People deserted the region in search of better opportunities. A sign near the airport read: "Will the last person leaving Seattle turn out the lights?" In spite of local economic conditions, Starbucks quickly attracted a faithful, growing clientele. Its reputation spread. Within eleven years of its founding, the company had eighty-five employees, five retail stores selling freshly roasted beans (known as whole-bean coffee to distinguish it from traditional canned or instant coffee), a small roasting facility, and a wholesale business that supplied coffee to local restaurants.

In 1974, three years after Starbucks opened for business, George Howell left San Francisco for Massachusetts. When he could not find quality coffee beans at Boston stores, he and his wife Laurie decided to open their own business. They chose a site in Harvard Square in Cambridge and called the establishment The Coffee Connection. The store specialized in whole beans, but it also served coffee by the cup or plunger pot. "We were an overnight success," Howell remembered. The Howells opened other stores in the Boston area. Their customers, he added, "were like parched people coming out of a desert and finding an oasis."[87]

In Denver, San Diego, Pittsburgh, and other cities, independent specialty coffee roasters sprang up. Most of these were small operations without large advertising budgets. But many companies, such as Peet's or

Starbucks, had an enthusiastic base of regular customers who told their family, friends, and colleagues about gourmet coffee. As was the case with microbreweries and their individual varieties of beer, consumer interest in specialty coffee grew principally by word of mouth.

On both the demand and supply sides, the fledgling specialty coffee market grew rapidly in the 1970s and early 1980s, rising from $45 million in annual revenues in 1969 to more than $750 million in 1980.[88] Despite such growth, specialty coffee remained a very small segment, accounting for less than a tenth of total industry sales in the early 1980s.[89] Nestlé, General Foods, and Procter & Gamble, nicknamed "the Big Three," controlled nearly 60 percent of roasted coffee and 80 percent of instant coffee sales.[90]

In 1981, however, the specialty coffee business captured the attention and talents of Howard Schultz. He had never worked in the industry. He had learned to drink coffee that came from a can purchased in a supermarket. Yet he had a strong hunch that the young, fragmented specialty coffee sector held tremendous opportunities. Many of these were on the demand side, and Schultz intended to seize them: to use his talents to build a strong company and a large market for high-quality coffee.

Schultz's Beginnings

Howard Schultz was born on July 19, 1953, in Brooklyn, the most populous borough of New York City. He was the oldest of three children of Fred and Elaine Schultz, both of whom were from Jewish working-class families. When Howard and his younger brother and sister were growing up, their father held a variety of jobs, among them cab driver, diaper-service truck driver, and factory laborer. Elaine stayed home to care for her young children and later worked as a receptionist.[91]

Money was tight in the Schultz household. In 1956, the family moved into a two-bedroom apartment in Bay View Projects, a federally subsidized housing development in Brooklyn's Canarsie section. At that time, Schultz remembered, the housing projects were not a formidable place, but "a friendly, large leafy compound with a dozen eight-story brick buildings, all brand new." The local elementary school was located on the housing projects' grounds, and it had a playground and basketball courts. "Still, no one was proud of living in the Projects; our parents were all what we now call 'the working poor.'"[92]

Howard was a bright, sociable, and energetic child. From an early age, he loved sports, organizing countless pickup games of baseball and basketball among neighborhood friends and competing in larger informal events on the school grounds nearby. "You had to be good there," Schultz recalled, "because if you didn't win, you'd be out of the game, forced to watch for hours before you could get back in. So I played to win." His teammates and opponents came from a range of ethnic backgrounds: "Jewish kids, Italian kids, black kids. Nobody ever had to lecture us about diversity; we lived it."[93]

When he was twelve, Howard began earning money as a paperboy. Later, he served food behind the counter of a Brooklyn luncheonette. At sixteen, he found an after-school job in Manhattan's garment district, stretching animal skins for a furrier. He also worked in a knitting factory steaming yarn. He always turned some of his income over to his mother. She did not ask him for money, he remembered, but "I felt bad for the position my parents were in."[94]

Howard attended Canarsie High School with almost six thousand other students.[95] Academic work did not captivate him, and he applied himself only sporadically to his courses. He directed the bulk of his time and ambition to playing football, seeing athletics as an escape route out of the projects, out of Brooklyn, away from the road his father had taken.[96] His diligence paid off when he became quarterback of the high school team. His school did not have a football field, Schultz remembered, "and all our games were away games. Our team was pretty bad, but I was one of the better players on it."[97]

In his senior year, he was offered a football scholarship to the University of Northern Michigan, where he enrolled in the fall of 1971. Howard majored in communications, taking courses in public speaking, business, and other subjects. Nights, weekends, and summers, he worked various jobs to help finance his education. In 1975, he received a B.S., becoming the first college graduate in his family.[98]

Schultz entered Xerox's sales training program in 1976. After completing the course, he returned to New York and started drumming up prospective business customers for the company's office equipment, going door to door in midtown Manhattan. Most days, he made fifty cold calls. It was not easy work. The process, Schultz said, "taught me to think on my feet. So many doors slammed on me that I had to develop a thick skin and a concise sales pitch for a then-newfangled machine called a word processor." But the twenty-three-year-old learned quickly, thriving on the competition that permeated professional selling. He sought "to be the best, to be noticed, to provide the most leads to my salesmen. I wanted to win."[99]

He was promoted to a full sales representative, outselling many of his peers. But in 1979 after three years with Xerox, Schultz grew restless. He sought a more challenging position. At twenty-six, he took a job with Hammerplast, a U.S. subsidiary of the Swedish housewares company Perstorp. He rose quickly to vice president and general manager of the subsidiary, responsible for U.S. operations and based in New York. With a team of twenty salespeople reporting to him, Schultz sold Hammerplast products to upscale retailers, and the manufacturer's revenues increased.

By 1981, he had come a long way from the projects. He had an executive job with a generous salary. Together with Sheri Kersch, an interior designer whom he had met three years earlier, he owned an apartment on Manhattan's Upper East Side. The couple enjoyed urban life, "going to the theater, dining at restaurants, and inviting friends to dinner parties."[100]

But at age twenty-eight, he was again restive, on the lookout for new possibilities. In 1981, Schultz decided to visit a small Hammerplast client in Seattle. He had never been to the city and was curious about why this customer—Starbucks Coffee, Tea and Spice—was ordering so many plastic cone filters from the housewares supplier. Schultz knew that the coffee retailer had only four outlets at the time. But it was buying more of the devices than Macy's department store chain or other big clients. He wondered why the Seattle retailer was using so many cone filters when most Americans made their coffee in electric percolators or drip coffee machines.

The trip was Schultz's first encounter with specialty coffee. His mother had drunk instant coffee when he was a child, and like most Americans in the early 1980s, he had grown up thinking of coffee as a commodity purchased along the inner aisles of supermarkets. In taste, smell, preparation, and overall appeal, Starbucks coffee was markedly different. It was also sold differently: with knowledgeable salespeople scooping coffee beans from bins behind a counter in a store devoted to coffee and tea. Schultz was impressed with the company's operation, management, and product. "I felt as though I had discovered a whole new continent," he said. "By comparison, I realized, the coffee I had been drinking was swill."[101]

He believed that people all over the country would have similar reactions. Specialty coffee, Schultz reasoned, could attract a much bigger group of consumers than devotees. Growing numbers of men and women were embracing natural foods, those that they perceived to be less processed and more nutritious.[102] At the same time, Americans, especially urbanites, were buying increasing quantities and varieties of ethnic foods: pesto, dim sum, focaccia, paella, hummus, burritos, and more.[103] Such consumers might enjoy Starbucks emphasis on a given coffee's origins and history. Most important from Schultz's vantage point, coffee drinkers everywhere who were accustomed to traditional blends and percolator brews would like the dark, full taste of specialty coffee.

He was immediately excited about the company's prospects. Starbucks, Schultz told Baldwin and Bowker, had the potential to become a national business with dozens or perhaps hundreds of stores. The enthusiastic New Yorker argued that Starbucks might one day become synonymous with the finest coffee, its brand a guarantee of world-class quality.[104] He wanted to be part of the retailer's growth. After many discussions with the managing partners, Schultz joined the company as director of operations and marketing in 1982.[105] His new salary was considerably lower than what he had earned at Hammerplast, but he was granted a small equity stake. In July, he and Sheri Kersch were married. That fall, the couple moved to Seattle, and Schultz started work at Starbucks.

Creating the Concept

In 1983, Schultz traveled to Milan, Italy, on a buying trip for the company. Once there, he was struck by the centrality of coffee in daily life. This was evident in the city's espresso bars, where trained *baristas* prepared espresso, cappuccino, and other drinks made from high-quality arabica beans. "I saw the relationship," Schultz explained, "that Italian culture has with coffee and the romance of the beverage. The Italian starts his day at the espresso bar and sees his friends there later on."[106] In the early 1980s, there were 1,500 espresso bars in Milan alone, 20,000 in Italy. "It seemed they were on every street corner, and all were packed," Schultz observed. He also noticed that although each establishment had a distinct character, all of them provided an inherently *social* experience—one that offered people community, comfort, and some sense of extended family.[107]

Intrigued, Schultz visited as many espresso bars as he could during his trip. In offerings, ambience, and service, they differed from U.S. diners or coffee shops. Italian coffee bars, he surmised, were not places where consumers went for an inexpensive, often solitary, cup of drip coffee or quick meal. Rather, they served as an extension of the front porch or home, a place that individuals frequented not only to enjoy custom-made coffee drinks but also to connect—however briefly—with others.[108]

Most Americans in the early 1980s, Schultz realized, had little access to the quality and sociability of coffee as it was served in Italian espresso bars. Even Starbucks, which was founded to roast and sell first-rate beans, did not provide coffee by the cup. "We treated coffee as produce," Schultz remembered, "something to be bagged and sent home with the groceries." He and other company managers had overlooked the connections that coffee drinking had to conversation and communal rituals. "We stayed one big step away from the heart and soul of what coffee has meant throughout the centuries."[109]

He saw a huge, untapped opportunity for Starbucks. He envisioned the company re-creating the Italian coffee bar culture in the United States; it would use its reputation for fine coffee to serve espresso drinks while providing a comfortable, appealing store experience. Schultz was convinced that such offerings would differentiate the Seattle roaster from the scores of other specialty coffee suppliers entering the U.S. market.

When he returned to Seattle, he tried unsuccessfully to convince his bosses that Starbucks should build a chain of Italian-style espresso bars. The managing partners were not interested in entering what they considered the restaurant business.[110] Moreover, Starbucks was in the process of purchasing Peet's Coffee & Tea in northern California. This acquisition would require substantial organizational resources, financial and otherwise, leaving few for other expansion or innovation.[111]

His Own Business

Schultz, however, could not let his idea go. In late 1985, he left Starbucks to start a chain of coffee bars, remaining on good terms with his former employers, Baldwin and Bowker. Both offered their advice and financial support to the entrepreneur, committing $150,000 in company funds to Schultz's venture. The thirty-two-year-old entrepreneur raised an additional $250,000 in seed capital from several private investors.[112] He planned to use the money to launch his first coffee bar. If the store was successful, he would seek an additional $1.25 million to demonstrate the viability of the concept, opening at least eight more outlets in and outside of Seattle with a view to more growth.

Schultz's initial store began business on April 8, 1986, in the Columbia Center, a Seattle skyscraper. The café was called *Il Giornale* after the Italian newspaper of the same name. It served espresso drinks, such as cappuccino and caffe latte, sandwiches, and pastries. The 700-square-foot store was designed to replicate an Italian coffee bar as closely as possible. Employees who made the specialty coffee drinks were called baristas and wore white shirts and bow ties. Opera music played in the background. Newspapers hung on rods on the walls. Customers ordered from a menu full of Italian terms, such as *grande* (a large drink) and *panini* (sandwiches). Like most coffee bars in Italy, there was no seating. Instead, customers stood at the bar or along narrow side counters while they drank, ate, talked, or read.

Former Starbucks employees, such as Dawn Pinaud, who had decided to join Schultz in his start-up, helped staff the store. So, too, did Dave Olsen, a new partner. Olsen, a native of Montana, had a decade of experience in the specialty coffee business. He ran a well-known Seattle coffeehouse, which bought beans from Starbucks. He had worked with the company's founders to develop an espresso roast (which is still used in all Starbucks espresso drinks).[113] At the time he met Schultz, Olsen was considering his own expansion plans. Specialty coffee, he believed, "needed to be taken out of the intellectual stratosphere and made more accessible."[114] Schultz's idea for a chain of coffee bars modeled on those in Italy made intuitive and economic sense to Olsen. He agreed to work for Il Giornale at an annual salary of $12,000 plus stock options.[115]

From their first meeting, the two men liked and respected each other.[116] Their experiences and talents fit well together. Schultz focused his energies outward: presenting the business concept, raising capital, locating real estate, creating the brand, and preparing for growth. Olsen was the operator: running the café, hiring and training baristas, buying and preparing fine coffee, and "just plain doing whatever was needed in the store."[117] This rough division of responsibility made sense to both partners.

But in the exigencies of managing a new business, they could not always adhere to this division. "Everyone did everything" in the small company, Olsen said. He sliced meats in the tiny business office, while his partner made phone calls at the desk next to him. Schultz waited on customers, wiped counters, and checked the speed of service in the store. Baristas, such as Jennifer Ames-Karreman, and Pinaud, who managed the store, took part in many decisions. "We agonized over all kinds of questions, big and small, trying to make the coffee bar experience as fine as possible," Olsen said. "We debated, for example, whether a particular napkin was as good in quality as the coffee we were serving."[118] The entire staff logged long hours.[119] "We lived and breathed the company and its possibilities," Olsen said. But it was not "workaholism" that drove the group. "It was risk, passion, investment, and opportunity all converging."[120]

One of the challenges that the Il Giornale staff confronted was gauging consumer opinion. An experienced salesman, Schultz appreciated the importance of this responsibility in virtually every company. It was even more crucial in the very early stages of building a business model, brand, and organization.[121] The Columbia Center store was the first of what the entrepreneur hoped would be scores, perhaps hundreds, of outlets. He was keen to understand which aspects of his coffee bar concept appealed to consumers and which were less interesting or desirable. He could then decide how to respond to this feedback, using the most relevant input to plan for future stores.

The entrepreneur and his team listened carefully to patrons and each other in the months after Il Giornale opened. Consumers, they discovered, did not like nonstop opera music. Those interested in lingering in the store desired chairs. Some asked for flavored coffee. A menu printed primarily in Italian was not accessible to many people. The baristas' bow ties were uncomfortable to wear and difficult to keep looking neat after hours in front of the espresso machine.[122]

Schultz considered each of these issues. He wanted to please consumers. But he had to do so in a way that was consistent with the offerings and distinct identity that he was trying to create. He adjusted many operating policies in response to customer and employee feedback. Il Giornale began providing chairs and playing more varied music. The baristas stopped wearing ties. "We fixed a lot of mistakes," Schultz said. But he decided not to honor some requests. For example, although the larger market for vanilla, hazelnut, and other artificially flavored beans was growing rapidly, the company consistently refused to sell coffee brewed from them.

Schultz believed the practice would compromise his organization's commitment to selling an authentic, high-quality product and thus its brand's developing image.[123]

Il Giornale quickly became popular, attracting more than one thousand customers a day within six months of the store's opening.[124] Schultz and Olsen attributed this success not only to the quality of the coffee but also to the people it hired and trained. Olsen worked with baristas and other employees to teach them about coffee, including its origins, varieties, and preparation. Schultz concentrated on selling techniques. Both partners recognized that building a market for coffee bars required educating consumers, introducing them to and helping them assess specialty coffee. They encouraged Il Giornale's employees to communicate their knowledge of and enthusiasm for coffee to store patrons.

Throughout 1986, Schultz continued to raise money. He spoke to dozens of people, explaining his plan to transform coffee from a commodity into a branded offering that consumers associated with quality, service, and community. Most were not interested in funding the venture and cited several reasons. Coffee sales were stagnant. Retail establishments, especially restaurants, were often precarious enterprises, particularly vulnerable to poor management and downturns in the business cycle. Many potential backers questioned whether in the absence of a proprietary technology, Schultz could construct a sustainable competitive advantage. Perhaps, some reasoned, high-technology companies were better investments. Of the 242 men and women whom Schultz approached, more than 217 decided not to fund the entrepreneur's venture.[125]

A number of people, however, did purchase equity in the young company. In this first round of financing, Schultz raised $1.65 million, including $400,000 in seed capital. He earmarked the funds for Il Giornale's growth, opening a second store in downtown Seattle in late 1986 and a third the next spring in Vancouver, British Columbia. Schultz knew it would be more difficult to build brand loyalty for Il Giornale in distant markets. It would also be harder to source and staff such outlets. But Schultz believed he had no choice. His business plan was based on multiple stores in various regions. He had to show investors that his concept was credible outside Seattle.

Revenues at all three stores grew rapidly. By mid-1987, sales totaled about $1.5 million. The company was not yet profitable. But it was meeting the financial and organizational targets that Schultz and others had set for the business.[126]

In early 1987, Schultz saw an opportunity to expand his concept even faster. The original founders of Starbucks, Bowker and Baldwin, were thinking about selling the Seattle coffee business in order to pursue other opportunities.[127] Bowker wanted to concentrate on a new microbrewery venture, Red Hook Ale, and Baldwin had decided to devote his time to managing Peet's Coffee & Tea, the San Francisco–based coffee company. Schultz learned that he might be able to acquire Starbucks, including the company's six retail stores and roasting plant in Seattle and the Starbucks name.

He saw a good fit between the two firms. Operationally, Il Giornale was growing fast enough that it would soon require its own roasting facilities. Buying Starbucks would supply this physical capital, allowing Schultz to integrate upstream and control coffee quality more rigorously. As important, he had firsthand experience with the Starbucks organization: its employees, policies, culture, strengths, and weaknesses. This knowledge would be invaluable as the two companies merged and then tried to expand quickly.

The acquisition also had strategic advantages. It would allow Schultz to unite Starbucks whole-bean sales with Il Giornale's beverage business, creating a combined offering that he believed would have strong appeal to consumers. The Starbucks name and powerful regional reputation would be equally valuable resources in attempting to make a large market for specialty coffee bars. In mid-1987, the older company had six stores to Il Giornale's three. Buying Starbucks would triple the number of outlets that Schultz's organization controlled. If these nine stores performed well, they would reinforce the viability of his business model and help him raise additional capital for more growth. Finally and perhaps most significant, the entrepreneur simply *wanted* to own Starbucks. Since 1981, the company had been the seedbed for his evolving ideas about the specialty coffee market. The chance to test these ideas by leading the organization that had helped shape them was irresistible.

In August 1987, Il Giornale bought the Seattle assets of Starbucks, including its name, for $3.8 million.[128] Schultz financed the purchase by selling equity to private investors, most of whom already owned stock in the acquiring business. The entrepreneur and his colleagues decided to call the new organization Starbucks Corporation, consolidating all the stores under the name.[129] The combined enterprise included almost 100 employees, nine outlets located in Seattle and Vancouver, and a roasting plant.

Schultz assumed the position of chief executive officer. Olsen took responsibility for coffee buying and roasting. Lawrence Maltz, an investor in Il Giornale, had run a multimillion-dollar beverage company before joining Starbucks as executive vice president in late 1987.[130] Ron Lawrence had extensive restaurant experience when Schultz hired him to handle finance and accounting. He now became controller of the new company. Christine Day, who had started working with Schultz in late 1985 in a myriad of functions, from inventory control to sales audits and payroll, continued with the bigger enterprise.

Starbucks Expands

The management team wasted no time in plotting a growth strategy for the company. Schultz's business plan called for opening 125 stores in five years with annual revenues rising to $60 million—a yearly average of almost $500,000 per store—at the end of the period. Measured by almost any standard, these were very ambitious targets. The average store revenue projections, for example, were considerably higher than those that the former Starbucks Coffee Company had achieved in sixteen years of operation.

But Schultz and his team thought that they *had* to move quickly. They believed that the potential market for specialty coffee was enormous. In 1987, however, this market was also largely undefined. On the demand side, the majority of consumers knew little about espresso drinks or whole beans. Few had encountered an Italian-style coffee bar. On the supply side, the vast majority of outlets selling specialty coffee were small, independent purveyors, mostly mom-and-pop coffeehouses or single-store retailers. A few other regional roasters like Starbucks were starting to expand in various areas of the country, opening additional bean stores, mail-order operations, or coffee bars. For example, Chicago-based Gloria Jean's Coffee Bean, which sold a range of specialty coffees, including flavored beans, had begun franchising some of its operations in 1985. Within two years, the company had twenty-three stores—eight company-owned and fifteen franchised—located primarily in malls and targeted at middle-class consumers.[131]

But a clear market leader had not yet emerged. In the late 1980s, none of these companies had developed a widely recognized brand or nationwide base of loyal customers. None had significantly affected most consumers' expectations regarding specialty coffee. No one single company influenced the way in which other players in the specialty coffee business competed.

Schultz wanted Starbucks to help shape this fledgling market. He was certain that his firm's offering—a particular retail experience built on premium quality coffee, responsive service, and inviting ambience—had broad appeal. To exploit this appeal, he and his colleagues would have to make the Starbucks experience available to millions of consumers. This, in turn, meant identifying and reaching households in specific areas all over the country, exposing them to the brand and its distinctive benefits, introducing them to new beverages and beans, and helping them associate Starbucks with fine coffee and community. Schultz and his team intended to do this before potential competitors—such as other specialty roasters, large food processors, or restaurant chains—did. In the context of these strategic goals, speed was essential.

By late 1988, Schultz and his team had opened fifteen new company-owned stores. Most of these outlets were concentrated in the Pacific Northwest, in cities such as Seattle and Portland, Oregon, and Vancouver, British Columbia, in Canada. The company also opened a store in Chicago. The northwestern locations had several advantages. Each was less than a three-hour drive from Starbucks headquarters and roasting plant, allowing executives to oversee operations and assess consumer reactions firsthand. The same proximity simplified the logistical problems that Starbucks managers faced as they tried to ensure an adequate supply of perishable, fresh-roasted coffee beans to each store.

Each of the northwestern cities also had a strong existing coffee culture, sustained by coffeehouses and roasters, such as Starbucks and Seattle-based Torrefazione Italia. Consumers in these areas bought coffee beans from local stores or by mail, grinding them at home. They also drank caffe lattes, cappuccinos, and other specialty coffee beverages on a regular basis. Schultz, Olsen, and others intended to capitalize on this regional interest and on Starbucks strong reputation in attracting customers to the company's espresso bars. The company's strategy, Schultz explained, was to establish a foothold in each new city, building a powerful identity there before entering the next market.[132]

The single exception to this plan was Schultz's decision to expand into Chicago. In October 1987, Starbucks opened a store in the center of the midwestern city, about a block from the Sears Tower. It was the company's first venture outside the Pacific Northwest. Board members and other experts had advised the entrepreneur against the move, arguing that the small enterprise did not have an adequate infrastructure to support growth 2,000 miles away. Not only would the company face problems in providing the store with fresh beans, it would also have to hire and train employees who were unfamiliar with Starbucks and specialty coffee more generally. It would face higher costs for rent, utilities, and other inputs than in western markets. Finally, Chicago consumers had little experience with specialty coffee. Even Schultz, who was committed to the move, wondered how Starbucks dark roast coffee would fare in the "heartland of Folgers and Maxwell House."[133]

Despite these potential obstacles, the entrepreneur decided to proceed. He was determined to test the feasibility of a national chain of coffee bars outside Seattle or "Latte Land" as some visitors dubbed the city. He viewed the Chicago venture as a pivotal experiment, which would help management assess the strengths and especially the weaknesses of Starbucks strategy early in its implementation. During the next two years, the company opened fifteen outlets in Chicago. Many of the problems that Schultz and his advisers had foreseen did, in fact, materialize. The company lost tens of thousands of dollars in its first years of midwestern operations.[134] Senior managers wondered "how far the business concept would travel."[135]

Despite these questions, the entrepreneur and his colleagues continued to pursue an aggressive expansion plan, concentrating on western markets. In fiscal 1989, Starbucks opened twenty stores and another thirty the following year. Each of these outlets was company owned. Each store opening represented a substantial financial investment, costing on average more than $200,000.[136] The organization's need for capital mounted.

In 1988, the business issued its first mail-order catalogue, targeting the publication at consumers in specific cities. Within a year, Starbucks was sending its catalogue to customers in all fifty states.[137] This distribution channel helped build brand awareness in regions where the company did not have stores. It also helped executives understand the emerging demand for specialty coffee: where it was growing quickly, where it was expanding more slowly, and where it was stagnant. This information was useful not only in trying to increase the company's mail-order business but also in selecting potential sites for new cafés. Since catalogue buyers made a special attempt to buy Starbucks products, Schultz explained, these customers were frequently very loyal. "It made sense to open stores in cities and neighborhoods where they were clustered."[138]

This strategy served the company well. In 1992, for example, Starbucks opened its first San Francisco outlet. Executives recognized that the new store would face serious competition from well-entrenched roasters such as Peet's and regional coffeehouse chains like Pasqua. But Starbucks managers also knew the company had a large base of mail-order customers in the Bay Area. They believed that the power of the brand would motivate these users to buy coffee beans, espresso drinks, and other items in person from a Starbucks store. These assumptions proved well founded, and the new outlet's revenues rose at unprecedented rates. More than a third of the store's early patrons had familiarity with the company through mail order.[139]

Wholesale distribution also enhanced consumer awareness. Since 1988, Starbucks specialty sales division had sold coffee to restaurants and other institutional purchasers located primarily in the Pacific Northwest. This line of business grew quickly as Starbucks expanded into new markets. By 1990, specialty sales revenues amounted to $4.5 million, climbing to over $9 million two years later.[140] In the early 1990s, Starbucks secured several key accounts, including Horizon Air (a subsidiary of Alaskan Airlines) and Nordstrom, the upscale department store chain. Powered by increasing revenues in all its distribution channels, Starbucks sales more than tripled in the company's initial years, from $10.2 million in 1988 to over $35 million in 1990.[141]

Building the Organization

Despite growing sales, losses also mounted as the business spent ahead of what it took in. The bulk of these expenditures was devoted to constructing an organizational infrastructure: to hiring seasoned executives for the company's retail, financial, human resources, and marketing functions; to constructing a much larger roasting facility; and to putting sophisticated management information systems (MISs) in place. Schultz and other managers were convinced that the enterprise needed to make such investments *proactively,* creating and marshaling resources that exceeded current needs in anticipation of future imperatives. For example, in 1989, Starbucks completed a new office and roasting plant in Seattle, which senior management predicted would last ten years. A year later, when the company had about

100 stores, it recruited an MIS expert from McDonald's to design a point-of-sale system capable of tracking consumer purchases across 300 outlets. In these early years, Schultz remembered, "we laid a solid base for national expansion." "It was expensive," he continued, "but without it, we would never have been able to accelerate our growth year after year, without stopping to catch our breath."[142]

Some of the most important investments that the company made were in management talent. In 1989, for example, Howard Behar, a retail veteran with twenty-five years' experience (mentioned early in this chapter), joined the company to oversee store operations. He immediately set about identifying organizational weaknesses and trying to correct them. He argued, for instance, that Starbucks was too product focused, that the business needed to pay more attention to the people who made, served, and bought coffee. Since baristas and other employees directly affected the quality of products and the consumer experience in stores, Behar argued, they exerted tremendous influence on the company's performance. Committed, enthusiastic employees were much more likely to deliver good service and provide an appealing environment for customers than disenfranchised staff. The success of the business thus depended significantly on motivating and sustaining employees' interest in Starbucks offerings, including its products, working environment, and culture.[143]

It also rested, Behar contended, on consistent attention to consumer priorities. He urged store workers to listen to and grant buyers' requests, instituting a "Just Say Yes" campaign for all Starbucks outlets. The retailer began distributing free-drink certificates to disgruntled buyers. Employees gave stickers to children. If a consumer brought another brand of whole-bean coffee into a Starbucks store, baristas ground it. "As long as it is moral, legal, and ethical," Behar said, "I thought Starbucks should do whatever it takes to please the customer."[144]

Some consumer preferences, however, seemed to threaten the brand's evolving identity. In 1989, for example, Behar noticed that some buyers were asking for skim milk in specialty coffee drinks. He knew that Starbucks' competitors were making cappuccino or caffe lattes with lowfat milk and urged Schultz to test the idea. But Schultz, Olsen, and other executives strongly resisted the proposed change, maintaining that anything but whole milk jeopardized the authentic Italian espresso bar experience that the organization was committed to providing. At that time, Schultz recalled, "even *mentioning* nonfat milk was tantamount to treason."[145] Some store managers worried about the operational logistics of handling more than one kind of milk.

In the face of such opposition, Behar continued to push the issue. Uncertain what to do, Schultz visited a Starbucks store one morning, stationing himself behind a newspaper close to the counter where customers ordered. He heard a woman ask for a nonfat latte. When the barista explained that he had only whole milk, she turned away, saying she could find what she wanted at a nearby competing café. In a young market, Schultz reasoned, lost customers were too high a price to pay for unjustified dogmatism in defense of the brand. The company started testing milk varieties at selected stores. Low- and nonfat milk quickly proved popular, and all outlets soon offered them. (In the mid-1990s, almost half of the lattes and cappuccinos served by Starbucks were made with low- or nonfat milk).[146]

In 1990, the company made another important appointment, hiring Orin Smith as chief financial officer (CFO). Like Behar, he was about ten years older than Schultz. Smith had been budget director for the state of Washington, a managing partner at the consulting firm Deloitte and Touche, and CFO for a freight company before coming to Starbucks. He had substantial experience managing complex enterprises, which Schultz hoped to exploit as Starbucks grew. Forging a large market for specialty coffee, a meaningful brand, and an effective organization, Schultz recognized, would require more than his own commercial imagination:

> Without romance and vision, a business has no soul, no spirit to motivate its people to achieve something great. But a successful company can't sustain itself on exhilarating ideas alone. Many business visionaries have failed as leaders because they could not execute. Processes and systems, discipline and efficiency are needed to create a foundation before creative ideas can be implemented and entrepreneurial vision can be realized.[147]

Schultz realized he alone did not have the skills to build such an infrastructure. He believed, however, that Smith did, granting him wide-ranging authority to accomplish the objective.[148] During the next five years, the CFO recruited talented professional managers from Taco Bell, Wendy's, and other retailers. Some of these individuals, like Deidra Wager, who joined

Starbucks in the early 1990s to help oversee retail operations, relinquished high-powered positions and executive perks to join the young business. "It was not easy to give up what I had learned and built in ten years at PepsiCo," Wager said. "The salary was lower at Starbucks, and there was no company car. But I was an early adopter of cappuccinos, and I knew many other consumers would respond similarly." She was struck by the entrepreneurial vision behind the organization. "I believed strongly in Schultz's dream and the powerful emotional connection that is possible between customers, partners (Starbucks employees), and a daily cup of coffee."[149] Like most of Schultz's early executive hires, Wager stayed with the company, taking on increasing responsibility as it grew.

During the late 1980s and early 1990s, Schultz and his young team worked to develop a range of systems—financial, accounting, legal, planning, and logistics—that the company would require if it were to become a national business. Achieving this goal was hardly a sure bet in 1990. Starbucks lost money in fiscal 1987, 1988, and 1989—more than $1.1 million in 1989 alone.[150] But investors, impressed by the company's sales growth and the expansion of the larger specialty coffee market, which was growing at more than 20 percent a year, continued to support Schultz and his organization.[151] Between 1988 and 1991, the entrepreneur raised $32 million in three rounds of private financing. Most of these funds were supplied by venture capitalists, with individual investors buying almost $4 million in Starbucks equity.[152]

Growth continued to accelerate. In 1991, the company entered the southern California market, opening kiosks in Hollywood, Beverly Hills, and West Los Angeles, followed by freestanding stores in Santa Monica, Brentwood, and Los Angeles. Unlike Seattle or Portland, Oregon, Los Angeles did not have an established specialty coffee culture based on well-known roasters or espresso bars. But Schultz and his colleagues saw other advantages to establishing a presence in southern California. The region exerted great influence on the nation's tastes and trends. Los Angeles was home to movie stars, media executives, and other opinion leaders. If Starbucks became a popular brand in Hollywood, it would attract consumers' interest all over the country.[153]

Starbucks was a hit in Los Angeles. Southern Californians welcomed the brand's coffee, espresso bar experience, and urban elegance.[154] In late 1990, the *Los Angeles Times* had named Starbucks coffee the best in America, fueling broad interest in the company and its products.[155] As in other markets, the company did not advertise its new locations heavily, relying instead on consumers' endorsements to family, friends, or colleagues to promote the brand. Word of mouth spread quickly, and lines formed outside stores in Santa Monica and other locations. Hollywood notables, such as director David Lynch and singer Paula Abdul, frequented company outlets.[156] Virtually overnight, Starbucks became fashionable, Schultz recalled.[157]

The early 1990s were a turning point for the firm. In Los Angeles, San Francisco, Chicago, and other cities, droves of consumers started drinking Starbucks coffee on a regular basis.[158] The markets that the company had been seeking to build by opening stores and educating customers took off, attaining new, sustained momentum. As Orin Smith recalled,

> One day it seemed . . . a critical mass of customers discovered Starbucks and stayed with the company. We had been working for a long time to interest people in our products and retail experience by relying on consumer word of mouth. This is a powerful, enduring way to create loyalty. But we did not know exactly when it would bear fruit. Then virtually overnight, it just popped.[159]

Revenues boomed. Between fiscal 1990 and 1992, Starbucks sales increased almost 300 percent to $103 million in the latter year. Earnings turned positive in 1990, climbing steeply to $4.4 million in 1992.[160] In July 1992, after several years of sound performance, the company conducted an initial public offering (IPO) of 1.5 million shares of common stock to raise the capital it needed to fund its rapid growth. Issued at $17 a share, the IPO yielded $29 million in net proceeds.[161] By late 1992, Starbucks had 154 outlets, employed more than 2,000 people, and was one of the most widely recognized companies in the young specialty coffee industry.[162]

Specialty Coffee Market

Other purveyors, too, tried to build a presence in the evolving market for specialty coffee. One of the largest companies was Gloria Jean's Coffee Beans, which in 1993 had 163 outlets in 33 states.[163] Most of these were franchised operations located in shopping malls. The privately held retailer had enjoyed rapid sales growth in the late 1980s, but encountered problems early in the next decade. Owner Ed Kvetko could not consistently control the quality of beans purchased or service provided by franchisees. As important, mall stores were closed early in the morning and late at night, peak hours for specialty coffee drink sales.[164] In late 1993, Brothers Gourmet Coffee, which sold bulk coffee beans in supermarkets, acquired Gloria Jean's.[165]

Like Gloria Jean's, most of the other large coffee bar companies in the late 1980s and early 1990s sold franchises as a way of quickly increasing their market presence.[166] Based in Orlando, Barnie's had eighty-five outlets in the southeastern United States. Second Cup, a fast-growing Canadian chain, had over two hundred stores in the early 1990s. Another Canadian company, Timothy's, also sold franchises. Smaller regional players in the United States, such as Java Centrale, which had stores in California and Nevada, expanded through a combination of company-owned and franchised cafés.[167] The Minneapolis-based Caribou Coffee and a few other young firms resisted franchising and, like Starbucks, grew by opening company-owned outlets.

As Starbucks, Gloria Jean's, and other retailers expanded into different regions of the country, the broader market grew. In 1990, for example, consumers bought $1 billion in specialty coffee, a 25 percent increase from the previous year.[168] Most of these purchases were beans or ground coffee, which households prepared at home. But as more and more Americans sampled espresso-based beverages, such as caffe lattes or cappuccinos, sales of ready-to-drink coffee surged, rising almost 3,000 percent in the early 1990s.[169] Households simultaneously reduced their consumption of regular canned and instant coffee.

The large coffee roasters, confronted with falling revenues and newly prominent competitors, scrambled to catch up. In the late 1980s and early 1990s, for example, Folgers, Maxwell House, and Chock Full o' Nuts each added "premium coffees" to their product lines, distributing them through supermarkets. Priced between $3.50 and $6.00 a pound, the new offerings, such as Maxwell House's Private Collection coffees, were aimed at consumers who wanted higher-quality coffee at relatively low cost. Some industry experts speculated that the leading roasters were too closely linked in buyers' minds with mediocre coffee to attract new users who wanted specialty grinds.[170] Others, including Schultz, argued that the marketing power of big roasters, such as Procter & Gamble, would enhance consumer interest in better grades of coffee and increase total sales of high-quality beans and beverages.[171]

Demand-side developments also increased the appeal of specialty coffee. Since the early 1980s, Schultz had realized that a growing number of Americans, especially on the West Coast, were buying more foods that they regarded as "natural" and of higher quality than most processed goods. In embracing natural products, such as arabica coffee beans, freshly baked bread, and organic vegetables, and turning away from highly processed foods such as canned coffee, white bread, and frozen vegetables, consumers, Schultz reasoned, were rejecting "the artificial for the authentic, the processed for the natural, the mediocre for the high quality."[172]

Underlying these emerging priorities were demographic and economic shifts. One of the most important was the rising influence of "baby boomers" in a wide range of consumer product and service markets. Almost 78 million Americans were born between 1946 and 1964.[173] Most of these men and women came of age during a period of unprecedented economic growth for the United States. By the late 1980s and early 1990s, their lives mirrored such prosperity. Compared to their parents, they had more education, higher incomes, and a lower incidence of poverty among their ranks. For example, almost 90 percent of boomers had high school diplomas. More than a quarter earned college degrees. The majority of boomers—more than 75 percent—held paying jobs, earning a median income of $43,000. Almost two-thirds owned their own home. About 10 percent of the cohort lived below the poverty line, a smaller fraction than that of the general population.[174]

Affluence molded these Americans' expectations and objectives. Sociological surveys, market research, and other polls revealed that most boomers grew into adulthood believing that their economic future was secure. They thus felt free, as two demographic experts noted, "to focus instead on themselves, on experimentation, on fulfillment," on what the sociologist and former political activist Todd Gitlin termed "the voyage to the interior."[175] Relative to older cohorts, boomers were interested in using consumption to assert their own agency and individuality.[176]

As the first wave of boomers entered their peak income-earning years in the 1980s, many began purchasing more natural foods such as free-range chickens, preservative-free cereals, and bulk grains. Some consumers associated these products with healthier lifestyles. Some sought additional control over what they ate. Many wanted food that they believed tasted better than canned vegetables, boxed macaroni and cheese, and other highly processed products.[177] Such motivations, noted one food industry executive, represented consumers' efforts "to do something good for themselves."[178] The perceived benefits of natural foods often came at a price. Organic fruits, like hormone-free poultry and arabica coffee beans, generally cost more than their traditional counterparts.

But for growing numbers of baby boomers, especially those with relatively high levels of education and income, the advantages of natural foods justified their higher price tags. Fueled by consumers' interest and spending power, sales of organic produce and other less processed, high-quality foods increased quickly—as much as 20 percent a year—in the 1980s and early 1990s.[179] Older and younger Americans followed the boomers' lead, helping create broad demand for goods once sold in small, niche segments and spurring the rise of dedicated retailers—natural foods supermarkets such as Whole Foods Markets and Wild Oats and specialty coffee distributors like Starbucks.[180]

Rising real incomes provided the means for millions of Americans to buy these and other consumer goods. In the last two decades of the twentieth century, real gross domestic product (GDP) increased almost twofold, with per capita income rising more gradually—about 50 percent.[181] Table 6-1 demonstrates this growth.

Not all Americans, however, shared equally in this economic expansion. Mounting evidence suggested that families in the top fifth of the nation's income distribution, especially those earning the largest amounts, gained disproportionately, while the fraction of income going to the remaining 80 percent of families fell. For example, the average income earned by the top 5 percent of households grew almost 40 percent in real terms between 1979 and 1994, to over $180,000 a year.[182] By contrast, households in the middle fifth of the distribution—the group that has traditionally been at the center of American conceptions of "middle class"—saw their real annual incomes decline slightly to an average of $32,385.[183]

As the richest Americans grew richer in the 1980s and 1990s, they spent lavishly on large houses, luxury cars, fine wines, and exclusive vacations. Lower down the economic ladder, other consumers hustled to emulate those on the top rung, buying bigger houses, higher-priced cars and sport utility vehicles, more private education, and more professional services than earlier generations had. Many families that could not afford a new

TABLE 6-1

U.S. Per Capita Income, 1910–1999
(1999 dollars)

Year	Per Capita Income
1910	7,287
1920	7,386
1930	8,358
1940	9,649
1950	13,138
1960	14,714
1970	19,427
1980	23,965
1990	28,800
1999	34,805

Sources: U.S. Department of Commerce, *Historical Statistics of the United States, Colonial Times to 1970* (Washington, DC: U.S. Government Printing Office, 1976), 1, p. 224; U.S. Department of Commerce, *Statistical Abstract of the United States, 1998* (Washington, DC: U.S. Government Printing Office, 1998), p. 456; U.S. Bureau of the Census, "U.S. Statistics in Brief—Income, Prices, Energy," http://www.census.gov/statab/www/part4.html (accessed 30 June 2000). Price indexes are from U.S. Department of Commerce, *Historical Statistics of the United States,* 1, p. 197, and Council of Economic Advisers, *Economic Report of the President* (Washington, DC: U.S. Government Printing Office, 2000), p. 373.

home or auto purchased other goods that reflected their aspirations to join the ranks of the wealthiest households: cell phones, Jacuzzis, Caribbean cruises, designer clothes, a third television.[184] Home computers, health club memberships, a second car, and other goods that had been considered luxuries by most consumers in the late 1970s were considered necessities for millions of households by the mid-1990s.[185]

In order to pay for such goods, most middle- and lower-income Americans saved less.[186] They also borrowed more. All but the highest income earners took on bigger credit card obligations. Between 1990 and 1996, total credit card debt in the United States doubled, climbing to $900 billion in 1996. By the end of the century, the average household owed $9,000 on credit card loans and was paying about $1,000 annually in interest payments on this sum.[187]

Yet not all emulative spending required long-term financing. By the mid-1990s, specialty coffee was one of an increasing number of goods that Americans regarded as "affordable luxuries."[188] Like premium cigars, prestige cosmetics, fine wines, and other items once purchased primarily by affluent households, specialty coffee products became more important for millions of middle- and lower-middle-class consumers. Many of these men and women had tasted a caffe latte, sampled a Chanel lipstick, or smoked a cigar in connection with a special occasion: a celebratory dinner, an elegant holiday party. Beginning in the late 1980s and early 1990s, however, goods that were previously regarded as exceptional indulgences became more common fare. Americans' growing interest in affordable luxuries enhanced the appeal of Starbucks and other specialty coffee companies' offerings. The company's stores, as Schultz realized, attracted policemen and taxi drivers as well as surgeons and stockbrokers. Not all customers could afford a luxury car, but each could "order the same $2.00 cappuccino. They're both giving themselves a reward and enjoying something world class."[189]

Increasing international travel also fed the specialty coffee market. In 1970, about 14 million Americans a year visited other countries. By 1980, this number had climbed to 22 million, by 1985, more than 34 million, and in 1997, 52 million.[190] Stimulated by more international flights, falling airfares, and rising incomes, leisure travelers ventured across the Atlantic in record numbers during the 1980s and 1990s. Europe, long the province of wealthy households and backpacking college students became a destination for middle-class consumers. The scope of business travel expanded at the same time, taking millions of men and women to other countries on a regular basis.[191] Many returned home with new interests in the cultures and products that they had sampled abroad, including soccer, samba music, and cappuccino.

Specialty coffee sales soared in the late 1980s and early 1990s, climbing to more than $1.2 billion annually in the United States in 1993.[192] The bulk of these revenues was generated in the proliferating coffee bars, cafés, carts, and roaster-retailers. In 1993, there were more than 4,500 such outlets selling dark-roast coffee beans, espresso drinks, and related food and beverages, a sixfold increase from 1979.[193]

Taking the Brand National

Human Resources

By the early 1990s, Starbucks had emerged as one of the leading specialty coffee purveyors in the country. Schultz, Smith, Behar, and other executives believed that the company's success was predicated on several organizational assets. The most important of these, from senior management's perspective, was Starbucks relationship with its employees. Schultz had long been concerned with what a given organization owed its workforce. Growing up in Canarsie, he had vowed that if he acquired significant responsibility, he would "do something that would guarantee that people would not be left behind." "I always wanted," he continued, "to build the kind of company that my father never got a chance to work for."[194]

As Starbucks expanded quickly in the late 1980s, the entrepreneur debated how to realize this commitment. In many respects, it was a personal obligation. Yet he was fairly confident that institutionalizing rewards and respect for employees also made *strategic* sense. "It's an ironic fact that, while retail and restaurant businesses live or die on customer service, their employees have among the lowest pay and worst benefits of any industry." By paying higher wages, offering better benefits, and treating employees with more respect than did most restaurant and retail businesses, Schultz hoped to help make Starbucks the company people wanted to work for. He was interested in attracting people who would communicate their enthusiasm for the coffee to customers.[195] Employee excitement and responsiveness had been critical factors in creating an appealing retail experience in Il Giornale and early Starbucks stores. These resources would become even more significant as Starbucks reputation grew.

How were Schultz and other executives to sustain employee interest in and loyalty to the business? In 1988, Schultz's father, Fred, died of lung cancer. This event helped crystallize Howard's thinking about his own life and work. When Fred Schultz was a blue-collar worker, his son remembered, he "didn't have health insurance or benefits, and I saw firsthand the debilitating effect that had on him and our family."[196] Howard Schultz resolved to create a different kind of environment at Starbucks. He proposed offering health care coverage to all employees who worked twenty hours or more a week. Board members were critical of the plan, citing its high costs and the company's mounting financial losses.

But Schultz was convinced that this was a smart investment in Starbucks identity, company culture, and future profitability. Paying better benefits helped build competitive advantage, he argued, by attracting strong, committed candidates. Once hired, these people would be well compensated and appreciated. They were more likely to offer responsive service than weaker candidates or disgruntled employees. Competent, enthusiastic workers were also likely to remain with the company longer. Greater worker retention, in turn, helped create a productive organizational culture and generally resulted in superior service to consumers, enhancing Starbucks relationships with consumers and its brand. Many Starbucks customers came so regularly to company stores, Schultz explained, that individual baristas began preparing their favorite drink as the person came in the door. "If that barista leaves, that strong connection is broken."[197]

Lower employee turnover also reduced the company's training costs. In the late 1980s, Starbucks spent about $3,000 to train each new retail hire. By contrast, providing each worker with full health benefits cost $1,500.[198] Based on this evidence and reasoning, the company's board approved Schultz's plan, and in late 1988, Starbucks began offering health benefits to employees—or "partners," as they were known within the organization—who worked twenty hours a week or more. Three years later, when a companywide survey revealed that many workers aspired to own a stake in the business, Starbucks instituted an employee stock option plan called Bean Stock.[199] Schultz regarded this policy, like the health benefits plan, as an investment both in the organization's relationship with consumers and its culture. "No one can afford to not provide these kinds of benefits," he said. "The desire to scrimp on these essentials helps reinforce the sense of mediocrity that seeps into many companies. Without them, people don't feel financially or spiritually tied to their jobs."[200]

To facilitate communication between management and employees, Behar initiated open forums at which company news and regional issues were discussed. At these meetings, held four times a year, employees were encouraged to ask questions, make suggestions, or air grievances. Senior executives regarded these company forums, like Starbucks stock option plan or employee health benefits, as more than "just the right thing to do."[201] They were an integral part of Starbucks brand creation and retail strategies, encouraging employee enthusiasm, reducing turnover and training costs, and improving service. By the mid-1990s, the company's turnover rate was about 60 percent, compared with rates of 140 to 300 percent for hourly workers in the fast-food industry.[202] The company's workforce grew quickly in the late 1980s and early 1990s (Figure 6-2).

Starbucks continued to invest in human resources, developing training programs for baristas and managers. Beginning in the late 1980s, all employees were required to complete a twenty-four-hour training program, in which they studied the history of coffee, product offerings, customer service, and the mechanics of beverage preparation. By the mid-1990s, this program, which ran over three days, included five subjects, ranging from "Brewing the Perfect Cup" to "Coffee Knowledge" to "Retail Skills." In "Brewing the Perfect Cup," new employees learned how to follow Starbucks exacting quality requirements. For example, milk for cappuccinos, caffe lattes, and other beverages had to be steamed to between 150° and 170°F. Each espresso shot had to be poured within twenty-three seconds of brewing or be thrown out.[203] In "Coffee Knowledge," new employees learned to distinguish between coffee made from distinct Starbucks beans

FIGURE 6-2

Starbucks Employees, 1987–1999

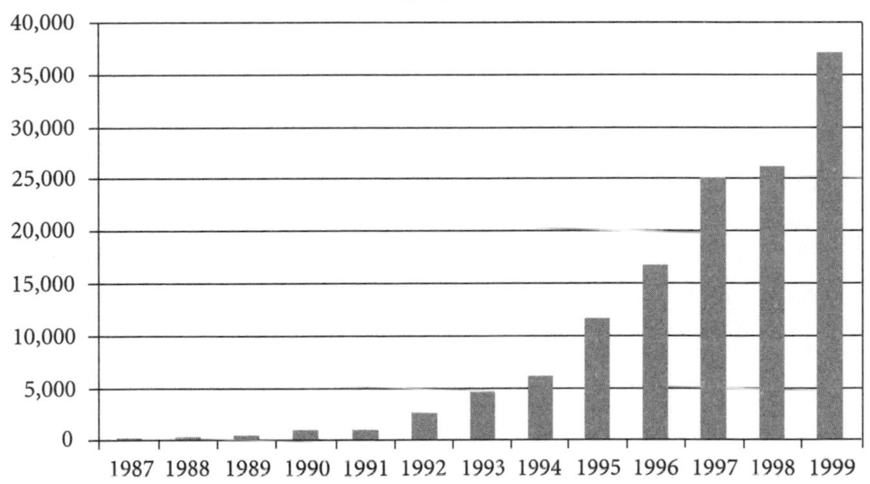

Sources: Starbucks Corporation, *Form 10Ks 1992,* p. 4; *1993,* p. 4; *1994,* p. 5; *1995,* p. 5; *1996,* p. 5; *1997,* p. 5; *1998,* p. 5; *1999,* p. 6.

Note: Employee numbers for 1988, 1989, and 1990 are author's estimates.

such as Ethiopian Sumatra and Costa Rica. In "Retail Skills," Starbucks trainers taught new hires how to clean counter equipment, weigh, measure, and grind beans, fill one-pound bags, and affix the sticker with the name of the specific coffee exactly one half inch over the Starbucks logo.[204] Like other human resources initiatives, senior executives regarded training programs as *strategic* commitments—critical components of the organization's identity and culture.

Quality Control

From senior management's perspective, the quality of coffee products was critical to the brand's strength. Unlike many competing chains that relied on wholesalers, Starbucks bought its own coffee direct from producing countries. Olsen, senior vice president of coffee, and his team traveled around the world to select beans. "We could operate from a home base," he explained:

> In a great many coffee companies, especially historically, the buyer sat in an office and waited for the samples to arrive, by telex or Morse code or whatever. A lot of coffee was bought by description. That kind of thing is still possible, although now it's augmented greatly by better communication. . . . But we take the whole process one big step further by insisting that we go to places and see for ourselves the circumstances that prevail. We want to learn about the problems and possibilities of growing coffee around the world. We don't generally buy coffee directly off the farm, but we want to meet the people who cultivate coffee and develop relationships with them . . . to learn about the problems and issues that confront them. This knowledge helps us understand what to plan for, and what to expect. This is true whether the coffee is fairly close by in Latin America or whether it's in Indonesia or East Africa.[205]

After purchase, the beans were roasted and blended by trained personnel in Starbucks facilities, according to specific standards.[206] They were then shipped to company stores or wholesale customers in FlavorLock bags, specially designed to preserve freshness without allowing moisture or air in. Once a bag was opened in a Starbucks outlet, company policy dictated that the coffee beans be used within seven days or donated to charity. By controlling as much of the value chain as possible—from buying the raw beans to the roasting process to selling specialty coffee in company-owned stores—Starbucks executives ensured high quality standards for its offerings in a young market.[207]

Similar reasoning dictated the company's consistent refusal to franchise. In the early 1990s, Schultz recognized that franchising was a logical way to finance swift growth. Most of the company's rivals, such as Gloria Jean's, used this structure to expand. But the entrepreneur was strongly opposed to it. He and his colleagues feared losing control of coffee quality, employee training and service levels, store atmosphere, and other components of the developing Starbucks identity if they contracted out operations. Orin Smith explained:

> This company is primarily about building a brand. Everything we do has an effect on the brand. . . . Certainly visual things have an initial impact and have to communicate pretty clearly the image we want to project. The quality of our products and the service levels we provide and the focus of our efforts are all crucially important in developing who and what this company is. . . . What we do with our people is another part of it. . . . How can we maintain such standards, the culture we have established in our Seattle markets, as we roll out stores rapidly in new markets? . . . We've developed and are continuing to build an infrastructure to meet these challenges. . . . Franchising makes growth far easier because you don't have to develop the infrastructure and your franchisees share the burden of recruiting and training people. But we decided that this was at the cost of maintaining control of the factors we saw as important.[208]

To meet its growth targets and maintain quality standards, Starbucks built an in-house team of real-estate managers, architects, designers, and construction managers. Schultz recruited Arthur Rubinfeld, an architect and commercial real estate broker, to manage this effort. He set high quality parameters for store design, which incorporated natural materials such as hardwood cabinetry and slate flooring. The objective was to ensure that the quality of the company's store design—including layout, lighting, and furnishings—reinforced Starbucks commitment to fine coffee products. Rubinfeld knew it was imperative to build loyal relationships with real estate representatives across the country who were experts in their markets and who would facilitate Starbucks entry into new markets by helping to identify the best locations early on, and he set about doing this.

In each city that the coffee purveyor entered, site selection was closely linked to building the young brand. "We want to be in highly visible locations," Rubinfeld said in 1995, "that provide easy access for our customers who value great coffee." "You want a store," he added, "located in the path of people's daily shopping experience, their route to work, or their way home from a movie. You want to be America's front porch, the place where people gather to meet neighbors and friends."[209] Other significant criteria in choosing store sites included population density, residents' median age and education level, estimated household income, and the state of local competition. "In some sense, we are cherry-picking all markets we go into," Smith noted in the mid-1990s. "[We're doing this] by going to highly visible areas and then working our way out as we build brand equity and general awareness."[210] In congested downtown districts that drew substantial weekday traffic, Starbucks opened kiosks, often in commercial buildings.

Continued Growth

In the mid-1990s, company executives remained committed to rapid expansion. By opening Starbucks stores in new and existing markets, they hoped to increase sales, expand brand awareness, and preempt potential competitors. During most of the 1990s, Starbucks continued to launch outlets at breakneck speed; by the end of the decade, the retailer averaged almost two store openings a day.[211] Most of these new outlets were company-owned cafés and kiosks, with licensed airport sites making up the remainder. Figure 6-3 shows this growth.

During the late 1980s and early 1990s, the company concentrated its expansion efforts in the Pacific Northwest and California; the Chicago stores were the retailer's only outlets not located on the West Coast. Beginning in 1993, however, Starbucks broadened the geographic scope of its customer base, moving into its first East Coast market, Washington, DC. In 1994, the company entered the Boston market by acquiring The Coffee Connection, a popular, local coffee bar chain; during the next two years, Starbucks converted these stores to its own cafés.[212] Starbucks also opened new stores in Boston, Minneapolis, New York, Atlanta, Dallas, and Houston in fiscal 1994. The next year, Starbucks established a presence in seven new cities: Baltimore, Cincinnati, Philadelphia, Pittsburgh, Las Vegas, Austin, and San Antonio.

When entering a new region, Starbucks typically opened in a major market that would also function as a logistical and managerial "hub" for

FIGURE 6-3

Starbucks Stores, 1987–1999

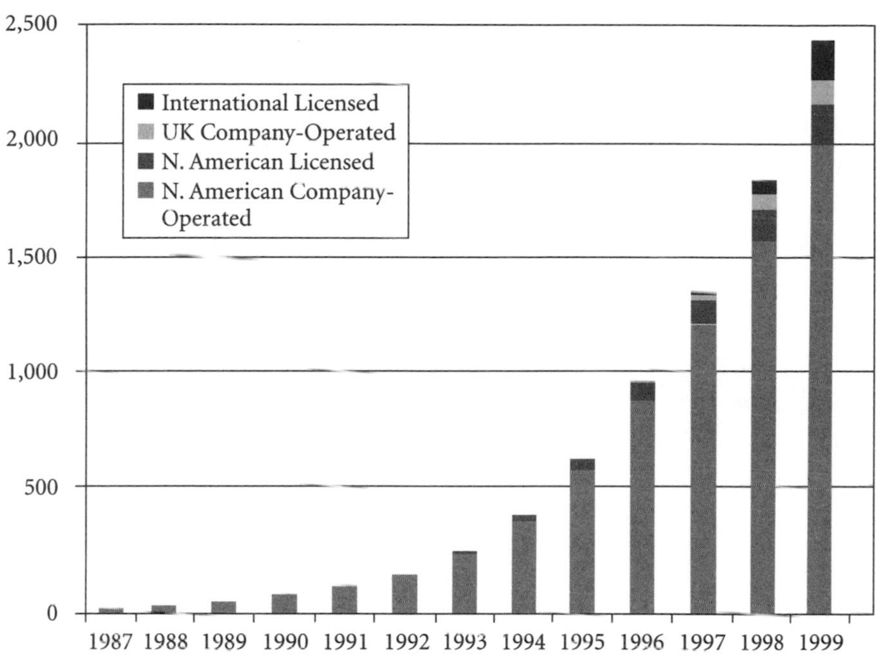

Sources: Starbucks Corporation, *Annual Reports 1992,* p. 12; *1994,* p. 13; *1995,* p. 21; and *Form 10K 1999,* Exhibit 13, p. 1.

further expansion. Chicago served as a center for the Midwest, while New York City and Boston played the same roles in the Northeast.[213] Atlanta was a regional hub for Starbucks southeastern growth. Once the hub had been established and management talent recruited to oversee regional and individual store operations, the company rolled out outlets in nearby markets.

A significant component of the company's retail expansion strategy was store clustering. To attract consumer attention, lock up market share, and deter other coffee retailers from entering important markets, such as DuPont Circle in Washington, DC, Starbucks opened several stores in close proximity to each other. In a fashionable area of downtown Vancouver, for example, Starbucks had stores on two of the corners at the intersection of Robson and Thurlow streets. By 1998, there were three company-owned cafés located in and around Harvard Square in Cambridge, Massachusetts.

Clustering in high-traffic areas helped increase consumer awareness of the brand and sales, but often at the cost of cannibalizing existing business. The growth of comparable store sales, which measured revenues at stores in operation a year or longer, frequently slowed as Starbucks saturated the markets in which it operated, occasionally depressing analysts' expectations and thus the company's stock price. Senior managers recognized this possibility, but believed that the strategic advantages of store clustering outweighed its potential drawbacks.

As the number of outlets increased, Starbucks sales exploded. Total sales surpassed $100 million for the first time in 1992. Four years later, they climbed to almost $700 million, a compound annual growth rate of 61 percent. Net earnings also rose during the period, to more than $42 million in 1996.[214] Table 6-2 shows sales growth.

TABLE 6-2

Starbucks Net Revenues, 1988–1999
(millions of dollars)

Year	Total Net Revenues
1988	10.2
1989	19.2
1990	35.4
1991	65.3
1992	103.2
1993	176.5
1994	284.9
1995	465.2
1996	697.9
1997	975.4
1998	1,308.7
1999	1,680.0

Sources: Starbucks Corporation, *Annual Reports 1992,* p. 1; *1995,* p. 22; *1998,* p. 17; *1999,* p. 17.

Note: These revenue numbers have been adjusted to reflect the 1994 acquisition of Coffee Connection.

A "Coffee Experience"

By the close of 1996, Starbucks was the most widely recognized brand of specialty coffee in the United States. Schultz and his colleagues remained convinced that retail stores were essential to the company's identity and success. Nominally, Starbucks was a coffee retailer. But executives believed that what the company actually provided was a consistent, satisfying "coffee experience" that combined premium coffee beverages with an inviting atmosphere and service that demonstrated respect for the individual. Since the mid-1980s, Schultz had been certain there was a need for such an environment:

> Across all channels of American society and culture, there is such a fracturing of values. There are no heroes. . . . There is little trust in a number of public institutions. . . . I am not saying Starbucks is going to save the world, because we can't. . . . What we've done is provide a safe harbor for people to go. I think the brand equity of the name Starbucks has supplied a level of trust and confidence, not only in the product, in the trademark, but in the experience of what Starbucks is about. At a time when there are very few things that people have faith in. It's a very fragile thing. You can't take it for granted. It's something that has to be respected and continually built upon.[215]

One of the company's major strategic objectives focused on maintaining and enhancing the customer's retail encounter. "In the longer run," Orin Smith said, "it is what distinguishes us to our customer. . . . The most enduring competitive advantage we have is that we are able to give our customers a better experience at store level . . . than any competitor we have out there."[216] This experience included not only what the coffee customers drank, the interactions they had with store employees, and the visual environment; it also encompassed the coffee aromas in the air, background music, and overall ambience of company stores. "There's a connection at Starbucks between consumers and baristas that works together naturally," Behar said. "People want this connection to work because coffee is such a big part of our lives. In this and other ways, the company works to fill souls, not bellies."[217]

Strong store operations increased business in other distribution channels, such as Starbucks specialty sales and mail-order divisions. In this context, executives believed that Starbucks outlets functioned as "brand validators" or company "billboards," augmenting and reinforcing the company's image as a premium purveyor of specialty coffee, related products, and an attractive experience.[218] Between 1987 and 1995 Starbucks spent very little on national advertising. "We don't devote huge sums to large scale ad campaigns," observed Jennifer Tisdel, who oversaw retail marketing in the mid-1990s:

> Our most important advertising vehicles, our key resources, have been our stores and our people. Consumers go through many retailers in the course of a week or month. Fortunately, they visit us frequently during these periods. So our in-store communication has to be fresh. Our partners need to be well-informed and enthusiastic in interacting with our customers.[219]

By the mid-1990s, Starbucks had become a recognized "third place"—a location apart from home or work, where people congregated for social interaction, refreshment, or a few moments of communal solitude.[220] In hundreds of cities and towns, company cafés became informal gathering places for mothers and young children, teenagers, students, shoppers, and couples. In 1995, for example, more than three million people visited a Starbucks store each week.[221]

Schultz was not surprised by the broad appeal of the Starbucks "coffee experience." Since he first traveled to Italy in the early 1980s, he had wanted to bring the sociability and romance of Italian coffee bars to the United States. He had long believed that time-pressed American consumers would respond to an opportunity to talk, relax, or think in an attractive, comfortable, and clean setting. "In an increasingly fractured society," he said, "our stores offer a quiet moment to gather your thoughts and center yourself." In Schultz's view, each café served as an oasis for harried individuals, offering "a small escape during a day when many other things are beating you down."[222]

Starbucks stores also became meeting places for businesspeople. Spurred on by improved communication technologies, rapid organizational restructuring, expanded entrepreneurial opportunities, and changing family commitments, growing numbers of white-collar Americans started working outside the traditional office in the late 1980s and 1990s. By 1999, 18 million men and women used their home as their primary place of business, a 400 percent increase from 1990.[223] For telecommuters and others seeking a setting outside company offices, Starbucks stores offered accessible, well-lit venues for meetings, phone calls, and professional companionship. Some telecommuters used morning trips to a local café as a means of structuring the day. Others sought an escape from the isolation of working alone. Many home-based entrepreneurs visited specialty coffee outlets to speak with clients and each other. "That's what Starbucks and those kinds of places are great for," noted the president of the International Telework Association & Council. "The local coffee shops and the local copy shops get a lot of business they wouldn't otherwise get if people were working downtown in an office."[224]

As consumer familiarity with the Starbucks experience increased, a new vocabulary developed. Caffe latte, espresso macchiato, and cappuccino had long been common terms in Italy. But the growing popularity of specialty coffees helped make these and other made-to-order beverages, such as *double skinny latte* (two shots of espresso with steamed low-fat milk), *decaf cappuccino* (decaffeinated espresso with steamed and foamed milk), and *espresso macchiato* (espresso with a dollop of milk foam) part of everyday parlance. Once considered an exotic request, ordering a cappuccino or other specialty coffee beverage became commonplace at restaurants, company cafeterias, and airport carts.

Leveraging the Brand

As Starbucks identity developed, Schultz and his colleagues confronted numerous brand extension possibilities. The company could "put its name on toothpaste and it would sell," Schultz observed. "But we would never do anything to dilute the integrity of the brand."[225] Senior managers debated how to use and enhance the power of the retailer's reputation without damaging its appeal to consumers.

In the mid-1990s, Starbucks introduced several new products, including a coffee named Blue Note Blend. The blend was the core of a marketing campaign that also featured jazz CDs, specially produced with Capitol Records Inc. and its Blue Note record label. This was not the first time Starbucks had combined coffee and music. In 1994, company stores had marketed CDs with the music of Seattle-based musician Kenny G, selling 50,000 copies in a six-week period around Christmas. Schultz was confident that music was "a major part of both the environment and the soul of the Starbucks retail experience."[226] The company continued to sell a limited number of CDs in its outlets, many of them produced in response to customers' requests for music that they heard playing in Starbucks stores. Each compilation was selected to interest consumers, enhance brand associations, or underscore seasonal themes.[227]

In 1995, the company launched Frappuccino, a sweet, cold, creamy drink combining coffee, milk, and ice. Consumer word of mouth about the beverage spread quickly, and Frappuccino sold well around the country. In its first full year on the market, the beverage accounted for $52 million in revenues or about 7 percent of the company's total.[228] Two years later, the company introduced Power Frappuccino® blended coffee drink, which included protein, carbohydrates, and vitamins and was targeted at health-conscious consumers. Through a joint venture with Pepsi-Cola, Starbucks also began selling a bottled version of Frappuccino in U.S. supermarkets. By 1998, bottled Frappuccino was the most popular ready-to-drink coffee in the United States.[229]

The company continued to expand its beverage menu. In 1998, Starbucks began selling several milder-tasting coffee blends. Marketed under the Milder Dimensions label, these blends were intended to increase Starbucks customer base by appealing to consumers who preferred more lightly roasted coffee than the company had historically offered. The retailer also broadened its other drink offerings, introducing Tiazzi® blended juiced tea in 1998, a cold drink available in mango citrus and wild berry flavors, targeted at consumers who did not drink coffee and those interested in a lighter beverage during the summer months. During the late 1990s, Starbucks also introduced Caramel Frappuccino® blended coffee drink; Chai Tea Latte, a combination of black tea, spices, honey, and milk; Caramel Apple Cider; and White Chocolate Mocha.

As Starbucks business and market position developed, Schultz, Smith, and their colleagues considered broadening their product offerings beyond beverages and related food sold in company-owned stores. In 1995, they decided to partner with Dreyer's Grand Ice Cream Company to produce premium coffee-flavored ice cream. Made with Starbucks coffee and distributed under the Starbucks name in a variety of flavors, the product innovation served several strategic goals for the coffee retailer. It introduced the Starbucks brand into supermarkets, enabling the company to build awareness among millions of consumers who had not previously visited a Starbucks café. Ice cream also allowed the coffee retailer to leverage its strong reputation across a related product. Consumers who trusted the Starbucks brand and associated it with quality coffee were likely to sample ice cream produced under the same name. Finally, the launch of Starbucks ice cream was part of an ongoing organizational commitment to innovation. "Innovation is a critical part of our business," according to Smith. "We depend on a pipeline of ideas—including products, concepts, themes—to keep our customers interested and intrigued."[230] The ice cream was immediately popular and remained so. Within a few months after the product's launch, it became the best-selling branded coffee ice cream in the country.

Ice cream was not the only product Starbucks offered outside its own stores. The vast majority of the company's sales continued to be generated in its retail outlets—cafés, kiosks, carts, and mail order. But by the end of the 1990s, the specialty sales division accounted for about 15 percent of total business.[231] Equally important, specialty sales agreements provided alternative distribution channels for the coffee retailer's products, helping build consumer interest outside the retail stores. For example, millions of Americans who shopped at Barnes & Noble bookstores or Nordstrom department stores encountered Starbucks beverages in small cafés located within these larger outlets. Passengers on Horizon Air and—after 1996—on United Airlines, sampled Starbucks coffee in the air. Customers at selected premium hotels and growing numbers of restaurants drank Starbucks coffee. So, too, did employees in the hundreds of offices across the country supplied with the company's core products. "We want to expand our brand franchise," explained Vincent Eades, head of Starbucks specialty sales division, "to be where consumers work, travel, relax, and to help increase our customer base as the overall market develops."[232]

A primary channel for reaching coffee consumers, as Schultz, Smith, and other senior executives realized, was supermarkets. In 1998, supermarkets and food stores accounted for almost half of total coffee sales in the United States.[233] With more than 26,000 stores in operation, grocery chains offered the possibility of much greater market penetration than Starbucks could achieve through its own retail and specialty sales operations, allowing the company to reach thousands—perhaps millions—of additional consumers. Selling through supermarkets also held out the possibility of increasing traffic in Starbucks stores and strengthening the company's retail franchise. Judy Meleliat, then Starbucks senior vice president of marketing, explained:

> Customers who are exposed to our coffee in supermarkets and take it home to try it may very well become interested in learning more about the brand, in trying other products and visiting our stores. In this way and others we can nurture our relationships with consumers and our brand across distribution channels—connecting with the consumer at home, in our cafés, and when he or she works, plays, or travels.[234]

But supermarket distribution also carried significant risks for the young brand. Starbucks had built its distinctive reputation around the retail experience in company-owned stores. Schultz, Smith, and other executives wondered how new customers would perceive the brand when they encountered it in a grocery store aisle—an environment and channel that Starbucks did not control? "Supermarkets don't have the kind of feel you get walking into a shop," commented one industry observer. "It's not the kind of romance consumers expect from a coffee bar."[235]

A second risk involved at-home coffee preparation. Rigorous quality controls and skilled baristas ensured the quality of Starbucks offerings in company-owned stores. Would first-time customers who bought the company's beans in grocery stores blame burned or weak-tasting coffee on the Starbucks brand? Finally, how would Starbucks fare against other, much bigger companies competing in the center aisles of U.S. supermarkets? "Without a doubt," Smith said, "this is the most formidable competition we have faced. You cannot get much tougher than Kraft, Procter & Gamble, and Nestlé."[236]

Despite these risks, Starbucks began test marketing coffee bean sales in selected grocery stores in 1997. Supermarket chains, such as Larry's in the Pacific Northwest and Jewel in the Midwest, were generally responsive to the possibility of offering Starbucks coffee beans. "From the grocery store perspective," said Jim Alling, Starbucks senior vice president of business alliances, "there is a whole new world going on in specialty coffee, and they have not had much news to report here. Selling our coffee provides them a means to be part of this world. And this outlook is a real testament to the power of the Starbucks brand."[237]

The test-market results were strongly positive, and based on these, Starbucks began selling its beans in specific grocery store chains in 1997. A year later, the company entered a long-term licensing agreement with Kraft to accelerate the growth of Starbucks brand into the grocery channel. Under the terms of the agreement, Kraft managed all distribution, marketing, and promotions for Starbucks whole-bean and ground coffee in grocery, warehouse club, and mass merchandise stores. In return, Starbucks sold Kraft the packaged products, receiving licensing fees as a percentage of sales. By late 1999, Starbucks beans and ground coffee were available in 8,500 supermarkets in fifteen states.[238]

Global Expansion

As Starbucks market position in the United States strengthened, Schultz and his colleagues moved rapidly to develop the company's international presence. Building on the company's early success in Japan, stores opened in Europe and the Middle East as well as Asia in the late 1990s. Senior managers followed similar strategies to those they had used in launching Starbucks first store outside North America in Tokyo. In most countries, they selected a local business partner to help them recruit talented individuals, set up supplier relationships, and understand market conditions. "We are only as good as the people on the ground, so choosing the right partner is really important," said Howard Behar, the first president of Starbucks International.[239]

Once Starbucks selected a joint-venture partner in a specific country, such as Sazaby in Japan, executives from the partnering company traveled to Seattle for an intensive training program on Starbucks products, brand, and organization. According to Behar, success in international outlets depended on effective communication among managers, employees, and customers in each market:

> If you want to put down real roots in a country and become part of a particular culture, you have to go in thinking "how can we *serve* people?" Not only in terms of meeting customers' needs, but also in terms of meeting our partners and Starbucks needs. This means responding to a wide range of priorities beyond purely financial issues.[240]

Starbucks pursued a different strategy in entering the United Kingdom in 1998. Instead of selecting a British joint-venture partner with which the retailer would work to build a national presence, Starbucks acquired a London-based coffee bar chain that Schultz and his colleagues hoped would serve as a launching pad for future expansion in Europe. Ironically, the fifty-six-store business was called Seattle Coffee Company. It had been founded by two American émigrés, who said they started the company because they missed drinking caffe lattes like those they had grown accustomed to from Starbucks stores in the Pacific Northwest.[241] To help build brand awareness in Britain and elsewhere in Europe, Schultz and his team planned to convert the Seattle Coffee Company outlets to Starbucks stores as well as open new Starbucks locations throughout the United Kingdom.[242]

In 1999, as table 6-3 shows, Starbucks had 264 stores outside North America. More than 10 million people a week visited Starbucks at more than 2,300 outlets.[243]

By late 1999, Starbucks sales totaled almost $1.7 billion. The company planned to open 400 new stores in North America in fiscal 2000 and more than 1,000 in Asia and Europe by 2003.[244] Measured by projected store openings, this was rapid-fire expansion. Schultz saw still more growth ahead for his organization of 37,000 people: "Adults all over the world drink approximately two cups of coffee every day. Most of that coffee is not very good." Starbucks, he continued, has "an unbelievable opportunity to build an enduring global brand."[245]

TABLE 6-3

Starbucks Worldwide Presence, 1999

Country	Total Stores
United States and Canada	2,038
United Kingdom	97
Japan	82
Taiwan	23
Singapore	21
Philippines	14
China	9
Thailand	7
New Zealand	6
Malaysia	2
Kuwait	2
South Korea	1

Source: Starbucks Corporation, *Form 10K 1999*, p. 4 and Exhibit 13, p. 1.

Conclusion

By 2000, the burgeoning market for specialty beans and beverages had permanently altered how American consumers thought about, purchased, and enjoyed coffee. More than 21 million men and women—about one in five daily drinkers—chose specialty coffee. Many ground it in their own kitchens using high-quality arabica blends, varietals, or single-country-of-origin beans.[246] Others bought dark-roast coffee, caffe lattes, or other specialty drinks away from home at restaurants, fast-food outlets, cafés, and kiosks. Whether they made it themselves or not, regular drinkers had become much more interested in and knowledgeable about coffee, including its sources, preparation, aroma, flavor nuances, and social possibilities.

Expanding distribution channels for specialty coffee outlets—particularly coffeehouses and cafés where people gathered to talk, read, even conduct business—attracted other consumers. In 1991, for example, 34 million Americans drank coffee occasionally; eight years later, 63 million did.[247] Many of these occasional consumers, especially men and women between the ages of eighteen and twenty-four, bought cappuccino, iced coffee, or other specialty drinks.[248] These beverages generally tasted better and cost more than most of the leading coffees sold in U.S. supermarkets. For many individuals, such consumption also encompassed an element of self-definition that had not been part of the traditional "cuppa Joe."[249]

The transformation of the U.S. coffee market during the 1990s, observed one expert, had been radical:

> The industry enlarged upon its traditional profile of being a staple beverage to become a social and even a gourmet beverage. It managed this transformation by offering premium blends, single country-of-origin varieties, a selection of roasts, and an expanded menu of coffee beverages. It increased the number of out-of-home distribution channels with the gourmet coffeehouse . . . transforming these distribution channels into attractive social settings for the upscale consumption of the beverage.[250]

For millions of consumers not only in the United States, but also in Canada, Japan, and the United Kingdom, coffee had ceased being a commodity that they evaluated primarily on the basis of price. Instead, it had become a differentiated offering that they assessed in relation to its quality, convenience, social ambience, and possibilities for self-expression.

How did so many people come to spend more time, energy, and money on this traditional beverage? Why did twenty-five-year-old software programmers, middle-aged academics, and retired firefighters all include double lattes in their everyday routines? How were these changes related to larger social and economic shifts and to business innovations that tapped into such shifts?

Howard Schultz had started thinking about the potential coffee market in the early 1980s. He could see that rising incomes, time constraints, increased airline travel, changing working patterns, and the growing use of high-technology products were creating new consumer priorities and enhancing the significance of specific older ones. As his ideas about the demand side of the specialty coffee market took shape, he envisioned an offering—a particular retail experience that revolved around high-quality coffee, but that also included personal, knowledgeable service and sociability—that met these emerging needs.

He and his colleagues set out to make this experience appealing to millions of people, constructing a compelling identity for Starbucks products, stores, and the larger organization. Relying on rigorous quality control, progressive employment policies, tightly controlled distribution, strategic store site selection and design, and careful merchandising, Schultz and his colleagues created a brand that quickly became the strongest in the business. By the late 1990s, consumers in a dozen countries associated the Starbucks brand with fine coffee, accessible elegance, individual expression, control, and community.

As the business grew, the entrepreneur and other managers worked to build a set of organizational capabilities that consistently delivered on the promises of the Starbucks brand. They also tried to enhance and leverage the powerful identity that they had created, broadening the company's product offerings and moving into new distribution channels. Most of these initiatives were successful, and many of the innovations that Starbucks developed to make a market for specialty coffee, such as made-to-order beverages and attractive cafés, rapidly became industry standards. At the beginning of the twenty-first century, the company was the leading global player in the young, growing market for specialty coffee. This position depended critically, as Howard Schultz and others realized, on Starbucks consistent ability to interest, understand, and empathize with consumers around the world.[251]

Preview to Chapter 7: Michael Dell

THE NEXT CHAPTER analyzes Michael Dell's efforts to make a mass market for personal computers in the 1980s and 1990s. The personal computer (PC) was introduced in 1975. During the following decades, it played a critical role in the Information Revolution, transforming a wide range of traditional business processes—from financial planning to intra-office communication—and creating new ones as well. As the PC market developed in the late 1980s and early 1990s, increasing numbers of consumers bought machines for their homes, using them to manage money, help their children with homework, and play video games. The extraordinary growth of the Internet in the 1990s was partly dependent on a large installed base of PCs. By the early twenty-first century, millions of Americans used their PCs—at work and at home—not only to process information for themselves, their colleagues, or family but also to create information on their own Web sites and send it around the globe.

But none of this, of course, was clear in the late 1970s and early 1980s when the PC market was in its infancy. Michael Dell was sixteen years old in 1981, the year when IBM launched its own PC and thereby multiplied the size of the market manyfold. But even as a teenager, Dell was fascinated with personal computers, which he enjoyed taking apart and reassembling. He was also a talented salesman, having built a profitable newspaper subscription business in Houston before graduating from high school in 1983.

During the next fifteen years, Michael Dell put his passion for computers together with his gifts for understanding and reaching consumers to build one of the most successful PC companies in the world. Like Josiah Wedgwood, who had worked to create a very different kind of market in the First Industrial Revolution more than two hundred years earlier, Dell realized that his own moment—the Information Revolution—had an important demand side to it. He recognized that how a new product was *marketed* to consumers was sometimes as significant as how it was *manufactured*. He used his insights about both the supply and demand sides of the young PC industry to forge a new offering, a new brand, and a new business model—based on efficient production and "mass customization."

Dell was not, of course, the only young entrepreneur to become interested in PCs. Hundreds of start-up and existing companies entered the young market in the ten years after the first machine was introduced. Steve Jobs and Steve Wozniak launched the Apple II in 1977. In 1982, Rod Canion, Jim Murto, and Bill Harris founded Compaq to make IBM-compatible machines. Others, such as Bill Gates and Paul Allen, became interested in developing software for the PC and set up vibrant businesses to do exactly this. Larger companies, including Xerox, Hewlett-Packard, Texas Instruments, Digital Equipment, and Wang, began manufacturing PCs in the 1980s. A few of these entrants, such as Apple, Compaq, and, of course, Microsoft, enjoyed tremendous success and remained market leaders at the beginning of the twenty-first century.

But these were exceptions, as was Dell's company. Most of the hundreds of firms that started making PCs in the late 1970s and early 1980s either failed or fled the business. As the industry consolidated in the 1990s, Dell leveraged his strong connections with customers to expand his company's product line and to respond with brilliant success to the emerging opportunities and uncertainties of the Information Revolution.

CHAPTER 7

Michael Dell

Prologue: Dell Computer's Quick Delivery to NASDAQ

On October 27, 1997, a financial crisis in Asia set off a frenzy of activity on the U.S. stock markets. By the end of the day, the New York Stock Exchange had fallen 554 points, and the NASDAQ Composite, representing stocks of small and medium-sized companies, had dropped 115.[1] These were unprecedented declines, fueled by record levels of trading activity in both markets.

The NASDAQ was the world's first electronic stock market, and a substantial portion of the trades made by individuals—in excess of 25 percent—were conducted on-line.[2] On October 27, the NASDAQ received more than twenty million hits at its Internet trading site, NASDAQ.com, straining its information-processing infrastructure. To handle the huge increase in on-line traffic, the NASDAQ ordered eight sophisticated new server systems from Dell Computer. Thirty-six hours later, Dell delivered the customized, fully tested systems to NASDAQ. Within three days, the exchange was using the Dell equipment to conduct on-line transactions.[3]

Even in the rapid-fire pace of the Information Age, this was an extraordinarily fast delivery of customized high-technology products. NASDAQ's director of interactive services was astonished that the exchange had received the systems so quickly and without being charged extra for the rapid turnaround. "Originally Dell got in with us on price," he explained, "but that's not the issue now. Their customer support and service [are] what's driving our relationship now."[4] In the ruthless competition that prevailed among computer makers, such loyalty was a decided strategic advantage.

The NASDAQ order of 1997 was an accomplishment Michael Dell could hardly have dreamed of in 1984 when, at age nineteen, he founded a small business to assemble personal computers. In the intervening years, his company's operating model, strategic position, and the broader PC industry had undergone tremendous change, much of it at breakneck speed.

The first microcomputer or personal computer was developed in 1974 by a small firm in New Mexico that did not long survive. The next year, PC makers in the United States shipped 43,000 machines. By 1995, annual shipments totaled almost 45 million.[5] Dell Computer's expansion was no less striking. During the company's first sixteen years, sales climbed at a compound annual rate of more than 50 percent.[6] By 1999, Dell had yearly revenues of more than $18 billion and was the fastest-growing major computer maker in the industry.[7] It employed more than 36,000 people in 33 countries and sold to customers in 170 nations.[8]

The U.S. capital markets consistently recognized Dell Computer's successful expansion. During the decade of the 1990s, the company's stock price surged 87,000 percent, making it the best performing stock on the Standard & Poor's 500.[9] Michael Dell's personal wealth soared with this appreciation. In 1991, at age twenty-six, he was worth $300 million, ranking 368th on the Forbes Four Hundred for the United States.[10] Seven years later, his wealth exceeded $13 billion, and he had become the fourth richest person on the *Forbes* ranking.[11] By the end of the century, Dell had a net worth of more than $21 billion and was the wealthiest American under the age of forty.[12]

Industry observers and other business leaders credited the company's founder with having revolutionized the PC market. Ford Motor Company CEO Jacques Nasser commented in 1999 that "occasionally, rarely, history is made when a gifted new leader, who has a vision of new processes and technologies, produces a brilliant new business model. Henry Ford did it in automobiles, Michael Dell has done it in PCs."[13]

Like Ford, Michael Dell was fascinated by a new technology. From the time he discovered personal computers as a teenager, he could not keep his hands off them, constantly taking the machines apart and reassembling them to improve their performance. The more he learned about how computers were made and what they could do, the more certain he became that the PC was a revolutionary innovation with wide-reaching applications for business and household consumers. "I knew," Dell said, remembering his initial perspective on the PC, "that if you took this tool, previously in the hands of a select few, and made it available to every big business, small business, individual, and student, it could become the most important device of this century."[14] From Dell's first experiences tinkering with computers, he wanted to exploit the technological, industrial, and other supply-side possibilities of the Information Revolution.

But Dell's key entrepreneurial vision came from the *demand side* of the market. In 1984, he realized that how a new product such as the PC was presented, sold, and serviced to consumers was just as critical as how it was made, and he used this insight to build strong, direct connections with customers. These connections were invaluable in helping Dell anticipate what buyers wanted and how to earn their loyalty. In tandem with Dell's insights about the supply side of the PC business, these relationships with consumers became the bedrock of his product offerings, operating strategy, and brand. By the early twenty-first century, Dell Computer's business model, which was based on efficient manufacturing and "mass customization," had become the industry standard.[15] Millions of business and home users around the world associated the Dell brand with quality information technology (IT) products, direct sales, customer control, and responsive service and support.

What exactly did Michael Dell see about the demand side of the fledgling PC market that others did not? How did he build meaningful connections with customers? What role did this communication and the entrepreneurial initiatives behind it play in the development of Dell Computer and the broader industry?

By 1998, there were almost 600 million PCs in use worldwide.[16] The majority of these machines were used in business applications. From banking to graphic design to chemical manufacture to fast food, few industries in the late 1990s were untouched by the PC. Spurred on by falling prices and by the broad range of applications associated with the Internet, the home market for PCs was also growing quickly.[17] By 1999, as figure 7-1 shows, over half of the 100 million households in the United States owned a PC.[18] More than three-quarters of these—approximately 39 million households—had Internet access.[19] Like cellular phones, answering machines, and other novel electronic devices, PCs rapidly became part of consumers' daily lives, creating new possibilities and, at times, problems in the midst of the Information Revolution.

FIGURE 7-1

U.S. Consumer Electronic Ownership, 1985–1999
(% of households)

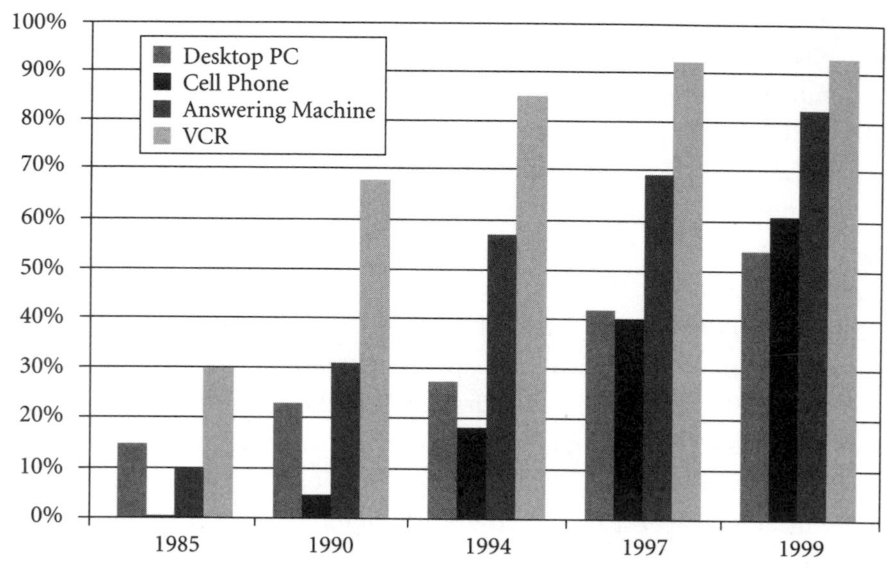

Sources: Ronald Alsop, ed., *The Wall Street Journal Almanac, 1999* (NY: Ballantine, 1998), p. 362; "Women and Consumer Electronics," *Dealerscope Consumer Electronics Marketplace,* 40 no. 1 (January 1998), p. 25; *Consumer Electronics Annual Review,* 1986 and 1990 eds. (Washington, DC: Electronic Industries Association), p. 59 and p. 62, respectively; "Comdex—The Home of the Future," *Newsbytes News Network,* No. 16 (16 Nov. 1994); Paul Andrews, "New Section to Keep You Online with the World," *Seattle Times,* 17 April 1994, p. D1; Paul Andrews, "So Many Choices, But Control Must Be with the Users," *Seattle Times,* 24 July 1994, p. D1; call to Consumer Electronics Association, Arlington, VA; "Home Networked Home," *Appliance* (March 2000), p. 49; "'Wired' Households Pick Bell Atlantic Home Voice Mail Over Low-Tech Answering Machines," *PR Newswire* (22 Sept. 1999), p. 670; U.S. Bureau of the Census, "National Population Estimates, 1980 to 2000," www.census.gov/population/estimates/uspop.html (accessed 30 June 2000).

Note: Percent of households using cell phones is the author's calculation based on total number of cell phone subscribers, U.S. population, and U.S. household data. 1999 calculations are based on 1998 household estimates. Percentages assume one cell phone per household.

The Evolution of the Personal Computer Industry

The first digital computers made in the United States dated back to the 1940s. One of the most advanced of the early machines was the Electronic Numerical Integrator and Computer (ENIAC), completed in 1945 at the

University of Pennsylvania.[20] Used in design calculations for atomic weapons and weather predictions, the ENIAC weighed thirty tons and consumed 1,800 square feet of floor space. Programming was accomplished with cables and switches and mandated rewiring for each new application. The ENIAC needed six full-time technicians to keep it running.[21]

In 1947, Thomas J. Watson Sr. (1874–1956), the charismatic leader of IBM, ordered his company's engineers to develop an alternative to the ENIAC. Created in 1911 from the merger of several small firms, IBM had by the 1940s become a leading manufacturer of business tabulating equipment. Watson and his son, Thomas J. Watson Jr., who was being groomed to lead IBM, intended to leverage the company's reputation and competitive position in the emerging computer industry.[22]

In 1948, IBM introduced its Selective Sequence Electronic Calculator (SSEC). A hybrid of the modern mainframe computer and the punch-card machine that IBM had marketed for decades, the SSEC was 120 feet long and the first large calculator to run on software.[23] Four years later, Remington Rand Corporation made the first Universal Automatic Computer or UNIVAC. The machine filled a twenty-five-by-fifty-foot room and performed calculations faster and more efficiently than its predecessors. Government agencies and insurance companies purchased almost fifty of the computers.[24] Other large organizations soon clamored for additional computing power.

The pressure on IBM mounted to manufacture faster, better computers. In the early 1950s, with urging from company engineers and his son, Thomas Watson Sr. led IBM into mainframe production. IBM devoted enormous resources to researching and developing this new technology. Company executives were equally committed to *marketing* these mainframes effectively to existing clients of its punch-card machines as well as new customers. As Tom Jr., who became company president in 1952, explained:

> In the history of IBM, technological innovation often wasn't the thing that made us successful. Unhappily there were many times when we came in second. But technology turned out to be less important than sales and distribution methods. . . . [W]e consistently outsold people who had better technology because we knew how to put the story before the customer, how to install the machines successfully, and how to hang on to customers once we had them.[25]

The company's early mainframes were a hit. The IBM 650, introduced in 1954, became the first electronic computer to be installed in more than 1,000 locations.[26]

By the early 1960s, the mainframe had become an essential piece of equipment in thousands of big corporate and governmental offices. Using its established relationships with scores of clients, IBM dominated the market.[27] In 1963, the company's revenues from electronic data processing were $1.2 billion. Its closest competitor, Sperry Rand, had revenues of $145.5 million.[28]

Despite IBM's market dominance, many executives and engineers within the company were anxious about the future. Most IBM mainframes were not compatible with each other, so software that ran on one computer might not on another. Designers also contended that as computing technology developed, company products were likely to be overtaken by cheaper, competing alternatives. IBM's response to these challenges—led by Thomas Watson Jr.—was to develop the revolutionary System/360 series. Named for its universal applicability (the 360 degrees of a circle), the initial 360 was a broad line, including five computers, an operating system, and peripherals such as card input/output equipment and a printer.[29] Producing the new line was an enormous gamble for IBM. The company invested $5 billion in the project, a sum equivalent to three times IBM's revenues in 1960.[30]

Tom Watson Jr.'s gamble paid off. Introduced in 1964, System/360 offered compatibility, power, and computing costs lower than anything on the market. Industrial and scientific customers hurried to replace their existing machines. The 360 took U.S. business by storm, becoming one of the most successful big-ticket products ever introduced.[31] The system's architecture quickly became the industry standard and helped fuel explosive growth in mainframe use.[32] IBM's revenues increased by 300 percent in the six years after it launched System/360, climbing to $7.5 billion in 1970.[33] For a multibillion-dollar corporation at that time, this was an astronomical rate of growth. Other players, such as Burroughs Adding Machines, Sperry Rand, National Cash Register, Control Data, and Honeywell began manufacturing mainframes for corporate and other institutional consumers. But none came close to challenging IBM's dominance.

Early PCs

While the mainframe market expanded, the possibility of manufacturing computers on a smaller scale moved forward. In the late 1950s, a young

Massachusetts company, Digital Equipment Corporation (DEC), began developing a line of smaller computers designed for specialized research and engineering uses. Over the next decade, DEC and other manufacturers, such as Varian Data Machines (later part of Sperry Univac), introduced a series of what they called "minicomputers." These machines, which weighed about 200 pounds, had fewer processing and storage capabilities than mainframes, but they carried considerably lower price tags. DEC's first major product, the PDP-8, was introduced in 1965 and sold for $15,000.[34] By contrast, one of IBM's less expensive System/360 mainframe computers carried a price tag of $75,000.[35]

In 1969, a young engineer, Marcian E. "Ted" Hoff, invented the microprocessor. With this creation, the technological potential for small-scale computing gathered momentum.[36] Working for the newly formed Intel Corporation in what became known as the Silicon Valley region of California, Hoff figured out how to create a silicon chip that would serve as a kind of functional headquarters or central processing center. The microprocessor or "computer on a chip" used software instructions to execute a wide range of operations for calculators, computers, and other machines. Because it eliminated the need to build hardwired circuits for each individual operation, the microchip laid the groundwork for radically decentralized computing capabilities.

The development of the microprocessor also initiated an intense race to install ever more power onto a silicon wafer. Gordon Moore, one of the founders of Intel, predicted that the number of transistors that could be put onto the same size chip would double every year. (He later extended the period to eighteen months.[37]) His prediction became known as Moore's Law, and unlike most prophecies, has proven remarkably accurate.[38]

As productivity galloped ahead, the cost of any function that a microchip could perform declined dramatically. Falling computing costs helped focus industry managers', engineers', and others' attention on exploiting the latest and most efficient microprocessing innovations. Declining costs also helped make hundreds of applications practicable that were once prohibitively expensive. In the last quarter of the twentieth century, microprocessing chips that automatically controlled a myriad of operations were incorporated into cars, cash registers, garage door openers, kitchen appliances, and hundreds of other products.[39]

The personal computer, of course, was the most important application of microchip technology. In 1974, Ed Roberts, an Albuquerque, New Mexico, businessman, developed the first PC. He designed the machine around the latest Intel microprocessor, the 8080, calling his invention the Altair after a star in the Aquila constellation.[40]

The Altair, a bulky box about the size of a case of beer or soda, had no keyboard, monitor, external memory, or printer.[41] Its internal memory was a scanty 256 bytes. (By contrast, most desktop PCs in the late 1990s contained 64 million bytes of memory.) Targeted at hobbyists, the Altair sold for $395 in kit form and $621 preassembled.[42] To enter programs and data, users flipped switches on the front of the computer. Results appeared as patterns of flashing lights above the switches. Roberts' innovation proved popular; within a few months, he had backlog of 4,000 orders.[43] Most of these customers were electronic hobbyists and programmers.[44]

A host of start-up companies, many of them based in northern California garages, emerged to produce machines similar to the Altair. Some of these enterprises, like Apple Computer, quickly became major players in the PC industry. Larger, established companies, including Tandy Radio Shack, Commodore, and Atari, also began producing PCs.

The most popular early machine was the Apple II, introduced in 1977. It was the brainchild of Steve Wozniak, Steve Jobs, and Mike Markkula. They hoped to build a market broader than hard-core enthusiasts and created the Apple II to be both functionally efficient *and* user friendly. The three entrepreneurs devoted considerable resources to naming, packaging, and marketing the new PC.[45]

The Apple II reflected its designers' ambitions. It was the first PC to look and feel like a consumer product. Unlike competing machines, the Apple II was aesthetically appealing. Housed in a sleek case of beige plastic, the computer included a full-sized keyboard and supported color graphics as well as text. A small television monitor and floppy disk drive were optional peripherals. Numerous software programs, such as games and word processing, could run on the machine. The Apple II enjoyed tremendous commercial success, opening a market that reached beyond hobbyists to include business customers, especially those in engineering-related industries.[46] At the end of 1980, more than 120,000 units had been sold, and Apple had established a leading position in the young PC industry.[47]

Meanwhile, continued improvements in microprocessing capacity enhanced the PC's memory, speed, and potential applications. Such efficiency gains, coupled with the PC's growing popularity, greatly stimulated software production, as hundreds of hobbyists created programs to run on the new machines. Most software inventors at the time were enthusiasts who created games and computer languages for their own use. Harvard undergraduate Bill Gates and his high school friend Paul Allen, however, saw significant commercial possibilities in manufacturing software.[48] When they first discovered the Altair in 1975, they decided to go into business adapting computer languages for the PC and perhaps other similar machines. Convinced that there was no time to lose in exploiting this window of opportunity, Gates dropped out of Harvard.[49] Allen quit his job at Honeywell. The two moved to New Mexico and began the business that was later to become Microsoft in an Albuquerque hotel room.

By early 1980, the worldwide installed base of PCs totaled almost 610,000 machines. About 65 percent of these—390,000 machines—were in the United States.[50] On both the supply and demand sides, the PC market remained a collection of dynamic, but disparate, cottage industries. Hardware and software manufacturers designed their products for one particular computer. Virtually every model on the market was incompatible with competing models.[51] For example, an engineer working with an Apple computer could not use calculations performed on a Radio Shack machine. An application that ran on an Atari computer would not work on a Commodore. In this scattered marketplace, early PC consumers had few industry standards or generally recognized attributes on which to base purchasing decisions. Most relied on word-of-mouth recommendations from colleagues, friends, and salespeople.

Individual manufacturers reached potential customers by advertising in specialty magazines, trade shows, and computer clubs. The Altair and other early PCs were distributed principally by mail order. But as the market expanded, new outlets developed, including retail stores dedicated to personal computers. During the late 1970s and early 1980s, PC retailers multiplied, stimulated partly by manufacturers' interest in distributing their products as efficiently as possible.[52] In 1975, for example, Roberts began creating a network of franchised distributors to sell the Altair.[53] Tandy Radio Shack, which began manufacturing PCs in 1977, wasted little time expanding its own PC distribution system, selling them through its national chain of 800 electronics stores. At the same time, the company opened Radio Shack Computer Centers, which were dedicated PC stores offering Tandy's products and those of leading manufacturers. Tandy Radio Shack's computer-related sales boomed, climbing from 1.8 percent of its North American revenues in 1978 to almost 13 percent in 1980.[54]

In the later-1970s, the California-based PC manufacturer IMSAI helped establish ComputerLand, a retail franchise operation for PCs, related hardware, and software applications. Unlike Altair dealers, which sold only Altair machines, ComputerLand stores carried machines made by several companies. Two years after the first store opened in 1977, ComputerLand had more than 100 outlets; four years later, in 1983, there were close to 460 of these outlets across the country.[55]

IBM's Entrance

By 1980, the personal computer industry was well established, especially among hobbyists and business users with engineering or computer experience.[56] Over 490,000 units were shipped that year, totaling more than $1 billion in sales.[57] This was a small market relative to those for mainframes and minicomputers, but it was growing at an annual rate of more than 30 percent.[58] New and existing companies wanted a piece of the action, and in the early 1980s, Osborne, Kaypro, Xerox, Hewlett-Packard, DEC, and Wang in the United States—along with European makers such as Olivetti and Philips and Japanese manufacturers NEC, Toshiba, and Fujitsu—began producing PCs.[59]

The most important entrant to the PC market, however, was IBM. More than any other single company in the 1980s, IBM transformed the PC industry. IBM broke open the business market for personal computers, making them essential equipment for a wide range of companies and inadvertently attracting a host of new competitors, such as Dell Computer.

The transformation unfolded fairly quickly. In 1980, an IBM task force was charged with developing a PC and building a national and global marketing organization for it.[60] The deadline for the IBM PC's introduction was fall 1981. Pressed for time, the task force decided that IBM would build its personal computer from components made by outside suppliers rather than developing its own proprietary hardware and applications. The task force also decided to leave the introduction of specific peripherals to third parties, basing the new computer on an open architecture, meaning system specifications would be made public.[61]

IBM contracted with Intel to produce the PC's microprocessor because the Intel 8088 was the best overall fit with other chips already chosen for the IBM machine. It was also compatible with more software than competing Motorola chips.[62] Intel executives welcomed the new business, but initially viewed IBM's choice merely as a "small design win," according to Gordon Moore. At the time, it was not seen as a major strategic or financial coup.[63]

IBM hoped to obtain the operating system that had become the standard for Intel-based microcomputers.[64] After an initial meeting between IBM planners and the system's developer, Gary Kildall, did not go well, IBM turned to Bill Gates and Paul Allen of Microsoft. Now based in Seattle, the two entrepreneurs had already agreed to supply IBM with a number of programming languages for the PC.[65]

Microsoft did not have an operating system in 1980, and there was no time to develop one from scratch. So Gates purchased the licensing rights to a viable product, QDOS (Quick and Dirty Operating System), from Seattle Computer Products, a local company. He and his Microsoft colleagues then made the system compatible with the PC that IBM was developing, renaming the operating system MS-DOS (Microsoft Disk Operating System).[66] In exchange for supplying IBM with an operating system, Microsoft received a one-time payment of $80,000.[67] Microsoft, however, maintained control of the software, retaining the right to license it to other companies. Although neither party realized it at the time, this was destined to be one of the most important (and one-sided) business deals of the twentieth century.

The IBM PC was officially launched in August 1981, right on schedule. Its base price was $1,595, which included one floppy drive, 64 kilobytes (K) of random-access memory (RAM), and a monitor. With software applications, a printer, and other peripherals, the entire package cost close to $3,000. The IBM PC was an extraordinary triumph. In the first full year of production, the company's microcomputing revenues topped $500 million. Three years later, they had skyrocketed to $5.5 billion, the fastest recorded revenue growth in industrial history.[68]

IBM's new product created the first truly mass market for the personal computer. In 1981, U.S. shipments of PCs totaled 760,000. The next year, shipments soared to 2.5 million, and in 1985, to over 6 million.[69] Most of these were IBM or IBM-compatible machines. But it was not individual consumers who fed the exploding market.[70] Less than one in six U.S. households owned a PC in 1985.[71] The vast majority of PCs—about 80 percent—were purchased by corporate and other business customers.[72] Figure 7-2 charts the growth in PC shipments.

How did IBM break open business demand for the PC? The company used a two-pronged approach to marketing its new product. With its large corporate clients, IBM chose to leverage its powerful brand, sales force, service organization, and established customer relationships to sell PCs.

FIGURE 7-2

Total Worldwide and U.S. Personal Computer Shipments, 1977–1999
(thousands of units)

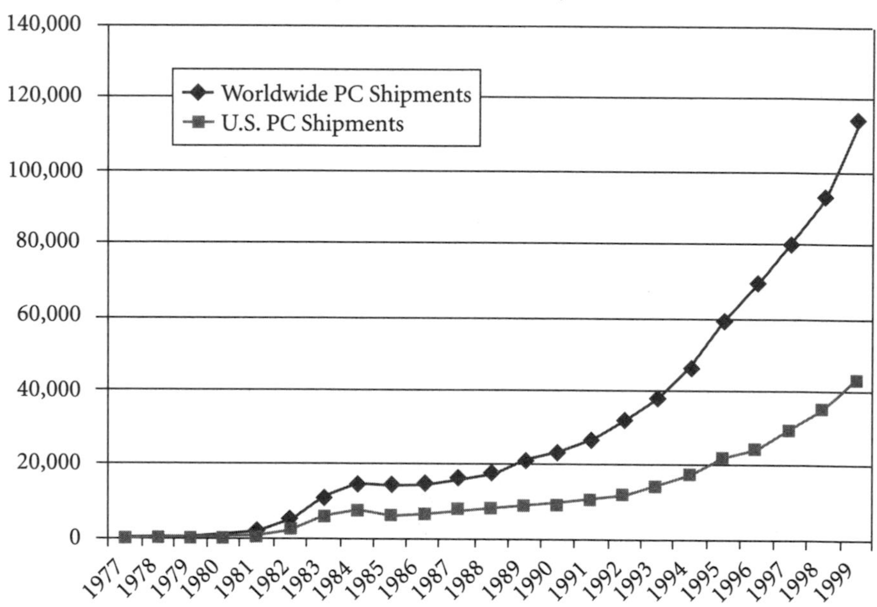

Sources: Courtesy of Leslie Robbins, GartnerGroup/Dataquest; Dan Balaban, "All Systems Go: Global Top Eight Regions by Mobile Commerce Market Size by Sales in U.S. Dollars Forecast for 2005," *Card Technology* (April 2000), p. 59; Doug Olenick, "Dell Takes over First Place; Compaq Slips to Two," *TWICE* (13 March 2000), p. 20.

Note: According to industry convention, PC shipments are counted with reference to the end market. "U.S. PC Shipments" refers to products shipped into or within the United States and then sold within the United States.

They were marketed as part of a larger network linked to customers' existing IBM mainframes. This tack proved effective in legitimizing the personal computer in the minds of data-processing managers, and PC sales accelerated in the mid-1980s.[73] By the end of the decade, the PC had largely replaced the typewriter, calculator, and other machines in large offices.

IBM did not rely on its direct sales force to distribute the PC to small and medium-sized businesses. This customer base was scattered geographically, and the average purchase not large enough to support the cost of the company's national sales force.[74] Thus, the second prong of IBM's marketing strategy was to sell its PC through retailers such as Sears and ComputerLand, each of which was charged with providing after-sales support.[75] To promote its PC, IBM ran a massive print and television advertising campaign featuring a Charlie Chaplin–like tramp who used the new machine to solve the problems of a small or medium-sized business.[76] The effort to build a large market for PCs among smaller companies was very successful, exceeding all expectations.[77]

The success of the IBM PC created a tremendous market opportunity. In the early and mid-1980s, hundreds of companies, mostly start-ups such as Compaq, Dell, and AST, began making IBM-compatible machines. They used IBM's open architecture as their blueprint, buying Intel chips and Microsoft operating systems. At the same time, countless software engineers and amateurs hurried to develop applications for IBM-compatible machines. As the market for such machines exploded in the 1980s, common standards emerged de facto for software and hardware production. By 1985, most PC-related development and production efforts were aimed at IBM-compatible PCs. (Apple Computer, which kept both its hardware and software proprietary, remained the most notable exception.)

Hundreds of computer makers, or "clones" as they came to be called, raced to bring the latest IBM-compatible technology to market. Without IBM's corporate overhead and sales expenses, most of these companies could sell their machines at lower prices. Price and thus manufacturing costs rapidly became the critical drivers of competition among the clones. It was fierce rivalry, determined principally by supply-side factors. In this environment, price wars erupted frequently, and relatively few companies earned consistent profits. Atari and Texas Instruments, for example, each lost tens of millions of dollars trying to produce low-cost computers for home users. In 1983, Texas Instruments announced it would exit the business.[78] Even Apple saw its early leadership erode, despite a vigorous advertising campaign and the 1984 introduction of the superb Macintosh computer. In 1982, Apple's market share was 22 percent; two years later, it had fallen to 11 percent.[79]

This was the stage on which Michael Dell made his entrance. The intensity of the competition in the PC industry did not intimidate him, even though he was only a college freshman. Nor did IBM's size or its remarkable success with the PC. Dell believed that he could capitalize on this triumph by assembling IBM-compatible computers and providing consumers better service, more choice, and a superior buying experience than was currently available.

Dell's Beginnings

Michael was born on February 23, 1965, the second of three sons of Alexander and Lorraine Dell. Alexander, an orthodontist, and Lorraine, a stockbroker, had met and married in Brooklyn, New York. In the early 1960s, they had moved to Houston and settled in an affluent suburb.

The Dell household was filled with the activities of three smart boys. Michael and his brothers, Steven and Adam, competed at Ping-Pong and other sports. When the games grew rowdy, Alexander Dell would admonish his sons to play civilly. Then, he would take each child aside and say, "But win."[80] Family dinner table discussions centered around economic subjects, such as the Federal Reserve's policies, the oil crisis, inflation, and promising stocks. "In our household," Michael Dell explained, "you couldn't help being aware of commercial opportunities."[81]

Michael was a curious child, interested in new pursuits and unafraid of the larger world. As a second-grader, he enjoyed selling candy to his classmates. Struck by his sales abilities, his teacher told the seven-year-old that he was destined to succeed in business.[82] A year later, Michael applied for a high school equivalency diploma, mailing in the appropriate form from the back of a comic book. He and his parents were surprised one Sunday evening not long after when a smartly dressed saleswoman from the company to which the boy had applied arrived at the family home looking for Mr. Michael Dell. "Am I in trouble?" the boy asked when he was called to meet the stranger.[83]

By the time Michael was age nine, he had a checking account. At twelve, he took up stamp collecting, working as a bus boy in a nearby Chinese restaurant to finance his purchases. Rather than buy stamps from retail dealers, who earned a fee, Michael decided to start his own small business buying and selling. "Then I could learn even more about stamps," he remembered, "*and* collect a commission in the process."[84] He obtained a reseller's license and lobbied neighbors to consign stamps from their collections to him.[85] Michael then advertised "Dell's Stamps" in a national trade journal, typing and mailing out a twelve-page catalogue to support the ad. "Much to my surprise, I made $2,000," he said. "And I learned an early powerful lesson about the rewards of eliminating the middleman."[86]

At age sixteen, he took a part-time job as assistant subscription coordinator for the *Houston Post.* The position involved cold-calling names from new listings provided by the telephone company. Michael began to notice a pattern to the responses he received during these conversations. Two kinds of people were especially interested in buying a newspaper subscription: newlyweds and those who had recently moved into a new residence.

In his first effort at customer segmentation, Michael devised ways of reaching these groups. He hired two friends to help him canvas courthouses in and around Houston. They collected names and addresses of couples who had recently applied for a marriage license. Michael also obtained lists of applicants from home mortgage companies. He contacted those with the highest mortgages first, using his Apple II computer to write each customer a personalized letter and offer them a newspaper subscription. These tactics worked well. Subscriptions came in by the thousands.[87] By the time he was seventeen, Michael was the *Post*'s top salesperson, earning commissions of $18,000 in a single year.[88]

Dell's Passion for Computers

Michael had bought his first electronic calculator at age seven, "fascinated by the idea of a machine that could compute things." As he grew older, computers absorbed more and more of his attention. He constantly sought opportunities to learn how they worked and what they could do. When his junior high school installed its first teletype terminal, Michael was hooked. "If you stayed after school," he recalled, "you could play around with it and write programs or input equations and get back answers. It was the most amazing thing I'd ever seen."[89]

His computer interests expanded. In high school, Michael worked as a student assistant to the principal, writing administrative programs to track student absences and plan school budgets.[90] He logged long hours on the school's mainframe terminals.[91] After classes and on weekends, he went to a local Radio Shack to use the PCs there. Michael also devoured computer magazines and became fascinated by the electronic architecture of the Apple II and other popular machines. He begged his parents to let him have his own PC, and for his fifteenth birthday, they consented. As soon as he got his hands on the new, expensive Apple II, he took it apart to see how it was made. His parents were furious.[92]

A short time after Michael had acquired his Apple II, IBM introduced its PC. The teenager was immediately struck by the new computer's commercial possibilities. Even though he had only recently started using his own Apple II, he switched machines when the IBM PC was launched in the fall of 1981. As Dell recalled, "while the Apple had lots of games," he said, "at the time, the IBM was more powerful. It had software and programs for business usage, and although I didn't have a lot of business experience, I had enough to know that this PC was going to be *the* choice for business in the future."[93]

In June 1982, unbeknownst to his parents, Michael skipped school for several days to attend a national computer conference held in the Houston Astrodome. For the first time, the sixteen-year-old got a real sense of the burgeoning PC industry. The conference opened his eyes to a world of component makers, PC manufacturers, related equipment suppliers, and distributors. The conference intensified his interest in understanding the economics of making and selling PCs, and Michael set up a computerized bulletin board—a forerunner of e-mail—to exchange notes with others interested in the business.

At the same time, he began purchasing components and peripherals, such as memory, disk drives, and monitors, to improve his own PC's performance. Then he began to buy and improve used machines. "I would enhance a PC the way another guy would soup up a car, and then I would sell it for a profit and do it again," said Dell.[94] This was the real beginning of Dell Computer.

Forging a Made-to-Order Model

Like many other American teenagers, Michael Dell enrolled in college in the fall of 1983. He attended premed classes at the University of Texas at

Austin. But he devoted most of his time and energy to computers. Working out of his dorm room, he continued to upgrade IBM PCs, buying machines from local dealers with excess inventory and enhancing their performance before selling them to Austin businesspeople at 10 to 15 percent below the retail price.[95]

Dell did not worry about finding a steady supply of stripped-down IBM PCs. As overall demand for PCs soared in the early 1980s, inefficiencies in the distribution system often left retailers with too many or too few machines. IBM required retailers to take a monthly quota of machines which frequently exceeded what the retailer could sell.[96] In other cases, the reverse was true. "A dealer," Dell explained, "would order 100 computers and receive only 10. So the next time, to get what he wanted, he would order 1,000. Maybe then he'd get 633, when he'd needed only 100."[97] In order to qualify for the discounts that IBM granted on large orders, retail dealers bought more PCs than customer demand warranted.

A "gray market" outside the established channels quickly developed to sell machines dealers were left with. Rather than carry excess inventories, distributors sold their extra IBM PCs at a reduced markup over wholesale cost to small resellers such as Dell. This tactic, explained an authorized IBM dealer, allowed an individual distributor to "show IBM that he was a 'high volume seller'" and entitled to "favorable treatment from the company when, in fact, he was a major conduit for the gray market."[98] Meanwhile, these informal outlets fueled the PC industry's expansion. "There was no discipline at all in the marketplace," the IBM dealer stated, "and so the gray market in the machines just took off."[99] Michael Dell was one of many aspiring entrepreneurs operating in this dynamic shadow market.

The PC industry was too young in the early 1980s to have generated extensive market research. What little evidence there was indicated that hardware prices mattered a great deal to potential consumers. Two-thirds of business buyers and 61 percent of home users polled in 1981 rated price as the chief criterion in selecting a PC. Ease of expansion, programming possibilities, and reliability ranked as other relevant factors affecting purchasing decisions.[100]

Michael Dell had little access to consumer surveys. The research was too new and too costly for all but the largest manufacturers, companies such as IBM and Tandy Radio Shack, to afford. But Dell did have considerable firsthand experience with computers and their users. He had been visiting computer stores for years, informally studying the industry. He knew that the IBM PC was fast becoming the industry standard. But with a retail price tag of $3,000, it represented a sizeable expenditure for individuals and small businesses. Was the IBM PC actually worth $3,000? Most first-time PC buyers, as Dell realized, could not readily answer this question. They were not well informed about how they would use the new machine and what benefits it might yield.

As Dell's knowledge of the broader industry grew, he saw several business opportunities. Some involved how PCs were priced. Despite the IBM PC's retail price tag of $3,000, Dell figured out that its components—which were not proprietary to IBM—wholesaled for only about $600 or $700. This meant that retailers typically paid $2,000 for an IBM machine, and then added a markup of about $1,000.[101]

Given the functions that retailers were actually performing, Dell viewed this markup as unreasonably high. He perceived that retailers and other distributors had a potentially vital role to play in the larger PC industry. Much more than component or PC manufacturers, distributors *interacted* with customers. Retailers and manufacturers' salespeople could thus serve as a two-way communication avenue between the supply and demand sides of the market. They could educate consumers about PCs, answering questions, allaying anxieties, and demonstrating how the complicated new product operated. They could also channel valuable information about consumer priorities, complaints, and reactions back to manufacturers. The feedback from these "human listening posts" could then be incorporated in production, marketing, and other supply-side decisions.[102]

From Michael Dell's vantage point in 1983 (he was then eighteen years old), PC distributors were falling far short of their potential. The majority of distributors offered PC consumers little or no product support, such as training or on-site testing and repairs. "The people operating the computer stores didn't even know much about PCs," Dell recalled. "For the most part, they had previously sold stereos or cars, and thought that computers represented the next 'big ticket' fad, so they figured 'Why not?'"[103]

Meanwhile, the rapid proliferation of PCs posed many problems for users. In the early 1980s, most secretaries and administrative assistants did not know how to set up a personal computer. Very few business managers understood what "system error" and other messages flashing across their monitors meant. Few medium-sized and virtually no small companies had an IT department with a dedicated help desk. Although many corporations had in-house technicians to service mainframes, most were not trained to deal with PCs.

Business consumers were clamoring for help. So were distributors. In the months after introducing its new machine, IBM received thousands of phone calls on the toll-free lines it had installed for quality complaints. Most of the callers were not concerned with quality problems, but instead sought operating information or technical support.[104] They called IBM because the retailers from whom they had purchased the computers were providing little or no help. Frustrated dealers themselves contacted IBM to learn how to respond to the queries they were receiving from consumers. The situation was even worse with companies that made IBM-compatible machines. Competing principally on price, most of the clones offered little or no customer support.

Michael Dell saw not only that people like himself could profit from this emerging chaos; he also perceived a huge opportunity in how PCs were sold. He became convinced that many business consumers cared about more than price and computing power. They also wanted knowledgeable, responsive service, after-sales support, and a say in how their machines were configured to meet specific needs. But in 1983, few manufacturers or retailers were providing these benefits to small and medium-sized companies. Dell's own informal, one-person PC assembly shop was an exception. Working from his dorm room, the college freshman was providing more computing capabilities, operating information, customer support, and control—often at a lower price—than were most established retailers in the Austin area. Not surprising, Michael had more orders than he could handle. If he expanded his operation, perhaps he could compete with larger distributors. A business organized around direct sales, customer input, and product support, he thought, could fill a significant opening in the market. This turned out to be the key business vision of Dell's career.

Michael first intended to target experienced users in small and medium-sized businesses, such as legal and medical offices, banks, manufacturing operations, and government agencies. Most of these consumers were not professionally trained to work with computers. But as a group, they knew enough to appreciate the broad applications of the PC. From Dell's perspective, there were other advantages to focusing on these users.

They understood the power of the emerging standard for PCs and were interested in acquiring IBM or IBM-compatible machines. Cost was often an important factor for these customers, many of whom wanted higher performance at lower prices than they could get from the PCs available through IBM-authorized dealers. The same buyers typically desired some control in configuring their machines. As experienced users, they required less information and product support than most first-time buyers, yet they still valued informed, responsive service. Dell believed that this consumer segment was underserved by most established PC makers and distributors.

In the fall of 1983, Dell began approaching potential customers. He applied for a vendor's license, enabling him to bid on computing contracts for the state of Texas. He won several government orders. He also placed ads in local newspapers and sold door-to-door at Austin law offices and other small businesses.[105] Word of Dell's enterprise spread. Sales climbed quickly. By early 1984, working from his dorm room, he was selling $50,000 to $80,000 a month in upgraded PCs and components.[106]

On His Own

Michael's parents grew increasingly worried that he was neglecting his academic work for business interests. In the fall, Alexander and Lorraine Dell flew to Austin for a surprise visit, calling Michael from the airport. He barely had time to hide the computers in his roommate's shower before they arrived.[107] Arguments erupted between parents and son. During one such discussion, Alexander Dell asked Michael what he wanted to do with his life. "I want to compete with IBM!" the son replied. As Michael remembered it, his father "was not amused."[108]

Despite his parents' objections, Michael could not resist the opportunity he saw before him. He moved his operation out of his dorm room and into a two-bedroom condominium. In January 1984, he registered his business as a company with the state of Texas, listing the firm as "PC's Limited" (which was how the enterprise was known for several years). Four months later, he incorporated the company as "Dell Computer Corporation" with an initial investment of $1,000. He hired several people to take phone orders and fulfill them. He moved his operation again—this time to a 1,000-square-foot office.

Estée Lauder, shortly after her marriage in 1930.
Photography courtesy of Estée Lauder Companies.

Estée's personal appearances at her cosmetics counters drew large crowds of shoppers who came to see the entrepreneur, have a makeover, and sample her products. She had learned early on that touching her customers was a very effective way of establishing a connection with them. *Photography courtesy of Estée Lauder Companies.*

A jar of "Flory Anna's Eczema Ointment"—one of John Schotz's skin care products, named after his wife. Estée learned much about the skin care and cosmetics business from Schotz, her uncle.

Courtesy of the private collection of Lucille Carlan Rottkov.

Estée Lauder at a cosmetics counter with some of the company's trained saleswomen, circa 1960s. The promotion was "Enter our Spring Garden of Fragrance from Estée Lauder...dozens of wonderful ways to wear and give Youth-Dew, Estée, Azuré, and Aliage." In her public appearances, Estée Lauder personified the confident, elegant image of her flagship brand.

Photography courtesy of Estée Lauder Companies.

Youth Dew, introduced in 1953, was Lauder's first blockbuster product. The bath oil, which doubled as a fragrance, helped to make her name in the beauty business.

Photography courtesy of Estée Lauder Companies.

When Estée started out in the beauty business, she mixed her formulas on the kitchen stove in her New York apartment. Later, she and Joe Lauder made most of their products in a former Manhattan restaurant. As the company grew in the 1950s and 1960s, they moved manufacturing to much larger facilities. But Estée remained very involved in quality control.

Photography courtesy of Estée Lauder Companies.

Estée and Joe Lauder cutting the ribbon at the entrance of the new Melville, Long Island Estée Lauder plant at its opening in 1967, with the staff of laboratory researchers. From the early years, Joe managed the company's manufacturing operations and finances, while Estée focused on product development, promotion, and merchandising.

Photography courtesy of Estée Lauder Companies.

The Estée Lauder plant in Melville, Long Island, circa 1967. The 1960s was a decade of growth for the company, and the business built this $2 million, 150,000-square-foot plant to handle expanding production. Shortly after it opened, the plant employed over 300 people.

Photography courtesy of Estée Lauder Companies.

An Estée Lauder Youth Dew ad, 1960. The copy beneath the striking image of the woman at her bath reads: "Live a little, darling. Romance begins at bathtime! Estée Lauder reveals the secret of the bath . . . a very French bath oil that perfumes every inch of you . . . the most luxurious bath oil in the world. . . . And darling, only a few drops perform to give you a silky-smooth body that glows with youth. Make Youth-Dew your secret."

Courtesy of Vogue, *Condé Nast Publications, Inc.* Vogue, *February 1960, p. 86.*

Estée Lauder executives worked to differentiate the company's second line of women's cosmetics, Clinique, from the Estée Lauder brand. This award-winning "Twice a day" ad, photographed by Irving Penn in 1974, emphasized the simplicity and benefits of using Clinique products daily and provided a contrast to the ads for the company's flagship line.

Photograph by Irving Penn. Courtesy of Clinique Laboratories, Inc.

Estée in her office, mixing perfume oils. She prided herself on being a keen "nose," someone with a talent for creating perfumes.

Photography courtesy of Estée Lauder Companies.

Estée with her two grown sons, Ronald (left) and Leonard, circa 1960s. Both worked for the family business, Leonard succeeding Estée as president in 1973. Several of Leonard and Ronald's children, in turn, followed their parents into the business in the 1980s and 1990s. The firm remained privately held by the family until 1995.

Photography courtesy of Estée Lauder Companies.

Leonard Lauder, Chairman of Estée Lauder Companies.
Photography courtesy of Estée Lauder Companies. Photograph by Trudy Schlachter.

An ad for Estée Lauder's Beautiful perfume, featuring the line's signature bridal theme.
Skrebneski Photograph. Courtesy of Estée Lauder Companies, Victor Skrebneski, Elite Model Management and Paulina Porizkova, and Tina Thomas, mother of beloved Nicholas Christy.

Illustration of a European—probably Viennese—coffeehouse of 1848. In nineteenth-century Europe, coffeehouses were places where men and occasionally women came together to debate politics, read the latest newspapers, play billiards, pool, or chess, and socialize.

Reprinted from Coffee: The Epic of a Commodity *by H. E. Jacob, courtesy Burford Books.*

A 1932 advertisement for Del Monte Coffee, a typical coffee ad from this period. Coffee ads for a variety of brands played on traditional husband-wife gender roles in the making and drinking of coffee. The husband in this ad complains, "My wife can't make good coffee!" The advice provided in the ad copy below says, "Friend, you *have* a problem on your hands! A real breakfast disaster! No reason for changing wives, but surely a reason for changing brands of coffee." And the recommended brand is of course Del Monte. The ad concludes, "Don't *blame* your wife, man—cooperate! Give her a chance with Del Monte Coffee!"

© Del Monte Foods; used with permission. Photograph from the Hartman Center for Sales, Advertising & Marketing History.

Howard Schultz in one of his Starbucks cafés. Schultz joined Starbucks in 1982 as director of operations and marketing. From the beginning, he was struck by the potentially broad appeal of the company's offerings. But it was not until the mid-1980s when he opened his own coffee bar and then bought Starbucks from its founders that he started actively creating a national market for specialty coffee served in a café setting.

Courtesy of Starbucks Coffee Company.

The exterior of the first Starbucks store in Seattle's Pike Place Market. In addition to the original mermaid logo and some of the interior décor, the Pike Place store at the end of the twentieth century still retained some of the counterculture spirit that helped inspire its founding in 1971.

Courtesy of Starbucks Coffee Company.

Inside the company's Kent, Washington warehouse, where thousands of bags of Starbucks coffee beans were received, roasted, and then distributed to Starbucks retail outlets around the world.

Courtesy of Starbucks Coffee Company.

A Starbucks Frappuccino® blended coffee drink, which was introduced in 1995.

Courtesy of Starbucks Coffee Company.

The "Robson I" Starbucks location in Vancouver, Canada in a view from behind the counter, where the baristas worked. Starbucks cafés were designed to ensure that the activity behind the counter was visible throughout the store.

Courtesy of Starbucks Coffee Company.

Starbucks first store outside North America opened in 1996 in the Ginza district of Tokyo. By the early twenty-first century, there were more than 100 Starbucks outlets in Tokyo.

Courtesy of Starbucks Coffee Company.

The ENIAC Computer, 1946. Completed a year earlier, the Electronic Numerical Integrator and Computer (ENIAC) was one of the first mainframe computers and the first electronic stored-program computer. The ENIAC weighed 30 tons, took up 1,800 square feet, and required six full-time technicians to keep it running. *Courtesy of IBM Archives.*

The IBM System/360, 1964. A broad line of compatible computers, the System/360 represented a significant improvement in computer system compatibility. The system's structure became the industry standard and propelled IBM's success through the late 1960s. *Courtesy of IBM Archives.*

Michael Dell, the founder of Dell Computer Corporation, in 1987, when the company was still known as "PC's Limited." This was just three years after he had started the business out of his University of Texas at Austin dorm room with $1,000 from his own pocket.

Zigy Kaluzny/Liaison Agency.

	20 MEG	33 MEG	42 MEG
Internal	$775	$1395	$1595
External	$975	$1495	$1695

An advertisement for "PC's Limited" that ran in *PC Week* in 1985. From early on, Michael Dell advertised his products in trade publications such as *PC Week,* emphasizing the capabilities and low cost of his machines and components. Between 1984 and 1985, company sales skyrocketed from $6 million to $33 million.

Courtesy of Dell Computer Corporation. PC Week, *April 2, 1985.*

Dell's product line has broadened considerably since the company's founding in 1984, developing with changes in technology and customer priorities. Here are two desktop personal computers: the top image is the Dell System 433 TE, a 1990 desktop PC. The bottom photo is the more recent Dimension L PC introduced in 1999.

Courtesy of Dell Computer Corporation.

At the top is the Inspiron 3800 laptop computer, introduced in 2000. At the bottom is Dell's PowerApp Web 100, a server appliance also introduced in 2000. Dell's products were made to order at facilities in Austin, Texas; Nashville, Tennessee; Eldorado do Sul, Brazil; Limerick, Ireland; Penang, Malaysia; and Xiamen, China.

Courtesy of Dell Computer Corporation.

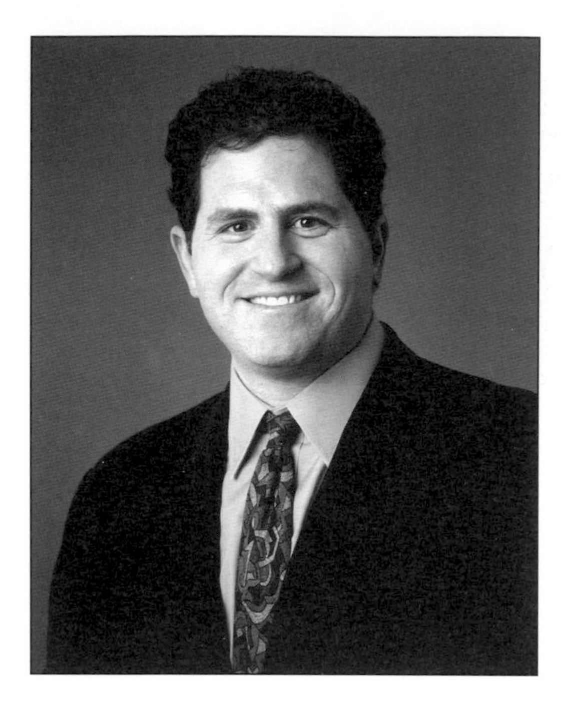

Michael Dell, chairman of the board and chief executive officer of the company he founded. Dell started the business in 1984, while a freshman in college. By the beginning of the twenty-first century, it was the second largest personal computer systems company in the world with daily online sales of $50 million and total annual sales of $25 billion.

Courtesy of Dell Computer Corporation.

The Dell corporate headquarters in Round Rock, Texas, near Austin, the company's birthplace. Round Rock was also home to Dell Americas, the regional business unit for the United States, Canada, and Latin America. Dell also had regional headquarters in England, Japan, and Hong Kong.

Courtesy of Dell Computer Corporation. Photograph by Bob Daemmrich Photo Inc.

In May 1984, the nineteen-year-old took his spring semester final exams at the University of Texas. As the academic term closed, Dell decided to devote all his energies to his growing business. The decision to leave school was not an easy one, and he arranged to take a leave of absence from the university. "Where I come from," he recalled,

> not going to college is not an acceptable option. Convincing my parents to allow me to leave school would have been impossible. So I just went ahead and did it, whatever the consequences. I finished my freshman year and left. After a while, my parents forgave me. A little bit after that, I forgave them, too.[109]

By the summer of 1984, Dell's monthly sales of upgraded IBM PCs had increased to $180,000.[110] They continued to rise at dizzying speeds. The company moved three times between June and late December 1984, outgrowing not only its headquarters, but its phone system, electronic infrastructure, and organizational design. By early 1985, the young company employed more than fifty people. In its first full year, Dell Computer Corporation's revenues totaled $6 million.[111]

Like most entrepreneurs running a new venture, Dell had his hands in everything—working the phone lines, planning product features, managing finances, and hiring new employees. There was little time to rest. He logged eighteen-hour days, often sleeping on a cot in the office.[112]

Mundane operating issues followed hard on the heels of broader strategic and organizational problems. What time in the morning should the office open? How should phone orders be taken, compiled, and relayed to employees assembling PCs?[113] By what criteria should the organization evaluate prospective and existing workers? How much inventory did the company need when sales were doubling monthly? Who were the chief competitors and what were they doing?

Much of what Dell and his colleagues accomplished early on was a result of learning by doing, of inventing solutions to problems as they occurred, and trying not to make the same mistake twice. Rapid growth meant constant change—in staff, financial management, supplier agreements, office infrastructure, and operating policies. Dell and his first employees experimented constantly with new processes, adapting many as the business grew and changed, jettisoning others that were no longer effective. Some, such as how the company recorded new orders, constantly evolved as the volume of business outpaced the enterprise's resources.[114]

Michael had gotten his start in the PC business by upgrading IBM machines. But in 1985, he decided that Dell Computer should begin making, marketing, and distributing its own brand of IBM-compatible machines. In July, the company's Turbo PC appeared under the "PC's Limited" name. The base price of the machine was $795—less than half the price of IBM's PC.[115] Two months later, the firm introduced its first 286 machine, based on the leading-edge technology at the time—Intel's 286 microprocessor.[116] New models followed in April and August of 1986.[117] Priced aggressively below IBM PCs and other compatibles, each new line outsold the previous one.[118] At the close of the 1985 business year, Dell's sales topped $30 million.[119]

As Michael understood, there were four major strategic advantages to his company's designing and making its own products from scratch. Dell Computer would no longer have to depend on supplies of stripped-down PCs from IBM dealers to meet growing demand. Producing its own PCs would also tighten the firm's control over product development and manufacturing, allowing Dell and his colleagues to better exploit the rapidly expanding capabilities and declining costs of computing technology.

This decision also helped the young company communicate with consumers more effectively by exploiting its direct sales model. Since Dell had begun taking apart computers at age fifteen, he had been skeptical of PC retailers' abilities to meet customers' needs. Most third-party sellers, he believed, were not well informed about the new and changing products they distributed. Many were also unsuccessful in relaying consumers' priorities back to manufacturers. This indirect channel, according to Dell, "was based on a marriage of the unknowing buyer and the unknowledgeable seller." As the PC market developed and users grew more familiar and demanding with the technology, Dell was certain that such a "marriage could not last."[120]

Manufacturing his own machines also provided Dell a means of differentiating his company's offerings from other clones. In 1985, there were hundreds of companies making IBM-compatible machines. Most of these were small start-ups. But a few were enjoying tremendous success simply by undercutting IBM's prices. The most prominent of these was Compaq Computer Corporation, founded in 1982 in Houston.[121] Three years later,

Compaq's annual sales topped $500 million, earning it a place in the Fortune 500.[122]

In contrast to Dell's start-up, Compaq chose to use third-party distribution networks to sell its products. Developed by a former IBM executive, Compaq's retail strategy relied on outlets such as ComputerLand and Sears to sell its machines. Many of these stores were already selling IBM PCs, but were willing to offer Compaq products because their profit margins were slightly higher than those on IBM machines. From the retailers' perspective, selling Compaq PCs had other benefits: unlike IBM, Compaq had no direct sales force that competed with stores, and Compaq promised a steady stream of inventory without IBM's frequent supply problems.[123]

In 1985, Michael Dell surveyed IBM, Compaq, and other PC makers' distribution strategies. Compaq's rapid growth was striking. Clearly a huge market existed for high-performance IBM-compatible machines. He was less impressed with how Compaq was putting its products in front of consumers. By selling through independent dealers that also offered IBM PCs, Compaq had to share retail space and salespeople with some of its strongest competitors. From Michael Dell's perspective, this meant that Compaq could not ensure that third-party representatives thoroughly understood its products and their distinctive attributes. Moreover, it could not *directly* target its product development, manufacturing, marketing, and distribution efforts to consumers' changing priorities.

Implementing the Direct Model

In the mid-1980s, Michael Dell began formalizing a different business model, one based on *personal* interaction with consumers. The vast majority of the firm's customers were reached by phone. Most individual customers placed orders by toll-free calls to company salespeople. Most institutional consumers were initially cold-called by Dell sales representatives, who were trained to work with particular customer segments. Once an order was taken, this information was relayed to the company's factory, located close to the firm's offices. There the computer was assembled according to customer specifications. An insurance company, for example, could purchase a hundred machines with varying processing speeds. A state agency could buy twenty PCs, each with two floppy drives, and fifteen additional PCs, each with one floppy and one hard drive. An academic, working on a book, could order a computer with additional hard-drive memory.

Once the factory had completed an order, it was shipped directly to the customer, arriving one to three weeks after the order was placed.[124] (By the late 1990s, Dell was able to fulfill orders, such as the NASDAQ servers, in one to two days.)

This "made-to-order" or direct sales and manufacturing model grew out of Michael Dell's insights about the demand side of the PC market. But it also yielded important supply-side benefits. By eliminating third-party salespeople (and their customarily high retail margins), Dell's company could reduce its distribution costs substantially below those of its rivals. Many of these savings were passed onto customers, enabling Dell Computer to profitably undersell IBM and others. In 1986, for example, a line of Dell's PCs based on the 286 microprocessor chip sold for between $2,500 and $3,900. Comparable machines from IBM were priced between $4,600 and $5,800; those from Compaq between $4,300 and $5,000.[125]

The direct model also resulted in lower inventory costs. Because Dell Computer built computers *after* customers ordered them, the company carried almost no inventory of finished machines. By contrast, PC makers such as IBM and Compaq had to maintain much larger product inventories to stock reseller and retail channels. Building to consumer order—rather than to demand forecasts as most manufacturers did—also kept Dell's materials inventories relatively low. In an industry based on rapid technological innovation, this resulted in considerable cost savings. As Michael Dell later explained:

> Component prices are always falling as suppliers introduce faster chips, bigger disk drives, and modems with ever-greater bandwidth. Let's say Dell has eight days of inventory. Compare that to an indirect competitor who has twenty-five days of inventory with another thirty in their distribution channel. That's a difference of forty-seven days, and in forty-seven days, the cost of materials will decline about 6 percent.[126]

In its broad outlines, Dell's model of direct selling was not entirely new. Corporate sales forces, like IBM's, had long dealt face-to-face with institutional customers. Consumer products companies such as Fuller Brush and Avon used door-to-door salespeople to market goods to individual consumers. Dell's model was perhaps most akin to mail-order or catalogue distribution in which consumers ordered clothes, household goods, and other products, sight unseen, directly from the manufacturer. By eliminating wholesalers and other related costs, many catalogue retailers, such as Sears, Roebuck, L.L. Bean, and Spiegel, had realized economies similar to those that Dell enjoyed. But none of these companies were in a position to offer products "made to order" for individual customers, as Dell was able to do.

Dell was not the only PC maker to harness the possibilities of direct selling by phone and mail. In the mid-1980s, a score of clones, such as TIPC Network (later renamed Gateway), distributed IBM-compatible machines by mail order. But most of these players competed solely on price. Only a handful offered reliable service or support for their products. Even fewer manufactured their computers to customer specifications. None invested the resources that Dell Computer did to build strong connections with consumers, understand their priorities, and earn their trust.

Building the Brand and Organization

Dell Computer's sales increased rapidly in the mid-1980s, climbing from $6 million in fiscal 1985 to $70 million two years later.[127] As the company's market presence expanded, industry experts were openly skeptical of its strategy. Some argued that businesses and individual consumers would not continue to buy costly new products they could not see from a manufacturer they did not know. Some pointed to the dubious public reputation of other direct sellers. "Most mail-order houses," wrote one industry reporter in 1987, "were fly-by-night outfits of marginal reputation that imported cheap [IBM] PC clones from the Far East and resold them at bargain basement prices."[128] Still others criticized Dell's underlying business model, asserting that direct marketing to PC users would devolve into a price war in which profit margins for manufacturers—and in some cases, distributors—would be competed away.

Michael Dell's response to these challenges was to build a powerful brand based on high-quality machines and outstanding service. He did not have many compelling examples to follow. Only a few computer companies, such as IBM, Hewlett-Packard, and Apple, had brands that had earned widespread consumer recognition and trust. Both IBM and Hewlett-Packard enjoyed the benefits of long-standing reputations and customer relationships that predated the PC. While Apple was a relatively young company, it had invested heavily in forging a strong brand based on user accessibility, elegant design, and the creative possibilities of technology.

Apple's name, logo, and products were well known to both business and home consumers.[129]

These strong brands, however, were exceptional. In 1985, the majority of PC makers had not established a meaningful name, symbol, or identity that consistently differentiated their offerings and commanded buyer loyalty. Most of the major IBM clone makers—including manufacturers like Compaq and Epson and larger mail-order firms such as Northgate and Compuadd—based their marketing appeals primarily on cost. They charged prices higher than those of very small PC makers but lower than those of IBM and Apple.[130]

Some of the clones emphasized specific functional attributes such as processing speed. "Megahertz wars" erupted frequently, as individual manufacturers scrambled to offer the fastest possible computer processing units (CPUs). In 1987, for example, many clones produced machines that ran at eight megahertz—eight million operations per second—ten, twelve, and even sixteen megahertz. (At the beginning of the twenty-first century, this rivalry continued as companies raced to introduce PCs with 900-megahertz processors.) Compaq, Leading Edge, and other producers also advertised their dealer networks and product support. But price remained the single most important feature that almost all IBM-clone makers chose to highlight in bringing their products to market.[131]

Michael Dell, however, believed that consumers wanted more than good technical quality at low prices. He was convinced that buyers wanted a satisfying buying experience with informed, helpful salespeople. He suspected that buyers also wanted a strong voice in configuring their computers and peripheral equipment, such as monitors and printers, for specific applications. He also believed that users desired effective service and product support after the sale. All of these issues, Dell reasoned, would only become more significant as the market matured and consumers gained more familiarity with PCs. He intended to develop an appealing brand that customers would associate with current technology, customer control, and responsive service.[132] As he put it years later:

> I'd much rather design the winning system to sell and support customers than design an incredibly technically proficient microprocessor that nobody wants to buy. I mean, that's the problem with our industry: There are a lot of technologists who will create wonderful

> things and then go try to find people who want to buy them. We started with the customer, and then worked our way back.[133]

This was the essence of demand-side thinking and strategic planning.

Segmenting the Market

This ambitious strategy, however, was not an easy one to implement, and it could be expensive. Training sales representatives, offering effective customer service and support, and configuring machines to buyer specifications generally increased operating costs and thus, potentially, PC prices. How was Michael Dell to create a distinctive brand *and* manufacture personal PCs that rivaled other IBM-compatibles in price?

His solution to this dilemma was to segment the market. He would first target buyers who could help develop his company's reputation among other consumers. In the late eighteenth century, Josiah Wedgwood had done something similar. Knowing that middle-class consumers coveted goods owned by their social betters, Wedgwood had marketed his china to the nobility. Once he had established a foothold in the aristocratic market, he quickly publicized these sales to the much broader group of middle-class customers.

Dell's own segmentation strategy, however, was based on his target consumers' familiarity with PC technology rather than on their incomes or social status. He knew that there were knowledgeable users, who, like himself, envisioned a growing number of applications for the PC. Based on his initial experience selling upgraded IBM machines, Dell suspected that these consumers were likely to be interested in configuring the computers they bought.[134] (They also wanted to work with expert salespeople and responsive service technicians.) Ever since Dell had started selling upgraded IBM machines in 1983, he had been most interested in targeting this segment of buyers. Three years later, as the leader of a multimillion-dollar business with 250 employees, he was ready to focus his strategic efforts directly on these knowledgeable customers.[135]

Dell Computer began introducing products, services, and other brand attributes that appealed specifically to these users. The majority of them were men who enjoyed keeping tabs on practical high-tech developments.[136] They were pragmatic people who read computer magazines and were generally more concerned with superior PC performance than was the case for first-time buyers.[137] Many of Dell's target customers were business buyers interested in computing capabilities tailored to specific needs.

This group's understanding of and facility with new technologies made them an influential source of information for additional purchasers. Colleagues, family members, and friends often took their high-tech cues from these knowledgeable people, watching what they bought and asking their advice.[138]

Dell chose to focus on these discerning customers for other reasons as well. Many members of the targeted group were managers in small and medium-sized companies, most of which were in the market for more than one machine. The vast majority of these buyers were too small to be served by IBM's sales force and bought PCs from third-party retailers or value-added resellers (VARs). These outlets typically could not offer the sales information, service, and specialized configuration that business consumers wanted.

But these kinds of benefits, Michael Dell reasoned, could be provided to targeted users on a cost-effective basis. Telephone ordering, for example, was ideally suited to knowledgeable business customers who did not require hands-on product demonstrations or extensive explanations. These same buyers generally had fewer product questions than less experienced buyers. When problems did arise for targeted consumers, the issues could often be resolved quickly by phone.

To serve this segment, Dell Computer hired and trained a growing sales force. For most of the company's first three years, these people worked primarily off toll-free telephone lines: making cold calls to potential business customers initially in the Southwest and later around the country, taking orders, and answering questions. By 1987, the telemarketing group was fielding more than 1,700 phone calls a day from across the country.[139] To allay consumers' fears about buying a PC sight unseen, the company offered a thirty-day money-back guarantee and a one-year limited warranty with free on-site repair and support for customers within 100 miles of designated service providers.[140]

To further enhance the company's commitment to responsive service, Dell Computer established toll-free technical support lines and a twenty-four-hour telephone number for questions and comments. If any customer dialing the support line had to wait more than five minutes for a technician, Dell Computer mailed the caller a check for twenty-five dollars.[141] Based in the company's Austin headquarters, the seventy-five technicians staffing these phone lines were generally assigned to particular consumer groups and trained to handle inquiries about specific products. Using a computerized database, Dell representatives tracked the service history of each machine mentioned during the phone call.[142] About 90 percent of these queries and problems were handled to the customer's satisfaction in a single telephone conversation.[143] To resolve other issues, the company provided a guaranteed forty-eight-hour shipment of replacement parts.[144] In early 1987, Dell began offering customers the option of purchasing a service agreement with Honeywell Bull, which repaired machines on site or at one of its 160 service centers in the United States. The agreement cost thirty-five dollars a year.[145]

Since his early days upgrading computers, Dell had relied on consumer word of mouth and newspaper ads to interest potential buyers. Once his organization began producing its own machines, the founder invested more heavily in print advertising, promoting his company's service, product support, and money-back guarantee as well as its products. Dell Computer advertised in computer magazines and other trade publications read by knowledgeable users.[146] In 1987, the company spent about $3 million—about 4 percent of sales—on advertising.[147]

Dell and his colleagues also made sure that analysts for *PC Week, Computerworld, Byte, InfoWorld,* and other special interest magazines would be given an opportunity to use and test the company's products personally. This tactic paid off, and by the late 1980s, computer magazines were giving Dell's products high marks for quality, performance, power, service, and support.[148]

These endorsements translated into increased consumer interest and sales. For example, *PC Week*'s rave review of Dell's first IBM-compatible machine, the Turbo, appeared shortly after the product was introduced in July 1985. Almost immediately, the company began selling more than 1,000 Turbo machines per month.[149] Continued praise from industry publications attracted still more consumers, as did the company's participation in computer trade shows and conferences. Dell's sales for the company's 1986 fiscal year were about $60 million—double those of 1985.[150] In less than thirty-six months, the firm that Michael Dell had started in his college dorm room had grown into a big business. Table 7-1 illustrates the company's growth. In 1986, about 40 percent of sales came from small and

TABLE 7-1

Dell Computer Corporation Sales, 1985–2000
(millions of dollars)

Year	Total Sales
1985	6
1986	34
1987	70
1988	159
1989	258
1990	389
1991	546
1992	890
1993	2,014
1994	2,873
1995	3,475
1996	5,296
1997	7,759
1998	12,327
1999	18,243
2000	25,265

Sources: Dell Computer Corporation, *Annual Reports 1989,* p. 21; *1991,* p. 15; *1993,* p. 1; *1998,* p. 2; *1999,* p. 20; *2000,* p. 20.

Note: These figures are for fiscal, not calendar years. The Dell fiscal year ends January 31.

medium-sized businesses, almost a third from larger companies such as Burlington Northern Motor Carriers and Price Waterhouse, and the remainder from sales to governmental and educational users and individual consumers.[151]

Listening to Customers

As sales climbed, the company's direct relationship with customers served as a primary source of demand-side intelligence, affecting a range of strategic and operating decisions.[152] Dell Computer's human resource executives and departmental heads based their staffing plans and production levels partly on market estimates gathered through thousands of daily customer interactions. Purchasing managers used the same estimates to place orders with suppliers, making every effort to reduce the firm's inventory costs.

Dell's sales and marketing executives used customer information to evaluate changes in demand and measure response rates from newspaper ads, catalogues, and other communication initiatives.[153] Equally important, sales representatives tracked a customer's order history to help configure a new purchase by the same customer. Because the sales division had access to a given buyer's previous purchases, explained Hershel Hochman, vice president of manufacturing in the late 1980s,

> we can determine what equipment they already have and their complete repair history. This gives us the opportunity to ensure that customers are ordering equipment appropriate for their needs. You have a sort of inventory control that you never have on the retail level. You can save yourself a bundle . . . [by not] building machines and buying parts nobody wants or needs.[154]

Consumer feedback also influenced research and product development directives, helping Dell Computer tailor its product innovation and offerings to changing industry conditions. In 1987, for example, IBM introduced its Personal System/2s (PS/2)(named for the second generation of PCs). The PS/2 machines came in four models and were designed with a new architecture, including a more powerful microprocessor, a new operating system called the OS/2, and a faster "bus" or data highway between the microprocessor and the rest of the machine. IBM intended for the PS/2 line to become the next standard in the PC industry, giving the company a new competitive advantage against the clones.

But most business customers were unenthusiastic about the PS/2 line. For one thing, the new computers cost more than other PCs. In addition, product analysts at *InfoWorld* and other trade publications criticized the performance of PS/2 models, contending that the new machines were no faster, and in some cases slower, than older PCs.[155] Most important, the new IBM machines were not compatible with some existing components and peripheral equipment used by customers of IBM clones.

Relying on its own market information, Dell Computer decided not to invest heavily in the PS/2 technology. Instead, the company expanded and upgraded its line of PCs based on Intel's existing 286 and 386 microprocessors. In 1988, a consortium of clone makers led by Compaq developed an alternative data highway for IBM-compatible machines. The new design proved to be not only more efficient than the one in the PS/2 line but also compatible with the installed base of clone PCs. The design quickly became the industry standard, and Dell produced several successful lines of computers based on it.[156]

Dell's management also used customer information from the technical support phones to remedy defects in individual customers' equipment and to rapidly improve Dell's overall product line. In responding to calls, technicians logged customer complaints into a database. If the same customer called the support hot line again, a Dell technician could instantly call up a record of the consumer's previous difficulties. Executives and engineers then used all of this accumulated information to improve computer assembly. When "we get more than a few complaints,"commented a Dell marketing manager in the late 1980s, "I go about 130 feet to the people who design the thing. Within five or six hours, engineering has fixed the design, and within two or three days, the factory's got that change incorporated on the line."[157]

Consumer feedback also helped Dell's manufacturing managers evaluate their suppliers and subcontractors. For example, if an institutional customer purchased fifty machines, and reported that ten of them had graphics problems, engineers in Dell's product division not only tried to solve the problem themselves but also alerted the vendor of the offending part.[158]

Constructing the Organization

In 1987, the twenty-two-year-old Michael Dell and his colleagues surveyed the company's prospects. Dell's business had come a long way very rapidly. Annual sales that fiscal year totaled $70 million, an elevenfold increase from the company's first-year sales. Net income had climbed to $2.1 million in fiscal 1987 from $32,000 in fiscal 1985—a 6,500 percent increase.[159]

An enormous expansion in company infrastructure and output underlay this financial performance. In late 1986, an 82,000-square-foot factory in north Austin had gone into operation. Six months later, it was turning out 7,000 machines a month, each one built to meet customers' specifications on an existing order. By 1987, Dell Computer employed more than 350 people working in marketing and distribution, service and support, research and development, and manufacturing.[160]

Private debt and retained earnings funded the company's early growth. Michael Dell's family members lent the firm $500,000 to fund its initial operations. By the end of 1986, the company had repaid these loans.[161] The business also took out bank loans, including a $10 million credit line.[162] In 1987, the company completed a private equity placement. The deal closed in the wake of the October stock market crash, but investors were relatively enthusiastic, and the firm raised more than $21 million.[163] As sales and net income increased in the late 1980s, the company also relied on retained earnings to finance its growth.

The young enterprise conserved its resources. Money was often tight, so employees improvised a range of cost-saving measures. "People didn't have wastebaskets," Michael Dell recalled, "instead, they used the cardboard boxes that computer parts came in."[164] As the organization exploded in size in its early years, space was in short supply, and employees often shared cubicles. When the factory had more orders than its staff could fulfill, engineers helped assemble the machines. When phone orders backed up, staff from all over the company pitched in to answer calls. "Our sales people would stuff RAM chips into tubes to ship to customers," Dell recalled, "even while they were taking more orders on the phone."[165]

Michael Dell himself, of course, oversaw the company's initial expansion. But he soon realized that he needed seasoned executive talent. In 1986, he recruited Lee Walker, an Austin investment banker and venture capitalist, to join the business as second in command with the title of president and chief operating officer. (Michael became chairman and CEO.) Walker, then forty-four years old, had experience in a number of start-up companies. One of his first achievements at Dell was to secure badly needed bank credit. He also recruited some nationally prominent executives to join Dell's board of directors, including George Kozmetsky, a cofounder of Teledyne, and Robert "Bobby" Inman, former head of the CIA and CEO of Westmark, a private defense company. Both men brought a wealth of experience and key contacts to Dell Computer.[166] Meanwhile, Lee Walker also instituted stronger financial controls, restructured lines of managerial responsibility, and reorganized the company's senior staff, demoting some managers and firing others.

It could not have been easy for Michael Dell to relinquish as much control as he did to Lee Walker. It must have been especially hard to watch a newcomer fire people whom Dell himself had once hired and promoted.

But he recognized the value of Walker's experience and perspective. Before founding the company, Dell admitted, "I was a little kid. I didn't run a division of Procter and Gamble."[167] "I didn't know everything there was to know about running a large business like this. But I knew how to hire people who did."[168] He stood firmly behind the new president's actions, knowing that "this had to be done for the company's future."[169]

Over the next several years, he and Walker recruited executives from companies such as Prudential Insurance and Standard Oil of Ohio. Some of these new leaders, such as Graham Beachum, who had worked at Tandy and IBM before joining Dell as senior vice president of marketing, and Glen Henry, who left IBM to head Dell's product development division, entered the organization at top management. Others, such as Morton Meyerson, former president of Electronic Data Systems, signed on as advisers. Dell Computer's hiring at all levels expanded rapidly, as figure 7-3 shows.

When Walker first came to the company, he was almost twice the age of the man who hired him. But Dell and Walker enjoyed working together.

FIGURE 7-3

Dell Computer Corporation Employees, 1985–2000

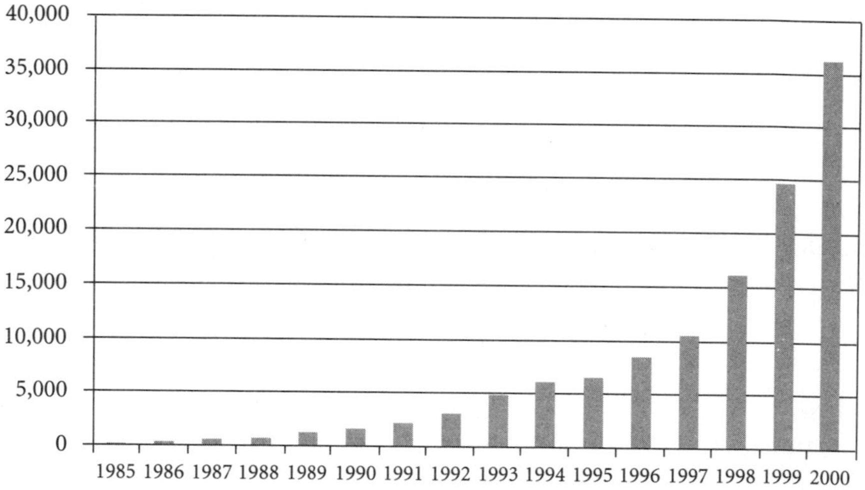

40,000
35,000
30,000
25,000
20,000
15,000
10,000
5,000
0

1985 1986 1987 1988 1989 1990 1991 1992 1993 1994 1995 1996 1997 1998 1999 2000

Sources: Dell Computer Corporation, *Annual Report 1989,* p. 6; *Form 10Ks 1990,* p. 9; *1991,* p. 12; *1992,* p. 9; *1993,* p. 10; *1994,* p. 8; *1995,* p. 10; *1996,* p. 8; *1997,* p. 8; *1998,* p. 8; *1999,* p. 9; Kimberly N. Hunt and AnnaMarie L. Sheldon, eds., *Notable Corporate Chronologies,* vol. 1, A–K (Detroit, MI: Gale Research, 1999), p. 531; Thomas C. Hayes, "Is Austin the Next Silicon Valley?" *The New York Times,* 13 Jan. 1988, p. D6.

"People might think the age difference would work against us," Walker said at the time. "But Michael and I discovered that just the opposite is true. We end up completing each other's sentences."[170] For Dell, the relationship worked on several levels. It freed him from direct responsibility for daily operations, allowing him to concentrate on broad strategic issues. Walker also acted as an invaluable sounding board for Dell's business ideas, helping him decide which to develop and which to discard. In this role as an adviser and confidant to the younger man, Walker tempered some of Dell's brashness. "Lee helped me get around the potholes," Dell remembered. "Sometimes he was my father, sometimes he was my brother. We were very, very close."[171] Like Josiah Wedgwood's partnership with Thomas Bentley or Howard Schultz's with Orin Smith, this relationship was based on mutual respect and complementary skills, and it served the young company very well.

Expanding the Market

Both Dell and Walker were committed to a strategy of rapid expansion. Dell Computer expected to sell 84,000 machines in 1987, earning revenues of more than $100 million. But as such a young entrant, it was not yet one of the top ten PC makers. Measured by total sales, Dell in 1987 had about 1 percent of the U.S. personal computer market. Zenith had about 4.4 percent, Olivetti 5 percent, Compaq 5.2 percent, Apple, 8.7 percent, and IBM almost 30 percent.[172] Yet Dell Computer was emerging as a recognized player in the industry. Its products continued to receive widespread media praise for their performance, reliability, service, and support. Building on Dell's growing reputation, senior managers now made two important decisions: to target large corporations and to expand internationally.

Targeting Large Corporations

First, Dell and Walker enlarged the company's field of target customers to include Fortune 2,000 and other large corporations. In 1987, Dell already had some big accounts—Dow Chemical and Arthur Andersen, for example. These purchasers had been attracted initially by Dell's customization capabilities as well as its competitive pricing.[173] But the bulk of Dell revenues at the time still came from small and medium-sized companies.

Dell's executives understood the strategic advantages in selling computers to big institutions. Many corporate customers bought fifty or more computers at a time, creating potential economies of scale for Dell in marketing and supporting its products. These same customers also upgraded their IT systems more frequently than did most household or small business buyers. The possibility of repeat sales to large corporations and government agencies thus had relatively high payoffs. For example, in 1987, Continental Grain Company first ordered PCs from Dell. From the perspective of Dell's management, this initial purchase might become—over time—a stream of future purchases. As Continental Grain managers' experience with Dell deepened and their trust in the manufacturer and its brand increased, they were likely to buy additional products and services. With each new order, Dell representatives would learn more about Continental Grain's priorities and how to satisfy them. This knowledge would make selling and servicing these products increasingly efficient, lowering Dell's operating costs on future sales and increasing its profit margins.[174] At the same time, the Dell brand might benefit from working successfully with more and more Fortune 2,000 customers. These new relationships would eventually make Dell a safer choice for chief information officers vis-à-vis their supervisors within corporate hierarchies—an advantage exploited by IBM and its globally known brand for several decades.

There were still other advantages to working with large institutional customers. Big companies and government agencies were often interested in purchasing computer-related products such as modems, disk drives, printers, and software packages. Like the options available on a new car, many of these products carried high profit margins and low distribution costs.

In targeting large institutions, Dell Computer was effectively taking on IBM, the acknowledged industry leader. Nicknamed "Big Blue" for the large blue panels that covered the company's mainframes, IBM had built its strategy, brand, and organization on selling to big corporations.[175] Since introducing the PC in 1981, Big Blue's share of the office PC market had climbed to almost 40 percent.[176]

But this did not dissuade Dell, Walker, and their colleagues. Since Michael had begun enhancing and selling IBM computers as a college freshman, he had wanted to beat Big Blue at its own game, at least in the PC market. He had long predicted that as this market matured, the number of sophisticated corporate buyers would grow. These customers, in turn, would be receptive to reliable, high-performance machines configured to user specifications, well supported, and priced below comparable IBM products.[177]

Dell executives planned to use both established and newer routes to reach large institutional consumers. Proven methods included launching a direct-mail initiative that would focus on administrators and purchasing agents in specific organizations, supplementing Dell's print ads in computer magazines. Dell also planned to assemble a team of people specializing in direct sales to major customers. Initially, the sales force would be small—about twenty-five people. Unlike IBM, Apple, and other manufacturers' representatives, Dell's salespeople would not spend most of their time in the field, staffing existing accounts or making in-person calls on specific clients. Instead, they would work from their homes, calling potential corporate customers by phone.[178] Senior management knew that this method would be much less expensive than supporting a traditional sales force in the field. In spite of such cost-saving measures, getting the company's products in front of large institutional buyers would hardly be an inexpensive proposition. In addition to hiring and training a larger sales group, Dell had to augment its on-site service and product support efforts.

Dell also had to convince big corporations that purchasing computers through the mail was as safe as buying them from an IBM representative or authorized dealer. Toward this end, Dell salespeople were trained to provide an abundance of relevant information to likely customers. Some of the salespeople's education in how to accomplish this came through formal coursework. Each Dell representative was required to complete a five-week program covering a range of subjects from the latest PC technology to the company's product lines. As reps advanced in the organization, they received additional training in specific skills, such as creating new sales territory or—in the case of corporate reps—handling big accounts.[179] Every Dell salesperson also participated in a range of hands-on exercises designed to enhance his or her abilities to provide efficient, effective customer service. For example, the company required each rep to unpack his or her own PC from its carton and set the machine up. Most salespeople, as Michael Dell explained, "probably didn't enjoy it, but it gave them (and us) a real sense of what the uneducated customer would go through to set up his system, and it helped them develop a more intimate understanding of the products they were selling." Such exercises were also designed to enable the sales force to help solve equipment problems and answer customer questions.[180]

Sales representatives were also trained to urge corporate and government users to tour the PC maker's plant in Austin. "The threshold issue for us," as Michael Dell put it in 1987, "is to get the customer into our factory and let them see our automated manufacturing system, show them we've got a professional operation here. If they see that, we've got a customer."[181]

Winning prominent corporate accounts also entailed new risks for the company's young brand. For most of its first three years, Dell Computer had received significant media attention. By 1987, several national business magazines were charting the firm's performance. Most of this coverage had been favorable, enhancing the Dell brand at little cost to the company. This same visibility, however, would become a liability if Dell did not succeed in satisfying large institutional customers. Yet, Michael Dell and his executive team believed targeting large consumers was critical to the company's future growth.[182] They knew that they had to take great care to minimize the chances of disappointing a major client and thereby damaging the Dell brand, but they were confident that their organization could meet or exceed their big new customers' expectations.

International Expansion

A second and equally important strategic decision Dell and his colleagues made in 1987 was to seek out international markets. By the late 1980s, almost half of all worldwide sales of PCs took place outside the United States.[183] The majority of this demand was concentrated in Europe and Asia, particularly in Japan. With the exception of the United States, Japan was the single largest national market for PCs.[184] But Dell executives realized that competing in Japan, as Michael put it, "was more of a longer-term dream. The investment we'd need to enter a market that was then dominated by entrenched Japanese companies was more than we could handle."[185]

By contrast, British and other European markets were more open. In the late 1980s, a number of companies were selling PCs in European markets at prices competitive with Dell's. But from the vantage point of Dell's senior management, most of these products were not as well made or as reliable as their own. Few of the players in European markets effectively serviced their machines. Virtually none provided free after-sales support. Dell and his colleagues were therefore confident that the company's products, services, and—eventually—its brand would appeal to European consumers. Equally important, demand in these markets was expanding rapidly. By 1990, total PC sales in Europe were expected to exceed $7.5 billion.[186]

Dell had been eyeing the British market since 1984, when he and his family had traveled to London during his spring break from the University of Texas. "I observed the same high markup/lousy service phenomenon in the United Kingdom as I had in the United States," he said.[187] These shortcomings, as Dell understood, represented strategic opportunities, and three years later he and his colleagues decided to exploit them.

Like Henry Heinz and Estée Lauder, he and his colleagues saw other advantages to starting in the United Kingdom. For one thing, there was no language barrier. As important, the United Kingdom had a large number of knowledgeable business users who might become interested in the Dell brand. In addition, the country might prove to be an excellent beachhead for future European expansion. In June 1987, Dell Computer's first international subsidiary opened for business in the United Kingdom, following the same broad strategies of its parent company. Telemarketing sales representatives backed by a national advertising campaign contacted potential customers and took orders for customized computers.[188]

Dell's overseas sales grew rapidly, and the subsidiary was profitable within seven months. By April 1988, the London-based telemarketing group was retailing $4 million in computers a month.[189] Revenues increased more than 60 percent in the subsidiary's second year of operation.[190] Much of this business came from *The Financial Times Top 1000* companies and from large public sector organizations.[191] During the next several years, Dell Computer built on this initial success, establishing subsidiaries in Germany, France, Sweden, and Canada. Less than three years after its first foray into international markets, almost a quarter of Dell Computer's annual sales were coming from outside the United States.[192]

Continued Growth

By early 1988, the company's annual sales had climbed to $159 million—a 129 percent increase over the previous fiscal year.[193] To keep pace with this rate of expansion, the company needed additional manufacturing, warehouse, and office facilities. It also needed more people. In 1988, Dell

Computer employed 650 men and women. Senior management expected this number to increase by at least 60 percent over the coming year.[194]

These requirements created a huge need for fresh capital. In the fall of 1987, as noted earlier, the company had raised $21 million in a private equity placement managed by Goldman Sachs. To fund new investments as well as working capital needs, senior management hoped to raise $38 million in 1988.[195] In May of that year, twenty-three-year-old Dell announced that he and his colleagues would take the company public. Financial analysts and business reporters expressed mixed reactions. Most were impressed with Dell's meteoric rise, but many doubted that the company could continue to grow rapidly *and* profitably. "Dell has just about tapped out the mail-order business," asserted the editor of the *Technologic PC Letter*.[196] Other writers predicted that the company's recent initiative to offer Dell computers through value-added resellers would force it to change its entire operating strategy.[197] Although Walker and other experienced executives helped Dell oversee the business, a few industry observers questioned the young founder's ability to share control, citing the recent departures of several top managers.[198]

Despite comments such as these, Dell Computer raised over $34 million when it went public in June 1988. The company sold about a quarter of its outstanding stock—some four million shares—at an average price of about $8.50 per share. In its first six months on the NASDAQ, the company's stock price fluctuated between 7¾ and 12⅝.[199] Dell employees were eligible to receive incentive stock options, but Dell himself owned more than half the company's equity.[200]

Dell Computer's expansion accelerated in the late 1980s and early 1990s. In fiscal 1991, sales exceeded $546 million. Net income totaled $27 million.[201] For the preceding four years, sales and profits had each grown at compound annual rates of more than 65 percent. Measured by market share, Dell Computer was now the sixth largest player in the U.S. PC industry—a fast climb from the number twenty-two position it held in 1989.[202] But it was not a leading company in terms of global sales. In 1991, the companies with the biggest shares of the PC world market were IBM, Apple, NEC, Compaq, and Fujitsu. Together, these five companies accounted for 52 percent of global sales.[203]

But Dell's market presence and brand recognition continued to develop, and by 1991, the company's strategy of targeting large institutional consumers had borne fruit. Almost half of Dell Computer's sales during that fiscal year were to major corporate, governmental, and educational customers. Small and medium-sized businesses accounted for 40 percent of sales, with individual consumers making up the remaining 12 percent.[204] The majority of Dell's customers—70 percent—were repeat purchasers, attracted by the company's products, service, and support.[205] In early 1991, Dell earned the top ranking for customer satisfaction among business users in J. D. Powers and Associates' first annual survey of PC consumers.[206] Other organizations, such as *PCWeek*, also awarded Dell Computer high marks in pleasing customers.[207]

Learning by Doing

The company had enjoyed remarkable growth during its first seven years in business. But in the intensely competitive PC market, past achievements hardly guaranteed future success. Rapid technological advances in hardware and software continued to characterize the industry. In the late 1980s and early 1990s, microprocessing capacity was still increasing rapidly. So, too, were other PC capabilities, such as graphics and network applications. Software innovation kept pace as Microsoft, Lotus, and other manufacturers rushed to market with applications designed to run on the next generation of machines. The most famous of these was Microsoft's Windows operating system, first launched in 1985 as an attempt to bring a graphical user interface (GUI)—in which users pointed to pictures rather than typing commands to give the computer instructions—to IBM-compatible PCs. The early versions of Windows were plagued by many problems, including huge memory requirements and frequent system crashes. But Microsoft continued to improve and upgrade its operating system, introducing three additional versions of Windows between 1985 and 1992.[208] Software developers such as Intuit hurried to offer applications compatible with the latest operating systems and the newest hardware.

In the late 1980s and early 1990s, scores of PC manufacturers worked to assimilate all this technological change. The leading companies included IBM, Compaq, Apple, Tandy, and Zenith.[209] Each firm used its own research and experience to assess the operating efficiencies, commercial viability, user appeal, and profitability of a never-ending stream of new product possibilities, many of which displaced earlier offerings or made them obsolete.

PC makers competed not only on how well they brokered technological innovation coming from all sides but also on product quality, and, of course, price.

Also in the late 1980s and early 1990s, PC prices plummeted, driven down by technological advances and a nationwide recession. As sales dampened, a price war broke out. Between 1987 and 1992, the average selling price of a PC declined from $2,760 to $2,309—a 32 percent decrease, adjusted for inflation.[210] Falling prices squeezed industry profitability, motivated most players to reduce operating costs, and forced some companies, such as Wang, out of the PC business altogether. One industry consultant described participation in the PC industry as akin to operating "inside a tornado," a metaphor that captured the speed and ruthlessness of rivalry in the sector.[211] Figure 7-4 traces the sales of PCs by leading manufacturers.

FIGURE 7-4

Selected Manufacturers' PC Sales, 1984–1998
(millions of dollars)

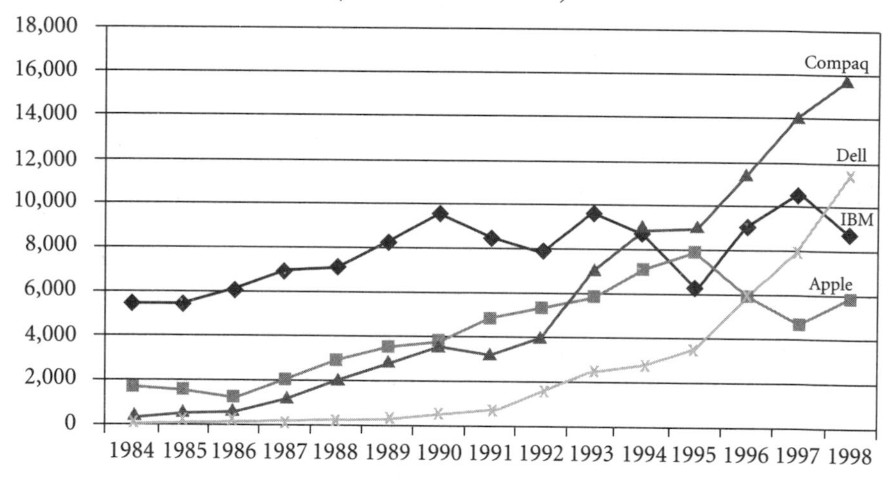

Sources: Datamation Special Issues (15 June 1986), p. 45; (15 June 1988), p. 160; (15 June 1990), p. 184; (15 June 1992), p. 26; (15 June 1994), p. 55; (1 June 1995), p. 62; *Computer Reseller News* (2 June 1997), p. 122; (20 April 1998), p. 112; (17 May 1999), p. 94; Peter Burrows, "A Baby Mac Attack," *Business Week* (10 Aug. 1998), p. 30.

Note: This information reflects calendar year, not fiscal year, results. 1998 sales for Apple Computer are the company's net sales for the year, including related software and peripherals.

Dell Computer—like other relatively low-cost manufacturers, including Packard Bell and AST—more than survived the price war of the late 1980s and early 1990s. For most of the period, the growth of Dell's sales and net income outpaced industry averages.[212] But neither this generally strong financial performance nor Dell's increasing market share in desktop PCs came easily. As the company struggled to develop its products and brand in a young, dynamic sector, senior managers made two significant mistakes—the first in 1989, the second in the early 1990s. Each resulted from Michael Dell and his colleagues' attempts to expand the firm's product lines, customer base, and market presence as rapidly as possible. Each represented a potentially serious threat to the company's reputation and its relationship with consumers. But Dell and his enterprise recovered quickly from both experiences, learning critical lessons that had lasting—and strategically beneficial—consequences for the brand, the organization, and the entrepreneur.

Managing Inventory

In Dell Computer's first four years of business (1984–1988), annual sales rose at a compound annual rate of more than 250 percent.[213] It was dizzying growth, and in early 1989, Dell managers were concerned about keeping pace with it as efficiently as possible. To meet what managers expected would be rapidly increasing demand for Dell products, the company invested in large quantities of components: semiconductors, disk drives, and memory chips. Memory chips were projected to be in short supply by late 1989, so Dell's management bought as many as possible.

Michael Dell and his colleagues quickly discovered that they had purchased many more memory chips than needed—at high prices. "And then prices plunged," Dell remembered. "To make matters worse, we also got caught 'crossing the street' technologically, as memory chip capacity went from 256K to 1 megabyte almost overnight."[214] The company found itself holding millions of dollars of memory chips that were rapidly becoming obsolete.[215] Dell went on to say, "inventory is the worst thing to own in an industry in which the value of the materials or information declines quickly. . . . As one of my colleagues in this industry likes to say, inventory has the shelf life of lettuce."[216]

It took the company almost a year to sell off its inventory of memory chips—at prices much lower than it paid for them. These losses affected strategic initiatives as the company postponed launching operations in new international markets. The losses contributed to a drop in Dell Computer's net income, which fell to $5 million in fiscal 1990 from $14 million a year earlier.[217] To preserve overall profit margins, Dell executives were forced to raise product prices, and this action, in turn, dampened consumer demand. It also raised doubts on the part of some financial analysts and reporters about the viability of Dell's direct business model.[218] Inside the company, most of the senior management team—including the founder—was deeply affected by the crisis. "For the first time in the company's history," recalled Dell, "we didn't deliver. To our stunned disbelief, we had quickly become known as the company with the inventory problem."[219]

It was the company's biggest mistake to date, and Dell and his colleagues were determined to learn all they could from it. Senior managers recommitted their efforts and resources to one of their own original operating principles—minimizing inventory. They devised new methods of monitoring the speed with which inputs flowed through the factory. As the firm expanded in the early and mid-1990s and its influence with vendors increased, it negotiated specific agreements with suppliers to deliver components on the day that Dell planned to use them. The company also improved its abilities to better predict future demand for its products. By the late 1990s, Dell Computer had lower inventories—an average of about eleven days—than virtually all rival firms. These leaner inventories not only freed up financial resources for other uses, they also helped the company respond quickly to changes on the demand or supply side of product markets. "If I've got 11 days of inventory," Michael Dell explained, "and my competitor has 80, and Intel comes out with a new 450-megahertz chip, that means I am going to get to market 69 days sooner."[220]

Recommitting to Direct Sales

In 1990, Dell executives made another decision that turned out to be a serious mistake. They decided to begin selling PCs in traditional retail outlets. This was a controversial choice within a business that had been founded partly on Michael Dell's skepticism regarding third-party dealers and their role in the PC market. Echoing Dell's own earlier thoughts, some managers expressed concern about mass merchandisers' abilities to deliver the service and support that many consumers had come to associate with the Dell brand. Others worried that the company would have to either raise prices or watch its profit margins shrink since retailers would add their own markups.

The senior management team weighed these potential risks against the possibility of reaching new consumer segments such as small office and household users, and thus expanding the overall demand for Dell products. In particular, they also hoped to capitalize on the recent growth in PC sales through discount retailers and superstores. In 1987, for example, PCs had generated $600 million in sales at stores such as Sam's Clubs and PriceClub; by 1990, these sales had climbed to $1.6 billion.[221] Dell executives thereupon decided that they could not afford to ignore these opportunities for growth, and they signed an agreement with CompUSA for the retailer to sell Dell PCs and peripheral equipment. In the next two years, Dell products also became available in Staples stores and PriceClub warehouse outlets. The company's PCs sold well in these retailers, helping fuel record increases in gross revenues, which climbed from $546 million in fiscal 1991 to more than $2 billion in 1993.[222]

Yet, as Michael Dell and his colleagues came to realize, selling in the traditional retail channel was not very profitable for the company. Dealers' markups, the return of unsold products, plus the administrative costs of dealing with middlemen all reduced the income Dell earned. Equally important, Dell had no direct line of communication with buyers who purchased PCs through retailers, and this prevented the manufacturer from gathering market intelligence about consumers' priorities and user feedback about product performance. Company executives became increasingly concerned that they were diluting the firm's brand equity by relying on salespeople and technicians whom it did not hire, train, or manage.

In late 1993, the company stopped distributing its products through mass merchandisers and superstores. Inside and outside the organization, the company was criticized for strategic vacillation. Some industry analysts and journalists expressed skepticism about the company's future prospects.[223] It could not have been easy for Michael Dell to listen to these assessments and harder still for him to reverse course. At age twenty-eight, his track record in understanding consumer wants and needs and how to meet them had been a stream of virtually uninterrupted successes. Yet here, he and his top executives had miscalculated.

Fortunately, however, Dell again proved to be a fast learner. In the aftermath of withdrawing from the traditional retail channel, his appreciation of the company's direct sales model deepened. During the mid-1990s, he and his colleagues dedicated the organization to building and maintaining strong, unmediated connections with consumers. They also began exploring new ways to broaden the company's customer base without resorting to third parties.

One such avenue involved distributing products directly to end users over the Internet. In the early 1990s, Dell had been attracted to the possibilities of reaching consumers this way, envisioning such communication as a powerful extension of the company's direct model. In 1995, he put together a small team of managers to begin exploring how Dell Computer might use the Internet to connect with customers, deliver information, and sell products.[224] Impressed with the growth of Internet access—especially among business users—in the United States, its potential synergies with Dell's existing customer relationships, and the projected increase in electronic commerce, Dell team members began planning an on-line technical interface and retail store in late 1995.[225]

In 1996, Dell Computer launched its Web site, www.dell.com. Financial analysts and journalists applauded the initiative, pointing to the advantages that Dell enjoyed in selling over the Internet relative to PC makers with third-party distribution networks. "Dell has been positioned for something like this since its beginning," noted one industry observer. "They can migrate what they do in the real world to the Web easily without upsetting any of these existing sales channels."[226] In its first four years, Dell's on-line initiative proved very successful, helping the company better understand user priorities and further customize service and product support offerings to them. The Web site quickly became a dynamic marketplace; by the early twenty-first century, company sales through its Web site averaged more than $40 million a day.[227]

As the speed of business and intensity of competition increased in the Information Revolution, Dell's commitment to using the Internet to build stronger connections with customers and suppliers was applauded by business leaders from different industries. So, too, were the company's inventory management practices. Less scrutinized was the relationship between Dell's direct model as it evolved in the late 1990s and earlier entrepreneurial learning. Michael Dell and his colleagues' ability to understand the causes of one-time stumbles, rectify them, and institutionalize this understanding in new organizational practices proved critical to the ongoing success of the direct model.

Conclusion

By the beginning of the twenty-first century, Dell Computer's yearly sales exceeded $25 billion. Measured by annual revenues, Dell was the second largest PC-systems company in the world. Its PC sales exceeded those of Apple and IBM, two of the industry's early leaders.[228] Many industry observers credited Dell's success to a range of supply-side initiatives: rigorous quality control, lean inventories, close relationships with suppliers, and efficient cash-flow management. Michael Dell had long recognized that producing quality goods at reasonable prices was essential to competing effectively in the Information Revolution.

But Dell also realized that such success depended on more than well-organized manufacturing. Sustained business achievement also rested on some critical demand-side capabilities. Since 1984, he had worked to understand what consumers wanted and needed in IT products. He used this understanding to build strong connections with consumers, a powerful brand and business model, and the organizational capabilities to support these vital resources.

CHAPTER 8

Historical Forces and Entrepreneurial Agency

This book is a work of history. It examines six individuals, the products and organizations they created, and the wider industrial and economic contexts in which they worked. The book spans three centuries and two countries. It contains lots of information about people, businesses, social developments, and macroeconomic conditions. Some details are directly relevant to the book's general arguments. Others relate to the environment in which a specific entrepreneur lived and worked. In this last chapter, I want to speak to some of the overarching historical themes that emerge from the six narrative chapters.

History is obviously a record of broad, sweeping forces: technological breakthroughs, mass migrations, wars, social needs, and so forth. But history also has a strong biographical component. It is a record of individual effort—of personal aspiration, success, and failure. This chapter traces first the sweeping historical forces and then the specifics of entrepreneurial *agency* (that is, individual choices and behavior) as they emerged in the careers of the six businesspeople analyzed. Taken together, these concluding thoughts underscore the broad significance of the dynamic interplay between historical forces and individual human agency and—equally important for my own argument in this book—the complex relationships between entrepreneurs and consumers.

Historical Forces

As is apparent in each of the six narrative chapters, accelerating economic change presented unusual opportunities for entrepreneurs to create new products and sell them in growing markets.

Since the onset of industrialization in the late eighteenth century, periods of rapid transition have affected both the supply and demand sides of national economies. The main sources of these changes were the following: greater productivity, population and urban growth, improved transportation and communication, and people's changing social and psychic needs.

Greater Productivity

During the three historical settings emphasized in this book—the Industrial Revolution, the Transportation and Communication Revolution, and the post–World War II era—the acceleration of technological change drove improvements in manufacturing, information exchange, and organizational capabilities. Productivity (that is, output as a proportion of hours worked and capital employed) increased significantly, almost across the board.

In eighteenth-century Britain, for example, technological change and other developments increased the productive capacity of both traditional industries and newer ones.[1] Agricultural output expanded quickly in the early 1700s. Output in commerce and manufacturing sectors also grew swiftly, climbing at a compound annual rate of 0.7 percent each year before 1760, then accelerating to annual growth rates of more than 1 percent for about 20 years, and quickening still again after 1780.[2] By the standards of that time, this was indeed rapid expansion. It was this context in which Josiah Wedgwood built his business.

The annual output of Staffordshire potteries as a whole rose by 1,400 percent between 1710 and 1760, and unit costs declined steadily.[3] On a broader level, technological innovation and other productivity improvements centering around canals and steam engines helped change the economic landscape of eighteenth-century and early-nineteenth-century Britain. The expansion was widespread, affecting a range of industries including coal mining, iron production, and eventually cotton textiles, and it continued for decades. These powerful forces increased the relative importance of industry and commerce as sources of output, income, and employment, in comparison to the long-standing dominance of agriculture. In 1700, farming had accounted for about 40 percent of national income, and industry and commerce about a third (the remainder was in transportation, construction, and especially in services of various kinds:

government, defense, and the upkeep of households). By 1800, these proportions were reversed: agriculture amounted to less than 30 percent of national income, industry and commerce composed 45 percent.[4]

More than a hundred years later, something remarkably similar in the statistical sense happened in the United States. Communications and transportation improvements, especially the telegraph and a burgeoning national rail system, transformed the national economy. In 1869, more than half of all goods produced in the United States were agricultural. About a third were manufactures, and the remaining fraction were products of mining and construction. But thirty years later, at the dawn of the twentieth century, more than half of the American economy's output was industrial. Farming products made up only 33 percent of commodity output.[5]

Widespread industrialization brought accelerated economic growth. From 1870 until the beginning of World War I in 1914, real gross national product (GNP) in the United States increased at a compound annual rate of 4 percent; on a per capita basis, it grew at an average rate of 2.2 percent.[6] This was the most dramatic and sustained expansion that the U.S. economy had ever experienced, and its effects stretched far and wide. One of the most visible results was the mass production and distribution of countless new goods: packaged meat, safety razors, sewing machines, bottled pickles, early models of automobiles, and much more. Some of the same technological and organizational improvements that created new things also helped make *established* products—such as revolvers, buckets, corsets, gloves, and locks—sturdier, less expensive, and more easily obtainable.[7] Much of this output was produced for huge new markets, many of them national in scope. This was the setting for the business successes of Henry Heinz and Marshall Field.

Still later, in the twenty-five years following World War II and in the last decade of the twentieth century, the U.S. economy again expanded very swiftly, fueled by emerging high-tech industries such as electronics, aircraft, chemicals, and computers. Between 1945 and 1970, real GNP in the United States more than doubled.[8] Although overall economic growth slowed considerably in the mid-1970s, it accelerated once more in the 1990s, growing by more than 35 percent in real terms during that decade.[9] Many of the goods and services that the U.S. produced in the late twentieth century, including antibiotics, microprocessors, personal computers (PCs), franchised fast food, and consulting services, were sold in huge national and international markets. Estée Lauder, Howard Schultz, and Michael Dell created their business successes during these times.

Population and Urban Growth

The sheer growth in the number of potential customers enlarged the markets that each of the six entrepreneurs confronted. The relationships among economic expansion, population growth, urbanization, and other demographic shifts in a given period are complex, of course, and scholars have often found it difficult to unravel the precise connections among them.[10] The six entrepreneurs analyzed here were not necessarily interested in understanding the *exact* relations among productivity improvements, population growth, and the size of emerging urban markets. Each, however, could see clearly that he or she was living through a moment when the absolute number of consumers was rising, especially in urban areas. Each well understood the rare opportunity that these changes represented.

Between 1680 and 1820, for example, the English population grew much faster than it had done in earlier periods. It more than doubled during the eighteenth century alone, climbing from 4.9 million people to 11.5 million. Much of this increase came in the late 1700s and continued on into the early nineteenth century.[11] As the population climbed and the pace of economic development quickened, urbanization leapt forward.[12] London, the nation's political, financial, and fashion capital, became one of the largest cities in the world, its population rising by 66 percent—from 575,000 in 1700 to 960,000 in 1801. Birmingham, a regional center for metalware manufacturing, and Manchester, a hub of textile production, each experienced population growth of more than 800 percent during the eighteenth century.[13] Thus, as Josiah Wedgwood's pottery works grew, so too did his potential national markets and—especially toward the end of the century—his international markets as well.

The United States experienced even more powerful demographic changes. In 1800, about 5.3 million people lived in the United States. In 1840, about 17 million did; by 1900, the U.S. population was more than 76 million.[14] New York, Cincinnati, Milwaukee, Henry Heinz's Pittsburgh, and many other cities grew very fast, buoyed by immigration and relentless industrialization. The number of people living in Marshall Field's Chicago climbed by more than 1,700 percent between 1856 and 1900.[15] This was an extraordinary rate of urban expansion, and it was hardly limited to

Chicago. In 1840, only 11 percent of the U.S. population had lived in towns of 2,500 or more.[16] The overwhelming majority of Americans lived in the country—often far removed from industry, commerce, rapid information flows, and each other. But six decades later—in 1900—40 percent of the nation's men, women, and children lived in urban areas. Here they encountered people, goods, and a range of personal opportunities previously unknown to them.

Population growth and urban concentration also helped expand markets in the twentieth century, particularly after 1945. In the three decades following World War II, the U.S. population swelled by 50 percent.[17] Much of this increase was fueled by a sharp surge in birthrates that began in 1945 and continued through the early 1960s, creating the postwar "baby boom."

As the nation's population and economy expanded during the postwar period, certain regions and cities grew at especially rapid rates. World War II had stimulated the growth of some southern and West Coast port cities, such as Norfolk, Charleston, San Diego, and greater Los Angeles, as well as other parts of the Sunbelt. The commercialization of air conditioning, the construction of the interstate highway system, and the emergence of high-tech industries such as aerospace and electronics, accelerated this development. California, Florida, Texas, and other Sunbelt states boomed. The population of California increased by more than 500 percent in the sixty years after 1940, climbing to 33 million people by the end of the century. The number of people living in Florida increased even faster, by a factor of eight.[18] Cities such as Austin, Seattle, and Miami rose to new prominence. In 1940, for example, about 88,000 people lived in Austin; at the end of the twentieth century, more than 550,000 did.[19]

The seventy-eight million "baby boomers" born in the United States between 1945 and 1964 were generally better educated and more affluent than preceding generations of Americans, and collectively they possessed tremendous purchasing power. Their tastes, incomes, and interest in using consumption as a means of self-expression did not escape the attention of Estée Lauder, Howard Schultz, and Michael Dell.[20]

Improved Transportation and Communication

In eighteenth-century Britain, as in the United States in the late nineteenth and entire twentieth centuries, transportation and communication became much better, faster, and more efficient. Driven by technological innovation as well as by public and private investment, improvements in each of the three eras described in this book allowed entrepreneurs to reach many more consumers than had previously been possible.

In 1751, a journalist described some of England's primitive roads as being "what God left them after the Flood."[21] But beginning at just this time, a series of local and parliamentary acts underwrote hundreds of miles of new turnpikes and the improvement of existing roads. Upgraded transportation, in turn, promoted interregional and national distribution of goods. It became possible for Josiah Wedgwood and other British merchants and manufacturers to move goods to market towns and cities *year-round.* "As to new markets at home," the political economist Josiah Tucker noted in 1758, "every Road well mended produces that Effect in one Degree or other."[22] The pace of trade quickened as linkages between traders and commercial centers became more efficient.[23]

Water transportation in Britain also improved, especially as canal building accelerated after 1760. During the last four decades of the century, this construction added more than a thousand miles of navigable waterways, radically lowering the cost and increasing the speed of transportation for industrial goods and raw materials such as coal.[24] These new efficiencies expanded the volume and geographic scope of potential markets and helped render the country "still more affluent, populous, and secure," as Wedgwood's partner Thomas Bentley put it in 1766.[25] By 1770, teapots and snuffboxes made in the British midlands were being advertised not only in London, Birmingham, and Bath, but also in New York and Philadelphia.[26]

In the nineteenth century, the United States experienced even more dramatic improvements in transportation and communication. These developments touched nearly all types of economic activity—from farming to financial innovation to mining to steel manufacturing. At their core lay the railroad and the telegraph, both of which mushroomed after the Civil War. In 1850, there were 9,000 miles of railroad track in operation. By 1890, this figure had climbed to more than 208,000 miles.[27] The new railroads allowed people, livestock, and goods to travel quickly and cheaply across states, regions, and—after 1869, when the first transcontinental link was completed—the entire country. Henry Heinz, like many other American entrepreneurs, understood how important railroads were in creating a huge market for processed food. He wasted no time in expanding his customer base in areas where new lines were being constructed.

As the railroad revolutionized transportation, so the telegraph and telephone transformed communication. By moving information almost instantaneously across millions of miles of wire, the telegraph tied people and organizations more closely together, thus laying the foundations for a brand new *national* economy. The telephone, which was patented in 1876, accelerated this process. By 1914, more than 10 million telephones were in operation, and calls averaged more than 40 million per day.[28] Marshall Field recognized that such advances in communication and transportation allowed him to buy and sell goods on a scale far larger than urban retailers had been able to do in earlier decades.

Next came the automobile, which made shopping much easier and thereby expanded consumers' opportunities (and entrepreneurs' initiatives) in still other ways. The first cars were built in Europe in the 1880s and 1890s. But it was not until 1908, when Henry Ford introduced the Model T, that the automobile came within the financial reach of middle-class Americans. During the next twenty years, production soared, prices fell, and the mass market for cars was born. In 1910, fewer than half a million families owned an automobile. By 1920, more than eight million did, and by 1930, nineteen million. At the time, there was one car for every 5.3 people in the United States. In France and Great Britain, by contrast, the ratio was one car per forty-four people.[29] The automobile, like the railroad before it, obviously had tremendous social and economic consequences. It decreased the isolation of rural families, helped create the suburbs and commuting, and provided the foundation for a range of new service businesses from supermarkets to shopping centers to amusement parks.

Other improvements in transportation also expanded markets. In the three decades after World War II, a major road-building program—notably the construction of the Interstate Highway System—added more than 500,000 miles of federal roads to the nation's infrastructure, many of them four- and six-lane freeways.[30] By 1970, almost 900,000 miles of federal highways crisscrossed America, allowing people and goods to move faster and more efficiently.

The rapid proliferation of air travel in the postwar period also helped build new outlets for goods and services and expand existing ones. With the advent of jet airliners after World War II, Americans took to the skies in growing numbers. In 1940, U.S. airlines had carried 3.2 million passengers. In 1960, they carried almost 58 million, and in 1980, almost 297 million. As ticket prices fell in the 1980s, following deregulation of the industry, still larger numbers began flying across the country and—by the last decade of the twentieth century—the world. In 1998, U.S. airlines carried 614 million passengers.[31] The accelerating geographic mobility of Americans via both cars and airplanes—and their exposure to new cultures and tastes—was part of the opportunity that Howard Schultz saw for spreading the word about Starbucks premium coffee and other products.

Communication and information technology also advanced markedly during and after World War II. Perhaps the two most influential innovations were the television and the computer. In 1940, there had been almost no TV stations. In 1950, there were 100, and by 1970, 680. This proliferation continued in the last decades of the century, intensified by the explosion of cable TV after 1980. By the end of the twentieth century, hundreds of stations and cable systems were broadcasting news, sports, movies, soap operas, situation comedies or "sitcoms," music videos, and—above all—advertising around the clock.[32]

Television ownership kept pace with the growth of stations and programming. In 1945, less than 0.1 percent of all U.S. households owned a television set. By 1970, 95 percent did, and by 1997, 98 percent.[33] More than any other innovation in the twentieth century, television influenced Americans' material expectations, exposing them to an endless variety of products, people, and lifestyles and creating fresh conceptions of what constituted "the good life." As consumers began to take many of their fashion cues from TV in the 1950s and 1960s, a new breed of entrepreneurs (exemplified by Estée Lauder, among others) worked to extend their product lines and expand their markets.

In the last quarter of the twentieth century, the development of the PC and the Internet proceeded to revolutionize communication, much as the telegraph and telephone had done in the nineteenth century. Modern mainframe computers such as the UNIVAC (which was about the size of an automobile) were first used in business during the early 1950s. But it took twenty-five years and a series of technological breakthroughs before the first PC was introduced in 1975. The young industry grew rapidly in the late 1970s as start-ups such as Apple Computer and larger, established companies, including Texas Instruments and Tandy Radio Shack, began manufacturing PCs.

By 1981, U.S. shipments of personal computers had reached 760,000.[34] In that same year, mighty IBM's introduction of its own PC broke open the mass market, and by 1985 U.S. shipments exceeded 6 million machines. Ten years later, in 1995, U.S. shipments totaled 20 million, and the PC had become standard operating equipment in most businesses—largely replacing the typewriter, calculator, paper spreadsheet, and mainframe computer terminal.[35] Although the PC market had developed principally through sales to industrial customers, growing numbers of consumers at the end of the twentieth century viewed the functions of the personal computer as essential in their everyday lives. In the year 2000, about 50 million American households owned a PC.[36]

From his adolescence during the 1970s, Michael Dell (and many other young entrepreneurs) had sensed that the PC had the potential to revolutionize business and consumer markets. As the PC market evolved, Dell worked to position his company as close to the center of these developing markets as possible. He saw in particular the possibilities of what came to be called "mass customization."

One of the most important changes of all, of course, was the growth of the Internet, which transformed the way business could be done. The Internet originated in the 1960s context of the Cold War when the Department of Defense had set up networks of mainframe computers to facilitate cooperation among scientists in the government and at universities. By the 1980s, scientists and researchers had begun accessing the increasing number of these networks from their PCs, using them to exchange ideas and organize "bulletin boards."[37] By 1990, several commercial service providers were supplying business and individual PC users with access to thousands of linked networks.

The diffusion of personal computers and the development of the World Wide Web made possible the flowering of the Internet, which became a uniquely powerful medium of communication. Beginning in 1993, Internet connections, usage, and content spread like wildfire, creating a cheap, instantaneous means of sending data, images, and sounds around the world. As the railroad and telegraph had created an infrastructure that facilitated the emergence of a national market and big business in the late nineteenth century, the Internet created a new infrastructure that gave rise to novel outlets and companies one hundred years later. For Michael

Dell—as well as many other information-technology entrepreneurs and organizations of all kinds—the emerging possibilities seemed endless, though difficult to predict.

People's Changing Social and Psychic Needs

Far-reaching economic growth, including huge increases in the quantity and variety of goods available, offered many new opportunities for consumers but imposed some significant dilemmas as well.

One set of both opportunities and dilemmas came through the proliferation of choices. During each of the three periods discussed in this book—the Industrial Revolution, the Transportation and Communications Revolution, and the post–World War II era—the choices confronting consumers mushroomed. People were exposed to vast new arrays of goods: in eighteenth-century Britain, to tea sets, clocks, brooches, curtains, books, and fine china; in nineteenth-century America, to ready-made clothing, processed meats, canned vegetables, and experiential shopping in department stores; toward the close of the twentieth century, to elegant skin creams, organic vegetables, specialty coffee shops, PCs, and the Internet. Some of these products and services, such as fine china and cosmetics, had existed for many decades but had been available only to the wealthy. Others really were brand new, such as canned baked beans during the late 1800s, department stores in the closing decades of the nineteenth century, and personal computers in the 1980s.

How could prospective buyers reduce the uncertainty and risk they faced in purchasing these novel or unfamiliar goods? How were potential customers to gather relevant knowledge about novel goods and services? How were shoppers to distinguish one maker's wares from those of another? By what criteria should they evaluate them?[38]

Consumers themselves played crucial roles in the evolution of new product markets. In millions of transactions annually, they embraced some products while rejecting a much larger number of others. Their daily experience with specific offerings shaped their attitudes toward a particular good, brand, and organization. Many purchasers expressed their thoughts to salespeople, entrepreneurs, and other company representatives. For each of the six entrepreneurs analyzed here, this ongoing communication was critical in helping understand and anticipate consumers' needs in young, changing markets.

Intensified socioeconomic change also raised thorny questions surrounding social and personal identity. How were men and women living amid rapid socioeconomic transition to make sense of its deep effects on their lives? What did the accelerating pace of economic life, shifting employment patterns, and the visible acquisition of unprecedented new wealth mean for contemporaries trying to understand their place in the social order? In increasingly mobile societies undergoing substantial change, to which emerging groups and subcultures did these consumers and their families belong? To whom, in such moments, was a person or group obligated—and exactly for what?

These problems were not, of course, entirely new to the Industrial Revolution, the Transportation and Communication Revolution, or the post–World War II economy. Status issues and questions of reciprocal responsibilities have plagued most societies.[39] What was novel about these concerns during the three periods covered in this book was their growing urgency among larger and larger numbers of people. As a British politician put it toward the close of the eighteenth century, "Everyone is flying from his inferiors, in pursuit of his superiors who fly from Him with equal alacrity."[40] Many late eighteenth-century Britons, like their counterparts in Marshall Field's Chicago a century later or in Howard Schultz's Seattle at the beginning of the twenty-first century, puzzled over their evolving social positions in a rapidly changing economic setting.

Among other means of adjustment available to them, consumers used their purchasing power to address the problems that accompanied accelerating social mobility. They tended to place their money where they felt their most pressing needs.[41] They selected goods and services that fed their aspirations—that bought them time or a feeling of at least some control over their lives—and helped them express their individual and collective identities.

Each of the entrepreneurs analyzed in this book understood a great deal about which kinds of priorities mattered most to consumers' lives at particular historical conjunctures. In one way or other, Josiah Wedgwood, Henry Heinz, Marshall Field, Estée Lauder, Howard Schultz, and Michael Dell created products and connections to buyers that offered not only quality, convenience, and reliability but also a powerful sense of self-expression, fashion, status, community, and control.[42]

Entrepreneurial Agency—What They Did and How They Did It

Many Were Called, Few Were Chosen

The six entrepreneurs analyzed in this book were not, of course, the only businesspeople to try to attract consumer interest, develop strong brands, and make markets for new offerings during moments of intensified socioeconomic change. Each of the six worked in a young industry characterized—at least, initially—by a large number of entrepreneurial players competing for customers and strategic advantage. Yet most of these other players failed. In Staffordshire, for example, the center of Britain's earthenware industry in the 1750s, more than 130 potteries competed, one of which was Josiah Wedgwood's. Many of these other firms did not survive the eighteenth century. Few, if any, pursued the full range of initiatives necessary to compete successfully with Wedgwood. As we have seen, these initiatives included communicating effectively with consumers, exploiting supply-side innovations, and constructing organizational capabilities in a changing economy.

In the 1860s, across the Atlantic in Maryland, the center of the U.S. canning business, something similar happened. Over thirty entrepreneurs vied, along with Henry Heinz, to create a regional market for processed produce.[43] Yet few of their firms survived the nineteenth century, and none came close to matching the success of the H. J. Heinz Company.

In Chicago at about the same time, Marshall Field confronted fierce competition in the distribution of dry goods. In the 1860s, scores of wholesalers in the city battled for the growing trade of midwestern retailers. In 1866, more than fifty of these wholesale companies had annual sales of more than $1 million. About thirty other large players in St. Louis and Cincinnati also competed with Field, as did big wholesalers from New York.[44] Field's company also faced rivals in the retail business. A few of Chicago's department stores, such as Carson Pirie Scott, prospered well into the twentieth century along with Marshall Field. But most local retailers, even some of the big ones (such as A. T. Stewart, which opened a Chicago store in 1876), failed in their first decade. None succeeded in matching the size, elegance, and sheer regional strength of Marshall Field.

Estée Lauder's company went through a similar competitive crucible. In the decade after World War II, at least 500 cosmetics companies marketed beauty products to American consumers.[45] Most of these firms were small manufacturers selling in local or regional markets. Several companies, such as Avon, Helena Rubinstein, Elizabeth Arden, Revlon, Helene Curtis, and Mary Kay became multimillion-dollar organizations with nationally known brands. In the 1940s and 1950s, a few of these players—Helena Rubinstein, Elizabeth Arden—offered prestige cosmetics in company-owned salons. But none pursued as distinctive a strategy as Estée Lauder's, based on upscale department-store distribution, complimentary make-overs, free samples, and the development of a brand specifically designed to communicate a sense of worldly sophistication. By the late 1960s, Estée Lauder was one of the most successful cosmetics companies in the United States. At the beginning of the twenty-first century, it was one of the leading players in the industry worldwide.

In the coffee business during the 1980s and 1990s, hundreds of regional roasters and other distributors tried to attract consumer interest in specialty coffees.[46] Some of these companies, such as Gloria Jean's, Barnie's, and Timothy's, expanded rapidly, working to build a national presence in the young market. But Howard Schultz and Starbucks outperformed them all. No other specialty coffee provider developed such a strategically effective connection to consumers—through high-quality products, a strong brand, and an appealing in-store "experience."

Analogously, a wide assortment of start-up and established companies began to manufacture PCs in the late 1970s and early 1980s. Some, like Apple and Compaq, quickly became major players in the industry. A few of the large manufacturers—most notably IBM—also enjoyed early success. But most of the companies that had led the sector in its first decade, including Atari, Commodore, and Kaypro, failed. Virtually none committed the resources that Michael Dell and his young business did to understanding what consumers needed and wanted from personal computers. At the beginning of the twenty-first century, Dell Computer was one of the three biggest PC manufacturers in the world and, in the view of many analysts, the one with the most savvy in marketing.

Elements of Entrepreneurial Success

Building markets, companies, and credible identities for new products based on evolving consumer wants was costly for each of the six entrepreneurs. So, too, was communicating the benefits of a new good or service to a group of target customers. Generally speaking, each of the six was willing to spend more time, energy, and money on brand creation, quality control, employee training, and innovative sales and distribution methods—initiatives that enhanced the reputations of their companies and helped earn consumers' trust. Many of the people and firms that competed with the six entrepreneurs analyzed here simply did not make comparable investments.

The individuals in this study, therefore, have hardly been "representative" of their particular sectors or lines of business. Each seemed to sense that he or she was living through a period of extraordinary opportunity, when windows were open and market leadership up for grabs. Each intended to make the most of the moment to construct a name, brand, and organization that would endure, and each succeeded brilliantly, in substantial measure, for the following five reasons:

- They had deep knowledge and personal experience of their product or service.
- They learned quickly from their mistakes and made rapid adjustments.
- They created meaningful brands that distinguished their offerings and responded to consumers' changing priorities.
- They initiated a process of reciprocal learning with their customers that resulted from ongoing two-way communication with them.
- They created a range of organizational capabilities that delivered on the promises of their respective brands.

Close, Hands-on Familiarity. Each of the six knew an extraordinary amount about the goods and services he or she was offering. Josiah Wedgwood started as a potter at the age of nine. Henry Heinz gardened and bottled horseradish as an adolescent. Marshall Field had his initial experience as a clerk in a dry goods store when he was seventeen. Estée Lauder, beginning at the age of sixteen, spent more than two decades mixing and selling skin care formulas before she undertook to build a national market for her products. Howard Schultz did not grow up drinking specialty coffee, but as soon as he was introduced to the business (he was twenty-nine at the time), he learned as much about it as he could. He even trained for months to learn how to roast beans—becoming one of only nineteen people in Starbucks first two decades as a company to be judged qualified to do so.

Michael Dell as a teenager amused himself by taking complex computers apart, repairing or upgrading them, then putting them back together.

This detailed personal knowledge yielded numerous secondary benefits. For one thing, it allowed each of the six to respond quickly and wisely to consumer input. In some instances, such as Marshall Field's decision to establish a travel agency in the State Street store, this understanding led to honoring customers' requests at little additional cost. In other cases, intimate knowledge of the business provided the basis for *not* granting certain requests, even if they seemed reasonable. Howard Schultz, for example, consistently refused to sell flavored coffee beans. He believed that the chemicals added to these beans would compromise the flavor and quality of the coffee and ultimately the Starbucks brand image.

Learning from Mistakes. In the early stages of any market's development, both the exact nature of the product and its position in the market are usually unresolved. In these circumstances, it is often difficult for an entrepreneur to figure out how to expand buyer interest in a new offering, enhance its identity, and stay in business while the market shakes out.

The six entrepreneurs analyzed here made mistakes, but each learned quickly from experience and made rapid adjustments. In 1769, for example, Josiah Wedgwood tried to increase vase production to meet an unexpected surge in demand. The firm's ensuing cash-flow crisis caused him to initiate a complete analysis of manufacturing expenses and to redirect his firm's production and marketing away from made-to-order sales. The crisis also motivated Wedgwood to learn much more about the vital difference in business between fixed and variable costs.

In 1875, Henry Heinz overreached himself to an even greater degree than Wedgwood had done. In the midst of a national depression, Heinz committed scarce financial resources to purchasing all the cucumbers and cabbages to be grown by a particular Illinois supplier. When a record harvest came in from the supplier, Heinz's purchasing costs unexpectedly soared, depleting the last of his firm's financial resources. Soon, both his business and he himself were bankrupt. Penniless and consumed with shame, Heinz blamed his former partners for not taking more responsibility for the company's fortunes. But he had the good sense to blame himself as well. And when he started over in 1876, it was with an enhanced awareness of the importance of managing future supply contracts, understanding cash outflows more precisely, and partnering only with people whom he trusted completely, which ultimately meant going into business for himself.

Marshall Field, too, grew disillusioned with some of his early colleagues. In 1879, he and partner Levi Leiter nearly lost a prime retail building on Washington and State Streets in downtown Chicago to a competing department store. To secure the building, Field and Leiter were forced to pay a much higher price than they had originally bargained for. Each of the two partners blamed the other for negotiating badly and causing the firm needless expense. Anxious to avoid similar mistakes in the future, Field resolved to increase his own control over the company. In 1881, with the agreement of his junior partners, he effectively forced Leiter to resign from the firm. During the next thirty-five years, Field himself continued to recruit new talent and to promote promising managers from within both the wholesale and retail operations. He maintained a tight rein on the terms and tenure of all partnerships, making sure no other person's ownership stake rivaled his own.

In 1965, Estée Lauder's company introduced Aramis, a new brand of toiletries for men. The initial line consisted of three similar products: fragrance, cologne, and an aftershave lotion. All were packaged in brown paper with a blue stripe. None sold well. For the first time in the company's history, it had misjudged the market. But Estée herself continued to believe that the underlying concept was sound. Male consumers, she reasoned, wanted high-quality toiletries just as female ones did. But perhaps they wanted more than scent and shaving products. In 1967, therefore, she, Joe, Leonard, and their colleagues relaunched Aramis as a complete line of skin care treatment products for men, including fragrances, moisturizers, hand cream, and even a deep-cleaning facial masque—all wrapped in tortoiseshell and gold packaging. Supported by an elaborate advertising campaign, the revamped Aramis line succeeded in helping create a major new market for men's prestige toiletries. Estée had remembered a lesson she had learned long before: the importance of offering a broad line of related items in elegant, distinctive packaging, and of introducing new products with fanfare and targeted advertising. In the future, she used these insights repeatedly in launching new lines of fragrances, such as Beautiful, and other products.

Howard Schultz also sometimes miscalculated the demand for his products. In mid-1995, Starbucks managers ordered a large assortment of coffee mugs, chocolates, and coffee gift sets in preparation for the upcoming Christmas season. By late fall, inventory levels were satisfyingly high, and so, too, were investor expectations regarding the company's sales performance. The previous year's holiday season had been a very successful one, and stock market analysts expected even better performance in 1995. But it soon became apparent that the rate of Christmas sales at most Starbucks stores was slowing down and that the company might not meet its quarterly financial targets.

Schultz knew that his business was not the only one suffering from lackluster consumer demand in 1995. Winter storms across much of the country were keeping shoppers at home. But he was determined to do as much as possible to improve Starbucks' sales in the short term while at the same time working to prevent similar problems in the future. He succeeded in doing both. Schultz, Orin Smith, and the rest of the senior management team tracked daily sales carefully and offered in-store promotions—serving free coffee after five in the afternoon. Meanwhile, they undertook a thorough review of the company's planning processes, noting where demand forecasts had erred and analyzing why. Schultz also intensified the organization's research and development initiatives in an effort to find new products and categories that would appeal to consumers' changing priorities.

In 1989, Dell Computer, buoyed by several years of skyrocketing sales and income growth, invested heavily in component inventories. Management placed especially heavy orders for memory chips. Not long after Michael Dell and his colleagues made this decision, the market demand for PCs suddenly dipped, pushing down the prices Dell and its competitors could charge. At the same time, memory-chip capacity within the industry surged ahead—from 256K to 1 megabyte. Dell Computer was stuck with a large inventory of chips that were rapidly becoming obsolete. Forced to dispose of these excess components at relatively low prices, the firm saw its sales and income growth slow considerably. As a result of this setback, Dell and his team undertook a thorough review of their company's inventory management, significantly improving the speed with which inputs moved into and out of its assembly plants. The company also increased its capabilities in the tricky art of demand forecasting. Partly as a result of learning from this major mistake, Dell Computer was the industry leader in inventory management by the start of the twenty-first century.

Meaningful Brands. Wedgwood, Heinz, and Field did not use the terms "brand creation" or "brand management." These did not enter business parlance until the twentieth century. Yet each of the three earlier entrepreneurs—like Lauder, Schultz, and Dell who came after them—recognized that building a distinct, appealing, and credible identity for their products was a strategic imperative. All six understood that developing and maintaining such an identity required constant and highly focused attention to both consumers' preferences and competitors' behavior.

Wedgwood, for example, realized how important status and novelty were in eighteenth-century markets for china. He took great care to associate his brand with contemporary aristocratic "legislators of taste."[47] He understood that new goods acquired by the aristocracy became appealing to middling Britons and he exploited this process. For thousands of households, buying and owning products with aristocratic associations were at least partial solutions to subtle psychological questions about social place. Possession of even one or two pieces bearing the Wedgwood *brand* seemed to make people feel better about themselves.

A hundred years later, Henry Heinz recognized a different kind of material and psychological need. He saw that nineteenth-century women, especially those living in cities without access to a family garden, might welcome food products that saved them time and energy. But, he reasoned, they would buy from a commercial producer only if they were convinced that the new processed foodstuffs were as tasty and healthy as those they could can and preserve themselves. From his earliest days selling bottled horseradish, Heinz therefore emphasized the *cleanliness* of his company's manufacturing methods and the *purity* of its products. By the turn of the century, his brand was closely connected in consumers' minds with "Pure Food for the Table." Partly because of this ingenious marketing, branded Heinz ketchup, pickles, and other goods replaced those once made in millions of homes.[48]

Similarly, Marshall Field suspected that many women and men in Chicago and other young midwestern cities wanted stylish goods—products that expressed their taste and social position. Toward this end, Field, Levi Leiter, and Harry Selfridge crafted a reputation for selling high-quality, dignified, and fashionable merchandise. Many of Chicago's wealthiest women became regular customers of Field's, buying scores of items from clothing to household furnishings to toys. Meanwhile, the broader ranks of the city's consumers in the late 1800s generally could not afford to do all their shopping at Marshall Field's. But many viewed the store's merchandise as symbols of social achievement and therefore did go to Field's for special-occasion purchases—a confirmation suit, a wedding gift. As these consumers moved up the social and economic ladder, their patronage became more regular and their purchases more numerous. Field's as a store had become a brand in itself.

In the late 1940s and early 1950s, Estée Lauder addressed a distinct set of consumer priorities. She saw that in the postwar U.S. economy both household incomes and female employment were on the rise. She reasoned that whether or not women worked outside the home, they were becoming much more important economic actors. They had more resources, more choices regarding their lives, and greater possibilities for individual self-expression than most women had possessed only a few decades earlier. Within their means, women were increasingly using consumption to deal with a range of issues that flowed from changes in their social position and sense of personal identity. Recognizing this, Lauder created a line of prestige cosmetics and a powerful *brand.* Working tirelessly, she shrewdly managed to associate her brand with elegance, control, and self-definition for her customers.

In the 1980s, Howard Schultz saw that "baby boomers" and other American consumers were becoming more and more interested in food and drink that they perceived to be more "natural" and of higher quality than most processed goods. Schultz also realized that many Americans wanted affordable luxuries—specialty coffee drinks, fine cigars, membership at a fitness club—that they could "experience" more frequently than an annual vacation or some other big-ticket purchase. These small indulgences, as Schultz appreciated, represented in consumers' minds more than an opportunity to enjoy high-quality products; they also served as a means of self-expression, a way for buyers to assert and exhibit their tastes, knowledge, and aspirations. Sensing that many Americans wanted a broader sense of community than that available at home or work, Schultz and his colleagues crafted the Starbucks brand to represent not just premium coffee, but also an upscale café, an inviting meeting place.

Working in Austin at about the same time, Michael Dell well knew that technology, organization, purchasing strategies, financial management, and other supply-side factors would play key roles in producing made-to-order

PCs. But he also knew that these were not, in themselves, sufficient conditions for entrepreneurial success. Competencies in marketing would be at least as important as those in manufacturing. In particular, Dell sensed that experienced PC users wanted some say in how their machines were configured; a satisfying buying experience with informed, responsive salespeople; and effective product support.

But unless Dell could actually make individually configured high-quality computers and quickly deliver them to consumers ordering the products sight unseen by phone or fax, the young company could not prosper. Dell realized that these operational issues would become more important as the PC market developed and consumer familiarity with computing technology increased. He therefore developed his machines, his business model, and his *brand* with these demand-side priorities in mind. He initially targeted knowledgeable users—particularly men—who were proud of their grasp of high-tech developments and wanted to customize their machines. As the reputation of the Dell brand became closely identified with knowledgeable, efficient service, customization, and rapid delivery, Michael Dell broadened his potential customers to include corporations and less experienced household users.

The Personal Art of Brand Creation. Building a powerful brand that offered tangible and intangible benefits was, as all six entrepreneurs came to appreciate, a very complicated process. It involved much more than guessing right just *once* about buyer preferences during some fortuitous moment of rapid economic growth and social change. Rather, each of the six had to pay consistent long-term attention to demand-side preferences, adjusting their offerings and strategic initiatives so that they could consistently deliver on the promises—explicit and implicit—that their brands were making to consumers.

Each of the six companies grew not only out of the entrepreneur's intimate knowledge of his or her product or service but also from personal sales experience. All six were involved in *selling* early in their careers. Each proved adept at it. Each also spent a good deal of time in a fast-growing urban center, one that figured prominently in the economic transition underway: Josiah Wedgwood continued to live in relatively rural Staffordshire, but he traveled frequently to Sheffield, Birmingham, and London; he also benefited from his partner Thomas Bentley's rich experience in Liverpool, London, and other commercial centers. Henry Heinz lived in Pittsburgh, Marshall Field in Chicago, Estée Lauder in New York, Howard Schultz in Seattle, and Michael Dell in Austin—all booming cities at the center of emerging industries. Coupled with their knowledge of selling, their residence in these rapidly growing urban environments gave them useful vantage points on the effects of social and economic changes and on consumers' responses to these shifts.

Even after leaving direct sales, each entrepreneur stayed in close touch with consumers. In 1774, Wedgwood convened an informal "focus group" of aristocrats to ask their opinions about his Etruscan vases before introducing them to the larger market.[49] Heinz made it a point to talk with consumers at fairs and other public expositions and always seemed to enjoy the experience. Marshall Field, long after his department store had become one of the leading retailers in the country, continued to walk the sales floors, conversing with shoppers and overseeing the arrangement of merchandise and quality of service. Estée Lauder, Howard Schultz, and Michael Dell constantly readjusted their offerings, working directly with consumers of lipsticks, caffe lattes, and PCs.

When each of the six entrepreneurs began to scale up production and sales, he or she still depended heavily on word-of-mouth *personal* communication networks. Wedgwood targeted his jasperware tea sets at British elites on the grounds that these customers would expose others to his wares. Heinz developed an elaborate training program for his "travelers" (salesmen) to enhance the brand's image with individual merchants, face-to-face. Field began hiring female clerks to serve women shoppers in the State Street store, sometimes training them himself on proper retail approaches. Lauder opened cosmetics counters herself, applying makeup to hundreds of women's faces and showing her representatives how to do the same thing. From Schultz's earliest days running a café, he believed investments in employee development and benefits were crucial to providing a distinctive café experience and developing a productive organizational culture. Dell personally trained company salespeople and customer support representatives to offer responsive, knowledgeable service over the telephone, in part as a way to distinguish the Dell *brand* from all others.

Longer-Term Functions of Brands. Each of the entrepreneurs analyzed in this book created a branded product initially to make or exploit a market.

Each used his or her brand as a tool to reach potential buyers and pique their interest in novel goods and services. As time went on and markets matured, brands began to serve additional, related functions that became critical to competing effectively. In every case, the six entrepreneurs used their brands to serve at least four distinct functions:

- To differentiate their offerings from those of rivals *over the long term.* To be meaningful to consumers, each brand had to connote quality, reliability, and other advantages, such as elegance or convenience.

- To control product quality inside the company and help set industry standards outside.

- To protect profit margins and avoid costly price wars.

- To facilitate the introduction of additional products carrying the same brand name or known to come from the same company.

Many firms often launch new products under an existing brand, hoping to capitalize on consumers' interest and trust. In 1960, for example, Colgate introduced a line of toothbrushes to accompany its toothpaste. The entrepreneurs analyzed in this book also engaged in "stretching their brands horizontally" (as it is often called in marketing jargon)—that is, across similar products. Wedgwood stretched his brand horizontally by introducing vases, commemorative plates, jewelry, chess sets, and other products under the Wedgwood name. In the 1880s and 1890s, Henry Heinz launched dozens of canned and bottled foods—baked beans, mango chutney, and mincemeat, for example—under his name. Estée Lauder sold not only facial cream and bath oil but also perfume, body lotion, and powder—all under the Lauder brand. Horizontal brand stretching could also be done under a new name promoted explicitly by a well-known company. In 1968, for example, Estée Lauder launched Clinique skin care and cosmetics products. In 1986, Levi-Strauss began selling Dockers pants as an extension of its informal clothing line. In the late twentieth century, Campbell's introduced a number of new soup lines, including Homestyle, Home Cookin,' and Cookbook Classics.

Some companies also engaged in "vertical stretching," extending their brand to different products and services. Howard Schultz successfully introduced a premium ice cream under the Starbucks name in 1996, selling it through supermarkets. Michael Dell launched network servers and began offering consulting services for Internet businesses. Field's brand in effect covered every product in his store.

In each of the three historical eras discussed here, the size and scope of markets and thus the potential reach of brands expanded enormously. Heinz and Field encountered a much larger group of consumers than Wedgwood had done a hundred years earlier. Yet Heinz and Field themselves would probably have been astonished at the range of possibilities available to twenty-first-century executives such as Estée Lauder, Howard Schultz, and Michael Dell. The art and science of brand creation and management in new, potentially gigantic world markets now confronts entrepreneurs with unprecedented (and often mind-boggling) opportunities and challenges.

Reciprocal Learning. Faced with proliferating choices, prospective consumers needed more information to guide their decisions, reduce the risks they faced, and enhance their confidence in purchasing new products. The businesspeople discussed in this book initiated and sustained *two-way* avenues of communication with their customers. The entrepreneurs used these channels to provide consumers with relevant and credible information. In the mid-1700s, when Josiah Wedgwood was getting started as an independent businessman, very few potters maintained sales showrooms. None guaranteed their wares. Nor did buyers expect these features. Wedgwood, by offering free shipping, a satisfaction-or-money-back guarantee, and urban salesrooms with knowledgeable staff, conveyed reassuring information to consumers and increased his goods' appeal relative to competitors' products. He elevated buyers' ideas of what they might expect from all earthenware makers and thus influenced other manufacturers' strategies.[50] By the end of the century, most large china makers had opened London showrooms, but Wedgwood remained the market leader.[51]

The other five entrepreneurs also created new means of communicating with buyers about new products. Henry Heinz, for example, was one of the first American manufacturers to open his Pittsburgh factory to the public, showing interested men and women exactly how his vegetables were processed. Marshall Field instituted an unusually liberal returns policy, which included paying postage or delivery costs on returned merchandise. Supported by this and other specific organizational commitments, the company's reputation—in effect, the Field brand name—came to represent fine, stylish merchandise and a pleasing, convenient shopping experience. Tens of thousands of Chicago shoppers used their identification with (and loyalty to) Field's to help them make buying decisions.

To increase consumers' knowledge of her product lines and earn their trust, Estée Lauder traveled across the United States year after year, talking to women about her cosmetics, providing free makeovers, and distributing samples. Howard Schultz created an elaborate training program for Starbucks employees to educate them in the art of making and enjoying specialty coffee themselves so as to better express their own enthusiasm for the product to consumers. Like the other aspects of Starbucks in-store experience, these initiatives were developed to provide relevant information to consumers about new products: caffe lattes, cappuccinos, and other specialty coffee drinks. Michael Dell also wanted to communicate effectively with potential buyers and to this end, he established toll-free phone lines for customer questions and orders, staffing the call centers with trained, educated salespeople. He, too, offered a money-back guarantee on his PCs, effectively reducing the risks of purchasing a computer sight unseen.

Information also flowed *from* consumers to companies. All six entrepreneurs paid close attention to customers' reactions in the markets they were helping to develop. Each realized that buyers used their financial resources as de facto votes. They endorsed products and services that most effectively met their needs at what they regarded as reasonable prices, rejecting those that did not. Each entrepreneur scrutinized broad purchasing patterns and responded accordingly. For example, in 1769 Wedgwood saw that elaborately decorated tableware was not selling well in London shops. He returned to Etruria with a "firm resolution to simplify" his own design, ordering flowered handles to be removed from virtually all products.[52] Similarly, Estée Lauder's experience giving women makeovers in the 1930s and 1940s afforded her ample time to observe what customers liked and did not like about her goods and sales pitch. She was not afraid to adjust her selling tactics, and occasionally even her product formulas, to better meet customers' preferences. Howard Schultz broadened Starbucks menu and altered the décor of its cafés after watching consumers' reactions. Michael Dell and his colleagues kept close tabs on customer feedback, talking constantly with company salespeople and technicians working the phone lines and using this information in product development and other decisions.

Each of the entrepreneurs also listened closely to individuals whom he or she believed understood evolving tastes. Each trained colleagues and employees to do the same. Henry Heinz, for instance, consulted frequently with family members on product design and marketing. Marshall Field urged saleswomen to take careful note of customer reactions to new items. He and other managers at Field's used this information to adapt product displays and advertising as well as to make future merchandising decisions. In the late 1980s, Michael Dell made certain that writers for *PCWeek* and other trade publications as well as consumers had a chance to evaluate the machines and then adjusted his products and manufacturing processes in response to the feedback that he received.

Obviously, entrepreneurs' and companies' ability to communicate back and forth with consumers has expanded tremendously since the eighteenth century. Josiah Wedgwood built his brand by targeting specific aristocrats, often by personal contact. As we have seen, he reached what at the time would have been considered large, concentrated groups of customers by opening showrooms in fashion centers such as London and Bath. Estée Lauder did much the same two hundred years later in New York and Miami Beach. The other entrepreneurs also realized how quickly new products and styles could take hold in fast-growing urban centers.

As the Transportation and Communication Revolution unfolded in the United States in the late 1800s, entrepreneurs tried to reach consumers all over the country. Heinz, for example, advertised "Pure Food for the Table" on thousands of subway car signs and billboards, shipping millions of units annually over a growing rail network. In the twentieth century, Lauder and Dell followed suit, advertising in national magazines. Both Lauder and Dell also purchased time on major television networks, which enabled each to put their brand names before millions of consumers simultaneously.

Schultz, by contrast, used almost no mass advertising to promote the Starbucks brand. He increased consumer awareness by constructing more stores, relying on word-of-mouth endorsements from customers and forging alliances with business partners such as Barnes & Noble and Nordstrom. His underlying strategy of rapid bricks-and-mortar expansion depended on sophisticated point-of-sale information systems and other computer-dependent technology to link transmission of data from company outlets to senior management and suppliers, and from one store to another. When Schultz believed that the Starbucks brand had achieved a discernible, attractive identity and a critical mass of loyal customers in the United States, he and his colleagues moved quickly to develop international markets. So, too, did Wedgwood, Heinz, Lauder, and Dell.

The absolute size of consumer markets has exploded, of course, since Josiah Wedgwood forged commercial connections with eighteenth-century households. Each of the five succeeding entrepreneurs analyzed in this book realized early on that technological innovations, economic growth, and demographic shifts might enable him or her to establish contact with millions of people. But each correctly sensed that making initial contact with potential customers was only a small part of the broad task of establishing a powerful brand. In particular, each understood that mass advertising alone could not motivate potential buyers to spend their money or change their habits for a new product. Mass advertising certainly could not earn consumers' trust over the long term. Much, much more was required. And the reciprocal learning that resulted from ongoing communication between entrepreneurs and consumers was critical to meeting this challenge.

Building Institutions. In order to provide the benefits that their brands promised consumers, each of the six entrepreneurs had to create a range of *organizational capabilities.* Each of the six entrepreneurs worked with colleagues and employees to build not only a brand but also a *company.* Earning consumers' trust through forging reputations that buyers regarded as desirable and credible necessitated specific capabilities in many other functions besides product innovation and creative marketing. The difficult process of institution building therefore required major investments of time and resources in areas such as manufacturing, product development, and finance.

Each entrepreneur, together with his or her colleagues, paid close attention to operating procedures. Their policies included what today we would call "efficiency" in research and development, quality control, human resource development, distribution, sales, and cash-flow management. Strategies and specific procedures in all of these areas were coordinated to support the company's product, brand, and other connections with consumers: to gain their attention not only in the short term but also—as noted earlier—their confidence and loyalty over the long term.

It would take a book many times the length of this one to do full justice to the complex organization building essential for entrepreneurial successes of the degree these six individuals achieved. Each of the narrative chapters contains a wealth of information, such as statistics on sales, number of employees, and so on, as each of the six businesses grew. This last section of the book provides six final illustrations of the institution-building necessary to turn each of the companies from an entrepreneurial start-up to a full-fledged *organization.*

Wedgwood. In order to produce useful and ornamental china of a consistently high quality that consumers associated with aristocratic fashion, Josiah Wedgwood and his partner Thomas Bentley needed skilled artists and craftsmen. As the market for their products grew, they found it increasingly difficult to find workers with the requisite abilities. In the 1770s and 1780s, the two men created a number of organizational initiatives to train both existing staff and new hires. The training initiatives included an apprenticeship program for artists and a modeling and drawing school for painters. Wedgwood and Bentley also created the position of foreman to oversee employees in individual workshops and an elaborate system of rules, regulations, rewards, and fines to motivate workers' behavior.

Heinz. When Henry Heinz was starting out in the 1860s and 1870s, he used independent wholesalers to sell his goods to grocers. As the market for processed food grew, Heinz realized that to support the integrity of his brand and communicate its reputation to retailers and consumers, he could no longer rely wholly on such "jobbers" to distribute his products. For one thing, many of them also sold competing goods. So, in the early 1880s, Henry and his brothers, John and Peter, began constructing a company-owned sales force and creating a series of regional selling offices and warehouses, each staffed with trained, full-time employees. By the end of the century, the Heinz company had more than 270 sales representatives or "travelers" drumming up business in America and abroad. Twenty years later, in 1919, almost a thousand travelers sold Heinz products around the world. In the jargon of economics and business administration, adding the function of sales to that of manufacturing is called "downstream vertical integration," and the Heinz company pursued it vigorously.

Marshall Field. "Upstream vertical integration" often occurred as well. In the 1860s and 1870s, Marshall Field, Levi Leiter, and their partners established a number of in-house workshops to make specific products to be sold by the firm's wholesale and retail divisions. Most of these goods, such as suspenders and fur coats, were manufactured solely for Field's and were marked with the company's name. In the 1880s and 1890s, as Harry Selfridge successfully broadened Field's product lines, the company expanded its manufacturing capabilities, constructing large workshops and off-site factories to supply products for its wholesale and especially retail divisions. In 1906, the business even began making its own golf balls. By 1920, Field's owned and managed a number of manufacturing plants, including several huge cotton textile mills located in the South that produced goods under the "Fieldcrest Mills" name for exclusive distribution by Field's.

By building manufacturing capabilities, Field and his partners increased the scope of the company's activities beyond its initial competencies, engaging in extensive upstream vertical integration. This kind of intrafirm expansion of functions, as Field and his colleagues appreciated, was risky and—at least in the short run—expensive. But, they believed, it was essential in order to preserve the firm's reputation of style and exclusivity. Owning and managing manufacturing plants allowed the company to respond quickly to changes in consumer demand and also indirectly reduced distribution costs.[53]

Estée Lauder. In building their own company step by step, the Lauders and their colleagues had also increased the range of their company's activities. In the mid-1960s, the founders and senior managers began developing new offerings distinct from those sold under the flagship "Estée Lauder" brand. Between 1965 and 1990, the company created four novel product lines and brands. Each was targeted at a specific customer segment and designed to meet that group's needs: Aramis (men over age twenty-five), Clinique (women between the ages of twenty and thirty-five), Prescriptives (career women between the ages of thirty and forty-five), and Origins (men and women between the ages of twenty-five and fifty interested in "natural," environmentally friendly products). Each brand carried its own line of goods, packaging design, and marketing and distribution strategies. Each was managed as a separate division within the larger parent organization. The process as a whole was as much akin to brand stretching as to vertical integration, but the addition of several functions did become necessary at the company.

As the pace of general socioeconomic change accelerated in the 1990s, Leonard Lauder and his colleagues worked to create and sustain close relationships with an increasingly diverse customer base. Toward this end, the

Estée Lauder Companies began acquiring other cosmetics brands such as Bobbi Brown, *jane*, and Aveda. Like the firm's other lines, each of these brands was directed at a specific consumer segment. Bobbi Brown was targeted at upper-middle-class working mothers between the ages of thirty-five and fifty, *jane* at teenage consumers, and Aveda at educated buyers interested in "lifestyle" products made from "pure flower and plant ingredients."[54]

Increasing the number and variety of the firm's product lines was a complex undertaking, as the Lauders well understood. Developing new goods and brands in-house required significant time, money, and managerial talent. Acquiring new lines by purchasing existing companies usually took less time, but often involved considerable monetary and organizational investments. Leonard Lauder, other family members, and their colleagues within the firm recognized that in order to keep pace with evolving consumer preferences and to maintain strong relationships with customers, the company had to broaden its markets and segment them more precisely.

Starbucks. Like the Lauders, Howard Schultz also encountered daunting organizational challenges as his company expanded. When he acquired Starbucks in 1987 and set out to create a large chain of specialty coffee bars, Schultz resisted the option of franchising, choosing instead to grow by opening company-owned stores. As the business expanded rapidly in the 1990s, this choice had profound consequences for the size and scope of Schultz's organization. Rather than relying on franchisees to help finance expansion, oversee individual stores, monitor product and service quality, and support the company's brand—as many competitors did—Starbucks built its own management infrastructure in the field. Organized by geographic markets, the new structure included district and regional offices, a managerial hierarchy, and sophisticated information systems to link stores, managers, and corporate headquarters. From the chief executive to the district manager to the *barista* (store server) level, each Starbucks employee had responsibilities that were clearly delineated.

Constructing this organizational structure was a complicated, costly process. So too was the rigorous training that Starbucks provided its employees. But from his first experience with the company, Schultz believed that increasing the firm's capabilities at every level made strategic sense. "We're so fanatical about quality control," he explained, "that we keep the coffee in our hands every step of the way from raw green beans to the steaming cup. We buy and roast all our own coffee, and we sell it in company-owned stores. That's vertical integration to the extreme."[55]

Dell Computer. Dell Computer was a different sort of business from Starbucks, of course, but Michael Dell shared some of the same kinds of challenges confronting Howard Schultz. In order to maintain strong connections with consumers, Dell needed knowledgeable, courteous, and responsive salespeople and service technicians. When he started out in the PC business, he dealt with many of the firm's potential customers himself. He also trained employees in how to engage and educate consumers about personal computers, promote products, and deal with questions or complaints. Dell emphasized the importance of quality service in exceeding customer expectations and creating a superior buying experience.

As the PC market expanded rapidly in the late 1980s and 1990s, Dell invested heavily in employees, establishing a range of programs to train the field-based sales force, telephone representatives, and customer service and support staff. These training sessions covered not only issues such as how to field questions, customize orders, and suggest other products; they also included instructions on how to listen effectively to consumers' comments—laudatory and critical—and convey this information back to the appropriate place in the company. A collective talent for *listening* became one of Dell Computer's salient organizational capabilities. For overseas markets, Dell created centralized customer support functions in its own regional centers, staffing them with technicians who were fluent in specific languages and routing incoming phone calls accordingly.

In building their organizations, each of the six individuals conceived a number of practices that eventually became established policies in many companies besides their own. A few of these initiatives, such as Josiah Wedgwood's inertia selling, were unprecedented. Others, such as Henry Heinz's promotional giveaways, had existed for decades, but had not previously been so creatively harnessed to a strategy focused on making a novel market.

As noted, most of these policies were directed toward the demand side, such as Wedgwood's aristocratic sanction, Heinz's fair exhibits, Marshall Field's money-back guarantees, Estée Lauder's gift-with-purchase, Howard Schultz's coffee bar "experience," and Michael Dell's made-to-order PCs. They were intended to differentiate the founder's offerings in ways that were meaningful to customers and likely to attract their interest. But some of the procedures that these entrepreneurs helped pioneer, such as Wedgwood's clocking-in system, Field's backward integration into manufacturing, and Dell's thoroughgoing inventory management, were on the supply side. They were aimed at affecting how efficiently the firm's goods were produced. In either case—whether on the demand or the supply side—nearly every innovation required substantial adjustment within the company: a new set of organizational capabilities, built piece by piece over several decades.

The six entrepreneurs in this book—from Wedgwood in the Industrial Revolution, to Henry Heinz and Marshall Field in the Transportation and Communication Revolution, to Estée Lauder, Howard Schultz of Starbucks, and Michael Dell in our own time—lived and worked in different contexts. Yet they all shared a powerful gift: the ability to discern how economic and social change affected consumer needs and wants. They also understood that these demand-side shifts presented critical business opportunities—opportunities that each exploited by creating new, best-of-class goods and strong brands.

But these individuals were more than savvy marketers. They were institution builders who were not interested in riding the wave of a short-lived trend or forcing their young brands on buyers. They wanted to *earn* consumers' trust and keep it. Achieving this objective, as each realized, meant that he or she had to use both empathy and commercial imagination not only to satisfy buyers' changing preferences, but to anticipate them as well. Earning and maintaining buyers' trust also involved forging organizational capabilities to support the product and brand. Finally, it required that these entrepreneurs listen carefully to customers' reactions and use this feedback to help improve their offerings.

These commitments, in combination with each individual's ambition and experience, yielded competitive advantages in their respective markets. By successfully introducing a novel product and demonstrating its value to consumers in terms that they regarded as meaningful, each of the six brands became a de facto standard for its young industry. Like other early-mover brands, such as Coke or Federal Express, they etched themselves in consumers' consciousness, altering their thinking and conversation about particular goods. At the beginning of the twenty-first century, we eat off Wedgwood; we pass the Heinz; we order a Dell.

An equally important source of competitive advantage flowed from the set of organizational capabilities that each of these entrepreneurs developed to support their brand. Tailored specifically toward making the most of particular possibilities on the demand side, these capabilities spanned virtually all company functions from operations to marketing to finance. Taken together, they functioned as a vital system of interdependent activities that frequently proved difficult for competitors to emulate.

Sustaining such strategic advantages over the long term, however, has required high levels of corporate investment, including conscientious brand and organizational stewardship, significant financial resources, and vigilant attention to the ceaseless change that has always defined competition in a capitalistic economy. Being early in the game has never guaranteed lasting success.

The individuals in this book had some sense of this. Nevertheless, each was determined to use his or her assets, especially the power of the brand, to lead their nascent industries: to set the terms of rivalry in the market, to create products and institutions that endured, and to enhance their respective company's position as much as possible.

Their actions toward these ends were important in bringing the fruits of industrial capitalism to millions of consumers. In developing new products, brands, and companies, each of these innovators changed people's daily priorities and behavior in small but significant ways. Their agency thus comprised a crucial part of the material and cultural shifts accompanying great economic turbulence. We cannot understand the birth of consumer societies in developing nations or the evolution of modern consumerism in industrialized economies today without understanding what these entrepreneurs did.

The work and times of these individuals also affords us a valuable perspective on our own moment in history. Like modern business leaders and consumers, the individuals in this book had no assurances about the future. They chased their dreams, fought their fears, and tried to place smart bets in the midst of extraordinary—sometimes seemingly overwhelming—change. The world of Wedgwood and eighteenth-century British buyers was vastly different from that of Heinz, Field, and their customers. In many respects, both eras were unlike that which we know today. But each entrepreneur acting within a particular historical context helped shape the possibilities and challenges of the next moment: Wedgwood's work in the

Industrial Revolution influenced the business landscape of the Transportation and Communications Revolution and thus affected the actions of Heinz and Field. Their efforts, in turn, had important consequences for companies and consumers throughout the twentieth century and for innovators in our time who, like Dell, have been concerned with capitalizing on the opportunities of the Information Age. The past, as William Faulkner wrote, "is not dead. It is not even past."

Notes

CHAPTER 1

1. Howard H. Stevenson, "A Perspective on Entrepreneurship," in *New Business Ventures and the Entrepreneur*, eds. H. H. Stevenson, Michael J. Roberts, and H. Irving Grousbeck (Homewood, IL: Richard D. Irwin, Inc., 1985), pp. 2–15. See also William A. Sahlman, Howard H. Stevenson, Michael J. Roberts, and Amar Bhidé, eds., *The Entrepreneurial Venture* (Boston: Harvard Business School Press, 1999), p. 1.

2. See, for example, Alfred D. Chandler Jr., *The Visible Hand: The Managerial Revolution in American Business* (Cambridge: Harvard University Press, 1977); Thomas C. Cochran and William Miller, *The Age of Enterprise: A Social History of Industrial America* (New York: Macmillan, 1942); N. F. R. Crafts, *British Economic Growth during the Industrial Revolution* (Oxford: Clarendon, 1985); Paul A. David and Gavin Wright, *Early Twentieth Century Productivity Growth Dynamics: An Inquiry into the Economic History of "Our Ignorance"* (Oxford: University of Oxford, 1999); Phyllis Deane, *The First Industrial Revolution* (Cambridge: Cambridge University Press, 1965); Leslie Hannah, *The Rise of the Corporate Economy* (London: Methuen, 1976); David A. Hounshell, *From the American System to Mass Production, 1800–1932: The Development of Manufacturing Technology in the United States* (Baltimore: Johns Hopkins University Press, 1984); R. P. T. Davenport-Hines and Geoffrey Jones, eds., *Enterprise, Management, and Innovation in British Business, 1914–80* (London: F. Cass, 1988); David S. Landes, *The Unbound Prometheus: Technological Change and Industrial Development in Western Europe from 1750 to the Present* (Cambridge: Cambridge University Press, 1969); William Lazonick, *Business Organization and the Myth of the Market Economy* (Cambridge: Cambridge University Press, 1991); Roland Marchand, *Advertising the American Dream: Making Way for Modernity, 1920–1940* (Berkeley: University of California Press, 1986); Thomas K. McCraw, ed., *Creating Modern Capitalism: How Entrepreneurs, Companies, and Countries Triumphed in Three Industrial Revolutions* (Cambridge: Harvard University Press, 1997); Glenn Porter and Harold C. Livesay, *Merchants and Manufacturers: Studies in the Changing Structure of Nineteenth-Century Marketing* (Baltimore: Johns Hopkins University Press, 1971); Robin Reilly, *Wedgwood* (New York: Stockton, 1989); Philip Scranton, *Endless Novelty: Specialty Production and American Industrialization, 1865–1925* (Princeton: Princeton University Press, 1997); Susan Strasser, *Satisfaction Guaranteed: The Making of the American Mass Market*

(New York: Pantheon, 1989); and Richard S. Tedlow, *New and Improved: The Story of Mass Marketing in America* (New York: Basic, 1990).

3. See, for example, David Aaker, *Managing Brand Equity: Capitalizing on the Value of a Brand Name* (New York: Free Press, 1991); Neil H. Borden, *The Economic Effects of Advertising* (Chicago: Richard D. Irwin, 1944); John Deighton, "The Future of Interactive Marketing," *Harvard Business Review* 74, no. 6 (November-December 1996), pp. 151–162; John Deighton and Kent Grayson, "Marketing and Seduction: Building Exchange Relationships by Managing Social Consensus," *Journal of Consumer Research* 21, no. 4 (March 1995), pp. 660–676; Susan Fournier, "Consumers and Their Brands: Developing Relationship Theory in Consumer Research," *Journal of Consumer Research* 24, no. 4 (March 1998), pp. 343–373; Jean-Noel Kapferer, *Strategic Brand Management: Creating and Sustaining Brand Equity Long Term* (London: Kogan Page, 1997); Kevin Lane Keller, *Strategic Brand Management: Building, Measuring, and Managing Brand Equity* (Upper Saddle River, NJ: Prentice Hall, 1998); Philip Kotler and Gary Armstrong, *Principles of Marketing* (Upper Saddle River, NJ: Prentice Hall, 1996); Theodore Levitt, *The Marketing Imagination* (New York: Free Press, 1986); John A. Quelch and David Kenny, "Extend Profits, Not Product Lines," *Harvard Business Review* 72, no. 5 (September-October 1994) pp. 153–160; John A. Quelch and David Harding, "Brands versus Private Labels," *Harvard Business Review* 74, no. 1 (January-February 1996), pp. 99–109; and Alvin J. Silk, "Marketing Science in a Changing Environment," *Journal of Marketing Research* 30 (November 1993), pp. 401–404.

4. The scholarly literature on the history of consumption is large and growing. Some of the important works include: Daniel J. Boorstin, *The Americans: The Democratic Experience* (New York: Vintage, 1973); John Brewer and Roy Porter, eds., *Consumption and the World of Goods* (London: Routledge, 1993); Lizabeth Cohen, *Making a New Deal: Industrial Workers in Chicago, 1919–1939* (Cambridge: Cambridge University Press, 1990), pp. 99–158; and "Embellishing a Life of Labor: An Interpretation of the Material Culture of American Working-Class Homes, 1885–1915," *Journal of American Culture* 3 (winter 1980), pp. 752–775; Richard W. Fox and T. J. Jackson Lears, eds., *The Culture of Consumption: Critical Essays in American History, 1880–1980* (New York: Pantheon, 1983); Andrew R. Heinze, *Adapting to Abundance: Jewish Immigrants, Mass Consumption, and the Search for American Identity* (New York: Columbia University Press, 1990); Daniel Horowitz, *The Morality of Spending: Attitudes toward the Consumer Society in America, 1875–1940* (Baltimore: Johns Hopkins University Press, 1985); T. J. Jackson Lears, *Fables of Abundance: A Cultural History of Advertising* (New York: Basic Books, 1994) and "Reconsidering Abundance," in Susan Strasser, Charles McGovern, and Mathias Judt, eds., *Getting and Spending: European and American Consumer Societies in the Twentieth Century* (Cambridge: Cambridge University Press, 1998), pp. 449–466; Stanley Lebergott, *Pursuing Happiness: American Consumers*

in the Twentieth Century (Princeton: Princeton University Press, 1993); Grant McCracken, *Culture and Consumption: New Approaches to the Symbolic Character of Consumer Goods and Activities* (Bloomington, IN: Indiana University Press, 1990); Neil McKendrick, John Brewer, and J. H. Plumb, *The Birth of a Consumer Society: The Commercialization of Eighteenth-Century England* (Bloomington, IN: Indiana University Press, 1982); David M. Potter, *People of Plenty: Economic Abundance and the American Character* (Chicago: University of Chicago Press, 1954); Juliet Schor, *The Overspent American: Upscaling, Downshifting, and the New Consumer* (New York: Basic Books, 1998); and Carole Shammas, *The Pre-Industrial Consumer in England and America* (Oxford: Oxford University Press, 1990). A number of scholars have analyzed the historiography of consumption. See, for example, Jean-Christophe Agnew, "Coming Up for Air: Consumer Culture in Historical Perspective," in Brewer and Porter, eds., *Consumption and the World of Goods*, pp. 19–39; Ben Fine and Ellen Leopold, *The World of Consumption* (London: Routledge, 1993); and Grant McCracken, "The History of Consumption: A Literature Review and Consumer Guide," *Journal of Consumer Policy* 10 (June 1987), pp. 139–166.

5. See, for example, Humberto Barreto, *The Entrepreneur in Microeconomic Theory: Disappearance and Explanation* (London: Routledge, 1989); Israel M. Kirzner, *Competition and Entrepreneurship* (Chicago: University of Chicago Press, 1973); Joseph A. Schumpeter, *Capitalism, Socialism and Democracy* (New York: Harper & Row, 1976); and Sahlman et al., *The Entrepreneurial Venture*. For an overview of recent scholarship on entrepreneurship and the relative dearth of systematic research about starting and growing new business, see Amar V. Bhidé, *The Origin and Evolution of New Businesses* (New York: Oxford University Press, 2000), pp. ix–xv, 6–7, 238–259, 319–337.

CHAPTER 2

All Wedgwood MSS references are to the Wedgwood collection deposited at Keele University or held at The Wedgwood Museum at Barlaston in Staffordshire. The author is grateful to The Trustees of The Wedgwood Museum for access to the collection. Quotations from its manuscripts are published by courtesy of The Trustees of The Wedgwood Museum, Barlaston, Stoke-on-Trent, Staffordshire, England, and copyright of this material remains vested in The Trustees of The Wedgwood Museum.

1. John J. McCusker, *How Much Is That in Real Money? A Historical Price Index for Use as a Deflator of Money Values in the Economy of the United States* (Worcester, MA: American Antiquarian Society, 1992) pp. 325, 332, and Council of Economic Advisers, *Economic Report of the President* (Washington, DC: U.S. Government

Printing Office, 2000), p. 373. There is some historical dispute about the total number of pieces included in the set ordered by the Russian empress. The standard company histories place the number between 950 and 1,000.

2. Creamware was a durable, lead-glazed earthenware first made in England in the 1730s and named for its cream color. The description of the service is from Mary Granville, Mrs. Delany, *Autobiography and Correspondence of Mrs. Delany* (London: Little, Brown, 1862), 1, p. 593.

3. Julia Wedgwood, *The Personal Life of Josiah Wedgwood* (London: Macmillan, 1915), p. 154.

4. Profit estimates vary from £200 to £500. See Wolf Mankowitz, *Wedgwood* (London: Dutton, 1953), p. 46, and Robin Reilly, *Wedgwood* (London: Stockton, 1989), 1, p. 72.

5. Josiah Wedgwood to Thomas Bentley, September 1767, E. 18167-25, Wedgwood Manuscripts, Keele University Library (original emphasis).

6. Nancy F. Koehn, *The Power of Commerce: Economy and Governance in the First British Empire* (Ithaca: Cornell University Press, 1994), pp. 26–50.

7. Henry Fielding, *An Enquiry into the Causes of the Late Increase of Robbers, with Some Proposals for Remedying this Growing Evil* (London: A. Millar, 1751), p. xi.

8. E. A. Wrigley and R. S. Schofield, *The Population History of England, 1541–1871: A Reconstruction* (Cambridge: Harvard University Press, 1981), pp. 249–253; Lawrence Stone, *The Family, Sex and Marriage in England, 1500–1800* (London: Weidenfeld & Nicolson, 1977), p. 68; and John Rule, *The Vital Century: England's Developing Economy, 1714–1815* (London: Longman, 1992), p. 9.

9. As Josiah wrote his partner in 1767, "I am in pursuit of so many objects, beside what my current run of business furnishes me with." Josiah Wedgwood to Thomas Bentley, 23 May 1767, E. 18147-25, Wedgwood Manuscripts.

10. Quoted in G. W. and F. A. Rhead, *Staffordshire Pots and Potters* (London: Hutchinson, 1906), p. 223.

11. Josiah Wedgwood to Thomas Bentley, 8 November 1766, E. 18132-35, Wedgwood Manuscripts (original emphasis).

12. Lorna Weatherill, *The Pottery Trade and North Staffordshire, 1660–1760* (Manchester: Manchester University Press, 1971), p. 112. As Weatherill writes, "When a place acquired a population of between 1,000 and 2,000, it was well within the ranges of population of small market towns, as a few instances show. . . . The second largest town in England [behind London with 675,000 inhabitants], Bristol, had a population of about 100,000 in the mid-eighteenth century, Birmingham 30,000, Manchester 45,000 and Norwich 50,000. . . . ," p. 115.

13. Ibid., pp. 124–125.

14. Ibid., p. 126. Relative to numerous other contemporary shops, those in Burslem were advanced. Throughout the eighteenth century, many shop premises

were informal. Sales across open windows of tradesmen's homes were common; so too were stalls in sheds or "bulks" set up against house or shop walls. "Some were only big enough to provide a seat and roof; some were slept in at night by vagrants; some had a door and a bed on the floor and their tenants had no other home. One cold night in 1768, for instance, a [London] cobbler was found frozen to death in his pavement stall." Dorothy Davis, *A History of Shopping* (London: Routledge & Kegan Paul, 1966), p. 191.

15. Eliza Meteyard, *The Life of Josiah Wedgwood* (London: Hurst and Blackett, 1865–1866), 1, p. 182.

16. Burslem's roads were comparable to others in Britain before 1750. As the essayist Daniel Defoe wrote in 1720, "I saw an ancient lady [near Brighton in southeast England], and a lady of very good quality, I assure you, drawn to church in her coach with six oxen; nor was it done in frolic or humour, but mere necessity, the way being so stiff and deep [with mud], that no horses could go in it." Daniel Defoe, *A Tour through the Whole Island of Great Britain* (London: P. Davies, 1927), 1, p. 129.

17. Robin Reilly, *Wedgwood: The New Illustrated Dictionary* (Woodbridge, Suffolk: Antique Collectors' Club, 1995), pp. 143, 336.

18. Weatherill, *The Pottery Trade,* p. 79. In the seventeenth and eighteenth centuries, the Dutch town of Delft became famous for the tin-glazed earthenware made there. Consequently, the name "Delftware" was often applied to English and Irish tin-glazed earthenware. Robin Reilly, *Wedgwood: The New Illustrated Dictionary,* p. 134.

19. Weatherill, *The Pottery Trade,* pp. 32–34. Before 1971 when Great Britain moved to decimalization—a coinage system based on 100 pence to the pound—the pound consisted of 20 shillings, and each shilling consisted of 12 pence; a pound was thus worth 240 pence.

20. Weatherill, *The Pottery Trade,* p. 44. By way of comparison, a baker in Burslem in 1724 had equipment and inventories valued at £12, while the capital and stock of the Coalbrookdale ironworks were worth £3,000 in 1718. Weatherill, *The Pottery Trade,* p. 48. Price indexes are from McCusker, *How Much Is That in Real Money?,* pp. 324, 332, and Council of Economic Advisers, *Economic Report of the President,* p. 373.

21. In 1740, a farm laborer earned between £12 and £17 annually, an unskilled nonfarm worker £20, and a collier less than £22 ($3,028 in today's dollars). A bushel of wheat in 1740 cost 4 shillings and a pound of beef 1 or 2 pence. A calf could be purchased for between 6 and 9 shillings. See Robin Reilly, *Josiah Wedgwood* (London: Macmillan, 1992), p. 2. Wage data are from Peter H. Lindert and Jeffrey G. Williamson, "English Workers' Living Standards During the Industrial Revolution: A New Look," *Economic History Review,* 2nd ser., 36 (1983), p. 4, and Thomas

Malthus, *Principles of Political Economy* (London: Reeves and Turner, 1836), pp. 241–251, quoted in Peter H. Lindert, "English Population, Wages, and Prices: 1541–1913" in Robert I. Rotberg and Theodore K. Rabb, eds., *Population and History: From the Traditional to the Modern World* (Cambridge: Cambridge University Press, 1986), p. 52. Price indexes are from McCusker, *How Much Is That in Real Money?*, pp. 324, 332, and Council of Economic Advisers, *Economic Report of the President*, p. 373. As several economic historians have pointed out, wage data, like other numbers for the early eighteenth century, are limited and subject to large margins of error.

22. As early as 1700, pottery manufacture bore more resemblance to medium- and larger-scale production than to domestic or cottage industries, such as lace making or straw plaiting. The term *cottage industry* or *putting-out system* refers to a variety of handicraft production processes undertaken for the market by rural households as a means of supplementing agricultural incomes during slack seasons. Maxine Berg, *Age of Manufactures, 1700–1820* (New York: Oxford University Press, 1986), p. 79.

23. On the historiographical debates surrounding the timing of the Industrial Revolution, see David Cannadine, "The Past and Present in the English Industrial Revolution, 1880–1980," *Past & Present* 103 (1984), pp. 131–172, and Julian Hoppitt, "Understanding the Industrial Revolution," *The Historical Journal* 30 (1987), pp. 211–224.

24. N. F. R. Crafts, "The Industrial Revolution," in Roderick Floud and Donald McCloskey, eds., *The Economic History of Britain since 1700* (Cambridge: Cambridge University Press, 1994), 1, p. 49.

25. Peter H. Lindert, "English Occupations, 1670–1811," *Journal of Economic History* 40 (1980), pp. 685–712. As Lindert notes, eighteenth-century occupational labels were often imprecise. "We know from literary evidence that persons with one label often had many occupations, both in a single year and (especially) over their adult lives. Weavers farmed and farmers wove, in unknown proportions," p. 693. See also Crafts, "The Industrial Revolution," p. 45; *British Economic Growth during the Industrial Revolution* (Oxford: Oxford University Press, 1985), pp. 12–14; and Peter Mathias, "The Social Structure in the Eighteenth Century: A Calculation by Joseph Massie," *Economic History Review*, 2nd ser., 10 (1957), pp. 30–45.

26. Koehn, *Power of Commerce*, p. 32. Agricultural output figure is from Crafts, "The Industrial Revolution," p. 47.

27. Crafts, "The Industrial Revolution," pp. 47–48.

28. See Cannadine, "The Past and Present in the English Industrial Revolution."

29. No other eighteenth-century European economy has received so much attention. See John Brewer, *Sinews of Power: War, Money, and the English State, 1688–1783* (New York: Alfred A. Knopf, 1989), p. 179.

30. According to recent research, farm output grew at an average rate of 0.1 or 0.2 percent per annum from 1760 to 1780. Crafts, "The Industrial Revolution," p. 47.

31. Crafts, *British Economic Growth during the Industrial Revolution*, p. 23.

32. Lindert, "English Occupations, 1670–1811," p. 709.

33. Simon Kuznets, *Modern Economic Growth* (New Haven: Yale University Press, 1966), pp. 88–89. There is scholarly controversy about the magnitude of Britain's industrialization. According to the economic historian W. A. Cole, industry accounted for half of real output in 1800. "Factors in Demand, 1700–1800," in Floud and McCloskey, eds., *The Economic History of Britain since 1700*, 1, pp. 40, 64. Crafts estimates industry's contribution to British output at about 20 percent in 1800, but he does not include commerce, services, or mining. Crafts, "The Industrial Revolution," p. 45, and *British Economic Growth*, pp. 62–63.

34. In 1800, about 80 percent of the U.S. labor force was engaged in agricultural activities. See Richard K. Vedder, *The American Economy in Historical Perspective* (Belmont, CA: Wadsworth Publishing Company, 1976), p. 227. In France, approximately 40 percent of the nation's output was nonagricultural. See Myron P. Guttman, *Toward the Modern Economy: Early Industry in Europe, 1500–1800* (Philadelphia: Temple University Press, 1988), p. 117.

35. In the 1750s and 1760s, an extensive division of labor developed in many of the larger metalware workshops and factories. Here is how the British statesman Shelburne described the organization of work he observed on a 1766 tour of a Birmingham manufactory:

> Instead of employing the same hand to finish a button or any other thing, they subdivide it into as many different hands as possible, finding beyond doubt that the human faculties by being confined to a repetition of the same thing become more expeditious and more to be depended on than when obliged or suffered to pass from one to another. Thus a button passes through fifty hands, and each hand perhaps passes a thousand in a day; likewise, by this means, the work becomes so simple that, five times in six, children of six or eight years old do it as well as men, and earn from ten pence to eight shillings a week. (Lord Shelburne to Lady Shelburne, 19 May 1766, quoted in Lord Fitzmaurice, ed., *Life of William Earl of Shelburne* [London: Macmillan, 1912], 1, pp. 276–277.)

36. Supplies of west country clay were limited and relatively expensive until the Weaver River canal opened in 1733. Reilly, *Wedgwood*, 1, p. 21.

37. Josiah C. Wedgwood, *Staffordshire Pottery and Its History* (New York: McBride, Nast, 1913), pp. 46–47.

38. Meteyard, *Life of Josiah Wedgwood*, 1, p. 142; Josiah Wedgwood, *Staffordshire Pottery*, p. 61; and A. H. Church, *Josiah Wedgwood: Master-Potter* (New York: Dutton, 1908), p. 21.

39. Weatherill, *The Pottery Trade*, p. 35.

40. Enoch Booth, a master potter in Tunstall, Staffordshire, is generally credited with pioneering these techniques.

41. Meteyard, *Life of Josiah Wedgwood*, 1, p. 203.

42. Reilly, *Wedgwood*, 1, pp. 25–26. See also Julia Wedgwood, *The Personal Life of Josiah Wedgwood*, pp. 8–9; Alison Kelly, *The Story of Wedgwood* (London: Faber & Faber, 1975), p. 11; Meteyard, *Life of Josiah Wedgwood*, 1, pp. 199–200; and Llewllynn Jewitt, *Life of Josiah Wedgwood* (London: Virtue Brothers, 1865), p. 89.

43. In the eighteenth century, *manufacturer* designated a workman or master, as well as an industrialist. P. Mantoux, *The Industrial Revolution in the Eighteenth Century: An Outline of the Beginnings of the Modern Factory System* (London: J. Cape, 1928), p. 375.

44. Anthony Burton, *Josiah Wedgwood: A Biography* (New York: Stein and Day, 1976), p. 19.

45. Ibid.

46. There is no documentary evidence regarding Josiah's employment between 1739 and 1744. Reilly, *Wedgwood*, 1, p. 26.

47. "[S]mallpox, unlike a disease such as influenza, did not sweep across the country as a national epidemic. Rather it seems to have been endemic at a regional level, returning to individual communities when there was a sufficient number of young children who had not previously been exposed to it." Wrigley and Schofield, *The Population History of England*, p. 669. Before 1800, about one in seven people infected with the disease died. Fernand Braudel, *The Structures of Everyday Life: The Limits of the Possible* (New York: Harper & Row, 1979), p. 79.

48. Reilly, *Wedgwood*, 1, p. 27; Meteyard, *Life of Josiah Wedgwood*, 1, pp. 228–230; Burton, *Josiah Wedgwood: A Biography*, p. 21; Jewitt, *Life of Josiah Wedgwood*, pp. 102–103; and Julia Wedgwood, *The Personal Life of Josiah Wedgwood*, p. 16. In 1779, Wedgwood drew up a list of books he wished to own. "Besides county and other histories," the list included "travel [logs], and books on mathematics and science, especially chemistry . . . a large number of works of general literature: Bacon's works, [Laurence] Sterne's Letters, Churchill's [the Duke of Marlborough] Works, Hesiod, Horace, Cicero, Caesar . . . Bolingbroke on History, [Scottish poet James] Beattie on Truth" and others. Julia Wedgwood, *The Personal Life of Josiah Wedgwood*, p. 18.

49. "As [Wedgwood] was later to prove," Robin Reilly writes, "there were few tasks performed by craftsmen in his factories which he was unable to perform himself, often rather better than those he employed." Reilly, *Wedgwood*, 1, p. 27.

50. Quoted in Meteyard, *Life of Josiah Wedgwood*, 1, p. 222.

51. A *journeyman* is a person who has served an apprenticeship at a trade and is certified to work at it assisting or under another person.

52. Reilly, *Wedgwood*, 1, p. 29. When Whieldon retired in 1780, his fortune was estimated at £10,000 ($1.3 million today). Mankowitz, *Wedgwood*, p. 27.

53. Weatherill, *The Pottery Trade*, p. 51.

54. According to estimates later drawn up by Josiah Wedgwood, annual sales at his father's pottery in 1715 were £185. Josiah C. Wedgwood, *Staffordshire Pottery*, p. 49. Price indexes are from McCusker, *How Much Is That in Real Money?*, pp. 324, 332, and Council of Economic Advisers, *Economic Report of the President*, p. 373.

55. Most of the ornamental goods Josiah sold in Birmingham and Sheffield were *agateware*, pottery made of various local clays, blended to imitate marble and other natural stones.

56. E. Anthony Wrigley, "Urban Growth and Agricultural Change: England and the Continent in the Early Modern Period," in Rotberg and Rabb, eds., *Population and History*, pp. 126, 133.

57. Ibid., p. 126.

58. On the expansion of consumer goods in the eighteenth century, see Eric L. Jones, "The Fashion Manipulators: Consumer Tastes and British Industries, 1660–1800," in Louis P. Cain and Paul J. Uselding, eds., *Business Enterprise and Economic Change: Essays in Honor of Harold F. Williamson* (Kent, OH: Kent State University Press, 1973), pp. 201–207; Lorna Weatherill, *Consumer Behaviour and Material Culture in Britain, 1660–1760* (London: Routledge, 1988), pp. 25–42; Neil McKendrick, "Home Demand and Economic Growth: A New View of the Role of Women and Children in the Industrial Revolution," in Neil McKendrick, ed., *Historical Perspectives: Studies in English Thought and Society* (London: Europa, 1974), pp. 152–210; Neil McKendrick, "The Consumer Revolution of Eighteenth-Century England," in Neil McKendrick, John Brewer, and J. H. Plumb, *The Birth of a Consumer Society: The Commercialization of Eighteenth-Century England* (Bloomington, IN: Indiana University Press, 1982), pp. 9–99; and D. E. C. Eversley, "The Home Market and Economic Growth in England, 1750–80," in E. L. Jones and G. E. Mingay, eds., *Land, Labour and Population in the Industrial Revolution: Essays Presented to J. D. Chambers* (London: Edward Arnold, 1967), pp. 206–259.

59. Lord Shelburne to Lady Shelburne, 19 May 1766, quoted in Fitzmaurice, *Life of Shelburne*, 1, p. 276.

60. Josiah Wedgwood's Experiment Book, E. 19121-29, Wedgwood Manuscripts.

61. The numerical code constituted a form of shorthand. It also had the advantage, as Josiah noted, "of not being intelligible without the key." Quoted in Burton, *Josiah Wedgwood: A Biography*, p. 25.

62. John Wedgwood's Account Book, City Museum & Art Gallery, Stoke-on-Trent, cited in Reilly, *Wedgwood*, 1, p. 42. Burton puts the annual rent at £10. *Josiah Wedgwood: A Biography*, p. 27. Price indexes are from McCusker, *How Much Is That in Real Money?*, pp. 324, 332, and Council of Economic Advisers, *Economic Report of the President*, p. 373.

63. Eversley, "The Home Market and Economic Growth," p. 257.

64. Weatherill, *Consumer Behaviour*, pp. 24–42.

65. McKendrick, "The Consumer Revolution of Eighteenth-Century England," p. 10.

66. Meteyard, *Life of Josiah Wedgwood,* 1, p. 215, and Jones, "The Fashion Manipulators," p. 206. Annual sugar consumption also rose rapidly during this period, from about 12 pounds per person annually in 1730 to 24 pounds per capita in 1790. Carole Shammas, "Changes in English and Anglo-American Consumption 1550 to 1800," in John Brewer and Roy Porter, eds., *Consumption and the World of Goods* (London: Routledge, 1993), p. 182.

67. Josiah Tucker, *Instructions for Travelers* (1758) reprinted in Robert L. Schuyler, ed., *Josiah Tucker: A Selection from His Economic and Political Writings* (New York: Columbia University Press, 1931), pp. 245–246.

68. In 1773, the Dissenting minister Richard Price bemoaned the creeping consumerism among laboring Britons: "The lower ranks of the people are altered in every respect for the worse, while tea, wheaten bread and other delicasies are necessaries which were formerly unknown to them." Bishop George Berkeley disagreed, applauding the fact that women and men were now purchasing items formerly only accessible to higher ranks. Quoted in Roy Porter, *English Society in the Eighteenth Century* (New York: Penguin, 1982), pp. 236–237.

69. Quoted in McKendrick, "The Consumer Revolution of Eighteenth-Century England," p. 10.

70. In 1768, Josiah commented on the importance of a single shade:

> With respect to the colour of my ware, I endeavour to make it as pale as possible to continue it *cream-colour,* and find my customers in general . . . think the alteration I have made in that respect a great improvement. But it is impossible that any one colour, even though it were to come down from heaven, should please every taste, and I cannot *regularly* make two cream colours . . . without having two works for that purpose. (Quoted in Mankowitz, *Wedgwood,* p. 44.)

71. Quoted in Ann Finer and George Savage, eds., *The Selected Letters of Josiah Wedgwood* (London: Cory, Adams & Mackay, 1965), p. 7.

72. Landscapes, commemorative scenes, foliage, flowers, and birds were all popular subjects in the late eighteenth century. Wedgwood used Sadler & Green, a Liverpool firm, for his escalating printing needs. As soon as possible, he insisted on exclusive designs for his creamware, and he consistently provided Sadler & Green engravers with new subjects for individual pieces and whole services. Mankowitz, *Wedgwood,* p. 53. The quantities of creamware sent to Liverpool for transfer-printing rose from £30 a month in 1763 to more than £600 a month in 1771. Reilly, *Wedgwood,* 1, p. 48.

73. Consignments intended for export were probably fired in Liverpool.

74. In addition to the growing number of molds he commissioned, Wedgwood also ordered large quantities of biscuit (unglazed) earthenware from other local potters for use with his own glazes.

75. Meteyard, *Life of Josiah Wedgwood,* 1, pp. 329–331.

76. As Wedgwood grew older and his success escalated, he became increasingly prone to psychosomatic ailments. His symptoms—rapid weight loss, blurred vision, shortness of breath—were real and consistently correlated with moments of frustration and anxiety, usually surrounding his business. See, for example, Josiah Wedgwood to Thomas Bentley, 12 October 1772, quoted in Reilly, *Wedgwood,* 1, p. 100.

77. In the 1760s, his fitness regime involved "riding on Horsback from 10 to 20 miles a day . . . [and eating] Whey and yolks of eggs in abundance, with a mixture of Rhubarb and soap just to keep my body open." Josiah Wedgwood to Thomas Bentley, 26 July 1767, E. 18160-25, Wedgwood Manuscripts.

78. Reilly, *Wedgwood,* 1, p. 46.

79. See Reilly, *Josiah Wedgwood,* pp. 98–99, 240–242, and Neil McKendrick, "Josiah Wedgwood and Thomas Bentley: An Inventor-Entrepreneur Partnership in the Industrial Revolution," *Transactions of the Royal Historical Society* 14 (1964), pp. 1–33.

80. Robert E. Schofield, *The Lunar Society of Birmingham: A Social History of Provincial Science and Industry in Eighteenth-Century England* (Oxford: Clarendon Press, 1963), p. 44.

81. Burton, *Josiah Wedgwood: A Biography,* pp. 36–37.

82. John Money analyzes the eighteenth-century political experience of the Midlands in *Experience and Identity: Birmingham and the West Midlands, 1760–1800* (Manchester: Manchester University Press, 1977). On the larger role of manufacturers and merchants in transportation initiatives, see Koehn, *The Power of Commerce,* pp. 42–43. On the financing of eighteenth-century turnpikes and canals, see G. R. Hawke and J. P. P. Higgins, "Transport and Social Overhead Capital," in Floud and McCloskey, eds., *Economic History of Britain since 1700,* 1, pp. 227–252.

83. Josiah Wedgwood to John Wedgwood, 1 February 1765, E. 18059-25, Wedgwood Manuscripts.

84. Thomas Bentley, *A View of the Advantages of Inland Navigation with a Plan of a Navigable Canal* (London: Becket and De Hondt, 1766), p. 42. The canal was completed in 1771 at a total cost of £300,000. It reduced transport costs for raw materials and finished goods from 10 pence per ton-mile to 1½ pence. Reilly, *Wedgwood,* 1, p. 57.

85. Wedgwood also served as treasurer for the canal's newly formed investment company, the Proprietors of the Navigation from the Trent to the Mersey. Before he assumed his (unpaid) post, he was required to post a £10,000 bond. Burton, *Josiah Wedgwood: A Biography,* p. 59.

86. Documentation of Josiah and Sarah's marriage settlement and other monetary arrangements between them has not survived. But there can be little doubt, as Reilly notes, that Josiah's marriage "was of great financial importance to him." In 1764, for example, Sarah's brother lent Josiah £500 for improvements to one of his

workshops. When Sarah's father died in 1782, she inherited £20,000 or about $1.2 million today. Reilly, *Josiah Wedgwood,* p. 36. Price indexes are from McCusker, *How Much Is That in Real Money?,* pp. 325, 332, and Council of Economic Advisers, *Economic Report of the President,* p. 373.

87. Reilly, *Wedgwood,* 1, p. 55.

88. George Stubbs's 1780 painting of the Wedgwood family captures a comfortable intimacy between Josiah and Sarah that is curiously at odds with the formal, genteel setting of the group portrait.

89. As Josiah wrote his brother:

> I have just begun a Course of experiments for a white body & glaze which promiseth well hitherto. Sally is my chief helpmate in this as well as other things, & that she may not be hurried by having too many *Irons in the fire* as the phrase is I have ordered the spinning wheel [brought] into the Lumber room. She hath learned my [code] characters, at least to write them, but can scarcely read them at present. (Josiah Wedgwood to John Wedgwood, 6 March 1765, E. 18070-25, Wedgwood Manuscripts [original emphasis].)

90. Josiah Wedgwood to Thomas Bentley, January 1768, E. 18183-25, quoted in Reilly, *Wedgwood,* 1, p. 55.

91. This estimate is based on Wedgwood's 4 February 1770 letter to Bentley, E. 18288-25, Wedgwood Manuscripts, and inventory figures from Wedgwood's accounts, W/M 1713, Wedgwood Manuscripts. Price indexes are from McCusker, *How Much Is That in Real Money?,* pp. 325, 332, and Council of Economic Advisers, *Economic Report of the President,* p. 373.

92. The construction costs for the factory and surrounding buildings amounted to almost £10,000. Accounts, 28632-43, Wedgwood Manuscripts.

93. In the 1760s it was a generally accepted, though mistaken, notion that much of the pottery unearthed in Italy was Etruscan.

94. Reilly, *Wedgwood,* 1, p. 57.

95. Davis, *A History of Shopping,* p. 193.

96. Josiah Wedgwood to Thomas Bentley, 31 May 1767, E. 18149-25, Wedgwood Manuscripts (original emphasis).

97. By the early 1770s, Wedgwood was worried about collection and sales costs, his sales representatives' initiative, and the general condition of his various showrooms. Josiah Wedgwood to Thomas Bentley, 1 September 1772, E. 18397-25, Wedgwood Manuscripts.

98. Josiah Wedgwood to Thomas Bentley, 14–18 June 1768, E. 18199-25, Wedgwood Manuscripts.

99. Burton, *Josiah Wedgwood: A Biography,* p. 82.

100. To commemorate the opening of the factory, six blackware vases were made in the classical style. Each bore the inscription: "One of the first Day's productions at Etruria in Staffordshire by Wedgwood and Bentley." On the reverse was

inscribed "Artes Etruriae Renascuntur" ("The art of Etruria is reborn"). In November 1769, Wedgwood and his family moved into their new mansion. They celebrated by hosting a dinner in the Burslem town hall for 120 of Wedgwood's workmen. Kelly, *The Story of Wedgwood*, p. 28.

101. Neil McKendrick, "Josiah Wedgwood and Factory Discipline," *The Historical Journal* 1 (1961), p. 31.

102. Josiah Wedgwood to Thomas Bentley, 19 September 1772, quoted in McKendrick, "Factory Discipline," p. 32.

103. Robin Reilly, "A Lifetime of Achievement," in Hilary Young, ed., *Genius of Wedgwood* (London: Victoria & Albert Museum, 1995), p. 48.

104. Josiah claimed to have introduced the engine-turning process to the pottery industry, Commonplace Book, 28408-39, Wedgwood Manuscripts. See also Reilly, *Wedgwood*, 1, pp. 691–693.

105. Reilly, *Wedgwood*, 1, p. 691.

106. Weatherill, *The Pottery Trade*, p. 82.

107. In 1765, Josiah noted to a member of Parliament that the "principal of [our export] markets are the [American] Continent & [the West Indian] islands." Josiah Wedgwood to William Meredith, 2 March 1765, E. 18067-25, Wedgwood Manuscripts. As Reilly points out, Wedgwood meant America not Europe, when he referred to the "Continent." Reilly, *Wedgwood*, 1, p. 95. Creamware, cauliflower ware, agate, and tortoiseshell were in great demand in colonial America during the 1760s. Josiah C. Wedgwood and Thomas H. Ormsbee, *Staffordshire Pottery* (London: R. M. McBride, 1947), pp. 49–50. See also T. H. Breen, "An Empire of Goods: The Anglicization of Colonial America, 1690–1776," *Journal of British Studies* 25 (1986), pp. 467–499.

108. R. P. Thomas and D. N. McCloskey, "Overseas Trade and Empire, 1700–1860," in Floud and McCloskey, eds., *The Economic History of Britain since 1700*, 1, p. 87.

109. Cole, "Factors in Demand," p. 39.

110. Ibid.

111. Thomas and McCloskey, "Overseas Trade and Empire," p. 91.

112. Josiah Wedgwood to Thomas Bentley, 13 September 1769, E. 18252-25, Wedgwood Manuscripts (original emphasis).

113. Josiah Wedgwood to Thomas Bentley, 11 February 1771, in Lady Farrar, ed., *The Letters of Josiah Wedgwood* (Manchester: E. J. Morten Publishers, 1973), 2, p. 7 (original emphasis).

114. Josiah Wedgwood to Thomas Bentley, 5 August 1772, E. 18384-25, Wedgwood Manuscripts (original emphasis).

115. McKendrick, "Josiah Wedgwood and the Commercialization of the Potteries," in McKendrick, Brewer, and Plumb, *Birth of a Consumer Society*, pp. 127–132. See also Reilly, *Josiah Wedgwood*, pp. 219–220. It is not clear how Wedgwood and Bentley financed this initiative. They were helped by a relatively swift and largely posi-

tive response on the part of their targeted customers. As Wedgwood wrote to Bentley in July 1772: "If a few more should turn up with letters as these promises of farther *commissions* we may in the end have no great reason to repent what we have done." Josiah Wedgwood to Thomas Bentley, 29 July 1772, E. 18383-15, Wedgwood Manuscripts, quoted in Reilly, *Josiah Wedgwood*, p. 220. Price indexes are from McCusker, *How Much Is That in Real Money?*, pp. 325, 332, and Council of Economic Advisers, *Economic Report of the President*, p. 373.

116. Quoted in Reilly, *Josiah Wedgwood*, p. 220.

117. Less than two years after the parcels were sent from England, all but three of the customers who had purchased the pottery had paid in full. McKendrick, "Josiah Wedgwood and the Commercialization of the Potteries," p. 130.

118. Josiah Wedgwood to Thomas Bentley, 7 June 1773, E. 18489-25, Wedgwood Manuscripts.

119. Reilly, *Josiah Wedgwood*, p. 213. See also Mankowitz, *Wedgwood*, pp. 149–150.

120. According to one eighteenth-century traveler to England, the extravagance of the lower and middling classes had "risen to such a pitch as never before seen in the world!" G. C. Lichtenberg, *Lichtenberg's Visits to England*, Margaret L. Mare and W. H. Quarrel, eds. (Oxford: Oxford University Press, 1938), p. 122.

121. Nathaniel Forster, *An Enquiry into the Causes of the Present High Price of Provisions* (London: J. Fletcher and Co., 1767), p. 41.

122. C. Knick Harley, "Reassessing the Industrial Revolution: A Macro View," in Joel Mokyr, ed., *The British Industrial Revolution: An Economic Perspective* (Boulder, CO: Westview Press, 1993), p. 194.

123. Peter H. Lindert and Jeffrey G. Williamson, "Reinterpreting Britain's Social Tables, 1688–1913," *Explorations in Economic History* 20 (1983), p. 102.

124. Josiah Wedgwood to Thomas Bentley, 2 August 1770, E. 18314-25, Wedgwood Manuscripts.

125. Josiah Wedgwood, *Catalogue of Cameos, Intaglios, Medals, Bas-Reliefs, Busts and Small Statues*, 6th ed. (1787), p. 1, Wedgwood Manuscripts.

126. Neil McKendrick, "Josiah Wedgwood: An Eighteenth-Century Entrepreneur in Salesmanship and Marketing Techniques," *Economic History Review*, 2nd ser., 12 (1960), pp. 353–379.

127. Ibid., p. 358.

128. Josiah Wedgwood to Thomas Bentley, 23 August 1772, E. 18392-25, Wedgwood Manuscripts (original emphasis).

129. The 1790 Travellers' Book instructed salesmen to "arrive [at a given dealer or residence] very early in the morning or at 6 in the evening." Travellers' Book, 1790, E. 23571-12, Wedgwood Manuscripts, p. 2. The book also contained information on the creditworthiness of individual customers.

130. Josiah Wedgwood to Thomas Bentley, 14 November 1773, E. 18498-25, Wedgwood Manuscripts.

131. "It has always been my aim," Wedgwood wrote in 1787, "to improve the quality of the articles of my manufacture, rather than to lower their price." Josiah Wedgwood to Charles Twigg, 18 June 1787, E. 8636-10, Wedgwood Manuscripts. See also Memorandum, 19 September 1772, E. 18407-25, Wedgwood Manuscripts.

132. In 1773, Wedgwood noted that his tableware prices were two to three times as high as the industry average and considered cutting prices. Josiah Wedgwood to Thomas Bentley, 14 April 1773, E. 18451-25, Wedgwood Manuscripts.

133. 1770 Price List, 9484-52, Wedgwood Manuscripts. Wedgwood offered retailers quantity discounts as well as a 5 percent price reduction for paying in cash. Price indexes are from McCusker, *How Much Is That in Real Money?*, pp. 325, 332, and Council of Economic Advisers, *Economic Report of the President*, p. 373.

134. Josiah Wedgwood to Thomas Bentley, 14 April 1773, E. 18457-25, Wedgwood Manuscripts.

135. In 1770, Wedgwood and twenty-five other master potters agreed to maintain specified minimum prices for a range of table and other useful ware products. This is one of the earliest recorded examples of industrial price collusion in the eighteenth century. E. 9484-52, Wedgwood Manuscripts.

136. Josiah Wedgwood to Thomas Bentley, 21 and 22 April 1771, quoted in Finer and Savage, *Selected Letters*, p. 106; Neil McKendrick, "Josiah Wedgwood: An Eighteenth-Century Entrepreneur," pp. 354–355 (original emphasis).

137. McKendrick, "Josiah Wedgwood and the Commercialization of the Potteries," 126. See also Ralph M. Hower, "The Wedgwoods—Ten Generations of Potters," *Journal of Economic and Business History* 4 (1932), p. 305.

138. The Chinese market presented significant challenges to Wedgwood. He was particularly concerned about porcelain manufacturers there copying his patterns and products and selling these new designs in Europe. Josiah Wedgwood to Thomas Bentley, 23 January 1771, W/M 1441, Moseley Collection, Wedgwood Manuscripts.

139. Arthur Young, *A Farmer's Tour through the East of England* (London: W. Strahan, 1771), 4, pp. 360–362. For Wedgwood's list of export destinations in 1786, see Wedgwood Ledger 10:200, Wedgwood Manuscripts.

140. McKendrick, "Josiah Wedgwood and the Commercialization of the Potteries," p. 135. See also Reilly, *Josiah Wedgwood*, p. 217.

141. On the organization of work in British and U.S. potteries, see Frank Burchill and Richard Ross, *A History of the Potters' Union* (Hanley: Ceramic and Allied Trades Union, 1977), pp. 28, 33; Marc Jeffrey Stern, *The Pottery Industry of Trenton: A Skilled Trade in Transition, 1850–1929* (New Brunswick, NJ: Rutgers University Press, 1994); John Thomas, *The Rise of the Staffordshire Potteries* (Bath: Adams & Dart, 1971); and Richard Whipp, *Patterns of Labour: War and Social Change in the Pottery Industry* (London: Routledge, 1990).

142. E. P. Thompson, "Time, Work-Discipline and Industrial Capitalism," *Past & Present* 38 (1967), pp. 71, 73.

143. Commonplace Book, E. 28408-39, Wedgwood Manuscripts.

144. E. 19114-26, p. 2, Wedgwood Manuscripts.

145. E. 28408-39, Wedgwood Manuscripts, quoted in McKendrick, "Factory Discipline," p. 41.

146. Professor Marc Stern has pointed out to me that the punch clock was not universally adopted by other eighteenth-century potters. As late as the 1920s, many U.S. potteries lacked time clocks.

147. Josiah Wedgwood to Thomas Bentley, 7 October 1769, E. 18265-25, Wedgwood Manuscripts.

148. McKendrick, "Factory Discipline," p. 38.

149. "Some Regulations and Rules made for this Manufactory more than Thirty Years Back," 1810, 4045-5, Wedgwood Manuscripts.

150. The fine for most offenses was 2 shillings, 6 pence, which amounted to about 12 percent of an apprentice's weekly pay and about a quarter of a less skilled worker's paycheck. Commonplace Book, 28409-39, Wedgwood Manuscripts. On Wedgwood's efforts to discipline his workforce in the context of modern organizational theory, see Steven Postrel and Richard Rumelt, "Incentives, Routines, and Self-Command," *Industrial and Corporate Change* 1 (1992), pp. 397–425.

151. Josiah Wedgwood to Thomas Bentley, 9 April 1773, E. 18455-25, Wedgwood Manuscripts, quoted in McKendrick, "Factory Discipline," p. 34.

152. Josiah Wedgwood to Thomas Bentley, 19 May 1770, E. 18301-25, Wedgwood Manuscripts (original emphasis).

153. Wedgwood began training female apprentices in the 1770s. Commonplace Book, 28409-39, Wedgwood Manuscripts.

154. Josiah Wedgwood to Thomas Bentley, 23 August 1772, E. 18392-25, Wedgwood Manuscripts.

155. Hamilton was honored to have his collection emulated and sent Wedgwood drawings and models of various vases:

> "It is with infinite satisfaction," he wrote the potter in 1786, "that I reflect on having been in some measure instrumental in introducing a purer taste of forms & Ornaments by having placed my Collection of Antiquities in the British Museum, but a Wedgewood and a Bentley were necessary to diffuse that taste so universally, and it is to their liberal way of thinking & . . . acting that so good a taste prevails at present in Great Britain." (Quoted in Reilly, "A Lifetime of Achievement," p. 59. See E. 22495-30, Wedgwood Manuscripts.)

156. Josiah Wedgwood to Thomas Bentley, 1 May 1769, E. 18240-25, Wedgwood Manuscripts (original emphasis).

157. Josiah Wedgwood to Thomas Bentley, 2 August 1770, E. 18314-25, Wedgwood Manuscripts (original emphasis).

158. Josiah Wedgwood to Thomas Bentley, 14 February 1769, quoted in Reilly, *Wedgwood*, 1, p. 349. Price indexes are from McCusker, *How Much Is That in Real*

Money?, pp. 325, 332, and Council of Economic Advisers, *Economic Report of the President*, p. 373.

159. Josiah Wedgwood to Thomas Bentley, 1 October 1769, E. 18264-25, Wedgwood Manuscripts (original emphasis).

160. Reilly, *Wedgwood*, 1, p. 350.

161. Josiah Wedgwood to Thomas Bentley, 19 November 1769, E. 18269-25, Wedgwood Manuscripts.

162. Josiah Wedgwood to Thomas Bentley, 4 February 1770, E. 18288-25, Wedgwood Manuscripts, quoted in Reilly, *Wedgwood*, 1, p. 351. Price indexes are from McCusker, *How Much Is That in Real Money?*, pp. 325, 332, and Council of Economic Advisers, *Economic Report of the President*, p. 373.

163. Price Book of Workmanship, E. 30023-54, Wedgwood Manuscripts.

164. Josiah Wedgwood to Thomas Bentley, 23 August 1772, E. 18392-25, Wedgwood Manuscripts (original emphasis).

165. Josiah Wedgwood to Thomas Bentley, 19 November 1769, E. 18269-25, Wedgwood Manuscripts.

166. Josiah Wedgwood, *An Address to the Young Inhabitants of the Pottery* (Etruria, 1783), p. 21.

167. In 1782, a riot broke out at Etruria. This was chiefly a result of a disastrous harvest that had resulted in escalating food prices and shortages. The uprising occurred when a barge loaded with cheese and flour and bound for the Staffordshire potteries was redirected to Manchester. Rioters seized the vessel and sold its contents at reduced prices. The protesters were finally dispersed by the local militia. Reilly, *Josiah Wedgwood*, pp. 142–143.

168. Josiah Wedgwood to Thomas Bentley, 25 October 1777, E. 18788-25, Wedgwood Manuscripts, quoted in Reilly, *Josiah Wedgwood*, p. 135.

169. McKendrick, "Josiah Wedgwood: An Eighteenth-Century Entrepreneur," p. 353. Price indexes are from McCusker, *How Much Is That in Real Money?*, pp. 326, 332, and Council of Economic Advisers, *Economic Report of the President*, p. 373.

CHAPTER 3

1. William Cronon, *Nature's Metropolis: Chicago and the Great West* (New York: W. W. Norton, 1991), pp. 341–342. On the World's Columbian Exposition, see R. Reid Badger, *The Great American Fair: The World's Columbian Exposition and American Culture* (Chicago: Nelson Hall, 1979); Donald Miller, *City of the Century: The Epic of Chicago and the Making of America* (New York: Simon & Schuster, 1996); and Robert W. Rydell, *All the World's a Fair: Visions of Empire at American International Expositions, 1876–1916* (Chicago: University of Chicago Press, 1984). Some of the best primary sources are guidebooks to the Exposition, including: *The Best Things to Be Seen at the World's Fair* (Chicago: Columbia Guide, 1893); *The*

Artistic Guide to Chicago and the World's Columbian Exposition (Chicago: R. S. Pearle, 1893); and *A Week at the Fair: Illustrating the Exhibits and Wonders of the World's Columbian Exposition* (Chicago: Rand, McNally, 1893).

2. Robert Rydell, a historian of the Exposition, has noted that it was not coincidental that Frederick Jackson Turner chose to articulate his frontier thesis at the American Historical Association's annual meeting, held that summer in conjunction with the world's fair, Rydell, *All the World's a Fair,* p. 47.

3. At the geographic center of the late-nineteenth-century U.S. economy, Chicago had not been spared the effects of the depression of 1893. Beginning the previous year, industrial output had slumped while unemployment rose and liquidity tightened in the wake of frequent bank failures. When a national bank with a branch on the Exposition grounds failed, fair managers decided this was not a desirable exhibition "among the interesting collection on the [main promenade known as] Midway Plaisance." F. C. James, *The Growth of Chicago Banks* (New York: Harper & Brothers, 1938), 1, p. 582. On the Panic of 1893, see Milton Friedman and Anna Jacobson Schwartz, *A Monetary History of the United States, 1867–1960* (Princeton: Princeton University Press, 1971), pp. 104–113.

4. William James to Henry James, 22 September 1893, quoted in Badger, *The Great American Fair,* p. 97.

5. Hubert Howe Bancroft, *The Book of the Fair: An Historical and Descriptive Presentation of the World's Science, Art, and Industry, as Viewed through the Columbian Exposition at Chicago in 1893* (New York: Bounty Books, 1894), p. 50.

6. Admission to the fairgrounds was fifty cents a person (about $9.00 today). *A Week at the Fair,* p. 42; U.S. Department of Commerce, *Historical Statistics of the United States: Colonial Times to 1970* (Washington, DC: U.S. Government Printing Office, 1975), 1, p. 211; and Council of Economic Advisers, *Economic Report of the President* (Washington, DC: U.S. Government Printing Office, 2000), p. 373.

7. "Men of science," Adams wrote, "can never understand the ignorance and naiveté of the historian, who, when he came suddenly on a new power, asked naturally what it was; did it pull or did it push? Was it a screw or thrust? Did it flow or vibrate? Was it a wire or a mathematical line?" Henry Adams, *The Education of Henry Adams,* ed. Ernest Samuels (Boston: Houghton Mifflin, 1974), p. 342. On Adams's trip to the Exposition, see Paul Nagel, "Twice to the Fair," *Chicago History* 14 (1985), pp. 4–19.

8. Adams, *The Education of Henry Adams,* pp. 339–340.

9. Ibid., p. 343.

10. Quoted in Robert C. Alberts, *The Good Provider: H. J. Heinz and His* 57 *Varieties* (Boston: Houghton Mifflin, 1973), p. 121.

11. Historian Susan Strasser estimates that U.S. consumer products companies each spent as much as $30,000 (about $553,000 today) on their individual displays at the Columbian Exposition. Susan Strasser, *Satisfaction Guaranteed: The Mak-*

ing of the American Mass Market (New York: Pantheon, 1989), p. 181. Given the relative size of the Heinz pavilion, it's reasonable to conclude that the Pittsburgh company devoted substantially more than this sum to its marketing efforts at the world's fair.

12. *A Week at the Fair*, p. 127.

13. As the *New York Times* reported two weeks after the Columbian Exposition closed, "It has just been discovered that the gallery floor of the Agricultural Building has sagged where the pickle display of H. J. Heinz stood, owing to the vast crowd which constantly thronged their goods." *New York Times*, 14 November 1893.

14. In 1897, the company officially adopted the pickle labeled with the company name as its logo. Eleanor Foa Dienstag, *In Good Company: 125 Years at the Heinz Table, 1869–1994* (New York: Warner Books, 1994), p. 38.

15. "H. J. Heinz Company Sales: Consolidated and by Company," p. 1, MSS 57, H. J. Heinz Company Collection [hereafter MSS 57], box 2, folder 4, Library and Archives Division, Historical Society of Western Pennsylvania, Pittsburgh, PA [hereafter HSWP].

16. 1 November 1893, "The Personal Diaries of Henry J. Heinz," Heinz Family Office, Pittsburgh, PA [hereafter Heinz Family Office].

17. As Senator John Sherman wrote to his brother, the Civil War hero General William Tecumseh Sherman, in 1865, "The truth is the close of the war with our resources unimpaired gives an elevation, a scope to the ideas of leading capitalists far higher than anything ever undertaken in this country before. They talk of millions as confidently as [they spoke] formerly of thousands." Quoted in John M. Blum et al., *The National Experience: A History of the United States since 1865* (San Diego: Harcourt Brace Jovanovich, 1989), 2, p. 417.

18. Simon Kuznets, "Changes in the National Income of the United States of America since 1870," *Income and Wealth Series II* (London: Bowes & Bowes, 1952), p. 55. See also Philip Scranton, *Endless Novelty: Specialty Production and American Industrialization, 1865–1925* (Princeton: Princeton University Press, 1997), pp. 10–19.

19. Kuznets, "Changes in the National Income of the United States," p. 55.

20. Sidney Ratner, James H. Soltow, and Richard Sylla, *The Evolution of the American Economy* (New York: Basic Books, 1979), p. 253.

21. In 1860, about 53 percent of the American labor force farmed; 14 percent labored in manufacturing; and the remaining 33 percent worked in trade, construction, fishing, transport, and professional and domestic services. By 1920, 26 percent of the labor force worked in agriculture, 27 percent in manufacturing, 14 percent in trade, 6 percent in transportation, and 27 percent in construction, fishing, and professional and domestic services. Ratner, Soltow, and Sylla, *Evolution of the American Economy*, p. 306.

22. U.S. Department of Commerce, *Historical Statistics of the United States,* 1, pp. 11–12.

23. Alberts, *The Good Provider,* preface.

24. James Mayo, *The American Grocery Store: The Business Evolution of an Architectural Space* (Westport, CT: Greenwood Press, 1993), pp. 51–52.

25. Anna and John Henry Heinz had nine children. One of them, a girl, did not live past her first birthday.

26. For most of his life, John Henry Heinz used his middle, rather than first, name. Like his oldest son, he was known as Henry Heinz. The younger Heinz was called Harry by some family members and friends. To distinguish the two, I refer to the younger Heinz as Henry and the elder Heinz as John Henry.

27. Anna's father, Jacob Schmitt, was an official of the Lutheran Church and Bürgermeister or mayor of Kruspis. *Pittsburgh Leader,* 30 January 1899.

28. "Henry J. Heinz," *Supplement to the Trade Review and Finance Record* (30 July 1897), Heinz Family Scrapbook, p. 65, Heinz Family Office.

29. When the British novelist Charles Dickens visited Pittsburgh in 1842, he noted that it "is like Birmingham in England, at least its townspeople say so. . . . It certainly has a great quantity of smoke hanging over it, and is famous for its iron works." Charles Dickens, *American Notes* (New York: Modern Library, 1996), p. 203. See also "Pittsburgh," *The Atlantic Monthly* 21 (January 1868), pp. 17–36, and "Pittsburgh," *Harper's Weekly* 15 (18 February 1871), p. 147.

30. U.S. Department of Commerce, *Historical Statistics of the United States,* 2, p. 666.

31. Quoted in Oscar Handlin, "The City Grows," in Stefan Lorant, ed., *Pittsburgh: The Story of an American City* (Garden City, NJ: Doubleday, 1964), p. 92. On the political history of Pittsburgh, see Michael Fitzgibbon Holt, *Forging a Majority: The Formation of the Republican Party in Pittsburgh, 1848–1860* (New Haven: Yale University Press, 1969).

32. "Pittsburgh," *The Atlantic Monthly,* p. 20. See also John N. Ingham, "Reaching for Respectability: The Pittsburgh Industrial Elite at the Turn of the Century," in Gabriel P. Weisberg et al., eds., *Collecting in the Gilded Age: Art Patronage in Pittsburgh, 1890–1910* (Hanover, NH: University Press of New England, 1997), pp. 3–8.

33. Handlin, "The City Grows," p. 101.

34. Ibid. See also Joseph F. Rishel, *Founding Families of Pittsburgh: The Evolution of a Regional Elite, 1760–1910* (Pittsburgh: University of Pittsburgh Press, 1990).

35. Handlin, "The City Grows," pp. 87, 101. By 1880, the city was home to more than 250,000 people. J. Cutler Andrews, "The Civil War and Its Aftermath," in Lorant, *Pittsburgh,* p. 161.

36. As an adult, Henry Heinz described his father as "a giant in strength and endurance" and very indulgent toward his children. Quoted in Alberts, *The Good Provider,* p. 3. But the entrepreneur always ascribed his professional success wholly to his mother. "Last Will and Testament of Henry Heinz," MSS 57, box 3, folder 6,

HSWP. See also Hugh Cork, "His Fifty-Eighth Variety," *Organized Work and Workers* (February 1911), pp. 55–56, and E. D. McCafferty, *Henry J. Heinz: A Biography* (New York: Bartlett Orr Press, 1923), p. 19.

37. Alberts, *The Good Provider,* p. 3.

38. John T. Faris, Interview with Henry J. Heinz (1901), published as "Sunday School Captains of Industry," *Sunday School Times* (13 June 1901), p. 288.

39. "My mother," Heinz wrote in middle age, "could handle me because she knew how to inspire me; because she knew what to say, when and how." Quoted in McCafferty, *Henry J. Heinz,* p. 30.

40. We don't know exactly when Henry began his formal education. Alberts implies the young man went to school before age twelve. *The Good Provider,* pp. 4–5. Dienstag notes that by his twelfth birthday, Henry was walking a mile and a half each way to school in a neighboring village. *In Good Company,* p. 22.

41. "A German farm," wrote a late-eighteenth-century observer, "may be distinguished from the farm of the other citizens of [Pennsylvania] by . . . the extent of their orchards; the fertility of their fields; the luxuriance of their meadows, and a general appearance of plenty and neatness in everything that belongs to them." Benjamin Rush, *An Account of the Manners of the German Inhabitants of Pennsylvania* (1789), reprinted in *Pennsylvania Dutch Studies* 1 (1974), p. 14.

42. Dienstag, *In Good Company,* p. 22. Heinz's fascination with gardening continued throughout his life. See, for example, his "Plans of Cultivating Certain Kinds of Vegetables and How to Raise Good Horseradish" (20 March 1871), in Henry J. Heinz, "Business-Account Book," H. J. Heinz & Son 1868–70, Heinz Family Office.

43. Henry Heinz's son, Howard, once suggested that reading gave his father a headache. Dienstag, *In Good Company,* p. 22.

44. Throughout his life, Heinz nurtured a strong interest in construction. He always carried a tape measure, which he liked to whip out at any moment to measure a doorway or other structure that intrigued him. Heinz also collected brick samples from a variety of locations. Stephen Potter, *The Magic Number: The Story of '57'* (London: Max Reinhardt, 1959), pp. 29–32. Heinz's early records for his food business include extensive notes on carpentry, the price of lumber, and construction plans. See, for example, "Specification for the Building of a Truck," in Henry John Heinz, "Records," Heinz Family Office, p. 174.

45. On nineteenth-century housework, see Ruth Schwartz Cowan, *More Work for Mother: The Ironies of Household Technology from the Open Hearth to the Microwave* (New York: Basic Books, 1983), and Susan Strasser, *Never Done: A History of American Housework* (New York: Pantheon Books, 1982). On late-twentieth-century time constraints and domestic responsibilities, see Arlie Russell Hochschild, *The Time Bind: When Work Becomes Home & Home Becomes Work* (New York: Metropolitan Books, 1997), and Juliet Schor, *The Overworked American: The Unexpected Decline of Leisure* (New York: Basic Books, 1991).

46. Cowan, *More Work for Mother,* p. 31.

47. "Manufacturers of Pennsylvania" (1875), p. 383, Alberts MSS 37, Alberts Collection [hereafter MSS 37], box 3, folder 6, HSWP; Alberts, *The Good Provider,* p. 7.

48. On food safety and adulteration in the late nineteenth century, see George T. Angell, *Autobiographical Sketches and Personal Recollections* (Boston: Franklin Press, Rand Avery, 1884), pp. 59–62; Edgar W. Martin, *The Standard of Living in 1860: American Consumption Levels on the Eve of the Civil War* (Chicago: University of Chicago Press, 1942), pp. 244–245; C. O. Bates, "Pure Food Laws," *Iowa Academy of Science Proceedings* 8 (1900), p. 209; and Department of Agriculture, Division of Chemistry, Bulletin 13, *Foods and Food Adulterants* (Washington, DC, 1887–1903). For secondary sources, see James Harvey Young, *Pure Food: Securing the Federal Food and Drugs Act of 1906* (Princeton: Princeton University Press, 1989), pp. 3–65; Earl Chapin May, *The Canning Clan: A Pageant of Pioneering Americans* (New York: Macmillan, 1937), pp. 318–328; and Richard Osborn Cummings, *The American and His Food: A History of Food Habits in the United States* (Chicago: University of Chicago Press, 1940), pp. 91–104.

49. Young, *Pure Food,* pp. 31–65, 107–112.

50. See, for example, Lewis Caleb Beck, *Adulteration of Various Substances Used in Medicine and the Arts* (New York, 1846).

51. On the evolution of food safety regulation and its broader nineteenth-century context, see Young, *Pure Food.* On canned foods, see K. P. McElroy and W. D. Bigelow, "Canned Vegetables," in Division of Chemistry, Bulletin 13, *Foods and Food Adulterants,* part 8 (Washington, DC, 1893).

52. Alberts, *The Good Provider,* p. 6. See also "Henry John Heinz," in *Story of Old Allegheny City,* compiled by the Writers' Program of the Works Project Administration, 1st ed. (Pittsburgh: Allegheny Centennial Committee, 1941), pp. 153–154, MSS 37, box 3, folder 7, HSWP. In 1861, the average annual wage for a skilled laborer—carpenter, blacksmith, etc.—was about $375. U.S. Department of Commerce, *Historical Statistics of the United States,* 1, p. 165. Price indexes are from ibid., 1, p. 211 and Council of Economic Advisers, *Economic Report of the President,* p. 373.

53. Dienstag, *In Good Company,* p. 24, and Alberts, *The Good Provider,* p. 8.

54. Harold F. Williamson and Arnold R. Daum, *The American Petroleum Industry,* vol. 1: *The Age of Illumination, 1859–1899* (Evanston, IL: Northwestern University Press, 1959).

55. Titusville, one writer observed in 1860,

> is now the rendezvous of strangers eager for speculation. They barter prices in claims and shares; buy and sell sites and report the depth, show, or yield of wells, etc. Those who leave today tell others of the well they saw yielding 50 barrels of pure oil a day. . . . The story sends more back tomorrow. . . . Never was a hive of bees in time of swarming more astir, or making a greater buzz. (Quoted in Daniel Yergin, *The Prize: The Epic Quest for Oil, Money and Power* [New York: Simon & Schuster, 1992], p. 29.)

56. The region's frantic boom fueled intense land speculation. In early 1865, for example, oil was discovered in Pithole Creek, a village fifteen miles from Titusville. By June of that year, a farm that had been virtually worthless in 1864 sold for $1.3 million. In September, it was resold for $2 million. Yergin, *The Prize,* p. 31.

57. Yergin, *The Prize,* p. 29. In 1871, Pittsburgh's sixty refineries had a combined total of 36,000 barrels a day. J. Cutler Andrews, "The Civil War and Its Aftermath," in Lorant, ed., *Pittsburgh,* p. 163.

58. Quoted in Harold C. Livesay, *Andrew Carnegie and the Rise of Big Business* (Boston: Little, Brown, 1975), p. 52.

59. Conversation with Frank Kurtik, Archivist, Heinz Family Office, 26 August 1996; Heinz Order books, 1869–1871, Heinz Family Office; Henry John Heinz Notebook, 1868–1869, Heinz Family Office; and Alberts, *The Good Provider,* p. 11.

60. Livesay, *Andrew Carnegie,* p. 57.

61. Alfred D. Chandler Jr., *The Visible Hand: The Managerial Revolution in American Business* (Cambridge: Harvard University Press, 1977), pp. 122–187.

62. Chandler, *The Visible Hand,* p. 79.

63. Andrews, "The Civil War," p. 147.

64. Between 1865 and 1880, coal production in Pittsburgh climbed more than 300 percent to about $13 million or one-fifth of the nation's total. Andrews, "The Civil War," p. 162.

65. T. Mellon & Sons opened in early 1870. A year later, the bank loaned Frick $10,000 to organize the Henry C. Frick Coke Company. By 1873, Frick was "selling all the coke he could produce. When the [depression of 1873] hit, he, like Carnegie . . . expanded rather than contracted his operations. With more of . . . Mellon's money he bought more coal lands at bargain prices. When prosperity returned, coke prices rose steadily, and he and Mellon rejoiced in their foresight." Livesay, *Andrew Carnegie,* p. 120.

66. Pittsburgh was also a center for glass production. In 1870, sixty-eight glass factories were producing more than half the nation's total output. In 1895, Pittsburgh Plate Glass was organized as a trust from an amalgamation of local manufacturing companies. Andrews, "The Civil War," p. 148.

67. There is little historical evidence on Sallie Sloan Young's family, save that in the 1860s, they were relatively prosperous. According to an early-twentieth-century history of Pittsburgh, the Youngs were a "highly esteemed" Presbyterian family from County Down, Ireland. John Jordan, *A Century and a Half of Pittsburgh and Her People* (Pittsburgh: Lewis Publishing, 1908), pp. 4, 302.

68. Sallie and Henry had five children: Irene Edwilda, Clarence Noble, Howard Covode, Robert Eugene, and Clifford Eugene. Their fourth, Robert Eugene Heinz, died in infancy.

69. Henry Heinz had worked with Noble in 1868, when they had organized a partnership to manufacture bricks in a small town north of Pittsburgh.

70. The anchor, Dienstag theorizes, was "probably chosen because it was a Christian symbol." *In Good Company,* p. 24.

71. May, *The Canning Clan,* p. 2. See also Laurence A. Johnson, *Over the Counter and on the Shelf: Country Storekeeping in America, 1620–1920* (Rutland, VT: Charles E. Tuttle, 1961), pp. 84–92, and Edward F. Keuchel, "Master of the Art of Canning: Baltimore, 1860–1900," *Maryland Historical Magazine* 67, no. 4 (winter 1972), pp. 352–355.

72. Henry John Heinz Order Book 1870–1871, Heinz Family Office.

73. See, for instance, Henry John Heinz Notebook of 1875 and 1876, Heinz, Noble & Co., Heinz Family Office.

74. "The Personal Diaries of Henry J. Heinz," March 1875, Heinz Family Office.

75. Ibid., 30 March 1875.

76. "Manufacturers of Pennsylvania," p. 385.

77. "Outline of the H. J. Heinz Company," p. 2, MSS 57, box 2, folder 7, HSWP.

78. Ibid., p. 2.

79. Angell, *Autobiographical Sketches,* p. 59.

80. "Outline of the H. J. Heinz Company," p. 2; May, *The Canning Clan,* pp. 8–11.

81. Chandler, *The Visible Hand,* especially pp. 363–368.

82. In 1875, for example, Heinz dealt with pickle manufacturers in Cleveland, Philadelphia, and other cities. Henry Heinz Notebook of 1876–1877, Heinz Family Office. See also "Manufacturers of Pennsylvania," p. 384.

83. "Manufacturers of Pennsylvania," p. 381.

84. See Heinz's notes on pickle preservation in Henry Heinz, "Recipe Book" (labeled "Records"), p. 27, Heinz Family Office. He credits his brother John with discovering a process for preserving pickles in vinegar without significantly softening or discoloring the cucumbers: "John [Heinz] by a number of experiments demonstrated beyond a doubt that by first heating the vinegar from 125 to 140 [degrees], heating the vinegar by turning straw into it . . . , and allowing it to gradually cool off, it would preserve pickles in a perfect condition. . . ." See also pp. 20–21, 40, 50, 65, 90, 95, 102, 122, 130; Henry Heinz Notebook of 1876–1877, Heinz Family Office; and Henry Heinz Notebook of 1868–1869, Heinz Family Office.

85. Chandler, *The Visible Hand,* p. 473. See also Alfred D. Chandler Jr., *Scale and Scope: The Dynamics of Industrial Capitalism* (Cambridge, MA: Belknap, 1990), pp. 14–18.

86. The word *brand* is a very old one, dating back to the Middle Ages, when it connoted a burning piece of wood or torch. By the fifteenth century, its meaning had widened to include distinctive marks on goods and more generally, farm animals, to designate origin or ownership. Marks on products also came to indicate specific quality standards and genuineness. In the early modern period, for example, trade guilds such as the Goldsmith's Company of London stamped all their

goods. But prior to the late nineteenth century, the concept of a brand had primarily defensive connotations when it was applied off the farm. Identifying marks on various products were used to protect buyers from fraudulent or defective goods. Only a few eighteenth-century manufacturers, such as Josiah Wedgwood, used their names or reputations as part of a focused marketing strategy to help interest consumers in their products. On the history of trademarks, see Neil Borden, *The Economic Effects of Advertising* (Chicago: Richard D. Irwin, 1944), pp. 21–24. On Josiah Wedgwood's branding strategy, see Nancy F. Koehn, "Josiah Wedgwood and the First Industrial Revolution," in Thomas K. McCraw, ed., *Creating Modern Capitalism: How Entrepreneurs, Companies, and Countries Triumphed in Three Industrial Revolutions* (Cambridge: Harvard University Press, 1997), pp. 37–42. See also Cummings, *The American and His Food,* pp. 104–109.

87. Richard S. Tedlow, *New and Improved: The Story of Mass Marketing in America* (New York: Basic Books, 1990), p. 14.

88. "Manufacturers of Pennsylvania," p. 384.

89. U.S. Department of Commerce, *Historical Statistics of the United States,* 1, p. 224. Price indexes are from the Council of Economic Advisers, *Economic Report of the President,* p. 373.

90. Donna R. Garbaccia, *We Are What We Eat: Ethnic Food and the Making of Americans* (Cambridge: Harvard University Press, 1998), pp. 46, 156.

91. Mayo, *The American Grocery Store,* pp. 51–52.

92. In 1890, the average American family spent only 5 percent of its food expenditures on vegetables other than potatoes. Fruit occupied a similarly small portion of food budgets. By contrast, the average family used almost a third of its food dollars on meat. U.S. Department of Commerce and Labor, *Eighteenth Annual Report of the Commissioner of Labor* (Washington, DC: U.S. Government Printing Office, 1903), p. 83. Lower expenditures on produce were partially attributable to family gardens, such as that Heinz tended. But with or without gardens, Americans did not eat significant amounts of fruits or vegetables. On nineteenth-century diets, see Dorothy S. Brady, "Consumption and the Style of Life," in Lance E. Davis et al., eds., *American Economic Growth: An Economist's History of the United States* (New York: Harper & Row, 1972), p. 65.

93. Of almost 400 working-class families surveyed in 1875 by the Massachusetts Bureau of Labor Statistics, 55 percent reported that they ate vegetables other than potatoes or cabbage at only one meal a day; 43 percent ate other vegetables less than once a day. U.S. Commissioner of Labor, *Sixth Annual Report: Costs of Production* (Washington, DC: U.S. Government Printing Office, 1891), p. 693.

94. Margaret Jarman Hagood, *Mothers of the South,* excerpted in Rosalyn Baxandall, Linda Gordon, and Susan Reverby, eds., *America's Working Women* (New York: Random House, 1976), pp. 228–230.

95. Cowan, *More Work for Mother,* pp. 16–39.

96. Hagood, *Mothers of the South*, pp. 229–230.

97. "Forty Years of Progress," *The 57* 10, no. 9 (1909), p. 9, Heinz Family Office.

98. Robert C. Alberts, "The Good Provider," *American Heritage* 23, no. 2 (February 1972), p. 27. In 1932, Howard Heinz, Henry's eldest son and then president of the company, commented on the sociological consequences of the rise of food processing. One of the greatest benefits of the food industry, he wrote,

> has been what it has done for women. It has released them from the drudgery of the kitchen, increased their leisure, and made it possible for them either to engage in business or to enjoy the social life of the community without seriously interfering with their duties and responsibilities as home makers. (Howard Heinz, "The Industry of Food," in Samuel Crowther, ed., *A Basis for Stability* [Boston: Little, Brown, 1932], p. 195.)

For a contrasting view of the effects of mass production on household work, see Cowan, *More Work for Mother*, pp. 69–101.

99. John Morton Blum, "The Entrepreneurs," in Lorant, ed., *Pittsburgh*, p. 234, and Alberts, *The Good Provider*, p. 12.

100. 19 August 1875, "The Private Diary of H. J. Heinz," Robert C. Alberts, ed., pp. 3, 10, MSS 37, box 4, folder 2, HSWP. Historians' estimates of the size of the company's local acreage vary from 100 to 150 acres. See E. D. McCafferty, *Henry J. Heinz*, p. 75; "Outline of the H. J. Heinz Company," p. 2; and "Manufacturers of Pennsylvania," p. 384.

101. 24 April 1875, 1 May 1875, 6 May 1875, "The Private Diary of H. J. Heinz," pp. 3–5.

102. 19 April 1879, "The Personal Diaries of Henry J. Heinz."

103. "Outline of the H. J. Heinz Company," p. 2, and "Manufacturers of Pennsylvania," p. 384.

104. "Manufacturers of Pennsylvania," p. 384.

105. Alberts, *The Good Provider*, p. 13.

106. 27 May 1875, "The Personal Diaries of Henry J. Heinz."

107. Ibid., 7 October 1875.

108. Ibid., 8 April 1875.

109. Ibid., 20 April 1875.

110. Ibid., 24 April 1875.

111. Ibid., 3 July 1875.

112. Ibid., 17 July 1875.

113. "Outline of the H. J. Heinz Company," p. 3.

114. Ibid.

115. 29 October 1875, "The Private Diary of H. J. Heinz," p. 13.

116. Ibid., 27 October 1875, p. 13.

117. Ibid.

118. 8 October 1875, "The Personal Diary of H. J. Heinz for the year 1875," transcribed by Frank J. Kurtik, p. 70, Heinz Family Office.

119. Francis G. Couvares, *The Remaking of Pittsburgh: Class and Culture in an Industrializing City, 1877–1919* (Albany: State University of New York Press, 1984), p. 101.

120. 2 October 1875, "The Personal Diary of H. J. Heinz for the year 1875," p. 69, and 8 October 1875, "The Private Diary of H. J. Heinz," p. 12.

121. 2 November 1875, "Personal Diary of H. J. Heinz," quoted in McCafferty, *Henry J. Heinz,* p. 80.

122. 29 November 1875, "The Private Diary of H. J. Heinz," p. 15.

123. 13 December 1875, "The Personal Diaries of Henry J. Heinz."

124. Heinz, Noble & Company was charged with hiding inventory and other goods for the purposes of defrauding creditors. In early 1876, the firm was acquitted of the charges.

125. Twelve other firms filed bankruptcy petitions in Allegheny County that week. In the bankruptcy documents, Heinz, Noble & Company's assets were listed as $110,000. Its liabilities totaled $160,000 (or about $1.6 million and $2.3 million, respectively, today). Alberts, *The Good Provider,* p. 22. Price indexes are from U.S. Department of Commerce, *Historical Statistics of the United States,* 1, p. 211, and Council of Economic Advisers, *Economic Report of the President,* p. 373.

126. 24 April 1876, 5 June 1876, "The Private Diary of H. J. Heinz," pp. 27–28.

127. Ibid., 25 December 1875, p. 17. After the bankruptcy, Heinz began to compile a list of names titled "M.O.," standing for moral obligations. The list was made up of Heinz's creditors and their claims. By the early 1880s, Heinz had paid all these debts.

128. "People will censure us," Heinz wrote on 7 January 1876, "no matter how or what we do, and we get no credit for anything good we have done, but censure for everything that they don't like." See also entries for December 14, 17, 23, 25–28, and 30 of 1875 and January 7, 12, 13, 15, and 28 of 1876, "The Personal Diaries of Henry J. Heinz."

129. 30 December 1875, "The Personal Diaries of Henry J. Heinz."

130. 13 January 1876, "The Private Diary of H. J. Heinz," p. 21.

131. Ibid. "People talk terribly," Heinz wrote at the end of January. "We find we have at our worst time but few friends left." Ibid., 28 January 1876.

132. 25 December 1875, 13 January 1877, "The Private Diary of H. J. Heinz," pp. 17, 35.

133. 13 April 1876, 24 June 1876, 11 November 1876, "The Private Diary of H. J. Heinz," pp. 27–28, 32.

134. See, for example, Heinz's diary entries for 26 January 1876 and 17 August 1876, "The Private Diary of H. J. Heinz," pp. 23, 29.

135. Ibid., 1 January 1876, p. 19.

136. See, for example, Andrew Carnegie, "How I Served My Apprenticeship as a Business Man" (23 April 1896), H. J. Heinz Scrapbook, Heinz Family Office:

> I never was quite reconciled to working for other people. At the most, the railway officer has to look forward to the enjoyment of a stated salary, and he

has a great many people to please; even if he gets to be president he has sometimes a board of directors who cannot know what is best to be done; and even if this board of directors be satisfied, he has a board of stockholders to criticise him, and as the property is not his own he cannot manage it as he pleases. I always liked the idea of being my own master, of manufacturing something and giving employment to many men.

137. According to the agreement, John and Frederick Heinz each had a one-sixth interest in the company; Henry and John's mother, Anna Schmitt Heinz, also had a one-sixth stake. Because Henry Heinz was prohibited from participating in any partnership, Sallie Young Heinz assumed the remaining 50 percent interest in the company.

138. McCafferty, *Henry J. Heinz,* p. 89.

139. 8 April 1876, "The Private Diary of H. J. Heinz," p. 27.

140. Ibid., 13 July 1876, p. 29.

141. To save money on the overnight trip, he slept in a chair. Ibid., 18 February 1876, p. 25.

142. Ibid., 14 June 1876, p. 28.

143. Ibid., 30 August 1876, p. 30.

144. Ibid., 30 September 1876, p. 30.

145. Ibid., 14 July 1876, p. 29.

146. On the relationship between industrial growth, managerial imagination, and customer satisfaction, see Theodore Levitt, "Marketing Myopia," *Harvard Business Review* 38, no. 4 (July-August 1960), pp. 45–56.

147. Ibid., p. 46. With reference to current business performance, Gary Hamel and C. K. Prahalad have argued that the organizational ability to imagine new markets and create core competencies to serve these markets is a critical factor of competitive success. "Corporate Imagination and Expeditionary Marketing," *Harvard Business Review* 69, no. 4 (July-August 1991), pp. 81–92.

148. Levitt, "Marketing Myopia," p. 56.

149. 25 August 1876, "The Private Diary of H. J. Heinz," p. 29. On the significance of fairs and trade shows in late-nineteenth-century marketing, see Strasser, *Satisfaction Guaranteed,* pp. 180–184.

150. 6 November 1876, "The Private Diary of H. J. Heinz," p. 32.

151. Ibid., 2 November 1876, p. 31, and 4 December 1876, p. 33.

152. Ibid., 14 December 1876, pp. 33–34.

153. "H. J. Heinz Company Sales: Consolidated and by Company," p. 1. Price indexes are from U.S. Department of Commerce, *Historical Statistics of the United States,* 1, p. 211, and the Council of Economic Advisers, *Economic Report of the President,* p. 373.

154. "The Private Diary of H. J. Heinz," 16 December 1876, p. 34.

155. In 1880, company sales exceeded $197,000, on which F. & J. Heinz earned income of $31,000. "H. J. Heinz Company Sales: Consolidated and by Company," p. 1, and "The Private Diary of H. J. Heinz," 28 May 1880, p. 79.

156. "Outline of the H. J. Heinz Company," p. 4. Andrew Smith, who has written on the history of commercial ketchup, dates Heinz's introduction of the product to the later years of Heinz, Noble & Company. Andrew F. Smith, *Pure Ketchup: A History of America's National Condiment* (Columbia, SC: University of South Carolina Press, 1996), p. 42.

157. "Outline of the H. J. Heinz Company," p. 22.

158. By the midpoint of the war, the Federal government and the Confederacy combined had over 400,000 men in the field, creating a huge, incessant demand for food that would remain edible over several weeks. May, *The Canning Clan,* pp. 23–24.

159. Smith, *Pure Ketchup,* pp. 33–58.

160. In the late nineteenth century, California also became a center of ketchup production. Ibid., p. 36.

161. Ibid.

162. Dienstag, *In Good Company,* p. 154.

163. "Outline of the H. J. Heinz Company," p. 4.

164. Ibid., p. 2.

165. 7 March 1877, "The Private Diary of H. J. Heinz," p. 35.

166. "H. J. Heinz Company Sales: Consolidated and by Company," p. 1. Price indexes are from U.S. Department of Commerce, *Historical Statistics of the United States,* 1, p. 211, and Council of Economic Advisers, *Economic Report of the President,* p. 373.

167. Alberts, *The Good Provider,* p. 51.

168. 21 September 1881, "The Personal Diaries of Henry J. Heinz."

169. 11 October 1881, "The Private Diary of H. J. Heinz," p. 99.

170. "H. J. Heinz Company Sales: Consolidated and by Company," p. 1. Price indexes are from U.S. Department of Commerce, *Historical Statistics of the United States,* 1, p. 211, and Council of Economic Advisers, *Economic Report of the President,* p. 373.

171. Alberts, *The Good Provider,* p. 34.

172. "It is part of the Company's policy," a Heinz newsletter noted in 1909, "to regard no article as completely sold until it has been consumed." "Our Branch Houses: The Heinz System of Distribution Direct to the Trade and How It Is Handled," *The 57* 10, no. 9 (1909), p. 18, Heinz Family Office.

173. In 1877, food advertising accounted for 1 percent of the revenues of the nation's biggest advertising firm, N. W. Ayer. Twenty-four years later, 15 percent of N. W. Ayer's revenues came from the food industry, the largest of any category.

Ralph Hower, *The History of an Advertising Agency* (Cambridge: Harvard University Press, 1939), pp. 634–642.

174. At the 1901 Pan-American Exposition in Buffalo, the company had three exhibits: one serving food, one displaying employee photographs, and one displaying the goods Heinz produced for the American and British armies. Strasser, *Satisfaction Guaranteed,* pp. 180–181.

175. These and other promotional materials represented substantial expenditures for the business. In 1892, for example, Heinz contracted for $10,000 in advertising matter (about $186,000 today). This was more, he noted, "than ever before in my life." 10–15 July 1892, "The Personal Diaries of Henry J. Heinz," Heinz Family Office. Price indexes are from U.S. Department of Commerce, *Historical Statistics of the United States,* 1, p. 211, and Council of Economic Advisers, *Economic Report of the President,* p. 373.

176. In 1904, for example, almost 100,000 retailers attended the three-week-long Cleveland Retail Grocers Association Food Show. According to the company newsletter, *The 57,* six employees staffed the company exhibit. Heinz "salesmen of the Cleveland Branch were on hand every night and made many friends among the visiting grocers. At the conclusion of the exhibition, all of the goods used in the Heinz Exhibit were sold intact to H. Klaustermeyer Co., whose store is one of the finest in the city of Cleveland." "Ohio Food Shows and Festivals," *The 57* 7, no. 8 (1904), p. 7, H. J. Heinz Company, Pittsburgh, PA [hereafter H. J. Heinz Co.]. On food industry trade shows more generally, see Strasser, *Satisfaction Guaranteed,* pp. 183–184.

177. Alberts, *The Good Provider,* p. 127.

178. Heinz prohibited company billboards in and around Pittsburgh.

179. Quoted in Blum, "The Entrepreneurs," in Lorant, ed., *Pittsburgh,* p. 235.

180. "Birth of Trade Mark Described in Article, Number 57 Turns Up in Many Weird Ways," *The 57 News* (9 March 1920), pp. 1, 3, H. J. Heinz Co.

181. Ibid., p. 3.

182. Madison Square, a company newsletter noted, "is a beautiful park covering several acres of ground in the center of the great metropolis, and the sign can be seen for quite a distance up Fifth Avenue and Broadway." "Heinz Electric Sign, New York," *Pickles* 5, no. 3 (May 1901), pp. 1–2, Heinz Family Office.

183. In 1901, the sign was dismantled to make way for the Flatiron Building, which still stands at the intersection of Fifth Avenue and 23rd Street.

184. 5 August 1880, "The Personal Diaries of Henry J. Heinz."

185. Alberts, *The Good Provider,* p. 132.

186. Ibid., p. 133. During a hurricane in 1944, the "5" on the "57" sign was cast into the sea, and the Heinz management decided to abandon the pier as a business endeavor.

187. "Visitors at the 'Home of the 57' in 1903," *The 57* 7, no. 9 (February 1904), p. 1, H. J. Heinz Co.

188. The company's manufacturing facilities, Henry Heinz noted, "are open every working day in the year for the inspection of the public. This has gained for us additional confidence, because it offers people an opportunity of finding out for themselves the true quality of our products, and the cleanliness that is observed in their manufacture." "A Gigantic Pickle Concern," *Pickles* 4, no. 5 (1900), p. 3, H. J. Heinz Co. See also Edward Earle Purinton, "The Plant that Made the Pickle Famous," *The Independent* 101, no. 3705 (17 January 1920), pp. 93–95, 116–117.

189. 10–15 July 1892, "The Personal Diaries of Henry J. Heinz."

190. Alberts, *The Good Provider,* p. 123.

191. Thomas O. Jones and W. Earl Sasser, "Why Satisfied Customers Defect," *Harvard Business Review* 73, no. 6 (November-December 1995), pp. 88–99.

192. 5 January 1893, "The Personal Diaries of Henry J. Heinz."

193. Alberts, *The Good Provider,* p. 139.

194. See, for example, 2 March 1878, 7 March 1878, "The Personal Diaries of Henry J. Heinz." The word *salesmanship,* as historian Timothy Spears has written, did not enter common usage until late in the nineteenth century. An earlier term, *fastening,* was used to describe the face-to-face interaction between *drummers,* wholesale agents hired to drum up customers, and provincial merchants who traveled to urban centers on purchasing trips. An 1832 commercial publication described the sales process:

> Drumming in a mercantile sense consists in fastening upon every man, whether stranger or otherwise, who labors under suspicion of having come to the city to purchase goods for the country market; and the object thereof is . . . to obtain as great a share as possible of the wholesale business. (Asa Greene, "Mercantile Drumming," *Constellation* [5 May 1832], quoted in Timothy B. Spears, 100 *Years on the Road: The Traveling Salesman in American Culture* [New Haven: Yale University Press, 1995], pp. 29–30.)

See also Walter A. Friedman, "The Peddler's Progress: Salesmanship, Science, and Magic, 1880 to 1940" (Ph.D. diss., Columbia University, 1996), and Strasser, *Satisfaction Guaranteed,* pp. 58–88.

195. 17 November 1881, "The Personal Diaries of Henry J. Heinz."

196. *The Licensed Victualler and Catering Trades' Journal* (21 June 1899), p. 645, MSS 37, series II, box 3, folder 6, HSWP. Establishing and maintaining such a distribution network was significantly more expensive than working with existing wholesalers. In the late nineteenth century, Heinz's selling costs exceeded 33 percent of gross revenues. John Connor et al., *The Food Manufacturing Industries: Structure, Strategies, Performance, and Policies* (Lexington, MA: Lexington Books, 1985), p. 47.

197. *Pickles* 4, no. 2 (1900), p. 2, H. J. Heinz Co.

198. *The 57* 8, no. 6 (1904), p. 9, H. J. Heinz Co. See also "Two Essential Points for a Successful Salesman," *Pickles* 2, no. 7 (1898), H. J. Heinz Co.

199. "Getting Close to the Buyer," *Pickles* 5, no. 12 (1902), p. 1, H. J. Heinz Co.

200. Strasser, *Satisfaction Guaranteed*, pp. 194–200; Chandler, *The Visible Hand*, pp. 290–299; and Thomas Horst, *At Home Abroad: A Study of the Domestic and Foreign Operations of the American Food Processing Industry* (Cambridge, MA: Ballinger, 1974), p. 17.

201. An early-twentieth-century Heinz company sales manual stated:

> There are grocers in every territory who are progressive up-to-date merchandisers and who are able to sell a large volume of Heinz products. These key stores are deserving of your special attention, and at every opportunity you should plan an outstanding Heinz sale which will not only increase the volume during the period of the sale but will help to make the dealer and the clerks more interested in the Heinz line and his customers better acquainted with the 57 Varieties. (H. J. Heinz Company, *57 Sales Manual* [Pittsburgh: H. J. Heinz Co., n.d.], MSS 57, box 21, p. 84, HSWP.)

202. "The Salesman as Advertiser," *Pickles* 2, no. 4 (May 1898), pp. 4–5, H. J. Heinz Co.

203. Company publications, such as "Superior Store Displays," outlined specific merchandising techniques and were intended to help strengthen relationships between Heinz sales representatives and grocers. As the early-twentieth-century booklet explained:

> The devices listed herein are the inventions of a corps of experts employed by the Company who devise ways and means of a practical nature for display purposes. They are intended to stimulate interest in interior store displays, which are recognized as the last link in the chain of advertising—the final reminder—necessary to influence the sale. ("Superior Store Displays," p. 1, MSS 57, box 4, folder 10, HSWP.)

On sales management at the turn of the century, see Walter A. Friedman, "The Science of Selling: Managers, Salesmen, Scientists, and Prospects, 1880 to 1920," (unpublished paper presented to the Business History Seminar, Harvard Business School, 1997), "The Peddler's Progress," and "John H. Patterson and the Sales Strategy of the National Cash Register Company, 1884 to 1922," *Business History Review* 72, no. 4 (Winter 1998), pp. 552–584.

204. *57 Sales Manual*, p. 81.

205. Strasser, *Satisfaction Guaranteed*, p. 196.

206. "From Day to Day: How the Convention Opened and How It Progressed," *Pickles* 5, no. 10 (1902), p. 7, H. J. Heinz Co.

207. "Our Annual Conventions," *Pickles* 4, no. 2 (1900), p. 8, H. J. Heinz Co.

208. "From Day to Day," p. 6.

209. See, for example, Henry Heinz's struggle with the Noble brothers in early 1876 to control the failed company's trademark, 20 March 1876, 1 May 1878, "The Private Diary of H. J. Heinz," pp. 26, 44.

210. On the relationship between brand equity and product extension, see David A. Aaker, "Should You Take Your Brand to Where the Action Is?" *Harvard Business Review* 75, no. 5 (September-October 1997), pp. 135–143; David A. Aaker, *Building Strong Brands* (New York: Free Press, 1996), pp. 269–302; Peter Farquhar, "Managing Brand Equity," *Journal of Advertising Research* 30, no. 4 (August/September 1990), pp. 7–12; Peter Farquhar, Julia Han, and Yuji Ijiri, "Strategies for Leveraging Master Brands," *Marketing Research* 4, no. 3 (September 1992), pp. 33–43; Stephen King, "Brand Building in the 1990s," *Journal of Consumer Marketing* 8, no. 4 (fall 1991), pp. 43–52; John M. Murphy, *Brand Strategy* (New York: Prentice Hall, 1990), pp. 110–114; and Alan Webber, "What Great Brands Do," *Fast Company* 10 (August-September 1997), pp. 96–103.

211. "Outline of the H. J. Heinz Company," p. 4.

212. Ibid., pp. 4–6.

213. Fruit jellies were an exception. Competition from the Campbell Soup Company, combined with housewives' preference for making their own preserves, depressed sales in the late nineteenth century. Stephen Potter, *The Magic Number*, pp. 49–50.

214. May, *The Canning Clan*, p. 2. See also Johnson, *Over the Counter and on the Shelf*, pp. 84–92, and Keuchel, "Master of the Art of Canning," pp. 352–355.

215. May, *The Canning Clan*, pp. 7–12.

216. Potter, *The Magic Number*, p. 49.

217. Keuchel, "Master of the Art of Canning," p. 359.

218. Alberts, *The Good Provider*, p. 49.

219. Chandler, *The Visible Hand*, p. 295.

220. The hole-in-cap can was used mainly for liquids, which were inserted through a small hole in the top of the can. The can was soldered shut after filling.

221. *The Licensed Victualler and Catering Trades' Journal*, (21 June 1899), p. 645. Heinz also worked with company farmers on the development of improved seed hybrids. "Pittsburgh—A Great City," *American Monthly Review of Reviews* 31, no. 1 (January 1905), p. 65.

222. Chandler, *The Visible Hand*, pp. 312, 349.

223. "Pittsburgh—A Great City," p. 65.

224. Connor et al., *The Food Manufacturing Industries*, p. 45. U.S. Department of Commerce, *Historical Statistics of the United States*, 2, p. 699. In 1900, food processing amounted to about 20 percent of U.S. GNP. Ibid.

225. Hollis Godfrey, "Food of the City Worker," *The Atlantic Monthly* 103 (February 1909), pp. 267–277.

226. Vivek Bammi, "Nutrition, the Historian, and Public Policy: A Case Study of the U.S. Nutrition Policy in the 20th Century," *Journal of Social History* 14, no. 4 (1980), p. 630.

227. Young, *Pure Food*, pp. 183–185.

228. "Pure Food," *The Outlook* (3 February 1906), p. 236.

229. Quoted in Young, *Pure Food,* p. 193.

230. P.L. 59-384. On the evolution of the final legislation, see Young, *Pure Food,* pp. 253–272.

231. In February 1906, Wiley made the same argument to an assembly of food canners and wholesalers. You must say to the American people, he said, that

> "there is absolutely nothing in the goods, which we present you, but what we say is in them;" and then instead of selling one can you will sell three before five years. But if you continue to try to deceive the American people, and to claim the right to use things that 95 percent of our people do not want you to use, your business is going to suffer. (Quoted in ibid., p. 177.)

232. Potter, *The Magic Number,* p. 52.

233. Alberts, *The Good Provider,* p. 74.

234. Ibid., p. 79.

235. 18 June 1886, in the Index to "The Private Diary of H. J. Heinz." As a result of this 1886 meeting, Heinz became a household word in the United Kingdom. Heinz baked beans on toast remains a staple in the English diet, and many modern British consumers assume Heinz is a British brand.

236. "Our European Progress," *The 57* 7, no. 6 (1903), p. 2, H. J. Heinz Co.

237. *H. J. Heinz Company: Producers, Manufacturers, and Distributors of Pure Food Products* (Pittsburgh, 1910), p. 22, Heinz Family Office.

238. "H. J. Heinz Company Sales," p. 1.

239. McCafferty, *Henry J. Heinz,* p. 171.

240. Ibid., p. 106. The company changed its name from F. & J. Heinz to H. J. Heinz in 1888.

241. See, for example, George Burton Hotchkiss and Richard B. Franken, *The Leadership of Advertised Brands: A Study of 100 Representative Commodities Showing the Name and Brands That Are Most Familiar to the Public* (Garden City, NY: Doubleday, Page, 1923), p. 113.

242. H. J. Heinz Co., *Heinz Annual Report* 1995, p. 7.

CHAPTER 4

1. "Marshall Field & Company, Retail," *Chicago Dry Goods Reporter* (11 October 1902), p. 1, Marshall Field & Co. Archives, Chicago, IL; Donald L. Miller, *City of the Century: The Epic of Chicago and the Making of America* (New York: Simon & Schuster, 1996), p. 254. For comparison, in 1997, the average size of a supermarket was about 27,000 square feet. *Progressive Grocer 1997 Annual Report* (April 1997), p. 38. In the same year, the average size of a Wal-Mart store was 92,000 square feet; a Wal-Mart Supercenter store measured 183,000 square feet. Moody's Investor Service, "Wal-Mart Stores—History and Debt Report," (6 October 1997), p. 9.

2. "Marshall Field & Company, Retail," p. 1.

3. Robert W. Twyman, *The History of Marshall Field & Co., 1852–1906* (Philadelphia: University of Pennsylvania Press, 1954), p. 158.

4. Lloyd Wendt and Herman Kogan, *Give the Lady What She Wants! The Story of Marshall Field & Company* (Chicago: Rand-McNally, 1952), p. 235. Price indexes are from U.S. Department of Commerce, *Historical Statistics of the United States: Colonial Times to 1970* (Washington, DC: U.S. Government Printing Office, 1976), 1, p. 211, and Council of Economic Advisers, *Economic Report of the President* (Washington, DC: U.S. Government Printing Office, 2000), p. 373.

5. The *Chicago Dry Goods Reporter* used a much higher figure, estimating opening week attendance at over two million or 350,000 a day. On a daily basis, the magazine pointed out, this number of visitors dwarfed that of the extraordinarily popular World's Columbian Exposition held in Chicago in 1893. "Marshall Field & Company, Retail," pp. 1–2. More than 150,000 visitors a day had come to the world's fair. William Cronon, *Nature's Metropolis: Chicago and the Great West* (New York: W. W. Norton, 1991), p. 343.

6. "Marshall Field & Company, Retail," p. 28. See also Hamilton Hull, *Marshall Field & Company: The World's Greatest Merchandiser* (Chicago: Marshall Field & Co., 1907), pp. 43–44, Chicago Historical Society, Chicago, IL [hereafter CHS].

7. "Marshall Field & Company, Retail," p. 28.

8. During the holiday shopping season, the number of employees rose to 8,000. "Marshall Field & Company, Retail," p. 2; *Chicago Evening Journal* (26 September 1903).

9. Marshall Field & Co., *Book of Rules*, quoted in Henry P. Williams, "Evolution of the Moral Idea in Business," *Interior* (18 December 1902), p. 7, Marshall Field & Co. Archives. See also Marshall Field & Co., *Employees Manual* (May 1927), CHS.

10. Quoted in Wendt and Kogan, *Give the Lady What She Wants!*, p. 235.

11. Hull, *Marshall Field & Company: The World's Greatest Merchandiser*, p. 19.

12. Record Book, "Rents, June 1, 1901," Marshall Field & Co. Archives, quoted in Twyman, *The History of Marshall Field & Co., 1852–1906*, p. 158. The *Chicago Dry Goods Reporter* estimated the building's cost at $2 million. "Marshall Field & Company, Retail," p. 2. Price indexes are from U.S. Department of Commerce, *Historical Statistics of the United States*, 1, p. 211, and Council of Economic Advisers, *Economic Report of the President*, p. 373.

13. Accounting Ledgers, 1874–1906, Marshall Field & Co. Archives.

14. Ibid. Price indexes are from U.S. Department of Commerce, *Historical Statistics of the United States*, 1, p. 211, and Council of Economic Advisers, *Economic Report of the President*, p. 373.

15. Accounting Ledgers, 1874–1906, Marshall Field & Co. Archives. Return on sales is calculated by dividing net profit by total net sales, which is gross sales minus returned merchandise. The resulting ratio is the company's overall profit margin. As a measure of profitability, return on sales is widely used in modern retailing.

Field's 5 percent return was higher than that of many stores at the end of the twentieth century. In 1997, for example, Wal-Mart earned 2.9 percent on total sales. Dayton Hudson, since 1990 the parent company of Marshall Field, earned 1.8 percent, and Sears 3.3 percent. The Gap, by contrast earned 8.6 percent. Wal-Mart, *Annual Report 1997;* Dayton Hudson Corporation, *Annual Report 1997;* Sears, Roebuck and Co., *Annual Report 1997;* and Gap Inc., *Annual Report 1997.*

16. "Marshall Field & Company," *Saturday Evening Review* (31 August 1904), Field Family Papers, box 2, Marshall Field I Correspondence, CHS.

17. Quoted in Herbert A. Gibbons, *John Wanamaker* (New York: Harper, 1926), 2, p. 206.

18. Elizabeth A. Perkins, "The Consumer Frontier: Household Consumption in Early Kentucky," *Journal of American History* 78, no. 2 (1991), pp. 494–497. In nineteenth-century retailing, see also Nancy F. Koehn, "Consumerism and Consumption," in Paul Finkelman, ed., *Encyclopedia of the United States in the Nineteenth Century* (New York: Charles Scribner's Sons, forthcoming).

19. Quoted in Ralph M. Hower, *History of Macy's of New York, 1858–1919: Chapters in the Evolution of the Department Store* (Cambridge: Harvard University Press, 1943), p. 79.

20. On the evolution of specialized retailing, see ibid., pp. 73–88, and Koehn, "Consumersim and Consumption."

21. Dorothy S. Brady, "Consumption and the Style of Life," in Lance E. Davis et al., eds., *American Economic Growth: An Economist's History of the United States* (New York: Harper & Row, 1972), p. 65. Price indexes are from U.S. Department of Commerce, *Historical Statistics of the United States,* 1, p. 211, and Council of Economic Advisers, *Economic Report of the President,* p. 373.

22. Lucy Larcom, *A New England Girlhood: Outlined from Memory* (New York: Houghton, Mifflin, 1889), pp. 149–150.

23. Alfred D. Chandler Jr., *The Visible Hand: The Managerial Revolution in American Business* (Cambridge: Harvard University Press, 1977), p. 86.

24. Robert E. Gallman, "Commodity Output, 1839–1899," in *Trends in the American Economy in the Nineteenth Century: A Report of the National Bureau of Economic Research* (Princeton: Princeton University Press, 1960), p. 26.

25. U.S. Department of Commerce, *Historical Statistics of the United States,* 1, p. 224.

26. On the growth of the mass market in the late nineteenth century, see Daniel J. Boorstin, *The Americans: The Democratic Experience* (New York: Vintage, 1974); Glenn Porter and Harold C. Livesay, *Merchants and Manufacturers: Studies in the Changing Structure of Nineteenth-Century Marketing* (Baltimore: Johns Hopkins University Press, 1971); Susan Strasser, *Satisfaction Guaranteed: The Making of the American Mass Market* (New York: Pantheon, 1989); and Richard S. Tedlow, *New and Improved: The Story of Mass Marketing in America* (New York: Basic Books, 1990).

27. Advertisements quoted in Robert C. Alberts, *The Good Provider: H. J. Heinz and His 57 Varieties* (Boston: Houghton Mifflin, 1973), p. 129; Tedlow, *New and Improved,* p. 50; and Boorstin, *The Americans,* p. 96.

28. See note 194 in chapter 3.

29. Daniel J. Boorstin, "A. Montgomery Ward's Mail-Order Business," *Chicago History* 2, no. 3 (spring/summer 1973), p. 149.

30. Quoted in Robert Hendrickson, *The Grand Emporiums: The Illustrated History of America's Great Department Stores* (New York: Stein and Day, 1979), p. 224.

31. William Leach, *Land of Desire: Merchants, Power and the Rise of a New American Culture* (New York: Pantheon, 1993), p. 44.

32. On the early history of New York department stores, see Hower, *History of Macy's of New York, 1858–1919,* pp. 67–98; Frank M. Mayfield, *The Department Store Story* (New York: Fairchild, 1949), pp. 35–55; Tom Mahoney and Leonard Sloane, *The Great Merchants: America's Foremost Retail Institutions and the People Who Made Them* (New York: Harper & Row, 1974); and John William Ferry, *A History of the Department Store* (New York: Macmillan, 1960), pp. 35–100.

33. Chandler, *The Visible Hand,* pp. 207–239.

34. Ibid., p. 209.

35. U.S. Department of Commerce, *Historical Statistics of the United States,* 1, p. 8.

36. The figure for 1856 is from Thomas Wakefield Goodspeed, "Marshall Field," *University of Chicago Biographical Sketches* 1 (April 1922), p. 6, Field Family Papers, box 1, folder 11, CHS. The figure for 1900 is from Campbell Gibson, "Population of the 100 Largest Cities and Other Urban Places in the United States: 1790 to 1990," Population Division Working Paper No. 27 (Washington, DC: U.S. Bureau of the Census, 1998), Table 13.

37. F. Herbert Stead, "The Civic Life of Chicago: An Impression Left on a Guest After a Visit of a Dozen Days," *Review of Reviews,* vol. 8 (July 1893), p. 96.

38. George W. Steevens, *The Land of the Dollar* (New York: Dodd, Mead, 1897), p. 144

39. Quoted in Wayne Andrews, *Battle for Chicago* (New York: Harcourt, Brace, 1946), pp. 11–12.

40. Twyman, *The History of Marshall Field & Co.,* p. 1.

41. Theodore Dreiser, "Life Stories of Successful Men—Interview with Marshall Field," *Success* (8 December 1898), p. 7, Field Family Papers, box 1, folder 6, CHS.

42. Ibid. In the 1898 interview, Field described his family in Conway, Massachusetts, as poor, "as all people were in those days, more or less."

43. Harold Irwin Cleveland, "Fifty-five Years in Business: The Life of Marshall Field—Chapter 1," *System* 13, no. 5 (May 1906), pp. 459–460.

44. Dreiser, "Life Stories of Successful Men," p. 7.

45. Ibid.

46. Quoted in Cleveland, "Fifty-five Years in Business," p. 462.

47. Goodspeed, "Marshall Field," p. 5; Wayne Andrews, *Battle for Chicago,* p. 9; and John Tebbel, *The Marshall Fields: A Study in Wealth* (New York: E. P. Dutton, 1947), pp. 20–21.

48. Dreiser, "Life Stories of Successful Men," p. 7.

49. Ibid. Biographers differ on how much money Field brought with him to Chicago. Estimates range from $1 to $1,000. It could not have been a large sum. His starting salary for Davis was $4 a week, and his family lacked the means to offer him significant financial help. See Twyman, *The History of Marshall Field & Co.,* p. 10; Andrews, *Battle for Chicago,* p. 19; Cleveland, "Fifty-five Years in Business," p. 464; Goodspeed, "Marshall Field," p. 7; and Tom Mahoney, "The Store that Stamina Built," *Midwest Magazine* (4 June 1967), p. 9.

50. In 1856, the firm's sales were $600,000 (about $11.2 million today). Goodspeed, "Marshall Field," p. 8. Price indexes are from U.S. Department of Commerce, *Historical Statistics of the United States,* 1, p. 211, and Council of Economic Advisers, *Economic Report of the President,* p. 373.

51. Gibson, "Population of the 100 Largest Cities and Other Urban Places in the United States: 1790 to 1990," Tables 8–15.

52. Andrews, *Battle for Chicago,* p. 18.

53. Dreiser, "Life Stories of Successful Men," p. 7.

54. Richard S. Tedlow, "Nineteenth-Century Retailing and the Rise of the Department Store," in Alfred D. Chandler Jr., Thomas K. McCraw, and Richard S. Tedlow, eds., *Management Past and Present: A Casebook on the History of American Business* (Cincinnati: South-western College Publishing, 1996), p. 3-7.

55. Frederika Bremer, quoted in Andrews, *Battle for Chicago,* p. 12. See also Julian Ralph, *Our Great West: A Study of the Present Conditions and Future Possibilities of the New Commonwealths and Capitals of the United States* (New York: Harper and Brothers, 1893), pp. 1–16.

56. Goodspeed, "Marshall Field," p. 8. Price indexes are from U.S. Department of Commerce, *Historical Statistics of the United States,* 1, p. 211, and Council of Economic Advisers, *Economic Report of the President,* p. 373.

57. Quoted in Harold Irwin Cleveland, "Fifty-five Years in Business: The Life of Marshall Field—Chapter II" *System* 13, no. 6 (June 1906), pp. 563–564.

58. Until the end of the nineteenth century, when the term *salesman* entered common parlance, wholesale agents such as Field were often known as *drummers,* a term derived from the practice of drumming up custom. See Timothy B. Spears, *100 Years on the Road: The Traveling Salesman in American Culture* (New Haven: Yale University Press, 1995), pp. 29–30. On Field's reputation in the late 1850s, see Cleveland, "Fifty-five Years in Business—Chapter II," pp. 563–564.

59. "Copy of Articles of Agreement Between Cooley, Farwell & Co. and Marshall Field, January 29, 1862," Marshall Field & Co. Archives. See also Marshall Field &

Co., "Brief Historical Outline of Marshall Field & Company," p. 1, Marshall Field & Co. Archives; Twyman, *The History of Marshall Field & Co.*, pp. 12–13.

60. Quoted in Cleveland, "Fifty-five Years in Business: The Life of Marshall Field—Chapter II," pp. 566–567.

61. Tebbel estimates that in 1863 Field was worth more than $30,000 (about $410 million today). *The Marshall Fields*, p. 27. Price indexes are from U.S. Department of Commerce, *Historical Statistics of the United States*, 1, p. 211, and Council of Economic Advisers, *Economic Report of the President*, p. 373.

62. Tebbel, *The Marshall Fields*, p. 25.

63. Twyman, *The History of Marshall Field & Co.*, p. 13.

64. Ibid., p. 15.

65. *Chicago Tribune* (16 March 1864).

66. "Mr. Leiter was a good financial manager," recalled John Farwell in 1906, years after Marshall Field's had become Chicago's most famous department store. "Mr. Field was the supreme goods manager and salesman. With these essential qualities possessed to the ultimate degree, it was only a question of time what the position of the firm would be in the business world." Quoted in Harold Irwin Cleveland, "Fifty-five Years in Business, The Life of Marshall Field—Chapter III," *System* 14, no. 1 (July 1906), p. 26.

67. Twyman estimates Field's savings at $200,000 and Leiter's capital at $100,000. *The History of Marshall Field & Co.*, pp. 15–16. Goodspeed's estimates are higher. He contends Field had $260,000, Leiter half that amount. "Marshall Field," p. 10. The sources on Field are silent as to how and where he earned over $200,000. Perhaps it was the accumulated total of his share in company profits over the four years since he had become a partner or the result of diligent saving, rising profits, and smart investments in other ventures. Later in life, Field became a savvy, successful investor in a wide range of what were then young new industries, including steel, railroads, and electricity, and other investors followed his movements closely. See, for example, Field's financial correspondence, 1875–1877, 1902–1903, 1903–1906, Field Family Papers, box 3 (3 vols.), CHS.

68. Field initially approached Cyrus and Willam McCormick, whose Chicago agricultural machinery business was well established in the 1860s. They delayed making an investment decision, and when Palmer offered to sell his business, Field felt he could not afford to wait any longer for the McCormicks.

69. Palmer & Company had three floors devoted to wholesale operations, including storage, and one floor dedicated to retail. The business occupied approximately 80,000 square feet. Twyman, *The History of Marshall Field & Co.*, p. 18.

70. Ibid., p. 3. On Palmer's early success in the broader context of Chicago retailing, see Joseph Siry, *Carson Pirie Scott: Louis Sullivan and the Chicago Department Store* (Chicago: University of Chicago Press, 1988), pp. 15–18, and S. H. Ditchett,

Marshall Field & Company: The Life Story of a Great Concern (New York: Dry Goods Economist, 1922), pp. 15–17.

71. Palmer kept costs low in both the retail and wholesale branches by eliminating the jobber and buying direct from manufacturers. As early as the 1850s, he made his own buying trips abroad. He also established direct connections with New England textile makers. Tedlow, "Nineteenth-Century Retailing," pp. 3–7, and Twyman, *The History of Marshall Field & Co.*, pp. 7–8. See also the *Chicago Press and Tribune* (8 June 1859).

72. Quoted in Cleveland, "Fifty-five Years in Business, The Life of Marshall Field—Chapter III," p. 24.

73. Twyman, *The History of Marshall Field & Co.*, p. 17; Goodspeed, "Marshall Field," p. 10; and Andrews, *Battle for Chicago*, p. 23.

74. "Articles of Co-Partnership," 4 January 1865, pp. 1–6, 12, Marshall Field & Co. Archives.

75. Ibid., p. 12.

76. Ibid., pp. 5–6.

77. Ibid., p. 15.

78. Carson, Pirie & Company added retail sales to their wholesale operations in 1867. John Vinci, "Carson Pirie Scott: 125 Years in Business," *Chicago History* 8, no. 2 (summer 1979), p. 92.

79. In 1866, the young ambitious Aaron Montgomery Ward clerked for Field, Palmer & Leiter. Boorstin, "A. Montgomery Ward's Mail-Order Business," p. 144.

80. Field, Palmer & Leiter letter to wholesale customers (10 August 1865), Marshall Field & Co. Archives.

81. In 1865, Dutch gingham sold wholesale was priced at twenty-four cents a yard, "gents" collars at twenty-three cents each, and Waterville shawls at $1.30 each. Twyman, *The History of Marshall Field & Co.*, p. 19.

82. See, for example, *Inter-Ocean* (28 January 1890). Quoted in Twyman, *The History of Marshall Field & Co., 1852–1906*, p. 35. There was room for exceptions, however. Leiter and Field were prepared to grant additional time to specific merchants who faced extenuating circumstances. They paid particular attention to promising retailers in new, growing communities. Retail customers were extended credit on an individual basis.

83. H. N. Higinbotham, "The Cash and Credit Systems Compared in Light of Experience," *Chicago Dry Goods Reporter* (20 February 1897).

84. Credit investigation at Field's and other large wholesalers, Higinbotham noted in 1906, was "so thorough and searching . . . that it is practically hopeless for [debtors] to attempt any concealment of unfavorable conditions. Again, the credit men of the wholesale houses are the keenest men in the business, and their judgment of human nature is quick and shrewd." Harlow N. Higinbotham, *The Making of a Merchant* (Chicago: Forbes, 1906), p. 41.

85. Twyman, *The History of Marshall Field & Co.*, p. 35.

86. U.S. Department of Commerce, *Historical Statistics of the United States*, 1, p. 201.

87. Four months after Field, Leiter & Palmer opened, the company's stock of goods was worth $300,000 less than when the partnership agreements had been drawn up. To help the company meet its financial obligations, Potter Palmer bought back $25,000 of Field's equity in the firm. Twyman, *The History of Marshall Field & Co.*, p. 20.

88. Ibid., p. 177. The company's return on sales was about 3 percent. Price indexes are from U.S. Department of Commerce, *Historical Statistics of the United States*, 1, p. 211, and Council of Economic Advisers, *Economic Report of the President*, p. 373.

89. Miller, *City of the Century*, p. 140.

90. Wendt and Kogan, *Give the Lady What She Wants!*, p. 89. Price indexes are from U.S. Department of Commerce, *Historical Statistics of the United States*, 1, p. 211, and Council of Economic Advisers, *Economic Report of the President*, p. 373.

91. Twyman, *The History of Marshall Field & Co.*, pp. 23–24.

92. *Chicago Tribune* (13 October 1868).

93. Ibid.

94. On the history of State Street's commercial development, see Siry, *Carson Pirie Scott*, pp. 12–63.

95. In 1881, the dry goods retailer Schlesinger & Mayer relocated to State Street. See Siry, *Carson Pirie Scott*, pp. 28–33, and Vinci, "Carson Pirie Scott: 125 Years in Business," p. 92.

96. See, for example, Alfred Theodore Andreas, *History of Chicago* (1886, reprint, New York: Arno Press, 1975), 3, p. 718.

97. The fire's destruction was extraordinary: more than 2,000 acres were devastated, almost 18,000 buildings were destroyed, and 9,000 people were left homeless. The Chicago Relief and Aid Society estimated total damages at $196 million. Bessie Louise Pierce, *A History of Chicago* (Chicago: University of Chicago Press, 1957), 3, pp. 5–6, 10. On the Great Fire, see ibid., pp. 1–19; Miller, *City of the Century*, pp. 143–171; and Herman Kogan and Robert Cromie, *The Great Fire: Chicago, 1871* (New York: Putnam, 1971).

98. The company collected almost $1.75 million in insurance on its lost inventory. Tedlow, "Nineteenth-Century Retailing," pp. 3–8.

99. The new structure cost the company $140,000. Its West Side location was influential in determining the reconstructed city's new wholesale center. When Field, Leiter & Company and J. V. Farwell's firm obtained sites in this area, other smaller jobbers moved into the West Side. Twyman, *The History of Marshall Field & Co.*, p. 42. See also Herman Kogan, "Grander and Statelier than Ever," *Chicago History* 1, no. 4 (fall 1971), p. 236.

100. *Chicago Tribune* (26 April 1872); *Chicago Times* (13 October 1868).

101. Quoted in Wendt and Kogan, *Give the Lady What She Wants!*, pp. 130–131.

102. *1883: Chicago's First Half Century* (Chicago: Inter Ocean Publishing, 1883), p. 87.

103. "This store," a company publication of 1900 noted, "has long been one of the most interesting sights of Chicago, and is probably visited by a greater number of people than any other place in the city." "Views of the Retail Store of Marshall Field & Company" (1900), p. 1, CHS.

104. In 1871, eleven major trunk lines converged in Chicago. David Buisseret, *Historic Illinois from the Air* (Chicago: University of Chicago Press, 1990), p. 135. See also Harold M. Mayer and Richard C. Wade, *Chicago: Growth of a Metropolis* (Chicago: University of Chicago Press, 1969), pp. 35–42.

105. On the ethnic composition of Chicago's population in the later nineteenth century, see Pierce, *A History of Chicago*, 3, pp. 20–63.

106. Theodore Dreiser, *A Book About Myself* (New York: Boni and Liveright, 1922), p. 20.

107. On Chicago's significance in the nation's late-nineteenth-century economic development, see Cronon, *Nature's Metropolis*, pp. 282–283.

108. Levi Leiter to William H. A. Spaulding, 21 November 1881, Leiter Papers, box 46, folder 4, CHS.

109. Accounting Ledgers, Marshall Field & Co. Archives. Price indexes are from U.S. Department of Commerce, *Historical Statistics of the United States*, 1, p. 211, and Council of Economic Advisers, *Economic Report of the President*, p. 373.

110. Richard Tedlow, *New and Improved*, p. 10.

111. Tedlow, "Nineteenth-Century Retailing," p. 3–6. "It was not unknown," a corporate historian has noted, for some merchants "to solder a one-ounce lead sinker on the appropriate side of the balance scale. Some miscreants put ground beans in the coffee, sand in the sugar . . . lard in the butter, and potato starch in the lard." Alberts, *The Good Provider: H. J. Heinz and His 57 Varieties*, p. 45. In 1892, Dreiser wrote several articles for the *Chicago Globe* on swindling auctioneers and retailers in the city. See the *Chicago Globe* (6 October 1892, 16 October 1892, and 19 October 1892), reprinted in Theodore Dreiser, *Journalism*, vol. 1: *Newspaper Writings, 1892–1985*, T. D. Nostwich, ed. (Philadelphia: University of Pennsylvania Press, 1988), pp. 8–15.

112. A. T. Stewart founded his New York dry goods store in 1823. Two decades later, he integrated backward and established a wholesale division. By the 1850s, his business had expanded significantly and was known as Stewart's Dry Goods Palace.

113. See, for example, Hower, *History of Macy's of New York*, pp. 98–110. On John Wanamaker's salesmanship, see Leach, *Land of Desire*, pp. 32–38.

114. In 1869, the partnership was reorganized to include Marshall Field, Levi Leiter, Joseph and Henry Field, Lorenzo Woodhouse, and Henry Willing, Copartnership Agreement, 1 January 1869, Marshall Field & Co. Archives.

115. In making company policy, explained John Shedd, a longtime partner and Field's chosen successor, "the founders and owners of this institution [have] always tried to govern their actions by their interpretation of the effect upon public morale." Quoted in Ditchett, *Marshall Field & Company,* p. 23.

116. Richard A. Easterlin, "Interregional Differences in Per Capita Income, Population, and Total Income, 1840–1950," in *Trends in the American Economy in the Nineteenth Century* (Princeton: Princeton University Press, 1960), p. 137.

117. Ibid., p. 137. See also Ralph Gray and John M. Peterson, *Economic Development of the United States* (Homewood, IL: Irwin, 1974), pp. 287–289, and U.S. Department of Commerce, *Historical Statistics of the United States,* 1, p. 242.

118. Henry Ward Beecher, *Eyes and Ears* (Boston: Ticknor & Fields, 1864), p. 100.

119. Quoted in Dreiser, "Life Stories of Successful Men," p. 7.

120. Ditchett, *Marshall Field & Company,* p. 23.

121. *Chicago Tribune* (27 January 1881); Twyman, *The History of Marshall Field & Co.,* pp. 63–64.

122. *Gross margin,* the difference between an item's sales price and its cost, is often used as a general indicator of the value added by the retailing environment, operations, and brand. In the 1880s, Field's retail gross margins averaged about 25 percent. Accounting Ledgers, Marshall Field & Co. Archives. Relative to modern retailers, this is comparable to those enjoyed by Dayton Hudson (renamed Target Corporation in 2000) today, higher than Wal-Mart's 1996 gross margins of 22 percent, and substantially lower than The Gap's 41 percent. Field's retail operating profit for the 1880s averaged almost 9 percent of sales, about the same as The Gap in 1996. Accounting Ledgers, Marshall Field & Co. Archives, and Wal-Mart, *Annual Report 1997;* Dayton Hudson Corporation, *Annual Report 1997;* Sears, Roebuck and Co., *Annual Report 1997;* and Gap Inc., *Annual Report 1997.* After the depression of the early 1890s, Marshall Field's gross margins and operating profits rose substantially as a result of a number of factors: brand development, increased operating efficiencies (including smarter pricing policies), and rising income levels in Chicago.

123. Field, Leiter & Co., *Wholesale Spring Catalogue* (1870), p. 15, CHS.

124. Marshall Field & Company, "View of the Retail Store" (1900), p. 1, CHS.

125. Accounting Ledgers, Marshall Field & Co. Archives.

126. Offerings continued to expand in the early twentieth century. In 1904, for example, when Selfridge left the company to found his own business, Marshall Field's had over 150 departments. Accounting Ledgers, Marshall Field & Co.; Tedlow, "Nineteenth-Century Retailing," pp. 3–8.

127. In 1871, Field and Leiter's combined sales from the wholesale and retail divisions were $13.5 million. Assuming the business enjoyed gross margins of 20 percent and received a 1 percent discount for paying promptly on these stocks, the

savings would have totaled $112,500 or 14 percent of net profits. Accounting Ledgers, Marshall Field & Co. Archives. In 1871, the commercial credit agency Hurst and Garlock attributed a considerable portion of Field and Leiter's profits to such discounts. *Hurst, Garlock and Company's Western Report* (1871), p. 521, quoted in Twyman, *The History of Marshall Field & Co.*, p. 37.

128. Field, Leiter & Company, *Wholesale Spring Catalogue* (1870), p. 72, CHS.

129. Twyman, *The History of Marshall Field & Co.*, pp. 97–103.

130. Field, Leiter & Company, *Wholesale Advertising Circular* (1877), Marshall Field & Co. Archives.

131. See, for example, the *Chicago Evening Journal* (27 April 1872).

132. *Wholesale Catalogue* (n.d.), Marshall Field & Co. Archives.

133. Twyman, *The History of Marshall Field & Co.*, p. 94.

134. Ibid., pp. 92–97.

135. Accounting Ledgers, Marshall Field & Co. Archives.

136. Twyman, *The History of Marshall Field & Co.*, p. 66. Retail buyers were expected to pay for goods on the same terms as outside wholesale customers. No credit was allowed between divisions.

137. Because of buying expertise, higher conversion rates, and increased leverage with suppliers, modern specialty stores usually attain higher turns. But even superior performers, such as The Gap, rarely achieve turnover rates higher than five; most average about four on clothing. National Retail Federation, *Merchandising and Operating Results of Retail Stores in 1995* (New York: John Wiley & Sons, 1996), p. 87.

138. Accounting Ledgers, Marshall Field & Co. Archives.

139. Quoted in Twyman, *The History of Marshall Field & Co.*, p. 117.

140. Ibid., p. 122.

141. Quoted in ibid., p. 113.

142. C. L. Drain Record Book, 1900–1907, Marshall Field & Co. Archives; Accounting Ledgers, Marshall Field & Co. Archives.

143. On wealthy and upper-middle-class women in late-nineteenth-century Chicago, see Wendt and Kogan, *Give the Lady What She Wants!*, pp. 153–161.

144. Ibid., pp. 228–229.

145. "In the larger cities," the *Dry Goods Reporter* noted in 1898, "there are well-defined gradations in department stores. One attracts to itself the better class trade, and handles the more expensive lines of goods. To another goes the medium-class trade, while the management of a third seeks to cater to the cheaper and lower class demand." "English View of Department Stores," *Chicago Dry Goods Reporter* 28 (12 February 1898), p. 51.

146. Quoted in Wendt and Kogan, *Give the Lady What She Wants!*, p. 230.

147. See, for example, the *Chicago Tribune* (26 October 1887).

148. Interview with Tony Jahn, Marshall Field & Co. Archivist (21 October 1997).

149. Marshall Field & Co. Archives.

150. Twyman, *The History of Marshall Field & Co.*, p. 28.

151. "Foreign Purchases, 1892–1900," Marshall Field & Co. Archives, quoted in Twyman, *The History of Marshall Field & Co.*, p. 99; *Chicago Evening Post* (16 January 1906).

152. In 1883, Field's wholesale inventory of kid gloves turned seven times. Accounting Ledgers, Marshall Field & Co. Archives.

153. Accounting Ledgers, Marshall Field & Co. Archives.

154. *Chicago Tribune* (21 November 1861).

155. J. V. Farwell & Co., Invoice (18 February 1868), quoted in Twyman, *The History of Marshall Field & Co.*, p. 30; Field, Leiter & Co., *Wholesale Spring Catalogue* (1870), p. 15, CHS.

156. Marshall Field & Co., *Employees Manual*, Retail (1927), p. 14, CHS.

157. By 1900, the company's return rate on retail merchandise was over 13 percent. Accounting Ledgers, Marshall Field & Co. Archives. Return rates at modern department stores average between 5 and 10 percent.

158. Quoted in Twyman, *The History of Marshall Field & Co.*, p. 123.

159. Quoted in ibid., p. 126.

160. *Chicago Dry Goods Reporter* (9 October 1897), p. 11.

161. "'Don'ts' for Employees," Marshall Field & Co. Archives.

162. Accounting Ledgers, Marshall Field & Co. Archives.

163. *Chicago Tribune* (11 April 1896).

164. Hull, *Marshall Field & Company: The World's Greatest Merchandiser*, p. 46.

165. *Chicago Tribune* (31 January 1865).

166. Ibid. (17 September 1867).

167. Quoted in Twyman, *The History of Marshall Field & Co.*, p. 144.

168. *Chicago Tribune* (1 February 1892).

169. Quoted in Wendt and Kogan, *Give the Lady What She Wants!*, p. 218.

170. Accounting Ledgers, Marshall Field & Co. Archives. Modern department stores' marketing expenses, including publicity, advertising, and special events typically total 3 to 4 percent of sales.

CHAPTER 5

1. Lisa Belkin, "Beauty: Creating New Scents," *New York Times Magazine* (23 February 1986), p. 61. In 1985, Estée Lauder Inc. was one of the most successful manufacturers of fragrances in the United States. "Women's Toiletries & Cosmetics," *Mediamark Research* (spring 1986), p. 305. See also Ira P. Schneiderman, Jeanette L. Driscoll, and Audrey S. Balchen, "Toiletries, Cosmetics, Fragrances, and Beauty Aids," Fairchild Fact File Market Research Division (New York: Fairchild Publications, 1988), p. 24.

2. Kennedy Fraser, "As Gorgeous As It Gets," *The New Yorker* (15 September 1986), p. 42.

3. Belkin, "Beauty: Creating New Scents," p. 61.

4. Maryln Schwartz, "Estée Lauder Uses Nose-How to Advantage," *Dallas Morning News* (9 September 1985), p. 1c. According to Leonard Lauder, who in the mid-1980s was president and chief executive officer of Estée Lauder Inc., the name "Beautiful" originated with Carol Phillips, president of the company's Clinique division. See Fraser, "As Gorgeous As It Gets," p. 54.

5. Schneiderman, Driscoll, and Balchen, "Toiletries, Cosmetics, Fragrances, and Beauty Aids," p. 24.

6. Ibid.

7. Ibid., p. 23.

8. On consumption and its relationship to self-identity, see Russell Belk, "Possessions and the Extended Self," *Journal of Consumer Research* 15, no. 2 (September 1988), pp. 139–168; Russell Belk, "Cultural and Historical Differences in Concepts of Self and Their Effects on Attitudes toward Having and Giving," in Thomas C. Kinnear, ed., *Advances in Consumer Research* (Provo, UT: Association for Consumer Research, 1984), pp. 753–760; Susan Fournier, "Understanding Consumer-Brand Relationships," working paper 96-018, Harvard Business School, Boston, 1995 and "The Consumer and the Brand: An Understanding within the Framework of Interpersonal Relationships," working paper, 97-024, Harvard Business School, Boston, 1996; Grant McCracken, *Culture and Consumption: New Approaches to the Symbolic Character of Consumer Goods and Activities* (Bloomington, IN: Indiana University Press, 1988); Thorstein Veblen, *The Theory of the Leisure Class* (New York: Macmillan, 1912); and Melanie Wallendorf and Eric J. Arnould, "My Favorite Things: A Cross-Cultural Inquiry into Object Attachment, Possessiveness, and Social Linkage," *Journal of Consumer Research* 14, no. 4 (March 1988), pp. 531–547.

9. See, for example, "Estée Lauder's Dazzling Duo," *Beauty Fashion* 82, no. 7 (July 1998), pp. 42, 125.

10. "You Are So Beautiful," *Beauty Fashion* 69, no. 8 (August 1985), p. 62. Even in the upscale market for prestige fragrances, perfume did not constitute the majority of sales. Most female and male buyers were not willing to pay $150 an ounce for scent. Instead, manufacturers relied on lower-priced products, such as eau de perfume or cologne, to drive revenues. In 1985, the suggested retail price for Beautiful Eau de Parfum was $45.00 for 3.3 ounces.

11. Bernice Kanner, "Here Comes the Bride," *New York* (9 September 1985), p. 26.

12. Ibid.

13. Estée Lauder, *Estée: A Success Story* (New York: Random House, 1985), p. 149.

14. The company went public in late 1995 when it sold a small fraction of the total equity to outside investors. The majority of the stock continued to be held by members of the Lauder family. See, for example, The Estée Lauder Companies Inc., *Prospectus* (16 November 1995).

15. Estée Lauder Companies Inc., *Annual Report 1996*, p. 7. See also Kathleen Deveny, "Leonard Lauder Is Making His Mom Proud," *Business Week* (4 September 1989), p. 68; "Lauder's Success Formula: Instinct, Timing, and Research," *Business Week* (26 September 1983), pp. 122–124; and Sandra Salmans, "Estée Lauder: The Scents of Success," *New York Times* (18 April 1982), pp. F1, F27.

16. Deveny, "Leonard Lauder Is Making His Mom Proud," p. 69, and Lisa Belkin, "Man Behind Estée Lauder Image Steps Out of His Mother's Shadow," *Palm Beach Post* (27 November 1987), p. 7D.

17. See, for example, Schwartz, "Estée Lauder Uses Nose-How to Advantage."

18. Quoted in Fraser, "As Gorgeous As It Gets," p. 68.

19. Robin Wiest, "Lauder Sets a Big and Beautiful Debut," *Women's Wear Daily* (28 June 1985), p. 13.

20. In the mid-1980s, Estée Lauder Inc. distributed about 120 million samples of its products each year. Kanner, "Here Comes the Bride," p. 28.

21. In 1985, Calvin Klein spent more than $17 million to launch "Obsession." Belkin, "Creating New Scents."

22. When Estée Lauder Inc. launched Pleasures in 1994, the company projected factory sales of $35 million for the inaugural year. "The Beauty Top 50," *Women's Wear Daily* (8 September 1995), p. S26.

23. "NPD Beauty Trends Semi-Annual Report," *Beauty Fashion* 82, no. 8 (August 1998), p. 28.

24. Estée Lauder Companies Inc., *Annual Report 1999*, p. 10.

25. Estée Lauder Companies Inc., *Annual Report 1998*, p. 6.

26. Gilbert Vail, *A History of Cosmetics in America* (New York: Toilet Goods Association, 1947), p. 138. Price indexes are from U.S. Department of Commerce, *Historical Statistics of the United States: Colonial Times to 1970* (Washington, DC: U.S. Government Printing Office, 1975), 1, p. 211, and Council of Economic Advisers, *Economic Report of the President* (Washington, DC: U.S. Government Printing Office, 2000), p. 373.

27. Population figures and historical price index are from U.S. Department of Commerce, *Historical Statistics of the United States*, 1, p. 8. More current price indexes are from Council of Economic Advisers, *Economic Report of the President*, p. 373.

28. Sales of prestige cosmetics accounted for about $16 billion of total global revenues. Estée Lauder Companies Inc., *Annual Report 1997*, p. 6.

29. Standard & Poor's, *Industry Surveys* (28 September 1995), p. T116.

30. "It's Personal," *American Demographics* 15, no. 7 (July 1993), p. 17.

31. As the twentieth century drew to a close, the company that Estée Lauder founded continued to ground its strategy on demand-side possibilities. "Tastes and styles are evolving on a world scale," noted her son and company CEO, Leonard Lauder, in 1999. These priorities are

> greatly influenced by what is happening in America. Improving global economies are making available and affordable products once reserved for a privileged few. The baby boom has come roaring into middle age with money to spend and a determination to fight the effects of growing older. U.S. teenagers have exploded into a major demographic group with a reported $122 billion in spending power. Growing, shifting populations are creating exciting new marketing opportunities. . . . As always, our philosophy is to have demand precede supply. (Estée Lauder Companies Inc., *Annual Report 1998*, p. 6.)

32. See, for example, Donaldson, Lufkin & Jenrette Securities, "Estée Lauder Companies" (27 November 1996), p. 2.

33. Maggie Angeloglou, *A History of Make-Up* (London: Macmillan, 1970), p. 25, and Richard Corson, *Fashions in Makeup: From Ancient to Modern Times* (London: Peter Owen, 1972), pp. 8–9.

34. Corson, *Fashions in Makeup*, pp. 25–38.

35. Quoted in ibid., p. 46.

36. Quoted in ibid., pp. 66–67.

37. Angeloglou, *A History of Make-Up*, p. 48.

38. Quoted in Corson, *Fashions in Makeup*, p. 196.

39. Initially designed as a means to conceal blemishes, the practice of wearing patches took on political connotations in the later eighteenth century. Before the American Revolution, for example, Tories wore patches on the right side of the face, Whigs on the left. Ibid., p. 38.

40. Vail, *A History of Cosmetics in America*, p. 68.

41. John F. Kasson, *Rudeness & Civility: Manners in Nineteenth-Century Urban America* (New York: Hill and Wang, 1990), p. 29.

42. Kathy Peiss, "Making Up, Making Over: Cosmetics, Consumer Culture, and Women's Identity," in Victoria de Grazia with Ellen Furlough, eds., *The Sex of Things: Gender and Consumption in Historical Perspective* (Berkeley: University of California Press, 1996), pp. 313–315. See also Karen Halttunen, *Confidence Men and Painted Women: A Study of Middle-Class Culture in America, 1830–1870* (New Haven: Yale University Press, 1982). In 1840, the political enemies of President Martin Van Buren attacked the contents of his dressing table, accusing the chief executive of effeminacy and artifice for using Corinthian Oil of Cream, Concentrated Persian Essence, and Extract of Eglantine. Vail, *A History of Cosmetics in America*, p. 95.

43. Kathy Peiss, *Hope in a Jar: The Making of America's Beauty Culture* (New York: Metropolitan Books, 1998), pp. 26–27.

44. Ibid., p. 13.

45. Ibid., p. 12.

46. Original emphasis. Madame Lola Montez, *The Arts of Beauty or, Secrets of a Lady's Toilet* (New York: Dick & Fitzgerald, 1858), p. xii. See also D. G. Brinton and George H. Napheys, *Personal Beauty: How to Cultivate and Preserve It* (Springfield, MA: W. J. Holland, 1870), pp. 214–215.

47. William Howard Shaw, *The Value of Commodity Output since 1869* (New York: National Bureau of Economic Research, 1947), pp. 110, 30, 31, 38.

48. On these entrepreneurs, see Nancy Shuker, *Elizabeth Arden: An American Dream* (Englewood Cliffs, NJ: Silver Burdett Press, 1989); Helena Rubinstein, *My Life for Beauty* (New York: Simon & Schuster, 1966); Helena Rubinstein, *The Art of Feminine Beauty* (New York: Horace Liveright, 1930); Patrick O'Higgins, *Madame: An Intimate Biography of Helena Rubinstein* (New York: Viking, 1971); and A'Lelia Perry Bundles, *Madam C. J. Walker: Entrepreneur* (New York: Chelsea House, 1991).

49. See, for example, Peiss, *Hope in a Jar,* p. 78.

50. A'Lelia P. Bundles, "Lost Women: Madam C. J. Walker—Cosmetics Tycoon," *Ms.* (July 1983), p. 93.

51. Working for Madam Walker, wrote one woman in 1913, enabled "hundreds of colored women to make an honest and profitable living where they make as much in one week as a month's salary would bring from any other position that a colored women can secure." Quoted in ibid., p. 93.

52. Bundles, "Lost Women: Madam C. J. Walker," pp. 91–94, and *Madam C. J. Walker.* See also Charles Latham Jr., "Madam Walker and Company," *Traces of Indiana and Midwestern History* 1, no. 3 (summer 1989), pp. 28–37.

53. Shuker, *Elizabeth Arden,* pp. 42, 48, and Sina Dubovoj, "Elizabeth Arden Co.," in Paula Kepos, ed., *International Directory of Company Histories,* (Detroit: St. James Press, 1994), 8, p. 168.

54. Helena Rubinstein, "Manufacturing—Cosmetics," in Doris E. Fleischman, ed., *An Outline of Careers for Women* (New York: Doubleday, Doran, 1929), p. 331.

55. In 1925, for example, Arden's sales exceeded $2 million. Four years later, revenues had doubled. Dubovoj, "Elizabeth Arden Co.," p. 168. In 1929, Arden was offered $15 million for her business. She refused to sell. Margaret Case Harriman, "Elizabeth Arden," *The New Yorker* (6 April 1935), p. 27. See also "Cosmetics: The American Woman Responds," *Fortune* (August 1930), pp. 40–41, 92. Rubinstein's business was also very successful. In 1928, she sold a two-thirds interest in her company to several investment houses for $7.5 million. After the stock market crashed in 1929, she bought back complete control of the business for $1.5 million. John N. Ingham, *Biographical Dictionary of American Business Leaders, N-U* (Westport, CT: Greenwood Press, 1983), p. 1212.

56. McConnell handed daily operating responsibility for the company over to a woman, Mrs. P. F. E. Albee, who implemented a strategy to have women sell

cosmetics and toiletries door-to-door in their communities. Peiss, *Hope in a Jar*, p. 72.

57. Vail, *History of Cosmetics in America*, p. 138.

58. Robert S. Lynd and Alice C. Hanson, "The People as Consumers," in *Recent Social Trends in the United States: Report of the President's Research Committee on Social Trends* (New York: McGraw-Hill, 1933), 2, p. 900.

59. Charles J. McGuirk, "A Subtle Something," *Saturday Evening Post* (4 December 1926), p. 72.

60. Vail, *History of Cosmetics in America*, p. 138. Price indexes are from U.S. Department of Commerce, *Historical Statistics of the United States*, 1, p. 211. The value added by cosmetics companies grew even faster, expanding more than four times from $33 million in 1919 to $135 million in 1929. Solomon Fabricant, *The Output of Manufacturing Industries, 1899–1937* (New York: National Bureau of Economic Research, 1940), p. 619.

61. Toiletry sales figure is from Vail, *History of Cosmetics in America*, p. 138. Population number and historical price indexes are from U.S. Department of Commerce, *Historical Statistics of the United States*, 1, pp. 8, 211. Current price indexes are from Council of Economic Advisers, *Economic Report of the President*, p. 373.

62. *Toilet Requisites* 1 (May 1916), pp. 22–23; *Toilet Requisites* 1 (June 1916), p. 12. Scripps-Howard Newspapers, "Buying Habits and Brand Preferences of Consumers in Sixteen Cities," *Market Records* 1 (1938), p. 206; and Neil H. Borden, *The Economic Effects of Advertising* (Chicago: Richard D. Irwin, 1944), pp. 294–295.

63. On rising incomes, working women, diffusion of photography, proliferation of mass-circulation magazines, and expansion of chain and department stores—and the roles of all these factors in making beauty products accessible and acceptable—see Peiss, *Hope in a Jar*, pp. 61–133, and Vincent Vinikas, *Soft Soap, Hard Sell: American Hygiene in an Age of Advertisement* (Ames, IA: Iowa State University Press, 1992).

64. Peiss, *Hope in a Jar*, pp. 168–171.

65. See, for example, a *New York World* reporter's assessment of Manhattan consumers. Writing in 1910, she was struck by how much makeup city women wore: "Eyelids can't be painted too blue nor lashes too heavily beaded." *New York World* (11 September 1910). In 1924, a reporter for *Toilet Requisites*, an industry trade journal, contrasted wealthy women's careful, conservative use of cosmetics with that of working women who "use it in astonishing quantities." Beth Brown, "Chicago—The Convention City," *Toilet Requisites* 9 (August 1924), p. 46. See also *Toilet Requisites* 8 (April 1923), p. 33.

66. Peiss, *Hope in a Jar*, pp. 168–170. See also Scripps-Howard Newspapers, "Buying Habits and Brand Preferences of Consumers in Sixteen Cities"; "Farmer's Daughter Big User of Cosmetics and Drugs," *Sales Management* 37, no. 4 (15 August

1935), p. 147; Brown, "Chicago—The Convention City"; McGuirk, "A Subtle Something"; and Merchandising Service Bureau of the Milwaukee Journal, *Survey of the Milwaukee Market*, vol. 3: *Cosmetics and Accessories* (Chicago: O'Mara & Ormsbee, 1924), pp. 198–207.

67. Peiss, *Hope in a Jar*, pp. 169–170. On rural retailing in the 1920s, see "What Do Our Rural Neighbors Buy," *J. Walter Thompson News Bulletin*, no. 120 (March 1926), pp. 1–35.

68. "Farmer's Daughter Big User of Cosmetics and Drugs," p. 147.

69. *A Table of Leading Advertisers: Showing Advertising Investments of Advertisers Spending $20,000 and over in Thirty-two Leading National Publications* (Philadelphia: Curtis Publishing, 1926), p. 220. Price indexes are from U.S. Department of Commerce, *Historical Statistics of the United States*, 1, p. 211, and Council of Economic Advisers, *Economic Report of the President*, p. 373.

70. Vinikas, *Soft Soap, Hard Sell*, p. 3.

71. Peiss, *Hope in a Jar*, p. 105.

72. See, for example, Hazel Rawson Cases, *Any Girl Can Be Good-Looking* (New York: D. Appleton, 1927), and Ethel Lloyd Patterson, "Why Grow Old? Face Do's and Don'ts," *Ladies Home Journal* (October 1922), pp. 153–154. See also Emma Walker, "Pretty Girl Questions," *Ladies Home Journal* (February 1912), p. 49; "On Her Dressing-Table," *Vogue* (1 January 1925), pp. 88, 90; "Mouthpiece: Lipsticks," *Harper's Bazaar* (January 1935), pp. 42–122; and Mme. Lina Cavalieri, *My Secrets of Beauty* (New York: Circulation Syndicate, 1914).

73. State of New York, *Certificate and Record of Birth*, no. 3352, 8 July 1908, Municipal Archives, New York, NY.

74. The history of Estée's family on both her maternal and paternal sides is obscure. According to one biographer, the name "Mentzer" means "the Jew from Mainz," Lee Israel, *Estée Lauder: Beyond the Magic* (New York: Macmillan, 1985), p. 9.

75. Ibid., p. 8.

76. U.S. Department of Commerce, *Historical Statistics of the United States*, 1, p. 105.

77. Rose Mentzer never spoke of her first husband. Did he desert his family or divorce his wife? Looking back on her childhood in 1985, Estée suspected the latter. Lauder, *Estée: A Success Story*, p. 7.

78. According to Lauder, her mother had six children, five sons and a daughter, when she married Max Mentzer. The young Esty grew up in a house with seven siblings. Ibid., p. 7.

79. Walter I. Willis, ed., *Queens Borough, New York City, 1910–1920* (New York: Chamber of Commerce of the Borough of Queens, 1920), p. 146.

80. Vincent F. Seyfried, *Corona: From Farmland to City Suburb, 1650–1935* (Queens: Edgian Press, 1986), pp. 12–14. See also Vincent F. Seyfried and William Asadorian, *Old Queens, N.Y. in Early Photographs* (New York: Dover, 1991), p. 92.

81. Steven Gregory, *Black Corona: Race and the Politics of Place in an Urban Community* (Princeton: Princeton University Press, 1998), p. 20.

82. See, for example, *Newtown Register*, 24 August 1916, quoted in Frank J. Cavaioli, "Corona's Little Italy: Past and Present," *Long Island Historical Journal* 8, no. 2 (spring 1996), p. 200.

83. One observer, writing in the *New York Times*, remembered the dumping grounds:

> Smoking by day, glowing by night, these city dumps threw off odors which gave offense for miles around. The entire section became infested with rats; river and bay were polluted by sewage, and the Meadow was a breeding place for mosquitoes that tormented communities far removed. . . . Nature could not have been more outrageously defiled, and for a long time the immediate vicinity of the dump was one of the ugliest, foulest sections of Greater New York. (Quoted in Matthew Kachur, "A Stadium for Flushing Meadows," *Long Island Historical Journal* 5, no. 2 [spring 1993], p. 179.)

The novelist F. Scott Fitzgerald echoed this image in *The Great Gatsby.* He described the ash piles of Corona as "a fantastic farm where ashes grow like wheat into ridges and hills and grotesque gardens; where ashes take the forms of houses and chimneys and rising smoke and finally, with a transcendent effort, of ash-grey men who move dimly and already crumbling through the powdery air." *The Great Gatsby* (New York: Charles Scribner, 1925), p. 23.

84. Lauder makes almost no mention of Corona in her autobiography, *Estée Lauder: A Success Story.*

85. Ibid., p. 12.

86. Ibid., p. 14.

87. Ibid., p. 16.

88. Decades later looking back on her girlhood, Lauder saw great value in the experience she gained in her father's store: Lipstick and dry goods are different products, she explained, "but just about everything has to be sold aggressively." Ibid., p. 14.

89. During the 1910s and 1920s, Plafker & Rosenthal was known as "The Macy's of Corona." Israel, *Estée Lauder: Beyond the Magic*, p. 14.

90. On the experience of urban women in late-nineteenth-century department stores, see Elaine S. Abelson, *When Ladies Go A-Thieving: Middle-Class Shoplifters in the Victorian Department Store* (New York: Oxford, 1989). See also Michael B. Miller, *The Bon Marché: Bourgeoise Culture and the Department Store, 1869–1920* (Princeton: Princeton University Press, 1981); Rosalind H. Williams, *Dream Worlds: Mass Consumption in Late Nineteenth-Century France* (Berkeley: University of California Press, 1982); William Leach, *Land of Desire: Merchants, Power, and the Rise of a New American Culture* (New York: Pantheon, 1993); and Robert Hendrickson, *The Grand Emporiums: The Illustrated History of America's Great Department Stores* (New York: Stein and Day, 1979).

91. Lauder, *Estée: A Success Story*, p. 14.

92. Ibid., pp. 12–13.

93. When she was in her late teens and early twenties, she was known as Esther, according to Israel, *Estée Lauder: Beyond the Magic*, pp. 18, 22.

94. See, for example, Lauder, *Estée: A Success Story*, p. 22. By 1937, Lauder was listed as "Estée" in the New York City telephone directory. Israel, *Estée Lauder: Beyond the Magic*, p. 24.

95. Ibid., pp. 15–16.

96. In 1929, Helena Rubinstein estimated that women in the cosmetic industry might earn from $5 to $500 a week. Rubinstein, "Manufacturing—Cosmetics," in *An Outline of Careers for Women*. Writing in 1910, the manufacturer William Woodbury estimated that the

> incomes of beauty culturists vary from one thousand to twenty thousand dollars a year, the average of a good operator being possibly between twenty-five and thirty dollars a week. This, mind you, for an employee working on a salary and commission. Those who employ themselves, whether "by apportionment" or as owners of beauty shops, may make even more, even double or treble this amount. There are scores who take in a clear profit the year round of one hundred dollars a week and over. (William A. Woodbury, *Beauty Culture: A Practical Handbook on the Care of the Person, designed for Professional and Private Use* [New York: G. W. Dillingham, 1910], p. 14.)

97. In the United States as a whole, 113,000 women were employed in the beauty business. Figures are for 1929 and are from Ethel Erickson, "Employment Conditions in Beauty Shops: A Study of Four Cities," *Bulletin of the Women's Bureau* no. 133 (Washington, DC: U.S. Government Printing Office, 1935); "Letter of Transmittal," by Mary Anderson, p. v; and Sophonisba P. Breckinridge, *Women in the Twentieth Century: A Study of Their Political, Social, and Economic Activities* (New York: McGraw-Hill, 1933), pp. 134–135. See also Lois W. Banner, *American Beauty* (New York: Knopf, 1983), p. 216; *Woman Beautiful* 3 (November 1908), p. 46; and Paul W. White, "Our Booming Beauty Business," *Outlook and Independent* 154 (22 January 1930), p. 143. To train hairdressers, manicurists, and skin specialists, enterprising women started beauty schools or academies. In 1904, for example, Ruth Marinello established the Marinello Company to educate women who wanted to work in the beauty business. See Peiss, *Hope in a Jar*, p. 75. See also Edmund Saalfeld, *Lectures on Cosmetic Treatment: A Manual for Practitioners* (New York: Paul B. Hoeber, 1911), and Woodbury, *Beauty Culture.*

98. Woodbury, *Beauty Culture*, p. 13. See also Peiss, *Hope in a Jar*, pp. 91–92.

99. In 1929, *The American Druggist Yearbook and Price List* contained a listing for New Way Laboratories. The company's address was 276 West 43rd Street in New York City. The 1937 edition of the *American Druggist Price Book* lists New Way Laboratories' address as 1472 Broadway. The later volume details Schotz's product line, which included astringent, cleansing oil, day cream, rouge, neck cream and "quick

flaking cream." *American Druggist Year Book and Price List* (New York: American Druggist, 1930), p. 280, and *American Druggist Price Book* (New York: American Druggist, 1937), pp. 69, 295.

100. John Schotz probably did not have a Ph.D. But he was generally known as "Dr. Schotz" for his experience working as a chemist. Israel, *Estée Lauder: Beyond the Magic*, p. 18.

101. Ibid.

102. Lauder, *Estée: A Success Story*, p. 18.

103. On the composition of various skin creams, see Francis Chilson, *Modern Cosmetics: The Formulation and Production of Cosmetics together with a Discussion of Modern Production and Packaging Methods and Equipment* (New York: Drug and Cosmetic Industry, 1938). See also Woodbury, *Beauty Culture.*

104. Lauder, *Estée: A Success Story*, p. 19.

105. Schotz's formulas for his skin care products survived and were passed down to relatives. In 1985, a chemist for Revlon analyzed them:

> They're obviously very old-fashioned, but probably they were very efficacious. They lubricate. They're heavy. And they're probably very good still, if you have very dry skin. They wouldn't be as nice aesthetically as what you can buy today. But they're quite good for their time. . . . [One] even contained a sunscreen. Whether Schotz recognized that or not, one doesn't know. (Quoted in Israel, *Estée Lauder: Beyond the Magic*, p. 21.)

106. Sales of passenger cars, for example, climbed almost 300 percent from 1.7 million units in 1917 to more than 4.5 million in 1929. Thomas K. McCraw and Richard S. Tedlow, "Henry Ford, Alfred Sloan, and the Three Phases of Marketing," in Thomas K. McCraw, ed., *Creating Modern Capitalism: How Entrepreneurs, Countries, and Companies Triumphed in Three Industrial Revolutions* (Cambridge: Harvard University Press, 1997), p. 284. Radio output rose even faster, from under 200,000 units in 1923 to almost 5 million in 1929. Cigarette production increased markedly as well, growing from 48 billion units in 1920 to 122 billion nine years later. Fabricant, *The Output of Manufacturing Industries, 1899–1937*, p. 573; U.S. Department of Commerce, *Historical Statistics of the United States*, 2, p. 696.

107. Adjusted for inflation, aggregate national wealth rose 68 percent between 1912 and 1929. U.S. Department of Commerce, *Historical Statistics of the United States*, 1, pp. 224, 256.

108. Ira Rosenwaike, *The Population History of New York City* (Syracuse: Syracuse University Press, 1972), pp. 63, 77.

109. U.S. Department of Commerce, *Historical Statistics of the United States*, 1, p. 11.

110. Lauder, *Estée: A Success Story*, p, 19.

111. Stanley Lebergott, *The American Economy: Income, Wealth and Want* (Princeton: Princeton University Press, 1962), pp. 248–299.

112. On the chain store revolution, see Richard Tedlow, *New and Improved: The Story of Mass Marketing in America* (New York: Basic, 1990), pp. 182–214. On the history of consumer credit, see Martha Olney, *Buy Now Pay Later: Advertising, Credit, and Consumer Durables in the 1920s* (Chapel Hill, NC: University of North Carolina Press, 1991). See also William E. Leuchtenburg, *Perils of Prosperity, 1914–1932* (Chicago: University of Chicago Press, 1993), pp. 195–202. On contemporary attitudes toward consumption in the 1920s, see David Horowitz, *The Morality of Spending: Attitudes Toward the Consumer Society in America, 1875–1940* (Baltimore: Johns Hopkins University Press, 1985), pp. 134–152.

113. Preston William Slosson, *The Great Crusade and After, 1914–1928* (New York: Macmillan, 1930), p. 162.

114. Lynd and Hanson, "The People as Consumers," p. 893.

115. In contrast, all the business-class families had a telephone. Robert S. Lynd and Helen Merrell Lynd, *Middletown: A Study in Contemporary American Culture* (New York: Harcourt, Brace, 1929), pp. 97, 173.

116. U.S. Department of Commerce, *Historical Statistics of the United States*, 1, pp. 131–132.

117. Ibid. See also Sophonisba C. Breckinridge, *Women in the Twentieth Century*, pp. 108–123, and Claudia Goldin, *Understanding the Gender Gap: An Economic History of American Women* (New York: Oxford University Press, 1990), pp. 10–56.

118. "Women's employers or their customers," observed Helena Rubinstein, "are often the audience they want to please." On Saturdays when offices and stores are closed, she continued, "scores of women come to us for treatments; not only those who are at the head of their own business, but stenographers, clerks, and even little office girls." Many of these consumers wished to be attractive, the beauty specialist concluded. "They also know that natural good looks are an asset in business." Quoted in Allison Gray, "People Who Want to Look Young and Beautiful," *American Magazine* 94 (December 1922), p. 33.

119. On the history of the advertising industry, see Roland Marchand, *Advertising the American Dream: Making Way for Modernity* (Berkeley: University of California, 1985); T. J. Jackson Lears, *Fables of Abundance: A Cultural History of Advertising in America* (New York: Basic, 1994); Neil Borden, *The Economic Effects of Advertising*; and William Leach, *Land of Desire*. See also Tedlow, *New and Improved*, and Susan Strasser, *Satisfaction Guaranteed: The Making of the American Mass Market* (New York: Pantheon, 1989).

120. Israel, *Estée Lauder: Beyond the Magic*, p. 22. Lauter may also have been involved in an export-import venture. According to a 1983 interview with both Estée and Joseph Lauder, he also studied accounting. Catherine Warren, "Estée and Joe," *Women's Wear Daily* (7 January 1983), p. 4.

121. Gene N. Landrum, "Estée Lauder—Impatient Overachiever," in *Profiles of Female Genius: Thirteen Creative Women Who Changed the World* (Amherst, NY: Prometheus Books, 1994), p. 248. Looking back on the event, the cosmetics

entrepreneur recalled that it was the first time that she had worn lipstick. Lauder, *Estée: A Success Story*, p. 22.

122. Marylin Bender, "Estée Lauder: A Family Affair," in *At The Top* (Garden City, NY: Doubleday, 1975), p. 218.

123. Israel, *Estée Lauder: Beyond the Magic*, p. 24. What relationship, if any, Esty's enterprise had with New Way Laboratories and John Schotz is unclear.

124. U.S. Bureau of the Census, *Census of Business: 1935, Service Establishments*, vol. 2: *Statistics for States, Counties, and Cities* (Washington, DC: U.S. Government Printing Office, 1935), p. 172.

125. On the culture and community of beauty parlors, see Frida Kerner Furman, *Facing the Mirror: Older Women and Beauty Shop Culture* (New York: Routledge, 1997), and Kathy Kemp, *Beauty Box: A Tribute to the Legendary Beauty Parlors of the South* (Birmingham, AL: Crane Hill, 1998).

126. Lauder, *Estée: A Success Story*, p. 26.

127. Ibid., p. 28.

128. Ibid., p. 30.

129. See, for example, *American Druggist Price Book*, p. 69.

130. Lauder, *Estée: A Success Story*, p. 27.

131. According to her autobiography, Lauder and her husband made the name change to reflect its Austrian origins. Ibid., p. 22. In 1937, when the entrepreneur first appears as Estée Lauder in the New York telephone directory, her husband's entry that year is Joseph Lauter. Israel, *Estée: Beyond the Magic*, p. 24.

132. Lauder, *Estée: A Success Story*, p. 28.

133. On the importance of brand names in creating strategic advantages, see Philip Kotler and Gary Armstrong, *Principles of Marketing* (New York: Prentice Hall, 1996), pp. 282–285; Kevin Lane Keller, *Strategic Brand Management: Building, Measuring, and Managing Brand Equity* (Upper Saddle River, NJ: Prentice Hall, 1998); Jean-Noel Kapferer, *Strategic Brand Management: Creating and Sustaining Brand Equity Long Term* (London: Kogan Page, 1997), pp. 9–53, 60–65; and Leslie de Chernatony and Malcolm McDonald, *Creating Powerful Brands in Consumer, Service and Industrial Markets* (Oxford: Butterworth-Heinemann, 1998), pp. 88–100. See also Peter Doyle, "Building Successful Brands: The Strategic Options," *Journal of Marketing Management* 5 (1989), pp. 77–95.

134. Lauder, *Estée: A Success Story*, p. 39.

135. Ibid., p. 29.

136. U.S. Department of Commerce, *Historical Statistics of the United States*, 1, pp. 225, 135, 229, respectively.

137. Figures for 1999 are from Patricia Keegan Nicolescu, ed., *International Motional Picture Almanac* (New York: Quigley, 1999), p. 8; 1936 information is from Terry Ramsaye, ed., *International Motional Picture Almanac* (New York: Quigley, 1936), p. 6.

138. On the influence of cinematic fashions in the 1930s, see Margaret Thorp, *America at the Movies* (New York: Arno Press, 1970), pp. 90–115.

139. Lauder, *Estée: A Success Story*, p. 39.

140. In constant (1929) dollars, Americans bought $378 million in cosmetics and toiletries in the earlier year, $510 million in 1939. Industry sales figures are from "Toiletry Sales for 50 Years," *Oil, Paint, and Drug Reporter* 186 (6 July 1964), p. 45. See also Vail, *History of Cosmetics in America*, p. 138. Price indexes are from John McCusker, *How Much Is That in Real Money? A Historical Price Index for Use as a Deflator of Money Values in the Economy of the United States* (Worcester: American Antiquarian Society, 1992), p. 348. See also U.S. Department of Commerce, *Historical Statistics of the United States*, 1, p. 211.

141. In the late 1930s, women accounted for about 10 percent of the total number of managers, officials, and proprietors in the United States. The vast majority of these women, like Lauder, did not consider enrolling in business schools. Frank Stickler, "Cookbooks and Law Books: The Hidden History of Career Women in Twentieth-Century America," in Nancy F. Cott, ed., *History of Women in the United States*, vol. 8: *Professional and White-Collar Employments*, part 2 (Munich: K. G. Saur, 1993), pp. 441–442.

142. Toward this end, she spent much of her adult life selling herself as creatively and aggressively as she marketed her beauty products. In 1966, for example, she wanted to meet Palm Beach's most sought-after couple, the Duke of Windsor and Wallis Simpson. The former monarch and his wife spent most winters in Florida, traveling by train to New York when the season was over. That April, Lauder booked tickets for herself and her husband on the same train. She also arranged to have a photographer waiting at the West Palm train station before departure. Lauder arrived early and walked over to the Duke's car. Placing her hand on his arm, she said, "Are you taking the train also?" A photographer snapped the picture, and it ran on the front page of the *Palm Beach Daily News*. Estée's social stock soared. Israel, *Estée Lauder: Beyond the Magic*, pp. 66–67.

143. Israel, *Estée Lauder: Beyond the Magic*, p. 28.

144. "Toiletry Sales for 50 Years," p. 45. On cosmetics sales during the war, see "Cosmetic Output Spirals," *Business Week* (24 August 1946), pp. 68–69, and "Cosmetic Sales at New Highs in War Years," *Barron's* 24, no. 38 (18 September 1944), pp. 25–29.

145. See, for example, "Is Beauty Worth Half a Billion?" *New York Times Magazine* (20 December 1942), p. 25, and I. C. Furnas, "Glamour Goes to War," *Saturday Evening Post* (29 November 1941), pp. 18–19, 56–58, 60.

146. Fannie Hurst, "Glamour As Usual?" *New York Times Magazine* (29 March 1942), p. 11. C. A. Williams, deputy chief of the Cosmetics Branch of the War Production Board (WPB), was even more emphatic. "Good heavens," he exclaimed, most of the money spent on beauty products "doesn't do any good

anyway! We'd hardly want to sacrifice the war effort to a tooth whitener." Quoted in "Is Beauty Worth Half a Billion?" p. 25.

147. Taking care with one's appearance demonstrated women's patriotism, according to Harrison. Would we help the brave men fighting for our country, she asked, if "we appear before them tear-stained and worn?" No, she concluded, "let's lift our heads and send them off with iron in our hearts, a smile on our red lips and a bloom in our cheeks." Mrs. Horace L. Harrison, "Glamour As Usual," Letters to the Editor, *New York Times Magazine* (26 April 1942), pp. 2–3.

148. Maison G. deNavarre, "Are Further Restrictions Necessary for Cosmetics?" *Advertising & Selling* (February 1943), p. 153 (original emphasis).

149. Quoted in "Is Beauty Worth Half a Billion?" p. 25.

150. Ibid.

151. According to a 1942 *New York Times* report, efficiency experts had discovered that

> a dressing room established for primping purposes in a busy factory may improve efficiency to the extent of 10 or 15 per cent. British experience substantiates this remarkable contention. At the beginning of the war, in an effort to effect economics in raw materials, the British Government restricted the manufacture of cosmetics to 25 per cent of peacetime production. It was discovered according to a survey made by British authorities and reported to the [U.S.] War Production Board, that the civilian population was growing depressed, and war factory records were steadily declining. . . . When cosmetic stations were established in the industries the production curve soared upward immediately and increased numbers of women came flocking to the war factories for work. The effect was so striking that the restricting order for the nation as a whole was relaxed to 50 per cent of the peacetime level. A recent regulation orders that girl workers in British munitions factories shall wash and reapply cosmetics three times a day. Cosmetics are supplied for the purpose by the government. (Ibid., p. 25.)

152. See, for example, Mary Hornaday, "Factory Housekeeping," in *American Women at War* (New York: National Association of Manufacturers of the United States of America, 1942), pp. 35–38, and Laura Nelson Baker, *Wanted: Women in War Industry: The Complete Guide to a War Factory Job* (New York: E. P. Dutton, 1943), pp. 84–95.

153. Karen Anderson, *Wartime Women: Sex Roles, Family Relations and the Status of Women during World War II* (Westport, CT: Greenwood, 1981), pp. 60–61.

154. In 1933, U.S. unemployment had climbed to 25 percent. By 1944, the proportion of jobless Americans had fallen to 1.2 percent. Within eleven years, Americans had witnessed the highest and lowest levels of unemployment recorded in the nation's history. U.S. Department of Commerce, *Historical Statistics of the United States*, 1, p. 135.

155. More than 11 million entered the military between 1939 and 1940. More than 7 million entered civilian jobs in the same period. Ibid., 1, 126.

156. Gary Walton and Hugh Rockoff, *History of the American Economy* (Fort Worth, TX: Dryden, 1998), p. 581. On women's labor force participation during and after World War II, see Claudia Goldin, "The Role of World War II in the Rise of Women's Employment," *American Economic Review* 81, no. 4 (September 1991), pp. 741–756. For a social history of working women during the war see Anderson, *Wartime Women,* and Sherna Berger Gluck, *Rosie the Riveter Revisited: Women, the War, and Social Change* (Boston: Twayne, 1987).

157. "To the Future," *Beauty Fashion* (January 1943), quoted in Richard S. Tedlow, "Charles Revson and Revlon," working paper 00-032, Harvard Business School, Boston, 1999, p. 29.

158. Peiss, *Hope in a Jar,* p. 240. A 1942 *New York Times* cartoon conveyed some of the possible connections between women's war work and collective interest in beauty products. In the background of the drawing, a woman in goggles uses a soldering iron while sitting atop a girder. Her female colleague in the foreground has pushed her goggles up on her head and confidently applies lipstick with the aid of a compact mirror. "Is Beauty Worth Half a Billion?" p. 25.

159. "Toiletry Sales for 50 Years," p. 45; "Cosmetic Output Spirals"; "Cosmetic Sales at New Highs in War Years"; and Maurice Zolotow, "Boom in Beauty," *Saturday Evening Post* (25 December 1943), pp. 22–23, 58–59. On female consumers' attitudes toward cosmetics during the war, see "Face Powder and Lipstick Tops Among 'Indispensables,'" *Printer's Ink* 199, no. 4 (April 24, 1942), pp. 13–15.

160. deNavarre, "Are Further Restrictions Necessary for Cosmetics?" pp. 119, 153. See also Zolotow, "Boom in Beauty," p. 59, and "Is Beauty Worth Half a Billion?"

161. "Beauty Carries On," *Business Week* (1 May 1943), pp. 77–80, and deNavarre, "Are Further Restrictions Necessary for Cosmetics?" pp. 118, 153–154.

162. Corson, *Fashions in Makeup,* p. 524.

163. *Vogue* (1 January 1943), p. 67. See also ads in *Vogue* (15 January 1943), p. 81; *Vogue* (1 February 1943), p. 105; *Vogue* (15 February 1943), p. 72; *Vogue* (1 March 1943), p. 85; and *Vogue* (15 April 1943), p. 8.

164. *Cosmopolitan* (January 1943), p. 93. Some advertisements emphasized the historical importance of women's role in supporting men during war. A 1943 ad for Avon cosmetics, for example, was dedicated to the "Heroines of America" and included a picture of Martha Washington. The nation's earliest First Lady, the ad explained, "did much to inspire her husband to greatness. Now, when men are again fighting for the survival of their nation, women are by their sides inspiring them to the greatness that is demanded by Total Victory." *Vogue* (15 April 1943), p. 89.

165. Lauder, *Estée: A Success Story,* p. 40. See also Estée Lauder Companies Inc., *Annual Report 1996,* p. 2. In 1960, the company was incorporated as Estée Lauder, Inc.

166. Bender, "Estée Lauder: A Family Affair," p. 219.

167. Lauder, *Estée: A Success Story*, p. 45.

168. Israel, *Estée Lauder: Beyond the Magic*, p. 28.

169. Lauder, *Estée: A Success Story*, p. 55.

170. Tedlow, "Charles Revson and Revlon," pp. 31–34.

171. The same survey found that 80 percent of women used makeup base and 71 percent cleansing cream. Lee H. Graham, "The Big Business of Beauty," *New York Times Magazine* (12 May 1946), p. 16.

172. Adjusted for price changes, total purchases in 1960 were 54 percent higher than those fourteen years earlier. Total cosmetics sales from "Toiletry Sales, 1914–1965," *Oil, Paint and Drug Reporter* 189 (20 June 1966), p. 50. Price indexes are from U.S. Department of Commerce, *Historical Statistics of the United States*, 1, p. 224.

173. U.S. Department of Commerce, *Historical Statistics of the United States*, 1, p. 224.

174. Ibid., 1, p. 49.

175. See, for example, Joseph E. North, "The Cosmetics and Toiletries Industry," *Financial Analysts Journal* 19, no. 1 (January-February 1963), pp. 40–41.

176. On the significance of female employment and demand for cosmetics, see Margherita Karo, "Revisiting the Cosmetics-Toiletries Industry," *Financial Analysts Journal* 24, no. 5 (September-October 1968), p. 36; Ann Lyon, "The Cosmetics Industry: Hot New Products," *Printers' Ink* 280, no. 1 (6 July 1952), pp. 24–31; and "Cosmetic Makers Peer at Market of '60s," *Oil, Paint and Drug Reporter* 178 (4 July 1960), pp. 47–58.

177. About half of the female workers that entered the paid labor force during the war dropped out by 1950. See Goldin, "The Role of World War II in the Rise of Women's Employment," p. 741. See also Anderson, *Wartime Women*, pp. 154–178, and Doris Kearns Goodwin, *No Ordinary Time: Franklin and Eleanor Roosevelt: The Home Front in World War II* (New York: Simon & Schuster, 1994), pp. 620–624.

178. Kearns Goodwin, *No Ordinary Time*, p. 623.

179. Goldin, "The Role of World War II in the Rise of Women's Employment," p. 748.

180. U.S. Department of Commerce, *Historical Statistics of the United States*, 1, pp. 129, 132, 140.

181. See, for example, Susan Hartmann, "Prescriptions for Penelope: Literature on Women's Obligations to Returning World War II Veterans," *Women Studies* 5 (1978), pp. 223–239.

182. Lauder, *Estée: A Success Story*, p. 41.

183. Ibid.

184. John N. Ingham and Lynne B. Feldman, *Contemporary American Business Leaders* (New York: Greenwood, 1990), p. 331.

185. One of the company's first very successful products was a "Home Facial Kit," priced at $5.00. Estée Lauder Companies Inc., *Annual Report 1996*, p. 2.

186. Olney, *Buy Now Pay Later,* p. 95.

187. Ibid., p. 98.

188. Lauder, *Estée: A Success Story,* pp. 43–44.

189. Diners Club was founded in 1949. For many years, it was used primarily by salesmen who charged meals with clients or while on the road. American Express entered the universal credit card business in 1958, as did Bank of America, which issued the BankAmericard (later renamed Visa). In 1966, a bank consortium called Interbank issued Master Charge (later MasterCard). Lewis Mandell, *The Credit Card: A History* (Boston: Twayne, 1990), pp. xiv, 22–51.

190. Olney, *Buy Now Pay Later,* pp. 105–112.

191. Figures are from 1948. Robert David Entenberg, *Changing Competitive Position of Department Stores in the United States by Merchandise Lines* (Pittsburgh: University of Pittsburgh Press, 1961), p. 34.

192. Lauder, *Estée: A Success Story,* p. 44.

193. Ibid.

194. S. L. Mayham, *Marketing Cosmetics: A Guide for the Manufacturer in Placing His Products before the Stores and the Public* (New York: McGraw-Hill, 1938), pp. 51–64.

195. In 1954, a financial analyst estimated that there were 750 manufacturers "trying to entice women-folk to spend more" for makeup and fragrance. Faye Henle, "Beauty Parade: Cosmetics Makers Run Hard to Stand Still," *Barron's* 34, no. 10 (8 March 1954), p. 15.

196. See Tedlow, "Charles Revson and Revlon."

197. Henle, "Beauty Parade," pp. 15–16, and Tedlow, "Charles Revson and Revlon," p. 33.

198. Association of National Advertisers, *Advertising Expenditure Trends* (New York: Association of National Advertisers, 1953), appendix.

199. David A. Loehwing, "Search for Beauty: Cosmetics Makers Profit from an Eternal Feminine Quest," *Barron's* 36, no. 35 (20 August 1956), p. 20.

200. In 1940, Avon's revenues totaled $10 million. In 1951, they exceeded $35 million. Earlier sales figure from Peiss, *Hope in a Jar,* p. 245. Later number from "Avon: How to Be the Biggest Cosmetic Company but Never Sell in Stores," *Advertising Age* 32, no. 42 (16 October 1961), p. 72. By the early 1950s, Avon was the number one cosmetics maker in the United States. The company advertised its products and distribution channel heavily in leading newspapers and women's magazines. In 1953, Avon first purchased television advertising, spending $85,000 for several spots in the New York City market. Its brand and tag line "Avon calling" quickly became household words. "Why Use TV When You Sell Door-to-Door," *Sponsor* 12, no. 8 (22 February 1958), pp. 35–36.

201. "Why Use TV When You Sell Door-to-Door," p. 34 and author's estimates.

202. Keller, *Strategic Brand Management,* pp. 616–617.

203. Quoted in Israel, *Estée Lauder: Beyond the Magic,* p. 30.

204. Quoted in ibid., p. 31.

205. Lauder, *Estée: A Success Story,* p. 44, and The Estée Lauder Companies Inc., "Estée Lauder Companies Chronology," p. 1

206. Quoted in Nina Munk, "Why Women Find Lauder Mesmerizing," *Fortune* (25 May 1998), p. 97. Munk cites 1950 as the date when Neiman Marcus first sold Lauder products.

207. Lauder, *Estée: A Sucess Story,* p. 52.

208. Today, it costs approximately $80,000 to construct a new cosmetics counter in a department store.

209. S. L. Mayham, *Marketing Cosmetics,* pp. 65–73. Retailers and cosmetics companies often jointly financed newspaper and radio advertising expenditures.

210. "About the Size of It: An Interview with Leonard Lauder," *Beauty Fashion* 56, no. 10 (October 1971), p. 34; Lauder, *Estée: A Success Story,* p. 55; and author's estimates.

211. Lauder, *Estée: A Success Story,* pp. 61–62.

212. Bender, "Estée Lauder: A Family Affair," p. 219.

213. No matter how powerful and effective career women are, she wrote, they "will always have the problem of juggling priorities." Lauder, *Estée: A Success Story,* p. 65.

214. Lauder was proud of the hold her business had over her. "I've never been bored a day in my life," she remembered, "partly because as a true business addict it's never been enough to have steady work; I had to love what I was doing." Ibid., pp. 65, 160.

215. Ibid., p. 161. See also Malcolm Gladwell, "The Science of Shopping," *The New Yorker* (4 November 1996), pp. 66–75.

216. Lauder, *Estée: A Success Story,* p. 161. On consumer movements through stores, see Paco Underhill, *Why We Buy: The Science of Shopping* (New York: Simon & Schuster, 1999), pp. 43–91.

217. Lauder, *Estée: A Success Story,* p. 60.

218. As business grew, the company refined its strategies for promoting its brand throughout the store, placing its soaps next to towels in linen departments and advertising its sun cream in sections where bathing suits were sold. Ibid., p. 60.

219. Ibid., p. 45.

220. Fraser, "As Gorgeous As It Gets," p. 71.

221. Lauder, *Estée: A Success Story,* p. 52.

222. On the significance of consumer endorsements in expanding market share, see Thomas O. Jones and Earl Sasser, "Why Satisfied Customers Defect," *Harvard Business Review* 73 (November-December 1995), pp. 88–99.

223. "Estée Lauder Inc.," in Kepos, ed., *International Directory of Company Histories,* 9, p. 201. See also Lauder, *Estée: A Success Story,* p. 52, and Israel, *Estée Lauder: Beyond the Magic,* p. 36.

224. Tedlow, "Charles Revson and Revlon," p. 33.

225. Daniel Seligman, "Revlon's Jackpot," *Fortune* (April 1956), pp. 137, 236, 239. On the broader issues involved in Revlon's sponsorship of the quiz show, see Tedlow, "Charles Revson and Revlon," pp. 44–58.

226. Quoted in Lauder, *Estée: A Success Story*, p. 53.

227. Quoted in Marylin Bender, "The Beautiful World of Estée Lauder," *New York Times* (14 January 1973), S3, p. 5.

228. Grace Mirabella, former editor of *Vogue*, remembered that early in her career she was invited to lunch with Estée. "Before the meal was finished," Mirabella wrote, "she made sure to give me three chicken recipes to help me interest the man I hoped to marry (And did)." Grace Mirabella, "Beauty Queen: Estée Lauder," *Time* (7 December 1998), p. 184.

229. See, for example, Bender, "Estée Lauder: A Family Affair," pp. 219–200, and Mirabella, "Beauty Queen: Estée Lauder," pp. 183–184.

230. Dell Modern Group, *18th Survey of Beauty* (New York: Dell Publishing, 1953), p. 80.

231. "Aerosols Seen Spur to Perfumes," *Oil, Paint and Drug Reporter* 172, no. 18 (28 April 1958), p. 4. Figure is from 1956. Total cosmetics sales from "Toiletry Sales," *Oil, Paint and Drug Reporter* 186 (6 July 1964), p. 45.

232. Anthony J. Bucalo, "Overview of the U.S. Cosmetics and Toiletries Market," *Drug & Cosmetic Industry* 162, no. 6 (June 1998), pp. 26–27.

233. Lauder, *Estée: A Success Story*, p. 78. See also "The Pink Jungle," *Time* (16 June 1958), p. 89. In 1990, fragrances accounted for more than 12 percent of the larger cosmetics market. "Cleaners and Cosmetics," *U.S. Industrial Outlook 1990* (Washington, DC: U.S. Government Printing Office, 1990), pp. 37–44.

234. Lauder, *Estée: A Success Story*, p. 79

235. *Vogue* (15 November 1953), pp. 125, 138.

236. Ibid.

237. Quoted in Israel, *Estée Lauder: Beyond the Magic*, pp. 41–42. Company sales for the new fragrance were $50,000 in its first year. Lauder, *Estée: A Success Story*, p. 81.

238. Israel, *Estée Lauder: Beyond the Magic*, p. 42.

239. Ibid. See also Belkin, "Man Behind Estée Lauder Image Steps Out of His Mother's Shadow," p. 1D.

240. Quoted in Israel, *Estée Lauder: Beyond the Magic*, p. 42.

241. Lauder, *Estée: A Success Story*, p. 99; "About the Size of It," p. 34. See also Belkin, "Man Behind Estée Lauder Image Steps Out of His Mother's Shadow," p. 7D.

242. Leonard Lauder, interview by author, New York, NY, 24 May 2000 [hereafter Lauder interview].

243. "What people don't realize," Leonard Lauder said in the early 1970s, "is that I—to borrow Dean Acheson's phrase—was present at the creation. There isn't a

single job in this company, with the exception of the IBM jobs, that I hadn't done. But it wasn't part of a training program. I would hire my own replacement." Quoted in Bender, "Estée Lauder: A Family Affair," p. 225.

244. "About the Size of It," p. 35.

245. Ibid.

246. Ibid., p. 34.

247. As the business grew and Leonard's responsibilities expanded, he continued to visit retailers on a regular basis. In 1997, for example, he logged more than 165,000 air miles visiting stores that sold Estée Lauder products around the globe. Leonard said:

> I'm in department stores all the time. . . . Probably no one travels the way I do. You speak to retailers around the world; no one else visits them. I am the only person in the cosmetics industry that the retailers around the world know. Because my competitors don't care. I care, personally. If you asked me what I would like to do on my vacation, I'd say, I'd like to go and visit stores. (Nina Munk, "Why Women Find Lauder Mesmerizing," p. 106.)

248. Lauder, *Estée: A Success Story,* p. 105.

249. Toilet Goods Association, "Toiletry Sales," *Oil, Paint and Drug Reporter* (6 July 1964, 20 June 1966), pp. 45, 50, respectively. Price indexes are from U.S. Department of Commerce, *Historical Statistics of the United States,* 1, p. 210.

250. John Sherman Porter, ed., *Moody's Industrial Manual* (New York: Moody's Investors Service, Inc., 1961), p. 697, and Roy H. Krause, ed., *Moody's Industrial Manual* (New York: Moody's Investors Service, Inc., 1966), p. 1535.

251. Sales numbers are estimated. Israel, *Estée Lauder: Beyond the Magic,* p. 61. See also Kepos, "Estée Lauder Inc.," p. 202.

252. Lauder interview. See also Leonard Lauder's comments in Bender, "Estée Lauder: A Family Affair," p. 225. In 1970, looking back on his first twelve years at the company, Leonard Lauder said his main contribution to Estée Lauder Inc. had been "bringing the very strong and able people who are the backbone of our business." "I don't feel," he added, "that I have any monopoly on brains. Most of these [managers and employees] can do their jobs much better than I can do them." "The War of the Rosebuds," *Women's Wear Daily* (13 February 1970), p. 26.

253. Lauder interview.

254. "About the Size of It," p. 35.

255. Quoted in Bender, "Estée Lauder: A Family Affair," p. 227.

256. Quoted in Bender, "The Beautiful World of Estée Lauder," S3, p. 1.

257. Quoted in Bender, "Estée Lauder: A Family Affair," p. 226. At work, according to Lee Israel, Leonard Lauder exhorted his colleagues, "I want you to be nervous. I want you to be nervous. Are you nervous?" "It would make you nervous," commented one company executive. Quoted in Israel, *Estée Lauder: Beyond the Magic,* p. 79.

258. Bender, "Estée Lauder: A Family Affair," p. 225; Israel, *Estée Lauder: Beyond the Magic,* p. 51.

259. Lauder interview.

260. Quoted in Israel, *Estée Lauder: Beyond the Magic,* p. 95.

261. Kepos, "Estée Lauder Inc.," p. 202.

262. Frank J. St. Clair, ed., *Moody's Industrial Manual* (New York: Moody's Investors Service, Inc., 1969), pp. 122, 106, respectively.

263. Helena Rubinstein's sales are from 1965. Frank J. St. Clair, ed., *Moody's Industrial Manual* (New York: Moody's Investors Service, Inc., 1966), p. 912; Elizabeth Arden's are for 1966 and are from Cat Ong, "It All Began in 1908," *The Straits Times* (4 December 1997), Life section, p. 11.

264. Quoted in Lorraine Baltera, "Rubinstein Shucks Queen Bee Image," *Advertising Age* (27 May 1974), p. 5.

265. Beginning in the late 1970s, Elizabeth Arden began to move its brand upmarket, trying to stake out a viable competitive position against Estée Lauder, Germaine Monteil, and other companies competing exclusively in the prestige segment. See Margaret Allen, *Selling Dreams: Inside the Beauty Business* (New York: Simon & Schuster, 1981), p. 101.

266. See, for example, Toni Kosover, "Magna Cum Lauder," *Women's Wear Daily* (12 September 1969), pp. 18–19; "The War of the Roses;" *Women's Wear Daily* (25 September 1969), pp. 16–17; Bender, "The Beautiful World of Estée Lauder"; Bernadine Morris, "Somehow They Survive, Unruffled by Current Social Whirl," *New York Times* (5 June 1975), p. 32; Kate Lloyd, "How to Be Estée Lauder," *Vogue* (January 1973), pp. 130–131, 173–174; "Estée Lauder's Golden Giveaways," *Forbes* (15 June 1975), p. 41; and "Hark, the Heralded Princesses," *Women's Wear Daily* (15 December 1980), pp. 4–5.

267. Estée Lauder Companies Inc., *Annual Report 1998,* p. 8.

268. Bender, "The Beautiful World of Estée Lauder," S3, p. 1. See also Allen, *Selling Dreams,* p. 172, and Estée Lauder Companies Inc., *Annual Report 1998,* p. 8.

269. Avon sales figures from Bender, "Estée Lauder: A Family Affair," p. 215. Revlon revenues from Robert P. Hanson, ed., *Moody's Industrial Manual* (New York: Moody's Investors Service, Inc., 1974), 2, p. 2077.

270. Israel, *Estée Lauder: Beyond the Magic,* p. 61, and Bender, "The Beautiful World of Estée Lauder," S3, p. 1.

271. Estée Lauder's fragrances, such as Youth Dew, were often priced lower than those of the competition. This pricing strategy, which continues today, helps attract consumers to the company's counters where they often purchase other products, including skin care and makeup. Price figures are from Bender, "The Beautiful World of Estée Lauder," S3, p. 5.

272. Ibid., p. 1.

273. Quoted in ibid.

274. Lauder, *Estée: A Success Story*, p. 45. In the first few years of the business, the Lauders probably outsourced the manufacture of makeup such as lipstick, rouge, and eye shadow to private label companies in and around New York City.

275. "About the Size of It," p. 35 and author's estimates.

276. "An Architectural Gem," *Drug & Cosmetic Industry* 101, no. 1 (1967), pp. 39–41. See also "Packaging Flow at Estée Lauder," *Drug & Cosmetic Industry* 102, no. 2 (1968), pp. 64–66.

277. "About the Size of It," p. 35

278. See, for example, Estée Lauder Companies Inc., *Annual Report 1996*, pp. 19–20.

279. Kepos, ed., "Estée Lauder Inc.," p. 202.

280. In 1995, approximately 30 percent of Estée Lauder Companies' sales came from products launched in the past three years. Dillon, Read & Co., "Estée Lauder Companies—Company Report," (13 December 1995), p. 5.

281. See, for example, *Vogue* (15 February 1958), p. 9; *Vogue* (1 March 1958), p. 12; and Israel, *Estée Lauder: Beyond the Magic*, pp. 47–48. In the late 1950s Estée Lauder's other skin care creams and lotions were listed at under ten dollars.

282. *Vogue* (May 1960), p. 16.

283. "Women's Toiletries & Cosmetics," *Mediamark Research*, p. 305

284. Lauder, *Estée: A Success Story*, p. 149.

285. Ibid.

286. Ibid, p. 150.

287. Ibid., pp. 150–151.

288. In 1964, the company had established a distinct division, Aramis, Inc., to oversee its new brand. Estée Lauder Companies Inc., *Annual Report 1996*, p. 9. See also Kepos, ed., "Estée Lauder Inc.," p. 202, and Lauder, *Estée: A Success Story*, p. 124.

289. Lauder, *Estée: A Success Story*, p. 123

290. Ibid., pp. 124–126.

291. See, for example, "Soaps and Cosmetics," Business and Defense Services Administration, *U.S. Industrial Outlook 1975* (Washington, DC: U.S. Government Printing Office, 1975), p. 119, and "Cosmetics," U.S. Department of Commerce, Industry and Trade Administration, *U.S. Industrial Outlook 1980* (Washington, DC: U.S. Government Printing Office, 1980), pp. 154–155. A substantial portion of this expansion came from women consumers buying for men. By the mid-1990s, women purchased as much as 40 percent of these products. Dillon, Read & Co., "Estée Lauder Companies—Company Report," p. 7.

292. Israel, *Estée Lauder: Beyond the Magic*, p. 106. By the mid-1990s, Aramis had a 13 percent market share among prestige toiletries targeted at men. Dillon, Read & Co., "Estée Lauder Companies—Company Report," p. 7.

293. Lauder, *Estée: A Success Story,* p. 134.

294. According to Israel, the cosmetics manufacturer lost $3 million on Clinique before the line became profitable. *Estée Lauder: Beyond the Magic,* p. 75. To expedite production of Clinique products, the company built separate manufacturing facilities. "About the Size of It," p. 34, and Lauder, *Estée: A Success Story,* pp. 142–143.

295. Allan G. Mottus, "Skin Care Products on Rise," *Advertising Age* 50, no. 9 (26 February 1979), p. S-22, and Israel, *Estée Lauder: Beyond the Magic,* p. 106.

296. Howard Rudnitsky with Janet Bamford, "Vanity, Thy Name Is Profit," *Forbes* (25 May 1981), p. 48.

297. Estée Lauder Companies Inc., *Annual Report 1996,* p. 4.

298. Quoted in Rudnitsky and Bamford, "Vanity, Thy Name Is Profit," p. 48.

299. Quoted in Bender, "The Beautiful World of Estée Lauder," S3, p. 5.

300. Deveny, "Leonard Lauder is Making His Mom Proud," p. 69. In the mid-1990s, the brand was positioned to emphasize color availability and skin care products for female consumers of diverse ethnic backgrounds. The line continued to be popular with its targeted consumer segment—professional women between the ages of thirty and fifty. In 1995, for example, Prescriptives sales increased 10 percent. The brand's distribution was tightly controlled. The line was available in about a third of the number of outlets as Estée Lauder and Clinique brands. Dillon, Read & Co., "Estée Lauder Companies—Company Report," p. 7.

301. Estée Lauder Companies Inc., *Annual Report 1998,* p. 29.

302. Donaldson, Lufkin & Jenrette Securities, "Personal Care & Household Products Preview 1997—Industry Report" (30 January 1997), p. 3

303. Lauder, *Estée: A Success Story,* p. 114.

304. Ibid., pp. 118–119.

305. Jeanette Sarkisian Wagner, interview by author, New York, NY, 24 May 2000.

306. Lauder, *Estée: A Success Story,* p. 120; Estée Lauder Companies Inc., *Annual Report 1996,* p. 3; and Estée Lauder Companies Inc., *Annual Report 1998,* p. 6.

307. Estée Lauder Companies Inc., *Annual Report 1998,* p. 6.

308. Sales figure is from the fiscal year ending 30 June 1999. Estée Lauder Companies, "Investor Information," www.elcompanies.com/newsroom/ (accessed 30 June 2000). Employee figure from www. globalbb.onesource.com (accessed 30 June 2000).

309. It ranked 312th among U.S. companies in the same ranking. Kimberly N. Hunt and AnnaMarie L. Sheldon, eds., *Notable Corporate Chronologies* (London: Gale Research, 1998), 1, p. 633.

310. Patricia Sellers, "The Billionairesses," *Fortune* (9 September 1991), pp. 53, 60.

311. Mirabella, "Beauty Queen: Estée Lauder," pp. 183–184.

312. Dillon, Read & Co., "Estée Lauder Companies—Company Report," p. 4, and author's estimates.

CHAPTER 6

1. Kevin Sullivan, "Breaking New Grounds: Starbucks Store Opens in Caffeine-Crazy Japan," *Washington Post* (1 August 1996), p. C1.

2. Howard Schultz and Dori Jones Yang, *Pour Your Heart Into It: How Starbucks Built a Company One Cup at a Time* (New York: Hyperion, 1997), p. 244.

3. The founders had originally considered calling the company Pequod after the ship in *Moby Dick.* They had also debated naming the business Starbo after turn-of-the-century mining camps on Mt. Rainier, near Seattle. They settled on Starbuck because it evoked the romance and excitement of the sailing tradition while maintaining a connection to the history of the northwestern United States. Ibid., pp. 32–33.

4. Ibid., p. 244.

5. Ibid.

6. Starbucks Corporation, *Annual Report 1996*, p. 3.

7. In mid-1996, Starbucks also licensed operations in dozens of airports and other locations. When fiscal 1996 closed at the end of September, for example, the company had 1,006 stores; the vast majority of these—more than 920 outlets—were company-owned stores. Ibid., pp. 3, 27.

8. See, for example, Adrian J. Slywotzky, *Value Migration: How to Think Several Moves Ahead of the Competition* (Boston: Harvard Business School Press, 1996), pp. 165, 171; C. J. Lawrence/Deutsche Bank Securities, "Starbucks Corporation—Company Report" (14 November 1995), p. 1; and Bill McDowell, "The Bean Counters," *Restaurants & Institutions* (15 December 1995), pp. 40–56.

9. Quoted in Darren McDermott, "Starbucks to Open Singapore Outlets in Asian Expansion," *Wall Street Journal* (12 August 1996), p. B6.

10. Howard Behar, interview by author, Seattle, WA, 22 June 1995 [hereafter Behar interview].

11. Starbucks Corporation, "Store Locator," http://locator.starbucks.com/starbucks/foreign.hm?FS=Japan (accessed 30 June 2000).

12. Measured in dollars, Japanese per capita gross domestic product (GDP) was $40,940 in 1996. World Bank Group, "Japan Data Profile," http://wbln0018.worldbank.org/psd/ (accessed 30 June 2000).

13. In 1994, for example, the United States consumed more 1 billion kilograms of coffee. Germany consumed more than 600 million kilos, and Japan more than 360 million. Norihiko Shirouzu, "Japan's Staid Coffee Bars Wake Up and Smell Starbucks," *Wall Street Journal* (25 July 1996), p. B1.

14. Coca-Cola Company alone maintained more than 800,000 vending machines that sold canned coffee in Japan. Ibid.

15. See, for example, "Starbucks Dips into Upscale Tokyo Market," *Chicago Tribune* (4 August 1996), p. C4.

16. Quoted in ibid.

17. Schultz and Yang, *Pour Your Heart Into It,* p. 244.

18. Shirouzu, "Japan's Staid Coffee Bars," p. B1.

19. Seth Sutel, "Tokyo Wakes Up and Smells the Latté: Starbucks Perks Up Japanese Market with 'the Coffee Lifestyle,'" *The Boston Globe* (4 August 1996), p. F5.

20. Schultz and Yang, *Pour Your Heart Into It,* p. 244.

21. Howard Behar, telephone interview with author, 14 April 1998 [hereafter Telephone interview with Behar].

22. Sullivan, "Breaking New Grounds," p. C1. According to Starbucks Corporation, *Annual Report 1996,* the company's financial outlay in Japan, including investments in the joint venture, capital contributions, guaranteed loans, and operating losses, totaled $6.7 million as of the close of fiscal 1996 (p. 40). See also Starbucks Corporation, *Annual Report 1997,* p. 11, and Starbucks Corporation, *Annual Report 1998,* p. 26.

23. McDowell, "Bean Counters," p. 50.

24. Howard Schultz, telephone interview with author, 26 March 1998 [hereafter Telephone interview with Schultz]. See also Schultz and Yang, *Pour Your Heart Into It,* pp. 243–266.

25. Telephone interview with Schultz.

26. This section is based on Geoffrey Verter and Nancy F. Koehn, "Starbucks Coffee Company," Case 1-796-134 (Boston: Harvard Business School, 1996), pp. 2–3.

27. On the early history of coffee, see Fernand Braudel, *The Structures of Everyday Life: The Limits of the Possible,* translated by Sían Reynolds (New York: Harper & Row, 1979), pp. 256–262; Gregory Dicum and Nina Luttinger, *The Coffee Book: Anatomy of an Industry from Crop to the Last Drop* (New York: New Press, 1999), pp. 2–9; and Mark Pendergrast, *Uncommon Grounds: The History of Coffee and How It Transformed Our World* (New York: Basic Books, 1999), pp. 3–12.

28. Dicum and Luttinger, *Coffee Book,* p. 3.

29. A late-tenth-century physician noted that coffee "fortifies the members. . . . cleans the skin, and dries up the humidities that are under it, and gives an excellent smell to all the body." Quoted in W. H. Ukers, *All About Coffee* (New York: Coffee and Tea Journal, 1935), p. 8.

30. It is not clear precisely when and where users began roasting and grinding coffee beans. "Finally, probably in the sixteenth century," Pendergrast writes, "someone roasted the beans, ground them, and made an infusion." *Uncommon Grounds,* p. 5.

31. Quoted in Dicum and Luttinger, *Coffee Book,* pp. 7–8. See also Heinrich Eduard Jacob, *Coffee: The Epic of a Commodity,* translated by Eden and Cedar Paul (New York: Viking Press, 1962), p. 282.

32. The drink assumed special significance in Turkey. Soldiers there used it to rekindle their energy. Women giving birth were allowed coffee—or kaveh—to reduce labor pains. National law allowed Turkish women to divorce their husbands

if they were refused the beverage. Dicum and Luttinger, *Coffee Book*, p. 7. See also Pendergrast, *Uncommon Grounds*, p. 7.

33. An anonymous treatise, which appeared in Lyon in 1671, argued that

> coffee dries up all cold and damp humours, drives away wind, strengthens the liver, relieves dropsies by its purifying quality; sovereign equally for scabies and impurity of the blood, it revives the heart and its vital beat, relieves those who have stomach ache and have lost their appetite. (Quoted in Braudel, *Structures of Everyday Life*, p. 257.)

In the late sixteenth century Pope Clement VIII had threatened to ban coffee because it was perceived as a Muslim beverage. But the pontiff liked the flavor so well, he changed his mind, deciding instead to baptize the beverage as a Christian one. "Why, this Satan's drink is so delicious," he purportedly said, "that it would be a pity to let the infidels have exclusive use of it." Quoted in Pendergrast, *Uncommon Grounds*, p. 8.

34. Coffee, tea, and cocoa took early modern England by storm. By 1715, for example, there were 2,000 coffeehouses in London. Dicum and Luttinger, *Coffee Book*, p. 10. See also Mark Schapiro, "Muddy Waters: The Lore, the Lure, the Lowdown on America's Favorite Addiction," *Utne Reader* (November-December 1994), p. 59; Pendergrast, *Uncommon Grounds*, pp. 12–14; and Carole Shammas, "Changes in English and Anglo-American Consumption, 1550 to 1800," in John Brewer and Roy Porter, eds., *Consumption and the World of Goods* (London: Routledge, 1993), pp. 177–205. On the political role of coffeehouses in early modern Britain, see Alison Olson, "Coffee House Lobbying," *History Today* 41 (1991), pp. 35–41.

35. In the eighteenth century, Voltaire, Diderot, Rousseau, Benjamin Franklin, and other notables frequented Café Procope.

36. John E. Wills Jr., "European Consumption and Asian Production in the Seventeenth and Eighteenth Centuries," in Brewer and Porter, eds., *Consumption and the World of Goods*, p. 141.

37. Verter and Koehn, "Starbucks Coffee Company," p. 14; Dicum and Luttinger, *Coffee Book*, p. 14.

38. For example, in the eighteenth century, the New York City Chamber of Commerce held sessions in the Merchants' Coffeehouse located at the corner of today's Wall and Water Streets. In 1775, the same coffeehouse also hosted public meetings after the Revolutionary War battles of Lexington and Concord. In 1790, the Merchants' Coffeehouse was the site of the first U.S. public sale of stocks by sworn stockbrokers. Ukers, *All About Coffee*, pp. 101–126.

39. T. H. Breen, "'Baubles of Britain': The American and Consumer Revolutions of the Eighteenth Century," *Past & Present* 119 (1988), p. 83. See also Carole Shammas, *The Pre-Industrial Consumer in England and America* (Oxford: Clarendon Press, 1990), pp. 83–86.

40. Quoted in Charles A. Beard and Mary R. Beard, *The Rise of American Civilization* (New York: Macmillan, 1927), 1, p. 266.

41. In 1830, the average American consumed about half a pound of tea annually, compared to three pounds of coffee. E. G. Montgomery and C. H. Kardell, *Apparent Per Capita Consumption of Principal Foodstuffs in the United States,* Department of Commerce, Domestic Commerce Series, no. 38 (Washington, DC: U.S. Department of Commerce, 1930), p. 48. On coffee and tea consumption in the southern United States, see James R. Comer, "Cups That Cheer: Folkways of Caffeinated Beverages in the Reconstruction South," *Gulf Coast Historical Review* 10, no. 1 (fall 1994), pp. 61–71.

42. Per capita coffee consumption rose steadily in the early nineteenth century, climbing from three pounds a year in 1830 to five and a half pounds in 1850 to eight pounds on the eve of the Civil War. Pendergrast, *Uncommon Grounds,* p. 46.

43. Ibid. On coffee's significance on the frontier, see Wesley L. Fankhauser, "Son-of-a-Gun to Pâté de Foie Gras: Chow on Early Great Plains Ranches," *Journal of the West* 16, no. 1 (January 1977), pp. 29–33.

44. Pendergrast, *Uncommon Grounds,* p. 47.

45. Ibid., pp. 48–49.

46. The coffee ration, Billings wrote, "was most heartily appreciated by the soldier. When tired and foot-sore, he would drop out of the marching column, build his little camp-fire, cook his mess of coffee, take a nap behind the nearest shelter, and when he woke, hurry on to overtake his company." John D. Billings, *Hardtack and Coffee: The Unwritten Story of Army Life* (Chicago: R. R. Donnelly & Sons, 1960), pp. 129–130 (original emphasis).

47. Quoted in Pendergrast, *Uncommon Grounds,* p. 49.

48. Folger got his start in the business selling preroasted coffee to miners during the California Gold Rush in the 1850s. Although his firm went bankrupt in 1865, he quickly started over, building one of the most successful coffee companies on the West Coast.

49. FIND/SVP, *The Market for Coffee and Tea: A Market Intelligence Report* (October 1994), p. 18.

50. Pendergrast, *Uncommon Grounds,* p. 54.

51. Kraft Foods Inc., "Maxwell House Coffee Break—Our Heritage," http://www.kraftfoods.com/maxwellhouse/mh_heritage.html (accessed 11 October 2000).

52. The company was originally founded as the Great American Tea Company. In 1869, Gilman and his partner George Huntington Hartford changed the firm's name to the Great Atlantic and Pacific Tea Company in honor of the first transcontinental railroad. On the history of A&P, see Richard S. Tedlow, *New and Improved: The Story of Mass Marketing in America* (New York: Basic Books, 1990), pp. 182–259.

53. Like A&P, other grocery store chains grew out of operations that originally specialized in tea and coffee. The Jewel Tea Company, for example, was established in late-nineteenth-century Chicago to sell tea and coffee. Salesmen in horse-drawn wagons peddled bulk-roasted coffee door-to-door. In the early twentieth century, Jewel increased its offerings to include groceries and household goods. By 1916, when the company went public, it had more than 800 wagon routes serving more than two million midwestern families. Approximately half its annual profit came from coffee sales. Pendergrast, *Uncommon Grounds*, pp. 120–121.

54. Ukers, *All About Coffee*, p. 521. Pendergrast attributes the invention of instant or soluble coffee to George Washington, a Belgian who was living in Guatemala in the early twentieth century. In 1906, Washington "conceived the idea of refining coffee crystals from brewed coffee." Four years later, he moved to New York and founded a business to market and distribute his invention, calling it the G. Washington Coffee Company. *Uncommon Grounds*, pp. 147–148.

55. By the end of the war, the U.S. Expeditionary Forces had used 75 million pounds of coffee, much of it instant. Fighting men depended on the convenience of instant coffee. "I am very happy," wrote one soldier from a European trench, "despite the rats, the rain, the mud, the draughts, the roar of the canon and the scream of the shells." "It takes only a minute," he continued, "to light my little oil heater and make some George Washington Coffee." Quoted in Pendergrast, *Uncommon Grounds*, p. 148.

56. Quoted in ibid., p. 149.

57. Children also got into the act: Almost one in six Americans between the ages of six and sixteen consumed coffee in 1939. Pendergrast, *Uncommon Grounds*, pp. 215–216. See also Elizabeth Waterman Gilboy, "Time Series and the Derivation of Demand and Supply Curves: A Study of Coffee and Tea, 1850–1930," *Quarterly Journal of Economics* 48, no. 4 (August 1934), pp. 667–685.

58. "Emotional Ersatz," *Time* (16 January 1939), p. 50 (original emphasis).

59. Pendergrast, *Uncommon Grounds*, p. 215.

60. The term "Joe," probably taken from "G.I. Joe," was applied to the drink, and "a cuppa Joe" entered everyday speech as a reference to coffee. See note 249.

61. Folgers, for example, lacked sufficient containers. Hills Brothers postponed investments in additional capacity. Most companies confronted at least periodic shortages of beans imported from countries such as Brazil.

62. Pendergrast, *Uncommon Grounds*, pp. 228–229.

63. "We feel that the postwar market will be even greater than has been estimated to date," said one regional roaster in 1945:

> People who formerly drank only an occasional cup are now using coffee regularly in place of carbonated soft drinks or ice cream, and finding it both stimulating and satisfying to the craving for a bit of sweet taste. Pure tension

> and "cussedness" of high-speed defense work has added many more coffee users during the war production emergence, and of course millions of servicemen, being supplied with coffee in messhalls in the country, have found a taste for it. (Quoted in Robert Latimer, "St. Louis Roaster Now Planning for Expanding Post-War Coffee Market," *Tea & Coffee Trade Journal* 88, no. 6 [June 1945], p. 11.)

64. A writer for the trade journal *Coffee Annual* was particularly confident. Pointing to a growing national population and leading roasters' abilities to "keep close watch on all trends and developments" in the market, the observer concluded, "there's every sign that coffee will remain the country's favorite beverage forever." "Coffee is 'Big Business' in the United States," *Coffee Annual 1952* (New York: George Gordon Paton, 1952), p. 53. See also W. J. Ganucheau Jr., "A Decade in Retrospect," *Coffee Annual 1948* (New York: George Gordon Paton, 1948), pp. 41–42, and "Coffee Consumption—Key to the Future," *Coffee Annual 1949* (New York: George Gordon Paton, 1949), pp. 87–89.

65. Measured in pounds, this was more than three times the per capita consumption level in 1870. Ukers, *All About Coffee*, p. 521. Conversion guidelines are from Specialty Coffee Association of America guidelines and author's calculations. See Steve Emmons, "Feeling Bitter about Bad Coffee? A Trade Group Is Spilling the Beans on How to Get the Best Flavor When You Brew," *Los Angeles Times* (22 April 1997), p. E1, and S. D. Smith, "Accounting for Taste: British Coffee Consumption in Historical Perspective," *Journal of Interdisciplinary History* 27, no. 2 (autumn 1996), p. 193.

66. International Coffee Organization, "United States of America—Winter Coffee Drinking Study" (1988). In 1963, the majority of the population, nearly 75 percent of Americans age ten and over, drank hot coffee. *Coffee Annual 1988* (New York: George Gordon Paton, 1988), p. 103. Beginning in the mid-1950s, coffee manufacturers and trade associations began to measure per capita consumption in cups per day rather than pounds per year. Unlike previous industry practice, which used national population to calculate per-person usage, the new convention counted only Americans over the age of ten. See Pendergrast, *Uncommon Grounds*, pp. 272–273. Per-cup consumption figures for the 1960s are based on a six-ounce container.

67. Schapiro, "Muddy Waters," pp. 60–61.

68. By 1960, there were about 850 coffee roasters in the United States. Pendergrast, *Uncommon Grounds*, p. 261.

69. Richard G. Hamermesh and Steven B. Silk, "How to Compete in Stagnant Industries," *Harvard Business Review* 57, no. 5 (September-October 1979), p. 162.

70. Pendergrast, *Uncommon Grounds*, p. 153. See also Schapiro, "Muddy Waters," p. 58–65.

71. On contemporary consumers' opinions about coffee, see Benson & Benson, Inc., "Survey of Consumer Attitudes on Coffee" (Princeton: Benson & Benson, 1955); James P. Quinn, *Scientific Marketing of Coffee* (New York: Tea & Coffee Trade Journal, 1960).

72. Pendergrast, *Uncommon Grounds*, p. 235.

73. By the late 1950s, for example, most instant coffee blends contained 50 percent robusta beans. Pendergrast, *Uncommon Grounds*, p. 262. On coffee supplies in the 1960s, see U.S. Department of Commerce, *Coffee Consumption in the United States, 1920–1965* (Washington, DC: U.S. Government Printing Office, 1961), pp. 39–51.

74. Quinn, *Scientific Marketing of Coffee*, p. 25.

75. Husbands in the commercials, Dicum and Luttinger noted, "would leave for work angry over having suffered through another breakfast with toxic coffee. The men are abusive and childlike, incapable of fixing their own coffee." *Coffee Book*, p. 137. General Foods ran television commercials that portrayed a husband lecturing his spouse on coffee preparation. "Be a good little Maxwell Housewife," he said, "and I think I'll keep you around."

76. Reproduced in ibid., p. 137.

77. "Review of Consumption of Coffee in the United States of America—1961 to 1964 and 1979 to 1989," *Coffee Annual 1989* (New York: George Gordon Paton, 1990), p. 103.

78. FIND/SVP, *Market for Coffee and Tea*, p. 89. On the postwar market for Coke and Pepsi, see Tedlow, *New and Improved*, pp. 91–106.

79. Matthew Grimm, "Iced Drinks Perk Up Coffee, But Where Are the Big Brands?" *Adweek's Marketing Week* 31, no. 20 (14 May 1990), p. 4. See also William C. Strunning, "Recent Study of Consumer Attitudes Show Coffee's Varying Appeal Around the World," *Tea & Coffee Trade Journal* 146, no. 1 (January 1974), pp. 76–83.

80. Percentage fall is based on price-adjusted sales of canned and instant coffee. "Annual Consumer Expenditures Study," *Supermarket Business* 36, no. 9 (September 1981), p. 50, and "Annual Consumer Expenditures Study," *Supermarket Business* 46, no. 9 (September 1991), p. 74. Price indexes are from Council of Economic Advisers, *Economic Report of the President* (Washington, DC: U.S. Government Printing Office, 2000), p. 373.

81. Ted R. Lingle, "Avenues for Growth: A 20-Year Review of the U.S. Specialty Coffee Market," *Specialty Coffee Association of America* (1993), p. 3.

82. As late as 1980, specialty coffee composed less than 10 percent of total coffee sales. Ibid.

83. Quoted in Pendergrast, *Uncommon Grounds*, p. 292.

84. Schultz and Yang, *Pour Your Heart Into It*, p. 30.

85. Ibid., p. 31.

86. Under this name, the Pike Place Market store sold various roasts, approximately thirty types of tea, and spices such as chicory, candied ginger, and catnip.

87. Quoted in Pendergrast, *Uncommon Grounds*, p. 312. See also Mark Robichaux, "Boom in Fancy Coffee Pits Big Marketers, Little Firms," *Wall Street Journal* (6 November 1989), pp. B1–2.

88. Lingle, "Avenues for Growth," p. 1. These figures include retail sales of beans, ground coffee, and specialty coffee drinks as well as specialty coffee served in restaurants, offices, and other food-service channels.

89. Supermarket sales of coffee totaled $7.3 billion in 1980. "Annual Consumer Expenditures Study," p. 50.

90. Schapiro, "Muddy Waters," p. 61. See also Kathleen Deveny, "For Coffee's Big Three, A Gourmet-Brew Boom Proves Embarrassing Bust," *Wall Street Journal* (4 November 1993), p. B1. Kraft General Foods sold coffee under the Maxwell House and Yuban names; Procter & Gamble controlled the Folgers brand; Nestlé owned the Nescafé, Hills Bros., and MJB names.

91. Schultz and Yang, *Pour Your Heart Into It*, pp. 12–13; Anthony and Diane Hallett, *Encyclopedia of Entrepreneurs* (New York: John Wiley & Sons, 1997), p. 409.

92. Fred Schultz's annual income never exceeded $20,000. At times, his oldest son remembered, Fred had "to take on two or three jobs just to put food on the table," Schultz and Yang, *Pour Your Heart Into It*, pp. 4, 12.

93. Ibid., pp. 13–14.

94. Ibid., p. 15.

95. Ibid., p. 17; David Bollier, "Howard Schultz and the Starbucks Coffee Company: Employees as Partners in Growth," in *Aiming Higher: 25 Stories of How Companies Prosper by Combining Sound Management and Social Vision* (New York: American Management Association, 1996), p. 212.

96. As he grew up, Howard often argued with his father. "I became bitter about his underachievement," he said, "his lack of responsibility. I thought he could have accomplished so much more, if only he had tried." Schultz and Yang, *Pour Your Heart Into It*, p. 4.

97. Ibid., p. 17.

98. Neither Fred nor Elaine Schultz had finished high school.

99. Schultz and Yang, *Pour Your Heart Into It*, p. 21.

100. Ibid., p. 23.

101. Ibid., p. 26.

102. On the emergence of markets for natural foods in the 1970s and 1980s, see Warren J. Belasco, *Appetite for Change: How the Counterculture Took on the Food Industry* (Ithaca: Cornell University Press, 1989), and Harvey Levenstein, *Paradox of Plenty: A Social History of Eating in Modern America* (New York: Oxford University Press), pp. 195–212.

103. Donna R. Gabaccia, *We Are What We Eat* (Cambridge: Harvard University Press, 1998), pp. 203–224.

104. Schultz and Yang, *Pour Your Heart Into It,* p. 41.

105. Hallett, *Encyclopedia of Entrepreneurs,* p. 409. Zev Siegl, one of the three founders of Starbucks, sold his interest in the business in 1980.

106. Quoted in Ingrid Abramovitch, "Miracles of Marketing—How to Reinvent Your Product," *Success* 40 (April 1993), p. 23.

107. Schultz and Yang, *Pour Your Heart Into It,* p. 51.

108. Bollier, "Howard Schultz and the Starbucks Coffee Company," p. 213.

109. Schultz and Yang, *Pour Your Heart Into It,* p. 52.

110. Abramovitch, "Miracles of Marketing," p. 23.

111. In 1984, Starbucks acquired Peet's Coffee & Tea.

112. The entire sum was raised at ninety-two cents a share. Schultz and Yang, *Pour Your Heart Into It,* p. 71.

113. Ibid., p. 84.

114. Dave Olsen, interview by author, Seattle, WA, 10 November 1998 [hereafter Olsen interview].

115. Schultz and Yang, *Pour Your Heart Into It,* p. 83. The original agreement required Olsen to work half time. This, Olsen remembered, "amounted to about 60 hours a week." Olsen interview.

116. "We hit it off immediately. There was very good karma and credibility between us," Olsen recalled. Ibid.

117. Ibid.; Schultz and Yang, *Pour Your Heart Into It,* pp. 82–83.

118. Olsen interview.

119. Ames-Karreman, for instance, arrived at Il Giornale at 4:30 A.M. on weekdays, leaving most evenings after 6:00. She was often on the phone nights talking with other colleagues. She worked more weekends than not. Jennifer Ames-Karreman, interview by author, Seattle, WA, 10 November 1998 [hereafter Ames-Karreman interview].

120. Olsen interview.

121. As Schultz later observed, many of the decisions that entrepreneurs make in the early days of a business play a crucial role in laying the foundation for the firm's future. See Schultz and Yang, *Pour Your Heart Into It,* p. 85.

122. Ibid. and Ames-Karreman interview.

123. Schultz and Yang, *Pour Your Heart Into It,* pp. 87, 165; FIND/SVP, *The Market for Coffee and Tea,* pp. 32, 71; and Liz Fader, "What's Happening in Flavored Coffees: The Growth Area of Specialty Coffee," *Tea & Coffee Trade Journal* 163, no. 11 (November 1991), pp. 32–46. On the importance of building and maintaining a clear, consistent brand identity, see Jean-Noel Kapferer, *Strategic Brand Management: New Approaches to Creating and Evaluating Brand Management* (New York: Free Press, 1992), pp. 31–53; Kevin Lane Keller, *Strategic Brand Management: Build-*

ing, Measuring, and Managing Brand Equity (Upper Saddle River, NJ: Prentice Hall, 1998), pp. 130–174, 593–601; and Kevin Keller, "The Brand Report Card," *Harvard Business Review* 78, no. 1 (January-February 2000), p. 148.

124. Schultz and Yang, *Pour Your Heart Into It,* p. 88. See also Donald N. Schoenholt, "Starbucks: Metaphor for Specialty Coffee," *Tea & Coffee Trade Journal* 166, no. 2 (February 1994), p. 28.

125. Abramovitch, "Miracles of Marketing," p. 23. See also Schultz and Yang, *Pour Your Heart Into It,* p. 73.

126. Schultz and Yang, *Pour Your Heart Into It,* p. 90.

127. Earlier in 1987, the company had sold Caravali, its wholesale coffee business, to a group of investors headed by Seattle executive Bart Wilson. "Starbucks Corporation," in Tina Grant, ed., *International Directory of Company Histories* (New York: St. James Press, 1996), 13, pp. 493–494.

128. Ibid., pp. 493–494. By the terms of the deal, Jerry Baldwin retained control of Peet's Coffee & Tea Company, becoming head of the business. Peet's Coffee & Tea, "Our History," http://www.peets.com/abtu/22/4.4.1_history.asp (accessed 30 June 2000).

129. Schultz considered calling the newly merged company Il Giornale. But the Starbucks name was more widely recognized. Il Giornale, as one of his advisers pointed out, was also harder to pronounce and spell. Consumers might find it obscure. Schultz and Yang, *Pour Your Heart Into It,* p. 107.

130. Maltz had been president and chief operating officer of ICEE-USA, which made flavored syrups for slushy, ice-based beverages sold in mass merchandisers such as K-Mart, other retailers, and gas stations. ICEE-USA also provided the machines that made the drinks, charging customers for the syrups, cups, and other supplies. In 1987, the company had 1,800 distribution points. "J&J Elects Chairman, 4 Directors to ICEE," *Wall Street Journal* (21 May 1987), p. A34, and "ICEE-USA Poised to Expand Operations," *Los Angeles Times* (20 January 1987), S4, p. 5.

131. Joe Agnew, "Regular Coffee Grinding Down as Gourmet Brands Percolate," *Marketing News* (23 October 1987), p. 6.

132. Schultz and Yang, *Pour Your Heart Into It,* p. 115.

133. Ibid., p. 111.

134. Ibid., p. 370.

135. Orin Smith, interview by author, Seattle, WA, 10 November 1998 [hereafter Smith interview].

136. Starbucks Corporation, *Annual Report 1992,* p. 16.

137. "Starbucks Corporation," p. 494.

138. Schultz and Yang, *Pour Your Heart Into It,* p. 115.

139. Matt Rothman, "Into the Black," *Inc.* (January 1993), p. 65.

140. Starbucks Corporation, *Annual Report 1992,* p. 13.

141. Ibid., p. 1.

142. Schultz and Yang, *Pour Your Heart Into It,* p. 142.

143. On the relationship between effective service delivery, customer loyalty, and employee morale, see James L. Heskett et al., "Putting the Service-Profit Chain to Work," *Harvard Business Review* 72, no. 2 (March-April 1994), pp. 164–174.

144. Howard Behar, interview by author, Seattle, WA, 10 November 1998.

145. Schultz and Yang, *Pour Your Heart Into It,* p. 167.

146. Ibid., p. 169.

147. Ibid., pp. 160–161.

148. By delegating substantial power and responsibility to the CFO, Behar, and other new managers, Schultz hoped to send a clear message to other executives and employees: "I hired you because you're smarter than I. Now go and prove it." Ibid., p. 155. As the company grew, so did many executives' roles. Orin Smith, for example, began his career at Starbucks as executive vice president and CFO. In 1994, he was promoted to president and chief operating officer. In 2000, he became CEO, and Schultz assumed the new role of chief global strategist overseeing Starbucks global expansion and international brand development.

149. Deidra Wager, interview by author, Seattle, WA, 10 November 1998.

150. Starbucks Corporation, *Annual Report 1992,* p. 1.

151. Agnew, "Regular Coffee Grinding Down as Gourmet Brands Percolate," p. 6.

152. Schultz and Yang, *Pour Your Heart Into It,* p. 143.

153. Ibid., p. 116.

154. According to Schultz, L.A. consumers immediately took to dark-roast coffee. "Unlike our experience in Chicago," he wrote, "we never had to struggle with a learning curve." Ibid.

155. Kathie Jenkins, "America's Best: Brews with Attitude," *Los Angeles Times* (1 November 1990), p. H1. See also Barbara Hansen, "Shopping: Coffee Bars, Yogurt Bars and Light Sour Cream," *Los Angeles Times* (30 May 1991), p. H39, and Laurie Ochoa, "The Coffee Revolution; Seattle—It's Latte Town, Jake Trends: Coffee Cultism, Washington-style, May Be Coming to Your Neighborhood," *Los Angeles Times* (12 September 1991), p. H14.

156. Laurie Ochoa, "The Coffee Revolution; Seattle—It's Latte Town, Jake Trends: Coffee Cultism, Washington-style, May Be Coming to Your Neighborhood," *Los Angeles Times* (9 December 1991), p. H14.

157. Schultz and Yang, *Pour Your Heart Into It,* p. 116.

158. By the close of fiscal 1992, Starbucks stores were handling almost 100,000 transactions a day, a 60 percent increase from the preceding year. In fiscal 1992, the company opened stores in San Francisco, San Diego, and Denver. Starbucks Corporation, *Annual Report 1992,* pp. 3, 12.

159. Smith interview.

160. Starbucks Corporation, *Annual Report 1995,* p. 23.

161. Starbucks Corporation, *Annual Report 1992*, p. 26. Starbucks conducted a two-for-one stock split in September 1993 and December 1995. The $17 IPO offering price is not adjusted to reflect the splits.

162. Ibid., p. 1; Starbucks Corporation, *Annual Report 1995*, p. 23; and Rothman, "Into the Black," p. 60. On Starbucks growing reputation, see John Balzar, "American Album: In Northwest, Specialty Coffee Is the Hot Drink," *Los Angeles Times* (31 December 1990), p. A5, and Dori Jones Yang and Julia Flynn Siler, "Fewer Cups, but a Much Richer Brew," *Business Week* (18 November 1991), p. 80.

163. Marjorie Shaffer, "All About Specialty Coffees: These Days, the Bean's the Thing," *New York Times* (24 January 1993), S3, p. 10. See also Brothers Gourmet Coffee Company, *Prospectus 1993*, p. 3.

164. Pendergrast, *Uncommon Grounds*, p. 383.

165. In 1995, Brothers Gourmet Coffee sold the coffee bar chain to Second Cup, a Canadian coffee bar chain.

166. In 1989, for example, franchised coffee bars comprised almost a fifth of the 1,200 specialty coffee outlets in North America. Many franchisers, however, confronted quality-control problems similar to those Ed Kvetko faced in managing Gloria Jean's. During the mid-1990s, established and new players turned increasingly to owner-operated cafés and stores. By 1999, franchised coffee bean and café outlets represented only a twentieth of a total of 12,000. Statistics courtesy of Ted Lingle, executive director of the Specialty Coffee Association of America.

167. Java Centrale, *Prospectus 1994*, p. 4.

168. FIND/SVP, *The Market for Coffee and Tea*, p. 30.

169. Ibid., pp. 78–79.

170. Robichaux, "Boom in Fancy Coffee Pits Big Marketers, Little Firms," p. B2.

171. One journalist noted that Schultz welcomed the "marketing muscle of the big companies because it increases awareness of better grades of coffee." Quoted in Shaffer, "All About Specialty Coffees: These Days the Bean's the Thing," p. 10.

172. Schultz and Yang, *Pour Your Heart Into It*, p. 32.

173. J. Walker Smith and Ann Clurman, *Rocking the Ages: The Yankelovich Report on Generational Marketing* (New York: HarperCollins, 1997), p. 44.

174. Ibid., pp. 19, 44, 78. In the late 1990s, about 13 percent of Americans lived below the poverty line, which was about $16,900 for a family of four. U.S. Department of Commerce, *USA Statistics in Brief*, http://www.census.gov/statab/www/part4.html, and www.census.gov/hhes/poverty/threshld/thresh99.html. (accessed 30 June 2000).

175. Smith and Clurman, *Rocking the Ages*, p. 46. See Todd Gitlin, *The Sixties: Years of Hope, Days of Rage* (New York: Bantam, 1989), pp. 420–438.

176. See, for example, Russell W. Belk, "Yuppies as Arbiters of the Emerging Consumption Style," in Richard J. Lutz, ed., *Advances in Consumer Research* 13

(Provo, UT: Association for Consumer Research, 1986), pp. 514–519; and Susan Fournier, David Antes, and Glenn Beaumier, "Nine Consumption Lifestyles," in John F. Sherry Jr., and Brian Sternthal, eds., *Advances in Consumer Research* 19 (Provo, UT: Association for Consumer Research, 1992), pp. 329–337. See also Geoffrey Colvin, "What the Baby-Boomers Will Buy Next," *Fortune* (15 October 1984), pp. 28–34; Peter J. Gallanis, "The Customer Connection: Middle of the Road," *Discount News* 38, no. 20 (25 October 1999), pp. 42–56; and Smith and Clurman, *Rocking the Ages,* pp. 42–69.

177. On consumer motivation in buying natural foods, see Terry Hennessy, "Organics: Banking on the Boomers," *Progressive Grocer* 76, no. 7 (July 1997), pp. 95–100; Barry Janoff, "Supermarkets Go Au Naturel," *Progressive Grocer* 78, no. 3 (March 1999), pp. 75–80; Phil R. Kaufman, "Natural Foods Supermarkets Gaining in Popularity," *Food Review* 21, no. 3 (September-December 1998), pp. 25–27; and Toni Mack, "Good Food, Great Margins," *Forbes* (17 October 1988), p. 112.

178. Quoted in Janoff, "Supermarkets Go Au Naturel," p. 76.

179. Sales of organic products rose at a compound annual rate of 20 percent between 1980 and 1994, climbing to $2.3 billion in the latter year. By 1998, they totaled $4 billion. Julie Alton Dunn, "Organic Foods Find Opportunity in the Natural Food Industry," *Food Review* 181, no. 3 (September-December 1995), p. 7, and S. C. Gwynne, "Thriving on Health Food," *Time* (23 February 1998), p. 53. See also Levenstein, *Paradox of Plenty,* pp. 195–212.

180. In 1997, these two supermarket chains had combined sales of $2.3 billion. Kaufman, "Natural Foods Supermarkets Gaining in Popularity," p. 25.

181. Council of Economic Advisers, *Economic Report of the President,* pp. 308, 341.

182. In 1979, for example, the top fifth of income earners received about 42 percent of aggregate income. In 1994, the top quintile received 47 percent. U.S. Bureau of the Census, "Income Inequality—Table 1," http://www.census.gov/hhes/income/incineq/p60tb1.html (accessed 30 June 2000). See also Robert H. Frank, *Luxury Fever: Why Money Fails to Satisfy in an Era of Excess* (New York: Free Press, 1999), pp. 33–34; Paul Krugman, "The Right, the Rich and the Facts," *The American Prospect* 11 (fall 1992), pp. 19–31; Juliet B. Schor, *The Overspent American: Upscaling, Downshifting and the New Consumer* (New York: Basic Books, 1998), pp. 12–14, 107–108; and Edward N. Wolff, "Recent Trends in the Size Distribution of Household Wealth," *Journal of Economic Perspectives* 12, no. 3 (summer 1998), pp. 131–150, and "How the Pie Is Sliced: America's Growing Concentration of Wealth," *The American Prospect* 22 (summer 1995), pp. 58–64.

183. Households in the lowest and second quintiles also experienced a decline in average real incomes. Adjusted for price changes, the mean income for the poorest households fell from $8,239 in 1979 to $7,762 in 1994. The mean income for households in the second quintile fell from $19,955 to $19,224 during the period. For households in the fourth quintile, average real incomes rose slightly, from

$48,281 in 1979 to $50,935 in the later year. U.S Bureau of the Census, "Income Inequality—Table 3," http://www.census.gov/hhes/income/incineg/p60t63.html (accessed 20 April 2000).

184. On emulative spending in the late twentieth century and collective interest in the top tier of the income distribution, see Schor, *The Overspent American,* pp. 3–21, and Frank, *Luxury Fever,* pp. 14–44. See also Susan Fournier and Michael Guiry, "'An Emerald Green Jaguar, A House on Nantucket, and an African Safari': Wish Lists and Consumption Dreams in Materialist Society," in Leigh McAlister and Michael L. Rothschild, eds., *Advances in Consumer Research* 20 (Provo, UT: Association for Consumer Research 1992), pp. 352–364.

185. See, for example, Roper Survey Organization, "How We Classify Ourselves," *American Enterprise* (May-June 1993), pp. 87, 88.

186. As Robert Frank notes, the personal savings rate fell 40 percent in the last two decades of the century. In 1999, it was about 5 percent. Frank, *Luxury Fever,* p. 45.

187. Ibid., p. 46, and Schor, *The Overspent American,* p. 72.

188. On the increasing importance of little luxuries or small indulgences in consumer priorities, see Faith Popcorn, *The Popcorn Report on the Future of Your Company, Your World, Your Life* (New York: Doubleday, 1991), pp. 39–42.

189. Schultz and Yang, *Pour Your Heart Into It,* p. 119.

190. By 1997, almost fifty-three million Americans traveled to foreign countries. U.S. Department of Commerce, *Statistical Abstract of the United States, 1987* (Washington, DC: U.S. Government Printing Office, 1987), p. 224, table 390, and U.S. Bureau of the Census, *Statistical Abstract of the United States, 1999* (Washington, DC: U.S. Government Printing Office, 1999), pp. 277–278. Figures cited here include visits by Americans to all foreign countries. On average, about 35 percent of Americans traveling abroad visited Canada and Mexico each year. The 1970 total is based on census data and author's estimates.

191. In 1997, for example, Americans made 443 million business trips. U.S. Department of Commerce, *Statistical Abstract of the United States, 1999,* p. 277.

192. FIND/SVP, *The Market for Coffee and Tea,* p. 4. See also "Gourmet Coffee Leads Growth in the U.S.," *Tea & Coffee Trade Journal* 171, no. 11 (November 1999), p. 18, and Specialty Coffee Association of America, "1999 Coffee Market Summary" (Long Beach California, 1999), p. 3.

193. FIND/SVP, *The Market for Coffee and Tea,* p. 64; Lingle, "Avenues for Growth," p. 5; and "1999 Coffee Market Summary," p. 4. The majority of outlets devoted to specialty coffee were coffeehouses. In 1998, according to the National Coffee Association, there were 7,000 coffeehouses in the United States. "Gourmet Coffee Leads Growth in U.S.," p. 20.

194. Quoted in Thomas J. Neff and James M. Citrin with Paul B. Brown, *Lessons from the Top* (New York: Random House, 1999), p. 260.

195. Schultz and Yang, *Pour Your Heart Into It,* p. 125. See also Neff, Citrin, and Brown, *Lessons from the Top,* pp. 260–261.

196. Quoted in Rothman, "Into the Black," p. 59.

197. Schultz and Yang, *Pour Your Heart Into It,* p. 127.

198. Ibid.

199. To qualify for Bean Stock options, a partner had to be employed with Starbucks from April 1 until the end of the fiscal year, work at least 500 hours during that period, and still be employed when options were distributed in January. The number of options available for a given employee depended on a partner's base pay, the option price, and Starbucks profitability. The more profitable the company, the higher the percentage of base pay that could be applied to options.

200. Quoted in Rothman, "Into the Black," p. 59.

201. Jennifer Tisdel, telephone interview with author, 21 February 1996 [hereafter Telephone interview with Tisdel].

202. McDowell, "Bean Counters," p. 50. See also Jennifer Reese, "Starbucks: Inside the Coffee Cult," *Fortune* (9 December 1996), p. 194.

203. Reese, "Starbucks: Inside the Coffee Cult," p. 192.

204. Ibid., p. 194.

205. Dave Olsen, interview by author, Seattle, WA, 21 March 1995.

206. Roasters trained for more than a year before being allowed to roast Starbucks beans. According to the company's 1992 annual report:

> Roasting at Starbucks is a unique combination of high technology and artistic interpretation. . . . Roasting is done in three gas-fired machines, capable of roasting batches from 200 to 600 pounds each, over a period of roughly fifteen minutes per batch. Each machine is operated by an experienced roaster trained in relating subtle changes in the coffee's color and temperature to the desired flavor characteristics for each specific variety. (Starbucks Corporation, *Annual Report 1992,* p. 7.)

In the company's first twenty years of business, only nineteen people had been deemed qualified to roast the company's coffee. "Starbucks Corporation," p. 494.

207. Unlike many brand-name consumer-products companies, Schultz noted, Starbucks controlled virtually all the processes of production and distribution involved in bringing specialty coffee drinks to consumers: from buying and roasting beans, to shipping them to individual stores, to training baristas and other store employees, to designing and opening company-owned cafés. Schultz believed that to maintain the quality of Starbucks coffee and the company's in-store experience, it had to invest in a range of capabilities and business functions beyond selling specialty coffee. Schultz and Yang, *Pour Your Heart Into It,* p. 171.

208. Orin Smith, interview by author, Seattle, WA, 21 March 1995 [hereafter Smith interview, 21 March 1995].

209. Arthur Rubinfeld, interview by author, Seattle, WA, 22 June 1995.

210. Smith interview, 21 March 1995.

211. Starbucks Corporation, *Annual Report 1999*, p. 1.

212. Starbucks acquired the Boston-based coffee retailer in a stock swap valued at $23.7 million.

213. At the beginning of the twenty-first century, Starbucks had an office in Boston that served as a hub for New England.

214. Starbucks Corporation, *Annual Report 1996*, p. 4.

215. Howard Schultz, interview by author, Seattle, WA, 21 March 1995 [hereafter Schultz interview, 21 March 1995].

216. Smith interview, 21 March 1995.

217. Behar interview.

218. Telephone interview with Tisdel.

219. Ibid. In fiscal 1995, Starbucks marketing expenditures totaled approximately 3 percent of retail sales.

220. Pendergrast, *Uncommon Grounds*, p. 380. On the cultural significance of communal meeting places, see Ray Oldenburg, *The Great Good Place: Cafés, Coffee Shops, General Stores, Bars, Hangouts, and How They Get You Through the Day* (New York: Paragon, 1991).

221. McDowell, "Bean Counters," p. 53.

222. Schultz and Yang, *Pour Your Heart Into It*, p. 119.

223. Dan Eggen, "Area Neighborhoods Buzz with Home Businesses," *Washington Post* (3 October 1999), p. A1. Between 1989 and 1999, the number of home offices in the United States increased almost threefold, climbing to 23.8 million. Sarah Schafer, "All Business at the Coffeehouse; The New Base for Out-of-Office Workers has a Symbiotic Side for Shop Owners," *Washington Post* (7 June 1999), p. F12.

224. Quoted in Eggen, "Area Neighborhoods Buzz with Home Businesses," p. A1.

225. Schultz interview, 21 March 1995.

226. Ibid.

227. As Holly Hinton, Starbucks' music specialist, explained, in 1999:

> It's our customers who give us permission to try something new—something beyond coffee. . . . We started with mostly jazz and some blues collections, but recently we've discovered that we can walk out a bit further. And these little surprises can be one of the most rewarding things for customers. So we're beginning to introduce different genres—Celtic, alternative country, Cuban. It's niche music that people don't get through regular commercial channels, but they're intrigued by it. (Quoted in Starbucks Corporation, *Annual Report 1999*, p. 9.)

228. Schultz and Yang, *Pour Your Heart Into It*, p. 209.

229. Starbucks Corporation, *Annual Report 1998*, p. 19.

230. Orin Smith, telephone interview with author, 9 April 1998 [hereafter Telephone interview with Smith].

231. Starbucks Corporation, *Annual Report 1999*, p. 21.

232. Vincent Eades, telephone interview with author, 26 March 1998.

233. Packaged Facts, *The Market for Coffee and Tea* (New York: Kalorama Information, 1999), p. 172.

234. Judy Meleliat, telephone interview with author, 20 March 1998.

235. Quoted in Robichaux, "Boom in Fancy Coffee Pits Big Marketers, Little Firms," p. B2.

236. Telephone interview with Smith.

237. Jim Alling, telephone interview with author, 30 March 1998.

238. Starbucks Coffee Corporation, *Form 10-K, 1999*, p. 4, and Robert F. Ohmes, "Starbucks: An Early-Stage Global Packaged Goods Company: Upgrade to Outperform," Morgan Stanley Dean Witter (19 April 1999), p. 3.

239. Telephone interview with Behar.

240. Ibid.

241. Marjorie Milller, "Revolution Brewing: Selling Coffee to Tea-Drinking Brits is Becoming a Hot Business as Espresso Bars Multiply and Starbucks Arrives to Win Converts," *Los Angeles Times* (7 August 1998), p. D1.

242. By autumn 1999, the U.S. retailer had converted all locations acquired from Seattle Coffee Company into Starbucks stores and opened an additional thirty-six locations in the United Kingdom. Starbucks Corporation, *Annual Report 1999*, p. 1.

243. Ibid.; Starbucks Corporation, *Form 10-K 1999*, Exhibit 13, p. 1; and Nelson D. Schwartz, "Still Perking after All These Years," *Fortune* (24 May 1999), p. 204. See also "Starbucks Coffee Company Timeline" (February 2000), p. 2.

244. Sales figures from Starbucks Corporation, *Form 10-K 1999*, p. 30. "Starbucks Lays Out Expansion Plan: Will Finance 400 More Coffee Shops," *Wall Street Journal* (23 December 1999), p. B1, and Robert Marshall Wells, "Starbucks International President Steps Down after Five Years of Growth," *Seattle Times* (1 September 1999), p. C1.

245. "CEO Interview: Howard Schultz, Starbucks Corporation," *Wall Street Journal* Transcript Corporation (27 April 1999), pp. 2–3.

246. In 1983, Americans bought 450,000 home coffee grinders. Nine years later, this number had climbed to 1.25 million. FIND/SVP, *The Market for Coffee and Tea*, p. 29.

247. "Gourmet Coffee Leads Growth in U.S.," p. 20. The National Coffee Association distinguished occasional drinkers from those who drank coffee daily. Occasional drinkers were defined as those who consumed coffee for social reasons or on a weekly basis. Gary Goldstein, National Coffee Association, telephone interview with author, 6 January 2000.

248. In the late 1990s, the consumption of specialty coffee drinks increased significantly. In 1997, for example, 80 million Americans, about 35 percent of the pop-

ulation, drank espresso-based drinks or iced coffee beverages. A year later, 108 million consumers, about 47 percent of the population, did. Specialty Coffee Association of America, "1999 Coffee Market Summary," pp. 3–4.

249. As Robert Nelson, the president of the National Coffee Association, said in 1999, "The younger occasional drinkers are more likely to identify with 'gourmet' coffees as being 'for people like me.' And they think these beverages are worth the price they pay." Quoted in "Gourmet Coffee Leads Growth," p. 20. The term "cuppa Joe" was first coined during World War II when the United States supplied soldiers with as much coffee as they could drink. Some Marines claimed to drink twenty cups a day. American soldiers stationed overseas became so closely identified with the beverage coffee that the term "G.I. Joe" came to be applied to the mostly instant coffee that they consumed. Pendergrast, *Uncommon Grounds,* p. 224. See also Dicum and Luttinger, *Coffee Book.* These authors maintain that the term "cup of Joe" was a naval invention that originated during World War II. According to Dicum and Luttinger, commander Josephus "Joe" Daniels banned the regular use of alcohol aboard ships, forcing seamen to resort to coffee, pp. 69–70.

250. "Gourmet Coffee Leads Growth in U.S.," p. 18.

251. See, for example, Kevin Keller, "The Brand Report Card," p. 148; Robert J. Thomas, "Starbucks Coffee Company," in *New Product Success Stories: Lessons from Leading Innovators* (New York: John Wiley & Sons, 1995), p. 19; and "Starbucks Corporation," Hambrecht & Quist (19 November 1999).

CHAPTER 7

1. Michael A. Hiltzik and Thomas S. Mulligan, "Market Sell-Off," *Los Angeles Times* (28 October 1997), p. A1.

2. In 1998, about 27 percent of retail trading by individuals in stocks and mutual funds shares was done on-line. For stocks alone, on-line brokerages accounted for almost 40 percent of all retail trading. Lynnley Browning, "The Rise of E-Wall Street," *Boston Globe* (7 March 1999), pp. G1, G5.

3. Dell Computer Corporation, *Annual Report 1998,* p. 15.

4. Quoted in Marcia Stepanek, "What Does No. 1 Do for an Encore," *Business Week* (2 November 1998), p. 112.

5. Ronald Alsop, ed., *The Wall Street Journal Almanac* (New York: Ballantine, 1997), p. 483, and Doug Lenick, "Dell Takes Over First Place; Compaq Slips to Two," *TWICE* (13 March 2000), p. 20.

6. Dell Computer Corporation, *Annual Report 1990,* p. 1; Dell Computer Corporation, *Annual Report 1998,* p. 2; and Richard Murphy, "Michael Dell's Billion-Dollar Secret," *Success* 46, no. 1 (January 1999), p. 50.

7. Louise Kehoe, "Survey—World's Most Respected Companies," *Financial Times* (7 December 1999), p. 4.

8. Dell Computer Corporation, "Five-Year Statistical Review," http://www.dell.com/html/us/corporate/annualreports/reportoo/statistical/index.htm (accessed 30 June 2000); Dell Computer Corporation, *Annual Report 1998*, p. 2; and Murphy, "Michael Dell's Billion-Dollar Secret," p. 52.

9. Eryn Brown, "America's Most Admired Companies," *Fortune* (1 March 1999), p. 70; Dell Computer Corporation, "Five-Year Statistical Review"; and "Internet Stocks Drove Record Year of IPOs, Led Market in '99," *Los Angeles Times* (1 January 2000), p. C1.

10. Jody Brennan et. al. "The Forbes Four Hundred: The Richest People in America," *Forbes* (21 October 1991), p. 264.

11. Peter Newcomb, "The Forbes Four Hundred: The Richest People in America," *Forbes* (12 October 1998), pp. 176–177.

12. Melanie Warner, "The Young and the Loaded," *Fortune* (27 September 1999), pp. 79–88, and Michael Borden and Suzanne Koudsi, "America's Forty Richest Under 40," *Fortune* (27 September 1999), pp. 90–95.

13. Quoted in Michael Dell with Catherine Fredman, *Direct from Dell: Strategies that Revolutionized an Industry* (New York: HarperCollins, 1999), jacket endorsement. See also Gary McWilliams and Joseph B. White, "Others Want to Figure Out How to Adopt Dell Model," *Wall Street Journal Interactive Edition* (1 December 1999), and Gregory L. White, "How GM, Ford Think the Internet Can Make Splash in Their Factories," *Wall Street Journal Interactive Edition* (3 December 1999).

14. Dell and Fredman, *Direct from Dell*, p. 10.

15. McWilliams and White, "Others Want to Figure Out How to Adopt Dell Model"; and White, "How GM, Ford Think the Internet Can Make Splash in Their Factories."

16. Estimate from Egil Juliussen and Karen Petska-Juliussen, *Internet Industry Almanac* (San Jose: Computer Industry Almanac, 1998), p. 313.

17. Tim Rhinelander et al., "Cheap PC Thrills," *The Forrester Report* 4, no. 8 (December 1997), pp. 6–7.

18. Robert J. Samuelson, "Have PCs Peaked?" *Washington Post* (1 April 1999), p. A27.

19. United States Internet Council, "State of the Internet: USIC's Report on Use & Threats in 1999," http://www.usic.org/stateoftheinternet99.htm (accessed 30 June 2000).

20. On the history of the computer industry, see James Beniger, *The Control Revolution: Technical and Economic Origins of the Information Society* (Cambridge: Harvard University Press, 1986); Manuel Castells, *The Rise of the Network Society* (Oxford: Blackwell, 1996), pp. 40–65; Alfred D. Chandler Jr., *Inventing the Electronic Century: The Epic Story of the Consumer Electronics and Computer Industries* (New York: Free Press, forthcoming); Kenneth Flamm, *Creating the Computer: Government, Industry, and High Technology* (Washington, DC: Brookings Institution, 1988); Peggy A. Kid-

well and Paul Ceruzzi, *Landmarks in Digital Computing* (Washington, DC: Smithsonian Institution Press, 1994), pp. 59–74; and Steven W. Usselman, "Computer and Communications Technology," in Stanley I. Kutler, ed., *Encyclopedia of the United States in the Twentieth Century* (New York: Simon & Schuster, 1996), 2, pp. 799–829.

21. Kidwell and Ceruzzi, *Landmarks in Digital Computing,* pp. 64–65.

22. Rowena Olegario, "IBM and the Two Thomas J. Watsons," in Thomas K. McCraw, ed., *Creating Modern Capitalism: How Entrepreneurs, Companies, and Countries Triumphed in Three Industrial Revolutions* (Cambridge: Harvard University Press, 1997), pp. 360–362.

23. Ibid., p. 362.

24. Kidwell and Ceruzzi, *Landmarks in Digital Computing,* p. 71.

25. Thomas J. Watson Jr., and Peter Petre, *Father, Son & Co.: My Life at IBM and Beyond* (New York: Bantam, 1990), p. 242.

26. Kidwell and Ceruzzi, *Landmarks in Digital Computing,* p. 73.

27. In 1960, IBM's revenues totaled two times those of all its competitors combined. Chandler, *Inventing the Electronic Century,* ch. 1, p. 3.

28. Olegario, "IBM and the Two Thomas J. Watsons," p. 366.

29. Emerson W. Pugh, Lyle R. Johnson, and John H. Palmer, *IBM's 360 and Early 370 Systems* (Cambridge: MIT Press, 1991), p.167.

30. Olegario, "IBM and the Two Thomas J. Watsons," p. 367.

31. Ibid., p. 368.

32. Ibid. By the end of the 1970s, more than two-thirds of the world's computer installations were centered around IBM equipment. Charles H. Ferguson and Charles R. Morris, *Computer Wars: How the West Can Win in a Post-IBM World* (New York: Random House, 1993), p. 15.

33. Olegario, "IBM and the Two Thomas J. Watsons," p. 368.

34. Chandler, *Inventing the Electronic Century,* ch. 1, p. 4. Kidwell and Ceruzzi cite a price of $18,000 for the PDP-8. *Landmarks in Digital Computing,* p. 77.

35. IBM offered customers the option of leasing System/360 machines for about $1,500 a month. Most business customers chose leasing over outright purchase. Bill Cully and Dave Forestner, IBM Systems Hardware Team, North American Sales Center, Atlanta, GA, telephone interview, 25 March 1999.

36. Carolyn Caddes, *Portraits of Success: Impressions of Silicon Valley Pioneers* (Palo Alto, CA: Tioga, 1986), p. 46.

37. Thomas K. McCraw, *American Business, 1920–2000: How It Worked* (Wheeling, IL: Harlan Davidson, 2000), p. 200.

38. By 1971, 2,300 transistors could be packed on a chip the size of a thumbtack. In 1993, this number had climbed to 35 million. Chip memory capacity grew even faster. In 1971, Intel's cutting-edge DRAM (dynamic random-access memory) chip held 1,024 bits of data. At the end of the twentieth century, capacity was 250 million bits. Processing speed also accelerated dramatically. Microprocessors in the late

1990s were more than 550 times faster than those available in 1972. Castells, *Rise of the Network Society,* pp. 42–43.

39. McCraw, *American Business,* p. 201. By the 1990s, microprocessors served many of the potential applications that developers in the 1960s and 1970s had envisioned for the technology. At that time, many were skeptical about the innovation's use in computers. Instead, some Intel executives and developers initially believed that microprocessors would find their main commercial uses in automobiles and household appliances. In the early 1970s, for example, programmers approached Intel head Robert Noyce about using the microprocessor to create a simple computer game. He dismissed the suggestion, saying the chip's future lay elsewhere. "It's in watches," he said. Quoted in Paul Freiberger and Michael Swaine, *Fire in the Valley: The Making of the Personal Computer Industry* (Berkeley: Osborne/McGraw-Hill, 1984), p. 138.

40. According to Castells, Roberts chose the name *Altair* because his daughter liked a Star Trek character by that name. *Rise of the Network Society,* p. 44.

41. The Altair measured 17" × 18" × 7". Kidwell and Ceruzzi, *Landmarks in Digital Computing,* p. 95.

42. Das Narayandas and V. Kasturi Rangan, "Dell Computer Corporation," Case 9-596-058 (Boston: Harvard Business School, 1996), p. 1. Kidwell and Ceruzzi contend the Altair's preassembled price was $498. *Landmarks in Digital Computing,* p. 94.

43. In early 1975, *Popular Electronics* ran a cover story on the Altair, proclaiming it the "first minicomputer kit to rival commercial models." Edward H. Roberts and William Yates, "Exclusive! Altair 8800: The Most Powerful Minicomputer Project Ever Presented—Can Be Built for Under $400," *Popular Electronics* 7, no. 1 (January 1975), pp. 33–38. See also Kidwell and Ceruzzi, *Landmarks in Digital Computing,* p. 94.

44. The Altair's popularity stimulated a range of technological innovations, inaugurating the first wave of personal computing. In the mid-1970s, for example, the development of a 5¼-inch disk drive for data storage replaced more cumbersome external cassette tape drives used in mainframes, and scores of manufacturers soon entered the disk-drive business. On the history of the industry, see Clayton M. Chistensen, *The Innovator's Dilemma: When New Technologies Cause Great Firms to Fail* (Boston: Harvard Business School Press, 1997), pp. 4–7.

45. The original idea for the company's name is unclear. As Freiberger and Swaine noted, "Jobs claims it was a random decision. . . . Friends of Jobs say that he named it after the Beatle's record label, Apple." Regardless of its beginnings, Markkula recognized the marketing benefits of the name: Apple put the company first in the phone book and the name had positive connotations. "Very few people don't like apples," he said. Finally, the incongruous pairing of Apple and computer was striking and memorable. Quoted in *Fire in the Valley,* pp. 212, 215.

46. The invention of VisiCalc, the first computerized spreadsheet, increased the Apple II's value to business customers. Initially coded to run only on the Apple II, the software replaced the tedium and potential mistakes of paper-and-pencil spreadsheets with instant, accurate computations. VisiCalc was the PC industry's first "killer app," and businesses and government agencies that could not previously justify the expense of a desktop computer wanted an Apple II in order to use it. On the software's development, see Robert X. Cringely, *Accidental Empires: How the Boys of Silicon Valley Make Their Millions, Battle Foreign Competition, and Still Can't Get a Date* (Reading, MA: Addison-Wesley, 1992), pp. 64–72.

47. Kidwell and Ceruzzi, *Landmarks in Digital Computing*, p. 99. When Apple Computer conducted its IPO in 1980, the company raised more than $80 million. At the time, it was the most successful public offering since Ford Motor Company went public in 1956 and one of the largest IPOs to date in Wall Street history. Lee Butcher, *Accidental Millionaire: The Rise and Fall of Steve Jobs at Apple Computer* (New York: Paragon House, 1988), p. 133.

48. In 1976, for example, Gates wrote an "Open Letter to Hobbyists," that was printed in a well-known hobbyist publication, *The Homebrew Computer Club Newsletter*. The letter attacked software piracy, arguing that for efficient, state-of-the-art software to be produced, developers must be paid for their time and effort. Reprinted in Freiberger and Swaine, *Fire in the Valley*, p. 169. See also Randall Stross, *The Microsoft Way: The Real Story of How the Company Outsmarts Its Competition* (Reading, MA: Addison-Wesley, 1996), pp. 48–52.

49. "The future," Gates remembered in his autobiography, "was staring us in the face from the cover of a magazine. It wasn't going to wait for us. Getting in on the first stages of the PC revolution looked like the opportunity of a lifetime, and we seized it." Bill Gates with Nathan Myhrvold and Peter Rinearson, *The Road Ahead* (New York: Penguin, 1995), p. 17.

50. Venture Development Corporation, *The Personal Computer Industry II: A Strategic Analysis, 1981–1985* (Wellesley, MA: Venture Development Corporation, 1981), pp. 58–59. See also John Steffens, *New Games: Strategic Competition in the PC Revolution* (Oxford: Pergamon Press, 1994), p. 101.

51. James Chposky and Ted Leonsis, *Blue Magic: The People, Power and Politics Behind the IBM Personal Computer* (New York: Facts on File, 1988), p. 16.

52. Freiberger and Swaine, *Fire in the Valley*, p. 193.

53. Roberts offered prospective retailers a 25 percent discount on every PC they sold regardless of quantity. In exchange, franchisees agreed to carry only the Altair. Ibid., pp. 188–189.

54. Ibid., p. 198.

55. Ibid., p. 195.

56. Almost 60 percent of all business users were engineers, systems programmers, and analysts, or employed in a computer-oriented occupation. Venture Development Corporation, *The Personal Computer Industry II,* p. 105.

57. Production numbers reflect units shipped into or within the United States and are from Gartner Group/Dataquest, "Personal Computer History: U.S. Shipments, 1999," courtesy of Lesley Robbins, Senior Business Analyst, Gartner Group/Dataquest. Revenue figures are from Narayandas and Rangan, "Dell Computer Corporation," p. 2. Venture Development Corporation cites total output for 1980 as 391,600 units. The total factory dollar value of these shipments was $1.2 billion. *The Personal Computer Industry II,* p. 6.

58. In 1980, mainframe sales totaled $7.6 billion and minicomputer revenues $2 billion. Narayandas and Rangan, "Dell Computer Corporation," p. 2. These figures probably represent the factory dollar value of computers shipped.

59. Narayandas and Rangan, "Dell Computer Corporation," p. 3. In the mid-1970s, DEC, H-P, and IBM had considered producing PCs. But all three companies rejected the idea because the projected market was too small. Kidwell and Ceruzzi, *Landmarks in Digital Computing,* p. 92.

60. Chandler, *Inventing the Electronic Century,* ch. 1, p. 10.

61. IBM planners believed that this decision would encourage other companies to build compatible circuit cards and other extensions for the IBM machine. According to Cringely, the expected margins on PC add-ons such as circuit cards were relatively unattractive to the IBM task force. "So the decision was made to leave those crumbs to outsiders. Other companies would have to assume the development and marketing costs of add-on cards, but the existence of such cards would only help sales of IBM PCs." *Accidental Empires,* p. 137.

62. Ferguson and Morris, *Computer Wars,* pp. 24–25.

63. Ibid., p. 25.

64. Ibid.; Chandler, *Inventing the Electronic Century,* ch. 1, p. 10.

65. For personal and strategic reasons, Allen and Gates had moved the company from Albuquerque to Seattle at the end of 1978. On this decision, see Stephen Manes and Paul Andrews, *Gates: How Microsoft's Mogul Reinvented an Industry and Made Himself the Richest Man in America* (New York: Simon & Schuster, 1993), pp. 119–121.

66. QDOS was also known as SCP-DOS or Seattle Computer Products Operating System. Without revealing IBM's interest, Gates paid $25,000 for the licensing rights to QDOS. He later purchased exclusive rights for $50,000. Seattle Computer Products later sued and won a $1 million judgment against Microsoft. Freiberger and Swaine, *Fire in the Valley,* p. 276; and Ferguson and Morris, *Computer Wars,* p. 26.

67. Gates with Myhrvold and Rinearson, *The Road Ahead,* p. 54.

68. Chandler, *Inventing the Electronic Century,* ch.1, p. 11. If IBM's PC division had been an independent business in 1984, it would have ranked 74th on the For-

tune 500 list. Chposky and Leonsis, *Blue Magic,* p. 172, and Ferguson and Morris, *Computer Wars,* p. 28.

69. Gartner Group/Dataquest, "Personal Computer History: U.S. Shipments." See also Alsop, *Wall Street Journal Almanac,* p. 483. In 1982, *Time* chose the IBM PC for its cover story on "Man of the Year." "There are some occasions when the most significant force in a year's news is not a single individual, but a process," wrote the magazine's editors. "*Time*'s Man of the Year for 1982, the greatest influence for good and evil is not a man at all. It is a machine, the computer." Quoted in Ferguson and Morris, *Computer Wars,* p. 28–29.

70. In 1985, only 10 percent of the PCs produced were used in homes. Venture Development Corporation, *Venturecasts: The 1985 Consumer Electronics Data Book* (Natick, MA: Venture Development Corporation, 1985), p. 5.

71. *World Almanac, 1996* (Mahwah, NJ: Funk & Wagnalls, 1995), p. 171.

72. Individuals bought 10 percent of PC output in 1985, and educational institutions the remaining 10 percent. Venture Development Corporation, *Venturecasts: The 1985 Consumer Electronics Data Book,* p. 5.

73. Narayandas and Rangan, "Dell Computer Corporation," p. 3.

74. Estimates of the size of IBM's domestic sales force in the early 1980s vary widely. Narayandas and Rangan put this number at 2,500 people. Ibid. According to Chposky and Leonsis, IBM had 8,400 people in the field at this time. *Blue Magic,* p. 14. IBM does not disclose the size of past sales forces.

75. IBM also promoted the development of a network of distributors that targeted small and medium-sized businesses. These dealers were known as value-added resellers (VARs), and, as the network developed, they assumed a range of functions for business customers, including after-sales service and support. Jan W. Rivkin and Michael E. Porter, "Matching Dell," Case 9-799-158 (Boston: Harvard Business School, 1999), p. 2.

76. Sears and other retailers that sold IBM PCs benefited greatly from the advertising campaign, earning average gross margins of 25 percent on each machine sold in the rapidly growing market. These returns made computer distribution an attractive opportunity, and in the early 1980s, scores of new dealerships began selling IBM-compatible machines. Narayandas and Rangan, "Dell Computer Corporation," p. 3.

77. Demand for PCs grew faster than IBM's ability to meet it. "We missed the preliminary sales forecast by almost 500 percent," recalled Dan Wilkie, who in the early 1980s was in charge of manufacturing for the IBM PC. "But by the same measure," he continued, "it skewed the bottom line in our favor since, with the volumes going up, the per-unit production costs kept heading down." Quoted in Chposky and Leonsis, *Blue Magic,* p. 113.

78. Freiberger and Swaine, *Fire in the Valley,* p. 281.

79. Venture Development Corporation, *Venturecasts: The 1986 Computer Data Book* (Natick, MA: Venture Development Corporation, 1986), p. 113. In 1980, Apple

was one of the three largest PC producers. In number of units shipped, it ranked second behind Radio Shack. In terms of the factory dollar value of units made, Apple followed Radio Shack and Hewlett-Packard. Venture Development Corporation, *The Personal Computer Industry II,* pp. 85, 92. At the end of the 1990s, Apple's share in the business desktop market was 1.4 percent. Joe Mullich, "Second Tier Stays Alive," *Information Week* (7 September 1998), p. 105. On Apple's response to the IBM PC, see Butcher, *Accidental Millionaire,* pp. 147–165.

80. Charles Boisseau, "The Company That Dell Built—Isn't Finished Yet," *Houston Chronicle Magazine* (25 February 1996), pp. 6–10.

81. Dell and Fredman, *Direct from Dell,* pp. 4–5.

82. Boisseau, "The Company That Dell Built," and Craig E. Aronoff and John L. Ward, "Michael Dell," *Profiles of Entrepreneurs and the Businesses They Started: Representing 74 Companies in 30 Industries* (Detroit: Omnigraphics, Inc., 1992), p. 119.

83. Boisseau, "The Company That Dell Built."

84. Dell and Fredman, *Direct from Dell,* p. 4.

85. Anthony Hallet and Diane Hallett, *Encyclopedia of Entrepreneurs* (New York: John Wiley, 1997), p. 160, and Dell and Fredman, *Direct from Dell,* p. 4.

86. Dell and Fredman, *Direct from Dell,* p. 4.

87. Ibid, p. 5.

88. As part of a high school economics project, Dell was required to file a tax return. When he listed $18,000, his teacher assumed Michael had misplaced the decimal point. She was even more dismayed, Dell remembered in his autobiography, when she realized that he had written the correct figure—he had made more money that year than the educator. He used some of this money to buy a new white BMW, writing a check for the car. Boisseau, "The Company That Dell Built," and Dell and Fredman, *Direct from Dell,* pp. 5–6.

89. Dell and Fredman, *Direct from Dell,* p. 6.

90. Boisseau, "The Company That Dell Built."

91. In his junior year of high school, Dell took a computer class. His performance, the teacher remembered, was not exceptional: "He's a super person, knows how to make money, and that's what people are interested in, but he didn't turn in super-ordinary work for me." Dell occasionally deviated from class assignments. One day, when students were supposed to be writing programs, Dell's teacher discovered him using the mainframe computer terminal to retrieve stock market information. The older man disconnected the call. Michael "became pretty angry with me," the teacher said. Quoted in ibid.

92. Dell and Fredman, *Direct from Dell,* p. 7.

93. Ibid.

94. Ibid.

95. Stanley W. Angrist, "Entrepreneur in Short Pants," *Forbes* (7 March 1988), p. 85.

96. Dell and Fredman, *Direct from Dell,* p. 14.

97. Ibid.

98. Quoted in Chposky and Leonsis, *Blue Magic,* p. 115.

99. Ibid.

100. Venture Development Corporation, *The Personal Computer Industry II,* pp. 112–113.

101. Dell and Fredman, *Direct from Dell,* p. 8.

102. Christopher W. L. Hart, James L. Heskett, and W. Earl Sasser Jr., "The Profitable Art of Service Recovery," *Harvard Business Review* 68, no. 4 (July-August 1990), p. 151. See also James L. Heskett, W. Earl Sasser, and Leonard A. Schlesinger, "Listening to Customers," videotape (Boston: Harvard Business School, 1 January 1994).

103. Dell and Fredman, *Direct from Dell,* p. 8.

104. Chposky and Leonsis, *Blue Magic,* p. 114.

105. Andrew E. Serwer, "Michael Dell Turns the PC World Inside Out," *Fortune* (8 September 1997), p. 80.

106. Dell and Fredman, *Direct from Dell,* p. 13.

107. Ibid., p. 10.

108. Ibid.

109. Ibid., p. 13.

110. Serwer, "Michael Dell Turns the PC World Inside Out," p. 84.

111. Geoff Lewis, "The Hottest Little Computer Maker in Texas," *Business Week* (2 February 1987), p. 72.

112. Michael Oneal with Thane Peterson, "25 Executives to Watch," *Business Week* (1992 Business Week 1000), p. 86.

113. Dell and Fredman, *Direct from Dell,* p. 18.

114. Ibid., pp. 17–18.

115. Mark Goldstein, "An Industry Legend—at 21," *Industry Week* 233, no. 2 (20 April 1987), p. 73.

116. Today, Intel's 300 megahertz Pentium II processor is about 100 times faster than the 12 megahertz 286. Dell Computer Corporation, "The Dell Story," www.dell.com/corporate/access/dellstory/page1.htm (accessed 27 October 1998).

117. Aronoff and Ward, "Michael Dell," p. 121.

118. Richard Poe, "It's Not Bragging If You Can Do It," *Venture* 9, no. 7 (July 1987), p. 26, and Aronoff and Ward, "Michael Dell," p. 121.

119. Dell Computer Corporation, *Annual Report 1989,* p. 22.

120. Dell and Fredman, *Direct from Dell,* p. 12.

121. As Cringely writes, Compaq's founders realized soon after the IBM PC's introduction that it was software, not hardware, that determined a particular model's fate:

> In order for their computer to be successful, it would have to have a large library of available software right from the start, which meant building a

computer that was compatible with some other system. The only 16-bit standard available that qualified under these rules was IBM's, so that was the decision—to make an IBM compatible PC—and make it *damn* compatible—100 percent. Any program that would run on an IBM PC would run on a Compaq. Any circuit board that would operate in an IBM PC would operate in a Compaq. The key to their success would be leveraging the market's considerable investment in IBM. (*Accidental Empires,* p. 172.)

122. Louise Kehoe, "Defying the Analysts' Predictions," *Financial Times* (21 February 1986), p. 13.

123. Cringely, *Accidental Empires,* p. 173.

124. Angrist, "Entrepreneur in Short Pants," p. 85.

125. Alice LaPlante, "Buyers Guide: AT Computers," *InfoWorld* 9, no. 4 (26 January 1987), p. 40.

126. Dell and Fredman, *Direct from Dell,* p. 80. See also Joan Magretta, "The Power of Virtual Integration: An Interview with Dell Computer's Michael Dell," *Harvard Business Review* 76, no. 2 (March-April 1998), pp. 75–77.

127. Dell Computer Corporation, *Annual Report 1989,* p. 21. The Dell fiscal year ends January 31 of the relevant calendar year.

128. Poe, "It's Not Bragging If You Can Do It," p. 26.

129. Apple spent heavily on advertising, marketing both the company and its products. The 1984 launch of the Macintosh, for example, was preceded by a $15 million media campaign intended to interest business and home users. Butcher, *Accidental Millionaire,* p. 182.

130. See, for example, LaPlante, "Buyers Guide," p. 40. In 1985, there were hundreds of PC manufacturers that distributed products by mail. One of these was Gateway—originally named TIPC Network—which was founded in 1985 in an Iowa farmhouse by Ted Waitt and Michael Hammond. Gateway's strategy was focused on aggressively underselling its rivals. Annual revenues in 1986 were almost $1 million; by 1990, they climbed to $275 million. Paula Kepos, ed., *International Directory of Corporate Histories,* 10 (Washington, DC: St. James Press, 1995), pp. 307–309.

131. See, for example, Rivkin and Porter, "Matching Dell," pp. 1–14.

132. As Michael Dell said in 1989, "I found the way to differentiate our company was to deliver a greater set of benefits—high performance and other [service-oriented] benefits. That is what has stripped Dell away from the rest of the 800 crowd." Quoted in Mark Brownstein, "Mail Order Arrives," *InfoWorld* 11, no. 39 (25 September 1989), p. 49.

133. Helen Thorpe, "Michael Dell," *Texas Monthly* (September 1997), p. 177.

134. See, for example, Rebecca Hurst, "Mail-Order Micros Win Stamp of Approval," *ComputerWorld* 21, no. 09A (4 March 1987), p. 30.

135. Employee numbers are for 1986 and are from the company's Web site as of summer 2000. Dell Computer Corporation, "The Dell Story." Sales figures are for the fiscal year ending in January 1987 and are from Dell Computer Corporation, *Annual Report 1989,* p. 22.

136. According to a 1984 survey, men accounted for more than 90 percent of computer users. Michael Schrage, "Computer Sales Lag for Women, Blacks," *Washington Post* (24 July 1984), p. D8.

137. More than 85 percent of *Personal Computing*'s readership, and 96 percent of *PC World*'s audience, were men. Ibid., p. D8.

138. On the diffusion of new high-tech products among different consumer groups, see Geoffrey Moore, *Crossing the Chasm: Marketing and Selling High-Tech Products to Mainstream Customers* (New York: HarperBusiness, 1991), pp. 9–25.

139. Dell Computer Corporation, "The Dell Story."

140. In 1987, Dell's on-site support and repair services were provided by Honeywell. Stephen Satchell, "Machine Outspeeds 386 Pack For Surprisingly Low Price Tag," *InfoWorld* 9, no. 31 (3 August 1987), p. 59. On business consumers' reactions to Dell Computer's service initiatives, see also Alan J. Ryan, "Buyers Skirt Clone Service Woes," *ComputerWorld* 21, no. 50 (14 December 1987), pp. 35, 41.

141. Julie Pitta, "Why Dell Is a Survivor," *Forbes* (12 October 1992), p. 84.

142. Poe, "It's Not Bragging If You Can Do It," p. 27. See also Dell Computer Corporation, *Annual Report 1989,* p. 12.

143. Joel Kotkin, "The Innovation Upstarts," *Inc.* (January 1989), p. 71. See also Dell Computer Corporation, *Annual Report 1989,* p. 12.

144. Narayandas and Rangan, "Dell Computer Corporation," p. 6.

145. Poe, "It's Not Bragging If You Can Do It," p. 27. Dell customers within 100 miles of a Honeywell service office received the on-site service contract free the first year. Satchell, "Machine Outspeeds 386 Pack for Surprisingly Low Price Tag," p. 59.

146. Aronoff and Ward, "Michael Dell," p. 121.

147. Charles Bermant, "PC's Limited: Making Mail-Order Pay Off," *InfoWorld* 9, no. 4 (26 January 1987), p. 8. The same year, Compaq's advertising budget for print media was between ten and fifteen million dollars or about 1 percent of sales. Paula Schorbus, "Business Adds Byte," *Marketing and Media Decisions* 23, no. 1 (January 1988), p. 57.

148. See, for example, Satchell, "Machine Outspeeds 386 Pack For Surprisingly Low Price Tag," pp. 56–59; Stephen Satchell with David Chalmers and Sally J. Douglas, "The Ten Most Wanted AT Compatibles," *InfoWorld* 10, no. 30 (25 July 1988), pp. 44–45; John Unger and Stan Miastkowski, "Outclassing the AT," *Byte* 13, no. 7 (July 1988), pp. 136–137, 139, 142–144; and William Zachmann, "The Price Is Right," *ComputerWorld* 21, no. 35 (31 August 1987), pp. 33–34. In 1988, Dell's System 325, based on the 386 microprocessor, was selected *PC Magazine*'s "Editor's Choice,"

outranking a field of other 25-megahertz systems, including the Compaq Deskpro 386/24. Dell Computer Corporation, *Annual Report 1989*, p. 14.

149. Goldstein, "An Industry Legend—at 21," p. 74.

150. Dell and Fredman, *Direct from Dell*, p. 26. Gross profits in 1986 were about 10 percent of sales. Goldstein, "An Industry Legend—at 21," p. 74.

151. Bermant, "PC's Limited: Making Mail-Order Pay Off," p. 8; Hurst, "Mail-Order Micros Win Stamp of Approval," p. 29; and Lewis, "Hottest Little Computer Maker in Texas;" p. 72. See also Narayandas and Rangan, "Dell Computer Corporation," p. 6, and "Dell Computer Corporation, Private Placement Memorandum," July 1987, quoted in Dell and Fredman, *Direct from Dell*, p. 30.

152. "Direct sales gives you fantastic market intelligence, commented one Dell manager." Quoted in Kotkin, "The Innovation Upstarts," p. 71.

153. V. Kasturi Rangan and Marie Bell, "Dell OnLine," Case 9-598-116 (Boston: Harvard Business School, 1999), p. 3.

154. Kotkin, "The Innovation Upstarts," p. 73.

155. See, for example, Cringely, *Accidental Empires*, pp. 284–286.

156. Ferguson and Morris, *Computer Wars*, p. 99.

157. Quoted in Kotkin, "The Innovation Upstarts," p. 72. See also "Dell Computer: It's in the Mail," *Economist* (2 March 1991), p. 66.

158. I am grateful to Joseph Maurin, who, in the late 1980s, worked as a staff engineer in Dell's product division for sharing this information.

159. Dell Computer Corporation, *Annual Report 1989*, p. 22. Net income as a percentage of sales also grew quickly. In fiscal 1985, the company's first year of operations, net income was 0.5 percent of sales; in 1987, it was 3 percent.

160. Poe, "It's Not Bragging If You Can Do It," p. 26.

161. Aronoff and Ward, "Michael Dell," p. 121.

162. Poe, "It's Not Bragging If You Can Do It," p. 27.

163. Dell and Fredman, *Direct from Dell*, p. 32.

164. Ibid., p. 20.

165. Ibid.

166. Dell and Fredman, *Direct from Dell*, p. 21. See also John Gantz, "Dell Computer: Is Success a Result of Luck or Vision?" *InfoWorld* 10, no. 25 (20 June 1988), p. 37.

167. Quoted in Goldstein, "An Industry Legend—at 21," p. 74.

168. Quoted in Bermant, "PCs Limited: Making Mail Order Pay Off," p. 8.

169. Quoted in Goldstein, "An Industry Legend—at 21," p. 74.

170. Quoted in ibid., p. 74.

171. Quoted in Claire Poole, "The Kid Who Turned Computers Into Commodities," *Forbes* (21 October 1991), p. 322.

172. "The Datamation 100," *Datamation* 34, no. 12 (15 June 1987), p. 31 and author's calculations.

173. Poe, "It's Not Bragging If You Can Do It," p. 26.

174. In 1987, Continental Grain Company began buying Dell computers to replace machines made by Compaq. Continental continued to buy from Dell in succeeding years. Stephanie Anderson Forest, "PC Slump? What PC Slump?" *Business Week* (1 July 1991), p. 67. On the relationship between customer loyalty and long-term profitability, see Frederick F. Reichheld and W. Earl Sasser Jr., "Zero Defections: Quality Comes to Services," *Harvard Business Review* 68, no. 5 (September-October 1990), pp. 106–108.

175. See, for example, Olegario, "IBM and the Two Thomas J. Watsons," pp. 351–393; Emerson W. Pugh, *Building IBM: Shaping an Industry and Its Technology* (Cambridge: MIT Press, 1995); Pugh, Johnson, and Palmer, *IBM's 360 and Early 370 Systems;* and James W. Cortada, *Before the Computer: IBM, NCR, Burroughs, and Remington Rand and the Industry They Created* (Princeton: Princeton University Press, 1993). The history of IBM's nickname is courtesy of Dawn Stanford of IBM's history department.

176. Venture Development Corporation, *Venturecasts: The 1986 Computer Data Book*, p. 114.

177. For an economic analysis of these general strategic issues, see Cynthia A. Montgomery and Birger Wernerfelt, "Risk Reduction and Umbrella Branding," *Journal of Business* 65, no. 1 (1992), pp. 31–50.

178. Pitta, "Why Dell Is a Survivor," pp. 86, 91.

179. Stephanie Anderson Forest, "Customers 'Must be Pleased, Not Satisfied,'" *Business Week* (3 August 1992), p. 52.

180. Dell and Fredman, *Direct from Dell*, p. 19.

181. Poe, "It's Not Bragging If You Can Do It," p. 27.

182. Dell and Fredman, *Direct from Dell*, p. 27.

183. Dell Computer Corporation, *Form 10-K 1989*, p. 2.

184. Venture Development Corporation, *Venturecasts: The 1987 Consumer Electronics Data Book* (Natick, MA: Venture Development Corporation, 1987), p. 10.

185. Dell and Fredman, *Direct from Dell*, p. 27.

186. Venture Development Corporation, *Venturecasts: The 1987 Consumer Electronics Data Book*, p. 7. European sales have been adjusted for inflation.

187. Dell and Fredman, *Direct from Dell*, p. 28.

188. Dell Computer Corporation, *Form 10-K 1989*, pp. 2–3.

189. Kevin Kelly, "Michael Dell: The Enfant Terrible of Personal Computers," *Business Week* (13 June 1988), p. 62.

190. Dell Computer Corporation, *Annual Report 1990*, pp. 8–9.

191. Dell Computer Corporation, *Annual Report 1989*, p. 20.

192. Dell Computer Corporation, *Annual Report 1990*, pp. 8–9.

193. Dell Computer Corporation, *Form 10-K 1989*, p. 13.

194. By March 1989, Dell had 1,016 full-time employees in the United States and 168 in other countries. Ibid., p. 7.

195. Kelly, "Michael Dell: The Enfant Terrible of Personal Computers," p. 61. See also Dell Computer Corporation, *Form 10-K 1989*, p. 6.

196. Quoted in Kelly, "Michael Dell: The Enfant Terrible of Personal Computers," p. 61.

197. Quoted in ibid. See also Gantz, "Dell Computer: Is Success Result of Luck or Vision?" p. 37; Angrist, "Entrepreneur in Short Pants," p. 85.

198. Kelly, "Michael Dell: The Enfant Terrible of Personal Computers," p. 61. See also Tom Richman, "The Entrepreneur of the Year," *Inc.* (January 1990), p. 44, Abby Livingston, "Growing Pains," *Venture* 10, no. 7 (July 1988), p. 96.

199. Dell Computer Corporation, *Form 10-K 1989*, pp. 9, 13. After paying related fees, the company's net proceeds from the IPO were about $31 million. Dell Computer Corporation, *Annual Report 1989*, p. 33.

200. Dell Computer Corporation, *Proxy Statement* (5 May 1989), p. 2.

201. Dell Computer Corporation, *Annual Report 1991*, p. 22.

202. Forest, "PC Slump? What PC Slump?" p. 66.

203. "Global Leaders," *Datamation* 38, no. 12 (15 June 1992), p. 26.

204. Dell Computer Corporation, *Annual Report 1991*, p. 7.

205. Ibid., p. 5.

206. Ibid., pp. 3–4.

207. Ibid., p. 3.

208. Microsoft Corporation, "Microsoft Museum—The Timeline," http://www.microsoft.com/MSCorp/Museum/timelines/microsoft/timeline.asp (accessed 30 June 2000).

209. Dell Computer Corporation, *Form 10-K 1989*, p. 7.

210. Steffens, *New Games*, p. 231, 232–236. Price indexes are from Council of Economic Advisers, *Economic Report of the President* (Washington, DC: U.S. Government Printing Office, 2000), p. 373.

211. Geoffrey A. Moore, *Inside the Tornado: Marketing Strategies from Silicon Valley's Cutting Edge* (New York: HarperCollins, 1995), pp. 6–7.

212. Between 1985 and 1991, Dell Computer's sales grew at annual rates of almost 75 percent, almost three times the estimated 20 to 30 percent annual growth for the PC industry as a whole. See R. Martin, "Dell Computer—Company Report," *Prudential Securities* (12 April 1991), p. 9, and Steffens, *New Games*, pp. 236–241.

213. Dell Computer Corporation, *Annual Report 1989*, p. 21.

214. Dell and Fredman, *Direct from Dell*, p. 36.

215. In fiscal 1989, Dell inventories increased almost $80 million, an almost eightfold rise over the increase in inventories in fiscal 1988. By fiscal 1990, Dell inventories had declined $35.7 million. Dell Computer Corporation, *Annual Report 1990*, p. 26.

216. Dell and Fredman, *Direct from Dell*, p. 37.

217. Dell Computer Corporation, *Annual Report 1990,* p. 17.

218. See, for example, E. C. Zimits, "Dell Computer Corporation—Company Report," Rauscher, Pierce, Refsnes, Inc. (23 October 1989), p. 3, and Stephanie Anderson Forest et al., "The Education of Michael Dell," *Business Week* (23 March 1993), p. 83.

219. Dell and Fredman, *Direct from Dell,* p. 37.

220. Magretta, "The Power of Virtual Integration: An Interview with Dell Computer's Michael Dell," p. 76.

221. In 1992, PC sales in superstores and big discounters totaled $2.8 billion. S. L. Eskenazi, "Dell Computer Corporation—Company Report," Alex Brown & Sons (8 May 1992), p. 5.

222. Dell Computer Corporation, *Annual Report 1993,* p. 4.

223. See, for example, Forest et al., "The Education of Michael Dell"; Peter Burrows and Stephanie Anderson Forest, "Dell Computer Goes Into the Shop," *Business Week* (12 July 1993), pp. 138–140; and Kidder, Peabody & Co., "Dell Computer Company Report" (1 June 1993), pp. 1–2.

224. Rangan and Bell, "Dell Online," p. 10.

225. Ibid., p. 11.

226. "Dell Tailors Web for Business," *Inter@ctive Week* (9 June 1997), p. 19.

227. Dell Computer Corporation, *Annual Report 2000,* p. 2.

228. Therese Poletti, "Computer Shipments Take Unexpected Leap," *Toronto Star* (26 April 1999); "Data Basics: Dell Tops Compaq in U.S. Sales," *Washington Post* (28 October 1999), p. E6; "Japan: Global PC Shipment Rises 15%—Data Quest," *Reuters English News Service* (4 April 2000); and Dell Computer Corporation, *Annual Report 2000,* p. 1.

CHAPTER 8

1. See, for example, Maxine Berg, *Age of Manufactures: Industry, Innovation and Work in Britain, 1700–1820* (New York: Oxford University Press, 1986), pp. 23–47; N. F. R. Crafts, *British Economic Growth during the Industrial Revolution* (Oxford: Clarendon, 1985), pp. 17–34; Peter Lindert, "English Occupations, 1670–1811," *Journal of Economic History* 40, no. 4 (1980), pp. 685–712; and E. Anthony Wrigley, "Urban Growth and Agricultural Change: England and the Continent in the Early Modern Period," in Robert I. Rotberg and Theodore Rabb, eds., *Population and History from the Traditional to the Modern World* (Cambridge: Cambridge University Press), pp. 123–168. On the importance of traditional industries in the eighteenth-century economy, see Pat Hudson, "The Regional Perspective," in Pat Hudson, ed., *Regions and Industries: A Perspective on the Industrial Revolution in Britain* (Cambridge: Cambridge University Press, 1989), pp. 5–38.

2. Crafts, *British Economic Growth,* pp. 22–23, 38–40.

3. Over this period, the number and average size of Staffordshire potteries also increased significantly. Lorna Weatherill, *The Pottery Trade and North Staffordshire, 1660–1760* (Manchester: Manchester University Press, 1971), pp. 1–9, 42–58.

4. W. A. Cole, "Factors in Demand, 1700–1780," in Roderick Floud and Donald M. McCloskey, eds., *The Economic History of Britain since 1700*, vol. 1: *1700–1860* (Cambridge: Cambridge University Press, 1983), pp. 40–41, 64, and Berg, *Age of Manufactures,* p. 45. See also Nancy F. Koehn, *The Power of Commerce: Economy and Governance in the First British Empire* (Ithaca: Cornell University Press, 1994), pp. 34–39.

5. Robert E. Gallman, "Commodity Output, 1839–1899," in *Trends in the American Economy in the Nineteenth Century,* National Bureau of Economic Research, Conference on Research in Income and Wealth (Princeton: Princeton University Press, 1960), p. 26.

6. U.S. Department of Commerce, *Historical Statistics of the United States: Colonial Times to 1970* (Washington, DC: U.S. Government Printing Office, 1975), 1, p. 225. See also Simon Kuznets, "Changes in the National Income of the United States of America since 1870," *Income and Wealth Series II* (London: Bowes & Bowes, 1952), p. 55.

7. On the revolution in production and distribution, see Alfred D. Chandler Jr., *The Visible Hand: The Managerial Revolution in American Business* (Cambridge: Harvard University Press, 1977); David Hounshell, *From the American System to Mass Production, 1800–1932* (Baltimore: Johns Hopkins University Press, 1984); and Philip Scranton, *Endless Novelty: Specialty Production and American Industrialization, 1865–1925* (Princeton: Princeton University Press, 1997).

8. U.S. Department of Commerce, *Historical Statistics of the United States,* 1, p. 224.

9. Council of Economic Advisers, *Economic Report of the President* (Washington, DC: U.S. Government Printing Office, 2000), p. 308.

10. See E. A. Wrigley's thoughtful analysis of these relationships and their historiographical significance in *People, Cities and Wealth: The Transformation of Traditional Society* (Oxford: Basil Blackwell, 1987), pp. 1–45, 157–193, and 215–241. See also Eric Monkkonen, *America Becomes Urban: The Development of U.S. Cities and Towns, 1780–1980* (Berkeley: University of California Press, 1988), pp. 9–30.

11. E. A. Wrigley and R. S. Schofield, *The Population History of England, 1541–1871: A Reconstruction* (Cambridge: Cambridge University Press, 1989), pp. 208–209.

12. In 1670, for example, less than one in seven Britons lived in a town with 5,000 or more inhabitants. By 1801, more than one in four did. Wrigley, *People, Cities and Wealth,* p. 162.

13. Ibid., p. 160.

14. U.S. Department of Commerce, *Historical Statistics of the United States,* 1, p. 8.

15. The figure for 1856 is from Thomas Wakefield Goodspeed, "Marshall Field," *University of Chicago Biographical Sketches,* 1 (April 1922), p. 6, Field Family Papers, box 1, folder 11, Chicago Historical Society, Chicago, IL. The figure for 1900 is from "Population of Chicago by Decades 1830–1990," *A Chronological History of Chicago, 1673–*, compiled by Chicago Municipal Reference Library, City of Chicago, updated by Municipal Reference Collection, Chicago Public Library (August 1997).

16. U.S. Department of Commerce, *Historical Statistics of the United States,* 1, pp. 11–12.

17. Ibid., 1, p. 10. U.S. Department of Commerce, *Statistical Abstract of the United States, 1992* (Washington, DC: U.S. Government Printing Office, 1992), p. 8.

18. U.S. Department of Commerce, *Historical Statistics of the United States,* 1, p. 25, and U.S. Bureau of the Census, "State Population Estimates," http://www.census.gov/population/www/estimates/state/st-99-2txt (accessed 30 June 2000).

19. 1940 figure is from U.S. Department of Commerce, *Statistical Abstract of the United States, 1946* (Washington, DC: U.S. Government Printing Office, 1946), p. 10; 1998 figure is from U.S. Bureau of the Census, "Population Estimates for Cities with Populations of 100,000 and Greater," http://www.census.gov:80/population/estimates/metro-city/SC100K98-T1-DR.txt (accessed 30 June 2000).

20. J. Walker Smith and Ann Clurman, *Rocking the Ages: The Yankelovich Report on Generational Marketing* (New York: HarperBusiness, 1997), p. 42. See also Russell W. Belk, "Yuppies as Arbiters of the Emerging Consumption Style," in Richard J. Lutz, ed., *Advances in Consumer Research* 13 (Provo, UT: Association for Consumer Research, 1986), pp. 514–519, and Susan Fournier, David Antes, and Glenn Beaumier, "Nine Consumption Lifestyles," in John F. Sherry Jr. and Brian Sternthal, eds., *Advances in Consumer Research* 19 (Provo, UT: Association for Consumer Research, 1992), pp. 329–337.

21. *Gentleman's Magazine* (21 May 1751), p. 208.

22. Josiah Tucker, *Instructions for Travellers* (Dublin: William Watson, 1758), p. 213.

23. On the scope of markets for Staffordshire pottery at midcentury, for example, see Weatherill, *The Pottery Trade,* pp. 76–95.

24. Paul Langford, *A Polite and Commercial People, 1727–1783* (Oxford: Clarendon Press, 1990), p. 414. See also G. R. Hawke and J. P. P. Higgins, "Transport and Social Overhead Capital," in Floud and McCloskey, eds., *Economic History of Britain,* 1, pp. 227–252, and Koehn, *The Power of Commerce,* pp. 24–60.

25. Thomas Bentley, *A View of the Advantages of Inland Navigation with a Plan of a Navigable Canal* (London: Becket and DeHondt, 1766), p. 42.

26. Over the course of the eighteenth century, Britain's exports to North America and the West climbed more than twenty times. R. P. Thomas and D. N. McCloskey, "Overseas Trade and Empire, 1700–1860," in Floud and McCloskey, eds., *The Economic History of Britain since 1700,* 1, p. 91. On North American

consumption of china and other British manufactures, see T. H. Breen, "'Baubles of Britain': The American and Consumer Revolutions of the Eighteenth Century," *Past & Present* 18, no. 119 (May 1988), pp. 73–104, and "An Empire of Goods: The Anglicization of Colonial America, 1690–1776," *Journal of British Studies* 25, no. 4 (October 1986), pp. 467–499.

27. Chandler, *Visible Hand,* p. 83, and Thomas K. McCraw, "American Capitalism," in Thomas K. McCraw, ed., *Creating Modern Capitalism: How Entrepreneurs, Companies, and Countries Triumphed in Three Industrial Revolutions* (Cambridge: Harvard University Press, 1997), p. 319.

28. Sidney Ratner, James H. Soltow, and Richard Sylla, *The Evolution of the American Economy: Growth, Welfare and Decision Making* (New York: Basic, 1979), p. 321.

29. Thomas K. McCraw and Richard S. Tedlow, "Henry Ford, Alfred Sloan, and the Three Phases of Marketing," in Thomas K. McCraw, ed., *Creating Modern Capitalism,* p. 283. In the mid-1990s United States had the highest per capita vehicle ownership ratios in the world, with a car, truck, or sport utility vehicle (SUV) for about every 1.3 people. U.S. Department of Commerce, *Statistical Abstract of the United States, 1999* (Washington, DC: U.S. Government Printing Office, 1999), pp. 845, 848.

30. Thomas K. McCraw, *American Business, 1920–2000: How It Worked* (Wheeling, IL: Harlan Davidson, 2000), p. 112.

31. U.S. Department of Commerce, *Statistical Abstract of the United States, 1999,* p. 885.

32. McCraw, *American Business,* p. 126, and U.S. Department of Commerce, *Statistical Abstract of the United States, 1999,* p. 885.

33. U.S. Department of Commerce, *Historical Statistics of the United States,* 2, p. 796 and 1, p. 41; and U.S. Department of Commerce, *Statistical Abstract of the United States, 1999,* p. 885.

34. GartnerGroup/Dataquest, "Personal Computer History: U.S. Shipments" (1999), courtesy of Leslie Robbins, Senior Business Analyst, GartnerGroup/Dataquest.

35. Ibid.

36. Robert J. Samuelson, "Have PCs Peaked?" *Washington Post* (1 April 1999), p. A27, and "Metrics: Half of U.S. Homes Now Have PCs," *The Industry Standard* (14 June 1999), p. 102.

37. McCraw, *American Business,* p. 203.

38. On predictability and its role in human behavior, see Howard H. Stevenson with Jeffrey L. Cruikshank, *Do Lunch or Be Lunch: The Power of Predictability in Creating Your Future* (Boston: Harvard Business School Press, 1998).

39. See, for example, Fernand Braudel, *The Wheels of Commerce* (New York: Harper & Row, 1979), pp. 472–478; Thomas K. McCraw, "Introduction," in McCraw, ed., *Creating Modern Capitalism,* pp. 1–16; and Max Weber, *The Protestant*

Ethic and the Spirit of Capitalism, translated by Talcott Parsons (New York: Scribner's, 1958), pp. 47–78.

40. Quoted in C. N. Cole, ed., *The Works of Soame Jenyns,* 4 vols. (London, 1790), 2, p. 93. See also Roy Porter, *English Society in the Eighteenth Century* (New York: Penguin, 1984), pp. 61–112, and Langford, *A Polite and Commercial People,* pp. 59–121. For contemporary perspectives on economic and social conditions in late-nineteenth-century Chicago, see Julian Ralph, *Our Great West: A Study of the Present Conditions and Future Possibilities of the New Commonwealths and Capitals of the United States* (New York: Harper & Brothers, 1893), pp. 1–63, and Theodore Dreiser, *A Book About Myself* (New York: Boni and Liveright, 1922), pp. 65–67.

41. Neil McKendrick, "The Consumer Revolution of Eighteenth-Century England," in Neil McKendrick, John Brewer, and J. H. Plumb, *The Birth of a Consumer Society: The Commercialization of Eighteenth-Century England* (Bloomington, IN: Indiana University Press, 1985), pp. 9–33.

The history of consumption, several scholars have argued, should be understood in more complex terms than those provided by traditional conceptions of the mass market or social emulation. See, for example, John Styles, "Manufacturing, Consumption, and Design in Eighteenth-Century England," in John Brewer and Roy Porter, eds., *Consumption and the World of Goods* (London: Routledge, 1993), pp. 321–343. On the role of consumption as an expression of individual identity, social and personal, see Russell Belk, "Possessions and the Extended Self," *Journal of Consumer Research* 15, no. 2 (September 1988), pp. 139–168; Russell Belk, "Cultural and Historical Differences in Concepts of Self and their Effects on Attitudes Toward Having and Giving," in Thomas C. Kinnear, ed., *Advances in Consumer Research* 11 (Provo, UT: Association for Consumer Research, 1984), pp. 753–760; Colin Campbell, *The Romantic Ethic and the Spirit of Modern Consumerism* (Oxford: Basil Blackwell, 1987); Susan Fournier, "Understanding Consumer-Brand Relationships," working paper 96-018, Harvard Business School, Boston, 1995, and "The Consumer and the Brand: An Understanding within the Framework of Interpersonal Relationships," working paper 96-018, Harvard Business School, Boston, 1996; Sidney Levy, "Dreams, Fairy Tales, Animals, and Cars," *Psychology and Marketing* 2 (summer 1985), pp. 67–81; Grant McCracken, *Culture and Consumption: New Approaches to the Symbolic Character of Consumer Goods and Activities* (Bloomington, IN: Indiana University Press, 1988), and "Who Is the Celebrity Endorser? Cultural Foundations of the Endorsement Process," *Journal of Consumer Research* 16, no. 3 (December 1989), pp. 310–321; and Melanie Wallendorf and Eric J. Arnould, "My Favorite Things: A Cross-Cultural Inquiry into Object Attachment, Possessiveness, and Social Linkage," *Journal of Consumer Research* 14, no. 4 (March 1988), pp. 531–547.

42. Using a framework called the "Total Product Concept," Theodore Levitt and other marketing scholars have analyzed products and brands by levels of potential

differentiation. According to this framework, at the core of every brand is the generic or tangible product. This is the commodity or rudimentary thing that meets a basic consumer need—for example, an earthenware plate, manufactured foods, or clothing. In most product markets, Levitt has noted, consumers expect more than the generic product. Manufacturers that distinguish their core products by meeting these expectations and offering convenient distribution, informative, attractive packaging, reliable quality, efficient design, or other features that appeal to buyers create meaningful differentiation and the basis for a brand. By meeting consumers' minimal expectations, such branded goods, which Levitt terms "expected products," win business away from producers selling generic products.

Manufacturers, Levitt asserts, can further distinguish their goods by offering consumers more than they expect—supplying services, guarantees, after-sales support, or other features that enhance the value of the product to the buyer. These offerings supplement those of the expected and core product and are termed the "augmented product." Each of the entrepreneurs analyzed in this book differentiated their products from competing ones by giving consumers more than they expected. Wedgwood, for example, supported his products with a money-back guarantee. Heinz opened his factory to public inspection. Field offered department store shoppers a tea room, lounges, and a library. Lauder supplied free makeovers. Schultz offered friendly, knowledgeable, and efficient customer service in Starbucks cafés. Dell backed his products with high levels of customer service and after-sales support. Theodore Levitt, *The Marketing Imagination* (New York: Free Press, 1983), pp. 78–85. See also Peter Doyle, "Building Successful Brands: The Strategic Options," *Journal of Marketing Management* 5, no. 1 (1989) pp. 85–86; Kevin Lane Keller, *Strategic Brand Management: Building, Measuring, and Managing Brand Equity* (Upper Saddle River, NJ: Prentice Hall, 1998), pp. 3–5; and Philip Kotler and Gary Armstrong, *Principles of Marketing* (Upper Saddle River, NJ: Prentice Hall, 1996), pp. 274–282.

43. Edward F. Keuchel, "Master of the Art of Canning: Baltimore, 1860–1900," *Maryland Historical Magazine* 67 (1972), pp. 355.

44. Robert W. Twyman, *History of Marshall Field, 1852–1906* (Philadelphia: University of Pennsylvania Press, 1954), p. 31.

45. Faye Henle, "Beauty Parade: Cosmetics Makers Run Hard to Stand Still," *Barron's* 34, no. 10 (8 March 1954), p. 15.

46. Ted R. Lingle, "Avenues for Growth: A 20-Year Review of the U.S. Specialty Coffee Market," Specialty Coffee Association of America (1993), p. 3.

47. Quoted in McKendrick, "The Commercialization of Fashion," in McKendrick, Brewer, and Plumb, *Birth of a Consumer Society*, p. 71.

48. On early twentieth-century consumption of processed foods, see Margaret F. Byington, *Homestead: The Households of a Mill Town* (Philadelphia: Russell Sage Foundation, 1910), pp. 75–77; Robert Coit Chapin, *The Standard of Living Among*

Workingmen's Families in New York City (New York: Charities Publication Committee, 1909), pp. 154–162; Richard Osborn Cummings, *The American and His Food: A History of Food Habits in the United States* (Chicago: University of Chicago Press, 1940), pp. 247–249; National Industrial Conference Board, Inc., *The Cost of Living in the United States* (New York: National Industrial Conference Board, 1925), pp. 72–74, 94–95; and U.S. Bureau of Labor Statistics, *How American Buying Habits Change* (Washington, DC: U.S. Government Printing Office, 1959), pp. 112–124.

49. Robin Reilly, *Josiah Wedgwood, 1730–1795* (London: Macmillan, 1992), pp. 207–208.

50. The process of offering the customer more than he or she thinks is needed, marketing scholar Theodore Levitt has written, "can, over time, educate the buyer about what is reasonable for him to expect from the seller." *Marketing Imagination*, p. 82.

51. Not all of these efforts, Robin Reilly has noted, succeeded. See *Josiah Wedgwood, 1730–1795*, pp. 210–211.

52. Quoted in ibid., p. 77.

53. In later times, particularly the 1980s and 1990s, a good deal of "vertical divestiture"—or "de-integration"—occurred throughout American business as the general markets for specialized services and functions matured. All of this was part of the "downsizing" and "reengineering" movements of the 1980s, 1990s, and early twenty-first century.

54. Estée Lauder Companies Inc., *Annual Report, 1999*, p. 4.

55. Howard Schultz and Dori Jones Yang, *Pour Your Heart Into It: How Starbucks Built a Company One Cup at a Time* (New York: Hyperion, 1997), p. 171.

Acknowledgments

Seven years ago when I began thinking about entrepreneurs and new markets, I had no inkling that these interests would lead me on the long, winding road to this book. In the midst of researching Josiah Wedgwood and the earthenware industry in eighteenth-century Britain, I had little idea that the next stop on my historical itinerary would be Pittsburgh in the late 1800s. Or that I would eventually find myself in early-twentieth-century New York, reconstructing the beauty business, and in Seattle in the 1980s, analyzing the young market for specialty coffee. At the beginning of this journey, I certainly did not foresee that I would spend years trying to understand the working lives of such distinct individuals as Marshall Field and Michael Dell.

What I *did* know was that historical research involves both serendipity and careful planning. In the early stages of my travels, this meant that I had to navigate—as Abraham Lincoln once said—"from point to point." It also meant that I tried to scrutinize each new destination as closely as I could before beginning the next leg of the trip. Despite my best efforts, I ended up taking several complicated detours as well as a couple of highways that proved to be dead ends. On a few occasions, I wondered where I was going and why.

Thankfully, I never had to travel alone. Many individuals and institutions offered guidance and support, helping me complete this sometimes frustrating, always fascinating expedition. I am grateful to the Trustees of the Wedgwood Museum for access to the Wedgwood collections in Staffordshire, England; to the Heinz Family Office and the H. J. Heinz Company for allowing me to use Henry Heinz's diaries, business records, and other related documents in my research; and to the public relations department of Marshall Field's for access to the early records of the store. I owe special debts to Gaye Blake-Roberts and Lynn Miller of the Wedgwood Museum, Frank Kurtik of the Heinz Family Office, Nancy Winstanley and Debbie Foster of the H. J. Heinz Company, and Lynne Galia and Tony Jahn of Marshall Field's. These women and men gave generously of their expertise and time. Frank Kurtik made a particularly large contribution to this project, sharing his extensive knowledge of H. J. Heinz, showing my research associate Laura Bureš and me around Pittsburgh, and providing a variety of historic photographs.

Other people and organizations helped me along. I thank Leonard Lauder, Jeanette Wagner, Karen O'Connor, and Nina LaRicchia at the Estée Lauder Companies for their firsthand observations on the history of the business. The insights of Howard Schultz, Orin Smith, Dave Olsen, Howard Behar, and other senior executives at Starbucks Coffee Company proved invaluable to the evolution of my thinking about institution building and modern brand creation. I am especially grateful to Deidra Wager, who moved my research on Starbucks forward in several important directions. In addition to offering her own thoughts about the company's early years, she facilitated my interviews with her colleagues and arranged for me to work in two Starbucks cafés. I also want to thank Deb Balogh and Sonja Gould for their help in completing the chapter on Starbucks. Chris Bates and Debbie McNair of Dell Computer reviewed my research and answered my queries on the company's history.

I also thank the staffs of the Baker and Kress Libraries at the Harvard Business School, the Houghton, Schlesinger, and Widener Libraries at Harvard College, the Keele University Library in England, the New York Public Library, the Historical Society of Western Pennsylvania, the Chicago Historical Society, the Queens Historical Society, the Queens Borough Public Library, and the Historical Society of Palm Beach County. With courtesy and efficiency, these people helped me track down hundreds of books, newspapers, business records, consumption statistics, and even nineteenth-century railroad maps.

I would never have undertaken the intellectual expedition that ended in this book had I not been based at the Harvard Business School, an institution with a rich history of interdisciplinary research and delicate experiments. I am grateful to the School's Division of Research, which provided financial support for all stages of the project. I also thank the four faculty directors of research who helped me to map out my evolving journey: Steven Wheelwright, Dick Vietor, Cynthia Montgomery, and Ken Froot. My debts to Cynthia Montgomery are especially large. From the first step of my travels to the end, her intelligence, advice, good faith, and kindness proved indispensable.

I have benefited significantly from the input and experience of other Harvard Business School colleagues. Teresa Amabile, Myra Hart, Bill Sahlman, Howard Stevenson, Ed Zschau, and other scholars in the Entrepreneurial and Service Management Area at the Harvard Business School have taught me much about entrepreneurs and young enterprises. I am thankful as well for their support and camaraderie. Al Silk, John Deighton, and Susan Fournier helped me hone my research on brands, consumer behavior, and marketing initiatives more generally. I am particularly grateful to Al Silk, whose insights were critical in helping me reconstruct the history of brand creation and its evolving place in modern corporations.

Since I first embarked on this project, my colleagues in the School's Business History Group have offered their time and expertise in full measure. I am thankful to the members of the Business History Seminar, who provided me input on five of the book's eight chapters. I owe an especially large debt to Walter Friedman, who brought his historical expertise and editorial gifts to bear on this project. I thank him as well for his encouragement during the last four years.

I am also grateful to my students in the two M.B.A. history courses at the Harvard Business School: Creating Modern Capitalism and The Coming of Managerial Capitalism. During the last decade, they helped me test my ideas about entrepreneurial agency, demand-side competition, and young markets, expanding my understanding of how today's business leaders think and their companies operate.

Among the history faculty, I have been privileged to work with Alfred Chandler, Tom McCraw, Richard Tedlow, and Dick Vietor. I thank these four scholars for helping me conceptualize and develop this project. I am also grateful for their commitment to rigorous scholarship and for the overall pleasure of their company during a decade of talking, teaching, and passing book chapters back and forth. I am especially indebted to Tom McCraw, who, more than any other scholar, has helped me appreciate the wonder and sustaining richness of historical discovery. His advice on all matters of substance made an important contribution to this book. So, too, did his keen understanding of narrative structure and literary grace.

Other experts at Harvard and elsewhere read earlier versions of this book. I am grateful to them for their insights. Carliss Baldwin, Sven Beckert, John Brewer, Fred Carstensen, Sally Clarke, Liz Cohen, Dwight Crane, Wendy Gamber, Bob Hayes, Bob Kennedy, Ted Levitt, Gary Loveman, Grant

McCracken, Kathy Peiss, Philip Scranton, Larry Sosnow, Debora Spar, Marc Stern, Karen Wruck, and Abe Zaleznik all took time away from their own work to offer useful suggestions.

The editors and production team at the Harvard Business School Press helped me complete the final legs of this journey. I was fortunate to work with senior editor Kirsten Sandberg, whose careful feedback and sustaining interest in this project helped me see it through to completion. I was also lucky to work with manuscript editor Jane Judge Bonassar and designer Joyce Weston, each of whom brought her talents to bear on this book. I am grateful to Orit Gadiesh and Tom Hout, who read earlier versions of this work for Harvard Business School Press and offered valuable advice. I thank Pat Denault, Max Chuck, and especially Max Hall for turning their editorial talents to this project. Max Hall read six of the book's eight chapters, making recommendations large and small. On more than one instance, his literary integrity and faith in this work helped me find my way off an exhausting detour and onto the main road again.

I could not have brought the book to publication without the research assistance of Felice Whittum, Geoffrey Verter, Rachel Hitch, and William Grundy. They helped me track down information from books, interviews, business records, market research data, company archives, and other sources. I benefited as well from their insights on the project. I also want to thank Vadim Brinzan for his guidance and time in obtaining permission to use specific photographs from the Hermitage Museum, Jake Cohen for his work on Marshall Field's financial records, Gary Goldstein of the National Coffee Association and Ted Lingle of the Specialty Coffee Association for a variety of information on the U.S. coffee market, and Joe Maurin for his help on the history of Dell Computer.

One of the greatest joys in writing this book has been the opportunity to work with Elizabeth Sampson and Laura Bureš. For more than four years, each of these women applied her intelligence, organization, and creativity to virtually every aspect of this project—from planning the early research strategy to locating the final photographs. I am no less thankful for the support and warmth they so consistently provided. I owe each more than I can say.

My biggest debts in making this journey are to those near to home. Judith Livingston helped me to choose among different paths, offering her perspective and integrity at a number of crossroads. Paula Throckmorton

Zakaria read the entire manuscript, making a range of suggestions that improved the work. Her ideas about modern consumption and social change in tandem with her entrepreneurial experience broadened my thinking about getting, spending, and creating personal identity. I thank her as well for her kindness and humor—rays of sunlight on overcast days. I could not have ventured far without the advice and generosity of spirit of Brenda Mounzer. From the moment I packed my first suitcase, she helped me understand that the journey itself had rewards over and above its ultimate destination. At the same time, she never let me doubt too deeply that I would wind up at an interesting location with good views. Throughout the past five years, she has been a savvy, loving travel guide.

I owe the most to Colin Davis. In Staffordshire, Chicago, and especially at home base in Boston, his insights improved the substance and structure of the book. His wisdom and "firmness in the right" lit my way at each step. And his music and wit enriched the entire journey. I could not have made this trip without him. Or without our beloved Monty and Conway.

I also want to thank my father, Don Koehn, whose energy for teaching and interest in ideas have helped fuel my academic expeditions for many years.

But this book is for my mother, Sally Koehn. For as long as I can remember, she has shared her contagious enthusiasm for the people, places, events, and even the sights and smells of moments gone by. She has been an equally avid student of entrepreneurship, consistently fascinated by how certain individuals have reinvented not only entire industries but also themselves in the process. She has always encouraged my sister, brother, and me to follow our own fascinations, offering her support and empathy for each of our endeavors. She was particularly generous in helping me write this book, discussing possible subjects, reading chapter drafts, and keeping me in laughter throughout my travels. For these and other gifts, I thank her wholeheartedly.

Nancy F. Koehn
Boston, Massachusetts

Index

About the Author

NANCY F. KOEHN is an historian at the Harvard Business School and a member of the school's Entrepreneurial and Service Management Unit. She is the author of *The Power of Commerce: Economy and Governance in the First British Empire* (1994) as well as a contributor to *Beauty and Business* (2000), *The Intellectual Venture Capitalist* (1999), *Creating Modern Capitalism* (1997), *Macroeconomic Decision Making in the World Economy* (1989), and the *Business History Review* and other academic journals.

At the Harvard Business School, she teaches The Entrepreneurial Manager, a required M.B.A. course, and The Coming of Managerial Capitalism, an M.B.A. elective in business history that is one of the school's most popular courses. In 1998, the HBS Student Association selected Koehn as one of two Outstanding Professors in the Elective Curriculum.

Before coming to HBS in 1991, Koehn was a member of Harvard University's Faculty of Arts and Sciences, first as a graduate student in history and then as a lecturer in the History and Literature concentration and the Department of Economics. She received the Allyn Young Prize in 1989 and numerous Danforth Commendations for excellence in teaching.

A graduate of Stanford University, Koehn earned a Master of Public Policy from Harvard's Kennedy School of Government and an M.A. and Ph.D. in European history from Harvard University.

She lives outside Boston with her husband, Colin Davis, a classical violinist.

JACKET PHOTO CREDITS

Front cover. Top: Dell Dimension L desktop PC. Courtesy of Dell Computer Corporation. Bottom: Josiah Wedgwood and family, 1780, by George Stubbs. By kind permission of the Trustees of the Wedgwood Museum, Barlaston, Staffordshire, England.

Back cover. Top left: H. J. Heinz Company wagon, circa 1890. Courtesy of H. J. Heinz Company. Top right: Starbucks Caffè Mocha. Courtesy of Starbucks Coffee Company. Bottom left: Estée Lauder, 1930. Photography courtesy of Estée Lauder Companies. Bottom right: Bottles of Youth Dew. Photography courtesy of Estée Lauder Companies.

Front flap. Top: H. J. Heinz, 1880. Courtesy of the Heinz Family Office. Bottom: Tiffany Dome in Marshall Field's State Street store, circa 1927. Courtesy of Marshall Field's.

Spine. Top: Josiah Wedgwood, 1782, by Sir Joshua Reynolds. By kind permission of the Trustees of the Wedgwood Museum, Barlaston, Staffordshire, England. Bottom: Michael Dell. Courtesy of Dell Computer Corporation.